# Theories of the Labor Movement

# Theories of the Labor Movement

EDITED BY SIMEON LARSON AND BRUCE NISSEN

 WAYNE STATE UNIVERSITY PRESS    DETROIT

**Library of Congress Cataloging in Publication Data**

Theories of the labor movement.

  Bibliography: p.
  Includes index.
  1. Trade-unions—History.   I. Larson, Simeon,
1925-    . II. Nissen, Bruce, 1948-
HD6476.T47   1987     331.88'09     86-32414
ISBN 0-8143-1815-0
ISBN 0-8143-1816-9 (pbk.)


ISBN-13: 978-0-8143-1816-4 (pbk.)
ISBN-10: 0-8143-1816-9 (pbk.)

# Contents

# *Preface*

Teaching classes on labor movement theories or introducing the topic in other classes is a particularly difficult task. Instructors and students are confronted with the problem that no single volume containing the works of all the relevant theorists is available. Students spend endless hours searching for relevant material, and instructors are forced to extract from each theorist's work that part which would be most illuminating in conveying central ideas to students.

This book attempts to overcome some of these problems by combining in one volume the writings of some of our most important labor theorists in a manner which enhances student understanding. We hope that this work will be a useful text to instructors and students alike. We have organized the labor theories into seven basic groups according to the primary social role each theorist assigns to the labor movement. Such a classification should better enable students to understand the similarities and differences between the various theorists.

We wish to thank a number of individuals who assisted us in this undertaking. Our special thanks to Professor Miles Galvin of Rutgers University, who read the entire manuscript and made many helpful suggestions, and to Professor Wells Keddie, also of Rutgers University, whose original unpublished work on this topic provided us with the inspiration to complete this book. Thanks are also due to Professor Ronald Filipelli of Pennsylvania State University who read parts of the manuscript and whose comments helped us improve the manuscript.

Finally, we wish to thank Ms. Katherine Schroeder and Ms. Julayne Moser for their patience and understanding in typing the manuscript and putting up with all our demands for corrections and changes. And a special thanks to Kathryn Wildfong, a most able editor with Wayne State University Press.

# General Introduction

Theorizing about labor movements has always been an elusive, complex task, in great part because the labor movement has taken widely different forms historically, even in the same country, and takes widely different forms currently in various parts of the world. Witness, for example, the disparate aims of the Knights of Labor, the Industrial Workers of the World, and the American Federation of Labor in the United States. The contemporary American labor movement, almost alone among the world's labor movements, ideologically accepts the capitalist system and bases its strategies on an assumption of the job consciousness of workers, in contrast with many European movements which reject the capitalist system and base their strategies on an assumption of the class consciousness of workers. To further compound the problem, the need for a theory of labor is seriously questioned, and theorizing about labor movements is often regarded as an irrelevant activity whose primary purpose is to serve as an engaging pastime of ivory-tower academics. Why, these individuals ask, do we need a theory of labor when a history of labor organizations or an economic study of their impact might suffice? The result is that, except for a brief period after World War II, no other area in the study of labor has received so little attention in the United States as theories of the labor movement. It is hoped that this volume will serve as a guide to help stimulate our thinking about labor theory and to clarify the nature of labor movement theories.

Perhaps a simple explanation of a theory and its component elements would be helpful as a preliminary to understanding the works of the theorists presented in this volume. A theory is a comprehensive, systematic interpretation or explanation, derived from scientific data or facts, of a particular phenomenon. One of the most important building blocks of a theory, and most often used interchangeably with it, is a hypothesis. A hypothesis is a guess or supposition put forth as a possible explanation of certain phenomena. This serves as a guide in a process of experimentation to arrive at the truth, at least for scientific theories. (Not all theories claim to be scientific—an example would be those theories which view the labor movement as a moral institution, as in Part VI of this volume.) Once a hypothesis is tested and the results verified a theory of the particular phenomenon observed can be developed.

Care should be taken not to confuse an ideology with a theory. The former is a body of ideas or beliefs held by a social group or movement. Ideologies provide a "world view"; they often play an important part in forming the background or context within

*1*

which one formulates a theory. But an ideology does not by itself constitute a theory. The Industrial Workers of the World, for example, pursued a particular ideology and the American Federation of Labor another, but neither was able to explain the relationship between each or to incorporate within its thinking an explanation of the origin, development, present status or ultimate goals of any of the other labor organizations. Ideological differences among scholars have also led to sharp disagreements over the content and function of labor movement theories.

The purpose of a theory is to put isolated facts together into a coherent whole, and attempt to explain the "how" and the "why" of whatever is being examined. A good theory will connect the various facts we know about something, and use the resulting whole to explain its origin, development, present state, and (possibly) future evolution. When Sherlock Holmes brilliantly solves another case, he is constructing a *theory* of how the murder happened by arranging available facts into a plausible explanation of how and why it occurred. Therefore a theory is at least one step removed from a simple description of bare facts. However, a worthwhile theory not only will provide general principles which are compatible with the "bare facts," but will actually explain them in the most comprehensive and simple manner.

The aim of theories which attempt to be scientific is to isolate the main causal factors which explain something's origin, development, and present state. If major causes can be isolated (a difficult task: most modern social science is moving in the direction of *multi*-causal explanations), predictions about future development should be possible. However, several warnings are in order: (1) in the social sciences, predictions are notoriously unreliable, while clear causal relationships are difficult to establish; and (2) assumptions and value judgements almost always play a large part in social science theories.

There are problems in trying to test, verify, and compare theories as broad and complex as labor movement theories. It is all but impossible to conduct scientific experiments which observe the effects of changing one variable while holding all others constant. Unique historical situations cannot be recreated; complex variables involving human interaction cannot be held constant. Given this, most "testing" of labor theories consists of after-the-fact analyses and comparisons of historical events and movements. Such testing is important and useful, but seldom decisive.

Moreover, we find strong disagreement among labor theorists, in part because establishing clear proofs and disproofs is so difficult, and in part because of differing value judgments and assumptions. This does not mean that all theories are equally good or bad, or that there is no basis for choosing one theory over another. But it does mean that no theory is likely to be value-free or closed to all challenges. Every theory will contain assumptions about workers and their motivations, the existence or nature of economic and social classes, and the like. These assumptions need to be carefully identified, examined, and evaluated before they are accepted. The reader is advised to be especially critical of the theory which most agrees with his preconceptions, for it is here that unexamined assumptions are likely to pass unnoticed.

Biases can even creep into how we define the subject matter. For example, should the term "labor movement" be confined only to unions engaging primarily in collective bargaining (roughly, the situation with the U.S. labor movement today), or should it also include noneconomic institutions set up by workers to pursue political and social objectives? If we exclude the latter by definition, a conservative bias toward a nonpolitical "business unionism" (see Part III) is introduced. On the other hand, if we include within the confines of the labor movement such institutions as the Knights of Labor, the Industrial Workers of the World, and the many labor organizations in Europe, Czarist Russia, and many Third World countries primarily engaged in political and social activities, theories of a more social activist and even revolutionary nature become more plausible. The reader is cautioned against the assumption that the U.S. labor movement in the second half of the Twentieth Century is the norm for all labor movements at all times. A comprehensive labor movement theory should be able to explain the variety of labor movements across national and historical boundaries.

This raises one further point: students of labor theories will need some knowledge of labor history and comparative labor movements to be able to judge theoretical adequacy. A real dilemma in compiling this book arose over whether to include historical and empirical data needed as examples and tests of the theories. For space and other reasons, we chose to stay fairly close to "pure" theories, but it should be noted that this leaves some gaps in the knowledge necessary for a complete theoretical understanding of a labor movement. For example, in the U.S., the "utopian," "land reform," "10-hour," and "8-hour" movements, "cooperatives," "currency reform," "labor party," and other labor organizations and movements of the nineteenth century are not included here, even though they were important labor movement developments. And even for the more familiar "business unionism" of the AFL, the "social activist" unionism of the early CIO, the "social Catholic" unionism of the Association of Catholic Trade Unionists (ACTU), and a host of other such movements, historical documentation is entirely lacking. We see this as unavoidable in a book of this nature, but supplemental readings and background in labor history can fill the gaps.

The task of labor economists and historians to classify labor theories according to some established criteria is not a simple one, for theorists have not responded to the same set of questions. Some have concerned themselves primarily with the origin of the labor movement while others have focused on worker motivation or labor union behavior and its role in a particular industrial society. Still others are concerned with the ideological direction of labor organizations or with their ultimate goals. Thus not only are there sharp differences over the function and content of labor movement theory, but it is virtually impossible to integrate the various theories into one overall theory of the labor movement. An effort to categorize the diverse theories promises greater success.

The typology of American labor theories developed by Professor Mark Perlman is probably best known.[1] He employs a fivefold classification:

(1) the Protestant Christian Socialist and the Roman Catholic social movements
(2) the Marxian Socialist movements
(3) the environmental psychology discipline
(4) the neoclassical economics discipline, and
(5) the legal or jurisprudential history discipline.

Perlman associates each of the theoretical groupings with the distinctive questions and assumptions linked with a particular academic discipline or social movement. While different theoretical interpretations exist within each classification, Perlman finds sufficient agreement on underlying assumptions and basic thrust so as to unite each group around a general theme and to clearly distinguish one category from the other.

Our intent in this volume is not to construct a neat classification of labor movement theories but to arrange those theories in a manner most likely to enhance the learning process. For this purpose we have found it more useful to group the theories according to the *overall social role* each assigns the labor movement. This arrangement brings out sharply the points of contention (and agreement) between theories. In general, theorists assign to the labor movement one of seven basic social roles. The labor movement may be (1) an agent of revolution, (2) a business institution for economic protection of its members, (3) an agent for extending industrial democracy, (4) an instrument for achieving the psychological aims of groupings of workers, (5) an agent for moral and spiritual reform, (6) an antisocial, destructive monopoly, or (7) a subordinate mechanism with "special interest" functions in a pluralist industrial society. The selections that follow are grouped in accordance with these seven roles.

Each theorist develops hypotheses about the origin, development, and future of the labor movement. As with most questions, labor theorists do not agree in their interpretations of the origin of labor movements. Karl Marx, the classic spokesman for revolutionary theory, holds that the modern industrial working class, the proletariat, is a product of the growth and development of industrial capitalism. Brought into close association by the factory system and subject to the most oppressive working conditions, workers seek to protect themselves by forming labor organizations. Unions, therefore, are a product of class consciousness of an elementary sort—a recognition by workers of the common aims they share with their fellow workers and an acknowledgement that it is the employer who thwarts their desire for improved working conditions and for a better life in general.

John R. Commons and Sidney and Beatrice Webb agree with Marx that class division generated by industrialization is the primary factor in the development of trade unions. However, neither Commons nor the Webbs draw revolutionary conclusions from this as Marx does. Commons believes it is the *extension of markets* brought on by commercial and industrial expansion which forces workers to band together into unions to protect themselves from the market's corrosive influences. The enemy, therefore, is the market, not the capitalist. The Webbs agree with Marx that it is the transformation of the independent producer into a permanent wage earner in the capitalist wage system which leads to unionization. But the unions do not develop as part of a growing revolutionary movement for the Webbs; they exist simply as economic protection devices for workers.

Selig Perlman, on the other hand, rejects the idea of class consciousness as an explanation for the origin of trade unions and substitutes for it the notion of "job consciousness." Perlman rejects the entire idea of class, insisting that all manual laborers—peasants, modern wage earners and medieval master craftsmen—be organized into a single category termed "manualists." It is not until the "manualists" become aware of a scarcity of opportunity, Perlman maintains, that they band together into unions for the purpose of protecting their jobs and apportioning available employment opportunities on an equitable basis.

Psychological theorists—Carleton Parker, Robert Hoxie, Frank Tannenbaum, and Thorstein Veblen—consider the rise of labor unions to be the result of the workers' psychological reactions to an individualist, industrial society. Parker sees collective worker action almost as a form of pathology, for which he prescribes a change in public policies. Hoxie believes that there is no *one* social psychology for workers; different groupings of workers will develop differing psychological outlooks. Each psychological outlook leads to a unique functional type of union. According to Tannenbaum, unions are formed in reaction to the alienation and loss of community in an atomized, individualistic society. Through the union, workers recreate a new society based on status rather than economic individualism. Veblen sees the modern industrial society, with its scientific mentality, undermining the workers' faith in private property and "natural rights." Thus he predicts unions will originate and develop as a subversive force, although he modifies his views in later writings. Unlike the revolutionary theorists, business unionists, and the Webbs, this group of thinkers rejects economic gain as the driving force in the movement toward unionization.

A number of theorists—moral, anti-union, and industrial pluralist—either do not develop a clear explanation of the origin of labor organizations or ignore the topic altogether. Based on their writings, we can only hazard a guess as to their views. It is likely that both Richard Ely and the authors of the papal encyclicals view labor movements as arising from the natural attempt by human beings to create organizations for human betterment under the existing social and economic conditions. The primary contention of the anti-union theorists would seem to be that labor organizations arise when there is both the ability and the opportunity to create a labor monopoly. Lacking these two circumstances, they imply, unions are unlikely to develop or prosper. Industrial pluralist theorists like Kerr, Dunlop, Harbison, and Myers imply that conditions for labor movement beginnings will vary depending on the nature of the ruling elite in society. Under all circumstances, the labor movement—whether created by or in opposition to the elite —will arise in reaction to pressure by that elite.

A broad diversity of views also characterizes the works of labor theorists on the essential function and behavior of the labor movement. Marxists advocate economic and independent political action as essential functions of labor unions: only by defending the interests of the workers at the workplace and simultaneously challenging the capitalist state can labor unions advance the thinking of their members from a narrower trade union consciousness to higher levels of class consciousness. Syndicalists, while espousing the revolutionary goals of Marxism and its appeal for continued economic struggle by the workers and their unions, strongly object to union involvement in politics. Working-class objectives can only be achieved by the direct action of the workers themselves at the point of production and not through any form of parliamentary or political intervention, syndicalists proclaim. New Left theorists such as André Gorz and Stanley Aronowitz demonstrate elements of both Marxist and syndicalist thinking. But however they combine or revise earlier theories, and whatever the role they assign to the working class, they see the labor movement as an instrument in the radical transformation of capitalist society.

John R. Commons and Selig Perlman, on the other hand, see the labor movement as a mechanism for workers to integrate into, rather than oppose, the capitalist system. The labor movement functions as an interest group for workers within a competitive market economy: the trade unions function to increase labor's bargaining power, particularly over matters of job control. Commons and Perlman therefore reject any kind of wide ranging political action by unions which is not directly related to their economic function.

The Webbs also see labor unions as concerned primarily with protecting the economic interests of their workers. However, the Webbs consider the labor movement an essential part of a broader movement to reform the system by humanizing working conditions and providing a livable wage for all. Nonetheless, the labor movement is not to take on a broad political agenda, but to enter the political arena only to help extend industrial democracy at the workplace and eventually throughout industrial society.

Psychological theorists view the labor movement as performing a number of social functions. They agree with the revolutionary and business unionist advocates that labor organizations advance the economic interests of their members, but they do not see this as their prime or sole function. Of greater importance to the psychological theorists is the

5

social-psychological role of the labor movement. What that role is varies with the theorist, but in all cases the group psychology of the workers determines the essential function which organized labor plays.

To the moral theorists labor organizations are basically ethical institutions designed to advance the morality and religious discipline of their members. This can best be achieved through trade union efforts to ensure that workers receive a just wage and through support of meaningful social reform. The papal encyclicals also emphasize that this requires guidance by the Catholic church for proper implementation.

Whereas all of the above groups see labor unions as performing a positive role in society, the anti-union theorists view labor organizations as an antisocial force inherently antagonistic to a capitalist economic system. Unions, they emphasize, are economic institutions with monopolistic control over the labor supply whose primary purpose is to raise wages, restrict output, and raise the cost of goods to the entire community. The result is that society suffers at the expense of a few. The solution is to restrict labor union behavior.

Unlike the revolutionary theorists who accorded labor a crucial role in societal change, the industrial pluralists see labor as a generally passive actor in the transformation of society. It is not the industrial work force which controls the levers of power but a new professional elite whose members are indispensable to the functioning of an advanced industrial society. They view unions as bargaining organizations capable of adapting to a new but probably diminished role in a changed industrial world.

Labor theorists also share different views on the ultimate goals of the labor movement. Marxists view trade unions as an essential and instrumental force in the revolutionary transformation of capitalism. Syndicalists share this vision, but place labor unions in an even more prominent role as *the* instrument of revolution. New Left theorists develop more complicated and intricate goals for labor organizations, but in all cases they relate the ultimate goals of organized labor to the fundamental transformation of capitalist society. Commons and Perlman argue that labor unions, unless captured by revolutionary intellectuals, will remain pragmatic and job-oriented, their activities centered at the workplace. Ultimately, unions want protection from the menace of the marketplace and a measure of job control. The Webbs agree that labor unions play an influential role in the evolutionary progress toward a society based on industrial democracy. Promoting industrial efficiency, elevating standards of life for workers, increasing skills and education, and engaging in political activities through the democratic state to ensure better standards for all will lead to this ultimate goal.

The psychological theorists perceive ultimate goals of labor organizations as entirely dependent on the social psychology of the workers within those organizations. Thus the ultimate goals vary with the theorist and can range from the reestablishment of an earlier, status-bound society (Tannenbaum) to revolutionary change of a syndicalist or socialist nature (early Veblen). Protestant and Catholic theorists regard unions as a vehicle to bring about the moral regeneration of society. Labor organizations should, therefore, protect workers' economic interests, seek social justice, promote peace and harmony, and strengthen family life. This is but a step leading to an eventual partnership between labor and management. Class harmony rather than class struggle is the eventual goal of this school of thought. Exactly how labor organizations will achieve this objective depends on the theorist, but the ultimate goal is the same.

The anti-union theorists see organized labor as having ultimate goals of only the narrowest, most selfish nature. In the milder version (Friedman), the ultimate goal is to gouge the public through artificially high labor costs. In the strongest version (Simons), the ultimate goal is the destruction of the entire economic system and all enterprises within it, with loss of freedom and democracy as the inevitable accompaniment. Pluralist industrialist theorists see labor organizations as eventually evolving into professional associations. Trade unions ultimately aim for the nonideological goals of a special interest group rather than the ideological goals of a class movement. Occupational status goals will predominate in the end. Galbraith also sees the unions' traditional, class-based goals disappearing in the future, but offers no clear-cut substitutes. For Galbraith, unions are losing their significance and reason for being. Any new ultimate goals will be forced upon them for their survival.

The broad range of possible explanations as indicated by .this brief overview of labor movement theories amplifies the extraordinary diversity of those theories which seek to interpret worker motivation and trade union behavior. In the following chapters, the theorists speak for themselves, and the reader may make his or her own judgment as to which theory or combination of theories best satisfies the criteria for an acceptable theory of the labor movement.

---

[1]Mark Perlman, *Labor Union Theories in America: Background and Development* (Evanston, Ill.: Row, Peterson, 1958).

# ONE

**Establishing the Framework for a Theory
of the Labor Movement**

## Introduction

Exactly what questions should a labor theorist attempt to answer? John Dunlop addresses this question in the following selection. According to Dunlop, a fully developed labor theory would answer the following four questions:

(1) How do we account for the labor movement's emergence?
(2) How do we explain its pattern of growth and development?
(3) What are the labor movement's ultimate goals?
(4) Why do workers join labor organizations?

The theories presented in this book can be evaluated by how well they answer these four questions. Many theorists will address only one or two of the questions; few will integrate into their theory a complete answer to all four. This merely demonstrates the rudimentary nature of labor theorizing at this time. Dunlop himself makes only a preliminary attempt to answer his four questions. He explains the origins of the labor movement in terms of the strategic role of workers, both in the market structure and technologically. Unions and labor organizations historically arise first in strategically important sectors. Favorable community institutions of control, such as the legal, educational, and communications systems, are also important determinants of labor organization. And finally, values and beliefs favorable to a labor movement are necessary and important influences. The pattern of growth and development of the labor movement is attributed to these same factors. Dunlop especially notes the influence of laws and community institutions in driving the labor movement into a more political or less political direction. Dunlop leaves the questions of ultimate goals and why workers join relatively unexplored in this essay. Nevertheless, his "scaffolding, or method of approach," provides a highly useful framework within which to view theories of the labor movement.

The reader who wishes to probe deeper may wish to expand upon Dunlop's framework by exploring a number of auxiliary questions. Question 1, for example, might lead one to situate the theory in a broader social and historical framework by asking: How does the theory explain the origin of the modern working class? What is the historical or sociological setting within which the labor movement arose? Answers to questions like these will relate the theory more closely to traditional questions and theories in the fields of history and the social sciences.

Question 2 invites questions of both a structuralist and functionalist nature: What is the labor movement's main function (or essential function) within our economic and social system? What factors explain the difference between the labor movements of different countries? How have changes in the economic system, the class structure, or the political system changed the labor movement? Here again the variety of questions raised for the different disciplines of the social sciences embeds the theory of the labor movement in a larger theoretical perspective.

Question 3 raises other questions: Is the labor movement fundamentally favorable to, or antagonistic to the capitalist economic system? Is the labor movement unitary enough to have *one* set of ultimate goals? Would the labor movement's goals change fundamentally under another economic system, such as socialism? Nearly all the theorists in this book grapple with questions of ultimate goals; their differing answers reveal a wide disparity of economic and political analyses. And perhaps more than elsewhere, it is here that we find basic differences in values and philosophical orientation—issues not easily answered by empirical evidence.

Question 4 brings up a whole host of questions: Do different categories of workers (skilled and unskilled, blue collar and white collar, etc.) have different expectations of, and uses for the labor movement? Are relationships between the leadership and the rank-

and-file important determinants of how unions are perceived? The social psychology of workers' attitudes toward unions involves these and a number of other questions.

Finally, we should note that a number of theorists go one step beyond Dunlop's framework by abandoning the attempt to view the labor movement from a detached, or "neutral" perspective. Instead they adopt the "internal" viewpoint of a participant, or of one attempting to promote the goals and interests of the labor movement. If one takes this partisan, normative point of view, a number of other important questions arise as part of one's theory. (The same is of course true if one takes a partisan, anti-union point of view.) Thus Dunlop's "value-free" approach is replaced by one which explicitly draws out the value judgments and political implications of each theory. This view is best illustrated by Professor Wells Keddie of Rutgers University. In a worksheet designed to help students understand and evaluate labor theories (not included in this volume),[1] Keddie raises the following questions:

(1) How is the origin of the working class explained by the theory?
(2) What are the circumstances which lead to the development of the labor movement?
(3) What is the essential function of the labor movement in a capitalist economy?
(4) What is the relationship between political and economic activities of unions, if any?
(5) Is the labor movement (or, are unions) favorable or antagonistic to capitalism?
(6) What factors account for observed differences between labor movements in different countries?
(7) What, if any, historic mission or predestined role is accorded the labor movement?

Of vital importance to Keddie are the assumptions made by the theorist about (a) the existence of a working class; (b) the existence or non-existence of "working class consciousness"; (c) the "basic nature" of human beings—are we acquisitive? violent? selfish or unselfish? (d) the influence of economic conditions on the outlook or thinking of humans; (e) the viability of the capitalist economic system; and (f) any other important areas. This framework for evaluating labor theories has a strongly valuative and political component. For precisely that reason it should be kept in mind in examining all theories in this volume since each, whether explicitly political or not, has an impact on the present structure of society. Thus the reader should make reference to both the framework developed by Dunlop and that developed by Keddie. Both are useful in highlighting features of the theories for purposes of comparison and evaluation.

---

[1]Wells Keddie, "Theories of the Labor Movement" (unpublished manuscript, Pennsylvania State University, University Park, Pa., 1969).

# 1
## The Development of Labor Organization:
## A Theoretical Framework

JOHN T. DUNLOP                                                                    1948

"The facts do not tell their own story; they must be cross-examined. They must be carefully analyzed, systematized, compared and interpreted."[1] This conclusion is an indictment of the all too frequent approach to the development of the labor movement, in which "history" and "theory" are separate and non-permeable compartments.

Under the caption of "history of labor" are chronicled what purport to be collections of fact and sequences of fact. Under the heading of "theory of labor organization" are found "explanations" conjured out of inner consciousness with only occasional and convenient reference to the past. The "history" and "theory" of the labor movement can have little meaning in isolation. But it is particularly the failure of theoretical apparatus that accounts for the lack of greater understanding of the development of the labor movement and the paucity of significant research. Indeed, despite all the epoch-making developments in the field of labor organization in the past fifteen years, there has been virtually no contribution to the "theory" and scarcely a reputable narrative of this period exists.

This essay constitutes a re-examination of fashions of thinking in theories of the labor movement. It proceeds from the initial conviction that any theory of the labor movement must first establish its criteria. Just what questions is a theory of labor organization supposed to answer? Only after this task has been explicitly recognized can there be critical discussion of the development of the labor movement.

The body of economic theory attempts to explain the allocation of resources. Business cycle theories present systems of propositions to make intelligible the fluctuations of the economic system. In similar terms, what is the *pièce de résistance* of a theory of the labor movement? By what standards or tests is it possible to prefer one theory to another? What behavior must such a theory explain to be judged a "closer fit" than another model?

### Explanations of the Labor Movement

The literature on theories of the labor movement, if carefully analyzed, reveals at least four questions which have been the concern of investigators. As far as can be determined however, nowhere are these questions posed explicitly.

1. How is one to account for the origin or emergence of labor organizations? What conditions are necessary and what circumstances stimulate the precipitation of labor organization? Why have some workers organized and others not?

2. What explains the pattern of growth and development of labor organizations? What factors are responsible for the sequence and form in which organizations have emerged in various countries, industries, crafts, and companies? Since there is great diversity in the patterns of development, any theory of the labor movement must account for these differences.

3. What are the ultimate goals of the labor movement? What is its relationship to the future of capitalism? What is its role in the socialist or communist state?

4. Why do individual workers join labor organizations? What system of social psychology accounts for this behavior of the employee?

Most writings on theories of the labor movement have in effect been concerned with one or several of these questions. They show a tendency to seek a single and usually oversimplified statement of the development of labor organization. But the labor movement is highly complex and many-sided. The "history" does not readily lend itself to any single formula.

■  ■  ■

### The Determinants of Labor Organization

The labor movement, or any similarly complex social organization, may be fruitfully explored by an examination of four interrelated factors: technology, market structures and the character of competition, community institutions of control, and ideas and beliefs.

1. Technology.   This term includes not only changes in machinery and in methods of production but concomitant developments in the size and organization of production and distribution units.

2. Market structures and character of competition.   The term comprehends the growth of markets, the changes in the locus of financial control as distinguished from the size of production units, the development of buying and selling institutions in both product and factor markets, and the emergence of specialized functions and personnel within these organizations.

3. Wider community institutions.   This phrase is intended to include among others the role of the press, radio, and other means of communication in the society, the formal educational system for both general and vocational training, the courts, governmental administrative agencies, and political parties and organizations.

4. Ideas and beliefs. This caption is a short cut for the value judgments and mores that permeate and identify a social system.

Such a comprehensive scaffolding or method of approach does not in itself constitute a theory of the labor movement. It claims only to facilitate the development of such a theoretical system. It compels reflection on the range of mutual influences operative in any society. Such a comprehensive framework of reference assists in asking significant questions; the complex interrelations between the labor movement and any society are sharpened. The labor movement as seen in the context of its "total" environment. This fourfold scheme is a set of preliminary tools through which the labor movement may be reconnoitered and analyzed. The facts of labor history may more readily be cross-examined.

It must be emphasized that these four factors are intended not merely to facilitate the cross-sectional study of the labor movement at any one given time but even more to assist in the analysis of the growth and change of the labor movement over time. The interaction among technological and market factors, community institutions, and ideas and beliefs must be used to account for the development of the labor movement.

Social systems or institutions go through periods of relative stability and through other periods of spectacular and tortuous change. Periods of stability may be regarded as involving a certain equilibrium among these four factors. That is, a given system of technology and markets requires or is compatible with only a limited number of community institutions and value judgments and ideas. The converse is equally true; a given system of ideas and community organization is compatible only with particular types of market and technological arrangements. In these terms, equilibrium in the social system may be said to exist when these four groups of factors are compatible one with another. Equilibrium may involve an unchanging condition or rates of change among the factors which are congruous. Change the technology of a system and there are required alterations in the other three factors, or change the value judgments and ideas of a community and there must be changes in market systems and technology.

The actual course of history does not disclose the isolated reaction to the change in a single factor any more than a series of prices reveals directly the unique effects of shifts in demand or movements along demand schedules. A comprehensive theory of a society should indicate the result of varying one of these factors—the others unchanged —when the system as a whole is in initial equilibrium. The actual course of events consists in continuous and inseparable interaction between the secondary effects of the initial change and new impacts on the social system.

The procedure suggested in this section would analyze the labor movement by indicating the change in each of these four factors over the past and the consequent impact on the emergence and the manner of growth of the labor movement. The labor movement is seen as the product of its total environment. As labor organizations grow they become an independent factor affecting the course of their own destiny.

### Long-run Trends in Union Growth

In thinking of the development of the labor movement, it will be helpful to distinguish between long-term trends and variations around these tendencies. The evolution of social institutions does not take place at uniform rates. The process is more like waves eating away at the base of a cliff, which eventually crashes into the sea. The present section will be concerned with the trend aspects of the development of the labor movement, while that which follows will adapt this analysis to the pulsation of growth of labor organization.

No working community is ever completely unorganized. Any group of human beings associated together for any length of time develops a community in which there are recognized standards of conduct and admitted leaders. ". . . in industry and in other human situations the administrator is dealing with well-knit human groups and not with a horde of individuals."[2] A group of workers which continues together will establish standards of a "fair" day's work and acceptable norms of behavior in the views of the working group as a whole. Not everyone, of course, will conform to these standards, but there will be recognized norms. In the same way one worker will soon be recognized as a person whose judgment is sought on personal problems; another will be regarded as having superior skill, whose advice on the technical aspects of the job is highly regarded; still another will be accepted as spokesman in expressing the feelings of the group to the management. At times these functions may be combined in the same person. Whenever human beings live or work together the informal group develops. This fact is true today; it no doubt preceded the first formal labor organization.

Formal trade union organization has on many occasions been precipitated out of this type of informal organization. Some danger to the stability and security of the informal group frequently serves as the immediate occasion for formalizing an organization. The threat may come from the management in the form of a wage reduction or a substitution of women on men's jobs, or the arbitrary discipline of a member of the work community. The threat may have its origin outside the firm, as in the introduction of machinery made necessary by competitive conditions. Very frequently the formal organization may last for a short time, only during the period of greatest immediacy of the danger.

The formal group may be assisted and encouraged by outside organizers. The initiative may be taken by the professional organizer, or he may be called in after an initial step. The congealing of these informal organizations into formal structures follows no uniform pattern. The "intellectual" does not here receive the prominence in the development of the labor movement subscribed to by some writers. There can be little doubt that, in any going institution, "rationalizations" are developed—a task necessarily intellectual in content. Such formal statements often help in extending organization. The processes of rationalization are here treated as an essential step in the growth of the union movement, but the "intellectual" does not have a dominant role.

Wage earners join unions for a great many different reasons. They generally involve various aspects of the relation of the individual workman to his immediate work community and, at times, his relation to the larger locality and national life. The fundamental point, however, is that any analysis of the development of labor organizations must proceed from the recognition that work communities, prior to formal organization, are not simply random aggregates of individual workmen. Typically, informal coagulations exist. While every labor organization probably has not grown out of nor adopted the leadership of the informal group, it is difficult to conceive of a labor organization which has not been substantially influenced by these basic facts of any work community.

There have been, no doubt, many cases in which the informal organization has been precipitated into dramatic formal action only to lapse quickly and pass away. There have been many such outbursts against arbitrary behavior and substantial grievances. But in some circumstances continuing organization has developed and in others it has lapsed. The discussion which follows suggests, with reference to the American scene, two factors that were necessary to the emergence of organization historically and two that have been decisive in determining the trend of development.

(1) How is the student of labor organization to account for the location in the productive process of the emergence of continuing unions? Successful organization has required that workmen occupy a *strategic* position in the technological or market structures. In any *technological* process for producing and distributing goods and services, there are some workers who have greater strategic position than others; that is, these workers are able to shut down, to interrupt, or to divert operations more easily than others. They furnish labor services at decisive points in the productive stream where the withdrawal of services quickly breaks the whole stream. The productive process has its bottlenecks. Frequently these workers are skilled. The term strategic, however, is not identical with skill. It means sheer bargaining power by virtue of location and position in the productive process. Locomotive engineers, loom fixers in the textile industry, molders in the casting industry, and cutters in the garment industry well illustrate the concept. The withdrawal of the services of these relatively few men almost immediately compels, for technological reasons, the complete shutting down or diversion of operations of the plant.

Analogously, in the *structure of markets* there are firms, and consequently there are employees, who are in strategic positions to affect the whole stream of production and distribution. Employees are technologically strategic by virtue of their position *within* an individual firm. Workers are in a strategic position, marketwise, by virtue of their position in the structure of markets. In the market framework they can most readily exact a price. Not only are the teamsters in a position to tie up operations (technological position), but also their employers are in a position to pass on cost increases to their customers (market position). Another illustration would be a craft, such as the bricklayers, where cost increases may be passed on to the small house-builder whose bargaining position is such as to force absorption. The musicians constitute probably an even better example. The technological and market strategic positions are never completely disassociated, although it is helpful to make the conceptual distinction.

Labor organization emerges among employees who have strategic market or technological positions. They have bargaining power. They can make it hurt. These strategic employees may be regarded as "points of infection" or "growth cones," to borrow the latter term from embryology, for the spread of labor organization.

How far will organization spread around the original "point of infection"? In some instances organization is confined to these most strategic workers and a pure craft union may result. In other instances, these workers become the nucleus of the organization that encompasses other workers in the same plant. The cell wall of the organization may be pushed coextensively with the plant, and an industrial union result. The boundary line may be drawn any place in between and may in fact fluctuate a good deal over time. The analogous point applies to the growth of unions in different types of firms. The boundary line of the union may be stopped from crossing into firms with different product market conditions. The phenomenon of a union organized in commercial building but unable or uninterested in pushing into housing is familiar in construction.

There are barriers to extending the cell wall of organization that arise within the strategic group of workers themselves as well as from the opposition of those outside this nucleus. On occasions, the most strategic group will prefer to remain so purist that developments resulting in differentiation of work among these strategic workers will produce a split in the cell and two organizations result. Expanding the group would dilute the gains of organization for the existing nucleus. Labor organizations in the printing industry in this country have taken this pattern of development. From the original group of strategically positioned printers have split off the pressmen, the photoengravers, the stereotypers, the bookbinders, and others, as specialized operations have developed.

Resistance to the expansion of the strategic group may arise from the fact that those outside the nucleus may have such high rates of turnover as to make organization impossible. Thus the butchers in retail outlets did not originally include part-time employees around these stores. The boundary line of the union may be confined because those outside may feel that they can enjoy any benefits won by the strategic group without the costs of organization. It is a mistake to interpret historically the structure (in the sense of boundary lines) of American trade unionism, primarily in terms of a slavish following of the "principle of craft unionism." This analysis suggests a more general view.

Necessary to the emergence and growth of permanent labor organizations have been workers who are located in strategic positions in the market or technological framework. Organization may be treated as expanding from these centers in different patterns and to varying extents. It may be helpful to illustrate this formal analysis with examples from the early growth of labor organizations. In both the men's and women's clothing industry the first group organized was the cutters. Their key position in the technological operation of the making of garments gave them a dominant position in early organizations in these industries. For a while, organization was concentrated in this group. Later the cutters became the nucleus in the women's garment industry for the International Ladies' Garment Workers' Union.

Consider the development of the coal mining industry. Organization was first significant among the contract miners. As a "petty contractor," the miner owned his own tools, purchased his own powder, and worked without supervision. Starting from these strategic employees in the early coal mining industry as a nucleus, organization among the miners gradually expanded to include in a single organization all employees, including those who worked above ground as well as underground.

In the cotton textile industry, the loom fixer has had a position of technological prominence. The failure to keep the looms in running order would soon force the shutdown of the weaving shed. There are other strategic groups of employees, such as the spinners and the slasher tenders. In a sense, one finds multiple points of organization in this industry. In some cases the craft-like union resulted and in others the nucleus expanded to include sufficient other groups to be designated as a semi-industrial arrangement.

In the steel industry, the Amalgamated Iron, Tin, and Steel Workers Union was formed out of strategically located groups in various branches of the industry. The boilers and puddlers in the making of iron, and the heaters, rollers, and roughers from the finishing operations, formed the bulk of organization. This nucleus failed to expand and in fact could not maintain its own position until the emergence of the CIO. These illustrations could be multiplied many times: the linemen in the growth of the Brotherhood of Electrical Workers, the jiggermen and kilnmen in the pottery industry, and the blowers, gatherers, flatteners, and cutters in the flat glass industry. A union leader described an organizing drive as follows: ". . . we had all of the polishing department, and those men were the core of our whole organization."[3] Such instances provide flesh and blood to the formal scheme outlined above. The simple notion again is a strategic nucleus, which may expand in different patterns, depending on conditions and ideas within the union and the environment without.

The analysis that has just been outlined must be thought of as applicable to the task of understanding the development of the American labor movement in the context of community institutions which prevailed prior to the Wagner Act. Organization by ballot rather than by the picket line places much less emphasis upon strategic employees in the technological and market scene. Organization may proceed instead from those most susceptible to union appeals for votes. Furthermore, the unit or boundary which a union would select for an election is apt to be quite different from that which it would select to defend on the picket line. It has not been generally recognized that the Wagner Act has had as much effect on the organizing strategy and structure of labor organizations as upon relations with the employer.

The concept of strategic workers cannot be as useful to an understanding of the development of the labor movement today as it is for the explanation of the past. Still it may help to explain stresses and strains within unions and particular wage policies.

(2) A second necessary condition in the emergence of organization is the view of the employees that they shall look forward to spending a substantial proportion of their lifetime as workmen. This factor has been gradually developing over the past hundred years and has been influenced by the rate of increase in gainful employment. It is also necessary that a substantial proportion in any given work community look forward to remaining in the same or similar work community. Negatively, organization is difficult, if not impossible, where individuals expect to work themselves out of the status of wage earners, or where they expect to remain wage earners but a short time because of anticipated withdrawals from the labor market, or where the rate of turnover and migration is so rapid and so erratic and random as to preclude stability in organization. In a period or in situations in which individual employees expect to become foremen and then owners of their own business, permanent and stable organization is virtually impossible. One of the problems of organizing women arises from the fact that they expect only a short

working life and then plan to retire to the more arduous duties of the household. Migratory labor has been notoriously difficult to form into permanent organizations.

(3) Certain types of community institutions stimulate, and others retard, the emergence and growth of labor organizations. ". . . there had developed, in effect a double standard of social morality for labor and capital. . . . The story of the gradual modification of this double standard can be read in the history of labor organization and in the record of social legislation on state and federal governments over the past fifty years."[4] The legal system may actually preclude organization, as would have been the case had the doctrine of the early conspiracy cases been generally applied. This is not to suggest that the passage of a law could have wiped out all organization. Such a legal doctrine, however, acted as an obstruction to the growth of organization. Analogously, a policy of government to encourage organization, such as adopted in the Wagner Act, tends to accelerate the growth of labor unions.

The role of the wider community influence on the emergence and pattern of growth of the labor movement must be more broadly conceived than the legal system. Both the struggle for free public schools and the impact of widespread general and technical education have left their mark on the American labor movement. The labor press has drawn heavily on the conventions of the daily newspaper. The hostility of the ordinary press to labor organizations over much of the past in this country in turn helped to set the tone of the labor press.

The *emergence* of labor organizations has been related in preceding pages to the strategic position of wage earners in a market and technological setting. But the subsequent form of the labor organization will be decisively molded by the environment of these wider community and national institutions. In some contexts the labor organization has developed into an almost exclusively political body; in others political activity is minor. Special local or industry conditions, such as prevail in the field of municipal employment, may lead to substantial political activity even though the dominant pattern in the country may involve little such action.

The relation of the labor movement to the future of capitalism (question 3) must not be viewed narrowly as an issue of the extent or character of political activity. The growth in modern technology in the setting of the business corporation has gradually yielded a society predominately made up of wage and salary earners. Wage earners have constituted a minor element in previous communities made up largely of self-employed farmers, serfs, slaves, or peasants. Unique in human history has been the creation of a society where the vast majority of persons earn a livelihood as wage and salary earners. (Two-thirds of the national income is wage and salary payment). Under these circumstances when wage earners organize into labor organizations, as traced in previous sections, these bodies may be expected to exercise considerable political power in the community. The center of political power ultimately shifts as the character of the groups within the community changes.

If the locus of political power shifts to the degree that the labor organization becomes the dominant political power, there is growing evidence that the function and role of the union changes. The attitude toward the right to strike, compulsory arbitration, and production drives shifts away from the customary patterns under capitalism. This transition cannot but involve serious controversy within the labor movement.

(4) Over and above these technological, market, and community influences on the labor movement has been the system of values, the ethos, and the beliefs of the community. Professor Schlesinger has summarized the traditional attributes of the American most noted by foreign observers: "a belief in the univeral obligation to work; the urge to

move about; a high standard of comfort for the average man; an absence of permanent class barriers; the neglect of abstract thinking and of the aesthetic side of life . . ."⁵ Many of these characteristics are to be traced to the "long apprenticeship to the soil."

It should not be hard to understand why labor organization would be difficult in a day in which men believed that individual advancement was to be achieved solely by work, where leisure was a vice, where economic destiny depended solely upon one's ability to work and save, where poverty could only be the reward for sloth, where the poor deserved their fate, and where the public care of the impoverished was regarded as encouragement of idleness. As Poor Richard says:

Employ thy Time well, if thou meanst to gain Leisure;
And, since thou art not sure of a Minute, throw not away an Hour.

Trouble springs from Idleness, and grievous Toil from needless Ease.

For Age and Want, save while you may,
No Morning Sun lasts a whole day.

I think the best way of doing good to the poor, is, not making them easy *in* poverty but leading or driving them *out* of it.

These admonitions of Benjamin Franklin are hardly the ideal text for the organization of a labor union. This set of ethical standards which has pervaded the ethos of the American community until recently places the economic destiny of a workman in his own hands rather than in a labor union.

The political and economic philosophy of the founding fathers, beyond standards of individual behavior, came to be adapted to the advancing order of corporate business. "This ideology was derived in part from deep-rooted folk ideas, in part from the sanctions of religion, in part from concepts of natural science. But whatever the source, its arguments rested upon the concepts of individualism, equality of opportunity, and the promise of well-being under a profit economy. The conservative defense, crystallized by business leaders and by allied members of the legal, educational, and literary professions, was popularized in sermons, speeches, novels, slogans, and essays. It became part and parcel of American popular thought."⁶

Moreover, the dominant economic thinking on the determination of wage rates (the wage-fund doctrine), by the community, could hardly have been favorable a hundred years ago to the growth of labor organizations. ". . . there is no use in arguing against any one of the four fundamental rules of arithmetic. The question of wages is a question of division. It is complained that the quotient is too small. Well, then, how many ways are there to make a quotient larger? Two ways. Enlarge your dividend, the divisor remaining the same, and the quotient will be larger; lessen your divisor, the dividend remaining the same, and the quotient will be larger."⁷ There was no place for a union; it could serve no legitimate function. The intellectual climate of political economy changed and became more conducive to labor organization over the years.

The *trend* of standards of personal morality and social and economic philosophy has moved in directions more congenial to the flowering of unionism. Contrast the entreaties of Poor Richard and Horatio Alger with the admonitions of Sir William Beveridge! Leisure is now a virtue rather than a vice; saving may be a community vice rather than the epitome of individual morality; the economically less fortunate are to be sustained by comprehensive social security rather than to be left to sink or swim. The trade union has a more nourishing ethos.

The dominant ethical judgments pervading the community have been a vital factor influencing the growth of labor organization not only as they affect the individual workman but also as they shape and mold the character of the labor organization itself. The primacy of property rights in the American tradition is partly responsible for the dominance of the concept of exclusive jurisdiction in the American Federation of Labor constitution. Each union "owns" its jurisdiction in the same way that a businessman owns a piece of property. These community values have also decisively determined the attitude of the community toward social insurance. It is no accident that the American Federation of Labor was opposed to a program of compulsory insurance until 1932.

The environment of ideas and beliefs in which the labor organization developed has included the special role of the labor intelligentsia or the intellectual. "Capitalist evolution produces a labor movement which obviously is not the creation of the intellectual group. But it is not surprising that such an opportunity and the intellectual demiurge should find each other. Labor never craved intellectual leadership but intellectuals invaded labor politics. They had an important contribution to make: they verbalized, supplied theories and slogans for it, . . . made it conscious of itself and in so doing changed its meaning."[8] The formulation of a creed or folklore or rationalization is an important function in the development of the labor movement, just as in any organization. The function needs to be kept in proportion. In the American scene this process seems not to have been the province of a special class nor fashioned through different means in labor organizations than in other groups in the community. The English and Continental experience is different in this respect.

This section has sketched some suggestions toward an analytical view of the emergence and development of the labor movement out of its total environment, regarding that environment as the technological processes, the market structure, the community institutions, and the value judgments of the society. The emphasis has been upon the long-term *trend* of development.

### Short-run Variations in Trade Union Membership

The growth of the labor movement has not been uniform and the four factors which have been used to approach the long-term trends in the labor movement were not all operative at the same rate. This section is concerned with the deviations from trend, in particular the periods of advance in labor organization.

Even a cursory view of the American labor movement identifies seven major periods of rapid expansion in organization. The following tabulation identifies these periods; it also notes the estimated membership of the organizations at the end of a given period.

| Periods | Dates | Membership |
|---|---|---|
| Awakening | 1827–1836 | 300,000 |
| Nationalism | 1863–1872 | 300,000 |
| Great Upheaval | 1881–1886 | 1,000,000 |
| Mass Advancement | 1896–1904 | 2,000,000 |
| First World War | 1917–1920 | 5,000,000 |
| New Deal | 1933–1937 | 8,000,000 |
| Second World War | 1941–1945 | 14,000,000 |

These seven periods can be divided into two distinct types. The dominant characteristics of a period do not preclude some elements of the opposite type. The first group of periods were years of wartime, with rapid increases in the cost of living and stringency in the labor market. This group includes the periods of Nationalism (1863–1872), Mass

Advancement (1896–1904), the First World War (1917–1920), and the Second World War (1941–1945). The rapid expansion in membership is to be explained almost entirely by developments in the labor market: the rapid rise in the cost of living and the shortage of labor supply relative to demand. Under these circumstances a trade union helped to enable wage earners to increase their wages to an extent more closely approximating the rise in prices. The individual worker joined unions to push up his wages; the tightness in the labor market and the general level of profits enabled the union to achieve results. Organization in these instances may be regarded as predominately a market reflex.

Contrasting with these years is the second type of period, to be regarded as one of fundamental unrest. Organization of unions represented a basic dissatisfaction with the performance of the economic system and the society in general. Such were the years of Awakening (1827–1836), the Great Upheaval (1881–1886), and the New Deal (1933–1937). It is these three periods which call for special explanation.

It is well established in the analysis of economic fluctuations that modern capitalism has moved in certain long waves. These long waves or Kondratieff cycles are generally regarded as approximately fifty years in length with twenty-five years of good times and twenty-five years of bad times, and are distinguished from the shorter business cycles. Professor Alvin H. Hansen's dating scheme is typical.[9]

| *Good Times* | *Bad Times* |
| --- | --- |
| 1787–1815 | 1815–1843 |
| 1843–1873 | 1873–1897 |
| 1897–1920 | 1920–1940 |
| 1940– | |

The long wave represents a fundamental structural period in modern capitalism. The first of these waves has been designated as that of the Industrial Revolution, the second the Age of Railroads, and the third the Electrical Period. The fourth may be known as that of the airplane and atomic power.

For the present purposes it is significant to note that each one of the three periods of major upheaval and fundamental unrest came at the bottom of the period of bad times in the long wave. The period of good times in the long wave is associated with a cluster of major innovations. There follows a period of generally declining prices (1815–43, 1873–97, 1920–40), during which the shorter business cycles are severe and intense. The three major periods of upheaval follow severe depressions. It is suggested that after prolonged periods of high unemployment for a substantial number in the work force and after years of downward pressure on wages exerted by price declines, labor organizations emerge which are apt to be particularly critical of the fundamental tenets of the society and the economy.

These three fundamental periods of upsurge in the labor movement must also be related to important developments in community institutions and ideas or value judgments. Thus, the first period was the Age of Jacksonian Democracy, the second the Populist, and the third the New Deal. The labor movement of 1827–1836 has been treated as an alignment of "producer classes." The Knights of Labor in the period 1881–1886 has been referred to as the last great middle-class uprising. The expansion of the labor movement in the New Deal period was primarily a working class movement. The first period rallied around the slogan of free education, the second used the watchword of shorter hours, the third was characterized by the accent on security.

## Concluding Remarks

The scaffolding may now be removed. In the distinctive pattern of growth of the labor movement in this country, one sees in outline form the way in which technology, market structure, community institutions, and the ethos factors have interacted together to yield the labor movement considered as a whole. Special types of these factors in operation in specific industries and localities account for the divergent types and forms of unionism which have developed within the generalized framework. For example, the migratory character of agricultural work and the lumber industry, together with the absence of stability of community, help to account for the type of unionism that originally emerged in this sector, illustrated by the IWW. The unions in the field of local or national government employment have become lobbying agencies by virtue of the practical prohibitions to effective collective bargaining. These specialized forms or species are variations from the main pattern of growth and development arising from special types of environments. In the same way, peculiar national characteristics shape the operation of these factors in comparing labor movements in various countries.

The framework of approach to the labor movement presented here is intended to be suggestive for a renewed interest in the writing of the history of the labor movement in general and in particular sectors. The emphasis upon the interrelations and mutual dependence of four groups of factors has served as the basis for this analysis. Not only is the analysis schematic, but it must be recognized that any simplified schemata must abstract from many complexities of behavior. The formal analysis must not leave the impression of the labor organization as primarily rationalistic. Professor Knight has well said that there is need for "some grasp of the infinitely complex, intangible, and downright contradictory character of men's interests, conscious and unconscious, and their interaction with equally intricate mechanical, biological, neural, and mental processes in forming the pattern of behavior. The great vice is over-simplification . . . ."[10]

---

[1]Talcott Parsons, *The Structure of Social Action* (New York, McGraw-Hill Book Co., 1937), p. 698. [*Reader note:* throughout this volume, editors' footnotes are identified as such and are enclosed in square brackets.]

[2]Elton Mayo, *The Social Problems of an Industrial Civilization* (Cambridge, Harvard Univ. Press, 1945), p. 111.

[3]"From Conflict to Cooperation," *Applied Anthropology*, V (Fall, 1946), p. 9.

[4]Samuel Eliot Morrison and Henry Steele Commager, *The Growth of the American Republic* (Revised and enlarged edition, New York, Oxford Univ. Press, 1937), Vol. II, p. 153.

[5]Arthur Meier Schlesinger, "What Then Is the American, This New Man," reprinted from the *American Historical Review*, XLVIII (January, 1943), pp. 3–4.

[6]Merle Curti, *The Growth of American Thought* (New York, Harper & Bros., 1943), p. 656.

[7]A. L. Perry, *Political Economy*, p. 123, quoted in Francis A. Walker, *The Wage Question* (New York, Henry Holt & Co., 1886), p. 143.

[8]Joseph A. Schumpeter, *Capitalism, Socialism and Democracy* (New York, Harper & Bros., 1942), pp. 153–54.

[9]Alvin H. Hansen, *Fiscal Policy and Business Cycles* (New York, W. W. Norton & Co., 1940), p. 30.

[10]Frank H. Knight, *Risk, Uncertainty, and Profit* (London, London School of Economics and Political Science, 1933), p. xxix.

# TWO

## The Labor Movement as an Agent of Revolution

## Introduction

A number of the earliest theories put forward to explain and provide guidance for the organized labor movement saw it as a component part of a revolutionary transformation of society. In particular, two revolutionary theories have been important historically in the theory and development of labor organizations: Marxism and revolutionary syndicalism. More recently, reevaluations of traditional left-wing theory on trade union and other questions constitute a loose grouping of thought which has come to be known as a "New Left" perspective.

The Marxist theory of the labor movement is a subsidiary part of a much broader theoretical outlook. According to Marx, capitalism is an exploitative economic system which is based upon class distinctions. Just as previous slave and feudal societies exploited and oppressed the actual producers (slaves, peasants, etc.) for the benefit of a dominant class of slaveholders or feudal lords, capitalism creates a numerically large class of propertyless workers (proletarians) who create all wealth but are systematically denied the full fruits of their labor. A small group of capitalists—owners of the major means of production such as factories, mines, businesses, etc.—control the economy and ultimately the political system through their private property rights. Workers are denied economic control and political power; they also are systematically robbed as the capitalists extract enormous wealth from them and live off their labor. According to Marx, then, capitalism is a system based on antagonistic class interests; class struggle between capitalists and workers is inevitable.

Drawing upon an economic analysis which is beyond the scope of our present inquiry, Marx argues that capitalism is beset by internal contradictions which cannot be solved except by the revolutionary overthrow of the system. This revolutionary transformation is possible because the working class has the potential and the need to carry it off. Capitalism creates modern large-scale industry; this in turn shapes the workers and prepares them to be agents of revolution. By causing extreme economic dependence and insecurity for workers, by concentrating workers together in large industrial and business establishments where commonality of interest becomes obvious, by increasing lines of communication between workers in different occupations and geographical areas, by destroying old bonds of intercourse and dependence based on family or nationality, and in a host of other ways, capitalism thus produces its own gravediggers in the modern working class.

The labor movement, according to Marx, has a positive contribution to make to the workers' struggle. Trade unions are the first and most elementary method of organization for self-defense undertaken by workers. In the long run these economic class struggles demand further organization along political lines. Ultimately the class struggle becomes a full-blown struggle over state power. When it wins this contest, the working class will socialize the means of production and create a socialist society. Within this scenario, the trade unions can play an important supportive role. They can provide elementary vehicles of resistance to capitalist control, can defend the immediate economic interests of the workers (within limits), can help workers develop class consciousness and class methods of organization, and can act as "schools" or training grounds for the self-education of workers in preparation for the revolution. *The Communist Manifesto,* written in 1848, is a concise exposition of Marx's views on the history and development of the modern-day working class. In the first part of the *Manifesto,* which is included in our readings, Marx makes brief reference to the origin and future goals of the labor movement. Readings by Marx and other authors further illustrate Marx's theory of the labor movement.

Marx's followers have split into several camps. One of these, which ultimately became known as the Bolshevik or communist camp, was led by V. I. Lenin. Lenin was a Russian revolutionary leader who successfully led the revolution in Russia in 1917. In a famous booklet written in 1902 entitled "What Is To Be Done?" Lenin developed a number of themes on the role of trade unions and the role of a revolutionary party. According to Lenin, workers spontaneously develop only a trade union consciousness that is defensive and limited to issues of economic betterment. The task of a revolutionary party is not to bow to this spontaneous development, but to carry out work to constantly broaden consciousness to a revolutionary critique of the entire society. "What Is To Be Done?" is a sustained polemic against the "Economists" within Lenin's own party who advocated making trade unionist economic agitation the main work of the party. In developing this polemic Lenin puts forth clear views on the role of the trade union, the role of the party, the difference between them and how both fit into the revolutionary process.

Criticisms of Marx and his theories abound. Most, however, attack his entire theory, not his specific role for trade unions within that theory. Probably the most forceful and influential critique of Marx on the question of the labor movement is that of Selig Perlman (see Part III). Perlman conceived his entire theory as an answer to and refutation of Marx. We conclude this section with a critique of Lenin's theory by Thomas T. Hammond. Hammond argues that Lenin has a purely instrumentalist and manipulative view of trade unions that is coupled with an immature impatience with history. The results, Hammond argues, have been negative for workers and trade unions.

The name syndicalism is derived from the French word *syndicalisme,* which means trade unionism. In France it is often referred to as *syndicalisme revolutionnaire.* The doctrine first surfaced during the latter part of the nineteenth century when it was advanced by some French labor leaders who were swayed by anarchist thinking. The movement made considerable headway among French trade unions and, by 1914, exerted a powerful influence on the French working class. It also flourished in a number of other countries, especially Italy and Spain. In the United States, a parallel movement, the Industrial Workers of the World (IWW), developed on a much smaller scale.

At the heart of syndicalist thought is a belief in the inherent unfairness of a system based on wage labor and the immorality of capitalism. An irreconcilable conflict of interests separates the worker from the capitalist and these differences cannot be reconciled even momentarily. The emancipation of the working class can be achieved only by the abolition of a system based on individual ownership of the means of production and distribution and by substituting for it a society whose foundation rests on the communal ownership of all productive forces.

Since the conflict has economic causes, it can be resolved only in the economic arena. Only the working class through its own efforts can deliver itself from wage slavery. Workers must engage in direct action, action taken directly at the point of production without parliamentary involvement or intervention by the state. Syndicalists insist that political power is dependent on and secondary to economic power. Besides, the cement which binds workers together and promotes solidarity is the common problems they face as employees. This bond is strong enough to override other differences and binds workers together as a fighting force. Politics, on the other hand, divides wokers, who all hold different opinions on events outside of the workplace. Political parties, furthermore, are composed of heterogeneous groups which make them incapable of fostering a proletarian fighting spirit or of protecting and defending working class interests. By contrast, labor unions are composed of homogeneous groups of workers whose similar interests and goals weld them into a tight-knit fighting group capable of waging effective class war against the capitalist oppressors. Finally, political parties are regarded as frauds which divert workers from their true interests and often betray them after making lavish promises for their votes.

Conversely, direct action enables workers to achieve immediate gains and prepares the way for the ultimate revolution or overthrow of capitalism. Its most common form of expression is the strike. Regardless of its scope and objective, its success or failure, the strike is an educational experience which inspires workers with a sense of power and helps develop the tactics and strategy for future campaigns. The general strike, the culmination of various forms of direct action, is to bring about an apocalyptic transformation of society. Everything will be changed by one sudden stroke, a cataclysmic encounter between the ruling class and the workers in which the former will be vanquished and the new society erected. Syndicalists conceive of the real driving force behind any working class movement to be a militant minority dedicated to promoting class consciousness and a revolutionary spirit among the workers. In the United States, the IWW thought of itself as occupying such a vanguard role.

Syndicalism shares with Marxism and other forms of revolutionary socialism the doctrine of class struggle and revolutionary transformation of capitalist society. However, there are two important respects in which syndicalists differ from Marxists. First, they disagree on the methods and vehicles of revolution. Marxists insist on the importance of political methods, political parties, and political struggle. To the syndicalist, as we have seen, this is a diversion from the main task, a trap which the workers should not fall into.

A second major disagreement with Marxism is over the nature of the future revolutionary society. Marxists see the immediate post-revolutionary society as one where the workers control the economy through state ownership and control. Only gradually will the state wither away as the necessary historical preconditions for a stateless, non-class, non-coercive society of abundance are slowly achieved. Syndicalists, in contrast, see the future society as an industrial commonwealth based on association of autonomous productive and distributive associations. The political state as we know it would not exist; the association would be entirely harmonious and non-coercive. In many respects, the syndicalist vision of the future society—with its immediate abolition of the state—so approximates classic left-wing anarchist thought that it is often referred to as anarcho-syndicalism. Marxists regard syndicalists as hopelessly utopian; syndicalists regard Marxists as promoters of a new form of oppression.

The IWW, the United States' closest example to pure syndicalism, differed from the continental syndicalists in several respects. First, the IWW favored dual unions, in opposition to the established American Federation of Labor, whereas their European counterparts worked within and controlled many established unions. Second, it supported industrial unionism while the European syndicalists were working within craft unions. Although the IWW produced no great theorists, the IWW documents, speeches, and articles by leaders such as William Haywood, Vincent St. John, and William Trautmann (all included in Part II) convey very clearly the syndicalist theory underlying their activities. Since the syndicalist vision of a future society is hazy and uncertain, we have included a short chapter from a book by Lewis Lorwin describing the French syndicalists' views on the future commonwealth. The final syndicalist reading is a piece by

French philosopher Georges Sorel. Sorel attempts to systematize syndicalist practice into a general theory, and argues for the central role of a social *myth* for this and other social movements. The myth of central importance to syndicalism, for Sorel, is that of the general strike.

This chapter closes with readings from modern-day left-wing thought that, for lack of a better term, we label "New Left." André Gorz, a Frenchman with a Marxist background, argues that modern conditions in the West call for a reevaluation of traditional socialist trade union theory. Material deprivation can no longer be the basis of either socialist or trade union activity. However, new needs have been created which capitalism cannot fulfil. Therefore Gorz argues that "quality of life" issues, issues of control over the work process, and issues which continually challenge and preempt capitalist hegemony in all spheres of life must become a central part of trade union programs if the labor movement is to play its part in basic structural change. That is, the labor movement must put forward "non-reformist reforms."

Stanley Aronowitz also calls for a reevaluation of traditional socialist theory. However, his critique is more sweeping: traditional left-wing allegiance to trade unions and unionism must be abandoned, he asserts. While unions can still act as minimal agents of economic defense, their main role now is to integrate workers into an oppressive, monopolistic, capitalist system. Unions have become so enmeshed within the system that they act as a regressive force, he argues. They must be circumvented by dual forms of struggle and whatever mechanisms the spontaneous workers' struggle develops. Aronowitz presents the most negative assessment of trade unions and their theoretical possibilities that any left-wing thinker has presented in recent times.

# MARXISM

# 2

## The Communist Manifesto, Part 1

KARL MARX AND FRIEDRICH ENGELS                                              1848

The history of all hitherto existing society is the history of class struggles.

Freeman and slave, patrician and plebeian, lord and serf, guild-master and journeyman, in a word, oppressor and oppressed, stood in constant opposition to one another, carried on an uninterrupted, now hidden, now open fight, a fight that each time ended, either in a revolutionary reconstitution of society at large, or in the common ruin of the contending classes.

In the earlier epochs of history, we find almost everywhere a complicated arrangement of society into various orders, a manifold gradation of social rank. In ancient Rome we have patricians, knights, plebeians, slaves; in the Middle Ages, feudal lords, vassals, guild-masters, journeymen, apprentices, serfs; in almost all of these classes, again, subordinate gradations. The modern bourgeois society that has sprouted from the ruins of feudal society has not done away with class antagonisms. It has but established new classes, new conditions of oppression, new forms of struggle in place of the old ones.

Our epoch, the epoch of the bourgeoisie, possesses, however, this distinctive feature: it has simplified the class antagonisms. Society as a whole is more and more splitting up into two great hostile camps, into two great classes directly facing each other: Bourgeoisie and Proletariat.

From the serfs of the Middle Ages sprang the chartered burghers of the earliest towns. From these burgesses the first elements of the bourgeoisie were developed.

The discovery of America, the rounding of the Cape, opened up fresh ground for the rising bourgeoisie. The East Indian and Chinese markets, the colonization of America, trade with the colonies, the increase in the means of exchange and in commodities generally, gave to commerce, to navigation, to industry, an impulse never before known, and thereby, to the revolutionary element in the tottering feudal society, a rapid development.

The feudal system of industry, under which industrial production was monopolized by closed guilds, now no longer sufficed for the growing wants of the new markets. The manufacturing system took its place. The guild-masters were pushed on one side by the manufacturing middle class; division of labor between the different corporate guilds vanished in the face of division of labor in each single workshop.

Meantime the markets kept ever growing, the demand ever rising. Even manufacture no longer sufficed. Thereupon, steam and machinery revolutionized industrial production. The place of manufacture was taken by the giant, Modern Industry, the place of the industrial middle class, by industrial millionaires, the leaders of whole industrial armies, the modern bourgeois.

Modern industry has established the world market, for which the discovery of America paved the way. This market has given an immense development to commerce, to navigation, to communication by land. This development has, in its turn, reacted on the extension of industry; and in proportion as industry, commerce, navigation, railways extended, in the same proportion the bourgeoisie developed, increased its capital, and pushed into the background every class handed down from the Middle Ages.

Karl Marx and Friedrich Engels, *Manifesto of the Communist Party* (Moscow: Foreign Languages Publishing House, 1948), pp. 40–58. Footnotes in the original have been eliminated.

We see, therefore, how the modern bourgeoisie is itself the product of a long course of development, of a series of revolutions in the modes of production and of exchange.

Each step in the development of the bourgeoisie was accompanied by a corresponding political advance of that class. An oppressed class under the sway of the feudal nobility, an armed and self-governing association in the medieval commune; here independent urban republic (as in Italy and Germany), there taxable "third estate" of the monarchy (as in France), afterward, in the period of manufacture proper, serving either the semifeudal or the absolute monarchy as a counterpoise against the nobility, and, in fact, cornerstone of the great monarchies in general, the bourgeoisie has at last, since the establishment of Modern Industry and of the world market, conquered for itself, in the modern representative State, exclusive political sway. The executive of the modern State is but a committee for managing the common affairs of the whole bourgeoisie.

The bourgeoisie, historically, has played a most revolutionary part.

The bourgeoisie, wherever it has got the upper hand, has put an end to all feudal, patriarchal, idyllic relations. It has pitilessly torn asunder the motley feudal ties that bound man to his "natural superiors," and has left remaining no other nexus between man and man than naked self-interest, than callous "cash payment." It has drowned the most heavenly ecstasies of religious fervor, of chivalrous enthusiasm, of philistine sentimentalism, in the icy water of egotistical calculation. It has resolved personal worth into exchange value, and in place of the numberless indefeasible chartered freedoms, has set up that single, unconscionable freedom—Free Trade. In one word, for exploitation, veiled by religious and political illusions, it has substituted naked, shameless, direct, brutal exploitation.

The bourgeoisie has stripped of its halo every occupation hitherto honored and looked up to with reverent awe. It has converted the physician, the lawyer, the priest, the poet, the man of science, into its paid wage laborers.

The bourgeoisie has torn away from the family its sentimental veil, and has reduced the family relation to a mere money relation.

The bourgeoisie has disclosed how it came to pass that the brutal display of vigor in the Middle Ages, which Reactionists so much admire, found its fitting complement in the most slothful indolence. It has been the first to show what man's activity can bring about. It has accomplished wonders far surpassing Egyptian pyramids, Roman aqueducts, and Gothic cathedrals; it has conducted expeditions that put in the shade all former Exoduses of nations and crusades.

The bourgeoisie cannot exist without constantly revolutionizing the instruments of production, and thereby the relations of production, and with them the whole relations of society. Conservation of the old modes of production in unaltered form was, on the contrary, the first condition of existence for all earlier industrial classes. Constant revolutionizing of production, uninterrupted disturbance of all social conditions, everlasting uncertainty and agitation distinguish the bourgeois epoch from all earlier ones. All fixed, fast-frozen relations, with their train of ancient and venerable prejudices and opinions are swept away, all new-formed ones become antiquated before they can ossify. All that is solid melts into air, all that is holy is profaned, and man is at last compelled to face with sober senses his real conditions of life, and his relations with his kind.

The need of a constantly expanding market for its products chases the bourgeoisie over the whole surface of the globe. It must nestle everywhere, settle everywhere, establish connections everywhere.

The bourgeoisie has through its exploitation of the world market given a cosmopolitan character to production and consumption in every country. To the great chagrin of

Reactionists, it has drawn from under the feet of industry the national ground on which it stood. All old-established national industries have been destroyed or are daily being destroyed. They are dislodged by new industries, whose introduction becomes a life and death question for all civilized nations, by industries that no longer work up indigenous raw material, but raw material drawn from the remotest zones; industries whose products are consumed, not only at home, but in every quarter of the globe. In place of the old wants, satisfied by the productions of the country, we find new wants, requiring for their satisfaction the products of distant lands and climes. In place of the old local and national seclusion and self-sufficiency, we have intercourse in every direction, universal interdependence of nations. And as in material, so also in intellectual production. The intellectual creations of individual nations become common property. National one-sidedness and narrow-mindedness become more and more impossible, and from the numerous national and local literatures, there arises a world literature.

The bourgeoisie, by the rapid improvement of all instruments of production, by the immensely facilitated means of communication, draws all, even the most barbarian, nations into civilization. The cheap prices of its commodities are the heavy artillery with which it batters down all Chinese walls, with which it forces the barbarians' intensely obstinate hatred of foreigners to capitulate. It compels all nations, on pain of extinction, to adopt the bourgeois mode of production; it compels them to introduce what it calls civilization into their midst, i.e., to become bourgeois themselves. In one word, it creates a world after its own image.

The bourgeoisie has subjected the country to the rule of the towns. It has created enormous cities, has greatly increased the urban population as compared with the rural, and has thus rescued a considerable part of the population from the idiocy of rural life. Just as it has made the country dependent on the towns, so it has made barbarian and semibarbarian countries dependent on the civilized ones, nations of peasants on nations of bourgeois, the East on the West.

The bourgeoisie keeps more and more doing away with the scattered state of the population, of the means of production, and of property. It has agglomerated population, centralized means of production, and has concentrated property in a few hands. The necessary consequence of this was political centralization. Independent, or but loosely connected, provinces with separate interests, laws, governments and systems of taxation, became lumped together into one nation, with one government, one code of laws, one national class-interest, one frontier and one customs tariff.

The bourgeoisie, during its rule of scarce one hundred years, has created more massive and more colossal productive forces than have all preceding generations together. Subjection of Nature's forces to man, machinery, application of chemistry to industry and agriculture, steam navigation, railways, electric telegraphs, clearing of whole continents for cultivation, canalization of rivers, whole populations conjured out of the ground— what earlier century had even a presentiment that such productive forces slumbered in the lap of social labor?

We see then: the means of production and of exchange, on whose foundation the bourgeoisie built itself up, were generated in feudal society. At a certain stage in the development of these means of production and of exchange, the conditions under which feudal society produced and exchanged, the feudal organization of agriculture and manufacturing industry, in one word, the feudal relations of property became no longer compatible with the already developed productive forces; they became so many fetters. They had to be burst asunder; they were burst asunder.

Into their place stepped free competition, accompanied by a social and political constitution adapted to it, and by the economical and political sway of the bourgeois class.

A similar movement is going on before our own eyes. Modern bourgeois society with its relations of production, of exchange and of property, a society that has conjured up such gigantic means of production and of exchange, is like the sorcerer, who is no longer able to control the powers of the nether world whom he has called up by his spells. For many a decade past, the history of industry and commerce is but the history of the revolt of modern productive forces against modern conditions of production, against the property relations that are the conditions for the existence of the bourgeoisie and of its rule. It is enough to mention the commercial crises that by their periodical return put on its trial, each time more threateningly, the existence of the entire bourgeois society. In these crises a great part not only of the existing products, but also the previously created productive forces, are periodically destroyed. In these crises there breaks out an epidemic that, in all earlier epochs, would have seemed an absurdity—the epidemic of overproduction. Society suddenly finds itself put back into a state of momentary barbarism; it appears as if a famine, a universal war of devastation had cut off the supply of every means of subsistence; industry and commerce seem to be destroyed; and why? Because there is too much civilization, too much means of subsistence, too much industry, too much commerce. The productive forces at the disposal of society no longer tend to further the development of the conditions of bourgeois property; on the contrary, they have become too powerful for these conditions, by which they are fettered, and so soon as they overcome these fetters, they bring disorder into the whole of bourgeois society, endanger the existence of bourgeois property. The conditions of bourgeois society are too narrow to comprise the wealth created by them. And how does the bourgeoisie get over these crises? On the one hand by enforced destruction of a mass of productive forces; on the other, by the conquest of new markets, and by the more thorough exploitation of the old ones. That is to say, by paving the way for more extensive and more destructive crises, and by diminishing the means whereby crises are prevented.

The weapons with which the bourgeoisie felled feudalism to the ground are now turned against the bourgeoisie itself.

But not only has the bourgeoisie forged the weapons that bring death to itself; it has also called into existence the men who are to wield those weapons—the modern working class—the proletarians.

In proportion as the bourgeoisie, i.e., capital, is developed, in the same proportion is the proletariat, the modern working class, developed—a class of laborers, who live only so long as they find work, and who find work only so long as their labor increases capital. These laborers, who must sell themselves piecemeal, are a commodity, like every other article of commerce, and are consequently exposed to all the vicissitudes of competition, to all the fluctuations of the market.

Owing to the extensive use of machinery and to division of labor, the work of the proletarians has lost all individual character, and, consequently, all charm for the workman. He becomes an appendage of the machine, and it is only the most simple, most monotonous, and most easily acquired knack that is required of him. Hence, the cost of production of a workman is restricted, almost entirely, to the means of subsistence that he requires for his maintenance, and for the propagation of his race. But the price of a commodity, and therefore also of labor, is equal to its cost of production. In proportion, therefore, as the repulsiveness of the work increases, the wage decreases. Nay more, in proportion as the use of machinery and division of labor increases, in the same proportion the burden of toil also increases, whether by prolongation of the working hours, by increase of the work exacted in a given time or by increased speed of the machinery, etc.

Modern industry has converted the little workshop of the patriarchal master into the great factory of the industrial capitalist. Masses of laborers, crowded into the factory, are organized like soldiers. As privates of the industrial army they are placed under the command of a perfect hierarchy of officers and sergeants. Not only are they slaves of the bourgeois class, and of the bourgeois State; they are daily and hourly enslaved by the machine, by the overlooker, and, above all, by the individual bourgeois manufacturer himself. The more openly this despotism proclaims gain to be its end and aim, the more petty, the more hateful and the more embittering it is.

The less the skill and exertion of strength implied in manual labor, in other words, the more modern industry becomes developed, the more is the labor of men superseded by that of women. Differences of age and sex have no longer any distinctive social validity for the working class. All are instruments of labor, more or less expensive to use, according to their age and sex.

No sooner is the exploitation of the laborer by the manufacturer, so far, at an end, that he receives his wages in cash, than he is set upon by the other portions of the bourgeoisie, the landlord, the shopkeeper, the pawnbroker, etc.

The lower strata of the middle class—the small tradespeople, shopkeepers, and retired tradesmen generally, the handicraftsmen and peasants—all these sink gradually into the proletariat, partly because their diminutive capital does not suffice for the scale on which Modern Industry is carried on, and is swamped in the competition with the large capitalists, partly because their specialized skill is rendered worthless by new methods of production. Thus the proletariat is recruited from all classes of the population.

The proletariat goes through various stages of development. With its birth begins its struggle with the bourgeoisie. At first the contest is carried on by individual laborers, then by the workpeople of a factory, then by the operatives of one trade, in one locality, against the individual bourgeois who directly exploits them. They direct their attacks not against the bourgeois conditions of production, but against the instruments of production themselves; they destroy imported wares that compete with their labor, they smash to pieces machinery, they set factories ablaze, they seek to restore by force the vanished status of the workman of the Middle Ages.

At this stage the laborers still form an incoherent mass scattered over the whole country, and broken up by their mutual competition. If anywhere they unite to form more compact bodies, this is not yet the consequence of their own active union, but of the union of the bourgeoisie, which class, in order to attain its own political ends, is compelled to set the whole proletariat in motion, and is moreover yet, for a time, able to do so. At this stage, therefore, the proletarians do not fight their enemies, but the enemies of their enemies, the remnants of absolute monarchy, the landowners, the nonindustrial bourgeois, the petty bourgeoisie. Thus the whole historical movement is concentrated in the hands of the bourgeoisie; every victory so obtained is a victory for the bourgeoisie.

But with the development of industry the proletariat not only increases in number; it becomes concentrated in greater masses, its strength grows, and it feels that strength more. The various interests and conditions of life within the ranks of the proletariat are more and more equalized, in proportion as machinery obliterates all distinctions of labor, and nearly everywhere reduces wages to the same low level. The growing competition among the bourgeois, and the resulting commercial crises, make the wages of the workers ever more fluctuating. The unceasing improvement of machinery, ever more rapidly developing, makes their livelihood more and more precarious; the collisions between individual workmen and individual bourgeois take more and more the character of collisions between two classes. Thereupon the workers begin to form combinations (Trades' Unions) against the bourgeois; they club together in order to keep up the rate of wages; they found permanent associations in order to make provision beforehand for these occasional revolts. Here and there the contest breaks out into riots.

Now and then the workers are victorious, but only for a time. The real fruit of their battles lies, not in the immediate result, but in the ever-expanding union of the workers. This union is helped on by the improved means of communication that are created by modern industry and that place the workers of different localities in contact with one another. It was just this contact that was needed to centralize the numerous local struggles, all of the same character, into one national struggle between classes. But every class struggle is a political struggle. And that union, to attain which the burghers of the Middle Ages, with their miserable highways, required centuries, the modern proletarians thanks to railways, achieve in a few years.

This organization of the proletarians into a class, and consequently into a political party, is continually being upset again by the competition between the workers themselves. But it ever rises up again, stronger, firmer, mightier. It compels legislative recognition of particular interests of the workes, by taking advantage of the divisions among the bourgeoisie itself. Thus the ten-hours' bill in England was carried.

Altogether collisions between the classes of the old society further, in many ways, the course of development of the proletariat. The bourgeoisie finds itself involved in a constant battle. At first with the aristocracy; later on, with those portions of the bourgeoisie itself, whose interests have become antagonistic to the progress of industry; at all times, with the bourgeoisie of foreign countries. In all these battles it sees itself compelled to appeal to the proletariat, to ask for its help, and thus, to drag it into the political arena. The bourgeoisie itself, therefore, supplies the proletariat with its own elements of political and general education, in other words, it furnishes the proletariat with weapons for fighting the bourgeoisie.

Further, as we have already seen, entire sections of the ruling classes are, by the advance of industry, precipitated into the porletariat, or are at least threatened in their conditions of existence. These also supply the proletariat with fresh elements of enlightenment and progress.

Finally, in times when the class struggle nears the decisive hour, the process of dissolution going on within the ruling class, in fact within the whole range of old society, assumes such a violent, glaring character that a small section of the ruling class cuts itself adrift, and joins the revolutionary class, the class that holds the future in its hands. Just as, therefore, at an earlier period, a section of the nobility went over to the bourgeoisie, so now a portion of the bourgeoisie goes over to the proletariat, and in particular, a portion of the bourgeois ideologists, who have raised themselves to the level of comprehending theoretically the historical movement as a whole.

Of all the classes that stand face to face with the bourgeoisie today, the proletariat alone is a really revolutionary class. The other classes decay and finally disappear in the face of modern industry; the proletariat is its special and essential product.

The lower middle class, the small manufacturer, the shopkeeper, the artisan, the peasant, all these fight against the bourgeoisie, to save from extinction their existence as fractions of the middle class. They are therefore not revolutionary, but conservative. Nay more, they are reactionary, for they try to roll back the wheel of history. If by chance they are revolutionary, they are so only in view of their impending transfer into the proletariat, they thus defend not their present, but their future interests, they desert their own standpoint to place themselves at that of the proletariat.

The "dangerous class," the social scum, that passively rotting mass thrown off by the lowest layers of old society, may, here and there, be swept into the movement by a proletarian revolution; its conditions of life, however, prepare it far more for the part of a bribed tool of reactionary intrigue.

In the conditions of the proletariat, those of old society at large are already virtually swamped. The proletarian is without property; his relation to his wife and children has no longer anything in common with the bourgeois family relations; modern industrial labor, modern subjection to capital, the same in England as in France, in America as in Germany, has stripped him of every trace of national character. Law, morality, religion, are to him so many bourgeois prejudices, behind which lurk in ambush just as many bourgeois interests.

All the preceding classes that got the upper hand sought to fortify their already acquired status by subjecting society at large to their conditions of appropriation. The proletarians cannot become masters of the productive forces of society, except by abolishing their own previous mode of appropriation, and thereby also every other previous mode of appropriation. They have nothing of their own to secure and to fortify; their mission is to destroy all previous securities for, and insurances of, individual property.

All previous historical movements were movements of minorities, or in the interest of minorities. The proletarian movement is the self-conscious, independent movement of the immense majority, in the interest of the immense majority. The proletariat, the lowest stratum of our present society, cannot stir, cannot raise itself up, without the whole superincumbent strata of official society being sprung into the air.

Though not in substance, yet in form, the struggle of the proletariat with the bourgeoisie is at first a national struggle. The proletariat of each country must, of course, first of all settle matters with its own bourgeoisie.

In depicting the most general phases of the development of the proletariat, we traced the more or less veiled civil war, raging within existing society, up to the point where that war breaks out into open revolution, and where the violent overthrow of the bourgeoisie lays the foundation for the sway of the proletariat.

Hitherto, every form of society has been based, as we have already seen, on the antagonism of oppressing and oppressed classes. But in order to oppress a class, certain conditions must be assured to it under which it can, at least, continue its slavish existence. The serf, in the period of serfdom, raised himself to membership in the commune, just as the petty bourgeois, under the yoke of feudal absolutism, managed to develop into a bourgeois. The modern laborer, on the contrary, instead of rising with the progress of industry, sinks deeper and deeper below the conditions of existence of his own class. He becomes a pauper, and pauperism develops more rapidly than population and wealth. And here it becomes evident that the bourgeoisie is unfit any longer to be the ruling class in society, and to impose its conditions of existence upon society as an overriding law. It is unfit to rule because it is incompetent to assure an existence to its slave within his slavery, because it cannot help letting him sink into such a state, that it has to feed him, instead of being fed by him. Society can no longer live under this bourgeoisie, in other words, its existance is no longer compatible with society.

The essential condition for the existence, and for the sway of the bourgeois class, is the formation and augmentation of capital; the condition for capital is wage labor. Wage labor rests exclusively on competition between the laborers. The advance of industry, whose involuntary promoter is the bourgeoisie, replaces the isolation of the laborers, due to competition, by their revolutionary combination, due to association. The development of Modern Industry, therefore, cuts from under its feet the very foundation on which the bourgeoisie produces and appropriates products. What the bourgeoisie, therefore, produces, above all, is its own gravediggers. Its fall and the victory of the proletariat are equally inevitable.

# 3
## Trades' Unions. Their Past, Present and Future

KARL MARX                                                                    1866

*(a)* Their past.

Capital is concentrated social force, while the workman has only to dispose of his working force. The *contract* between capital and labour can therefore never be struck on equitable terms, equitable even in the sense of a society which places the ownership of the material means of life and labour on one side and the vital productive energies on the opposite side. The only social power of the workmen is their number. The force of numbers, however, is broken by disunion. The disunion of the workmen is created and perpetuated by their *unavoidable competition amongst themselves.*

Trades' Unions originally sprang up from the *spontaneous* attempts of workmen at removing or at least checking that competition, in order to conquer such terms of contract as might raise them at least above the condition of mere slaves. The immediate object of Trades' Unions was therefore confined to everyday necessities, to expediencies for the obstruction of the incessant encroachments of capital, in one word, to questions of wages and time of labour. This activity of the Trades' Unions is not only legitimate, it is necessary. It cannot be dispensed with so long as the present system of production lasts. On the contrary, it must be generalised by the formation and the combination of Trades' Unions throughout all countries. On the other hand, unconsciously to themselves, the Trades' Unions were forming *centres of organisation* of the working class, as the mediaeval municipalities and communes did for the middle class. If the Trades' Unions are required for the guerilla fights between capital and labour, they are still more important as *organised agencies for superseding the very system of wages labour and capital rule.*

*(b)* Their present.

Too exclusively bent upon the local and immediate struggles with capital, the Trades' Unions have not yet fully understood their power of acting against the system of wages slavery itself. They therefore kept too much aloof from general social and political movements. Of late, however, they seem to awaken to some sense of their great historical mission, as appears, for instance, from their participation, in England, in the recent political movement, from the enlarged views taken of their function in the United States, and from the following resolution passed at the recent great conference of Trades' delegates at Sheffield:

> "That this conference, fully appreciating the efforts made by the International Association to unite in one common bond of brotherhood the working men of all countries, most earnestly recommend to the various societies here represented, the advisability of becoming affiliated to that body, believing that it is essential to the progress and prosperity of the entire working community."

*(c)* Their future.

Apart from their original purposes, they must now learn to act deliberately as organising centres of the working class in the broad interest of its *complete emancipation.* They must aid every social and political movement tending in that direction. Considering themselves and acting as the champions and representatives of the whole working class, they cannot fail to enlist the non-society men into their ranks. They must look carefully after the interests of the worst paid trades, such as the agricultural labourers,

---

*The General Council of the First International, 1864–1866* (Moscow: Progress Publishers, 1962), pp. 347–349.

rendered powerless by exceptional circumstances. They must convince the world at large that their efforts, far from being narrow and selfish, aim at the emancipation of the downtrodden millions.

# 4
## Marxism and the Sociology of Trade Unionism
RICHARD HYMAN                                                                  1971

Socialists (and in particular revolutionary socialists), embracing the tasks of working-class mobilisation and social transformation, have of necessity confronted the theoretical problems posed by trade union activities—impinging as these so obviously do on their own objectives.

The perspectives which socialist theorists have generated may be roughly divided into two categories: those approaches which discern significant revolutionary potential in trade union activity; and those which argue that such activity does not in itself facilitate (or even that it inhibits) the revolutionary transformation of capitalist society. In this respect, the development of socialist analyses of trade unionism has displayed a certain dialectic. The early writings of Marx and Engels articulated in a pure form the "optimistic" assessment of unionism; subsequently they noted aspects of the British labour movement in the latter half of the nineteenth century which conflicted with this interpretation. In the present century, as trade unionism became extensively established without leading naturally to the overthrow of capitalism, various elements of a more "pessimistic" theory were elaborated; these in turn have exerted considerable influence on current academic orthodoxy. . . .

### The Optimistic Tradition: Marx and Engels

#### The Early Analysis

Historically the most significant exponents of the optimistic interpretation (though their optimism was by no means unqualified) were Marx and Engels. Given their long joint involvement, both theoretically and practically, with the labour movements of Britain and Europe, a rigorous and sustained analysis of the role of trade unions would not have been unexpected. In fact, their attention to this question is remarkably slight; and their most detailed discussion is to be found in their earliest works. Nevertheless, Marx and Engels clearly wrote sufficient to be considered as a coherent theory of trade unionism.

In economic terms, they saw the value of trade union action as extremely limited. Engels stated this point strongly in 1845:

> The history of these Unions is a long series of defeats of the working-men, interrupted by a few isolated victories. All these efforts naturally cannot alter the economic law according to which wages are determined by the relation between supply and demand in the labour market. Hence the Unions remain powerless against all *great* forces which influence this relation. In a commercial crisis the Union itself must reduce wages or dissolve wholly; and in a time of considerable increase in the demand for labour, it cannot fix the rate of wages higher than would be reached spontaneously by the competition of the capitalists among themselves. But in dealing with minor, single influences they are powerful. If the employer had no concentrated, collective opposition to expect, he would in his own interest gradually reduce wages to a lower and lower point; indeed, the battle of competition which he has to wage against his fellow-manufacturers would force him to do so, and wages would soon reach the minimum. But this competition of the manufactur-

ers among themselves is, *under average conditions,* somewhat restricted by the opposition of the working-men.[1]

This thesis was elaborated by Marx two decades later. The level of wages, he argued, was "only settled by the continuous struggle between capital and labour, the capitalist constantly tending to reduce wages to their physical minimum, while the working man constantly presses in the opposite direction."[2] In the absence of union organisation, the capitalist would cut wages during economic recessions even more severely than actually occurred, and would fail to restore these cuts when trade improved.[3] In the longer run, collective action imposed some constraint on capitalist encroachments on the *conditions* of labour.[4] Yet at the same time, "in its merely economic action capital is the stronger side"; and "the very development of modern industry must progressively turn the scale in favour of the capitalist against the working man."[5] Union achievements were also limited, for Marx and Engels, by long-run economic laws tending towards the increasing immiseration of the worker.

Despite—or, perhaps more correctly, because of—the restricted economic power attributed to trade unionism, Marx and Engels considered its *political* potential to be highly significant. For Engels, workers' combinations struck at the very fundamentals of capitalist "Political Economy."

What gives these Unions and the strikes arising from them their real importance is this, that they are the first attempt of the workers to abolish competition. They imply the recognition of the fact that the supremacy of the bourgeoisie is based wholly upon the competition of the workers among themselves; i.e., upon their want of cohesion. And precisely because the Unions direct themselves against the vital nerve of the present social order, however one-sidedly, in however narrow a way, are they so dangerous to this social order. The working-men cannot attack the bourgeoisie, and with it the whole existing order of society, at any sorer point than this. If the competition of the workers among themselves is destroyed, if all determine not to be further exploited by the bourgeoisie, the rule of property is at an end.[6]

Such a challenge to "the rule of property" was, initially at least, unconscious and indirect: but Engels saw unionism as preparing workers for a direct onslaught on capitalist class society.

That these Unions contribute greatly to nourish the bitter hatred of the workers against the property-holding class need hardly be said. . . . Strikes . . . are the military school of the working-men in which they prepare themselves for the great struggle which cannot be avoided; they are the pronunciamentos of single branches of industry that these too have joined the labour movement. . . . And as schools of war, the Unions are unexcelled.[7]

Shortly afterwards Marx, in his first detailed discussion of trade unions, defined precisely their role as integral to the process of social revolution. Analysing current British experience, he noted that the workers

have not stopped at partial combinations which have no other objective than a passing strike, and which disappear with it. Permanent combinations have been formed, *trades unions,* which serve as ramparts for the workers in their struggles with the employers.[8]

Such organisation was seen as a natural consequence of the development of capitalist industry:

> The first attempts of workers to *associate* among themselves always take place in the form of combinations. Large-scale industry concentrates in one place a crowd of people unknown to one another. Competition divides their interests. But the maintenance of wages, this common interest which they have against their boss, unites them in a common thought of resistance—*combination*.[9]

Marx argued that collective organisation, at first adopted merely as a means of defending wages, came to be pursued for its own sake; and that the ensuing conflict—'a veritable civil war'—served to generate among workers a consciousness of class unity, transforming them from a class "in itself" to a class "for itself."

> Economic conditions had first transformed the mass of the people of the country into workers. The combination of capital has created for this mass a common situation, common interest. This mass is thus already a class as against capital, but not yet for itself. In the struggle, of which we have noted only a few phases, this mass becomes united, and constitutes itself as a class for itself. The interests it defends become class interests.[10]

To underline the significance of this process as a preliminary to revolution, Marx drew an explicit analogy with the rise of the bourgeoisie as a revolutionary class.

> In the bourgeoisie we have two phases to distinguish: that in which it constituted itelf as a class under the regime of feudalism and absolute monarchy, and that in which, already constituted as a class, it overthrew feudalism and monarchy to make society into a bourgeoius society. The first of these phases was the longer and necessitated the greater efforts. This too began by partial combinations against the feudal lords.[11]

In the *Communist Manifesto*, the separate insights of Marx and Engels were synthesised:

> With the development of industry the proletariat not only increases in number, it becomes concentrated in greater masses, its strength grows, and it feels that strength more. The various interests and conditions of life within the ranks of the proletariat are more and more equalised, in proportion as machinery obliterates all distinctions of labour, and nearly everywhere reduces wages to the same low level. The growing competition among the bourgeois, and the resulting commercial crises, make the wages of the workers ever more fluctuating. The unceasing improvement of machinery, ever more rapidly developing, makes their livelihood more and more precarious; the collisions between individual workmen and individual bourgeois take more and more the character of collisions between two classes. Thereupon the workers begin to form combinations (Trades' Unions) against the bourgeois; they club together in order to keep up the rate of wages; they found permanent associations in order to make provision beforehand for these occasional revolts. Here and there the contest breaks out into riots.
> Now and then the workers are victorious, but only for a time. The real fruit of their battles lies, not in the immediate results, but in the ever-expanding union of the workers. This union is helped on by the improved means of communication that are created by modern industry and that place the workers of different localities in contact with one another. It was just this contact that was needed to cen-

tralise the numerous local struggles, all of the same character, into one national struggle between classes. But every class struggle is a political struggle. And that union, to attain which the burghers of the Middle Ages, with their miserable highways, required centuries, the modern proletarians, thanks to railways, achieve in a few years. This organisation of the proletarians into a class, and consequently into a political party, is continually being upset again by the competition between the workers themselves. But it ever rises up again, stronger, firmer, mightier.[12]

This analysis of the rise of the labour movement concluded with the famous assertion of the inevitable culmination of the process in social revolution.

The essential condition for the existence, and for the sway of the bourgeois class, is the formation and augmentation of capital; the condition for capital is wage-labour. Wage-labour rests exclusively on competition between the labourers. The advance of industry, whose involuntary promoter is the bourgeoisie, replaces the isolation of the labourers, due to competition, by their revolutionary combination, due to association. The development of Modern Industry, therefore, cuts from under its feet the very foundation on which the bourgeoisie produces and appropriates products. What the bourgeoisie, therefore, produces, above all, is its own grave-diggers. Its fall and the victory of the proletariat are equally inevitable.[13]

The above analysis, developed by Marx and Engels during the 1840s, may be briefly summarised as follows. The evolution of industrial capitalism provides the preconditions of collective organisation by throwing workers together in large numbers, and creates the deprivations which spur them to combination. This unity, by transcending competition in the labour market, in itself threatens the stability of capitalism: it also develops workers' class consciousness and trains them in methods of struggle. The limited economic achievements of their unions lead workers to adopt political forms of action, and ultimately to challenge directly the whole structure of class domination.

### The Later Reservations

One need scarcely document the failure of subsequent experience to validate this optimistic prognosis; yet Marx and Engels never produced a comprehensive revision of their early analysis. Rather, they tended to treat the development of trade unionism in the second half of the nineteenth century as a deviation from the natural course; a process occurring "by way of exception, under definite, special, so to say local, circumstances."[14] As Marx and Engels experienced the various phases of the British labour movement's development—the collapse of the revolutionary hopes of Chartism, the consolidation of craft unionism, the broader perspectives of the 1860s, the demoralisation of the Great Depression, and the revival of optimism with the "New Unionism"—their response varied; but three main arguments were used.

First, existing unions represented not the whole of the working class but "an aristocratic minority" of "privileged workers,"[15] able to achieve material concessions in principle unattainable by workers generally. This factor was seen as eventually self-correcting; as organisation was embraced by the lower-skilled, the conservative and inward-looking characteristics of minority unionism would be swept away. And indeed, Engels saw the "New Unionism" as the proof of this assertion:

Unlike the old trade unions, they greet every suggestion of an identity of interest between capital and labour with scorn and ridicule. . . . Thus we see now these new Unions taking the lead of the working-class movement generally, and more and more taking in tow the rich and proud "old" Unions.[16]

The absence of revolutionary activity was also blamed on the corruption—material or ideological—of treacherous leaders: a charge based, with considerable justice, on the experience of the 1868 General Election.[17]

> The leadership of the working class of England has wholly passed into the hands of the corrupted leaders of the trade unions and the professional agitators. . . . It seems to be a law of the proletarian movement everywhere that a section of the workers' leaders should become demoralised.[18]

Insofar as any explanation was offered for such a development, it was that the corruption of the leaders was made possible by the passivity of the rank and file.[19]

This leads to the third argument of Marx and Engels: the embourgeoisement of the British working class, a consequence of the monopoly position of British capitalism in the world economy. "The English proletariat is becoming more and more bourgeois, so that this most bourgeois of all nations is apparently aiming ultimately at the possession of a bourgeois aristocracy and a bourgeois proletariat *as well as* a bourgeoisie. For a nation which exploits the whole world this is of course to a certain extent justifiable."[20] This situation too could be seen as essentially temporary; as the British economy faced increasing international competition, so the privileged position of British workers would be undermined.[21]

Such special (and, it was assumed, transitory) factors were typically seen as explaining the absence of revolutionary initiative in the country where unionism had its deepest roots. Yet there are aspects of the writings of Marx and Engels which could be taken as evidence of a natural tendency for union activities to be restricted to those which posed no serious threat to capitalist stability.

> The British labour movement is to-day and for many years has been working in a narrow circle of strikes for higher wages and shorter hours without finding a solution; besides, these strikes are looked upon not as an expedient and not as a means of propaganda and organisation but as an ultimate aim. The trade unions exclude on principle and by virtue of their statutes, all political action and consequently also the participation in the general activity of the working class as a class. . . . We must not pass in silence over the fact that at the present moment no real labour movement, in the continental meaning of the word, exists here.[22]

Marx himself argued, before the International Working Men's Association in 1865, that organised workers "ought not to forget that they are fighting with effects, but not with the causes of those effects; that they are retarding the downward movement, but not changing its direction; that they are applying palliatives, not curing the malady."[23] In the following year he suggested, in draft resolutions for the Geneva Congress of the International, that the unions had unintentionally become focal points in the class struggle. But, he insisted, they

> must now learn how to act consciously as focal points for organising the working class in the greater interests of its complete emancipation. They must support every social and political movement directed towards this aim. . . . They must con-

vince the whole world that their efforts are far from narrow and egoistic, but, on the contrary, are directed towards the emancipation of the down-trodden masses.[24]

That such exhortations were considered necessary was eloquent testimony that trade unions *could* forget that they were "fighting with effects" and thus become accommodated to a restricted economic role; and therefore that their "local and direct struggle against Capital" did not lead automatically to a broader political movement. Another implication was that collective industrial action could be narrowly sectional in inspiration and thus in no way indicative of *class* consciousness.

[1] F. Engels, *The Condition of the Working Class in England in 1844,* English edn. 1892, pp. 216–7. In this, as in all other quotations in this paper the emphasis is in the original.

[2] K. Marx, "Wages, Price and Profit" (1865), in K. Marx and F. Engels, *Selected Works,* 2 Vol. edition 1958, Vol. I, p. 443.

[3] *Ibid,* p. 440.

[4] *Ibid.*

[5] *Ibid,* pp. 444, 446.

[6] *Condition of the Working Class,* pp. 218–9.

[7] *Ibid,* pp. 219, 224.

[8] Marx, *The Poverty of Philosophy* (1847), 1955 edn., p. 149.

[9] *Ibid,* p. 150.

[10] *Ibid.*

[11] *Ibid,* pp. 150–1.

[12] "Manifesto of the Communist Party," *Selected Works,* Vol. I, pp. 42–3.

[13] *Ibid,* p. 45.

[14] Marx, *Capital,* Vol. II, 1957 edn., p. 340.

[15] Collins and Abramsky, *Marx and the British Labour Movement,* p. 51; Engels, letter to Bebel, 28 October 1885.

[16] Engels, letter to Sorge, 7 December 1889 and Preface to the 1892 English edition of the *Condition of the Working Class,* p. xix. Engels died before it was wholly apparent that such high expectations of the "new unionism" were misplaced.

[17] See R. Harrison, "The Reform League and the General Election of 1868," in his *Before the Socialists,* 1965.

[18] Marx, letter to Liebknecht, 11 February 1878; Engels, letter to Marx, 30 July 1869.

[19] Engels remarked that the leaders of the "new unions" were themselves affected by "bourgeois 'respectability,' " but insisted that "it will not help the bourgeoisie much if they do succeed in enticing some of the leaders into their toils. The movement has been far enough strengthened for this sort of thing to be overcome." (letter to Sorge, 7 December 1889).

[20] Engels, letter to Marx, 7 October 1858.

[21] As Engels argued in the same letter, "the only thing that would help here would be a few thoroughly bad years." He repeated this argument in several letters in the 1880s, as well as in the 1892 Preface to the *Condition of the Working Class.*

[22] Engels, letter to Bernstein, 17 June 1879.

[23] "Wages, Price and Profit," *Selected Works,* Vol. I, p. 446.

[24] Cited in Lozovsky, *Marx and the Trade Unions,* pp. 16–8; see also Collins and Abramsky, *Marx and the British Labour Movement,* pp. 116–8.

# 5

## Rôle of the Trade Unions in the General Class Struggle of the Proletariat

A. LOZOVSKY                                                                    1935

Marx, first and foremost, considered the trade unions *organising centres*, centres for collecting the forces of the workers, organisations for giving the workers an elementary class training. What was most important for Marx? The fact that *the scattered workers, competing with one another, were now beginning to close their ranks and come out jointly.* In this he saw a guarantee that the working class would develop into an independent power. Marx and Engels repeatedly refer in their works to the idea that the trade unions are schools of solidarity, schools of socialism. . . .

The trade unions are schools of socialism. But Marx does not confine himself to formulas. He develops his idea, he approaches the problem of trade unions from all angles. Karl Marx was the author of the resolution on the question of the past, present and future of the trade unions, adopted at the Geneva Congress of the First International. What, then, is the past of the trade unions?

Capital is concentrated social power, while the worker has only his individual labour power at his disposal. Therefore the agreement between Capital and Labour can never be based on just terms, just not even in the sense of a society that places on one side the possession of the material means of life and production, and on the opposite side sets down the live productive forces. The only social force possessed by the workers is their numerical strength. This force, however, is impaired by the absence of unity. The lack of unity among the workers is caused by the inevitable competition among themselves, and is maintained by it. *The trade unions developed originally out of the spontaneous attempts of the workers to do away with this competition, or at least to restrict it, for the purpose of obtaining at least such contractual conditions as would raise them above the status of bare slaves.*

The immediate aim of the trade unions, therefore, was limited to waging the day-to-day struggle against Capital, as a means of defence against the continuous abuses of the latter, *i.e.,* questions concerning wages and working hours. This activity of the trade unions is not only justified, but also necessary. It is not advisable to dispense with it so long as the present system of production exists. On the contrary, it must become general by means of creating and uniting the trade unions in all countries.

On the other hand, *the trade unions, without being aware of it, became the focal points for the organisation of the working class*, just as the medieval municipalities and communities became such for the bourgeoisie. If trade unions have become indispensable for the guerilla fight between Capital and Labour, *they are even more important as organised bodies to promote the abolition of the very system of wage labour.*[1]

In this resolution a number of questions deserve special attention, particularly those concerning the *origin* and significance of the trade unions. Marx emphasises that the trade unions

> without being aware of it, became the focal points for the organisation of the working class, just as the medieval municipalities and communities became such for the bourgeoisie.

This comparison bears witness to the fact that Marx considered the trade unions not only "focal points" for the economic organisations; for the municipalities and communities in the Middle Ages were a weapon of the bourgeoisie in their struggle against feudalism, a weapon for the political struggle against the medieval system. Marx did not limit himself to this comparison, and already in this part of the resolution he says that the trade unions are *"even more important as organised means to promote the abolition of the very system of wage labour."* From this we see that Marx attached great political significance to the trade unions, that he regarded them least of all as neutral organisations, as non-political organisations. Every time that the trade unions closed themselves up in a narrow corporative framework, Marx would come out in sharp, lashing criticism of them.

This same Geneva Congress of the First International characterised the trade union movement of that period in the second part of that resolution, entitled *Their Present:*

> The trade unions hitherto concentrated their attention too exclusively on the local and direct struggle against Capital. *They have not yet completely realised their power to attack the very system of wage slavery and present-day methods of production.* This is why they kept aloof from social and political movements. However, lately they are evidently *awakening and beginning to understand their great historical mission,* as can be seen, for example, from their participation in the recent political movement in England, from their higher conception of their functions in the United States and from the following resolution adopted at the enlarged conference of trade union delegates recently held at Sheffield:
> "This Conference, fully approving of all the efforts made by the International Workingmen's Association to unite the workers of all countries into one fraternal union, urgently recommends the different societies whose representatives are present at the Conference to join the International, in the conviction that this is necessary for the progress and welfare of the whole working class."[2]

In this part of the resolution we already see sharp criticism of all the trade unions that divorce themselves from politics, and here the significance of the trade unions that begin to understand their great historical mission is sharply emphasised.

■    ■    ■

But Marx did not limit himself to defining the past and the present of the trade unions. In this resolution he says the following about their *future:*

> In addition to their original tasks, the trade unions must now learn how to act consciously as focal points for organising the working class in the greater interests of its complete emancipation. They must support every social and political movement directed towards this aim. By considering themselves champions and representatives of the whole working class, and acting accordingly, the trade unions must succeed in rallying round themselves all workers still outside their ranks. They must carefully safeguard the interests of the workers in the poorest-paid trades, as, for example, the farm labourers, who due to especially unfavourable circumstances have been deprived of their power of resistance. They must convince the whole world that their efforts are far from narrow and egoistic, but on the contrary, are directed towards the emancipation of the down-trodden masses.[3]

Here it is necessary to call attention to the fact that Marx again stresses the significance of the trade unions as *organising centres of the working class*. It is extremely important to note that the tasks set before the trade unions are: The struggle for the *complete*
emancipation of the working class, the support of every social-political movement of the
proletariat and the drawing of all workers into their ranks. Already in 1866 Marx emphasised the importance for the trade unions of defending the interests of the lower-paid
workers, for example, the agricultural labourers. He expected the trade unions not to be
"narrow and egoistic," that "their activities be directed towards emancipating the
oppressed millions." . . .

The question of the relationship between economics and politics was continuously
before Marx and the First International. . . . In this connection his resolution adopted at
the 1871 London Conference of the International Workingmen's Association is very
characteristic and instructive. Here we read the following:

In the presence of an unbridled reaction which violently crushes every effort at
emancipation on the part of the working men, and pretends to maintain by brute
force the distinction of classes and the political domination of the propertied classes
resulting from it;

considering that against this collective power of the propertied classes the
working class cannot act, as a class, except by constituting itself into a political
party, distinct from, and opposed to, all old parties formed by the propertied classes;

that this constitution of the working class into a political party is indispensable in order to ensure the triumph of the social revolution and its ultimate end—
the abolition of classes;

that the combination of forces which the working class has already effected
by its economical struggles ought at the same time to serve as a lever for its struggles against the political power of landlords and capitalists;

the Conference recalls to the members of the *International:*

That in the militant state of the working class, its economic movement and
its political action are indissolubly united.[4]

■    ■    ■

Two months after this, in his letter to Bolte, Marx again raises the question of the
relationship between politics and economics, and it is here that he defines the rôle of the
economic struggle in the general class struggle of the proletariat. Marx writes:

The 'political movement' of the working class naturally has as its final aim the
conquest of 'political power' for it; for this a 'previous organisation' of the working
class, an organisation developed to a certain degree, is naturally necessary, which
grows out of its economic forces themselves.

But on the other hand every movement in which the working class, as a class,
opposes the ruling classes and seeks to compel them by 'pressure from without' is a
*'political movement.'* For example, the attempt to obtain forcibly from individual
capitalists a shortening of working hours in some individual factory or some individual trade by means of a strike, etc., is a purely economic movement. On the
other hand a movement forcibly to obtain an eight-hour *law*, etc., is a political
movement.

And in this way a *political* movement grows everywhere out of the individual
economic movement of the workers, *i.e.*, a movement of the *class* to gain its ends in
a general form, a form which possesses compelling force in a general social sense. If

these movements presuppose a certain previous organisation, they in their turn are just as much means of developing the organisation.

■　　■　　■

It was necessary not only to give an answer to the question of the significance of the economic struggle, but also on the mutual relationship between the economic and political organisations of the working class. The decision of the Hague Congress of the International Workingmen's Association (held September 2 to 7, 1872), is very characteristic in this regard. The Hague Congress, upon the proposal of Marx, adopted a resolution "on the political activity of the proletariat." In this resolution we read that in its struggle against the collective power of the possessing classes, the proletariat can take action, as a class, only after having organised its own political party as opposed to all the old parties founded by the possessing classes. Such organisation of the proletariat into a political party is necessary to ensure the victory of the social revolution and its ultimate aim—the abolition of classes.

*The consolidation of the workers' forces attained in the economic struggle will also have to serve as a lever in the hands of this class for the struggle against the political power of its exploiters.* In view of the fact that the owners of the land and of capital always utilised their political privileges to guard and perpetuate their economic monopolies and to enslave labour, the conquest of political power comes to be the great task of the proletariat.[5]

---

[1]Resolution of the I.W.A. on Trade Unions, Geneva, 1866.
[2]*Ibid.*
[3]Resolution of the I.W.A. on Trade Unions, Geneva, 1886.
[4]*Resolution of the Conference of Delegates of the International Workingmen's Association, Assembled at London from 17th to 23rd September, 1871.* London, International Printing Office, 1871, p. 3.
[5]Excerpt from James Guillaume, *Documents et Souvenirs (L'International)*. My Italics.—*A. L.*

# 6
## *What Is To Be Done?*

V. I. LENIN 1902

### Political Agitation and Its Restriction by the Economists[1]

Everyone knows that the economic[2] struggle of the Russian workers underwent widespread development and consolidation simultaneously with the production of "literature" exposing economic (factory and occupational) conditions. The "leaflets" were devoted mainly to the exposure of the factory system, and very soon a veritable passion for exposures was roused among the workers. As soon as the workers realised that the Social-Democratic[3] study circles desired to, and could, supply them with a new kind of leaflet that told the whole truth about their miserable existence, about their unbearably hard toil, and their lack of rights, they began to send in, actually flood us with, correspondence from the factories and workshops. This "exposure literature" created a tremendous sensation, not only in the particular factory exposed in the given leaflet, but in all the factories to which news of the revealed facts spread. And since the poverty and want among the workers in the various enterprises and in the various trades are much the same, the "truth about the life of the workers" stirred *everyone*. Even among the most backward workers, a veritable passion arose to "get into print"—a noble passion for this rudimentary form of war against the whole of the present social system which is based upon robbery and oppression. And in the overwhelming majority of cases these "leaflets" were in truth a declaration of war, because the exposures served greatly to agitate the workers; they evoked among them common demands for the removal of the most glaring outrages and roused in them a readiness to support the demands with strikes. Finally, the employers themselves were compelled to recognise the significance of these leaflets as a declaration of war, so much so that in a large number of cases they did not even wait for the outbreak of hostilities. As is always the case, the mere publication of these exposures made them effective, and they acquired the significance of a strong moral influence. On more than one occasion, the mere appearance of a leaflet proved sufficient to secure the satisfaction of all or part of the demands put forward. In a word, economic (factory) exposures were and remain an important lever in the economic struggle. And they will continue to retain this significance as long as there is capitalism, which makes it necessary for the workers to defend themselves. Even in the most advanced countries of Europe it can still be seen that the exposure of abuses in some backward trade, or in some forgotten branch of domestic industry, serves as a starting-point for the awakening of class-consciousness, for the beginning of a trade union struggle, and for the spread of socialism.

The overwhelming majority of Russian Social-Democrats have of late been almost entirely absorbed by this work of organising the exposure of factory conditions. Suffice it to recall *Rabochaya Mysl*[4] to see the extent to which they have been absorbed by it—so much so, indeed, that they have lost sight of the fact that this, *taken by itself*, is in essence still not Social-Democratic work, but merely trade union work. As a matter of fact, the exposures merely dealt with the relations between the workers *in a given trade* and their employers, and all they achieved was that the sellers of labour-power learned to sell their "commodity" on better terms and to fight the purchasers over a purely commercial deal. These exposures could have served (if properly utilised by an organisation of revolutionaries) as a beginning and a component part of Social-Democratic activity; but they could

V. I. Lenin, *On Trade Unions* (Moscow: Progress Publishers, 1970), pp. 94–116, 126–130, 134–135. Footnotes in the original have been eliminated or renumbered.

also have led (and, given a worshipful attitude towards spontaneity, were bound to lead) to a "purely trade union" struggle and to a non-Social-Democratic working-class movement. Social-Democracy leads the struggle of the working class, not only for better terms for the sale of labour-power, but for the abolition of the social system that compels the propertyless to sell themselves to the rich. Social-Democracy represents the working class, not in its relation to a given group of employers alone, but in its relation to all classes of modern society and to the state as an organised political force. Hence, it follows that not only must Social-Democrats not confine themselves exclusively to the economic struggle, but that they must not allow the organisation of economic exposures to become the predominant part of their activities. We must take up actively the political education of the working class and the development of its political consciousness. . . .

The question arises, what should political education consist in? Can it be confined to the propaganda of working-class hostility to the autocracy? Of course not. It is not enough *to explain* to the workers that they are politically oppressed (any more than it is *to explain* to them that their interests are antagonistic to the interests of the employers). Agitation must be conducted with regard to every concrete example of this oppression (as we have begun to carry on agitation round concrete examples of economic oppression). Inasmuch as *this* oppression affects the most diverse classes of society, inasmuch as it manifests itself in the most varied spheres of life and activity—vocational, civic, personal, family, religious, scientific, etc., etc.—is it not evident that *we shall not be fulfilling our task* of developing the political consciousness of the workers if we do not *undertake the organisation of the political exposure* of the autocracy *in all its aspects*? In order to carry on agitation round concrete instances of oppression, these instances must be exposed (as it is necessary to expose factory abuses in order to carry on economic agitation).

One might think this to be clear enough. It turns out, however, that it is only in words that "all" are agreed on the need to develop political consciousness, *in all its aspects*. It turns out that *Rabocheye Dyelo*,[5] for example, far from tackling the task of organising (or making a start in organising) comprehensive political exposure, is even trying *to drag Iskra*,[6] which has undertaken this task, *away from it*. Listen to the following: "The political struggle of the working class is merely [it is certainly not "merely"] the most developed, wide, and effective form of economic struggle." . . . "The Social-Democrats are now confronted with the task of lending the economic struggle itself, as far as possible, a political character" (Martynov,[7] *Rabocheye Dyelo* . . .). "The economic struggle is the most widely applicable means of drawing the masses into active political struggle." . . . As the reader will observe, all these theses permeate *Rabocheye Dyelo* from its very first number to the latest "Instructions to the Editors," and all of them evidently express a single view regarding political agitation and struggle. Let us examine this view from the standpoint of the opinion prevailing among all Economists, that political agitation must *follow* economic agitation. Is it true that, in general, the economic struggle "is the most widely applicable means" of drawing the masses into the political struggle? It is entirely untrue. *Any and every* manifestation of police tyranny and autocratic outrage, not only in connection with the economic struggle, is not one whit less "widely applicable" as a means of "drawing in" the masses. The rural superintendents[8] and the flogging of peasants, the corruption of the officials and the police treatment of the "common people" in the cities, the fight against the famine-stricken and the suppression of the popular striving towards enlightenment and knowledge, the extortion of taxes and the persecution of the religious sects, the humiliating treatment of soldiers and the barrack methods in the treatment of the students and liberal intellectuals—do all these and a thousand other similar manifestation of tyranny, though not directly connected with the "econom-ic" struggle, represent, in general, *less* "widely applicable" means and occasions for polit-ical agitation and for drawing the masses into the political struggle? The very opposite is true. Of the sum total of cases in which the workers suffer (either on their own account or on account of those closely connected with them) from tyranny, violence, and the lack of rights, undoubtedly only a small minority represent cases of police tyranny in the trade union struggle as such. Why then should we, beforehand, *restrict* the scope of political agitation by declaring only *one* of the means to be "the most widely applicable," when Social-Democrats must have, in addition, other, generally speaking, no less "widely appli-cable" means?

■  ■  ■

What concrete, real meaning attaches to Martynov's words when he sets before Social-Democracy the task of "lending the economic struggle itself a political charac-ter"? The economic struggle is the collective struggle of the workers against their employers for better terms *in the sale of their labour-power*, for better living and working conditions. This struggle is necessarily a trade union struggle, because working condi-tions differ greatly in different trades, and, consequently, the struggle *to improve* them can only be conducted on the basis of trade organisations (in the Western countries, through trade unions; in Russia, through temporary trade associations and through leaf-lets, etc.). Lending "the economic struggle itself a political character" means, therefore, striving to secure satisfaction of these trade demands, the improvement of working condi-tions in each separate trade by means of "legislative and administrative measures." . . . This is precisely what all workers' trade unions do and always have done. Read the works of the soundly scientific (and "soundly" opportunist) Mr. and Mrs. Webb[9] and you will see that the British trade unions long ago recognised, and have long been carrying out, the task of "lending the economic struggle itself a political character"; they have long been fighting for the right to strike, for the removal of all legal hindrances to the co-operative and trade union movements, for laws to protect women and children, for the improvement of labour conditions by means of health and factory legislation, etc.

Thus, the pompous phrase about "lending the economic struggle *itself* a political character," which sounds so "terrifically" profound and revolutionary, serves as a screen to conceal what is in fact the traditional striving *to degrade* Social-Democratic politics to the level of trade union politics. Under the guise of rectifying the one-sidedness of *Iskra*, which, it is alleged, places "the revolutionising of dogma higher than the revolutionising of life," we are presented with the *struggle for economic reforms* as if it were something entirely new. In point of fact, the phrase "lending the economic struggle itself a political character" means nothing more than the struggle for economic reforms. Martynov him-self might have come to this simple conclusion, had he pondered over the significance of his own words. "Our Party," he says, training his heaviest guns on *Iskra*, "could and should have presented concrete demands to the government for legislative and adminis-trative measures against economic exploitation, unemployment, famine, etc." . . . Con-crete demands for measures—does not this mean demands for social reforms? Again we ask the impartial reader: Are we slandering the *Rabocheye Dyelo*-ites (may I be forgiven for this awkward, currently used designation!) by calling them concealed Bernsteinians[10] when, as their point of *disagreement* with *Iskra*, they advance their thesis on the necessity of struggling for economic reforms?

Revolutionary Social-Democracy has always included the struggle for reforms as part of its activities. But it utilises "economic" agitation for the purpose of presenting to the government, not only demands for all sorts of measures, but also (and primarily) the demand that it cease to be an autocratic government. Moreover, it considers it its duty to present this demand to the government on the basis, *not* of the economic struggle *alone*, but of all manifestations in general of public and political life. In a word, it subordinates the struggle for reforms, as the part to the whole, to the revolutionary struggle for freedom and for socialism. Martynov, however, resuscitates the theory of stages in a new form and strives to prescribe, as it were, an exclusively economic path of development for the political struggle. By advancing at this moment, when the revolutionary movement is on the upgrade, an alleged special "task" of struggling for reforms, he is dragging the Party backwards and is playing into the hands of both "Economist" and liberal opportunism.

To proceed. Shamefacedly hiding the struggle for reforms behind the pompous thesis of "lending the economic struggle itself a political character," Martynov advanced, as if it were a special point, *exclusively economic* (indeed, exclusively factory) *reforms*. As to the reason for his doing that, we do not know it. Carelessness, perhaps? Yet if he had in mind something else besides "factory" reforms, then the whole of his thesis, which we have cited, loses all sense. Perhaps he did it because he considers it possible and probable that the government will make "concessions" only in the economic sphere? If so, then it is a strange delusion. Concessions are also possible and are made in the sphere of legislation concerning flogging, passports, land redemption payments, religious sects, the censorship, etc., etc. "Economic" concessions (or pseudo-concessions) are, of course, the cheapest and most advantageous from the government's point of view, because by these means it hopes to win the confidence of the working masses. For this very reason, we Social-Democrats *must not* under any circumstances or in any way whatever create grounds for the belief (or the misunderstanding) that we attach greater value to economic reforms, or that we regard them as being particularly important, etc. . . .

■ ■ ■

### Political Exposures and "Training in Revolutionary Activity"

In advancing against *Iskra* his theory of "raising the activity of the working masses," Martynov actually betrayed an urge *to belittle* that activity, for he declared the very economic struggle before which all Economists grovel to be the preferable, particularly important, and "most widely applicable" means of rousing this activity and its broadest field. This error is characteristic, precisely in that it is by no means peculiar to Martynov. In reality, it is possible to "raise the activity of the working masses" *only* when this activity *is not restricted* to "political agitation on an economic basis." A basic condition for the necessary expansion of political agitation is the organisation of *comprehensive* political exposure. *In no way* except by means of such exposures *can* the masses be trained in political consciousness and revolutionary activity. Hence, activity of this kind is one of the most important functions of international Social-Democracy as a whole, for even political freedom does not in any way eliminate exposures; it merely shifts somewhat their sphere of direction. Thus, the German party is especially strengthening its positions and spreading its influence, thanks particularly to the untiring energy with which it is conducting its campaign of political exposure. Working-class consciousness cannot be genuine political consciousness unless the workers are trained to respond to *all* cases of tyranny, oppression, violence, and abuse, no matter *what class* is affected—unless they are trained, moreover, to respond from a Social-Democratic point of view and no other. The consciousness of the working masses cannot be genuine class-consciousness, unless the workers learn, from concrete, and above all from topical, political facts and events to observe *every* other social class in *all* the manifestations of its intellectual, ethical, and political life; unless they learn to apply in practice the materialist analysis and the materialist estimate of *all* aspects of the life and activity of *all* classes, strata, and groups of the population. Those who concentrate the attention, observation, and consciousness of the working class exclusively, or even mainly, upon itself alone are not Social-Democrats; for the self-knowledge of the working class is indissolubly bound up, not solely with a fully clear theoretical understanding . . . it would be even truer to say, not so much with the theoretical, as with the practical, understanding—of the relationships between *all* the various classes of modern society, acquired through the experience of political life. For this reason the conception of the economic struggle as the most widely applicable means of drawing the masses into the political movement, which our Economists preach, is so extremely harmful and reactionary in its practical significance. In order to become a Social-Democrat, the worker must have a clear picture in his mind of the economic nature and the social and political features of the landlord and the priest, the high state official and the peasant, the student and the vagabond; he must know their strong and weak points; he must grasp the meaning of all the catchwords and sophisms by which each class and each stratum *camouflages* its selfish strivings and its real "inner workings"; he must understand what interests are reflected by certain institutions and certain laws and how they are reflected. But this "clear picture" cannot be obtained from any book. It can be obtained only from living examples and from exposures that follow close upon what is going on about us at a given moment; upon what is being discussed, in whispers perhaps, by each one in his own way; upon what finds expression in such and such events, in such and such statistics, in such and such court sentences, etc., etc. These comprehensive political exposures are an essential and *fundamental* condition for training the masses in revolutionary activity.

Why do the Russian workers still manifest little revolutionary activity in response to the brutal treatment of the people by the police, the persecution of religious sects, the flogging of peasants, the outrageous censorship, the torture of soldiers, the persecution of the most innocent cultural undertakings, etc.? Is it because the "economic struggle" does not "stimulate" them to this, because such activity does not "promise palpable results," because it produces little that is "positive"? To adopt such an opinion, we repeat, is merely to direct the charge where it does not belong, to blame the working masses for one's own philistinism. . . . We must blame ourselves, our lagging behind the mass movement, for still being unable to organise sufficiently wide, striking, and rapid exposures of all the shameful outrages. When we do that (and we must and can do it), the most backward worker will understand, or *will feel*, that the students and religious sects, the peasants and the authors are being abused and outraged by those same dark forces that are oppressing and crushing him at every step of his life. Feeling that, he himself will be filled with an irresistible desire to react, and he will know how to hoot the censors one day, on another day to demonstrate outside the house of a governor who has brutally suppressed a peasant uprising, on still another day to teach a lesson to the gendarmes in surplices who are doing the work of the Holy Inquisition, etc. As yet we have done very little, almost nothing, *to bring* before the working masses prompt exposures on all possible issues. Many of us as yet do not recognise this as our *bounden duty* but trail spontaneously in the wake of the "drab everyday struggle," in the narrow confines of factory life. Under such circumstances to say that "*Iskra* displays a tendency to minimise the significance of the forward march of the drab everyday struggle in comparison with the propaganda of brilliant and completed ideas" . . . means to drag the Party back, to defend and glorify our unpreparedness and backwardness.

As for calling the masses to action, that will come of itself as soon as energetic political agitation, live and striking exposures come into play. To catch some criminal red-handed and immediately to brand him publicly in all places is of itself far more effective than any number of "calls"; the effect very often is such as will make it impossible to tell exactly who it was that "called" upon the masses and who suggested this or that plan of demonstration, etc. Calls for action, not in the general, but in the concrete, sense of the term can be made only at the place of action; only those who themselves go into action, and do so immediately, can sound such calls. Our business as Social-Democratic publicists is to deepen, expand, and intensify political exposures and political agitation.

■   ■   ■

Our Economists, including *Rabocyeye Dyelo*, were successful because they adapted themselves to the backward workers. But the Social-Democratic worker, the revolutionary worker (and the number of such workers is growing) will indignantly reject all this talk about struggle for demands "promising palpable results," etc., because he will understand that this is only a variation of the old song about adding a kopek to the ruble. Such a worker will say to his counsellors from *Rabochaya Mysl* and *Rabocheye Dyelo*: you are busying yourselves in vain, gentlemen, and shirking your proper duties, by meddling with such excessive zeal in a job that we can very well manage ourselves. There is nothing clever in your assertion that the Social-Democrats' task is to lend the economic struggle itself a political character; that is only the beginning, it is not the main task of the Social-Democrats. For all over the world, including Russia, *the police themselves often take the initiative in lending* the economic struggle a political character, and the workers themselves learn to understand whom the government supports.[11] The "economic struggle of the workers against the employers and the government," about which you make as much fuss as if you had discovered a new America, is being waged in all parts of Russia, even the most remote, by the workers themselves who have heard about strikes, but who have heard almost nothing about socialism. The "activity" you want to stimulate among us workers, by advancing concrete demands that promise palpable results, we are already displaying and in our everyday, limited trade union work we put forward these concrete demands, very often without any assistance whatever from the intellectuals. But *such* activity is not enough for us; we are not children to be fed on the thin gruel of "economic" politics alone; we want to know everything that others know, we want to learn the details of *all* aspects of political life and to take part *actively* in every single political event. In order that we may do this, the intellectuals must talk to us less of what we already know and tell us more about what we do not yet know and what we can never learn from our factory and "economic" experience, namely, political knowledge. You intellectuals can acquire this knowledge, and it is your *duty* to bring it to us in a hundred- and a thousand-fold greater measure than you have done up to now; and you must bring it to us, not only in the form of discussions, pamphlets, and articles (which very often—pardon our frankness—are rather dull), but precisely in the form of vivid *exposures* of what our government and our governing classes are doing at this very moment in all spheres of life. Devote more zeal to carrying out this duty and *talk less about "raising the activity of the working masses."* We are far more active than you think, and we are quite able to support, by open street fighting, even demands that do not promise any "palpable results" whatever. It is not for you to "raise" our activity, because *activity is precisely the thing you yourselves lack.* Bow less in subservience to spontaneity, and think more about raising *your own* activity, gentlemen!

### The Working Class as Vanguard Fighter for Democracy

We have seen that the conduct of the broadest political agitation and, consequently, of all-sided political exposures is an absolutely necessary and a *paramount* task of our activity, if this activity is to be truly Social-Democratic. However, we arrived at this conclusion *solely* on the grounds of the pressing needs of the working class for political knowledge and political training. But such a presentation of the question is too narrow, for it ignores the general democratic tasks of Social-Democracy, in particular of present-day Russian Social-Democracy. In order to explain the point more concretely we shall approach the subject from an aspect that is "nearest" to the Economist, namely, from the practical aspect. "Everyone agrees" that it is necessary to develop the political consciousness of the working class. The question is, *how* that is to be done and what is required to do it. The economic struggle merely "impels" the workers to realise the government's attitude towards the working class. Consequently, *however much we may try* to "lend the economic struggle itself a political character," we *shall never be able* to develop the political consciousness of the workers (to the level of Social-Democratic political consciousness) by keeping within the framework of the economic struggle, for *that framework is too narrow*. The Martynov formula has some value for us, not because it illustrates Martynov's aptitude for confusing things, but because it pointedly expresses the basic error that all the Economists commit, namely, their conviction that it is possible to develop the class political consciousness of the workers *from within*, so to speak, from their economic struggle, i.e., by making this struggle the exclusive (or, at least, the main) starting-point, by making it the exclusive (or, at least, the main) basis. Such a view is radically wrong. Piqued by our polemics against them, the Economists refuse to ponder deeply over the origins of these disagreements, with the result that we simply cannot understand one another. It is as if we spoke in different tongues.

Class political consciousness can be brought to the workers *only from without*, that is, only from outside the economic struggle, from outside the sphere of relations between workers and employers. The sphere from which alone it is possible to obtain this knowledge is the sphere of relationships of *all* classes and strata to the state and the government, the sphere of the interrelations between *all* classes. For that reason, the reply to the question as to what must be done to bring political knowledge to the workers cannot be merely the answer with which, in the majority of cases, the practical workers, especially those inclined towards Economism, mostly content themselves, namely: "To go among the workers." To bring political knowledge to the *workers* the Social-Democrats must *go among all classes of the population*; they must dispatch units of their army *in all directions*.

We deliberately select this blunt formula, we deliberately express ourselves in this sharply simplified manner, not because we desire to indulge in paradoxes, but in order to "impel" the Economists to a realisation of their tasks which they unpardonably ignore, to suggest to them strongly the difference between trade-unionist and Social-Democratic politics, which they refuse to understand. We therefore beg the reader not to get wrought up, but to hear us patiently to the end.

Let us take the type of Social-Democratic study circle that has become most widespread in the past few years and examine its work. It has "contacts with the workers" and rests content with this, issuing leaflets in which abuses in the factories, the government's partiality towards the capitalists, and the tyranny of the police are strongly condemned. At workers' meetings the discussions never, or rarely ever, go beyond the limits of these subjects. Extremely rare are the lectures and discussions held on the history of the revolutionary movement, on questions of the government's home and foreign policy, on questions of the economic evolution of Russia and of Europe, on the position of the various classes in modern society, etc. As to systematically acquiring and extending contact with other classes of society, no one even dreams of that. In fact, the ideal leader, as the majority of the members of such circles picture him, is something far more in the nature of a trade union secretary than a socialist political leader. For the secretary of any, say English, trade union always helps the workers to carry on the economic struggle, he helps them to expose factory abuses, explains the injustice of the laws and of measures that hamper the freedom to strike and to picket (i.e., to warn all and sundry that a strike is proceeding at a certain factory), explains the partiality of arbitration court judges who belong to the bourgeois classes, etc., etc. In a word, every trade union secretary conducts and helps to conduct "the economic struggle against the employers and the government." It cannot be too strongly maintained that *this is still not* Social-Democracy, that the Social-Democrat's ideal should not be the trade union secretary, but *the tribune of the people*, who is able to react to every manifestation of tyranny and oppression, no matter where it appears, no matter what stratum or class of the people it affects; who is able to generalise all these manifestations and produce a single picture of police violence and capitalist exploitation; who is able to take advantage of every event, however small, in order to set forth *before all* his socialist convictions and his democratic demands, in order to clarify for *all* and everyone the world historic significance of the struggle for the emancipation of the proletariat. . . .

■  ■  ■

Just picture to yourselves the following: a Social-Democrat comes to the "contingent" of Russian educated radicals, or liberal constitutionalists, and says, We are the vanguard; "the task confronting us now is, as far as possible, to lend the economic struggle itself a political character." The radical, or constitutionalist, if he is at all intelligent (and there are many intelligent men among Russian radicals and constitutionalists), would only smile at such a speech and would say (to himself, of course, for in the majority of cases he is an experienced diplomat): "Your 'vanguard' must be made up of simpletons. They do not even understand that it is our task, the task of the progressive representatives of bourgeois democracy to lend the workers' economic struggle *itself* a political character. Why, we too, like the West-European bourgeois, want to draw the workers into politics, *but only into trade-unionist, not into Social-Democratic politics.* Trade-unionist politics of the working class is precisely *bourgeois politics* of the working class, and this 'vanguard's' formulation of its task is the formulation of trade-unionist politics! Let them call themselves Social-Democrats to their heart's content, I am not a child to get excited over a label. But they must not fall under the influence of those pernicious orthodox doctrinaires, let them allow 'freedom of criticism' to those who unconsciously are driving Social-Democracy into trade-unionist channels."

And the faint smile of our constitutionalist will turn into Homeric laughter when he learns that the Social-Democrats who talk of Social-Democracy as the vanguard, today, when spontaneity almost completely dominates our movement, fear nothing so much as "belittling the spontaneous element," as "underestimating the significance of the forward movement of the drab everyday struggle, as compared with the propaganda of brilliant and completed ideas," etc., etc.! A "vanguard" which fears that consciousness will outstrip spontaneity, which fears to put forward a bold "plan" that would compel general recognition even among those who differ with us. Are they not confusing "vanguard" with "rearguard"?

∎　　∎　　∎

### Organisation of Workers and Organisation of Revolutionaries

It is only natural to expect that for a Social-Democrat whose conception of the political struggle coincides with the conception of the "economic struggle against the employers and the government," the "organisation of revolutionaries" will more or less coincide with the "organisation of workers." This, in fact, is what actually happens; so that when we speak of organisation, we literally speak in different tongues. I vividly recall, for example, a conversation I once had with a fairly consistent Economist, with whom I had not been previously acquainted. We were discussing the pamphlet, *Who Will Bring About the Political Revolution?* and were soon of a mind that its principal defect was its ignoring of the question of organisation. We had begun to assume full agreement between us; but, as the conversation proceeded, it became evident that we were talking of different things. My interlocutor accused the author of ignoring strike funds, mutual benefit societies, etc., whereas I had in mind an organisation of revolutionaries as an essential factor in "bringing about" the political revolution. As soon as the disagreement became clear, there was hardly, as I remember, a single question of principle upon which I was in agreement with the Economist!

What was the source of our disagreement? It was the fact that on questions both of organisation and of politics the Economists are forever lapsing from Social-Democracy into trade-unionism. The political struggle of Social-Democracy is far more extensive and complex than the economic struggle of the workers against the employers and the government. Similarly (indeed for that reason), the organisation of the revolutionary Social-Democratic Party must inevitably be of *a kind different* from the organisation of the workers designed for this struggle. The workers' organisation must in the first place be a trade union organisation; secondly, it must be as broad as possible; and thirdly, it must be as public as conditions will allow (here, and further on, of course, I refer only to absolutist Russia). On the other hand, the organisation of the revolutionaries must consist first and foremost of people who make revolutionary activity their profession (for which reason I speak of the organisation of *revolutionaries*, meaning revolutionary Social-Democrats). In view of this common characteristic of the members of such an organisation, *all distinctions as between workers and intellectuals*, not to speak of distinctions of trade and profession, in both categories, *must be effaced.* Such an organisation must perforce not be very extensive and must be as secret as possible. Let us examine this threefold distinction.

In countries where political libery exists the distinction between a trade union and a political organisation is clear enough, as is the distinction between trade unions and Social-Democracy. The relations between the latter and the former will naturally vary in each country according to historical, legal, and other conditions; they may be more or less close, complex, etc. (in our opinion they should be as close and as little complicated as possible); but there can be no question in free countries of the organisation of trade unions coinciding with the organisation of the Social-Democratic Party. In Russia, however, the yoke of the autocracy appears at first glance to obliterate all distinctions between the Social-Democratic organisation and the workers' associations, since *all* workers' associations and *all* study circles are prohibited, and since the principal manifestation and weapon of the workers' economic struggle—the strike—is regarded as a criminal (and sometimes even as a political!) offence. Conditions in our country, therefore, on the one hand, strongly "impel" the workers engaged in economic struggle to concern themselves with political questions, and, on the other, they "impel" Social-Democrats to confound trade-unionism with Social-Democracy (and our Krichevskys, Martynovs, and Co., while diligently discussing the first kind of "impulsion," fail to notice the second). Indeed, picture to yourselves people who are immersed ninety-nine per cent in "the economic struggle against the employers and the government." Some of them will never, during the *entire* course of their activity (from four to six months), be impelled to think of the need for a more complex organisation of revolutionaries. Others, perhaps, will come across the fairly widely distributed Bernsteinian literature, from which they will become convinced of the profound importance of the forward movement of "the drab everyday struggle." Still others will be carried away, perhaps, by the seductive idea of showing the world a new example of "close and organic contact with the proletarian struggle"—contact between the trade union and the Social-Democratic movements. Such people may argue that the later a country enters the areana of capitalism and, consequently, of the working-class movement, the more the socialists in that country may take part in, and support, the trade union movement, and the less the reason for the existence of non-Social-Democratic trade unions. So far the argument is fully correct; unfortunately, however, some go beyond that and dream of a complete fusion of Social-Democracy with trade-unionism. . . .

The workers' organisations for the economic struggle should be trade union organisations. Every Social-Democratic worker should as far as possible assist and actively work in these organisations. But, while this is true, it is certainly not in our interest to demand that only Social-Democrats should be eligible for membership in the "trade" unions, since that would only narrow the scope of our influence upon the masses. Let every worker who understands the need to unite for the struggle against the employers and the government join the trade unions. The very aim of the trade unions would be impossible of achievement, if they did not unite all who have attained at least this elementary degree of understanding, if they were not very *broad* organisations. The broader these organisations, the broader will be our influence over them—an influence due, not only to the "spontaneous" development of the economic struggle, but the direct and conscious effort of the socialist trade union members to influence their comrades. But a broad organisation cannot apply methods of strict secrecy (since this demands far greater training than is required for the economic struggle). How is the contradiction between the need for a large membership and the need for strictly secret methods to be reconciled? How are we to make the trade unions as public as possible? Generally speaking, there can be only two ways to this end: either the trade unions become legalised (in some countries this preceded the legalisation of the socialist and political unions), or the organisation is kept secret, but so "free" and amorphous, *lose*[12] as the Germans say, that the need for secret methods becomes almost negligible as far as the bulk of the members is concerned.

■ ■ ■

A small, compact core of the most reliable, experienced, and hardened workers, with responsible representatives in the principal districts and connected by all the rules of strict secrecy with the organisation of revolutionaries, can, with the widest support of the masses and without any formal organisation, perform *all* the functions of a trade union organisation, in a manner, moreover, desirable to Social-Democracy. Only in this way can we secure the *consolidation* and development of a *Social-Democratic* trade union movement, despite all the gendarmes.

It may be objected that an organisation which is so *lose* that it is not even definitely formed, and which has not even an enrolled and registered membership, cannot be called an organisation at all. Perhaps so. Not the name is important. What is important is that this "organisation without members" shall do everything that is required, and from the very outset ensure a solid connection between our future trade unions and socialism. Only an incorrigible utopian would have a *broad* organisation of workers, with elections, reports, universal suffrage, etc., under the autocracy.

The moral to be drawn from this is simple. If we begin with the solid foundation of a strong organisation of revolutionaries, we can ensure the stability of the movement as a whole and carry out the aims both of Social-Democracy and of trade unions proper. If, however, we begin with a broad workers' organisation, which is supposedly most "accessible" to the masses (but which is actually most accessible to the gendarmes and makes revolutionaries most accessible to the police), we shall achieve neither the one aim nor the other.

---

[1][The term "economists" is applied by Lenin to those in the Russian revolutionary movement who argued that propaganda and agitation among the workers should center on questions of economic betterment at the workplace, trade union issues, rather than on calling for the abolition of the social system or on raising questions about the relationship of the working class to all other classes and to the state as an organized political and military force.—*Eds.*]

[2]To avoid misunderstanding, we must point out that here, and throughout this pamphlet, by economic struggle, we imply (in keeping with the accepted usage among us) the "practical economic struggle," which Engels . . . described as "resistance to the capitalists," and which in free countries is known as the organised labour, syndical, or trade union struggle.

[3][Revolutionary Marxist groups in Russia at this time whose objective was the overthrow of the Czarist state. The term Social Democrat should not be confused with current usage to designate groups which are primarily reformist and do not seek the overthrow of the state.—*Eds.*]

[4][*Worker's Thought*, a newspaper expressing the views of the Economists and against which Lenin directed his polemics.—*Eds.*]

[5][*Worker's Cause*, a magazine published by the Economists.—*Eds.*]

[6][*The Spark*, a Russian Marxist newspaper founded by Lenin which played a critical role in the struggle against the Economists.—*Eds.*]

[7][A prominent Economist in the Russian Social Democratic movement and Lenin's major opponent in this polemic.—*Eds.*]

[8][Administrators for the landed nobility in czarist Russia.—*Eds.*]

[9][Sidney and Beatrice Webb were British Fabian socialists who opposed revolution and advocated peaceful and gradual social reform (see Part IV).—*Eds.*]

[10][Followers of Eduard Bernstein, a leader in the German Social Democratic Party who renounced revolutionary Marxism and espoused an evolutionary path to socialism based on gradual social reforms.—*Eds.*]

[11]The demand "to lend the economic struggle itself a political character" most strikingly expresses *subservience to spontaneity* in the sphere of political activity. Very often the economic struggle *spontaneously* assumes a political character, that is to say, without the intervention of the "revolutionary bacilli—the intelligentsia," without the intervention of the class-conscious Social-Democrats. The economic struggle of the English workers, for instance, also assumed a political character without any intervention on the part of the socialists. The task of the Social-Democrats, however, is not exhausted by political agitation on an economic basis; their task is *to convert* trade unionist politics into Social-Democratic political struggle, to *utilise* the sparks of political consciousness which the economic struggle generates among the workers, for the purpose of *raising* the workers to the level of *Social-Democratic* political consciousness. The Martynovs, however, instead of raising and stimulating the spontaneously awakening political consciousness of the workers, *bow to spontaneity* and repeat over and over *ad nauseam*, that the economic struggle "impels" the workers to realise their own lack of political rights. It is unfortunate, gentlemen, that the spontaneously awakening trade-unionist political consciousness does not *"impel"* you to an understanding of your Social-Democratic tasks.

[12][German word meaning "loose."—*Eds.*]

# 7
## *Lenin on Trade Unions*

THOMAS TAYLOR HAMMOND                                                     1957

Let us . . . summarize the basic points of Lenin's views on trade unions under capitalism.

First for the preliminary question: *Are trade unions necessary under capitalism?* There is no doubt about Lenin's views on this subject. On many, many occasions he emphasized the importance of trade unions and called upon his fellow Social-Democrats to help organize them and strengthen them. He felt that trade unions were especially important during the early stages of the labor movement because they helped to educate and train the workers, made them conscious of the evils of capitalism, and taught them how to organize and to fight against the employers. When certain Social-Democrats during the Revolution of 1905 argued that trade union work was relatively unimportant, Lenin insisted that such an attitude was mistaken, since trade unions were "always necessary under capitalism."

Another question, one that Lenin argued heatedly with the Economists, was this: *Which is more important, the economic struggle or the political struggle?* The Economists, charged Lenin, believed that the repressive conditions of tsarist autocracy made a successful political struggle impossible, and that the workers, therefore, should concentrate their energies on the economic struggle.

In reply Lenin insisted that the economic struggle alone could not possibly bring any significant improvement in the condition of the working class. He argued that the economic and political struggles could not be separated, that the fight of the workers against the capitalists would inevitably bring them into conflict with the government, and that the workers could achieve emancipation only through exerting their influence in the political field. This did not mean that the trade unions could be neglected. The proper course of action, said Lenin, was to combine the economic struggle with the political struggle and to make both of them revolutionary.

Closely related to this is another question: *Can trade unions take the place of the Party?* This subject was debated between Lenin and the Economists, and it came up again following the Revolution of 1905, when the Liquidators argued that the illegal revolutionary Party should be liquidated in favor of a legal Party and such legal organizations as trade unions.

Lenin was of course completely opposed to such views, since for him the most important organization was always the Party, which, he felt, should maintain its underground apparatus as long as capitalism continued to exist. Such an underground nucleus, he argued, could serve as a directing center for organizing and controlling the various legal societies. Lenin attacked both the Liquidators who wished to do away with the illegal Party and the Boycotters who boycotted such legal organizations as trade unions. The only way to overthrow capitalism, he said, was by extending and strengthening Social-Democratic work in all phases of the labor movement, both legal and illegal.

Lenin's insistence upon the importance of the Party was partly a result of his views on the next question: *Do the workers become socialist spontaneously?* That is, do conditions under capitalism inevitably lead the workers to believe in the necessity of revolution, or does this idea have to be instilled in their minds by a Vanguard of "conscious" intellectuals?

Reprinted from Thomas Hammond, *Lenin on Trade Unions and Revolution, 1893–1917,* pp. 123–129. New York: Columbia University Press, 1957. By permission. Footnotes in the original have been eliminated.

On this subject Lenin's views are not so clear; at times he said yes, and at other times he said no. In his famous pamphlet, *What Is to Be Done?* he argued that the workers by themselves would never develop real socialist consciousness, since this consciousness could be brought to them "only from without." But in 1905 he reversed himself and declared that "the working class is instinctively, spontaneously Social-Democratic." It may be that the 1905 Revolution showed Lenin that the workers were more inclined toward socialism than he had suspected. Apparently he felt that the workers become socialists because of the conditions of capitalism *and also* because the Vanguard of "conscious" Marxists organize them, educate them, and lead them in the right direction. The Party Vanguard was an essential element which he emphasized over and over.

If in Lenin's scheme of things the leadership of the Party Vanguard was so important, how could this leadership assert itself? Or, more specifically: *What sort of relationship should exist between the Party and the trade unions?*

On this point Lenin insisted, first of all, that the two organizations were different and should be kept separate. In normal times membership in the Party would be restricted to professional revolutionaries, whereas the trade unions would open their doors to all workers who understood the need for organization. During 1905 Lenin temporarily reversed himself and advocated the admission into the Party of hundreds and thousands of workers who had become infected with the revolutionary spirit. But this was merely a momentary lapse. Within a few months he was once again writing about a small underground Party and attacking those Social-Democrats who wanted to transform the Party into a mass organization.

If then in normal times Lenin wanted the Party Vanguard to consist of only a relatively small group of professional revolutionaries, the popular support for the revolutionary movement would have to be found elsewhere. Trade unions and other mass organizations would meet this need. They would act as auxiliaries to the Party, serving as forums for the dissemination of Social-Democratic doctrine, and providing a mass following for the Party in its struggle for revolution.

It is perfectly clear in Lenin's writings that from the first he wanted the trade unions to be under the influence of, and if possible controlled by, the Party. He did not want the unions to be neutral toward the Party; he wanted them to be *Social-Democratic* in ideology and in actions. But he was willing, under some circumstances, for the unions to *appear* neutral, so as to attract nonsocialists to membership and to avoid interference by the police.

Lenin urged Party members to join the unions and strive to achieve the dominant role in them. Each union, he said, should establish connections with the local organizations of the Party, and the unions could, under certain conditions, affiliate directly to the Party. To ensure firm control by the Party over union activities, Party cells should be established in the unions. These Party cells would be expected to secure the election of Party members to all important offices, and see to it that the unions followed the Party line. Lenin felt that unless the unions were firmly under Party control there was always the danger that the workers would succumb to bourgeois ideology, that they would neglect politics in favor of the economic struggle, and would look for their salvation to the trade unions rather than to the revolutionary Party.

■　　■　　■

Finally, there is that highly important problem: *the relation between reform and rev-*

*olution.* Which is the better way to achieve progress and improve the lot of mankind—gradual reform, or violent revolution? Lenin stoutly maintained that fundamental improvements were possible only through revolution. He was critical of English "trade union politics" on the ground that the English workers had renounced the goal of revolution in return for piecemeal reforms. This, of course, is exactly the path that England has followed for centuries. Russia, on the other hand, adopted the path of revolution and has been reaping the unfortunate consequences ever since.

For Lenin, revolution was a dogma. He felt that the struggle for petty reforms ordinarily carried on by trade unions under capitalism was a blind alley. Reforms were the crumbs that the capitalists offered to the workers in place of the whole loaf that could be won through revolution. Hence the struggle for reforms should be subordinated to the fight for revolution.

Lenin's ideological blinders prevented him from seeing or admitting that at least in some countries the condition of the working class was rather steadily improving over the long run, and that the proletariat was not inevitably doomed to Increasing Misery. But the condition of the working class in Russia in the early twentieth century was far worse than that of the workers in England, Germany, or the United States, and many of the reforms won in the Revolution of 1905 were lost in the succeeding years. This makes it easier to understand why Lenin was dubious about the method of reform and insisted that revolution was the only solution. But if Lenin and the other revolutionaries had been willing to concentrate on such methods as building up a strong trade union movement and winning piecemeal reforms, Russia might have been spared dictatorship, and the subsequent fate of the Russian working class would probably have been considerably better.

Marx had taught that certain "objective factors" in capitalist society (such as the factory system, the proletarianization of the population, depressions, and unemployment) would create a situation in which the proletariat out of desperation would rise up in revolt. Although he considered the revolution to be inevitable, Marx still worked to bring it about. He labored to create an international organization of workingmen whose leaders, after waiting for the necessary objective factors to develop, would take advantage of the situation to lead the proletariat to victory. These leaders were to be the subjective factor in the revolution.

Lenin was in too much of a hurry to wait for the objective factors of history to develop as Marx had prescribed. Like Zheliabov he might have said: "History moves too slowly. It needs a push." Lenin refused to be delayed by the fact that the objective conditions in Russia were not yet ripe—at least not in accordance with Marx's formula. What he emphasized, therefore, was the subjective factor—the role of leadership. Since the Russian proletariat was pitifully small, and since it was comparatively uneducated and unorganized, the leaders would have to be better trained and disciplined and more determined. They would make use not only of the proletariat, but also of the peasantry, and thus would greatly speed up the coming of the socialist revolution. In this manner, Russia could be made to move more quickly from an era that was still largely precapitalist to the era of socialism. In other words, the subjective factor (the Party Vanguard) would bring about the revolution, in spite of the fact that the objective factors had not sufficiently matured.

Lenin's insistence upon a Bolshevik revolution in November, 1917, despite the fact that the majority of the people did not share the aims of the Bolsheviks, meant that the new government had to impose its program upon the country by force and terror. The "dictatorship of the proletariat" became in fact the dictatorship of the Party which had led the revolution—a Party which was itself antidemocratic in tradition and organization.

Lenin was the epitome of the impatient radical who cannot wait for reforms to be instituted bit by bit, but insists that everything must be completely transformed in one great bloody cataclysm. He was the very embodiment of the self-confident religious zealot who feels that a handful of courageous converts, armed with the "true" dogmas, can remake human nature and worldly institutions in a few years. He was convinced that he and a few other revolutionaries (the Vanguard), through their determination and self-sacrifice, could bend the course of history to their will and create a paradise on earth. He deluded himself into believing that Russia could be transformed in a short while into a utopian wonderland, despite the fact that most of the "objective factors" of Russian society and Russian tradition indicated just the opposite. As far as freedom for the Russian people is concerned, the results of his impatience can perhaps best be summarized by the title of one of his own works: "One Step Forward, Two Steps Back."

■　　■　　■

One result that the revolution did bring was Lenin's aim of a trade union movement dominated by the Party Vanguard and used for Party ends. Although Soviet trade unions make some pretense of being genuine, independent bodies, Lenin himself admitted as early as 1920 that "all the controlling bodies of the overwhelming majority of the unions . . . consist of Communists and carry out all the instructions of the Party." While trade unions in "capitalist" countries are still winning such reforms as higher wages, shorter hours, and better working conditions, the unions in the USSR have become Party tools, completely powerless to champion the interests of the workers who comprise their membership and whom they supposedly represent.

# REVOLUTIONARY SYNDICALISM
## 8
### *I.W.W. Manifesto*

1905

Social relations and groupings only reflect mechanical and industrial conditions. The *great facts* of present industry are the displacement of human skill by machines and the increase of capitalist power through concentration in the possession of the tools with which wealth is produced and distributed.

Because of these facts trade divisions among laborers and competition among capitalists are alike disappearing. Class divisions grow ever more fixed and class antagonisms more sharp. Trade lines have been swallowed up in a common servitude of all workers to the machines which they tend. New machines, ever replacing less productive ones, wipe out whole trades and plunge new bodies of workers into the ever-growing army of tradeless, hopeless unemployed. As human beings and human skill are displaced by mechanical progress, the capitalists need use the workers only during that brief period when muscles and nerves respond most intensely. The moment the laborer no longer yields the maximum of profits, he is thrown upon the scrap pile, to starve alongside the discarded machine. A *dead line* has been drawn, and an age-limit established, to cross which, in this world of monopolized opportunities, means condemnation to industrial death.

The worker, wholly separated from the land and the tools, with his skill of craftsmenship rendered useless, is sunk in the uniform mass of wage slaves. He sees his power of resistance broken by craft divisions, perpetuated from outgrown industrial stages. His wages constantly grow less as his hours grow longer and monopolized prices grow higher. Shifted hither and thither by the demands of profit-takers the laborer's home no longer exists. In this helpless condition he is forced to accept whatever humiliating conditions his master may impose. He is submitted to a physical and intellectual examination more searching than was the chattel slave when sold from the auction block. Laborers are no longer classified by differences in trade skill, but the employer assigns them according to the machines to which they are attached. These divisions, far from representing differences in skill or interests among the laborers, are imposed by the employers that workers may be pitted against one another and spurred to greater exertion in the shop, and that all resistance to capitalist tyranny may be weakened by artificial distinctions.

While encouraging these outgrown divisions among the workers the capitalists carefully adjust themselves to the new conditions. They wipe out all differences among themselves and present a united front in their war upon labor. Through employers' associations, they seek to crush, with brutal force, by the injunctions of the judiciary, and the use of military power, all efforts at resistance. Or when the other policy seems more profitable, they conceal their daggers beneath the Civic Federation and hoodwink and betray those whom they would rule and exploit. Both methods depend for success upon the blindness and internal dissensions of the working class. The employers' line of battle and methods of warfare correspond to the solidarity of the mechanical and industrial concentration, while laborers still form their fighting organizations on lines of long-gone trade

Reprinted with permission of the author from *Rebel Voices: An I.W.W. Anthology* by Joyce L. Kornbluh, pp. 7–9. Ann Arbor: University of Michigan Press, 1964. Copyright ● 1964 by Joyce L. Kornbluh. The Manifesto was drafted in 1905 and sent to all unions in the United States and to the industrial unions in Europe. A new edition of Joyce Kornbluh, *Rebel Voices: An I.W.W. Anthology* was published in 1985 by Charles H. Kerr Co., Chicago.

divisions. The battles of the past emphasize this lesson. The *textile* workers of Lowell, Philadelphia and Fall River; the *butchers* of Chicago, weakened by the disintegrating effects of trade divisions; the *machinists* on the Santa Fe, unsupported by their fellow-workers subject to the same masters; the long-struggling *miners* of Colorado, hampered by lack of unity and solidarity upon the industrial battle-field, all bear witness to the helplessness and impotency of labor as at present organized.

This worn-out and corrupt system offers no promise of improvement and adaptation. There is no silver lining to the clouds of darkness and despair settling down upon the world of labor.

This system offers only a perpetual struggle for slight relief within wage slavery. It is blind to the possibility of establishing an industrial democracy, wherein there shall be no wage slavery, but where the workers will own the tools which they operate, and the product of which they alone will enjoy.

It shatters the ranks of the workers into fragments, rendering them helpless and impotent on the industrial battle-field.

Separation of craft from craft renders industrial and financial solidarity impossible.

Union men scab upon union men; hatred of worker for worker is engendered, and the workers are delivered helpless and disintegrated into the hands of the capitalists.

Craft jealousy leads to the attempt to create trade monopolies.

Prohibitive initiation fees are established that force men to become scabs against their will. Men whom manliness or circumstances have driven from one trade are thereby fined when they seek to transfer membership to the union of a new craft.

Craft divisions foster political ignorance among the workers, thus dividing their class at the ballot box, as well as in the shop, mine and factory.

Craft unions may be and have been used to assist employers in the establishment of monopolies and the raising of prices. One set of workers are thus used to make harder the conditions of life of another body of laborers.

Craft divisions hinder the growth of class consciousness of the workers, foster the idea of harmony of interests between employing exploiter and employed slave. They permit the association of the misleaders of the workers with the capitalists in the Civic Federations, where plans are made for the perpetuation of capitalism, and the permanent enslavement of the workers through the wage system.

Previous efforts for the betterment of the working class have proven abortive because limited in scope and disconnected in action.

Universal economic evils afflicting the working class can be eradicated only by a universal working class movement. Such a movement of the working class is impossible while separate craft and wage agreements are made favoring the employer against other crafts in the same industry, and while energies are wasted in fruitless jurisdiction struggles which serve only to further the personal aggrandizement of union officials.

A movement to fulfill these conditions must consist of one great industrial union embracing all industries,—providing for craft autonomy locally, industrial autonomy internationally, and working class unity generally.

It must be founded on the class struggle, and its general administration must be conducted in harmony with the recognition of the irrepressible conflict between the capitalist class and the working class.

It should be established as the economic organization of the working class, without affiliation with any political party.

All power should rest in a collective membership.

Local, national and general administration, including union labels, buttons, badges, transfer cards, initiation fees, and per capita tax should be uniform throughout.

All members must hold membership in the local, national or international union covering the industry in which they are employed, but transfers of membership between unions, local, national or international, should be universal.

Workingmen bringing union cards from industrial unions in foreign countries should be freely admitted into the organization.

The general administration should issue a publication representing the entire union and its principles which should reach all members in every industry at regular intervals.

A *central defense fund,* to which all members contribute equally, should be established and maintained.

*All workers, therefore, who agree with the principles herein set forth, will meet in convention at Chicago the 27th day of June, 1905, for the purpose of forming an economic organization of the working class along the lines marked out in this Manifesto.*

Representation in the convention shall be based upon the number of workers whom the delegate represents. No delegate, however, shall be given representation in the convention on the numerical basis of an organization unless he has credentials—bearing the seal of his union, local, national or international, and the signatures of the officers thereof—authorizing him to install his union as a working part of the proposed economic organization in the industrial department in which it logically belongs in the general plan of organization. Lacking this authority, the delegate shall represent himself as an individual.

Adopted at Chicago, January 2, 3 and 4, 1905.

| | |
|---|---|
| A. G. Swing | John Guild |
| A. M. Simons | Daniel McDonald |
| W. Shurtleff | Eugene V. Debs |
| Frank M. McCabe | Thos. J. DeYoung |
| John M. O'Neil | Thos. J. Hagerty |
| Geo. Estes | Fred D. Henion |
| Wm. D. Haywood | W. J. Bradley |
| Mother Jones | Chas. O. Sherman |
| Ernest Untermann | M. E. White |
| W. L. Hall | Wm. J. Pinkerton |
| Chas. H. Moyer | Frank Kraffs |
| Clarence Smith | J. E. Fitzgerald |
| William Ernest Trautmann | Frank Bohn |
| Jos. Schmidt | |

# 9
## Preamble of the Industrial Workers of the World

1908

The working class and the employing class have nothing in common. There can be no peace so long as hunger and want are found among millions of working people and the few, who make up the employing class, have all the good things of life.

Between these two classes a struggle must go on until the workers of the world organize as a class, take possession of the earth and the machinery of production, and abolish the wage system.

We find that the centering of management of the industries into fewer and fewer hands makes the trade unions unable to cope with the ever growing power of the employing class. The trade unions foster a state of affairs which allows one set of workers to be pitted against another set of workers in the same industry, thereby helping defeat one another in wage wars. Moreover, the trade unions aid the employing class to mislead the workers into the belief that the working class have interests in common with their employers.

These conditions can be changed and the interest of the working class upheld only by an organization formed in such a way that all its members in any one industry, or in all industries if necessary, cease work whenever a strike or lockout is on in any department thereof, thus making an injury to one an injury to all.

Instead of the conservative motto, "A fair day's wage for a fair day's work," we must inscribe on our banner the revolutionary watchword, "Abolition of the wage system."

It is the historic mission of the working class to do away with capitalism. The army of production must be organized, not only for the every-day struggle with capitalists, but also to carry on production when capitalism shall have been overthrown. By organizing industrially we are forming the structure of the new society within the shell of the old.

Reprinted with permission of the author from *Rebel Voices: An I.W.W. Anthology* by Joyce L. Kornbluh, pp. 12–13. Ann Arbor: University of Michigan Press, 1964. Copyright © 1964 by Joyce L. Kornbluh. The Preamble was approved by the 1908 I.W.W. Convention.

# 10
## *Why Strikes Are Lost*

WILLIAM TRAUTMANN                                                    CA. 1911

After a tremendous epidemic of strikes a few years ago, conflicts expressive of a general discontent finding its outlet in vehement eruptions, but ending only with a pitiful exhaustion of vitality, there seems to be at present a relapse all around. "The workers have gone to sleep" thinks the superficial observer and the uninformed outside world.

This seems, indeed, to be the truth. However, a relapse in numerical strength would amount to little: economic depression could be attributed as the cause.

But deplorable would it be if there were in reality a relapse in the aggressive attitude, in the revolutionary feelings of the workers.

This spirit of revolt manifesting itself a few years ago in somewhat rough actions and expressions seemed to mark the beginning of a general awakening of large masses of workers, and yet there seems to be nothing left of the spontaneous, widespread tendency of revolt.

For this there must be reasons. Such powerfully exploding forces cannot be destroyed altogether, or be dammed in by repressive measures.

Time flies quickly; here and there one hears again of rapid flaring up, of a volcanic eruption of accumulated discontent, but in most of the cases it is only a last flicker of a light before it goes out altogether.

If occasionally larger bodies of workers become involved in these demonstrations of revolt, politicians and labor (mis)leaders are quickly on hand to suggest termination of the conflict, with the promise of speedy arbitration. These leaders of labor often even threaten to engage union strikebreakers if the workers refuse to obey their mandates. In some cases the places of striking workers have been filled by other members of these so-called unions so as to suppress any rebellion against the leaders and the capitalist class whom they serve. But seldom is anything more heard of the results of such conciliatory tactics, or of any determined stand on the part of the workers to enforce the terms of such settlements. Their power once crushed after having been exercised with the most effective precision, also destroys their confidence; and the organization through which they were able to rally the forces of their fellow workers for concerted action disappears.

After an apparent awakening of three or four years duration (1901 to 1905), during which some of the largest conflicts were fought on American soil, a general indifference superseded the previous activity. A lethargy prevails now, even to the extent that many workers with eyes still shut are marching into the pitfalls laid for them. Blindfolded by false theories they are being prevented from coming together into organization in which the workers would be able to profit from the lessons of the past, and prepare for the conflicts with the capitalist class with better knowledge of facts and more thoroughly equipped to give them better battle.

In the period mentioned the general clamor for an advance in wages, and the shortening of the workday, had to find its expression. Prices of the necessities of life had been soaring up, as a rule, before the workers instinctively felt that they, too, had to make efforts to overcome the increased poverty attendant upon increased prices for life's necessities. Powerless as individuals, as they well knew, they were inclined to come together for more collective and concerted action. With great displays and much oratory the beauties and the achievements of such action on craft union lines, as exemplified by the American Federation of Labor and the eight independent national Brotherhoods of Railway Workers, were presented to them.

Not knowing better, seeing before their eyes immediate improvement of their conditions, or at least a chance to advance the price of their labor power in proportion to the increased cost of living, the workers flocked into the trades unions in large numbers. At the same time the relative scarcity of available workers in the open market, at a period of relative good times, forced the employers of labor to forestall any effort to cripple production. Consequently, in the epidemic of strikes following one another, the workers gained concessions. Such concessions, however, were as much the combined result of a decreased supply of labor to an increasing demand, as to the spontaneously developed onrush into the trade unions.

One thing, also, contributed largely to the success of these quickly developed strikes. The workers would come together shortly before walking out of the shops. In the primary stage of organization thus formed they knew nothing of craft distinctions. Unaware of what later would be used as a barrier against staying together, they would usually strike in a body and win in most cases. Anxious to preserve the instrument by which alone they could obtain any results, they found in most cases that certain rules were laid down by a few wise men in bygone years, which were to govern the organizations and force them to admit to, or reject from membership, anyone who did not strictly fit into the measure of "craft autonomy."

**What Is Craft Autonomy?**

It is a term used to lay down restrictive rules for each organization which adheres to the policy of allowing only a certain portion of workers in a given industry to become members of a given trade union. Formerly, as a rule, a craft was determined by the tool which a group of workers used in the manufacturing process. But as the simple tool of yore gave way to the large machine, the distinction was changed to designate the part of a manufacturing process on a given article by a part of the workers engaged in the making of the same.

For instance, in the building of a machine the following crafts are designated as performing certain functions, namely:

The workers preparing the pattern are patternmakers.

The workers making cores are core makers.

The workers making molds and castings are molders.

The workers molding the brass bearings are brass molders.

The helpers working in the foundry are foundry helpers.

The workers preparing and finishing the parts of machines are machinists.

The workers polishing up the parts of machines are metal polishers.

The workers assembling the parts of machines are assemblers.

The workers putting on copper parts are coppersmiths.

The workers putting on the insulation parts are steamfitters.

This line of demarkation could thus be drawn in almost every industry.

Now these various crafts, each contributing its share in the production of an article, are not linked together in one body, although members of these crafts work in one plant or industry.

They are separated in craft groups. Each craft union zealously guards its own craft interests. The rule is strictly adhered to that even if the protection of the interests of a craft organization is detrimental to the general interests of all others no interference is permitted. This doctrine of non-interference in the affairs of a craft union is what is called "craft or trade autonomy."

## Evil Effects of Craft Autonomy

Now, as observed in the beginning, a body of workers, only recently brought together, may walk out on strike, before they have learned to know what craft autonomy implies. In such cases they usually win. As soon as they begin to settle down to do some constructive or educational work, to keep the members interested in the affairs of the organization and prepare for future conflicts with the employers, they learn to their chagrin that they have done wrong in allowing all to be together.

They are told that they had no right to organize all working at one place into one organization. The splitting-up process is enforced, trade autonomy rules are applied, and what was once a united body of workers without knowledge of the intricate meaning of "autonomy" is finally divided into a number of craft organizations.

The result is that no concerted action is possible in the conflicts following. Many a time the achievements of one strike, won only because the workers stood and fought together, are lost in the next skirmish. One portion of workers, members of one craft union, remain at work, while others, members of another trade union, are fighting either for improved working conditions, or in resistance against wrongs or injustice done them by the employing class.

Take, for example, the first street car workers' strike in San Francisco, in the first year of Mayor Schmidt's administration. Not only were all motormen, conductors and ticket agents organized in one union, but the barnmen, the linemen and repairers, and many of the repair shop workers enlisted in the union, also the engineers, the firemen, the electricians, the ashwheelers, oilers, etc., in the power stations. They all fought together. The strike ended with a signal victory for the workers; this was accomplished because the workers had quit their work spontaneously. But hardly had they settled down to arrange matters for the future, and to make the organization still stronger, when they found themselves confronted with the clamor of "craft autonomy rules."

They were told that the electricians in the power houses, linemen and line repairers had to be members of the International Brotherhood of Electrical Workers. The workers heard to their amazement that the engineers had to be members of the International Union of Steam Engineers.

The firemen, ashwheelers and oilers were commanded to withdraw at once from the Street Car Employes' Union, and join the union of their craft. The workers in the repair shops were not permitted under trade autonomy rules to form a union embracing all engaged therein. They had to join the union of their craft, either as machinists, molders, polishers or woodworkers, and would not be permitted to be members of any other organization. *They are restrained by the rules of craft autonomy from being members of a union embracing all in the industry, even if they had chosen to remain members by their own free choice. They were not allowed to think that their place would be in such an organization through which the best results with the least of sacrifices for the workers could be obtained.*

In the second strike of street car workers in 1907 the absolute failure, the complete disaster, was solely due to the fact that the workers, separated in several craft groups, could not strike together and win together. Similar cases, by the hundreds, could be enumerated to show what grave injuries craft autonomy inflicts upon the workers. And if the investigator will follow the investigation of facts and underlying causes, he will be surprised to see how the employers take advantage of this dividing-up policy. He will see how the capitalist gleefully helped to pit one portion of the workers against others in the same or other industries, so that the latter, while kept busy fighting among themselves, had no time nor strength to direct their fights against the employers and exploiters.

The most striking example was given recently in the two strikes of street car workers in Philadelphia. In July 1909, they went on strike. Only a portion of them were then organized. But the workers all made the fight a common cause of all. Not only did workers on the subway lines begin to quit, but also the power house workers in several stations walked out, shutting off the power, thus forcing the company to make a settlement.

The Philadelphia street car lines are controlled by the same corporation that operates and owns the lines in San Francisco, in Pittsburgh, in Cincinnati, in Louisville, in Detroit, and other cities, the Elkins-Widener-Dolan Syndicate. The same trick was played in Philadelphia as in San Francisco after the first victorious contest. The separation process began. The power-house men, members of the National Union of Steam Engineers and the Brotherhood of Stationary Firemen, 1,800 of them, according to Tim Healy, one of the head labor fakirs of these organizations, and the electricians were tied down by contracts.

The street car company forced the second strike in February, 1910, and of course the craft union engineers, the union firemen, and the union electricians remained at work, protecting their craft union interests.

When, in the course of rapidly developed events, it was found necessary to call a general strike in all industries, what was the real result? The A.F. of L. unions who had declared the strike were the ones to ignore the strike orders. They had to protect their "contracts," by order from the national labor lieutenants. The Brewery Workers, the Printers, the Molders, later the Cigarmakers, and scores of other "union men" scabbed it on their own order, while the *big bulk of unorganized again responded nobly.*

Now that the real facts are known it is ascertained that out of approximately 320,000 wage workers in that city, 45,000 responded to the strike call, of whom there were 32,000 so-called "unorganized" workers, or partly organized in independent unions or in the Industrial Workers of the World. The balance, 13,000, were either building trades workers, who were not working anyway at the time of the strike order, or were members of radical, progressive unions.

But the body of approximately 45,000 workers, organized in the A. F. of L. unions, who had issued the strike call, remained at work, protecting their contracts. *The real union-made scabs*—the 1,800 union engineers, firemen, electricians, in the power houses—failed to respond; they *union-labeled scabs* by order of the labor lieutenants! And all other street car workers in other cities, where the same syndicate operates the street car service, remained at work, although a farcical general strike was pulled off, so as to discredit forever the general strike idea.

In the Baldwin Locomotive Works thousands of so-called "unorganized" workers had gone out in response to the general strike call. They were ready to form an organization embracing all in that industry. First they were urged not to insist on having *one union*. Their reply was: "Either all into one, or none at all!"

Finally, in a meeting attended by most of the "great" leaders of the strike, they were promised a charter as "Baldwin Locomotive Workers' Association"; but at the moment that the promise was made, William Mahon, "president of the Amalgamated Association of Street and Electric Car Employes," A. F. of L., turned around and remarked: "They can be assorted to their respective craft unions after this strike is over." (Authentic reports, corroborated by editorials in the Philadelphia Tageblatt, the official organ of the German Trades Union Council of Philadelphia.)

What more is needed to convince the workers of the reason: "Why Strikes Are Lost"?

## The Sacredness of Contracts

Perhaps the workers, although compelled in most of the cases to adhere to the outlined plan of organizing in craft unions, would have made common cause with other crafts in any one industry in their conflicts with the capitalists, if they had realized that the defeat of one ultimately meant the defeat of all"—such may be said in rebuttal.

But with the separation from other groups of workers a craft or sectarian spirit was developed among members of each of the trade organizations. A spirit manifested itself, and does so now, in their relations to other groups of workers as well as to the employers of labor. "Gains at any price" even at the expense of others, has become the governing rule. The rule of "non-interference" made sacred by the decrees of those who blatantly pose as leaders of labor, permitted one craft union to ride roughshod over the others. "Let us go ahead; the devil take the hindmost," has drowned the old idea of the "injury to one is the concern of all." Woe to anyone who would try to throw himself against this current. He will be drowned and buried under mud thrown upon him by all the vultures and vampires.

A great victory is proclaimed in print and public when one or the other of such craft organizations succeeds in getting a contract signed with an individual employer, or, what is considered still better, if it is consummated with an association of employers in a given industry. But actuated by that sectarian spirit these contracts are considered to be inviolable. Not so much by the employers, who will break them any time when it will be to their advantage; but by the workers who are organized in craft unions. Imbued with their sectarian ideas, by the terms of such a contract they are in duty bound to protect the interests of the employers if the latter should have controversies with other craft unions. Thus the workers consent to being made traitors to their class.

Small wonder, therefore, that in that period between 1901 and 1905, the time that these lessons and conclusions are drawn from, the employers were able to check first, then to retard, and finally to paralyze the workers in any efforts to secure by their organized efforts permanently improved conditions in their places of employment. The employers, supported by such lieutenants of labor as Gompers, Mitchell, Duncan and others (as they were rightly called by Marcus Aurelius Hanna when he organized the Hanna-chist Civic Federation), would harp continually on the sanctity of contracts with some of the craft unions, while at the same time slaughtering piece-meal other craft unions with whom they were in conflict.

Of the thousand and odd strikes that took place in that period and since, none bears better testimony of the impotency of the craft unions; not one has presented better proof of the shameless betrayal of working class interests than the gigantic strike of workers in the meat packing and slaughter houses in Chicago, Omaha and other places in the country.

### A Horrible Example

The meat wagon drivers of Chicago were organized in 1902. They made demands for better pay and shorter hours. Unchecked by any outside influence, they walked out on strike. They had the support of all other workers in the packing houses. They won. But before they resumed work the big packing firms insisted that they enter into a contract. They did. In that contract the teamsters agreed not to engage in any sympathetic strike with other employes in the plants or stockyards. Not only this, but the drivers also decided to split their union into three. They then had the "Bone and Shaving Teamsters," the "Packing House Teamsters," and the "Meat Delivery Drivers."

Encouraged by the victory of the teamsters, the other workers in the packing houses then started to organize. But they were carefully advised not to organize into one body, or at the best into one National Trades Union. They had to be divided up, so that the employers could exterminate them all whenever opportunity presented itself.

Now observe how the dividing-up process worked. The teamsters were members of the "International Union of Teamsters." The engineers were connected with the "International Union of Steam Engineers." The firemen, oilers, ashwheelers were organized in the "Brotherhood of Stationary Firemen." Carpenters employed in the stockyards permanently had to join the "Brotherhood of Carpenters and Joiners." The pipe and steam fitters were members of another "National Union." The sausage makers, the packers, the canning department workers, the beef butchers, the cattle butchers, the hog butchers, the bone shavers, etc., each craft group had a separate union. Each union had different rules, all of them not permitting any infringements on them by others. Many of the unions had contracts with the employers. These contracts expired at different dates. Most of the contracts contained the clause of "no support to others when engaged in a controversy with the stockyard companies."

The directory of unions of Chicago shows in 1903 a total of 56 different unions in the packing houses, divided up still more in 14 different national trades unions of the American Federation of Labor.

What a horrible example of an army divided against itself in the face of a strong combination of employers. This was best displayed in the last desperate and pitiful struggle of the stock yard laborers against the announced wage reduction from 17 to 16 cents an hour in 1904.

These oppressed workers, mostly Poles and Lithuanians, who have so often helped others when called upon, could have reasonably expected the support at least of those who were working with them in the same industry.

Nor would their expectations have failed of realization, if the other workers had been given a free hand.

No wage worker, if he has any manhood in him, likes to be a strikebreaker of his own free will. That there are thousands of strikebreakers in America is due to the discriminative rules of the American Federation of Labor unions. Due also to the high initiation fees, as high as $500.[1] But the history of strikes proves that where no restrictive measures are enforced, the workers in one plant instinctively make common cause; they stand together in every conflict with their employers.

Not so when the lash of a sacred contract is held over their head. The breaking of a contract, in most of the cases, means suspension from the union. It means that the union agrees to fill the places of men or women who suspend work in violation of contracts. This is so stipulated in most of the agreements with the employers. In more than one case labor leaders have helped the employers to fill the places of the rebellious workers.

Now in that strike of butcher workmen in the stock yards they looked to the engineers, the firemen and others to quit their jobs. They expected the teamsters to walk out in their support as the latter themselves had gained their demands only by the support of all. And really all the members of these craft unions were prepared and ready to lay down their tools. The strike would have been won within 24 hours if all had stood together. The employers realized that. They sent for their labor lieutenants. Over 25 labor leaders conjointly helped to force the workers back to their stations. Drivers already walking out were told to return or their places would be filled by other union men. The engineers were commanded to abide by their contract with the companies. Union printers, members of the Typographical Union, employed in the printing plants of the stock yards, were escorted every day through the picket lines of the poor strikers with permit badges pinned to their coats, issued by their union, so that the strikers' pickets would not molest these "licensed" strikebreakers. These aristocrats of labor even looked down with contempt on the men and women whom an ill fate compelled to be slaves of the magnates of

"Packingtown." All appeals to the manhood of these union strikebreakers were in vain. Stronger than their sense of duty and of solidarity in the struggle of members of their own class, was the "iron gag and chain of craft union non-interference." *The contracts* were the weapons in the hands of the capitalists, by which the craft unionists were forced to wear the stigma of strikebreakers. They were made union scabs at the moment when concerted action would have pulled down the flag of boastful, defiant triumph from the palaces of the bosses, and would have raised up the banner of working class victory on the miserable pest houses in which men and women and children are compelled to drudge for a pitiful, miserable existence. Yes! these were the weapons used by the meat barons of America to ultimately extinguish all unions of workers in their employ.

*The capitalists could not defeat the workers, not they!* The craft unionists, forced by the lieutenants of the employing class—because most of the craft union leaders are indirectly their servants—defeated themselves. They shattered not only their own hopes, but the hopes, the confidence, the aspirations of thousands and tens of thousands, who had thought, after all, that unionism meant: "Solidarity, Unity, Brotherly Support in Hours of Strike and Struggle."

This is why and how the workers lost! Not only in Packingtown, but in almost every industrial place of production in that period referred to. That was the way the employers did, and still do, rally their forces in their successful efforts to defeat labor. By slashing piecemeal the Giant, tied hand and foot by a paper contract, they throttled him, threw his members out of joint, so that his enormous strength could not be used against his oppressors. Oh, but they would not kill him, oh, no! He who is so useful to them to create everything, so that they who do nothing may abound in luxury and debauchery; he must only be kept in his cage, within his dungeon where he drudges in the sweat of his brow, bent over in blunt indifference, carrying stupidly his burden, the weight of a world that depends on him for its existence. Believing that he is eternally condemned to be a slave he perishes and falls by the wayside when his usefulness for the master class ceases. In "Organized Labor," John Mitchell, one of the "great leaders," begins his first sentence with the words: "The workers never hope to be more than wage earners."

Craft unionism, fostered by the American Federation of Labor, has made him the pathetic wage slave, always contented to be no more than a wage slave, with no higher ideals and sublime hopes for a better life on earth.

Can you hear the curses and condemnation, intermingled with the outcries of despair when the burdens become too heavy? Not so much hatred is expressed against those and their class who Shylock like, only ask for and take their good pound of flesh, as against the vampires who suck the life blood of the workers, destroy their hopes and energies, stultify their manhood! The labor traitors who live and dwell in debaucheries akin to the masters', whose pliant dirty tools they are, more than any other force are responsible that the workers have so often lost their battles for a higher station in life.

### Labor Vultures

They, whether their names be Gompers, Mitchell, Duncan, Tobin, Golden, Grant Hamilton, or what else, are the vultures, because they exist only by dividing the workers and separating one from another. They have been and are doing the bidding of the master class. Upon them falls the awful curse of a world of millions. They have made America the land of the lost strikes—the land where from the mountains and the hills, and in the plains and vales resound the echoes of the curse of an outraged working class. They are the dark forces that the world should know as the traitors, the real malefactors, the real instigators of the appalling defeats and betrayals of the proletarians. The land in which the depravity of these vultures has driven thousands back into despair and distrust, and aroused their suspicion—thousands who only lost because they placed implicit confidence in those who were agents of their oppressors—thousands who never were shown what they had come together for—thousands who had confided, only to be betrayed, to be thrown back into the desert from where there is no escape from the penalty for blind confidence: all those hundreds of thousands have lost faith in the ability of their own class to release themselves from the grasp of the oppressors. But what does it concern the labor leaders? It is on these conditions that they are allowed to exist in their debaucheries, to continue their destructive work in the interests of the capitalists.

This great country furnishes the most valuable object lesson to the working class movement of the universe. Let us hope, let us trust, that the workers everywhere may profit from the tragedies of this land, so that, enlightened by such experiences, they may throw their efforts into one cause and so enable the proletariat to free themselves from the chains of economic slavery and prepare themselves for the historic mission, for the real, final struggle, for their industrial freedom, the only freedom worth while fighting for.

---

[1]This amount is charged by the National Association of Green Bottle Blowers. In August, 1908, there was held in the city of Paris, France, an international congress of delegates of the ceramic trades. Delegates from the Green Bottle Blowers' Association of America were present. They were requested to at least waive that initiation fee for union men from other countries, at the same trade. To this the delegates of the Green Bottle Blowers' Association replied with the withdrawal of their two delegates, and with the announcement that they would work for the increase of that initiation fee to $1,000 for anybody who wants to get work in that industry. (See records published in Paris.) Dennis Hayes, the General President of that Association, is fourth Vice President of the American Federation of Labor.

# 11
## *Political Parties and the I.W.W.*

**VINCENT ST. JOHN**                                                    CA. 1910

I am in receipt of many inquiries relative to the position of the I.W.W. and political action. One fellow worker wants to know, "How is this revolutionary body going to express itself politically?" and "is it going to hop through the industrial world on one leg?"

A little investigation will prove to any worker that while the workers are divided on the industrial field it is not possible to unite them on any other field to advance a working class program.

Further investigation will prove that with the working class divided on the industrial field, unity anywhere else—if it could be brought about—would be without results. The workers would be without power to enforce any demands. The proposition, then, is to lay all stress in our agitation upon the essential point, that is upon the places of production, where the working class must unite in sufficient numbers before it will have the power to make itself felt anywhere else.

Will it not follow that, united in sufficient numbers at the workshops and guided by the knowledge of their class interests, such unity will be manifested in every field wherein they can assist in advancing the interest of the working class? Why then should not all stress be laid upon the organization of the workers on the industrial field?

The illustration used by our fellow worker in which he likens the economic organization to a one-legged concern because it does not mention political action, is not a comparison that in any way fits the case. As well might the prohibitionist, the anti-clerical, or any other advocate of the many schools that claim the worker can better his condition by their particular policy, say that because the declaration of principles of the economic organization makes no mention of these subjects, the I.W.W. is short a leg on each count.

The Preamble of the I.W.W. deals with the essential point upon which we know the workers will have to agree before they can accomplish anything for themselves. Regardless of what a wage worker may think of any question, if he agrees upon the essential thing we want him in the I.W.W. helping to build up the organized army of production.

The two legs of the economic organization are *Knowledge* and *Organization*.

It is impossible for anyone to be a part of the capitalist state and to use the machinery of the state in the interest of the workers. All they can do is to make the attempt, and to be impeached—as they will be—and furnish object lessons to the workers, of the class character of the state.

Knowing this, the I.W.W. proposes to devote all of its energy to building up the organization of the workers in the industries of the country and the world: to drilling and educating the members so that they will have the necessary power and the knowledge to use that power to overthrow capitalism.

I know that here you will say: what about the injunction judges, the militia and the bull pens? In answer, ask yourself what will stop the use of these same weapons against you on the political field if by the political activity of the workers you were able to menace the profits of the capitalist?

If you think it cannot be done, turn to Colorado where in 1904 two judges of the supreme court of that state, Campbell and Gabbert, by the injunction process assumed original jurisdiction over the state election and decided the majority of the state legislature, the governorship and the election of the United States senator.

Turn to the Coeur d'Alenes where the military forces of the United States put out of office all officials who would not do the bidding of the mining companies of that region.

Turn to Colorado, where a mob did the same thing in the interest of the capitalist class.

The only power that the working class has is the power to produce wealth. The I.W.W. proposes to organize the workers to control the use of their labor so that they will be able to stop the production of wealth except upon terms dictated by the workers themselves.

The capitalists' political power is exactly the measure of their industrial power—control of industry; that control can only be disputed and finally destroyed by an organization of the workers inside the industries—organized for the every day struggle with the capitalists and to carry on production when capitalism shall have been overthrown.

With such an organization, knowing that an injury to one member of the working class is an injury to every member of that class, it will be possible to make the use of injunctions and the militia so costly that the capitalist will not use them. None of his industries would run except for such length of time as the workers needed to work in order to get in shape to renew the struggle.

A stubborn slave will bring the most overbearing master to time. The capitalists cannot exterminate a real labor organization by fighting it—they are only dangerous when they commence to fraternize with it.

Neither can the capitalists and their tools exterminate the working class or any considerable portion of it—they would have to go to work themselves if they did.

It is true that while the movement is weak they may victimize a few of its members, but if that is not allowed to intimidate the organization the employers will not be able to do that very long.

Persecution of any organization always results in the growth of the principle represented by that organization—if its members are men and women of courage. If they are not, there is no substitute that will insure victory.

The I.W.W. will express itself politically in its general convention and the referendum of its members in the industries throughout the land, in proportion to its power.

The work before us is to build up an organization of our class in the field wherein our power lies. That task must be accomplished by the workers themselves. Whatever obstacles are in the way must be overcome, however great they seem to be. Remember that the working class is a great class and its power is unbounded when properly organized.

The sooner all the members of the working class who agree with this program lend their efforts to bring it about—by joining the I.W.W.—the sooner will the struggle be ended in spite of all the machinations of the capitalist and his judges and armies.

We are forced, however, to point out the limitations of political action for the working class in order that the workers be not led into a cul de sac by the politician, and because of that lose all idea of ever being anything but slaves for generations to come.

This we can only do by devoting our entire effort in the work of organization and education to the industrial field.

To those who think the workers will have to be united in a political party, we say dig in and do so, but do not try to use the economic organization to further the aims of the political party.

# 12
## *The General Strike*

WILLIAM HAYWOOD                                                    1911

I came to-night to speak to you on the general strike. And this night, of all the nights in the year, is a fitting time. Forty years ago to-day there began the greatest general strike known in modern history, the French Commune; a strike that required the political powers of two nations to subdue, namely, that of France and the iron hand of a Bismarck government of Germany. That the workers would have won that strike had it not been for the copartnership of the two nations, there is to my mind no question. They would have overcome the divisions of opinion among themselves. They would have re-established the great national workshops that existed in Paris and throughout France in 1848. The world would have been on the highway toward an industrial democracy, had it not been for the murderous compact between Bismarck and the government of Versailles.

We are met to-night to consider the general strike as a weapon of the working class. I must admit to you that I am not well posted on the theories advanced by Jaures, Vandervelde, Kautsky, and others who write and speak about the general strike. But I am not here to theorize, not here to talk in the abstract, but to get down to the concrete subject whether or not the general strike is an effective weapon for the working class. There are vote-getters and politicians who waste their time coming into a community where 90 per cent of the men have no vote, where the women are disfranchised 100 per cent and where the boys and girls under age, of course, are not enfranchised. Still they will speak to these people about the power of the ballot, and they never mention a thing about the power of the general strike. They seem to lack the foresight, the penetration to interpret political power. They seem to lack the understanding that the broadest interpretation of political power comes through the industrial organization; that the industrial organization is capable not only of the general strike, but prevents the capitalists from disfranchising the worker; it gives the vote to women, it reenfranchises the black man and places the ballot in the hands of every boy and girl employed in a shop, makes them eligible to take part in the general strike, makes them eligible to legislate for themselves where they are most interested in changing conditions, namely, in the place where they work.

I am sorry sometimes that I am not a better theorist, but as all theory comes from practice you will have observed, before I proceed very long, that I know something about the general strikes in operation.

Going back not so far as the Commune of Paris, which occurred in 1871, we find the great strike in Spain in 1874, when the workers of that country won in spite of combined opposition against them and took control of the civil affairs. We find the great strike in Bilboa, in Brussels. And coming down through the halls of time, the greatest strike is the general strike of Russia, when the workers of that country compelled the government to establish a constitution, to give them a form of government—which, by the way, has since been taken from them, and it would cause one to look on the political force, of Russia at least, as a bauble not worth fighting for. They gave up the general strike for a political constitution. The general strike could and did win for them many concessions they could gain in no other way.

---

While across the water I visited Sweden, the scene of a great general strike, and I discovered that there they won many concessions, political as well as economic; and I happened to be in France, the home of all revolutions, during the strike on the railroads, on the state as well as the privately owned roads. There had been standing in the parliament of France many laws looking toward the improvement of the men employed on the railroads. They became dissatisfied and disgruntled with the continued dilatory practices of the politicians and they declared a general strike. The demands of the workers were for an increase of wages from three to five francs a day, for a reduction of hours and for the retroaction of the pension law. They were on strike three days. It was a general strike as far as the railroads were concerned. It tied up transportation and communication from Paris to all the seaport towns. The strike had not been on three days when the government granted every demand of the workers. Previous to this, however, Briand had issued his infamous order making the railroaders soldiers—reservists. The men went back as conscripts; and many scabs, as we call them over here (I don't know what the French call them; in England they call them "blacklegs"), were put on the roads to take the places of 3,500 discharged men.

The strike apparently was broken, officially declared off by the workers. It's true their demands had all been granted, but remember there were 3,500 of their fellow-workers discharged. The strikers immediately started a campaign to have the victimized workers reinstated. And their campaign was a part of the general strike. It was what they called the "grève perlée," or the "drop strike"—if you can conceive of a strike while everybody is at work; everybody belonging to the union receiving full time, and many of them getting overtime, and the strike in full force and very effective. This is the way it worked—and I tell it to you in hopes that you will spread the good news to your fellow-workers and apply it yourselves whenever occasion demands—namely, that of making the capitalist suffer. Now there is only one way to do that; that is, to strike him in the place where he carries his heart and soul, his center of feeling—the pocketbook. And that is what those strikers did. They began at once to make the railroads lose money, to make the government lose money, to make transportation a farce so far as France was concerned. Before I left that country, on my first visit—and it was during the time that the strike was on—there were 50,000 tons of freight piled up at Havre, and a proportionately large amount at every other seaport town. This freight the railroaders would not move. They did not move it at first, and when they did it was in this way: they would load a trainload of freight for Paris and by some mistake it would be billed through Lyons, and when the freight was found at Lyons, instead of being sent to the consignee at Paris it was carried straight through the town on to Bayonne or Marseilles or some other place—to any place but where it properly belonged. Perishable freight was taken out by the trainload and sidetracked. The condition became such that the merchants themselves were compelled to send their agents down into the depots to look up their consignments of freight—and with very little assurance of finding it at all. That this was the systematic work of the railroaders there is no question, because a package addressed to Merle, one of the editors of *"La Guerre Sociale,"* now occupying a cell in the Prison of the Saint, was marked with an inscription on the corner, "Sabotagers please note address." This package went through posthaste. It worked so well that some of the merchants began using the name of "La Guerre Sociale" to have their packages immediately delivered. It was necessary for the managers of the paper to threaten to sue them unless they refrained from using the name of the paper for railroad purposes.

Nearly all the workers have been reinstated at the present time on the railroads of France.

That is certainly one splendid example of what the general strike can accomplish for the working class.

Another is the strike of the railroaders in Italy. The railroaders there are organized in one great industrial union, one card, taking into membership the stenographers, train dispatchers, freight handlers, train crews and section crews. Everyone who works on the railroad is a member of the organization; not like it is in this country, split up into as many divisions as they can possibly get them into. There they are all one. There was a great general strike. It resulted in the country taking over the railroads. But the government made the mistake of placing politicians in control, giving politicians the management of the railroads. This operated but little better than under private capitalism. The service was inefficient. They could make no money. The rolling stock was rapidly going to wreck. Then the railroad organizations issued this ultimatum to the government, and it now stands: "Turn the railroads over to us. We will operate them and give you the most efficient service to be found on railroads in any country." Would that be a success for the general strike? I rather think so.

And in Wales it was my good fortune to be there, not to theorize but to take part in the general strike among the coal miners. Previous to my coming, or in previous strikes, the Welsh miners had been in the habit of quitting work, carrying out their tools, permitting the mine managers to run the pumps, allowing the engine winders to remain at work, carrying food down to the horses, keeping the mines in good shape, while the miners themselves were marching from place to place singing their old-time songs, gathering on the meeting grounds of the ancient Druids and listening to the speeches of the labor leaders; starving for weeks contentedly, and on all occasions acting most peaceably; going back to work when they were compelled to by starvation. But this last strike was an entirely different one. It was like the shoemakers' strike in Brooklyn. Some new methods had been injected into the strike. I had spoken there on a number of occasions previous to the strike being inaugurated, and I told them of the methods that we adopted in the West, where every man employed in and around the mine belongs to the same organization; where, when we went on strike, the mine closed down. They thought that that was a very excellent system. So the strike was declared. They at once notified the engine winders, who had a separate contract with the mine owners, that they would not be allowed to work. The engine winders passed a resolution saying that they would not work. The haulers took the same position. No one was allowed to approach the mines to run the machinery. Well, the mine manager, like the mine managers everywhere, taking unto himself the idea that the mines belonged to him, said "Certainly the men won't interfere with us. We will go up and run the machinery." And they took along the office force. But the miners had a different notion and they said, "You can work in the office, but you can't run this machinery. This isn't your work. If you run that you will be scabbing; and we don't permit you to scab—not in this section of the country, now." They were compelled to go back to the office. There were 325 horses underground, which the manager, Llewellyn, complained about being in a starving condition. The officials of the union said, "We will hoist the horses out of the mine."

"Oh, no," he said, "we don't want to bring them up. We will all be friends in a few days."

"You will either bring up the horses now or you will let them stay there."

He said, "No, we won't bring them up now."

The pumps were closed down on the Cambria mine, 12,000 miners were there to see that they didn't open. Llewellyn started a hue and cry that the horses would be drowned, and the king sent the police, sent the soldiers and sent a message to Llewellyn asking "if the horses were still safe." He didn't say anything about his subjects, the men. Guarded by soldiers, a few scabs, assisted by the office force, were able to run the pumps. Llewellyn himself and his bookkeeping force went down and fed the horses.

Had there been an industrial organization comprising the railroaders and every other branch of industry, the mines of Wales would be closed down to-day.

We found the same condition throughout the West. We never had any trouble about closing the mines down; and could keep them closed down for an indefinite period. It was always the craft unions that caused us to lose our fights when we did lose. I recall the first general strike in the Coeur d'Alenes, when all the mines in that district were closed down to prevent a reduction of wages. The mine owners brought in thugs the first thing. They attempted to man the mines with men carrying sixshooters and rifles. There was a pitched battle between miners and thugs. A few were killed on each side. And then the mine owners asked for the soldiers, and the soldiers came. Who brought the soldiers? Railroads manned by union men; engines fired with coal mined by union men. That is the division of labor that might have lost us the strike in the Coeur d'Alenes. It didn't lose it, however. We were successful in that issue. But in Leadville we lost the strike there because they were able to bring in scab labor from other communities where they had the force of the government behind them, and the force of the troops. In 1899 we were compelled to fight the battle over in a great general strike in the Coeur d'Alenes again. Then came the general strike in Cripple Creek, the strike that has become a household word in labor circles throughout the world. In Cripple Creek 5,000 men were on strike in sympathy with 45 men belonging to the Millmen's Union in Colorado City; 45 men who had been discharged simply because they were trying to improve their standard of living. By using the state troops and the influence of the Federal government they were able to man the mills in Colorado City with scab millmen; and after months of hardship, after 1,600 of our men had been arrested and placed in the Victor Armory in one single room that they called the "bullpen," after 400 of them had been loaded aboard special trains guarded by soldiers, shipped away from their homes, dumped out on the prairies down in New Mexico and Kansas; after the women who had taken up the work of distributing strike relief had been placed under arrest—we find then that they were able to man the mines with scabs, the mills running with scabs, the railroads conveying the ore from Cripple Creek to Colorado City run by union men—the connecting link of a proposition that was scabby at both ends! We were not thoroughly organized. There has been no time when there has been a general strike in this country.

There are three phases of a general strike. They are:

A general strike in an industry;

A general strike in a community;

A general national strike.

The conditions for any of the three have never existed. So how any one can take the position that a general strike would not be effective and not be a good thing for the working class is more than I can understand. We know that the capitalist uses the general strike to good advantage. Here is the position that we find the working class and the capitalists in. The capitalists have wealth; they have money. They invest the money in machinery, in the resources of the earth. They operate a factory, a mine, a railroad, a mill. They will keep that factory running just as long as there are profits coming in. When anything happens to disturb the profits, what do the capitalists do? They go on strike, don't they? They withdraw their finances from that particular mill. They close it down because there are no profits to be made there. They don't care what becomes of the working class. But the working class, on the other hand, has always been taught to take care of the capitalist's interest in the property. You don't look after your own interest, your labor power, realizing that without a certain amount of provision you can't reproduce it. You are always looking after the interest of the capitalist, while a general strike would displace his interest and would put you in possession of it.

That is what I want to urge upon the working class; to become so organized on the economic field that they can take and hold the industries in which they are employed. Can you conceive of such a thing? Is it possible? What are the forces that prevent you from doing so? You have all the industries in your own hands at the present time. There is this justification for political action, and that is, to control the forces of the capitalists that they use against us; to be in a position to control the power of government so as to make the work of the army ineffective, so as to abolish totally the secret service and the force of detectives. That is the reason that you want the power of government. That is the reason that you should fully understand the power of the ballot. Now, there isn't any one, Socialist, S. L. P., Industrial Worker or any other workingman or woman, no matter what society you belong to, but what believes in the ballot. There are those—and I am one of them—who refuse to have the ballot interpreted for them. I know, or think I know, the power of it, and I know that the industrial organization, as I stated in the beginning, is its broadest interpretation. I know, too, that when the workers are brought together in a great organization they are not going to cease to vote. That is when the workers will *begin* to vote, to vote for directors to operate the industries in which they are all employed.

So the general strike is a fighting weapon as well as a constructive force. It can be used, and should be used, equally as forcefully by the Socialist as by the Industrial Worker.

The Socialists believe in the general strike. They also believe in the organization of industrial forces after the general strike is successful. So, on this great force of the working class I believe we can agree that we should unite into one great organization— big enough to take in the children that are now working; big enough to take in the black man; the white man; big enough to take in all nationalities—an organization that will be strong enough to obliterate state boundaries, to obliterate national boundaries, and one that will become the great industrial force of the working class of the world. (Applause.)

I have been lecturing in and around New York now for three weeks; my general topic has been Industrialism, which is the only force under which the general strike can possibly be operated. If there are any here interested in industrial unionism, and they want any knowledge that I have, I will be more than pleased to answer questions, because it is only by industrial unionism that the general strike becomes possible. The A. F. of L. couldn't have a general strike if they wanted to. They are not organized for a general strike. They have 27,000 different agreements that expire 27,000 different minutes of the year. They will either have to break all of those sacred contracts or there is no such thing as a general strike in that so-called "labor organization." I said, "so-called"; I say so advisedly. It is not a labor organization; it is simply a combination of job trusts. We are going to have a labor organization in this country. And I assure you, if you could attend the meetings we have had in Philadelphia, in Bridgeport last night, in Haverhill and in Harrison, and throughout the country, you would agree that industrialism is coming. There isn't anything can stop it. (Applause.)

**Questions by the Audience**

Q.—Don't you think there is a lot of waste involved in the general strike in that the sufferers would be the workers in larger portion than the capitalists? The capitalist class always has money and can buy food, while the workers will just have to starve and wait. I was a strong believer in the general strike myself until I read some articles in *The Call* a while ago on this particular phase.

A.—The working class haven't got anything. They can't lose anything. While the capitalist class have got all the money and all the credit, still if the working class laid off, the capitalists couldn't get food at any price. This is the power of the working class: If the workers are organized (remember now, I say "if they are organized"—by that I don't mean 100 per cent, but a good strong minority), all they have to do is to put their hands in their pockets and they have got the capitalist class whipped. The working class can stand it a week without anything to eat—I have gone pretty nearly that long myself, and I wasn't on strike. In the meantime I hadn't lost any meals; I just postponed them. (Laughter.) I didn't do it voluntarily, I tell you that. But all the workers have to do is to organize so that they can put their hands in their pockets; when they have got *their* hands there, the capitalists can't get theirs in. If the workers can organize so that they can stand idle they will then be strong enough so that they can take the factories. Now, I hope to see the day when the man who goes *out* of the factory will be the one who will be called a scab; when the good union man will stay in the factory, whether the capitalists like it or not; when we lock the bosses out and run the factories to suit ourselves. That is our program. We will do it.

Q.—Doesn't the trend of your talk lead to direct action, or what we call revolution? For instance, we try to throw the bosses out; don't you think the bosses will strike back?

Another thing: Of course, the working class can starve eight days, but they can't starve nine. You don't have to teach the workingman how to starve, because there were teachers before you. There is no way out but fight, as I understand it. Do you think you will get your industrialism through peace or through revolution?

A.—Well, comrade, you have no peace now. The capitalist system, as peaceable as it is, is killing off hundreds of thousands of workers every year. That isn't peace. One hundred thousand workers were injured in this state last year. I do not care whether it's peaceable or not; I want to see it come.

As for starving the workers eight days, I made no such program. I said that they could, but I don't want to see them do it. The fact that I was compelled to postpone a few meals was because I wasn't in the vicinity of any grub. I suggest that you break down that idea that you must protect the boss's property. That is all we are fighting for—what the boss calls his "private property," what he calls his private interest in the things that the people must have, as a whole, to live. Those are the things we are after.

Q.—Do the Industrial Unionists believe in political action? Have they got any special platforms that they support?

A.—The Industrial Workers of the World is not a political organization.

Q.—Just like the A. F. of L.?

A.—No.

Q.—*They* don't believe in any political action, either, so far as that is concerned.

A.—Yes, the A. F. of L. does believe in political action. It is a political organization. The Industrial Workers of the World is an economic organization without affiliation with any political party or any non-political sect. I as an Industrialist say that industrial unionism is the broadest possible political interpretation of the working-class political power, because by organizing the workers industrially you at once enfranchise the women in the shops, you at once give the black men who are disfranchised politically a voice in the operation of the industries; and the same would extend to every worker. That to my mind is the kind of political action that the working class wants. You must not be content to come to the ballot box on the first Tuesday after the first Monday in November, the ballot box erected by the capitalist class, guarded by capitalist henchmen, and deposit your ballot to be counted by black-handed thugs, and say, "That is political action." You must protect your ballot with an organization that will enforce the mandates of your class. I want political action that counts. I want a working class that can hold an election every day if they want to.

Q.—By what means could an Industrial Unionist propagate Industrial Unionism in his organization of the A. F. of L.? He would be fired out and lose his job.

A.—Well, the time is coming when he will have to quit the A. F. of L. anyway. And remember, that there are 35,000,000 workers in the United States who can't get in the A. F. of L. And when you quit you are quitting a caste, you are getting back into your class. The Socialists have been going along maintaining the Civic Federation long enough. The time has almost arrived when you will have to quit and become free men and women. I believe that the A. F. of L. won't take in the working class. They don't want the working class. It isn't a working-class organization. It's a craft organization. They realize that by improving the labor power of a few individuals and keeping them on the inside of a corral, keeping others out with initiation fees, and closing the books, and so on, that the favored few are made valuable to the capitalists. They form a little job trust. It's a system of slavery from which free people ought to break away. And they will, soon.

Q.—About the political action we had in Milwaukee: there we didn't have Industrial Unionism, we won by the ballot; and while we haven't compelled the government to pass any bills yet, we are at it now.

A.—Yes, they are at it. But you really don't think that Congressman Berger is going to compel the government to pass any bills on Congress? This Insurgent bunch that is growing up in the country is going to give you more than the reform Socialists ever asked for yet. The opportunists will be like the Labor party in England. I was in the office of the *Labor Leader* and Mr. Whiteside said to me: "Really, I don't know what we are going to do with this fellow, Lloyd-George. He has taken every bit of ground from under our feet. He has given the working class more than the Labor party had dared to ask for." And so it will be with the Insurgents, the "Progressives" or whatever they propose to call themselves. They will give you eight-hour laws, compensation laws, liability laws, old-age pensions. They will give you eight hours; that is what we are striking for, too—eight hours. But they won't get off the workers' backs. The Insurgents simply say, "It's cruel, the way the capitalists are exploiting the workers. Why, look! whenever they go to shear them they take off a part of the hide. We will take all the wool, but we will leave the hide." (Laughter.)

Q. (By a woman comrade)—Isn't a strike, theoretically, a situation where the workingmen lay down their tools and the capitalist class sits and waits, and they both say, "Well, what are you going to do about it?" And if they go beyond that, and go outside the law, is it any longer a strike? Isn't it a revolution?

A.—A strike is an incipient revolution. Many large revolutions have grown out of a small strike.

Q.—Well, I heartily believe in the general strike if it is a first step toward the revolution, and I believe in what you intimate—that the workers are damn fools if they don't *take* what they want, when they can't get it any other way. (Applause.)

A.—That is a better speech than I can make. If I didn't think that the general strike was leading on to the great revolution which will emancipate the working class I wouldn't be here. I am with you because I believe that in this little meeting there is a nucleus here that will carry on the work and propagate the seed that will grow into the great revolution that will overthrow the capitalist class.

# 13
## *Some Definitions: Direct Action—Sabotage*

**FRANK BOHN**                                                              1912

*Direct Action:*—Of all the terms made use of in our discussion during the last six months, this has been the most abused. By direct action is meant any action taken by workers directly at the point of production with a view to bettering their conditions. The organization of any labor union whatever is direct action. Sending the shop committee to demand of the boss a change of shop rules is direct action. To oppose direct action is to oppose labor unionism as a whole with all its activities. In this sense, the term has been used by those who made use of it down to the time of the late controversy. It was the misuse of this expression by the comrades who oppose class-labor unionism which has caused so much uneasiness in the Socialist Party. When we come to the question as to what direct action shall be taken and when and how—that is for the organization on the job to determine. For the Socialist Party to try to lay down rules for the conduct of unions or one union in this matter would be as ridiculous as for the Socialist Party to seek to determine what the workers shall eat for breakfast. It is the business of the Socialist Party to organize and conduct political education activity. This does not imply, however, that in a lecture dealing with unionism conducted by the Socialist Party, these matters shall not be discussed. On the contrary, it is of the highest importance that the Socialist Party shall keep its membership informed through its press and its lecture courses of the latest developments in the field of labor.

*Sabotage:*—Sabotage means "strike and stay in the shop." Striking workers thus are enabled to draw pay and keep out scabs while fighting capitalists. Sabotage does not necessarily mean destruction of machinery or other property, although that method has always been indulged in and will continue to be used as long as there is a class struggle. More often it is used to advantage in a quieter way. Excessive limitation of output is sabotage. So is any obstruction of the regular conduct of the industry. Ancient Hebrews in Egypt practiced sabotage when they spoiled the bricks. Slaves in the South practiced it regularly by putting stones and dirt in their bags of cotton to make them weigh heavier. An old cotton mill weaver in Massachusetts once told me that when baseball was first played, the boys in his mill stuck a bobbin in the running gear of the water wheel and so tied up the shop on Saturday afternoon that they could go and see the ball game. . . . When the workers face a specific situation, they will very likely continue to do as their interests and intelligence dictate.

---

Reprinted with permission of the author from *Rebel Voices: An I.W.W. Anthology* by Joyce L. Kornbluh, pp. 52–53. Ann Arbor: University of Michigan Press, 1964. Copyright © 1964 by Joyce L. Kornbluh.

# 14
## *Big Bill Haywood Testifies*

COMMISSIONER WEINSTOCK. Now, will you tell this commission, Mr. Haywood, as an authority on the subject, wherein, assuming that you and the Socialists and the American Federationists have the same objective in mind; that is, the betterment of the worker—will you point out to this commission as clearly and concisely as you can wherein your methods differ and are better than the method of the Socialists, and of the American Federationists?

MR. HAYWOOD. Well, I do not like to set myself up as a critic.

COMMISSIONER WEINSTOCK. We have a right to your opinion, I think. You were invited here for that purpose and have certainly given the matter a great deal of thought and study and ought to be able to point out clearly to us the comparative advantages and disadvantages.

MR. HAYWOOD. Without saying—without criticizing trade-unions, which I regard as having accomplished great good in their time, there are many things in the workings of trade-unions where they recognize the right of the bosses. The Industrial Workers of the World do not recognize that the bosses have any rights at all. We have founded the organization on the basis of the class struggle, and on that basis it must work out its ultimate.

The trade-union says, "Well, the boss has some rights here, and we are going to enter into a contract with him." How long is it going to take to solve this problem if you have continuity of contracts? That is the thing we say.

The trade-union is organized on the basis of the tools they work with. Now, the tools are changing, and it is driving trade-unions out of business. For instance, the glass-blowers—glass was made by workmen who blew through a tube. A glass maker, a glass blower himself contrived a machine whereby this blowing is done automatically, and the glass blower, he is wheeling sand to that machine now.

We believe that everybody that works around that machine ought to be organized just as before; we believe that everybody that works around the glass factory ought to be organized, organized with regard to the welfare of each other. That is the reason I pointed out to you that in the Western Federation of Miners there was small differentiation in the wage scale. It is not true with the glass blower; he was paid from eight to ten dollars a day, while the boy off-bearer got a few dollars a week. Now, with us there was no boy went into the mine younger than 16 years of age, and when he went into the mine he got a man's wages, because we thought he was old enough to do a man's work. It was not a matter of skill; he did not have to serve any apprenticeship; we just took the position when the boy was old enough for the boss to exploit he was old enough to draw full pay.

After the Socialist Party—

COMMISSIONER WEINSTOCK. Let us make this point, Mr. Haywood, before we take up the Socialist Party: I gather, then, from your statement that the two fundamental points in which I.W.W.'s differ from American Federationists is you are opposed to contracts with employers on the one hand, and you believe in one great union instead of craft unions. Does that make the difference?

MR. HAYWOOD. That makes two differences.

Commission on Industrial Relations, Final Report and Testimony, 64th Congress, 1st Session, Document 415 (Washington, D.C.: Government Printing Office, 1916), vol. XI, pp. 10581–10589.

COMMISSIONER WEINSTOCK. In other words, you believe that by the adoption of the methods adopted by the I.W.W. that the ends can be achieved better and more quickly than under the methods followed by the American Federationists?

MR. HAYWOOD. Can you conceive of anything that labor can not do if they were organized in one big union? If labor was organized and self-disciplined it could stop every wheel in the United States tonight—every one—and sweep off your capitalists and State legislatures and politicians into the sea. Labor is what runs this country, and if they were organized, scientifically organized—if they were class conscious, if they recognized that the worker's interest was every worker's interest, there is nothing but what they can do.

COMMISSIONER WEINSTOCK. Granting an organization so colossal in its character would have great power for good, would it not have great power for ill?

MR. HAYWOOD. Yes; it would have great power for ill—that is, it would be ill for the capitalists. Every one of them would have to go to work.

COMMISSIONER WEINSTOCK. Would it not also have great power in doing this—in establishing a new slavery? If the wage earner claims that under present system of things he is in slavery, would not the colossal power of your plan simply be slavery with new masters?

MR. HAYWOOD. Such a labor organization would be a fine sort of slavery. I would like to work for my union in a shop that I owned best.

COMMISSIONER WEINSTOCK. If you were the "big Injun" chief?

MR. HAYWOOD. No; to go right back in the mine that I came from. That is the place that I would like to go, right tomorrow, and receive for my labor, without any stockholder, without any Rockefeller taking off any part of it, the social value of what my labor contributed to society.

COMMISSIONER WEINSTOCK. To that degree, then, I take it, the I.W.W.'s are Socialistic?

MR. HAYWOOD. All right.

COMMISSIONER WEINSTOCK. Let me see if I understand the distinction correctly between socialism and I.W.W.'ism.

As I understand it, I.W.W.'ism is socialism, with this difference—

MR. HAYWOOD (interrupting). With its working clothes on. . . .

COMMISSIONER WEINSTOCK. Now, would you confine this great army of workers, organized in one body, would you confine their functions and their efforts to industrial matters pure and simple, or would you at the same time have them also deal with the political conditions, with the government of our municipalities, of our Commonwealths, or our Republic?

MR. HAYWOOD. There would be neither county or State or National lines.

COMMISSIONER WEINSTOCK. There would be no political subdivision?

MR. HAYWOOD. Only what existed in the community.

COMMISSIONER WEINSTOCK. That is incomprehensible to me, Mr. Haywood; you will have to explain it a little more definitely.

MR. HAYWOOD. What is the government of the city? The government of many cities has been changed to the commission form.

COMMISSIONER WEINSTOCK. Yes, sir.

MR. HAYWOOD. The commissioner has the fire department, the public safety, and public improvement. Those are the different divisions. Why not have that same thing under industrial—

COMMISSIONER WEINSTOCK. Have it nationally?

MR. HAYWOOD. You have no community that is national in scope.

COMMISSIONER WEINSTOCK. How, then, would you have it?

MR. HAYWOOD. Have this group or this community wherever the industry was located. Do you suppose under normal conditions there would be communities like New York or Chicago with great skyscrapers sticking up in the air?

COMMISSIONER WEINSTOCK. What would you say would be the size of the community?

MR. HAYWOOD. Some 50,000 or 60,000, where the people in that industry would dwell. There would be no lawyers or preachers or stockholders like built New York.

COMMISSIONER WEINSTOCK. What would you do with the city of New York?

MR. HAYWOOD. Tear it down, or leave it as a monument to the foolishness of the present day.

COMMISSIONER WEINSTOCK. How long do you think it will be, Mr. Haywod, knowing the conditions as you know them, before your ideals will be realized, before cities like New York and Chicago will be wiped out and replaced by urban communities?

MR. HAYWOOD. Well, Mr. Weinstock, if some one had asked me a year ago how long it would be before a world-wide war would take place I would not have answered them; but you see the people of many nations now pitted against each other, committing murder by the wholesale, and I would say that this can come just as quick as the war. I don't know when, but I know that there are people that are interested in bringing about a change of society; whether it will be the change that I have suggested here, or whether that is the right change—and I feel that it is—still I feel that it could come just as quick as other grave things have come.

COMMISSIONER WEINSTOCK. You think it will be an overnight affair?

MR. HAYWOOD. I think so; that is, as you mean overnight affairs, as war was an overnight affair....

COMMISSIONER WEINSTOCK. Let me make sure, Mr. Haywood, that I clearly understand the objective of I.W.W.'ism. I have assumed—I will admit that I have assumed in my presentation to you that I.W.W.'ism was socialism with a plus; that is, that I.W.W.'ism in—

MR. HAYWOOD (interrupting). I would very much prefer that you would eliminate the reference to socialism in referring to I.W.W.'ism, because from the examples we have, for instance, in Germany, socialism has, or at least the Social Democratic Party, has been very much discredited in the minds of the workers of other countries. They have gone in for war, and those of us who believe we are Socialists are opposed to war. So if you don't mind we will discuss industrialism on its own basis.

COMMISSIONER WEINSTOCK. Well, in order that I at least may better understand the purpose, aims, and objects of industrialism, I must, in order to bring out the differences and to compare it with the socialistic doctrine—you may not believe in the socialistic doctrine any more, and I do not; but my purpose is, so that we do not have a misunderstanding of the meaning of words. Now, let me briefly state to you what I understand socialism stands for, and what I understand the I.W.W.'ism stands for. The Socialist, as I understand it, is striving for the cooperative commonwealth, striving to bring about a situation whereby all the machinery of production and distribution shall be owned by all the people, where there shall be but one employer, and that employer shall be all the people, and everything shall be conducted substantially as the Army and Navy are conducted under our form of Government. I understand that I.W.W.'ism believes in exactly the same objectives but differs in the methods—....

MR. HAYWOOD. No; the ends are not the same. Now, Socialists, while they present an industrial democracy, they hope to follow the files of existing governments, having industries controlled by the Government, eventually, however, sloughing the State. They will tell you the State is of no further use; that when industries are controlled by the workers the State will no longer function.

COMMISSIONER WEINSTOCK. Well, then, am I to understand this, Mr. Haywood? I want that made very clear to me, because if the objective is as I understand you have tried to indicate, then I have been laboring under a misapprehension. Am I to understand that it is not the objective of the I.W.W. to have the State-owned industries?

MR. HAYWOOD. It certainly is not.

COMMISSIONER WEINSTOCK. I see. Then there is a radical difference between the I.W.W.'s and the Socialists, Mr. Haywood?

MR. HAYWOOD. Yes.

COMMISSIONER WEINSTOCK. The Socialist wants the State to own all the industries.

MR. HAYWOOD. Yes, sir.

COMMISSIONER WEINSTOCK. And the I.W.W., then, as you now explain it, proposes to have those industries not owned by the State but by the workers—

MR. HAYWOOD (interrupting). By the workers.

COMMISSIONER WEINSTOCK. (continuing). Independent of the State.

MR. HAYWOOD. Independent of the State. . . .

COMMISSIONER WEINSTOCK. Well, then, will you briefly outline to us, Mr. Haywood, how would you govern and direct the affairs under your proposed system of 100,000,000 of people, as we are in this country today?

MR. HAYWOOD. Well, how are the affairs of the hundred million people conducted at the present time? The workers have no interest, have no voice in anything except the shops. Many of the workers are children. They certainly have no interest and no voice in the franchise. They are employed in the shops, and of course my idea is that children who work should have a voice in the way they work—in the hours they work, in the wages that they should receive—that is, under the present conditions children should have that voice, children who labor. The same is true of women. The political state, the Government, says that women are not entitled to vote—that is, except in the 10 free States of the West; but they are industrial units; they are productive units; from millions of women. My idea is that they should have a voice in the control or disposition of their labor powers, and the only place where they can express themselves is in their labor union halls, and there they express themselves to the fullest as citizens of industry, if you will, as to the purposes of their work and the conditions under which they will labor. Now, you recognize that in conjunction with women and children.

The black men of the South are on the same footing. They are all citizens of this country, but they have no voice in its government. Millions of black men are disfranchised, who if organized would have a voice in saying how they should work and how the conditions of labor should be regulated. But unorganized they are as helpless and in the same condition of slavery as they were before the war. This is not only true of women and children and black men, but it extends to the foreigner who comes to this country and is certainly a useful member of society. Most of them at once go into industries, but for five years they are not citizens. They plod along at their work and have no voice in the control or the use of their labor power. And as you have learned through this commission there are corporations who direct the manner in which those foreigners shall vote.

Certainly you have heard something of that in connection with the Rockefeller interests in the southern part of Colorado. You know that the elections there were never carried on straight, and these foreigners were directed as to how their ballot should be placed.

They are not the only ones who are disfranchised, but there is also the workingman who is born in this country, who is shifted about from place to place by industrial depressions; their homes are broken up and they are compelled to go from one city to another, and each State requires a certain period of residence before a man has the right to vote. Some States say he must be a resident 1 year, others say 2 years; he must live for a certain length of time in the county; he must live for 30 days or such a matter in the precinct before he has any voice in the conduct of government. Now, if a man was not a subject of a State or Nation, but a citizen of industry, moving from place to place, belonging to his union, wherever he went he would step in the union hall, show his card, register, and he at once has a voice in the conduct of the affairs pertaining to his welfare. That is the form of society I want to see, where the men who do the work, and who are the only people who are worth while—understand me, Mr. Weinstock, I think that the workingman, even doing the meanest kind of work, the workingman is a more important member of society than any judge on the Supreme Bench; than any other of the useless members of society. I am speaking for the working class, and I am a partisan to the workers.

# 15
## Revolutionary Syndicalism

LEWIS LORWIN                                                                    1914

*(Editors' Note: Syndicalists were often vague and uncertain about the details of the political and economic organization they wished to form after the overthrow of capitalism. The result is that very little has been written about this topic. This selection is taken from a book on the French syndicalists during the early part of this century. Since there is no authoritative account of the social organization syndicalists wished to construct, the author develops an outline of their views by compiling the ideas of syndicalists taken from reports submitted at a congress of syndicalist unionists in 1902.)*

What are the forms of the social organization which will take the place of those now in existence? The Congress of Lyons (1901) had expressed the wish to have this question on the program of the next Congress. In order that the answer to this question should reflect the ideas prevalent among the workingmen, the Confederal Committee submitted the question to the syndicats[1] for study. A questionnaire was sent out containing the following questions:

(1) How would your syndicat act in order to transform itself from a group for combat into a group for production?

(2) How would you act in order to take possession of the machinery pertaining to your industry?

(3) How do you conceive the functions of the organized shops and factories in the future?

(4) If your syndicat is a group within the system of highways, of transportation of products or of passengers, of distribution, etc., how do you conceive its functioning?

(5) What will be your relations to your federation of trade or of industry after your reorganization?

(6) On what principle would the distribution of products take place and how would the productive groups procure the raw material for themselves?

(7) What part would the *Bourses du Travail*[2] play in the transformed society and what would be their task with reference to the statistics and to the distribution of products?

At the Congress of Montpellier, in 1902, a number of reports were presented answering the above questions. The reports were in the name of the syndicats and came from different parts of France. Only a limited number of them were printed as appendices to the general report of the Congress. Among them, it may be interesting to note, was the report of the syndicat of agricultural laborers. The rest were summed up in the official organ of the Confederation, *La Voix du Peuple*.

The reports differed in details. Some emphasized one point more than another and *vice versa*. But the general character of the reports was identical and showed a consensus of opinion on the main outlines of that "economic federalism" which is the ideal of the syndicalists.

According to this ideal, the syndicat will constitute the cell of society. It will group the producers of one and the same trade who will control their means of production. Property, however, will be social or collective, and no one syndicat will be the exclusive

Reprinted from Lewis Lorwin, *Syndicalism in France*, pp. 133–140. New York: Columbia University Press, 1914. By permission.

owner of any portion of the collective property. It will merely use it with the consent of the entire society.

The syndicat will be connected with the rest of society through its relations with the Federation of its trade, the *Bourse du Travail*, and the General Confederation. With the National Federation relations will be mainly technical and special, and the rôle of the Federation will be insignificant. With the General Confederation relations will be indirect and mainly by mediation of the *Bourse du Travail*. Relations with the latter will be of permanent importance, as the *Bourses du Travail* will be the centers of economic activity.

The *Bourse du Travail*—in the ideal system of the syndicalists—will concentrate all local interests and serve as a connecting link between a locality and the rest of the world. In its capacity as local center it will collect all statistical data necessary for the regular flow of economic life. It will keep itself informed on the necessities of the locality and on its resources, and will provide for the proper distribution of products; as intermediary between the locality and the rest of the country it will facilitate the exchange of products between locality and locality and will provide for the introduction of raw materials from outside.

In a word, the Bourse will combine in its organization the character both of local and of industrial autonomy. It will destroy the centralized political system of the present State and will counterbalance the centralizing tendencies of industry.

To the General Confederation will be left only services of national importance, railways for instance. However, even in the management of national public utilities the National Federation and the Bourses will have the first word. The function of the General Confederation will consist mainly in furnishing general information and in exerting a controlling influence. The General Confederation will also serve as intermediary in international relations.

In this social system the State as now constituted will have no place. Of course, one may call the ideal system of the syndicalists a State. All depends on the definition given to the term. But when the syndicalists speak of the State, they mean an organization of society in which a delegated minority centralizes in its hands the power of legislation on all matters. This power may be broken up and divided among a number of governing bodies, as in the federal system of the United States, but it does not thereby change its character. The essential characteristic of the State is to impose its rule *from without*. The legislative assemblies of the present State decide upon questions that are entirely foreign to them, with which they have no real connection in life and which they do not understand. The rules they prescribe, the discipline they impose, come as an external agency to intervene in the processes of social life. The State is, therefore, arbitrary and oppressive in its very nature.

To this State-action the syndicalists oppose a discipline coming *from within*, a rule suggested by the processes of collective life itself, and imposed by those whose function it is to carry on those processes. It is, as it were, a specialization of function carried over into the domain of public life and made dependent upon industrial specialization. No one should legislate on matters unless he has the necessary training. The syndicats, the delegates of the syndicats to the *Bourses du Travail*, and so on, only they can properly deal with their respective problems. The rules they would impose would follow from a knowledge of the conditions of their social functions and would be, so to speak, a "natural" discipline made inevitable by the conditions themselves. Besides, many of the functions of the existing State would be abolished as unnecessary in a society based on common ownership, on co-operative work, and on collective solidarity. The necessary functions of local administration would be carried on by the *Bourses du Travail.*

In recent years, however, revolutionary syndicalists have not expatiated upon the forms of the future society. Convinced that the social transformation is inevitable, they have not thought it necessary to have any ready-made model upon the lines of which the social organization of the future should be carved. The revolutionary classes of the past had no idea of the new social system they were struggling for, and no ready-made plan is necessary for the working-class. Prepared by all preliminary struggle, the workingmen will find in themselves, when the time comes, sufficient creative power to remake society. The lines of the future, however, are indicated in a general way by the development of the present, and the syndicalist movement is clearly paving the way for an "economic federalism."

The workingmen are being prepared for their future rôle by the experiences of syndicalist life. The very struggle which the syndicats carry on train the workingmen in solidarity, in voluntary discipline, in power and determination to resist oppression, and other moral qualities which group life requires. Moreover, the syndicats, particularly the *Bourses du Travail*, are centers where educational activities are carried on. Related to the facts of life and to the concrete problems of the day, this educational work, in the form of regular courses, lectures, readings, etc., is devised to develop the intellectual capacities of the workingmen.

The struggle of the present and the combat of the future imply the initiative, the example and the leadership of a conscious and energetic minority ardently devoted to the interests of its class. The experience of the labor movement has proven this beyond all doubt. The mass of workingmen, like every large mass, is inert. It needs an impelling force to set it in motion and to put to work its tremendous potential energy. Every strike, every labor demonstration, every movement of the working-class is generally started by an active and daring minority which voices the sentiments of the class to which it belongs.

The conscious minority, however, can act only by carrying with it the mass, and by making the latter participate directly in the struggle. The action of the conscious minority is, therefore, just the opposite of the action of parliamentary representatives. The latter are bent on doing everything themselves, on controlling absolutely the affairs of the country, and are therefore, anxious, to keep the masses as quiet, as inactive and as submissive as possible. The conscious minority, on the contrary, is simply the advance-guard of its class; it cannot succeed, unless backed by the solid forces of the masses; the awareness, the readiness and the energy of the latter are indispensable conditions of success and must be kept up by all means.

The idea of the "conscious minority" is opposed to the democratic principle. Democracy is based upon majority-rule, and its method of determining the general will is universal suffrage. But experience has shown that the "general will" is a fiction and that majority-rule really becomes the domination of a minority—which can impose itself upon all and exploit the majority in its own interests. This is inevitably so, because universal suffrage is a clumsy, mechanical device, which brings together a number of disconnected units and makes them act without proper understanding of the thing they are about. The effect of political majorities when they do make themselves felt is to hinder advance and to suppress the progressive, active and more developed minorities.

The practice of the labor movement is necessarily the reverse of this. The syndicats do not arise out of universal suffrage and are not the representatives of the majority in the democratic sense of the term. They group but a minority of all workingmen and can hardly expect ever to embrace the totality or even the majority of the latter. The syndicats arise through a process of selection. The more sensitive, the intellectually more able, the more active workingmen come together and constitute themselves a syndicat. They begin to discuss the affairs of the trade. When determined to obtain its demands, the syndicat enters into a struggle, without at first finding out the "general will." It assumes leadership and expects to be followed, because it is convinced that it expresses the feelings of all. The syndicat constitutes the leading conscious minority.

The syndicat obtains better conditions not for its members alone, but for all the members of the trade and often for all the workingmen of a locality or of the country. This justifies its self-assumed leadership, because it is not struggling for selfish ends, but for the interests of all. Besides, the syndicat is not a medieval guild and is open to all. If the general mass of workingmen do not enter the syndicats, they themselves renounce the right of determining conditions for the latter. Benefiting by the struggles of the minority, they cannot but submit to its initiative and leadership.

The syndicat, therefore, is not to be compared with "cliques," "rings," "political machines," and the like. The syndicat, it must be remembered, is a group of individuals belonging to the same trade. By this very economic situation, the members of a syndicat are bound by ties of common interest with the rest of their fellow-workingmen. A sense of solidarity and an altruistic feeling of devotion to community interests must necessarily arise in the syndicat which is placed in the front ranks of the struggling workingmen. The leadership of the syndicalist minority, therefore, is necessarily disinterested and beneficent and is followed voluntarily by the workingmen.

Thus, grouping the active and conscious minority the syndicats lead the workingmen as a class in the struggle for final emancipation. Gradually undermining the foundations of existing society, they are developing within the framework of the old the elements of a new society, and when this process shall have sufficiently advanced, the workingmen rising in the general strike will sweep away the undermined edifice and erect the new society born from their own midst.

---

[1][Trade unions.—*Eds.*]

[2][Local federations of trades corresponding somewhat to the central labor unions in the U.S.—*Eds.*]

# 16
## *Reflections on Violence*

GEORGES SOREL                                                                    1906

The revolutionary Syndicates argue about Socialist action exactly in the same manner as military writers argue about war; they restrict the whole of Socialism to the general strike; they look upon every combination as one that should culminate in this catastrophe; they see in each strike a reduced facsimile, an essay, a preparation for the great final upheaval.

The *new school*, which calls itself Marxist, Syndicalist, and revolutionary, declared in favour of the idea of the general strike as soon as it became clearly conscious of the true sense of its own doctrine, of the consequences of its activity, and of its own originality. It was thus led to leave the old official, Utopian, and political tabernacles, which hold the general strike in horror, and to launch itself into the true current of the proletarian revolutionary movement; for a long time past the proletariat had made adherence to the principle of the general strike the *test* by means of which the Socialism of the workers was distinguished from that of the amateur revolutionaries.

Parliamentary Socialists can only obtain great influence if they can manage, by the use of a very confused language, to impose themselves on very diverse groups; for example, they must have working-men constituents simple enough to allow themselves to be duped by high-sounding phrases about future collectivism; they are compelled to represent themselves as profound philosophers to stupid middle-class people who wish to appear to be well informed about social questions; it is very necessary also for them to be able to exploit rich people who think that they are earning the gratitude of humanity by taking shares in the enterprises of Socialist politicians. This influence is founded on balderdash, and our bigwigs endeavour—sometimes only too successfully—to spread confusion among the ideas of their readers; they detest the general strike because all propaganda carried on from that point of view is too socialistic to please philanthropists.

In the mouths of these self-styled representatives of the proletariat all socialistic formulas lose their real sense. The class war still remains the great principle, but it must be subordinated to national solidarity. Internationalism is an article of faith about which the most moderate declare themselves ready to take the most solemn oaths; but patriotism also imposes sacred duties. The emancipation of the workers must be the work of the workers themselves—their newspapers repeat this every day,—but real emancipation consists in voting for a professional politician, in securing for him the means of obtaining a comfortable situation in the world, in subjecting oneself to a leader. In the end the State must disappear—and they are very careful not to dispute what Engels has written on this subject—but this disappearance will take place only in a future so far distant that you must prepare yourself for it by using the State meanwhile as a means of providing the politicians with tidbits; and the best means of bringing about the disappearance of the State consists in strengthening meanwhile the Governmental machine. This method of reasoning resembles that of Gribouille, who threw himself into the water in order to escape getting wet in the rain.

Whole pages could be filled with the bare outlines of the contradictory, comical, and quack arguments which form the substance of the harangues of our great men; nothing embarrasses them, and they know how to combine, in pompous, impetuous, and nebulous speeches, the most absolute irreconcilability with the most supple opportunism. . . .

■   ■   ■

Against this noisy, garrulous, and lying Socialism, which is exploited by ambitious people of every description, which amuses a few buffoons, and which is admired by decadents—revolutionary Syndicalism takes its stand, and endeavours, on the contrary, to leave nothing in a state of indecision; its ideas are honestly expressed, without trickery and without mental reservations; no attempt is made to dilute doctrines by a stream of confused commentaries. Syndicalism endeavours to employ methods of expression which throw a full light on things, which put them exactly in the place assigned to them by their nature, and which bring out the whole value of the forces in play. Oppositions, instead of being glozed over, must be thrown into sharp relief if we desire to obtain a clear idea of the Syndicalist movement; the groups which are struggling one against the other must be shown as separate and as compact as possible; in short, the movements of the revolted masses must be represented in such a way that the soul of the revolutionaries may receive a deep and lasting impression.

These results could not be produced in any very certain manner by the use of ordinary language; use must be made of a body of images which, *by intuition alone*, and before any considered analyses are made, is capable of evoking as an undivided whole the mass of sentiments which corresponds to the different manifestations of the war undertaken by Socialism against modern society. The Syndicalists solve this problem perfectly, by concentrating the whole of Socialism in the drama of the general strike; there is thus no longer any place for the reconciliation of contraries in the equivocations of the professors; everything is clearly mapped out, so that only one interpretation of Socialism is possible. . . .

The possibility of the actual realisation of the general strike has been much discussed; it has been stated that the Socialist war could not be decided in one single battle. To the people who think themselves cautious, practical, and scientific the difficulty of setting great masses of the proletariat in motion at the same moment seems prodigious; they have analysed the difficulties of detail which such an enormous struggle would present. It is the opinion of the Socialist-sociologists, as also of the politicians, that the general strike is a popular dream, characteristic of the beginnings of a working-class movement. . . .

■   ■   ■

Neither do I attach any importance to the objections made to the general strike based on considerations of a practical order. The attempt to construct hypotheses about the nature of the struggles of the future and the means of suppressing capitalism, on the model furnished by history, is a return to the old methods of the Utopists. There is no process by which the future can be predicted scientifically, nor even one which enables us to discuss whether one hypothesis about it is better than another; it has been proved by too many memorable examples that the greatest men have committed prodigious errors in thus desiring to make predictions about even the least distant future.

And yet without leaving the present, without reasoning about this future, which seems for ever condemned to escape our reason, we should be unable to act at all. Experience shows that the *framing of a future, in some indeterminate time*, may, when it is done in a certain way, be very effective, and have very few inconveniences; this happens when the anticipations of the future take the form of those myths, which enclose with them, all the strongest inclinations of a people, of a party or of a class, inclinations which recur to the mind with the insistence of instincts in all the circumstances of life; and which give an aspect of complete reality to the hopes of immediate action by which, more easily than by any other method, men can reform their desires, passions, and mental activity. We know, moreover, that these social myths in no way prevent a man profiting by the observations which he makes in the course of his life, and form no obstacle to the pursuit of his normal occupations.

The truth of this may be shown by numerous examples.

The first Christians expected the return of Christ and the total ruin of the pagan world, with the inauguration of the kingdom of the saints, at the end of the first generation. The catastrophe did not come to pass, but Christian thought profited so greatly from the apocalyptic myth that certain contemporary scholars maintain that the whole preaching of Christ referred solely to this one point. The hopes which Luther and Calvin had formed of the religious exaltation of Europe were by no means realised; these fathers of the Reformation very soon seemed men of a past era; for present-day Protestants they belong rather to the Middle Ages than to modern times, and the problems which troubled them most occupy very little place in contemporary Protestantism. Must we for that reason deny the immense result which came from their dreams of Christian renovation? It must be admitted that the real developments of the Revolution did not in any way resemble the enchanting pictures which created the enthusiasm at its first adepts; but without those pictures would the Revolution have been victorious? Many Utopias were mixed up with the Revolutionary myth, because it had been formed by a society passionately fond of imaginative literature, full of confidence in the "science," and very little acquainted with the economic history of the past. These Utopias came to nothing; but it may be asked whether the Revolution was not a much more profound transformation than those dreamed of by the people who in the eighteenth century had invented social Utopias. . . .

A knowledge of what the myths contain in the way of details which will actually form part of the history of the future is then of small importance; they are not astrological almanacs; it is even possible that nothing which they contain will ever come to pass, —as was the case with the catastrophe expected by the first Christians. In our own daily life, are we not familiar with the fact that what actually happens is very different from our preconceived notion of it? And that does not prevent us from continuing to make resolutions. Psychologists say that there is heterogeneity between the ends in view and the ends actually realised: the slightest experience of life reveals this law to us. . . .

The myth must be judged as a means of acting on the present; any attempt to discuss how far it can be taken literally as future history is devoid of sense. *It is the myth in its entirety which is alone important:* its parts are only of interest in so far as they bring out the main idea. No useful purpose is served, therefore, in arguing about the incidents which may occur in the course of a social war, and about the decisive conflicts which may give victory to the proletariat; even supposing the revolutionaries to have been wholly and entirely deluded in setting up this imaginary picture of the general strike, the picture may yet have been, in the course of the preparation for the Revolution, a great element of strength, if it has embraced all the aspirations of Socialism, and if it has given to the whole body of Revolutionary thought a precision and a rigidity which no other method of thought could have given.

97

To estimate, then, the significance of the idea of the general strike, all the methods of discussion which are current among politicians, sociologists, or people with pretensions to political science, must be abandoned. Everything which its opponents endeavour to establish may be conceded to them, without reducing in any way the value of the theory which they think they have refuted. The question whether the general strike is a partial reality, or only a product of popular imagination, is of little importance. All that it is necessary to know is, whether the general strike contains everything that the Socialist doctrine expects of the revolutionary proletariat.

To solve this question we are no longer compelled to argue learnedly about the future; we are not obliged to indulge in lofty reflections about philosophy, history, or economics; we are not on the plane of theories, and we can remain on the level of observable facts. We have to question men who take a very active part in the real revolutionary movement amidst the proletariat, men who do not aspire to climb into the middle class and whose mind is not dominated by corporative prejudices. These men may be deceived about an infinite number of political, economical, or moral questions; but their testimony is decisive, sovereign, and irrefutable when it is a question of knowing what are the ideas which most powerfully move them and their comrades, which most appeal to them as being identical with their socialistic conceptions, and thanks to which their reason, their hopes, and their way of looking at particular facts seem to make but one indivisible unity.

Thanks to these men, we know that the general strike is indeed what I have said: the *myth* in which Socialism is wholly comprised, *i.e.* a body of images capable of evoking instinctively all the sentiments which correspond to the different manifestations of the war undertaken by Socialism against modern society. Strikes have engendered in the proletariat the noblest, deepest, and most moving sentiments that they possess; the general strike groups them all in a co-ordinated picture, and, by bringing them together, gives to each one of them its maximum of intensity; appealing to their painful memories of particular conflicts, it colours with an intense life all the details of the composition presented to consciousness. We thus obtain that intuition of Socialism which language cannot give us with perfect clearness—and we obtain it as a whole, perceived instantaneously.

We may urge yet another piece of evidence to prove the power of the idea of the general strike. If that idea were a pure chimera, as is so frequently said, Parliamentary Socialists would not attack it with such heat; I do not remember that they ever attacked the senseless hopes which the Utopists have always held up before the dazzled eyes of the people. . . . But when it is a question of the general strike, it is quite another thing; our politicians are no longer content with complicated reservations; they speak violently, and endeavour to induce their listeners to abandon this conception.

It is easy to understand the reason for this attitude: politicians have nothing to fear from the Utopias which present a deceptive mirage of the future to the people, and turn "men towards immediate realisations of terrestrial felicity, which any one who looks at these matters scientifically knows can only be very partially realised, and even then only after long efforts on the part of several generations." . . . The more readily the electors believe in the *magical forces of the State*, the more will they be disposed to vote for the candidate who promises marvels; in the electoral struggle each candidate tries to outbid the others: in order that the Socialist candidates may put the Radicals to rout, the electors must be credulous enough to believe every promise of future bliss; our Socialist politicians take very good care, therefore, not to combat these comfortable Utopias in any very effective way.

They struggle against the conception of the general strike, because they recognise, in the course of their propagandist rounds, that this conception is so admirably adapted to the working-class mind that there is a possibility of its dominating the latter in the most absolute manner, thus leaving no place for the desires which the Parliamentarians are able to satisfy. They perceive that this idea is so effective as a motive force that once it has entered the minds of the people they can no longer be controlled by leaders, and that thus the power of the deputies would be reduced to nothing. In short, they feel in a vague way that the whole Socialist movement might easily be absorbed by the general strike, which would render useless all those compromises between political groups in view of which the Parliamentary regime has been built up.

The opposition it meets with from official Socialists, therefore, furnishes a confirmation of our first inquiry into the scope of the general strike.

# NEW LEFT THEORY
## 17
### *Strategy for Labor*

ANDRÉ GORZ                                                                    1964

That socialism is a necessity has never struck the masses with the compelling force of a flash of lightning. There has never been direct transition from primitive revolt to the conscious will to change society. Discontent with their condition has never spontaneously led even the most organized workers to attack those structures of society which made their lives unbearable. In this regard, nothing has changed since Lenin, Marx, or Pécqueur.[1]

What has changed, however, is that in the advanced countries the revolt against society has lost its *natural base*. As long as misery, the lack of basic necessities, was the condition of the majority, the need for a revolution could be regarded as obvious. Destitute proletarians and peasants did not need to have a model of a future society in mind in order to rise up against the existing order: the worst was here and now; they had nothing to lose. But conditions have changed since then. Nowadays, in the richer societies, it is not so clear that the status quo represents the greatest possible evil.

Permanent misery still exists, but in France as in the United States, this is the condition of only a fifth of the population. This population, moreover, is not homogeneous. It is concentrated in certain regions and in certain strata which are not representative of their class: for example, among small peasants in isolated regions, the aged, the unemployed, unskilled laborers, etc. These strata are incapable of organizing themselves for decisive action against society and the State. They have the same needs, but no common point of view on how these needs should be satisfied.

This is one reason why poverty can no longer be the basis of the struggle for socialism.

There is a second reason: the workers whose vital needs are insufficiently satisfied are for all practical purposes a rear guard. Advanced capitalism needs skilled workers more than the unskilled, and it also needs consumers for its products. While it is still necessary to demand the satisfaction of immediate needs, this struggle no longer brings the entire social order into radical question.

That is why I will not dwell on misery as the basis for a challenge to capitalism. I will, rather, attempt to determine what new needs capitalist development creates; to determine to what extent these new needs, when we have gauged their depth, are comparable in their urgency to the old needs; and to what extent they too imply a radical critique of capitalism, that is to say a critique of the reasons why these needs remain permanently unsatisfied.

Thus the essential problem will be to determine in which needs the necessity for socialism is rooted now that the urgency born of poverty is blunted; and under what conditions these needs can lead to the consciousness that society must be radically transformed.

This line of thought necessarily leads one to question numerous aspects of the traditional strategy of the working class movement. Not those who question it, however,

Reprinted from *Strategy for Labor* by André Gorz, pp. 3-14, 16-18, 20-24, 26, 30-38, 43-45, 56-57, 60-62, 90-94. Boston: Beacon Press, 1967. By permission of the author. Footnotes in the original have been eliminated or renumbered.

but reality itself has made that strategy obsolete. In the developed societies, where the pressure of vital needs is attenuated, it is no longer possible to base the necessity for socialism on an immediate negation, rejection, of the status quo. Because the intolerability of this system is no longer absolute, but relative, supplementary mediations are necessary to make the intolerability felt. And these mediations must be *positive:* they must reveal the urgency of the qualitative needs which neo-capitalist ideology ignores or represses; they must make these needs conscious by demonstrating the possibility and the positive conditions of their satisfaction.

It is no longer enough to reason as if socialism were a self-evident necessity. This necessity will no longer be recognized unless the socialist movement specifies what socialism can bring, what problems it alone is capable of solving, and how. Now more than ever it is necessary to present not only an overall alternative but also those "intermediate objectives" (mediations) which lead to it and foreshadow it in the present.

The weakness of the working class and socialist movement in all capitalist countries and particularly in France has up to the present been its more or less pronounced inability to link the struggle for socialism to the everyday demands of the workers. This inability is rooted in historical circumstances. For at least the past thirty years, the Communist movement has propagated the prophecy that capitalism would inevitably, catastrophically collapse. In the capitalist countries, its policy has been to "wait for the revolution." The internal contradictions of capitalism were supposed to sharpen, the condition of the toiling masses to worsen. Inevitably the working class would rise up.

This period has left deep marks. Working class leaders continue to fear that too great a victory in their everyday struggles will remove—or blunt for a long time—the workers' discontent and their revolutionary spirit. These leaders fear that a tangible amelioration in the workers' condition, or a partial victory within the capitalist framework, will reinforce the system and render it more bearable.

These fears, nevertheless, only reflect fossilized thinking, a lack of strategy and theoretical reflection. On the assumption that partial victories within the system would inevitably be absorbed by it, an impenetrable barrier has been erected between present struggles and the future socialist solution. The road from one to the other has been cut. These leaders act as if the solution to all problems could wait until the working class had seized power, and as if in the meantime there were nothing to do but to stoke the flames of revolutionary discontent.

However, this kind of attitude leads to an impasse. Lacking perspectives and positive accomplishments, the revolutionary flame begins to dim. Certainly, capitalism is incapable of fundamentally resolving the essential problems which its development has brought about. But capitalism can resolve these in its own way, by means of concessions and superficial repairs aimed at making the system socially tolerable. At present the working class and socialist movement finds itself cornered and on the defensive: having failed to impose its own solutions, it has lost the initiative. Having failed to anticipate the foreseeable problems and to define the solutions beforehand, the working class ceases to assert itself as the potential ruling class. Quite the contrary, it is capitalism itself which then grants the workers half-solutions. And with each of these concessions, capitalism—left at liberty to define for itself the nature and scope of its measures—strengthens its lead and consolidates its power.

This is also true of the problems arising from the Common Market, of the imbalances and disparities between regions, of the problems of reconversion, development, economic planning, job-creation, training, and professional adaptation to technological evolution. Capitalism does not have a solution to any of these problems, much less a satisfactory solution. But the European labor movement (with the exception, sometimes, of the Italian) has not yet been able to define its own solutions concretely and to fight for them. This is why the movement has hardly advanced at all toward the seizure of power and has not increased in strength. That also is why the movement does not convince those who are not already convinced that, once in power, it will be able to offer a fundamental solution to all problems. The movement behaves as though the question of power were resolved: "Once we're in power . . ." But the whole question is precisely to get there, to create the means and the will to get there.

Is it possible *from within*—that is to say, without having previously destroyed capitalism—to impose anti-capitalist solutions which will not immediately be incorporated into and subordinated to the system? This is the old question of "reform or revolution." This was (or is) a paramount question when the movement had (or has) the choice between a struggle for reforms and armed insurrection. Such is no longer the case in Western Europe; here there is no longer an alternative. The question here revolves around the possibility of "revolutionary reforms," that is to say, of reforms which advance toward a radical transformation of society. Is this possible?

Straight off we must rule out the nominalist objection. All struggle for reform is not necessarily reformist. The not always very clear dividing line between reformist reforms and non-reformist reforms can be defined as follows:

A reformist reform is one which subordinates its objectives to the criteria of rationality and practicability of a given system and policy. Reformism rejects those objectives and demands—however deep the need for them—which are incompatible with the preservation of the system.

On the other hand, a not necessarily reformist reform is one which is conceived not in terms of what is possible within the framework of a given system and administration, but in view of what should be made possible in terms of human needs and demands.

In other words, a struggle for non-reformist reforms—for anti-capitalist reforms— is one which does not base its validity and its right to exist on capitalist needs, criteria, and rationales.[2] A non-reformist reform is determined not in terms of what can be, but what should be. And finally, it bases the possibility of attaining its objective on the implementation of fundamental political and economic changes. These changes can be sudden, just as they can be gradual. But in any case they assume a modification of the relations of power; they assume that the workers will take over powers or assert a force (that is to say, a non-institutionalized force) strong enough to establish, maintain, and expand those tendencies within the system which serve to weaken capitalism and to shake its joints. They assume structural reforms.[3]

Nevertheless, is it not inevitable that powers gained by the workers within the capitalist framework be reabsorbed by the system and subordinated to its functioning? This question is essential for the Marxist movement, and the only possible answer (which is the answer of the great majority of Italian Marxists, whether Communists or, such as Lelio Basso and Vittorio Foa, left wing Socialists) is the following: the risk of subordination exists, but subordination *is not inevitable*. The risk must be run, for there is no other way. Seizure of power by insurrection is out of the question, and the waiting game leads the workers' movement to disintegration. The only possible line for the movement is to seize, from the present on, those powers which will prepare it to assume the leadership of society and which will permit it in the meantime to control and to plan the development of the society, and to establish certain limiting mechanisms which will restrict or dislocate the power of capital.

It is not, therefore, the opportuneness of "counter-powers" which is in question, but their nature and their relationship to the power of the capitalist State. The alternative is not between the conquest, exercise, and constant enlargement of powers by the workers, on the one hand, and the necessarily abstract will to seize power, on the other. The choice is between subordinate powers and autonomous powers.

By subordinate powers must be understood the association or participation of workers in an economic policy which urges them to share the responsibility on the level of results and execution, while at the same time it forbids them to become involved in the decisions and the criteria according to which this policy has been decreed. For example, the union is invited to "participate" in a policy predetermined by others on the company level and to "share" in carrying out this policy. The union is permitted to "challenge" the implementation, or even the effects of capitalist administration. But it is hoped at the same time that it will in fact not be able to challenge the *effects,* since it has been made an accomplice to the premises from which they follow. And as an additional precaution, management provides for an "arbitrator" to make sure that the challenge to the effects does not place these premises in question.

By *autonomous* power, on the other hand, must be understood the power of the workers to challenge, in opposing the effects and the methods of implementation, the very premises of the management's policy; to challenge them even in anticipation, because they control all the particulars on the basis of which the management's policy is elaborated. We shall return to this at greater length later on. Such autonomous power is a first step toward the subordination of the exigencies of production to human exigencies, with the conquest of the power of autonomous control as an ultimate goal.

The exercise of this kind of autonomous power cannot be restricted to purely negative opposition. But it is also clear that this power will never be granted, nor even conceded, by the employers without a struggle. This power must be won by force. And even when it is won . . . , this power can be exercised only at the price of constant mobilization. Moreover, it will inevitably tend to extend beyond the framework of the large enterprise, because the policy of a monopoly or of an oligopoly is in such close reciprocal relation with the economic policies of the State, the life of the city, the community, and the region.

Far, then, from leading toward the integration and subordination of the labor movement to the State, the autonomous power of the workers—in the large enterprises, but also in the cities, the towns, public services, regional bodies, cooperatives, etc.—prepares the way for a dialectical progression of the struggle to a higher and higher level. Autonomous power is at once the generator and the indispensable relay station for the elaboration and pursuit of the integral objectives of a policy aimed at replacing capitalism.

Moreover, this autonomous power is an indispensable element in the training and education of the masses, making it possible for them to see socialism not as something in the transcendental beyond, in an indefinite future, but as the visible goal of a praxis already at work; not a goal which the masses are supposed to wish for abstractly, but one to aim for by means of partial objectives in which it is foreshadowed.

What is involved here is indeed a strategy of *progressive* conquest of power by the workers, a strategy which does not, however, exclude the possibility of or even the necessity for a revolutionary seizure of power at a later stage.

Is such a strategy a step backward, because it abandons the idea of seizing power right away, of installing socialism with one blow? That would be the case if a revolutionary seizure of power were possible, or if the preparation for this seizure maintained the masses in a state of mobilization. But such is not the case. It is impossible—above all for Marxists—to pretend to explain the masses' present state of demobilization by the absence of revolutionary fervor on the part of their leaders. In truth, the state of demobilization today is due to the fact that neither the possibility nor the form nor the content of the workers' potential political power has been defined.

As long as the condition of the workers was immediately and absolutely unbearable, the conquest of power was an immediate end in itself. At present, however, the conquest of power is not a goal which will gain support unless it is made clear toward what ends—unrealizable under capitalism—the workers' power will be *the means.* Why socialism? How will it be achieved?

The answer to these questions is today a necessary first step. Mobilization for the conquest of power and of socialism—abstract terms which no longer in themselves serve to mobilize the masses—must pass through the "mediation" of intermediate, mobilizing objectives. The struggle for partial objectives which arise from deep needs and bring into question the capitalist structure, the struggle for partial autonomous powers and their exercise should present socialism to the masses as a living reality already at work, a reality which attacks capitalism from within and which struggles for its own free development. Instead of dichotomizing the future and the present—future power and present impotence, like Good and Evil—what must be done is to bring the future into the present, to make power tangible *now* by means of actions which demonstrate to the workers their positive strength, their ability to measure themselves against the power of capital and to impose their will on it.

Certainly, socialism can be no less than the hegemony of the working class, the public ownership of the means of production. But in order to reach this goal, it is necessary first to aim at intermediate objectives by means of which socialism can be seen as possible, as having a concrete significance, as being within reach. If socialism is to result from the prolongation of the present day struggles and demands, it cannot be presented straight off as a whole system, as a solution which precedes all problems. It should be presented instead as the general direction in which concrete solutions to specific problems move. In this respect, nationalization, like power, is no longer today, as in the days of Pécqueur, an end in itself: to achieve it there must be a struggle, but before there can be a struggle it must first be clear toward what end nationalization is the means.[4]

Politically, socialism can mean no less than power to the working class; economically, it can mean nothing but collective ownership of the means of production, that is to say the end of exploitation. But socialism is also more than that: it is also a new type of relationship among men, a new order of priorities, a new model of life and of culture. If it is not all this also, it loses its meaning. This meaning, to define it in one sentence, is: the subordination of production to needs, as much for *what* is produced as for *how* it is produced. It is understood that in a developed society, needs are not only quantitative: the need for consumer goods; but also qualitative: the need for a free and many-sided development of human faculties; the need for information, for communication, for fellowship; the need to be free not only from exploitation but from oppression and alienation in work and in leisure.

. . . We deal more with labor union strategy than with political strategy because the union, much more than the party, is the body in which class consciousness in a neo-capitalist society is catalyzed and elaborated. In fact, in all its aspects, neo-capitalist civilization tends to be a mass civilization. Its propaganda, which is above all commercial, subordinates the means which individuals have for informing themselves and for being in touch with one another, to commercial criteria. In order to sell newspapers, radio time, or products of mass consumption, capitalist civilization aims at the common and average characteristics in men, seeking to efface and mask the conflicts which oppose them to each other and the barriers which separate them: the big brands, the big corporation, the big press must gain the favor of a heterogeneous and varied public. They will therefore ignore everything which divides and differentiates this public, conjure away the burning problems which confront it, and address it as a mass of "consumers" above class frontiers. The negation of classes is an ideology founded on mercantilism.

It is normal that this ideology, the carrier of "mass culture," should invade the public domain, and that political parties (or rather, men) seeking clients should appropriate the mass ideology and its methods of commercial seduction. It is even more normal that monopoly- and state-capitalism should work toward the concentration and continuity of power, and that, once the presidential regime is in place, the political parties are forced to regroup in two camps in their competition for supreme power.

"Mass culture" tends thus to be followed by "mass democracy," that is to say the competition of all groups for the support of the "center," of the "masses," of those least politicized. Thus, during an electoral or pre-electoral period, the two camps take turns in smoothing the edges, attenuating the conflicts, divisions, and differences.

Union autonomy, then, assumes prime importance. For the labor union becomes the only mass organization to escape the imperatives of mass democracy; far from becoming weaker, it is reinforced as it reveals the true concreteness of problems. In the factory, the community, and the region, the union becomes the only place where class consciousness—the consciousness of needs, of demands, and of ends to be pursued—are elaborated, the sanctuary where the conflict between labor and capital continues to be experienced in all its sharpness. The union struggle inevitably assumes a political context, because the link between the workers' condition on the job and the organization of society, between the specific demands of the workers and the economic, political, and social conditions necessary to satisfy them, is so evident.

That is why we must firmly reject all attempts to subordinate the union to the party, to limit or discipline the union's autonomy of action, to submit its action to objective criteria such as economic fluctuations, the evolution of productivity, of production, or of profits. This firm defense of the union's freedom of action must be unconditional and permanent, no matter what the political color of the government, no matter what type of economic planning there is and what its goals are.

Even among those who sympathize with socialism, it is often objected that in order to achieve a new economic orientation—for example, democratic or socialist planning—the union should accept as part of the bargain a limit on its freedom of action, a wage discipline. I cannot agree.

The permanent role of the union is to express the workers' real needs and to work toward their satisfaction; the role of the national Plan, in whose elaboration the union has every interest in participating, is to organize *the means* for this satisfaction. The tension between the needs and the means to satisfy them is indeed the driving force of economic planning and therefore of democracy. The tension between the union and the Plan should be accepted as a permanent fact.

■   ■   ■

A national incomes policy is not at all a necessary element in economic planning. The incomes policy merely expresses the political will of organized capitalism to integrate the union into the system, to subordinate consumption to production, and production to the maximization of profit. The union cannot defend itself against this political will except by an opposite and autonomous political will which is independent of party and State, and is rooted in the specific demands of the workers.

Bastion of class realities in the face of mass ideologies and their myths, the union—to the extent that it functions properly—becomes a center which radiates political energy.[5] It is through the union that the fundamental contradiction of capitalism—the contradition inherent in property relations—is continually manifest in its concrete, living reality. It is in the union, within the sphere of alienated labor, that the truth and the meaning (if not the immediate content) of revolutionary demands take shape: the demand that production be subordinated to needs, the manner of producng be subjected to the human exigencies of the producers, capital subordinated to society. Only in the union can socialist man be forged in the present: the worker organized with other workers to regulate production and exchange, the producer dominating the production process instead of being subordinated to it, the man of creative praxis. Socialism will be little—or nothing at all—if it is not first these men, if it is not a new order of priorities, a new model of consumption, of culture, of social collaboration.

This model has yet to be defined in any of the advanced industrialized societies. It does not yet exist anywhere. Until now, socialist societies also have subordinated consumption to production; creative needs, culture, and education to the needs of accumulation. This subordination has even been, in certain regards, more systematic and relentless than in the advanced phase of capitalism.

For socialism has until now been no more than a gigantic and systematic effort at public accumulation, impelled by the acute shortage of everything and by external menaces. This is now generally admitted. But above all, the problem is to determine how this wartime socialism, this socialism of scarcity which has little to do with the socialism conceived by Marx, can overcome its alienations and return to its original goals.

For when we begin by considering individuals as means of production, society as an instrument of accumulation, and work as a tool for producing other tools (which is what the socialist states have undeniably done up to now) then we are not preparing men to emancipate themselves and to construct a society in which production is a means and man is the end.

■   ■   ■

There is no crisis in the workers' movement, but there is a crisis in the theory of the workers' movement. This crisis (in the sense of reexamination, critique, broadening of strategic thought) arises principally from the fact that immediate economic demands no longer suffice to express and to make concrete the radical antagonism of the working class to capitalism; and that these demands, no matter how hard the struggle for them, are no longer enough to bring capitalist society to the point of crisis, nor to strengthen the autonomy of the working class within the society of which it is a part.

Now, the explicit and positive affirmation of class autonomy is one essential precondition for the attainment of revolutionary perspective in the working class movement. And by class autonomy one must understand first of all that the working class, in its everyday actions as well as in its attitude toward society, considers itself the permanent challenge not only to the capitalist economic system and social order, but also and equally to capitalist power and civilization (its priorities, its value hierarchies, its culture) in the name of a different power and a different civilization of which the working class, as the potential ruling class, makes itself daily the author and the prefiguration.

■  ■  ■

When I say that the struggle over the paycheck no longer suffices to express the fundamental antagonism of the classes, I mean above all that, in the mature capitalist societies, the problems of the standard of living, of wages and of the simple reproduction of labor power no longer possess an urgency great enough to allow one to envisage the overthrow of the system and the end of exploitation as their necessary outcome. For the working class, the intolerability of the capitalist system has become relative, and the overthrow or transformation of that system no longer appears as a clear and vital necessity, as was the case thirty or fifty years ago. As a result, struggles for immediate economic demands, even very bitter ones, no longer by themselves open up perspectives of revolutionary social change; they even accommodate themselves to the most insipid trade-unionist and reformist ideology.

To maintain the theory of absolute impoverishment in these conditions is entirely useless. . . .

■  ■  ■

The needs that are unsatisfied today are of a different nature from those of fifty or one hundred years ago: then, it was a question of unsatisfied elementary needs (misery); today, it is a question of historical needs, or historical-fundamental needs. . . . And the latter do not have the same absolutely imperative urgency as the former. They no longer assert the categorical exigency for life, but the infinitely elastic demand for a better life or for "human" life. And if revolution is an immediate necessity when the possibility of living can only be bought at that price, the same cannot be said when what is at stake is the possibility of living better, or differently.

I do not mean to say that one cannot make a revolution for a better or different life. I mean only that the urgency of revolution is no longer given, in this case, in the nature of consumer needs themselves, and that, if the existing dissatisfactions are to acquire a similar urgency, a higher than ever level of consciousness and of theoretical and practical elaboration are necessary. The error of those who have recourse to modernized forms of the theory of impoverishment has been to try to do without this necessary elevation of the level of consciousness and the level of struggle, without the new mediations necessary to lead from immediate dissatisfaction to the conscious will to bring about a radical transformation. This theory has become a crutch: like the theory of the inevitability of catastrophic crises which was current in the Stalinist era, it bases itself on the *growing discontent of the masses* as if that were an absolute impasse toward which capitalism were headed. Convinced that capitalism can only lead from bad to worse, the theory foresees its absolute intolerability. This allows it to dispense with the elaboration of a strategy of progressive conquest of power and of active intervention into capitalist contradictions.

The impasse predicted for capitalism becomes finally the impasse of the revolutionary waiting game. For while the developed capitalist societies, for better or for worse, integrate the struggles of the working classes as one factor amid others in their pursuit of economic equilibrium, the strategy of the working class, on the other hand, deals with the modern tendencies of mature capitalism only imperfectly in its calculations. Accustomed to find the source of its strength in the immediate intolerability of the system, in its "negative negation," the working class is not always conscious of a number of factors: in mature capitalist society the differences between the classes pertain less to the quantity than to the quality of consumption, and the same "model of affluence" is upheld by the sources of public information and education as suitable for all "consumers"; in such a society it is important to oppose the capitalist model itself with a "positive negation," with a model that is essentially qualitative, one which opposes the priorities of the "affluent society" with different and truer priorities; one which opposes less immediate but more profound needs to those induced by capitalist civilization, needs which no amount of consumption can satisfy. In other words, the revolutionary break between the classes is no longer located within the sphere of consumer needs; quite the contrary.

In effect, with its idle productive capacity and its liquid capital searching for outlets, mature capitalism is in a position to oppose the most flexible line of defense precisely to general demands for greater consumption and leisure. It can absorb both nominal wage increases and a reduction in working hours without harming either profits or above all, the power of the monopolies, and without increasing in any way the power of the working class, despite its victories.

■   ■   ■

The conclusion to be drawn from this argument is not that struggles over wages are useless; rather, it is that their effectivensss, insofar as mobilization, unification, and education of the working class are concerned, has become very limited. These struggles by themselves, even if they sometimes succeed in creating a crisis within capitalism, nevertheless succeed neither in preventing capitalism from overcoming its difficulties in its own way, nor in preparing the working class sufficiently to outline and to impose its own solutions to the crises it has provoked. On the contrary, the working class runs the risk of provoking a counteroffensive by the governmental technocracy, an attack leveled not only in the economic, but equally in the ideological, social, and political realms; and the working class, because it did not also wage a fight in these spheres, would be unable to respond with the necessary alertness and cohesion.

■   ■   ■

In a system whose intolerability is no longer absolute, but relative, one cannot make a revolution for a little more well-being any more than one can begin *and win* the political battle for the autonomy of the working class with quantitative arguments about the level of wages. Also, rather than enter battle on the question of percentages, why not rely on the working class's radical rejection of capitalist society on the level (that of the capitalist relations of production) where this rejection is permanently experienced? And why not from the beginning do battle on fundamental questions, that is to say, on the basis of this fundamental contradiction, of the qualitative rather than quantitative needs which capitalism will never succeed in satisfying? These needs, of a potentially revolutionary urgency, exist. While the development of capitalism has made the living standard of the worker relatively more tolerable as far as individual consumption is concerned, it has made the worker's condition still more intolerable as regards the relationships of production and of work, that is to say as regards his alienation in the largest sense, the sense not only of exploitation, but also of oppression, of dehumanization. It is this intolerable alienation that needs to be brought more profoundly into consciousness, because it implies the negation of the worker not only as a consumer and as "generic man" but also as producer, as citizen, as a human being; and because it calls for the refusal of capitalism not only as a system of exploitation, but also as an authoritarian society with deeply rooted anti-democratic social relations, as a civilization with inverted priorities, as a system of waste and destruction. . . .

■ ■ ■

In all these cases the possibility of designing a strategy which links the condition of the workers at the place of work with their condition in society, thus shifting the struggle away from the purely economic level (trade unionist level, which facilitates the adversary's maneuvers to divide the movement into industries and crafts, as well as permitting the "consensus" counteroffensive) toward the level of the class struggle—this possibility is inherent in the close connection which exists in the life of every worker between the three essential dimensions of his labor power:

1. *The work situation:* that is to say, the formation, evaluation, and utilization of labor power in the enterprise.

2. *The purpose of work:* i.e., the ends (or productions) for which labor power is used in society.

3. *The reproduction of labor power:* i.e., the life style and milieu of the worker, the manner in which he can satisfy his material, professional, and human needs.

No wage concession, no redistributive "social justice" can reconcile the worker with the conditions imposed on him by capital in these three dimensions. On the contrary . . . : to the extent that the workers are younger, better educated, better paid, that their vital needs are better satisfied, that they have more leisure and less fear of permanent unemployment, to that extent they become more demanding on the qualitative, non-wage aspects of their condition.

Still, their demands, arising out of experience, must be made explicit and conscious so that their subjective force may become objective power. The necessarily general themes of political propaganda (or even of industrial struggles) cannot suffice; they cannot be taken as the point of departure but only as the end point, by linking the concrete condition of the worker in his work to his condition in society. The weakness of the programs of the Left has often been that even in victory its action on the institutional and legislative level has scarcely modified the condition of the workers in the productive cycle. Its result for the workers has been neither an even partial liberation within their work, nor the conquest of power, a power which would have to be extended or risk losing its substance, a power which could not be defended except by constant struggles for ever more advanced objectives.

Now, the question of workers' power is precisely what distinguishes a reform in a reformist spirit from a reform in a non-reformist spirit. To assert that every reform, so long as political hegemony does not belong to the working class, is of a reformist character and only results in a preservation of the system, making it more tolerable, is to argue from a fallacious schematicism insofar as workers' power is concerned. For while it is true that every reform (for example, nationalization and economic planning) is absorbed by the system and ends up by consolidating it so long as it leaves the power of the capitalist state intact, and as long as it leaves the execution and administration of the reform in the hands of the State alone, it is also true, inversely, that every conquest of *autonomous* powers by the working class, whether these powers be institutionalized *or not*, will not attenuate class antagonisms but, on the contrary, will accentuate them, will yield new opportunities for attacking the system, will make the system not more but less tolerable by sharpening the conflict between the human demands of the workers and the inert needs of capital. One must indeed be a poor Marxist to believe that in the framework of the capitalist relationships of production, the fundamental contradiction between labor and capital can be attenuated to the point of becoming acceptable when the workers' local conquest of power gives them a richer and more concrete consciousness of their power as a class.

■　　■　　■

Quite apart from the actual capitalist exploitation of labor power, the work situation is characterized in form and in content by the oppressive subordination of labor to capital.

At no matter what level and under whose direction, workers' training tends in fact to produce men who are mutilated, stunted in knowledge and responsibility. The dream of large industry is to absorb the worker from cradle to grave (from the layette at birth to the coffin at death, with job training, housing, and organized leisure in between), so as to narrow his horizon to that of his job. It is important, to begin with, not to give the worker (and not to permit him to acquire) skills superior to those which his specialized job requires. (This is "in order to avoid problems of adaptation," as an important French industrialist candidly explained at a recent management forum.) The worker must not be permitted to understand the overall production process, nor to understand work as an essentially creative act; for such thoughts might lead him to reflect, to take the initiative, and to make a decision, as for example the decision to go sell his labor power elsewhere.

For its repetitive tasks, whether those of clerks in the banks and insurance houses or those of solderers in electronics, industry requires passive and ignorant manpower. Recruited on leaving school (in a rural area, by preference) and trained either on the job or in the trade schools, this manpower will not acquire a trade which will give it professional autonomy and human dignity, but merely the skills required in the individual company which hires it. In this way the company exercises over its workers not only a kind of perpetual property right, but also the right to regulate qualifications, wages, hours, quotas, piecework, etc., as it sees fit.

Even for skilled workers, the production process nevertheless remains obscure. For the semi-skilled workers, the dominant contradiction is between the active, potentially creative essence of all work, and the passive condition to which they are doomed by the repetitive and pre-set tasks dictated by assembly line methods, tasks which transform them into worn-out accessories to the machine, deprived of all initiative. For the highly skilled workers, on the other hand, the dominant contradiction is between the active essence, the technical initiative required in their work, and the condition of passive performers to which the hierarchy of the enterprise nevertheless still condemns them.

With the exception of certain industries employing chiefly unskilled labor—industries which are rapidly declining in importance—the level of technical training required for the average job is rising; but along with his increasing technical responsibility, the worker gains no correspondingly greater mastery over the conditions to which he is subjected and which determine the manner of his work (nor, of course, is there a greater mastery over the product). Responsible for his work, he is not master of the conditions under which he carries it out. The company which hires him requires of him both creativity in the execution of his task and passive, disciplined submission to the orders and standards handed down by management.

On the margin of civil society, with its formal liberties, there thus persists behind the gates of factories, a despotic, authoritarian society with a military discipline and hierarchy which demands of the workers both unconditional obedience and active participation in their own oppression. And it is only normal that this militarized society should, on suitable occasions, assert itself as the true face of capitalist society. It tends to break out of the factory walls and to invade all domains of civil life, championing the principle of authority, the suppression of thought, criticism, speech, and assembly. In its social model, the ideal man is active but limited and submissive, having extensive skills but restricting their application to the technical domain only. . . .

The oppression of the worker, the systematic multilation of his person, the stunting of his professional and human faculties, the subordination of the nature and content of his working life to a technological evolution deliberately hidden from his powers of initiative, of control, and even of anticipation—the majority of wage demands are in fact a protest against these things. Wage demands are more often motivated by a revolt against the workers' condition itself than by a revolt against the rate of economic exploitation of labor power. These demands translate the desire to be paid as much as possible for the time being lost, the life being wasted, the liberty being alienated in working under such conditions; to be paid as much as possible not because the workers value wages (money and all it can buy) above everything else, but because, at the present stage of union activity, only the price of labor power may be disputed with management, but not control over the conditions and nature of work.

In short, even when highly paid, the worker has no choice but to sell his skin, and therefore he tries to sell it as dearly as possible. And inversely, no matter what price he receives for selling his liberty, that price will never be high enough to make up for the dead loss which he suffers in qualitative and human terms; even the highest pay will never restore to him control over his professional life and the liberty to determine his own condition.

The simple wage demand thus appears as a distortion and a mystification of a deeper demand; exclusive concentration on the pay envelope is an impasse into which the labor movement is headed. For the movement is going in precisely the direction management wants: it is abandoning to management the power of organizing the production process, the quantitative and qualitative content of working hours and of working conditions as they see fit, in exchange for bonuses to "compensate" for the increased multilation of the working man. The movement thus accepts the fundamental criteria of the profit economy, namely that everything has a price, that money is the supreme value, that any and everything may be done to men provided they are paid. The movement is becoming increasingly "Americanized," as the European management wants it to be: the workers abandon all efforts to control and transform the relations of production, the organization of the productive process and capitalist control of the enterprise; they leave the company free to pursue its maximum profit and to reign unchallenged over society, receiving in exchange occasional large crumbs from capital's head table. The working class movement is allowing industry to produce a new mass of lobotomized proletarians whom eight hours of daily degradation and of work by the clock leaves with only a weary desire for escape, an escape which the merchants and manipulators of leisure time and culture will sell them on credit even in their homes, persuading them in the bargain that they are living in the best of all possible worlds.

In truth, if the working class wishes to preserve its potential as the ruling class, it must first of all attack the workers' condition on the job, because it is there, where the worker is most directly alienated as producer and citizen, that capitalist society can be most immediately challenged. Only by a conscious rejection of oppressive work conditions, by a conscious decision to submit these conditions to the control of the associated workers, by an unceasing effort to exercise autonomous self-determination over the conditions of labor, can the working class maintain or assert permanently the autonomy of its consciousness as a class, and the human emancipation of the worker as a supreme end.

■    ■    ■

The first task of the working class movement today is to elaborate a new strategy and new goals which will indivisibly unite wage demands, the demand for control, and the demand for self-determination by the workers of the conditions of work. The only way to unite and mobilize a differentiated working class at present is to attack the class power of the employers and of the State; and the only way to attack the class power of the employers and the State is to wrest from each employer (and from the State) a vital piece of his power of decision and control.

Concretely, the goal of this attack should not be to achieve modifications and accommodations of the workers' condition within the framework of a given management policy and a given stage in the technological development of the industry; for such a victory, besides being non-generalizable beyond the individual company, could rapidly be taken away from the workers, as rapidly as improvements in techniques and in the organization of production permit. On the contrary, the working class movement must demand permanent power to determine, by contract, all aspects of the work situation and the wage scale, so that all modifications in the productive process must be negotiated with the workers, and so that the workers can materially influence the management of the enterprise and orient it in a given direction.

For example:

—The union should be able to control the training schools to ensure that they do not train robots, multilated individuals with limited horizons and a life burdened by ignorance, but professionally autonomous workers with virtually all-sided skills, capable of advancing in their jobs at least as fast as technological development.

—The union should be able to control the organization of work and the personnel system, to guarantee that personnel and organizational changes are made with the aim of developing the workers' faculties and professional autonomy, and not the contrary. Young workers especially should not be confined to one particularly degrading task.

—The union should thus exercise its power over the division of labor, on the company and industry level, to keep abreast of the given techniques of production and their foreseeable evolution. It should be able to impose on the employers, in each enterprise, that level and structure of employment which will result in the adoption of optimum production techniques and organization from the workers' point of view, thus guaranteeing that technological and human progress will coincide.

—The union should be able to negotiate the speed or rhythm of work, the piecework rate, the qualifications required for a job, the hours—all of which implies a continuous surveillance and negotiation of technological changes and their effects on the workers' condition, as well as the power to influence them.

—Finally, the union should demand a collective output bonus, that is to say a premium which is dependent neither on individual productivity nor on profits, but on production accomplished in a fixed number of working hours. This premium, which should be added to the basic wage (and a raise in this wage should be demanded simultaneously) constitutes a first step toward workers' control over the distribution of company revenue among labor costs, investments, and amortization—that is to say, a first step toward workers' self-management.

■  ■  ■

The struggle against exploitation does not take on its full meaning until it becomes a conscious struggle against the social consequences of exploitation, that is to say, a struggle against the false priorities, the waste and deprivation that monopoly capitalism in its mature phase imposes on society as the so-called model of "affluent consumption." To struggle against the exploitation of labor is necessarily to struggle also against the purposes for which labor is exploited.

The separation of these two aspects is less possible than ever if the labor movement wants to conserve its autonomy. In effect, a labor organization which, on the pretext that politics is none of its business, tries to channel the workers' actions solely into demands for higher consumption, and, implicitly, into the struggle against exploitation, would logically be led to look with favor—or at least without principled hostility—on proposals made by the capitalist state to integrate labor organizations into the system, to discuss with them an eventual ceiling on the profit rate, eventually to link the level of wages to the expansion of the national income, without challenging either the overall cost of capitalist accumulation, or the driving role of profit, either the political-economic power of the monopolies or the orientations and priorities forced upon all economic activity by the urge to maximize profits.

In addition, to struggle against exploitation and in favor of demands for greater consumption, but without challenging the purposes of exploitation (i.e., accumulation) and the model and the hierarchy of consumption in advanced capitalist society, is to place the working class in a subordinate position with regard to the fundamental decisions, the values, the ideology of this society, and to reinforce the latter even with the minor successes achieved by the unions. In effect, these successes—increase in wages, in vacation time, in the amount of individual consumption—will rapidly be made into a paying proposition by those (government and monopolies) who granted them; they rapidly become a source of additional profits (with or without a rise in prices) for the consumer goods industry. So long as they remain only quantitative and not also qualitative, economic struggles remain unable to affect the system profoundly, and contribute very little to forging and raising class consciousness.

■  ■  ■

In other words, an alternative line must appear as a concrete and positive possibility, attainable through the pressure of the masses on all levels:

—On the shop level, through the conquest by the workers of power over the organization and condition of work;

—On the company level, by the conquest of a workers' counter-power concerning the rate of profits, the volume and orientation of investments, technical level and evolution;

—On the industry and sector level, by the fight against overinvestment, fraught with future crises; and the fight against the shortcomings of capitalist initiative as regards the development of socially necessary production; both fights having to be linked to a program of industrial reorientation and/or reconversion;

—On the level of the city, by the struggle against the monopolies' stranglehold over the entire life of the town (cultural, social, economic), over public transports, real estate and housing, city administration, the organization of leisure, etc.;

—On the provincial level, by the struggle for new industries which are necessary to the survival and the equilibrium of the region, the absorption of open or hidden unemployment, the creation of jobs for the workers whose industries undergo crises or are about to disappear. This fight should mobilize farmers as well as workers, should be based on an alternate program of regional development, directed by the unions and the labor parties jointly, and should aim at the establishment of regional centers of decision making which are independent both of monopoly capital and of the centralizing tendencies of the state;

—On the level of the national Plan,[6] that is to say on the level of society, finally, by the elaboration of an alternative Plan which modifies the orientation given to the economy by State and monopoly capitalism, which reestablishes real priorities that conform to social needs, and which challenges the purposes of private accumulation and of the "consumers' society" by developing the human resources (education, research, health, public installations, city planning) and the material resources of the nation.

■    ■    ■

Now the nature of capitalist society is to constrain the individual to buy back individually, as a consumer, the means of satisfaction of which the society has socially deprived him. The capitalist trust appropriates or uses up air, light, space, water, and (by producing dirt and noise) cleanliness and silence gratuitously or at a preferential price; contractors, speculators, and merchants then resell all of these resources to the highest bidder. The destruction of natural resources has been social; the reproduction of these vitally necessary resources is social in its turn. But even though the satisfaction of the most elementary needs now must pass through the mediation of social production, service, and exchange, no social initiative assures or foresees the replacement of what has been destroyed, the social reparation of the spoliation which individuals have suffered. On the contrary, once its social repercussions and its inverted priorities have aggravated the conditions in which social individuals exist, private enterprise then exploits at a profit the greater needs of these same social individuals. It is they as individual consumers who will have to pay for the growth of the social cost of the reproduction of their labor power, a cost which often surpasses their means.

The workers understand the scandal inherent in this situation in a direct and confused manner. The capitalist trust, after having exploited them and multilated them *in* their work, comes to exploit them and multilate them *outside* of their work. It imposes on them, for example, the cost, the fatigue, and the long hours lost on public transportation; it imposes on them the search for and the price of housing, made scarce by the trust's manpower needs and made more expensive by the speculations which increasing scarcity produces.

The same thing holds for air, light, cleanliness, and hygiene, whose price becomes prohibitive. . . .

On the level of collective needs, and only on this level, the theory of impoverishment thus continues to be valid. . . . The workers' social standard of living tends to stagnate, to worsen, even if their individual standard of living (expressed in terms of monetary purchasing power) rises. And it is extremely difficult, if not impossible, for urban workers to obtain a qualitative improvement in their living standards as a result of a raise in their direct wages within the framework of capitalist structures. It is this quasi-impossibility which gives demands in the name of collective needs a revolutionary significance.

■　■　■

Among these needs are:

—Housing and city planning, not only in quantitative but in qualitative terms as well. An urban esthetic and an urban landscape, an environment which furthers the development of human faculties instead of debasing them, must be recreated. Now it is obvious that it is not profitable to provide 200 square feet of green area per inhabitant, to plan parks, roads, and squares. The application of the law of the market leads, on the contrary, to reserve the best living conditions for the privileged, who need them least, and to deny them to the workers who, because they do the most difficult and the lowest-paid work, need them profoundly. The workings of this law also push the workers farther and farther from their place of work, and impose on them additional expense and fatigue.

—Collective services, such as public transportation, laundries and cleaners, child day care centers and nursery schools. These are non-profitable in essence: for in terms of profit, it is necessarily more advantageous to sell individual vehicles, washing machines, and magical soap powders. And since these services are most needed by those who have the lowest incomes, their expansion on a commercial basis presents no interest at all for capital. Only public services can fill the need.

—Collective cultural, athletic, and health facilities: schools, theatres, libraries, concert halls, swimming pools, stadiums, hospitals, in short, all the facilities necessary for the reestablishment of physical and intellectual balance for the development of human faculties. The non-profitability of these facilities is evident, as is their extreme scarcity (and usually great cost) in almost all of the capitalist countries.

—Balanced regional development in terms of optimum economic and human criteria, which we have already contrasted to neo-colonialist "slummification."

—Information, communication, active group leisure. Capitalism not only does not have any interest in these needs, it tends even to suppress them. The commercial dictatorship of the monopolies cannot in fact function without a mass of passive consumers, separated by place and style of living, incapable of getting together and communicating directly, incapable of defining together their specific needs (relative to their work and life situation), their preoccupations, their outlook on society and the world—in short, their common project. Mass pseudo-culture, while producing passive and stupefying entertainments, amusements, and pastimes, does not and cannot satisfy the needs arising out of dispersion, solitude, and boredom. This pseudo-culture is less a consequence than a cause of the passivity and the impotence of the individual in a mass society. It is a device invented by monopoly capital to facilitate its dictatorship over a mystified, docile, debased humanity, whose impulses of real violence must be redirected into imaginary channels.

■　■　■

Collective needs are thus objectively in contradiction to the logic of capitalist development. This development is by nature incapable of giving them the degree of priority which they warrant. This is why demands in the name of collective needs imply a radical challenge of the capitalist system, on the economic, political, and cultural levels.

---

[1][Constantin Pécqueur (1801–1887) was a French socialist theorist.—*Eds.*]

[2]The "counter-plan," i.e., an alternative plan advocated in France by a minority of socialists, is an ambiguous notion. French Communists criticize its reformism. It is impossible to decide *a priori* if this criticism is well founded or not.

■ ■ ■

Is it reformist, for example, to demand the construction of 500,000 new housing units a year, or a real democratization of secondary and higher education? It is imposible to know beforehand. One would have to decide first whether the proposed housing program would mean the expropriation of those who own the required land, and whether the construction would be a socialized public service, thus destroying an important center of the accumulation of private capital; or if, on the contrary, this would mean subsidizing private enterprise with taxpayers' money to guarantee its profits.

One must also know whether the intention is to build workers' housing anywhere that land and materials can be cheaply bought, or if it is to construct lodgings as well as new industry according to optimum human and social criteria.

Depending on the case, the proposal of 500,000 housing units will be either neo-capitalist or anti-capitalist.

[3]Each time I use the term structural reform, it should be understood that this does not mean a reform which rationalizes the existing system while leaving intact the existing distribution of powers; this does not mean to delegate to the (capitalist) State the task of improving the system.

Structural reform is by definition a reform implemented or controlled by those who demand it. Be it in agriculture, the university, property relations, the region, the administration, the economy, etc., a structural reform *always* requires the creation of new centers of democratic power.

Whether it be at the level of companies, schools, municipalities, regions, or of the national Plan, etc., structural reform always requires a *decentralization* of the decision making power, a *restriction on the powers of State or Capital,* an *extension of popular power,* that is to say, a victory of democracy over the dictatorship of profit. No nationalization is *in itself* a structural reform.

[4]Nationalization of the steel industry, for example, which was once a political aim, is today the least interesting of the foreseeable nationalizations, for this ancient industry is losing speed, its profitability is low, and it is already virtually controlled by the State. Nationalization, instead of changing the power relations and opening a breach in the capitalist system, can also strengthen this system: a neo-capitalist government, in purchasing the steel industry, could render a service to its present owners by permitting them to invest their capital much more profitably in growing industries.

The aim must rather be to nationalize the latter, the principal centers of capital accumulation, such as the chemical, oil, electronic, and mechanical and electrical construction industries; for the workers in these industries—including the technicians—suffer the consequences of the anarchic way they are run.

[5]Union action, however, can break through only if the class contradictions which it reveals are translated into a unifying political perspective and struggle by radical parties. Working class parties are powerless in the absence of the laboring masses' struggle, but the latter can get nowhere in the absence of a radical political force.

[6]["The Plan" in France refers to French governmental economic planning which commenced in 1946. Government economic plans are not mandatory, but the government does use tax and monetary policies to support them. Most French plans have concerned themselves with the direction of public and private investment.—*Eds.*]

# 18
## *Trade Unionism: Illusion and Reality*
STANLEY ARONOWITZ                                                                    1973

The configuration of strikes since 1967 is unprecedented in the history of American workers. The number of strikes as a whole, as well as rank-and-file rejections of proposed union settlements with employers, and wildcat actions has exceeded that in any
similar period in the modern era.

The most notable feature of the present situation is that the unions are no longer in
a position of leadership in workers' struggles; they are running desperately to catch up to
their own membership. There are few instances in which the union heads have actually
given militant voice to rank-and-file sentiment. In many cases, union sanctions for walkouts have followed the workers' own action. In others, the leadership has attempted to
thwart membership initiative and, having failed, has supported a strike publicly while
sabotaging it behind the scenes. For the most part, the national bureaucracies of the
unions have sided with employers in trying to impose labor peace upon a rebellious membership. What is remarkable is that the rebellion has been largely successful despite enormous odds.

The unions are afraid to oppose the rank and file directly. Their opposition has
taken the form of attempting to channel the broad range of rank-and-file grievances into
bargaining demands which center, in the main, on wages and benefits, while the huge
backlog of grievances on issues having to do with working conditions remains unsolved.
Rank-and-file militancy has occurred precisely because of the refusal of the unions to
address themselves to the issues of speedup, health and safety, plant removal, increased
workloads, technological change, and arbitrary discharges of union militants.

Wages have, of course, also been an enormously important factor in accounting for
the rash of strikes. Since 1967, workers have suffered a pronounced deterioration in living standards. Despite substantial increases in many current settlements, real wages for
the whole working class have declined annually, for there are few contracts which provide for cost-of-living increases in addition to the negotiated settlements. Even where
C-o-L clauses have been incorporated into the contracts, there is usually a ceiling on the
amount of increase to which the company is obligated. In many contracts, the first-year
increase is equal to the cost of living increase as tabulated by the Bureau of Labor Statistics for the previous year. But the second- and third-year increases are usually not as
great and during these years workers' real wages are diminished significantly.

Long-term contracts, which have become standard in American industry, have
robbed the rank and file of considerble power to deal with their problems within the
framework of collective bargaining. Workers have been forced to act outside of approved
procedures because instinctively they know that the union has become an inadequate tool
to conduct struggles, even where they have not yet perceived the union as an outright
opponent to their interests.

For most workers, the trade union still remains the elementary organ of defense of
their immediate economic interests. Despite the despicable performance of labor movement leadership during the past thirty years, and especially in the last two decades, blue-
and white-collar workers regard their unions as their only weapons against the dete-

Reprinted with permission of the publisher from *False Promises* by Stanley Aronowitz, pp. 214–223, 226,
251–257. 259–262. Some of the material originally appeared in *Liberation*. Copyright © 1973 by McGraw-Hill
Book Co.

rioration of working conditions and the rampant inflation responsible for recent declines in real wages.

In part, trade unions retain their legitimacy because no alternative to them exists. In part, workers join unions because the unions give the appearance of advancing workers' interests, since they must do so to some extent to gain their support. A national union bureaucracy can betray the workers' elementary demands for a considerable period of time without generating open opposition among the rank and file. Even when workers are aware of the close ties that exist between the union leaders and the employers, rebellion remains a difficult task for several crucial reasons.

First, in many cases, the union bureaucracy is far removed from the shop floor because membership is scattered over many plants or even industries. In unions like the United Steelworkers, only half the 1.2 million members are employed in the basic steel sector of the industry. The rest of the membership spans the nonferrous metals industry, steel fabricating plants, stone-working, can companies, and even a few coal mines. Most of the membership is in large multiplant corporations that have successfully decentralized their operations so that no single plant or cluster of factories in a single geographic region is capable of affecting production decisively. The problem of diffusion is complicated by the recent trend of U.S. corporations to expand their manufacturing operations abroad rather than within this country. In these circumstances, many workers, unable to communicate with workers in other plants of the same corporation since the union has centralized communications channels, feel powerless to improve their own conditions.

Second, the structure of collective bargaining enables the national union to transfer responsibility to the local leadership for failures of the union contract on working conditions issues, while claiming credit for substantial improvements in wages and benefits. This practice has been notable in the Auto Workers, the Rubber Workers, and others that have national contracts with large corporations.

Although the last decade has been studded with examples of rank-and-file uprisings against the least responsible of the labor bureaucrats, in nearly all cases, the new group of elected leaders has merely reproduced the conditions of the old regime. In the steel, rubber, electrical, government workers and other important unions one can observe some differences in sensitivity to the rank and file among the newer leaders. They are more willing to conduct strike struggles and their political sophistication is greater. But these unions can hardly be called radical nor have they made sharp breaks from the predominant policies of the labor movement in the contemporary era.

Some radicals explain this phenomenon in a purely idealistic way. According to them, the weakness of the factional struggles within the unions over the past decade has been that they have been conducted without an ideological perspective that differs from the procapitalist bias of the prevailing leadership. The left has been largely irrelevant to them. Therefore, if the new leadership merely recapitulates "the same old crap" (Marx's words), radicals should blame their own failure to concentrate their political work within the working class. Presumably, a strong left could have altered the kind of leadership and the program of the rank-and-file movements.

There is undoubtedly some truth in these assertions. Yet the disturbing fact is that the Communist left was very much a part of the trade union leadership for several decades prior to 1950; in some unions there are remnants of the left still in power. There is a tendency to explain the failure of the old Communist left by reference to its "revisionist" policies. Such superficial explanations assume that if only the politics of radical labor organizers had been better, the whole picture would have been qualitatively different. This will be shown not to be the case.

If the trade union remains an elementary organ of struggle, it has also evolved into a force for integrating the workers into the corporate capitalist system. Inherent in the modern labor contract is the means both to insure some benefit to the workers and to provide a stable, disciplined labor force to the employer. The union assumes obligations as well as wins rights in the collective bargaining agreement.

Under contemporary monopolistic capitalism, these obligations include: (1) the promise not to strike, except under specific conditions, or at the termination of the contract, (2) a bureaucratic and hierarchical grievance procedure consisting of many steps during which the control over the grievance is systematically removed from the shop floor and from workers' control, (3) a system of management prerogatives wherein the union agrees to cede to the employer "the operation of the employer's facilities and the direction of the working forces, including the right to hire, suspend, or discharge for good cause and . . . to relieve employees from duties due to lack of work," and (4) a "checkoff" of union dues as an automatic deduction from the workers' paychecks.

The last provision, incorporated into 98 percent of union contracts, treats union dues as another tax on workers' wages. It is a major barrier to close relations between union leaders and the rank and file. Workers have come to regard the checkoff as another insurance premium. Since they enjoy little participation in union affairs, except when they have an individual grievance or around contract time, the paying of dues in this manner—designed originally to protect the union's financial resources—has removed a major point of contact between workers and their full-time representatives. This procedure is in sharp contrast to former times when the shop steward or business agent was obliged to collect dues by hand. In that period, the dues collection process, however cumbersome for the officials, provided an opportunity for workers to voice their complaints as well as a block against the encroachment of bureaucracy.

The modern labor agreement is the principal instrument of the class collaboration between the trade unions and the corporations. It mirrors the bureaucratic and hierarchical structure of modern industry and the state. Its provisions are enforced not merely by law, but by the joint efforts of corporate and trade union bureaucracies. Even the most enlightened trade union leader cannot fail to play his part as an element in the mechanisms of domination over workers' rights to spontaneously struggle against speedup or *de facto* wage cuts, either in the form of a shift in the work process or by inflationary price increases.

The role of collective bargaining today is to provide a rigid institutional framework for the conduct of the class struggle. This struggle at the point of production has become regulated in the same way as have electric and telephone rates, prices of basic commodities, and foreign trade. The regulatory procedure in labor relations includes government intervention into collective bargaining, the routinization of all conflict between labor and the employer on the shop floor, and the placing of equal responsibility for observing plant rules upon management and the union.

The objective of this procedure is to control labor costs as a stable factor of production in order to permit rational investment decisions by the large corporations. The long-term contract insures that labor costs will be a known factor. It guarantees labor peace for a specified period of time. The agreement enables employers to avoid the disruption characteristic of stormier periods of labor history when workers' struggles were much more spontaneous, albeit more difficult.

An important element in the labor contract is that most of the day-to-day issues expressing the conflict between worker and employer over the basic question of the division of profit are not subject to strikes. In the automobile and electrical agreements as well as a few others, the union has the right to strike over speedup, safety issues, or a few other major questions. In the main, however, most complaints about working conditions and work assignments are adjusted in the final step of the grievance procedure by an "impartial" arbitrator selected by both the union and management. Even in industries where the strike weapon is a permitted option, the union leaders usually put severe pressure on the rank and file to choose the arbitration route since strikes disrupt the good relations between the union bureaucracy and management—good relations which are valued highly by liberal corporate officials and union leaders alike.

With few exceptions, particularly in textile and electrical corporations, employers regard labor leaders as their allies against the ignorant and undisciplined rank and file. This confidence has been built up over the past thirty-five years of industrial collective bargaining.

The trade unions have become an appendage of the corporations because they have taken their place as a vital institution in the corporate capitalist complex. If union leaders are compelled to sanction and often give at least verbal support to worker demands, it is most often because the union is a political institution whose membership selects officials. However, almost universally the democratic foundations of the trade unions have been undermined.

The left understood that the old craft unions were essentially purveyors of labor power, controlling both the supply of skilled labor and its price. The most extreme expression of their monopoly was the terror and violence practiced by craft union leadership against the rank and file. Since the old unions were defined narrowly by their economic functions and by their conservative ideology, the assumption of the Socialists and Communists who helped build industrial unions which included the huge mass of unskilled and semiskilled workers was that these organizations would express broader political and social interests, if not radical ideologies.

On the whole, despite corruption and bureaucratic resistance to the exercise of membership control, many unions in the United States have retained the forms but not the content of democracy. It is possible to remove union leaders and replace them, but it is not possible to transcend the institutional constraints of trade unionism itself.

Trade unions have fallen victim to the same disease as the broader electoral and legislative system. Just as the major power over the state has shifted from the legislative to the executive branch of government, power over union affairs has shifted from the rank and file to the corporate leaders, the trade union officials, and the government. Trade unions are regulated by the state both in their relations with employers and in their internal operations. Moreover, the problems of union leadership have been transformed from political and social issues to the routines of contract administration and internal bureaucratic procedures, such as union finances. The union leader is a business executive. His accountability is not limited to the membership—it is extended to government agencies, arbitrators, courts of law, and other institutions which play a large role in regulating the union's operations.

The contradictory role of trade unions is played out at every contract negotiation in major industries. Over the past several years the chasm between the leadership and membership has never been more exposed. During this period, a rising number of contract settlements have been rejected by the rank and file; in 1968 the proportion of rejection was nearly 30 percent. In contract bargaining the rank and file has veto power, but no means of initiative. In the first place, many major industries have agreements which are negotiated at the national level. There is room for local bargaining over specific shop issues, but the main lines of economic settlements are determined by full-time officials of the company and the union. One reason for this concentration of power is the alleged technical nature of collective bargaining in the modern era. Not only leaders and representatives of the local membership sit on the union's side of the bargaining table, but lawyers, insurance and pension experts, and sometimes even management consultants as well; the rank-and-file committees tend to be relegated to advisory or window-dressing functions or simply play the role of bystander. The product of the charade that is characteristic of much of collective bargaining today is a mammoth document which reads more like a corporate contract or a mortgage agreement than anything else. In fact, it is a bill of sale.

The needs of the membership only partially justify the specialization of functions within the trade unions. Insurance and pension plans do require a certain expertise, but the overall guidance of the direction of worker-employer relationships has been centralized as a means of preventing the direct intervention of the rank and file. More, the domination of specialists within the collective bargaining process signals the removal of this process from the day-to-day concerns of the workers. The special language of the contract, its bulk and its purely administrative character put its interpretation beyond the grasp of the rank and file and help perpetuate the centrality of the professional expert in the union hierarchy.

In this connection, it is no accident that the elected union official has only limited power within the collective bargaining ritual (and, in a special sense, within the union itself). Few national union leaders make decisions either in direct consultation with the membership or with fellow elected officials. It is the hired expert who holds increased power in union affairs and who acts as a buffer for the union official between the corporate hierarchy and the restive rank and file. As in other institutions, experts have been used to rationalize the conservatism of the leadership in technical and legal terms, leaving officials free to remain politically viable by supporting the sentiments expressed by the membership while, at the same time, rejecting their proposed actions. The importance of the experts has grown with the legalization of collective bargaining, especially the management of labor conflict by the courts and the legislatures, with legislation, and restraining orders limiting strikes, picketing, and other traditional working class weapons. In industries considered public utilities, such as the railroads, a strike is almost always countered by a court order enjoining the workers from taking direct action on the grounds that such action constitutes a violation of the national interest. The lawyer has become a key power broker between the workers, their unions, and the government. He is considered an indispensable operative in contemporary labor relations.

Some unions have promoted their house counsels from staff to officers. The secretary-treasurer of the Amalgamated Clothing Workers of America was formerly general counsel; its president began his career as counsel for the Detroit Joint Board of the union. The president of the United Packinghouse Workers was also its counsel for many years. But even without holding executive office the labor lawyer is placed in a position of both influence and ultimately of power within the organization by the increasing volume of government regulation of all types of trade union affairs. The same tendency can be observed within corporations where, together with financial experts, attorneys are replacing production men as the new men of power.

During the past decade in the auto, steel, rubber and other basic manufacturing industries, the critical issues of working class struggle have been those related to control over the workplace. The tremendous shifts in plant location, work methods, job definitions and other problems associated with investment in new equipment, expansion, and the changing requirements of skills to operate new means of production, have found the union bureaucracies unprepared. The reasons for trade union impotence at the workplace go beyond ideology. They are built into the sinews of the collective bargaining process.

Many important industries have national contracts covering most monetary issues, including wages. In the electrical, auto, and steel industries, negotiations are conducted with individual companies, but in reality there is "pattern" bargaining. A single major producer is chosen by the union and corporations to determine wage and fringe benefit settlement for the rest of the industry. All other negotiations stall until the central settlement is reached.

National union leadership always poses wage demands as the most important negotiating issues. Problems such as technological changes, work assignments, job classifications, and pace of work are usually negotiated at the local level after the economic package has been settled. And by the time the local negotiations begin—often conducted between rank-and-file leaders and middle managers—the national union has lost interest in the contract. Its entire orientation is toward the narrowly defined "economic" side of the bargaining. Although many agreements stipulate that resumption of work will not take place before the resolution of local issues, the international representatives and top leaders of the union put enormous pressure on the membership to settle these issues as quickly as possible. It is at the plant level that most sellouts take place. The local feels abandoned, but resentment is diverted to the failure of the shop leadership rather than that of the top bureaucracy, because the national union has "delivered the goods" on wages and benefits.

For example, after every national auto settlement, a myriad of local walkouts are called over workplace issues. These strikes are short-lived and usually unsuccessful. In the main, in struggles against speedup, young workers and Blacks are the spearhead. The impatience of the bureaucracy with this undisciplined action is usually expressed in long harangues to local leaders and the rank and file by international representatives who are employees of the national union. When persuasion fails, the rebellious local is sometimes put into receivership and an administrator is sent from the head office to take it over until order is restored.

Among radicals the conventional wisdom of today is to admit the conservative character of trade unions in the era of monopoly capitalism—their integration and subordination to the large corporations. At the same time, many radicals stress the important defensive role trade unions perform during the periods when growing capitalist instability forces employers to launch an offensive against workers' living standards and working conditions. Despite the conservative ideology of labor leaders and legal constraints upon them, rank-and-file pressure today is occasionally able to force unions to lead the fight against employer efforts to transfer to the working class the burdens of recessions or the dislocations of the labor force that occur during periods of technological change.

■    ■    ■

But the trade union structure has become less able to solve elementary defensive problems. Higher wages for organized workers since the end of World War II have been purchased at a high price. One result of the close ties between unions and corporations has been the enormous freedom enjoyed by capital in transferring the wage increases granted to workers in the shop to the shoulders of workers as consumers. Wage increases have been granted with relative ease under these circumstances in the largest corporations and the most monopolized industrial sectors.

Equally significant has been the gradual increase of constraints in the collective bargaining agreement on the workers' freedom to oppose management's imposition of higher production norms, labor-saving technologies, and policies of plant dispersal. (The last left millions of textile, steel, auto, shoe, and other workers stranded in the forties and fifties.) The bureaucratization of grievance procedures has robbed shop stewards of their power to deal with management on the shop floor. The inability of workers to change their working conditions through the union has had two results: workers limit their union loyalty to the narrow context of wage struggles, and they go outside the union to solve their basic problems in the plant. Thus the wildcat strike has become a protest not only against the brutality of industrial management, but also against the limits imposed by unionism. The conditions pertaining to the role of trade unions during the rise of industrial capitalism in the United States no longer apply in the monopoly epoch.

■   ■   ■

The bureaucratization of the trade unions, their integrative role within production, their conservative political ideology and their dependence on the Democratic Party are not primarily the result of the consciousness of the leading actors in the rise of industrial unionism. To the extent that the left participated in redefining the trade unions as part of the corporate system, it must now undertake a merciless critique of its own role before a new working class strategy can be developed.

It is not enough to admit bureaucratic tendencies in the unions or in their left leadership, however. The strategy flowing from this focus is to reform the unions from within in order to perfect their fighting ability and rank-and-file class consciousness. This line of thinking categorically denies that the unions can remain a dependent variable within the political economy dominated by corporate capitalism.

One of the important concepts of Marxist orthodoxy is that economic crisis is an inevitable feature of capitalist development, and that the tendency of employers will be to attack and reduce the power of trade unions during periods of declining production. Accordingly, it is believed that the government-employer attempts to circumscribe workers' power by restricting trade union functions will produce rank-and-file pressure confronting the leadership with the choice of struggle against capital or their own displacement. Thus the unions become objectively radical in their view despite their conservative consciousness.

However, strategies for rank-and-file reform ignore the bureaucracy and conservatism inherent in the present union structure and function, as well as the role of the unions in the division of labor. The growth of bureaucracy and the decline of rank-and-file initiative is built into the theory and practice of collective bargaining.

■   ■   ■

There is a . . . structural difficulty confronting trade unions in dealing effectively with the day-to-day issues on the shop floor. An increasing tendency can be observed in many unions toward the elimination, or the severe modification, of the shop steward system. One of the most progressive features of the CIO at its inception was the insistence of many of the new unions such as the Auto Workers and Electrical Workers that the members' basic grievances should be resolved at the workplace, since it was at the point of production that workers came face to face with problems of working conditions. Shop stewards were elected in each department, or even in each section of a department, on the basis of one steward for every twenty-five to thirty workers. The steward was not paid for union business either by the company or by the union and only left his/her work station when there was a grievance. In the early days of industrial management, foremen were still accorded more than marginal authority over the work forces. Foremen often performed the hiring and firing functions as well as distributing work and overtime to employees. Even as late as the early 1950s line supervisors and stewards fought out "beefs" right on the shop floor; failing a settlement, workers sometimes took "job actions," that is, refused to work or slowed down until the grievance was settled.

The centralization of management in the 1950s relieved the foremen of a great deal of their decision-making power. Nearly all decisions affecting production, including discipline, were now defined as policy issues reserved for professional personnel, directors or middle supervisors. Now nothing could be settled on the shop floor without direct independent action by the workers. Such action was opposed by union hierarchies.

In some instances, this opposition was not the result of venality or class betrayal by the union officials. For one thing, the Taft-Hartley Labor Relations Act imposed severe penalties for walkouts in violation of the terms of the labor agreement. Even when the walkout is not authorized by the union officials, the union is held responsible for penalties that may be ordered by a court. Some unions that have refused to order members to return to their jobs during wildcat strikes have been subjected to heavy fines and imprisonment of union officials by courts. Most union leaders have rejected the job action or the "quickie" as a self-defeating measure that can solve nothing and, on the contrary, make more problems.

Labor leaders attempted to adjust the grievance machinery to the realities of corporate power that removed decision-making from the work station. The rank-and-file steward was replaced by the "committeeman" in the United Auto Workers agreement with the "Big Three" manufacturers of the industry in 1946. The committeeman is employed virtually full time on union business and is paid by the company to deal with grievances. Instead of representing a small group of workers who do the same or similar labor in a relatively small area, the typical committeeman represents several hundred workers scattered over many different jobs and even geographic locations in the shop. He becomes the organizing force in the shop instead of the workers themselves. The argument for this system relies on the perception that the company will not deal with a steward because it has robbed its own line supervisor of real power.

The early version of the committeeman or business agent, the "walking delegate," was a post originally invented by craft unions whose membership was scattered over a large number of small shops. The commonly held belief among these workers in the latter half of the last century was that they must have a representative who was not paid by the company and was not required to work all day at the bench. But the introduction of the committee system into industrial plants can only have bureaucratic justifications. In large workplaces, this system has produced a union structure that is as alien to the line worker as to the company. The committeeman is perceived as a "man in the middle," having interests that are neither those of the rank and file nor those of management. His structural position is untenable from any point of view other than the performance of his main task: to police the union contract as well as possible and prevent both the rank and file and the management from going outside of it to solve problems. Many committeemen are sincerely interested in the welfare of union members and are frequently able to thwart the most arbitrary of management's actions against individuals. But they are powerless to deal with the issues that have produced the unauthorized job actions and wildcat strikes: the speedup of production, introduction of labor-saving machinery, plant removal, and disciplinary layoffs that do not result in immediate discharge.

The last thirty-five years of industrial unionism have failed to effect any substantive change in the distribution of income. Trade unionism under conditions of partial unionization of the labor force can do no more than redistribute income *within* the working class. Workers in heavily organized industries such as auto, rubber, and steel have relatively high wages compared to workers in consumer goods industries such as garments and shoes (which have migrated to the South), retail and wholesale workers, and most categories of government and agricultural workers.

The high wages of certain categories of industrial workers depend as much on the high proportion of capital to living labor and the monopoly character of basic industries as they do on trade union struggle. The tendency for employers in heavy industry to give in to union wage demands presupposes their ability to raise prices and productivity. In competitive industries such as light manufacturing, the unions have been transformed into stabilizers of industrial conflict in order to permit high rates of profits where no technological changes can be introduced. The result has been low wages for large numbers of Blacks, Puerto Ricans, and poor whites locked into these jobs.

Since advanced capitalism requires consumerism both as ideology and as practice to preserve commodity production, its payment of high wages to large segments of the working class—and minimum income to those excluded from the labor markets—is not objectively in the workers' interest. It is a means to take care of the market or demand side of production.

The ability of workers to purchase a relatively large quantity of consumer goods is dependent on the forces of production, which include the productivity and skill of the labor force and the scale and complexity of technology. Technological development, in turn, is dependent on the availability of raw materials and the degree of scientific and technical knowledge in society.

The most important issue to be addressed in defining the tasks ahead is not the question of inflation, wages, or general economic conditions. No matter how inequitable the distribution of income, no matter how deep the crisis, these conditions will never, by themselves, be the soil for revolutionary consciousness.

Revolutionary consciousness arises out of the conditions of alienated labor, which include economic conditions but are not limited to them. Its starting point is in the production process. It is at the point of mental and manual production, where the world of commodities is produced, that the worker experiences his exploitation. Consumption of waste production, trade union objectives in the direction of enlarging wages and social benefits, and the division of labor into industries and sections are all medications which stand between the workers' existential exploitation at the workplace and their ability to comprehend alienated labor as class exploitation.

Radicals of most persuasions have tended to address the problem of consciousness from the wrong end. Some believe that racism, trade unionism, conservatism, will be dissolved by discussion and exhortation alone, while others believe that "objective" conditions will force new understandings among workers. The notion that ideologies can be changed through ideological means or that capitalist contradictions will change consciousness with an assist from ideologically correct lines or propaganda is a nonrevolutionary position: in both cases, the role of practice is ignored. Nor will workers' struggles against economic hardship necessarily raise political consciousness.

In this connection one must reevaluate the rise of industrial unionism in the 1930s. Many radicals and labor historians have interpreted the failure of the CIO to emerge as an important force for social change as a function of the misleadership of its officials and the opportunism of the Communist Party and other radical parties that participated in its formation. According to a recent work on the development of the CIO by Art Preis, a contemporary labor reporter writing from a Trotskyist position, the 1930s were a pre-revolutionary period. Preis writes: "The first stage of awakening class consciousness was achieved, in fact, with the rise and and consolidation of the CIO. The second stage will be marked by a further giant step, the formation of a new class party based on the unions.

No important left-wing critique exists of unionism itself. Left-wing evaluations of the 1930s find the economic crisis a necessary condition for the development of class consciousness, but blame the Communist and Socialist policies for the fact that no significant radical force developed among the mass of workers.

I would dispute this theory since there is no genuine evidence that the CIO could ever have become an organized expression of a new class politics in America, or that trade unionism in the era of state capitalism and imperialism can be other than a force for integrating workers. After the disappearance of the IWW from the labor scene, there was no radical alternative offered within the working class. The trade union activists who belonged to Marxist parties functioned, in the main, as instruments for liberal union leaders. Their political thrust was dissipated by two factors. First, they were unwilling to become pariahs by opposing the rise of industrial unionism within the liberal consensus. Instead, they hoped to gain an operational foothold in the mass industrial unions from which to develop radical politics later on. Second, radical politics gradually became more rhetorical than practical for the left-wingers who entered the CIO. And it did not matter whether the left-winger was in the CP or anti-CP; the central thread was the same. Most radicals were all too willing to follow John L. Lewis. To them, he was performing the necessary preparatory work for socialism, later—despite his procapitalist bias, now.

Most non-Communist radicals within the labor movement refused to follow the CIO leadership into the New Deal coalition. It was the one distinguishing feature separating their politics from those of the CP. But insofar as they supported the CIO itself and subordinated themselves to its program, they could not but aid the despised Democratic Party.

In sum, radical ideologies and organizations played virtually no independent role in the trade unions after 1935. The few dissenters were swiftly cast aside in the triumphant march of industrial unionism.

■    ■    ■

It cannot be denied that working class militancy has generally been ambivalent in the United States. Workers are no less anti-employer than any other working class in the world. Strikes are bloodier, conducted for longer periods, and often manifest a degree of solidarity unmatched by any other group of workers. But working class consciousness is industry-oriented, if not always job-oriented. Workers will fight their unions and the companies through wildcat strikes and other means outside the established framework of collective bargaining. But they are ideologically and culturally tied to the prevailing system of power, because until now it has shown the capacity to share its expansion with a large segment of the working class.

These ideological ties, however, are much weaker among those segments of the working class that have historically been excluded from these shares—Black workers, women, and youth. But since 1919 it has not been accurate to claim that Black workers are not integrated at all into the industrial work force. Although they are excluded from unions representing skilled construction workers and underrepresented within the top echelons of union leadership, Blacks constitute between ⅓ and ⅔ of the work force in the auto and steel industries, and smaller but significant proportions of other mass production industries. Most union response to the large number of Black workers has been characterized at best by tokenism.

Union discrimination against Blacks and, to a lesser extent, young white workers, has led to the formation of caucus movements, particularly inside the auto and steel unions, based on the specific sectoral demands of these groups. Some Black caucuses seek more union power and, at the same time, demand upgrading to better-paying skilled jobs. Youth caucuses have been organized within the UAW making similar demands, but have gone further to suggest that the rigidity of industrial labor be relaxed. Some caucuses have asked that the uniform starting time of most workplaces be rescinded, that supervision be less severe, and that ways be found to enlarge job responsibility so that the monotony and meaninglessness of most assembly line tasks be mitigated. Young workers are groping for ways to control their own work, even though they are making piecemeal demands. Black workers are demanding liberation from the least satisfying of industrial tasks and more control over union decision-making processes.

But these are only tentative movements toward a different kind of working class consciousness. Workers are still oriented toward making demands on companies and unions, and do not aim at taking autonomous control over their own lives. Within the American working class, no significant movement or section of workers defines itself as a class and sees its mission to be the same as the liberation of society from corporate capitalist social relations.

Such consciousness will never arise in America from abject material deprivation. The position of the United States in the world has become more precarious since the end of World War II, but workers know that American capitalism has not reached dead end. However, the consciousness that most work in our society is deadening and much of it unnecessary has permeated the minds of young people, including the new entrants into the factories and offices. The growing awareness of the need for new forms of labor manifests itself in spontaneous ways. Corporations are becoming more concerned that young workers are not sufficiently disciplined to come to work on time or even every day. The new ideas for fewer workdays, even if the 40-hour work week is retained, are not likely to catch fire in the near future. But they indicate that corporations are searching for new methods of coping with the manifest breakdown of industrial discipline among the millions of workers who have entered the labor force in the past decade and have not experienced the conservatizing influence of the Depression. After all, if poverty is really not a threat for large numbers within our society, how can they be expected to endure the specialization of work functions and their repetitive character? The specter that haunts American industry is not yet the specter of Communism, as Marx claimed. It is the specter of social breakdown leading to a new conscious synthesis among workers.

It is the practice of trade unions and their position within production that determines their role in the social process. The transformation of the working class from one among many competing interests groups to capitalism's revolutionary gravedigger depends on whether working class practice can be freed from the institutions which direct its power into bargaining and participation with the corporate structure and can move instead toward workers' control.

The trade unions are likely to remain both a deterrent to the workers' initiative and a "third party" force at the workplace, objectively serving corporate interests both ideologically and in the daily life of the shop, and remaining a diminishing instrument of workers' struggles to be employed selectively by them. But the impulse to dual forms of struggle—shop committees, wildcat strikes, steward movements—may become important in the labor movements of the future.

The rise of new instruments of workers' struggle would have to reject the institutionalization represented by the legally sanctioned labor agreement administered by trade union bureaucracies. Workers would have to make conscious their rejection of limitations on their freedom to take direct action to meet their elementary needs at the workplace. Although many wildcat strikes are implicitly caused by issues which go beyond wage demands, these remain hidden beneath the more gross economic issues. Labor unions are not likely to become formally committed to the ideas of workers' control over working conditions, investment decisions, and the objects of labor. On the contrary, they will remain "benefits"-oriented, fighting incessantly to improve the economic position of their own membership in relation to other sections of the work force rather than in relation to the employers. They will oppose workers' efforts to take direct action beyond the scope of the union agreement and to make agreements with the boss on the informal basis of power relations on the shop floor.

The forms of consciousness that transcend trade unionism within the working class are still undeveloped and have not caught up with practice. Moreover, the perception that unions have become less useful institutions in the defensive as well as offensive struggles of workers, is confined to long-organized sections of the working class that have experienced the deterioration of the labor bureaucracies into instruments for the suppression of independent workers action. But barely 25 percent of the work force are members of trade unions. Workers in service industries and government employment who have been without union representation often regard trade unionism as a social mission.

For example, trade unionism still appears as a progressive force among the mass of working poor, such as farm and hospital workers, who labor under conditions of severe degradation. At first, unionization seems to be a kind of deliverance from bondage. But after the initial upsurge has been spent, most unions fall back into patterns of class collaboration and repression. At the point when grinding poverty has been overcome and unions have settled into their conservative groove, their bureaucratic character becomes manifest to workers.

We are now in the midst of a massive reevaluation by organized industrial workers of the viability of the unions. However, it is an action critique, rather than an ideological criticism of the union's role and the legal implications of it. It is still too early to predict its precise configuration in the United States. In the end, the spontaneous revolt will have to develop its own alternative forms of collective struggle and demands.

# THREE

**The Labor Movement as "Pure and Simple":
Business Unionism**

## Introduction

The theories in Part III present a direct contrast to those in the preceding chapter, especially Marxism. Whereas the previous theorists view unions in terms of antagonistic class struggles and revolutionary reconstruction of society, the following theorists see the labor movement as a nonantagonistic interest group among others competing in a pluralistic society for only restricted goals which are very far removed from revolution. Trade unions are a mechanism for *fitting in,* rather than *opposing* the system, say these theorists.

John R. Commons, a professor of economics at the University of Wisconsin during the early part of the twentieth century, developed the first systematic academic program concerned with labor. Together with pupils and scholars such as Selig Perlman, Philip Taft, and Don Lescohier, Commons founded what later became known as the Wisconsin school of labor history. The group compiled an exhaustive collection of labor material which would eventually illuminate our understanding of the development of labor unions in the United States and serve as an invaluable resource for further study in the field. Many of these original documents were published in a ten-volume *Documentary History of American Industrial Society.* It later led to the publication of the detailed four-volume *History of Labor in the United States.*

In this latter work, Commons and associates developed a pragmatic theory of the American labor movement. So great was its influence that until recently few books on American labor have challenged their interpretation. Essentially, they held, the unique characteristics of the American environment—free land, universal manhood suffrage, the absence of feudal obligations, and a democratic political system, among others—profoundly affected American workers and moved them in a direction different from that of their European counterparts. Whereas the unifying principle which mobilized European workers was class consciousness, in the United States it was job consciousness. The bond which held American workers together was derived from common job site problems and unions were seen as instruments to improve working conditions. In a pluralistic society such as the United States, workers held an infinite number of views on political, economic, and social issues. Labor unions which concerned themselves with issues outside of the employer-employee relationship, therefore, would sow disunity among their members and face eventual extinction. It was this fact, Commons and his associates claimed, which explained the ability of the AFL to survive and the absence of any radical alternatives.

Within this broad framework, members of the Wisconsin school developed several interpretations of the origin and development of labor unions. Like Marx, Commons sees the labor movement as developing from the emergence of a working class with its own distinct role in the economy. However, the resemblance ends there. Both in his general theory and in a particularly famous article on the history of the shoeworkers (partially reprinted here), Commons claims that it is the *extension of markets*—not a class struggle between employers and employees—that led to the growth and evolution of unionism.

Commons sees seven stages in the development of the U.S. industrial system, each corresponding to a level of development of the market (see table, p. 141). At each stage the expanding market forces a specialization of functions; the producer who was formerly the financier, wholesaler, retailer, manufacturer, and worker all combined in one person now finds more and more of these functions assumed by others. Competitive pressure from the expanded product market squeezes the manufacturer or "boss," forcing him to cut labor costs. Workers respond to the undermining of working conditions and wages by forming unions to protect themselves. Each stage further differentiates the functions involved in producing and marketing shoes, with everybody competing and bargaining with everybody else to obtain the best position possible.

The labor movement thus takes different forms and assumes different alliances as industrialism proceeds apace. These forms and alliances are dictated by the changing market structure. Always the enemy is the market and its competitive menace, not the employer. Labor struggles center, therefore, not on class struggles against the capitalist, but on protecting skills, maintaining wages, and preventing unskilled "green hands" from encroaching on one's work jurisdiction. To the extent there are class differences and antagonisms, Commons asserts, they are between labor and the market, or between producer and consumer, not between capitalist and worker. Marx's theories don't fit the historical facts: unionists are nothing more than another sector of producers organizing for the best price when faced with an encroaching market. This is no different from the American wholesalers or manufacturers or retail merchants attempting to protect themselves from ruination by the market.

In the following selection historian Alan Dawley strongly criticizes Commons's theory. According to Dawley, Commons is historically inaccurate in his contention that the early labor movement was a rearguard action directed against an encroaching market and inexperienced "green hands" fellow workers. Furthermore, Commons's procedure is methodologically flawed: circular reasoning forms the basis of the theory. Finally, Dawley argues, Commons fails completely to account for structural power differences between owners of property and propertyless workers. Such a theory is suspect on all accounts and can not be relied upon.

Without a doubt, the most influential (and controversial) theory of the labor movement was put forth by Commons's pupil Selig Perlman. Perlman developed the initial theoretical underpinnings of Commons's work into a fairly comprehensive theory, adding several distinctive features of his own. Perlman's theory was an explication of (and justification for) the practice of the AFL under Samuel Gompers. Eschewing all but the most minimal political involvements, Gompers's AFL organized almost exclusively on a *craft* basis according to skill. Exclusive craft union jurisdiction was a paramount principle of the early AFL; collective bargaining agreements for each craft became the main goal. Schemes for reconstructing society, labor parties and third parties, alliances with farmers or others in the political arena, government intervention into labor relations, or strong reliance on classwide labor solidarity were all rejected by Gompers and other top AFL leaders. Instead the labor movement was to be run along conservative, pragmatic lines that stayed with bread-and-butter issues solely. This form of unionism (which was the unique contribution of the U.S. to the worldwide labor movement) became known as "pure and simple" trade unionism, or "business unionism."

Perlman is the theorist *par excellance* of business unionism. His theory concludes that business unionism is the natural path for the labor movement if certain other factors do not get in the way. In brief, Perlman explains the state of the labor movement according to three factors: (1) the resistance power of capitalism (or the capitalists' "will to power"), (2) the role and influence of the intellectual, and (3) the maturity of the home-grown trade union movement. If capitalism's power of resistance is great, the trade union movement mature, and the influence of intellectuals in the labor movement minimal, then a stable and enduring business unionism will follow, as it has in the U.S. On the other hand, if the intellectuals gain influence over an immature labor movement, then a revolution—such as the 1917 revolution in Russia—could occur if the resistance power of the capitalists is low. Perlman also analyzes Germany and England using the same explanatory scheme.

Perlman argues that a mature labor movement will naturally turn to business unionism if left to itself because there is a natural psychology of "scarcity consciousness" on the part of all "manualists" (workers, peasants, etc.). In contrast with the "abundance consciousness" of capitalists displaying an entrepreneurial bent, workers know that they are incapable of managing economic enterprises, according to Perlman. Therefore they naturally display an interest only in the more restricted questions of job security, wages and hours, etc. Only if they are at an immature stage of organization and are misled by intellectuals will they demonstrate a more "social activist" or politically minded form of unionism, Perlman feels.

Charles Gulick and Melvin K. Bers argue that Perlman's threefold explanatory scheme lacks even the rudimentary prerequisites of a theory. Instead, they maintain, it reduces theory to definitions and descriptions that beg the very questions he purports to answer. Gulick and Bers also argue that Perlman's claim of "scarcity consciousness" among workers is poorly grounded. He relies on weak or irrelevant evidence, uses faulty logic to make his conclusion, and so idealizes workers and businessmen into psychological stereotypes that he badly distorts reality. Thus we have an ideological bias masquerading as an objective theory.

# 19
## *American Labour History*

**JOHN R. COMMONS** 1918

Labour movements in America have arisen from peculiar American conditions, and it is by understanding these conditions that we shall be able to distinguish the movements and methods of organisation from those of other countries. Out of these conditions have sprung certain philosophies, or certain modifications of imported philosophies, and it is the union of these conditions and philosophies that explains the movements. . . .

The condition which seems to distinguish most clearly the history of labour in America from its history in other countries is the wide expanse of free land. As long as the poor and industrious can escape from the conditions which render them subject to other classes, so long do they refrain from that aggression on the property rights or political power of others, which is the symptom of a "labour movement."

But even here we are likely to ascribe to the bounty of nature what proceeds from the struggle of classes. Like the *laissez-faire* philosophers, we trace back to a benevolent physical nature what springs directly from our social nature, and shows itself in organisation and political effort. Nature, in the physical sense, has been as bountiful to the poor and industrious of Australia, in proportion to their numbers, as it has been in America. But how different the outcome! In Australia the land has been locked up in great holdings, and labourers have been forced to fight the battles of organisation in the cities and on the ranches, rather than escape as individuals to lands that are free. Thus trade-unionism, socialistic politics, governmental coercion of employers, a parliament dominated by a labour party, characterise the labour movement of Australasia.

America, under the constitution of 1787, started off with a similar seizure of its western lands by speculators and slave owners. The masses of the people gradually awakened, then resisted, finally revolted, and a political struggle of half a century over the land laws ended in a Civil War, with its homestead law. The struggle was renewed when the railroad land grants of the Civil War brought back again in a new form the seizure by speculators, and again was renewed under the name of "conservation of natural resources." Free land was not a mere bounty of nature; it was won in the battle of labour against monopoly and slavery. . . . In the realm of philosophies, it was individualism rather than socialism, individual labour rather than trade unionism, political organisation rather than economic organisation, the laws of Congress rather than the "laws of nature"—a labour movement based on the ideas of a "middle class" or the "producing classes" rather than the "wage-class." In this sense, the free-land struggle, from George Henry Evans in the decade of the thirties of the nineteenth century to Henry George in the eighties, was as characteristic, for the time being, of American labour movements, as trade unionism in England, socialism in Germany, anarchism in Spain, nihilism in Russia, or labourism in Australia.

Even more fundamental than free land is that political institution which alone could make land a political issue. At least two or three generations before labour in other countries, whether peasant or wage-earner, had won the first great point of vantage for which it fought, labour in America had received with scarcely a struggle the boon of universal manhood suffrage. Almost unnoticed, the decade of the twenties, with straggling exceptions, completed the endowment of the mechanic and labourer in the North with his equal share in sovereignty, regardless of property, religion or origin. When, therefore, in the thirties, the first glimmerings of his condition as an unprivileged class awakened him from sleep, the "working man" entered promptly into that political struggle, which has ever been his hope and his undoing. The tragedy, the credulity, the fiasco, the lessons learned, forgotten, learned again, the defection of leaders, the desperate reaction to violence or anarchism, the disintegration of unions—these are the moving picture of eight decades of that universal suffrage, for which the labourer would give his life, but by which he has often followed a mirage. The repeating cycle of politics and trade unionism, political struggle and economic struggle, political organisation and economic organisation, marks out the course of this history of labour.

The vast area of the United States, coupled with free trade within that area and a spreading network of transportation, has developed an unparalleled extension of the competitive area of markets, and thereby has strikingly distinguished American movements from those of other countries. It is almost as though the countries of Europe, from Ireland to Turkey, from Norway to Italy, had been joined in a single empire like China, but, unlike China, had passed through a century of industrial revolution. Here, indeed, we have had at first thirteen, and now forty-eight sovereign states within a single empire —their laws as widely different as those of petty democracies in New England and slave aristocracies in the South, their industries as divergent as the manufacturers of Old England, the gold mines of Australia, the agriculture of the semi-tropics. It is the historical extension of markets over this broad expanse, from colonial times to the present, that has changed the character of competition, intensified its pressure, separated manufactures from agriculture, introduced the middleman, produced new alignments of social classes, and obliterated the futile lines that distinguish the jurisdiction of States. Without realising this extension of competitive areas, it is impossible to perceive either the characteristic features of American movements or the peculiar philosophies that distinguish them from the contemporaneous movements in Europe. Even the wonderful progress in the control of natural resources, summed up by economists as the "production of wealth," appears as but an after effect proceeding from this extension of markets which determines more directly the "distribution of wealth." For, it is not so much the mechanical inventions and the growth of industrial technique, which more properly belongs to the physical and engineering sciences, that have given character to American industrial movements, as it is the development and concentration of bargaining power over immense areas, whether in the hands of the merchant, the banker, the employer or the employé. The struggles with which we have to do are struggles to strengthen this bargaining power of one element against another, showing their results in the movement of prices, values and rates, whether for commodities, land, stocks, bonds, interest or wages. It is the emergence of these various struggles involved in the emergence of bargaining classes that we see when we follow the extension of markets. Beginning with the earliest colonial period, when the artisan was an itinerant, travelling laboriously to the farm or plantation of his employer who was also the consumer of his product, we next come to the custom-order stage and retail-shop stage, when the consumer travelled to the town, and it was the merchant or pedlar, not the artisan, who travelled to the consumer. In these stages, covering practically the entire colonial period, the interests of the small merchant, employer, and journeyman were identical, and, so far as they formed organisations to protect or strengthen their bargaining power, these organisations included, often in the same individual, all of the economic functions of wage-earning, price-fixing, and profit-making. Such was the typical organisation of the guild, whose occasional appearance is noted in our colonial period, and of the charitable and benevolent societies of the early decades of the nineteenth century.

It was not until after the constitution of 1787, and its levelling down of the market barriers which each colony had erected against the others, that a new stage began to appear with its wholesale markets, its credit system, and its separation of the merchant-capitalist, or capitalist-wholesaler, from the manufacturer on the one hand and the retailer on the other. In this stage the "manufacturer" was merely an incipient employer without capital—the "boss," the contractor,—the successor of the master workman—whose function was mainly that of driving the wage-bargain. The distinction between the employer and the wage-earner at the time was not so much the amount of his income or his possession of capital, as the contingent and speculative character of his income. His profit was the margin between the prices he paid for labour and the prices he received from the wholesale-merchant, or merchant-capitalist, for his product. The wage-earner, on the other hand, received a stipulated income for his physical exertion. The prices received by the contractor or employer were at the mercy of the merchant-capitalist and his main source of profit was his ability to reduce the prices which he paid to labour. This "sweated" condition, produced by the widening of the labour market and seen for the first time in a few trades at the beginning of the century, but seen most clearly in the decade of the thirties, drove the wage-earner as such to his first conscious union with competing labourers in defence against the master-workman who had now become the "boss." This was the signal for the breakup of the guild-like industrial stage which united master, journeyman and apprentice, and the substitution of the trade union of journeymen and the employers' union of masters, each contending for control of the apprentice. Different trades experience this break-up at different periods, and belated trades repeat the industrial history of older ones. Even to-day, we often find, in so-called trade-unions supplying a narrow local market with small investment in tools, like teamsters and musicians, what is really a guild of masters, owners and wage-earners.

Accompanying this separation of merchant, employer, and wage-earner, and called forth in order to aid the merchant in his extension of credits, a banking system arose, with a new bargainer in the social stratification, the financier. Later, in the sixties, with the railroad and its thousand-mile separation of producer from consumer, this middleman and this financier arose to such a position of power in industry and politics, that the movements of farmers, wage-earners and even small manufacturers focussed their attack on the symptoms or sources of this power. The peculiar philosophy of "greenbackism" emerged, as the American form of Europe's socialism and anarchism.

Not until this tri-century extension of markets had practically reached its limit in the decade of the eighties, and the nation had become a single market menaced at every point of its vast expanse by every competitor, no matter where situated, did the strictly modern movement, similar to that of older nations, take form and animus. And now it has rapidly gone even beyond the movements of other nations, for, on the one side, the huge corporation, on the other side, the trade union, have each reached a stage of centralisation under a single head that brooks no competitor—far beyond the loose and tolerant syndicates of capital or unions of labour in foreign lands. . . .

While economic forces have widened competitive areas to the limits of the nation, a system of government by States has covered these areas by widely divergent laws and administration. At the same time, the courts, blocking the way of a new aggressive class with precedents created to protect a dominant class, have had, in this country, a high authority unknown in other lands. By vetoing the laws which labour in its political struggles has been able to secure, the courts, joined to divergent state policies, have excluded or delayed labour from legislative influence. Consequently the energies of organisation are turned to the economic field, and often, in the latter decades, a trade union, by the force of its bargaining power, has exacted over a competitive area wider than any State more drastic regulations than those previously vetoed by the courts or even adopted by the most responsive legislatures. In this way has our Federal and judicial system of government added its pressure on labour and forced it to acquire by trade union action what in other countries has been granted by legislation. Furthermore, at the culmination of each aggressive labour movement, the courts have become a refuge for employers fleeing from the attacks of unions, until finally, by the weapon of the injunction newly applied in the eighties, they have even taken to themselves legislative and executive functions which the more popular branches of government had hesitated to exercise. In this way, the Federal Constitution with its self-government of the States and its threefold separation of the branches of government has been as powerful as economic conditions in giving to American labour movements their peculiar character.

More profound than any other condition distinctive of American movements have been the influx of immigrants and the unequalled variety of races, nationalities, and languages thrown together into a single competitive area. The problem of assimilation and Americanisation is thrust directly upon labour as a class, for immigrants and races come first as wage-earners, and it is only by the assimilating power of labour organisations that they can be brought together in a movement that depends for success on their willingness to stop competition and espouse co-operation. Property values, business profits, and professional incomes are elevated by the very competition of immigrants which depresses the wage-earning classes, and, while the beneficiaries may look with complacency on the incoming multitudes, the labourers themselves are reduced either to the invidious necessity of resisting their coming, or to the patriotic burden of assimilating them after they come. . . . The emancipation of the Negro meanwhile added, in effect, another race to the list of immigrants. It is in meeting this problem of races and immigration that American labour movements have displayed their most violent exclusiveness and their most humane fraternity. At the one extreme are the exclusion of the Chinese by law and the exclusion of immigrants by the "closed shop," at the other is the affiliation in the same union of whites and blacks. Circumstances, conditions, necessity, determine these extremes and the intermediate policies. From the very beginning of organised labour at the close of the eighteenth century, to its situation at the beginning of the twentieth, we find these swelling problems of immigration, race conflict, and race assimilation giving character to American movements and distinguishing them from foreign.

While the area of market competition has extended more widely than in other countries, the level of prices and wages across this area has arisen and fallen more excessively. Cycles of prosperity and depression have characterised all lands during the expansion of industry and credit in the nineteenth century, but the American cycles have touched higher peaks and lower depths. To the speculative character of American credit have been added the vagaries of paper money. . . . The two peaks of paper money, in the thirties and sixties, indicate two periods of excited, aggressive organisation, forced up in advance of their time, if measured only by industrial evolution. In these and other periods of rising prices, when the cost of living was outleaping the rise of wages, when business was prosperous and labour in demand, then aggressive strikes, trade unionism, class struggle, suddenly spread over the industrial sections of the country. At the other extreme, in the periods of falling prices, with their depression of business and distress by unemployment, labour, in its helplessness and failure of defensive strikes, has turned to politics, panaceas, or schemes of universal reform, while class struggle has dissolved in humanitarianism. . . .

It is by viewing the broad perspective of these various forces outstanding in American conditions, that we are able to distinguish separate historical periods and to characterise the movements of each period. The colonial, or dormant, period extends properly to the decade of the twenties, for such occasional awakenings as we find prior to 1827 do not take the form of concerted action by workmen of different occupations, but are fitful contests in separate trades. But in the thirties the public was suddenly awakened, and a new term, *trades' union,* appeared, signifying a *union of the trades,* where formerly there had been only "societies" of journeymen, or guild-like "associations" of masters, journeymen, and apprentices. The face-mark of this period is distinctly that of awakened *citizenship*—the first appearance in the history of modern nations of wage-earners as a class exercising the privilege of suffrage. Here appears the first newspaper published in their interest, and a study of the period shows the first painful efforts of wage-earners to extricate themselves both from the existing political parties and from the guild-like organisations which their employers controlled. The legislative measures which they put forward were not so much the trade-union measures of the later decades of the century, as those individualistic measures which assert the *rights of persons* against the *rights of property.* Free education supported by taxes on property, mechanics' liens on property in order to secure the wage-earner as a creditor, prohibition of seizure for debt by the capitalist creditor of the body of the propertyless debtor, followed in the next decade by the actual exemption of wages and tools from execution for the wage-earners' debts—these were the new jurisprudence by which, for the first time in the modern world, manhood suffrage created personal rights superior to property rights. Slow-moving as were these legislative reforms and beneficial as they might be to later generations, the wage-earners of the thirties soon forgot them in their trades' union effort of 1835 and 1836 to force wages up with the cost of living.

The panic of 1837 brought to a sudden stop these aggressions, and, for the next dozen years we find the most astonishing junction of humanitarianism, bizarre reforms and utopias, protective tariffs and futile labour legislation, known to our history. Swallowed, as these were in the rising prices of the gold discoveries and in the anti-slavery agitation, which approached its crisis in the early fifties, this *humanitarian* period slipped away into a second trade union period of the middle of the decade of the fifties, scarcely noticed beneath the absorbing premonitions of civil war.

The *nationalisation* period, from the War to the end of the seventies, repeats on a bigger scale of prosperity and depression and a wider area of competition, the events of the thirties. During the sixties the railroads, paper money and mechanical invention join together to throw up agitated organisations, and then, during the succeeding depression following 1873, to throw back their constituents into disorganisation, secret unions, or criminal aggression.

This agitational period of the sixties and seventies pointed to what, during the halting prosperity of the eighties, may be truly designated as the *Great Upheaval.* For, never before had organisation reached out so widely or deeply. New areas of competition, new races and nationalities, new masses of the unskilled, new recruits from the skilled and semi-skilled, were lifted up temporarily into what appeared to be an organisation, but was more nearly a procession, so rapidly did the membership change. With three-fourths of a million members on the books of the Knights of Labour at the height of its power, a million or more passed into and soon out from its assemblies.

Finally is a more constructive period slowly developing before us. Strengthened by many who enlisted during the enthusiasm of the eighties, then withdrawing from the weaker elements of unskilled and semi-skilled, the skilled trades began to preface the way for this period by building up stable and nation-wide organisations, and by winning such recognition from employers' associations that they were able to establish more or less enduring systems of arbitration or trade agreement, and to retain their membership during a period of depression. At the same time, the recurring problem of the unskilled, the semi-skilled, and the immigrant is again threatening an upheaval. In the field of legislation the crude and unconstitutional laws of earlier movements are now being followed by laws more carefully studied and drafted, while greater attention is given to the methods of administration.

■  ■  ■

As long as the wage-earning class accepts the existing order and merely attempts to secure better wage bargains, its goal must eventually be some form of the "trade agreement," which recognises the equal bargaining rights of the organised employers. Its union is not "class conscious" in the revolutionary sense of socialism, but "wage-conscious" in the sense of separation from, but partnership with, the employing class.

■  ■  ■

By a kind of natural selection a more "pragmatic" or "opportunistic" philosophy, based on the illogical variety of actual conditions and immediate necessities, has taken form in the American Federation of Labor, the railway brotherhoods, and industrial unionism, which is neither anarchism nor socialism but a species of protectionism combining both, and is analogous to the "solidarisme" of recent movements in France, and the "labourism" of England and Australasia.

Political movements, too, have changed in character, and, with them, the significance of the word politics. They differ from trade unionism in that, under the system of majority elections, they usually require coalition with other classes, whereas a union can act independently as a minority, without the consent of others. The first attempt to form a "labour party" in the early thirties resulted rather in a party of the "producing classes" as against the "aristocracy" or capitalist classes. The "capitalists" of the time were the money lenders, bankers, holders of public securities, wholesale and shipping merchants, great landowners and speculators, but not the farmers nor even the employers. The latter, together with the journeymen, composed the "working men" and "mechanics." It was not until the trades' unions of the middle thirties and their rejection of politics that wage-earners as a class separated themselves definitely in the larger cities from their employers. The political movements that followed were again mainly coalitions with the farmers, and only as the various socialist parties began to arise after the sixties, did politics take on a strictly wage-earning form. Meanwhile, from time to time, a kind of trade union politics appeared, not revolutionary in the socialistic sense, but directed to the narrower and more anarchistic object of relieving unions from the pressure of legislatures and courts controlled by hostile employers. In this way political movements have reflected the evolution of classes and policies, ranging all the way from the individualistic politics of small capitalists or wage-earners seeking to become capitalists, to the opportunistic politics of trade unions and the revolutionary politics of socialism or anarchism.

# 20
## *American Shoemakers, 1648–1895*

JOHN R. COMMONS                                              1909

The boot and shoe makers, either as shoemakers or "cordwainers," have been the earliest and the most strenuous of American industrialists in their economic struggles. A highly skilled and intelligent class of tradesmen, widely scattered, easily menaced by commercial and industrial changes, they have resorted with determination at each new menace to the refuge of protective organizations. Of the seventeen trials for conspiracy prior to 1842 the shoemakers occasioned nine. Taking the struggles of this harassed trade, it is possible to trace industrial stages by American documents from the guild to the factory. Organizations whose records give us this picture of industrial evolution under American conditions are the "Company of Shoomakers," Boston, 1648; the "Society of the Master Cordwainers," Philadelphia, 1789; the "Federal Society of Journeymen Cordwainers," Philadelphia, 1794; the "United Beneficial Society of Journeymen Cordwainers," Philadelphia, 1835; the Knights of St. Crispin, 1868; the Boot and Shoe Workers' Union, 1895. Each of these organizations stands for a definite stage in industrial evolution, from the primitive itinerant cobbler to the modern factory; each represents an internal contention over the distribution of wealth provoked by external conditions of marketing or production; each was productive of written documents preserving to us the types of social organization that struggled for adaptation to the evolving economic series.

## I
### "The Company of Shoomakers," Boston, 1648

Probably the first American guild was that of the "shoomakers of Boston," and its charter of incorporation, granted by the Colony of the Massachusetts Bay, on October 18, 1648, is the only complete American charter of its kind, of which I have knowledge. The coopers were granted a similar charter on the same date. The act recited that on petition of the "shoomakers" and on account of the complaints of the "damage" which the country sustained "by occasion of bad ware made by some of that trade," they should meet and elect a master, two wardens, four or six associates, a "clarke," a sealer, a searcher, and a beadle, who should govern the trade. The "commission" was to continue in force for three years.

■   ■   ■

In the charter of the Boston guild, the main object of the shoemakers was the suppression of inferior workmen, who damaged the country by "occasion of bad ware." The officers were given authority to examine the shoemakers, and to secure from the courts of the colony an order suppressing any one whom they did not approve "to be a sufficient workman." They were also given authority to regulate the work of those who were approved, and thus to "change and reforme" the trade and "all the affayres thereunto belonging." And they were erected into a branch of government with power to annex "reasonable pennalties" and to "levie the same by distresse."

At the same time it is evident that the colonial authorities took pains to protect the inhabitants from abuse of these powers by placing their determination "in cases of difficultie" in the hands of the judges of the county, and by allowing appeals to the county

*Quarterly Journal of Economics* 24 (November 1909), pp. 39–50, 58–64, 72–81. Footnotes in the original have been eliminated.

## Industrial Stages, Classes and Organizations of American Shoemakers

| | 1 Extent of Market | 2 Kind of Bargain | 3 Capital Ownership — Customer, Merchant, Employer, Laborer | 4 Industrial Classes | 5 Kind of Work | 6 Competitive Menace | 7 Protective Organizations | 8 Case |
|---|---|---|---|---|---|---|---|---|
| 1 | Itinerant | Wages | Customer-Employer: Material, Household, Board and Lodging — Journeyman: Hand tools | Farm family, Skilled helper | Skilled supervision | Family workers | None | Itinerant individuals 1648 |
| 2 | Personal | Custom order | Merchant-Master-Journeyman: Material, Hand tools, Home shop | Merchant-Master-Journeyman | "Bespoke" | "Bad Ware" | Craft guild | Boston "Company of Shoemakers" 1648 |
| 3 | Local | Retail | Merchant-Master: Material, Finished stock, Short credits, Sales shop — Journeyman: Hand tools, Home shop | Merchant-Master-Journeyman | "Shop" | "Market" Work, "Advertisers" Auctions | Retail Merchants Association | Philadelphia "Society of the Master Cordwainers" 1789 |
| 4 | Waterways | Wholesale order | Merchant-Master: Material, Finished stock, Long credits, Store-room — Journeyman: Hand tools, Home shop | Merchant-Master / Journeyman | "Order" | "Scabs", Interstate producers | Journeymen's Society, Masters' Society | Philadelphia "Federal Society of Journeymen Cordwainers" 1794–1806 |
| 5 | Highways | Wholesale speculative | Merchant-Capitalist: Material, Finished stock, Bank credits, Warehouse, "Manufactory" — Contractor: Work Shop — Journeyman: Hand tools | Merchant-Capitalist / Contractor / Journeyman | Team work | Prison sweatshop, "Foreigner", "Speeding up" | Journeymen's Society, Manufacturers' Association•, Employers' Association | Philadelphia "United Beneficial Society of Journeymen Cordwainers" 1835 |
| 6 | Rail | Wholesale speculative | Merchant-Jobber: Material, Finished stock, Bank credits, Warehouse, "Manufactory" — Contract Manufacturer: Work shop — Journeyman: Footpower machines | Merchant-Jobber / "Manufacturer" / Journeyman | Team work | Green hands, Chinese, Women, Children, Prisoners, Foreigners | Trade Union, Employers' Association, Manufacturers' Association• | "Knights of St. Crispin" 1863–1872 |
| 7 | World | Factory order | Manufacturer: Material, Stock, Credits, Power machinery, Factory — Laborer: None | Manufacturer / Wage-earners | Piece work | Child labor, Long hours, Immigrants, Foreign products | Industrial Union, Employers' Association, Manufacturers' Association• | "Boot and Shoe Workers' Union." 1893 |

•The "Manufacturers' Association" is the association based on the merchant or price-fixing function.

court. The two substantial reservations which the colony withholds from the company are the "inhancinge the prices of shooes, bootes, or wages," and the refusal to make shoes for inhabitants "of their owne leather for the use of themselves and families," if required by the latter.

From these reservations we are able to infer the industrial stage which the industry had reached at the time of incorporation. It was the transition from the stage of the itinerant shoemaker, working up the raw material belonging to his customer in the home of the latter, to the stage of the settled shoemaker, working up his own raw material in his own shop to the order of his customer. The reservation for the protection of inhabitants is suggestive of statutes of the fifteenth and sixteenth centuries imposing penalties on guild members who refused to work in the house of their customer. The fact that the colony, while granting power to reform the trade, nevertheless thought it necessary to require the shoemaker to continue to work up the leather owned by his customer, although conceding that he need not go to the house of the customer, indicates the source of the abuses from which the shoemakers were endeavoring to rid themselves. The itinerant was likely to be poorly trained, and he could escape supervision by his fellow craftsmen. He was dependent on his customer who owned not only the raw material, but also the work-place, the lodging, and the food supplies of the shoemaker, leaving to the latter only the mere hand tools. He worked under the disadvantage of a new work-place for each new order, without the conveniences and equipment necessary for speedy and efficient work. He had to seek the customer, and consequently was at a disadvantage in driving a bargain. This made him, however, a serious menace to the better trained shoemaker, working in his own shop and on his own material, but waiting for the customer to come.

The Boston guild represented the union in one person of the later separated classes of merchant, master, and journeyman. Each of these classes has a different function. The merchant function controls the kind and quality of the work, and its remuneration comes from ability to drive the bargain with the customer in the process of adjusting price to quality. The master-function, on the other hand, controls the work-place and the tools and equipment, and passes along to the journeyman the orders received from the merchant. Its remuneration comes from management of capital and labor. The journeyman-function, finally, is remunerated according to skill and quality of work, speed of output and the amount and regularity of employment.

Thus, from the standpoint of each of the functions that later were separated, did this primitive guild in self-interest set itself against the "bad ware" of the preceding itinerant stage. From the merchant standpoint the exclusion of bad ware removed a menace to remunerative prices for good ware. From the master standpoint the exclusion of the itinerant transferred the ownership of the workshop and the medium of wage payments from the consumer to the producer. From the journeyman standpoint, this exclusion of the itinerant eliminated the truck-payment of wages in the form of board and lodging by substituting piece wages for a finished product. And this control of the finished product through all the stages of production gave a double advantage to the craftsman. It transferred to him the unskilled parts of the work hitherto done by the customer's family, thus enabling him at one and the same stroke both to increase the amount of his work and to utilize the bargaining leverage of his skill to get skilled wages for unskilled work.

By this analysis we can see that when the three functions of merchant, master and journeyman were united in the same person, the merchant-function epitomized the other two. It is the function by which the costs of production are shifted over to the consumer.

The master looks to the merchant for his profits on raw material, workshop, tools and wages, and the journeyman looks to him for the fund that will pay his wages.

Now, there is a prime consideration in the craft-guild stage that enhances the power of the merchant to shift his costs to the consumer. This is the fact that his market is a personal one, and the consumer gives his order before the goods are made. On the other hand, the bargaining power of the merchant is menaced by the incapacity of customers accurately to judge of the quality of goods, as against their capacity clearly to distinguish prices. Therefore, it is enough for the purposes of a protective organization in the custom-order stage of the industry, to direct attention solely to the quality of the product rather than the price or the wage, and to seek only to exclude bad ware and the makers of bad ware. Thus the Boston shoemakers and coopers, though enlisting the colonial courts only in the laudable purpose of redressing "the damage which the country sustaynes by occasion of bad ware," succeeded thereby in "inriching themselves by their trades very much." In this they differed from later organizations, based on the separation of classes, to whom competition appeared as a menace primarily to prices and wages, and only secondarily to quality.

## II
## The Society of Master Cordwainers, 1789, and the Federal Society of Journeymen Cordwainers, 1794, Philadelphia

The separation of classes first appears in the case of the cordwainers of Philadelphia, a century and a half later. Here appeared the first persistent discord that broke the primitive American harmony of capital and labor. So intense were the passions aroused, and so widespread was the popular irritation, that they have left their permanent record in one hundred and fifty-nine pages of "The Trial of the Boot and Shoemakers of Philadelphia, on an indictment for a combination and conspiracy to raise their wages." Here we have a fairly full record of the first American association of employers and the first trade union. They were the "Society of the Master Cordwainers of the City of Philadelphia," 1789, and the "Federal Society of Journeymen Cordwainers" of the same city, organized in 1794.

■    ■    ■

The indictment charged the journeymen with conspiring not to work except at prices and rates in excess of those "which were then used and accustomed to be paid and allowed to them"; with endeavoring "by threats, menaces and other unlawful means" to prevent others from working at less than these excessive prices; and with adopting "unlawful and arbitrary by-laws, rules and orders" and agreeing not to work for any master who should employ any workman violating such rules, and agreeing "by threats and menaces and other injuries" to prevent any workman from working for such a master.

The conspiracy and strike occurred in November, 1805, and the matter came to trial in the Mayor's court in March, 1806. The court permitted the witnesses to recite the entire history of this and the preceding strikes, as well as the history of the preceding combinations both of journeymen and employers. Consequently we are able to trace from the year 1789 to the year 1806 the development of the boot and shoe industry in Philadelphia, along with the accompanying separation of the interests of the journeymen from those of the masters.

I do not find any record of a guild organization like that in Boston, but there had been a "charitable society" to which both employers and journeymen belonged, and this was still in existence in 1805. It was the masters who first formed themselves, in April,

1789, into a separate organization. Their early constitution was laid before the court, showing the purpose of their organization to be that of "taking into consideration the many inconveniences which they labour under, for want of proper regulations among them, and to provide remedies for the same." They were to "consult together for the general good of the trade, and determine upon the most eligible means to prevent irregularities in the same." . . .

Apparently the masters had at that time just two kinds of "inconveniences": the competition of cheap grades of goods offered for sale at the "public market," and the competition of masters who offered bargain prices by public advertisement. This is shown by their qualifications for membership. "No person shall be elected a member of this society who offers for sale any boots, shoes, etc., in the public market of this city, or advertises the prices of his work, in any of the public papers or hand-bills, so long as he continues in these practices."

Evidently this society of masters was not organized as an employers' association, for nothing is said of wages or labor. It was organized by the masters merely in their function of retail merchant. The attorneys for the journeymen tried to make out that when the latter organized separately in 1794 they did so in self-defence, as against the masters' association, and they contended that in the masters' constitution were to be found "ample powers" not only to regulate prices, but also "to form a league to reduce the wages of their journeymen." And, although they admitted that the association had terminated in 1790, yet they held "it was a Phoenix that rose from its ashes." But it was brought out clearly in evidence that the subsequent resurrections in 1799 and 1805 were provoked by the journeymen's aggressive society and were but temporary organizations. The Phoenix that kept on repeatedly rising was not the one that had disappeared. In 1789 it had been an organization of masters in their function of retail merchant. In its later stages it was an organization of masters in their function of employer. The distinction, fundmental in economics, caused a re-alignment in *personnel,* as will be shown presently. The early organization regulated prices and followed the vertical cleavage between producer and consumer. The later organization regulated wages and followed the horizontal cleavage between employer and laborer. In the early organization the journeyman's interest was the same as the master's. In the later ones the journeyman's interest was hostile to both consumer and master.

The foregoing considerations, as well as the transition to later stages, will become more apparent if we stop for a moment to examine the economic conditions that determine the forms of organization. These conditions are found, not so much in the technical "instruments of production," as in the development of new markets. The economic development of the market proceeded as follows: The cordwainer of the Boston guild made all his boots and shoes to the order of his customer, at his home shop. His market was a custom-order market, composed of his neighbors. His product, in the terminology of 1806, was a "bespoke" product. He was in his own person master, custom-merchant, and journeyman.

Next, some of the master cordwainers begin to stock up with standard sizes and shapes, for sale to sojourners and visitors at their shops. They cater to a wider market, requiring an investment of capital, not only in raw material, but also in finished products and personal credits. They give out the material to journeymen to be made up at their homes and brought back to the shop. In addition to "bespoke work," the journeyman now makes "shop work" and the master becomes retail merchant and employer. This was the stage of the industry in Philadelphia in 1789—the retail-shop stage.

Next, some of the masters seek an outside or foreign market. They carry their samples to distant merchants and take "orders" for goods to be afterwards made and delivered. They now become wholesale merchant-employers, carrying a larger amount of capital invested in material, products and longer credits, and hiring a larger number of journeymen. In addition to "bespoke" and "shop" work the journeyman now makes "order work" for the same employer. This is the wholesale-order stage of the industry.

This was the stage in Philadelphia in 1806. At that time we find the journeyman engaged on one kind and quality of work, with the same tools and workshops, but with four different destinations for his product. Each destination was a different market, with a different level of competition, leading ultimately, after a struggle, to differences in quality. The terms employed at the time recapitulate the evolution of the industry. "Bespoke work," recalls the primitive custom market of the Boston guild, now differentiated as the market offered by the well-to-do for the highest quality of work at the highest level of competition. "Shop work" indicates the retail market of less particular customers at a wider but lower level of competition and quality. "Order work" indicates a wholesale market made possible by improved means of transportation, but on a lower level of strenuous competition and indifferent quality projected from other centres of manufacture. "Market work"— *i.e.* cheap work sold in the public market—indicates the poorest class of customers, and consequently the lowest level of competition, undermining especially the shop-work level, and, to a lesser degree, the order-work level, but scarcely touching the "bespoke" level.

It was the widening out of these markets with their lower levels of competition and quality, but without any changes in the instruments of production, that destroyed the primitive identity of master and journeyman cordwainers and split their community of interest into the modern alignment of employers' association and trade union. The struggle occurred, not as a result of changes in tools or methods of production, but directly as a result of changes in markets. It was a struggle on the part of the merchant-employer to require the same *minimum quality* of work for each of the markets, but lower rates of wages on work destined for the wider and lower markets. It was a struggle on the part of the journeyman to require the same *minimum wage* on work destined for each market, but with the option of a higher wage for a higher market. The conflict came over the wage and quality of work destined for the widest, lowest and newest market. . . .

In the Boston guild it does not appear that there were any journeymen. Each "master" was at first a traveller, going to the homes of his customers and doing the skilled part of the journeyman's work. Next he was the all-round journeyman, not only "his own master" but, more important, his own merchant. The harmony of capital and labor was the identity of the human person. The market was direct, the orders were "bespoke."

Even in Philadelphia, in 1789, when the masters had added "shop work" and had separated themselves out as an association of retail merchants, the interests of the journeymen coincided with theirs. The journeymen were even more distressed by "market work" than were the masters. At the "market" there was no provision for holding back goods for a stated price. Everything had to be sold at once and for cash. Goods were not carried in stock. Consequently, the prices paid were exceedingly low. . . .

The two other kinds of work that prevailed in 1789 were "shop" work and "bespoke" work. The prices paid to the journeymen for these two kinds of work were originally the same. If they differed in quality, the difference was paid for at a specific price for extra work. . . . But the payment for extras was the same for shop work as it was for "bespoke" work. The same workman made both, and made them in the same way, with the same tools. One of the grievances of the journeymen was the innovation attempted in 1789 by one of the employers to reduce the price of shop work. . . . The society demanded similar pay for similar work, whether shop or bespoke. . . .

Thus the journeymen were at one with the masters in their opposition to "market work." For the journeyman it was a menace to his wages on shop work. For the master it was a menace to his business as a retail storekeeper.

It was the third, or "export" stage of the market, with its wholesale "order" work, that separated the interests of the journeyman from those of the master. Here the retail merchant adds wholesale orders to his business. . . .

■ ■ ■

On the other hand, employers who were not branching out for export work were willing to pay the wages demanded and unwilling to join the employers' association. . . .

Likewise, the journeymen who did only bespoke and shop work, were not inclined to stand by the union for the increase in prices. . . .

■ ■ ■

Notice now the characteristic features of the retail and wholesale-order stages of the industry. The master workman at the retail stage has added a stock of finished goods to his business of custom work. This requires a shop on a business street accessible to the general public, with correspondingly high rents. It involves also a certain amount of capital tied up in short credits and accounts with customers. In his shop he has a stock of raw material, besides finished and partly finished goods. The merchant-function has thus become paramount, and has drawn with it the master-function. The two functions have equipped themselves with capital—merchant's capital in the form of finished stock, retail store, and short credits; employer's capital in the form of raw material undergoing manufacture by workmen under instructions. The journeymen are left with only their hand tools and their home workshop.

Thus the retail market has separated the laborer from the merchant. Labor's outlook now is solely for wages. The merchant's outlook is for quality and prices. But the separation is not antagonism. The employer-function is as yet at a minimum. Profit is not dependent on reducing wages so much as increasing prices. Indeed, the journeymen are able almost to double their wages without a strike, and the merchants pass the increase along to the customers.

But it is different when the merchant reaches out for wholesale orders. Now he adds heavy expenses for solicitation and transportation. He adds a storeroom and a larger stock of goods. He holds the stock a longer time and he gives long and perilous credits. At the same time he meets competitors from other centres of manufacture, and cannot pass along his increased expenses. Consequently the wage-bargain assumes importance, and the employer-function comes to the front. Wages are reduced by the merchant as employer on work destined for the wholesale market. The conflict of capital and labor begins.

■ ■ ■

### III
### The United Beneficial Society of Journeymen Cordwainers, Philadelphia, 1835

The organizations of masters and journeymen of 1805 continued more or less until

1835. Then a new and more revolutionary stage of the industry is ushered in. This time it is the merchant-capitalist, who subdues both the master and the journeyman through his control of the new widespread market of the South and West. . . .

■   ■   ■

At this stage of the industry we have reached the market afforded by highway and canal, as well as ocean and river. The banking system has expanded, enabling the capitalist to convert customers' credits into bank credits and to stock up a surplus of goods in advance of actual orders. The market becomes speculative, and the warehouse of the wholesale-merchant-master takes the place of the store-room of the retail capitalist. The former master becomes the small manufacturer or contractor, selling his product to the wholesale-manufacturer, the merchant-capitalist. The latter has a wide range of option in his purchase of goods, and consequently in his ability to compel masters and journeymen to compete severely against each other. He can have his shoes made in distant localities. . . .

The merchant-capitalist can also discover new fields for the manufacture of cheap work, and for the first time we read of the competition of convict labor. . . .

The merchant-capitalist has also the option of all the different methods of manufacture and shop organization. He can employ journeymen at his warehouse as cutters, fitters and pattern makers; he can employ journeymen at their homes to take out material and bring back finished work; but, more characteristic of his methods, he can employ small contractors, the specialized successors of the master cordwainer, who in turn employ one to a dozen journeymen, and by division of labor and "team work" introduce the sweating system.

Through these different methods of manufacture we are able to see how it is that the merchant-capitalist intensifies and even creates the antagonism of "capital and labor." He does this by forcing the separation of functions and classes a step further than it had been forced in the wholesale-order stage. First, he takes away from the retail merchant his wholesale-order business. He buys and sells in large quantities; he assembles the cheap products of prison labor, distant localities, and sweat-shops; he informs himself of markets, and beats down the charges for transportation. Thus he takes to himself the wholesale business and leaves to the merchant the retail trade.

Second, he drives off from the retail merchant his employer-function. The retail merchant can no longer afford to employ journeymen on "shop" work, because he can purchase more cheaply of the merchant-capitalist. . . .

Thus the merchant-capitalist strips the former merchant-master both of his market and his journeymen. The wholesale market he takes to himself; the journeymen he hands over to a specialist in wage-bargaining. This specialist is no longer known as "master," —he takes the name of "boss," or employer. He is partly a workman, having come up through the trade, like the master, and continuing to work alongside his men. He is an employer without capital, for he rents his workshop, and the merchant-capitalist owns the raw material and the journeymen own the tools. His profits are not those of the capitalist, neither do they proceed from his ability as a merchant, since the contract-prices he gets are dictated by the merchant-capitalist. His profits come solely out of wages and work. He organizes his workmen in teams, with the work subdivided in order to lessen dependence on skill and to increase speed of output. He plays the less skilled against the more skilled, the speedy against the slow, and reduces wages while enhancing exertion. His profits are "sweated" out of labor, his shop is the "sweatshop," he the "sweater."

Thus the merchant-capitalist, with his widespread, wholesale-speculative market, completes the separation and specializes the functions of the former homogeneous craftsman. The merchant-function, which was the first to split off from the others, is now itself separated into three parts,—custom merchant, retail merchant, wholesale merchant,—corresponding to the three levels of market competition. The journeyman-function is now segregated on two levels of competition, the highest level of custom work and the lowest level menaced by prison and sweatshop work. The employer-function, the last to split off, makes its first appearance as a separate factor on the lowest level of market competition. Evidently the wide extension of the market in the hands of the merchant-capitalist is a cataclysm in the position of the journeyman. By a desperate effort of organization he struggles to raise himself back to his original level. His merchant-employers at first sympathize with him, and endeavor to pass over to their customers his just demand for a higher wage. But they soon are crushed between the level of prices and the level of wages. From the position of a merchants' association striving to hold up prices, they shift to that of an employers' association endeavoring to keep down wages. The result of these struggles of protective organizations will appear when we analyze more closely the economic forces under which they operate. These forces turn on the nature of the bargain, the period and risk of investment and the level of the competitive menace.

### I. The Nature of the Bargain

We have to do with two classes of bargains, the wage-bargain and the price-bargain. Each is affected by the increasing distance of the ultimate purchaser, the actual consumer, from the worker, the manual producer. In the primitive "bespoke," or custom-order stage, the market is direct and immediate. The producer is the seller to the consumer. The work is priced by means of a separate bargain for each article. The price-bargain is made before the work is done. The customer pays according to the quality, and if he desires an improved quality, he stands the increased price; or, if the producers are able to exclude an inferior quality, he pays the price of the quality supplied. Hence an increase of wages is shifted directly to the purchaser. The wage-bargain and price-bargain are identical.

In the retail-shop stage, the producer is removed one step from the ultimate purchaser. The merchant intervenes as a price-bargainer. This bargain is made after the work is done. The purchasers are now separated into two classes, those who are particular about quality and adhere to the custom-order bargain, and those who are particular about price and pass on to the "shop" bargain. To the latter is transferred a certain advantage, and the merchant is less able to shift upon them an increase in wages. The wage-bargain is made for a stock of shoes rather than an individual purchaser, and the goods are to be sold with reference to price rather than quality.

In the wholesale-order stage the market is removed a second step. There are two price-bargains that intervene between the worker and the market, one between the wholesaler and retailer and one between retailer and consumer. The wholesale price-bargain is indeed made before the work is done, and to that extent the wages, if previously known, can be shifted. But the retailer, as shown above, is himself restricted in his ability to shift an increase upon the purchasers, and he is more concerned than they as to price because his profit turns thereon, while he is concerned with quality only indirectly as their representative and not directly as the actual user. Consequently, the wholesale merchant is less able than the retail merchant to shift his wages. Of course, if an increase in wages is demanded after the orders are taken, he is compelled at once to make a fight against the workers. It was the opportunity offered by the wholesale-order stage to take this unfair advantage of the employer that provoked the first bitter struggle of capital and labor in 1806.

The wholesale-speculative stage of 1835 intrudes yet another step on the road from producer to market. The employer is now separated out from both the merchant and the worker, and, besides the wage-bargain, we have three price-bargains,—the employer-capitalist, capitalist-retailer and retailer-consumer. The second bargain, that of capitalist-retailer, is made after the work is done, and it is this that constitutes its speculative character. It transfers the advantage of position to the retailer, just as shop work had transferred the advantage to the consumer. Consequently, the employer, or "contractor," the sweatshop "boss," is now introduced as a specialist in driving the wage-bargain, with reference to the increased obstacles in the way of shifting wages along to the ultimate purchaser.

Thus it is that the ever-widening market from the custom-order stage, through the retail-shop and wholesale-order to the wholesale-speculative stage, removes the journeyman more and more from his market, diverts attention to price rather than quality and shifts the advantage in the series of bargains from the journeymen to the consumers and their intermediaries.

### 2. *The Period and Risk of Investment*

Throughout the four stages here described there have been no changes in the tools of production. The factory system with its "fixed capital" has not yet appeared, and the only capital invested is "circulating capital" in the form of raw material, finished stock and bills receivable. Upon this circulating capital the owner incurs the threefold expense of interest, risk and necessary profit. The amount of capital, per unit of product, remains the same, but the period during which it is locked up is lengthened in proportion as the market area is extended. In the custom-order stage this period is at its minimum; in the retail-shop stage the period is lengthened; in the wholesale-order stage, on account of long credits, the period is at its maximum; in the wholesale-speculative stage the average period is perhaps reduced, but this is more than offset by the increase in the rate of risk. This increase of expense for "waiting" and risk, owing to the lengthening of the period of investment, must either be added to the price paid by the consumer or deducted from the wage paid to the producer. But since the position of purchasers in the price-bargains is improved with the progress of the stages, the increased expense on account of circulating capital must be met by deductions from the rates of wages. This might not have been necessary if fixed capital had been introduced, bringing with it a greater speed of output at the old amount of earnings. But, in lieu of this cheapening by improved tools of production, the only way of meeting the increased expense of waiting is by reducing the rate of pay on each unit of product. The wholesale market is a market for "future goods," the custom-order market is a market for "present goods." The premium on "future goods" appears, therefore, as a reduction below the wages paid at the same time on "present goods." Shop work, order work and speculative work must be manufactured at a lower wage-cost than bespoke work of the same kind and quality.

### 3. *The Level of the Competitive Menace*

Defining the "marginal producer" as the one with the lowest standards of living and cost and quality of work, he is the producer whose competition tends to drag down the level of others toward his own. It is not necessary that he be able actually to supply the entire market or even the greater part of it. His effect on others depends on the extent to which he can be used as a club to intimidate others against standing out for their side of the bargain. He is a menace rather than an actual competitor. Now, the extension of the market for the sale of goods is accompanied by an extension of the field for the production of goods. This extension brings into the competitive area new competitors who are essentially a series of lower marginal producers. The capitalist who can reach out for these low-level producers can use them at will to break down the spirit of resistance of the high-level producers. In the custom-order stage there was but one competitive menace, the shoemaker who made "bad ware." In the retail-shop stage there is added the "advertiser," the "public market" and the auction system. In the wholesale-order stage there is added the foreign producer and in the wholesale-speculative stage the labor of convicts and sweatshops. Thus, the extension of the field of production increases the variety and discovers lower levels of marginal producers, and the merchant-capitalist emerges as the generalissimo, menacing in turn every part of the field from his strategic centre.

### 4. Protective Organizations

. . . We now proceed to notice the resistance of protective organizations and their ultimate effect in bringing about a segregation of work and workers on non-competing levels.

This may be seen by following again the movement of wages in Philadelphia from 1789 to 1835, on the different classes of work. Prior to 1792, on common boots, the journeyman's wages were $1.40 a pair on both bespoke and shop work. In the course of fifteen years the price advanced to $2.75, and this price was paid for both bespoke and shop work, but a concession of 25 cents was made on wholesale-order work, bringing that price to $2.50. In 1835 the price had fallen to $1.12½ for wholesale work, while retail work had dropped out or had come down to the same price as wholesale work, leaving custom work at a higher figure. In the course of this movement, the better class of workmen restricted themselves as much as possible to custom work, and the quality of this kind of work was improved. On the other hand, the wholesale-order and wholesale-speculative work tended throughout to fall into the hands of inferior workmen, and this brought about an inferiority in quality. These inferior goods, made by inferior workmen, became more and more a menace to the superior goods and the superior journeymen, both on account of the lower levels of the marginal producers and on account of the smaller demand relatively for the production of superior goods.

Herein was the necessity of protective organizations. In order that these organizations might succeed, it was just as necessary to set up protection against inferior goods as against low wages. In the guild stage of the industry, when the three functions of journeyman, master and workman were united in one person, the protection sought was against the "bad ware" made by some of the trade. By "suppressing" those who made bad ware, the customers would be compelled to turn to those who were "sufficient" workmen and made good ware. Since the bargain was a separate one for each article, so that the price could be adjusted to the quality before the work was done, nothing more was needed on the part of the guild members for the purpose of "inriching themselves by their trades very much."

But in the later stages of the industry, the merchant-function, and afterwards the employer-function, were separated from the journeyman-function. It is the special function of the merchant to watch over and guard the quality of the work, because his bargain with the consumer is an adjustment of the price to the quality demanded. The journeyman's function is simply that of making the kind and quality of goods ordered by the merchant. The merchant, in his function as employer, gives these orders to the journeyman, and consequently, when the employer-function is separated from the journeyman-function, the employer, as the representative of the merchant, attends to the quality of the work. In this way the journeyman has lost control over quality, and is forced to adapt his quality to his price, instead of demanding a price suited to his quality. So, when he forms his protective organization, his attention is directed mainly to the compensation side of the bargain. In proportion as the quality of his work depends on his rate of pay, he indirectly controls the quality, but the primary purpose of his organization is to control the rate of pay. This he does, first, by demanding the same minimum rate of pay for all market destinations of the same kind of work. It was this demand that forced the alignment of classes, and drove the sympathetic merchant over into the hostile employers' association. The employer could yield if he confined himself to the narrow field of the "bespoke" market, but not if he was menaced by the wider field of the wholesale market. On this account it was possible in the retail-shop stage for the interests of employer and workmen to be harmonious. But the employer could not yield in the merchant-capitalist stage, on that part of the field menaced by prison and sweatshop labor. Consequently, the outcome of the strikes of 1835 was the differentiation of the market into two non-competing levels, the higher level of custom and high-grade shop work, controlled more or less by the cordwainers' societies for the next twenty-five years and the lower level of inferior work controlled by prison and sweatshop competition.

## IV

### Knights of St. Crispin, 1868

We come now to an entirely different step in the progress of industrial stages. Hitherto, the only change requiring notice has been that produced by the extension of the market and the accompanying credit system. These changes were solely external. The next change is internal. Prior to 1837 there had been scarcely a hundred inventions affecting the tools used by the cordwainer. All of these may be described as "devices" rather than machines. Even as late as 1851 all of the labor in the manufacture of shoes was hand labor. In 1852, the sewing machine was adapted to the making of uppers, but this did not affect the journeyman cordwainer, because the sewing of uppers had been the work of women. Even the flood of inventions that came into use during the decade of the 'fifties were aids to the journeyman rather than substitutes for his skill. Indeed, some of them probably operated to transfer the work of women to men, for they required greater physical strength and endurance in order to develop their full capacity. Whether operated by foot power or merely facilitating the work of his hands, they were essentially shop tools and not factory machines. . . . Quite different were the pegging machine, introduced in 1857, and especially the McKay sole-sewing machine, introduced in 1862. These usurped not only the highest skill of the workman, but also his superior physique. The McKay machine did in one hour what the journeyman did in eighty. These machines were quickly followed by others, either machines newly invented or old ones newly adapted, but all of them belted up to steam. The factory system, aided by the enormous demand of government for its armies, came suddenly forth, though it required another fifteen years to reach perfection. It was at the middle of this transition period, 1868 to 1872, that the Knights of St. Crispin appeared, and flourished beyond anything theretofore known in the history of American organized labor. Its membership mounted to 40,000 or 50,000, whereas the next largest unions of the time claimed only 10,000 to 12,000. It disappeared as suddenly as it had arisen, a tumultuous, helpless protest against the abuse of machinery. For it was not the machine itself that the Crispins were organized to resist, but the substitution of "green hands" for journeymen in the operation of the machines. There was but one law which they bound themselves by constitutions, rituals, oaths and secret confederacy to enforce and to support each other in enforcing: refusal to teach green hands except by consent of the organization. This at least was the object of the national organization. When local unions once were established, they took into their own hands the cure of other ills, and their strikes and lockouts were as various as the variety of shops and factories in which they were employed. The Knights of St. Crispin were face to face with survivals from all of the preceding stages of industrial evolution, as well as the lusty beginnings of the succeeding stage. They were employed in custom shops, in retail and wholesale-order shops, in the shops of the merchant-capitalist and his contractors, in the factories of the manufacturer-capitalist. A comparison of the objects of their strikes reveals the overlapping of stages. All of their strikes turned directly or indirectly on two issues, resistance to wage reductions and refusal to teach "green hands." The wage strikes took place mainly in the shops of the merchant-capitalist, the "green hand" strikes in the factories. The merchant-capitalist was forced by the competition of the manufacturer, either to become a manufacturer himself (or to purchase from the manufacturer), or to cut the wages of his journeymen and the prices paid to his contractors. Neither the journeyman's devices nor his foot power machines yielded a sufficient increase of output to offset his wage reductions. His aggravation was the more intense in that the wage reductions occurred only on shop work and not on custom work. The anomaly of different prices for the same grade of work, which had showed itself with the extension of markets, was now still more exaggerated and more often experienced under the competition of factory products. Even prison labor and Chinese labor were not cheap enough to enable the merchant-capitalist to compete with the product of green hands and steam power.

The factory succeeded also in producing a quality of work equal or even superior to that produced by the journeyman. Consequently its levelling agencies reached upwards to all but the topmost of the noncompeting levels on which the journeymen had succeeded in placing themselves, and brought them down eventually to its own factory level. The Grand Lodge of the Knights of St. Crispin was the protest of workmen whose skill of work, quality of product and protective unions had for a generation preceding saved for themselves the higher levels of the merchant-capitalist system against the underwash of prison and sweatshop competition. It was their protest against the new menace of cheap labor and green hands utilized by the owners of steam power and machinery.

■   ■   ■

## V

### Industrial Evolution in Europe and America. Organization and Legislation for Protection.

The foregoing sketch of industrial evolution in America brings into prominence the part played by the ever-widening area of competition, and the effort of protective organizations to ward off the peculiar competitive menace of each stage of development. From this standpoint the sketch may be compared with the investigations of Marx, Schmoller and Bücher. Karl Marx was the first to challenge the world with a keen analysis of economic evolution, but his standpoint is that of the mode of production and not the extension of the market. His two assumptions of a given "use value" and a given "average social labor" serve to obliterate, the one the part played by the price-bargain, the other the part played by the wage-bargain. With these assumptions out of the way he is able to concern himself with the production of "surplus value" by his theory of the working day and the cost of living. But these are secondary factors, results, not causes. The primary factors are on the side of the market where competition is carried on at different levels. Instead of "exploitation," growing out of the nature of production, our industrial evolution shows certain evils of competition imposed by an "unfair" menace. Instead, therefore, of an idealistic remedy sought for in common ownership, the practical remedy always actually sought out has been the elimination of the competitive menace through a protective organization or protective legislation.

Schmoller and Bücher have both avoided the narrow abstractions of Marx, because they have traced out the actual development of industry through access to a wealth of historical material not available to their predecessor. Schmoller, with his ever-widening area of village, town, territory and state under a single political control leading to extension of markets, and Bücher with his ever-widening area of the markets leading to political extension, have cultivated the field where the true explanation of industrial evolution shall be found. But there are certain considerations in European history which have obliterated or confused the pure economic facts. Industrial evolution, considered as a mere economic process, had to work its way up through superimposed racial, military, tribal, feudal, ecclesiastical and guild regulations and restrictions. These have been especially disturbing to Schmoller, but have been delightfully brushed aside by Bücher. At the same time, in both cases they have operated to cover up certain significant stages and factors. For example, the retail-shop and the wholesale-order stages of the American shoe industry are not as strikingly apparent in the European process, probably because the powerful guild regulations served to maintain a uniform price for custom work, retail work and wholesale-order work. But the guilds were unable to cope with the cut prices of wholesale-speculative work. Consequently, Schmoller and Bücher pass over with slight emphasis from the primitive guild stage of Boston, 1648, to the merchant-capitalist stage of 1835. But it is not enough to say that the retail-merchant and wholesale-order stages were only "transitional," for they bring to light the fundamental economic forces at work. They reveal the segregation of the merchant-function and the joint effort of both employer and journeyman to extend markets. They modify materially Bücher's modified theory of exploitation through intermediary merchants, by concentrating attention on the competitive menace and the function of protection. It is this bald simplicity of American individualism, without much covering of races, armies, guilds or prelates, that permits us to trace out all of the economic sutures in their evolution from infancy to manhood.

The menace of competition may conveniently be described as internal and external. The former arises within the area of the existing market, the latter proceeds from cheap producers abroad. With the ever-widening area of political control these external menaces become internal, and it is this moving frontier that determines the scope and character of protective organization and protective legislation.

Throughout the course of industrial evolution the part played by the merchant stands out as the determining factor. The key to the situation is at all times the price-bargain. It is the merchant who controls both capital and labor. If the merchant has a market, he can secure capital. Even the modern "manufacturer" is first of all the merchant. The "conflict of capital and labor" is a conflict of market and labor, of merchant and wage-earner, of prices and wages. With the extension of the market the merchant-function is the first to separate, unless prevented by guild or other regulations, and with each further extension the separation is greater. Just as the first "masters' society" of 1789 was really a retail merchants' association, so the modern "manufacturers' association" is a price-regarding association. Capital follows the merchant, and the manufacturers' protective organization is an organization to protect prices. When the extension of the market provokes the conflict of prices and wages, the wage-earners resort to independent protective policies. Then the manufacturer turns, for the time, from the market and faces the workman. His "employers' association" is wholly different in method, object and social significance, and usually in *personnel* from his "manufacturers' association."

The conflict is ultimately one between the interests of the consumer and the interests of the producer. Wherever the consumer as such is in control, he favors the marginal producer, for through him he wields the club that threatens the other producers. Consequently, the producers resort either to private organizations equipped with coercive weapons to suppress their menacing competitor, or else they seek to persuade or compel the government to suppress him. In this way the contest of classes or interests enters the field of politics, and the laws of the land, and even the very framework of government, are the outcome of a struggle both to extend markets and to ward off their menace.

In the early stages the agricultural, as distinguished from the "industrial" interests, are in control, and they stand to the shoemakers as consumers. Consequently, if the industrial interests secure protection, they must do it by carving out a jurisdiction of their own, enfranchised with political immunities and self-governing organizations. In this struggle did the guilds of Europe rid themselves of feudal agriculture. But in colonial America only the soft petition of the Boston shoemakers and coopers in 1648 shows the high-water mark of the guild. Here protection was grudgingly granted against the internal menace of bad ware and itinerant cobblers. In later times, a manufacturing colony, like Pennsylvania, enacted protective tariffs against external menace, and in 1787 the commercial and manufacturing interests, now reaching out for wholesale trade, secured in the Federal Constitution the political instrument of their mercantile aspirations. Forthwith, as we have seen, the shoemakers of Philadelphia experienced the stimulus of this extension of markets and entered the wholesale-order stage of their industry. At once what had been an external menace now became internal on this wider and lower level of competition, resulting in the separation and struggle of classes. The wage-class began its long contest for the political immunity of a private organization to suppress the "scab" in his many forms of non-unionist, sweatshop worker, green hand, Chinaman and immigrant. But, prior to the merchant-capitalist stage, this separation of labor from merchant was sporadic and reconcilable. The employer, as such, with his specialized wage-bargain, had only occasionally appeared. Merchant and journeyman were at one in their effort to protect the price-bargain. Together they joined in their century-long effort, ever more and more successful, to use the federal constitution for the suppression of the cheap ware of the foreign producer. But after the merchant-capitalist period, the slogan of the protective tariff became protection for labor, where formerly it had been protection for capital. Eventually, with the further separation of labor under its own leaders, protection took the additional form of suppressing the Chinaman and the alien contract-laborer. Turning to the state governments, labor has summoned its political strength for the suppression of the internal menace of long hours, prison labor, child and woman labor. And finally, where neither politics nor organizations suffice to limit the menace of competition, both "manufacturers" and workmen in the shoe trade strive to raise themselves above its level by cultivating the good will of the consumers, the former by his trade mark, the latter by the union label.

Thus have American shoemakers epitomized American industrial history. Common to all industries is the historical extension of markets. Variations of form, factors and rates of progress change the picture, but not the vital force. The shoemakers have pioneered and left legible records. Their career is "interpretative," if not typical.

# 21
## *Who Were the Knights of St. Crispin?*

ALAN DAWLEY                                                                          1976

With the aim of organizing all who labored in the trade, industrial workers in Lynn's shoe industry established a local of the Knights of St. Crispin in 1868 and a local of the Daughters of St. Crispin shortly thereafter. They enrolled a representative cross section of the new factory work force and sustained the organizations against the disintegrating effects of seasonal unemployment, high rates of labor migration, diverse social backgrounds, occupational jealousies, and sexual divisions for all but two of the next ten years.

This picture of the Crispins as modern industrial workers conflicts sharply with the bulk of historical scholarship, which paint Crispins as oldtime artisans outside the new working class. The fountainhead of misinterpretation is none other than the founder of American labor history, John Commons. Commons attempted to relate successive types of labor organization to a sequence of stages in the development of the shoe industry in America. His method was to begin with labor documents—the constitution of a journeyman's society, the transcript of a trade union conspiracy trial—and read back from there the nature of industrial organization at the time. His scheme of stages in economic history was derived directly from Carl Bücher's *Industrial Evolution*, his documentary method replicated the work of George Unwin's *Industrial Organization in the 16th and 17th Centuries*, and his approach was conceived as an alternative to Marxian analysis.

He redefined the conflict between labor and capital as a conflict between labor and the market. From the seventeenth century onward, the ever-widening market reduced prices, brought increasing numbers of people into production, and depressed their wages. Thus he argued the basic fight of the nineteenth-century shoeworker was with the forces of the market, not with his boss. In his view, the Knights of St. Crispin were less concerned with waging a struggle against the bosses than with preventing green hands from taking their jobs. Under the terms of this green hands theory, the more experienced shoemakers felt their jobs threatened by new machinery and new workers, and they organized the Knights of St. Crispin to protect themselves against both.

■    ■    ■

The theory is wrong on two counts. First, it mistakenly construes the question of hiring new hands as a central issue; in fact, it was only a peripheral matter. Not a single strike was undertaken in Lynn over the issue of green hands. Wage disputes were always of primary concern locally, and more recent scholarship has demonstrated that the same was true in other towns where Crispins were active. The second fault of the theory is that it incorrectly locates the sources of Crispin strength among workers who were either outside the factories or else did not yet accept the permanence of factory organization. The Commons' view of the Crispins as "lifetime" shoemakers battling the inrush of "newcomers" is no longer tenable.

Reprinted with permission of the publishers from *Class and Community: The Industrial Revolution in Lynn* by Alan Dawley, pp. 143–148, 180–184. Cambridge, Mass.: Harvard University Press. Copyright © 1976 by the President and Fellows of Harvard College.

■  ■  ■

*The bulk of the Crispins were factory workers.* Three-fourths of the members were so listed in the 1870 census. Factory workers joined the union at a higher rate than nonfactory workers; the latter made up one-third of the labor force, but only one-fourth of the union membership. Perhaps one-half the 1870 factory work force signed up and payed their dues, and, in addition, hundreds more participated in Crispin mass meetings and strike actions. The major dichotomy in the work force was not between lifetime shoemakers and green hands but between factory and nonfactory workers. Indeed, most of the lifetime shoemakers who resided in Lynn did not even become Crispins; only 22 percent of the residents who remained in the trade from 1860 to 1870 joined the union (248 of 1152). The previous conception of Crispins as stable craftsmen trying to protect their skilled position against the competition of unskilled machine workmen breaks apart on these facts alone. The decision whether or not to join the union was made by and large along lines of industrial cleavage opposite to those suggested by the green hands theory.

■  ■  ■

In every measurable category, the Crispins contained a cross-section of the factory work force. They did not represent the highly paid, highly skilled labor aristocracy. They did not represent old-time, stable members of the community. Thus, in order to understand who the Crispins did represent, it is first necessary to recognize that they were factory workers. To the extent that the factory work force was recruited among "lifetime" shoemakers, these old-timers would in turn be present in the union. It is not so much that the green hands theory is wrong in describing the Crispins as lifetime shoemakers, but that the whole division of shoemakers into newcomers and lifetime workers is confusing and misses the point. Ex-artisans, both rural shoemakers and urban mechanics, undoubtedly made up of the bulk of the Crispin membership, but that is because they first made up the bulk of the factory work force.

Knowing who joined the union makes it possible to understand *why* they joined. Writers in the Commons' tradition answered this second question through a process of circular reasoning. They made assumptions about the membership of the KOSC on the basis of Crispin speeches and by-laws. Then they turned around and interpreted the speeches and by-laws in terms of their assumptions about membership. Take the study by Lescohier.[1] He assumed from the green hands theory that the Crispins were skilled artisans losing their jobs to machines and factory workers. Then he argued that the old artisans joined the union to protest against the competition for jobs and the resulting economic hardship. To be sure, Crispins hated competition and suffered hardship, but they identified the manufacturers as the prime cause of their troubles and organized to fight them, not green hands.

Commons articulated [his] theory in his long 1907 article "American Shoemakers, 1648–1895: A Sketch of Industrial Evolution," in which he outlined seven historical stages of production, from the simple stage of itinerant craftsmen through the complex and highly developed factory system. Presiding over the progression from lower to higher stages was the omnipotent, impersonal power of the market. The essential dynamic of the marketplace was the war of all against all. However, people entered the marketplace through different doors according to their different economic functions. Some individuals bought labor, others sold. In each functional unit, people shared an overriding common interest, and they could unite to form what Commons called a "bargaining class" for collective bargaining with other classes. A trade union was simply labor's legitimate bargaining agent. It haggled with an employer over wages just the way a manufacturer haggled with a wholesaler, a wholesaler with a retailer, a retailer with a consumer. Economic history was largely a series of struggles among bargaining classes "to strengthen this bargaining power of the one element against another, showing their results in the movement of prices, values and rates, whether for commodities, land, stocks, bonds, interest or wages. It is the emergence of these various struggles involved in the emergence of bargaining classes that we see when we follow the extension of markets."

Whatever merits Commons' theory may have in elucidating the trials of prefactory artisan shoemakers, the history of the artisan encounter with the factory system, as we have seen, tends to prove the theory wrong. Evidence compels one to ask what is the merit in a theory that regards the power of industrial employees on the same plane as their employers, as if the ownership of property in a marketplace economy did not confer power on the owners? What is the value in a view which regards the wage bargain between employers and employees as essentially the same thing as the price bargain between a manufacturer and a merchant, and the same as the terms of a loan between a manufacturer and a banker? But where is there an example of a manufacturer settling a dispute with a merchant by kicking the merchant out of his home, and when has a manufacturer bargained for better terms with the bank by sending Pinkertons to shoot up the board meeting? What in American history is the businessmen's counterpart of the workers' experience at Ludlow? When has an American corporation been destroyed by federal troops the way the American Railway Union was destroyed in the Pullman strike? Merchants, manufacturers, and bankers have been callous and ruthless with one another's fortunes and reputations, but the denial of food and shelter and bullet bargaining have been reserved for disputes between those who sell their labor and those who buy it.

Commons sought a place in classical economics for the labor movement. He hoped to legitimate collective bargaining by bringing it under the aegis of Adam Smith. In the same effort, he was hoping to rescue the labor movement from the clutches of Marxian socialism. The effort to refute Marx was a steady undercurrent in his writing. He relegated the Marxian categories of surplus value and the mode of production to the status of "secondary factors, results, not causes." He denied the reality of class conflict and exploitation, at least for American history, on the grounds that the ownership of the means of production and the income gap between owners and wage earners were simply a reflex of the market. "Instead of 'exploitation,' growing out of the nature of production, our industrial evolution shows certain evils of competition imposed by an 'unfair' menace." Since Marx was wrong to assert that ownership was the source of oppression, Commons held that appropriation of the means of production was no answer to the laborers' needs. "Instead, therefore, of an idealistic remedy sought for in common ownership, the practical remedy always actually sought out has been the elimination of the competitive menace through a protective organization or protective legislation."

Commons' history of American shoemakers, his attack on Marxism, his development of the notion of "bargaining classes," indeed, the whole of his intellectual contribution were intended to take class conflict out of the arena of irreconcilable struggle and transfer it to the bargaining table, where some compromise could be worked out. He argued that both sides would gain in the transfer: workers, by peacefully winning material improvements, owners, by securing the existing distribution of property. If this required some change in the status quo, the ultimate end was conservative: "Recognition of unions through collective bargaining would protect business and the nation against politics, radicalism and communism, by placing a conservative labor movement in the strategic position."

Like so many middle-class labor reformers before him and like so many Progressives of his own day, Commons' overriding objective was to achieve social harmony without disturbing basic property relations. He outlined his position in "Economists and Class Partnership" and presented it to the 1899 session of the American Economic Association, an organization founded by Commons' teacher and mentor Richard T. Ely. "Recognition of social classes," he contended, "means self government based on legalized justice between classes." Such recognition should take place in politics, as well as economics, where bona fide labor leaders should be brought into the process of decision making. "What is needed is a representative assembly which will bring together these leaders with the leaders of all other classes, so that they can make similar compromises in politics." In a grand proposal that harks back to the foundation of representative government in the United States, Commons proposed a national assembly of delegates from the various social interests. Labor would choose men like Gompers and Debs, business would pick such captains of industry as Morgan and Rockefeller, and likewise farmers, and even economists would choose their own representatives.

Taken as a whole, Commons' ideas were a restatement of classical liberalism in the context of industrial and corporate capitalism. His emphasis on the primacy of the marketplace restated the economic doctrines of Adam Smith; his view of politics as a field for compromise between contending economic interests reiterated the Madisonian philosophy of the *Federalist* # 10, which spoke of "a landed interest, a manufacturing interest, a mercantile interest, a moneyed interest, with many lesser interests" as the basis of politics.

In Commons' national assembly of bargaining classes there would be no question of the basic rights of ownership. The framework of a marketplace economy was assumed; only the relative advantage within it was up for discussion. With this conservative aim in mind, Commons assiduously promoted liberal reforms through his teaching and academic empire building at the University of Wisconsin, his voluminous writing in both popular and scholarly publications, and his practical work on such agencies of class partnership as the Industrial Commission of Wisconsin, the U.S. Commission on Industrial Relations, and the National Civic Federation. Commons never separated his scholarship from his activism and was a living embodiment of John Dewey's concept of "instrumentalism," the notion that ideas are plans of action. The scholar provided grist for the reformer's mill.

Commons shuttled back and forth between the labor movement and the Progressive movement. To the middle-class Progressives, he advocated collective bargaining as the surest means of resolving industrial strife and promoted the type of bread-and-butter unionism best represented by Samuel Gompers. To the labor movement, he preached the evil of revolutionary unionism of the sort represented by the IWW and urged acceptance of the employing class as a permanent and legitimate interest group. As an ambassador of reform, Commons traveled widely in labor and Progressive circles, enlisting in Robert La Follette's campaign to bring honest government to the state of Wisconsin, supporting the German socialists in Milwaukee in a project to improve the efficiency of municipal government, and serving as a member of Woodrow Wilson's Commission on Industrial Relations.

The consistency in these travels was his faith that America's industrial problems could be solved at the bargaining table where third parties like himself could offer their expertise to help resolve disputes peaceably and thereby serve the mutual interest of both sides while promoting the welfare of the general public. Though he gained a reputation as an advocate of labor, his basic ideas were in full accord with the philosophy of corporate liberalism. Like the leading proponent of that philosophy, Herbert Croly, Commons advocated the large-scale organization of both capital and labor, distinguished between good and bad unionism, as between good and bad capitalists, and proposed that technical experts working for the government oversee disputes among private economic interests. A self-conscious opponent of revolution, Commons was an efficiency expert in finessing class struggle. His influence on the field of labor history is a fact of history and can not be discounted, but historians must recognize and weigh carefully the scholarly prejudices of his personal political orientation.

-----

[1][Don Lescohier was a student of Commons who wrote parts of the four-volume *History of Labor in the United States* and also published an article entitled "The Knights of St. Crispin 1867–1874: A Study on Industrial Causes of Trade Unionism" (*Bulletin of the University of Wisconsin* no. 355, 1910).—*Eds.*]

# 22
## A Theory of the Labor Movement

SELIG PERLMAN                                                      1928

Twenty years ago the author of this book, like most of his college generation in Russia, professed the theory of the labor movement found in the Marxian classics. "Labor" was then to him—he realized afterwards—mainly an abstraction: an abstract mass in the grip of an abstract force. For, despite the copiousness of the statistical and sociological evidence adduced by Marxism for the view that the workman is bound, in the very nature of capitalism, to espouse the cause of revolution,—and despite Marxism's intense concern with concrete labor movements, from Chartism to date,—it remains true that, at bottom, the Marxian theory of the labor movement rests upon a species of faith, —namely the faith that history has appointed the labor movement to be the force which eventually will bring society to the third and final step in the Hegelian dialectical scheme of evolution.

Shortly afterwards (having in the meantime transferred himself to the American environment), by an unusual stroke of good luck, the author joined the research staff of Professor John R. Commons. Here he became acquainted with Professor Commons' method of deducing labor theory from the concrete and crude experience of the wage earners. This method is brilliantly demonstrated in his article on the *American Shoemakers*,[1] where a theory of industrial evolution as well as a theory of the labor movement were evolved from the testimony (in a series of reported conspiracy cases) given by sweat shop bosses, "scabs," strikers, merchant capitalists, and manufacturers. In this approach the Hegelian dialectic nowhere occurs, nor is cognizance taken of labor's "historical mission." What monopolizes attention is labor combatting competitive menaces—"scabs," "green hands," and the like; labor bargaining for the control of the job.

On joining in Professor Commons' pioneering undertaking of a history of American industrial society, the author started with the socialistic movements among immigrant workmen during the sixties and seventies. Here, in a field apparently of little significance, the author stumbled upon a veritable gold mine: he discovered that out of these overlooked movements among the German and other foreign wage-earners there finally emerged the non-socialistic program of the American Federation of Labor. What an absurd and topsy-turvy order of things! (For to the Marxian and to the socialist in general it is "normal" for a labor movement to "ascend" from "pure and simple" unionism to a socialistic class consciousness; never to "descend" from the second to the first.) Yet that was, clearly, the product of the genuine and prolonged experience of the Strasser-Gompers group of unionists who fell away from their original faith reluctantly indeed. This discovery gave the author another impulse in the same direction. Obviously, working people in the real felt an urge towards collective control of their employment opportunities, but hardly towards similar control of industry. The events of the day in the American labor movement—the failure of the socialists within the American Federation of Labor and of the Industrial Workers of the World without, to hold their own after auspicious débuts shortly before, added strength to the author's new convictions in formation.

When, at the outbreak of the European War, the German labor movement espoused the national cause, with the trade unions unexpectedly calling the tune to the Social-Democratic piper, the author set himself to studying the inter-relationships

Reprinted with permission of the author's estate from *A Theory of the Labor Movement* by Selig Perlman, pp. vii–x, 4–10, 237–247, 272–285, 299–302. New York: A. M. Kelley, 1970. Footnotes in the original have been eliminated or renumbered.

between the economic and the political movements in that country. Here he stumbled upon the idea that there is a natural divergence in labor ideology between the "mentality" of the trade unions and the "mentality" of the intellectuals; and that, given the opportunity to exist legally and to develop a leadership from among its own ranks, the trade union's mentality will eventually come to dominate. In Germany the trade unions had emancipated themselves from the hegemony of the intellectual revolutionists in 1906 —with the "Mannheim Agreement." That a trade unionism so emancipated will be deaf to the call of revolutions and will think in terms of its national industry from which spring both wages and profits has been proved over again by the events in Germany since 1918.

The Russian Revolution and the ease with which the Bolshevists seized power sent the author reviewing his Russian history to account for the weakness of the "ruling" classes of Russia—a weakness which was psychological and profoundly in contrast with the strength of German capitalists in 1918–1920 and with the fighting prowess of British capitalists in 1926.

■  ■  ■

Three dominant factors are emerging from the seeming medley of contradictory turns and events in recent labor history. The first factor is the demonstrated capacity, as in Germany, Austria, and Hungary, or else incapacity, as in Russia, of the capitalist group to survive as a ruling group and to withstand revolutionary atack when the protective hand of government has been withdrawn. In this sense "capitalism" is not only, nor even primarily, a material or governmental arrangement whereby one class, the capitalist class, owns the means of production, exchange, and distribution, while the other class, labor, is employed for wages. Capitalism is rather a social organization presided over by a class with an "effective will to power," implying the ability to defend its power against all comers—to defend it, not necessarily by physical force, since such force, however important at a crisis, might crumble after all—but to defend it, as it has done in Germany, through having convinced the other classes that they alone, the capitalists, know how to operate the complex economic apparatus of modern society upon which the material welfare of all depends.

The second factor which stands out clearly in the world-wide social situation is the rôle of the so-called "intellectual," the "intelligentsia," in the labor movement and in society at large. It was from the intellectual that the anti-capitalist influences in modern society emanated. It was he who impressed upon the labor movement tenets characteristic of his own mentality: the "nationalization" or "socialization" of industry, and political action, whether "constitutional" or "unconstitutional," on behalf of the "new social order." He, too, has been busily indoctrinating the middle classes with the same views, thus helping to undermine an important prop of capitalism and to some extent even the spirit of resistance of the capitalists themselves.

The third and the most vital factor in the labor situation is the trade union movement. Trade unionism, which is essentially pragmatic, struggles constantly, not only against the employers for an enlarged opportunity measured in income, security, and liberty in the shop and industry, but struggles also, whether consciously or unconsciously, actively or merely passively, against the intellectual who would frame its programs and shape its policies. In this struggle by "organic" labor[2] against dominance by the intellectuals, we perceive a clash of an ideology which holds the concrete workingmen in the center of its vision with a rival ideology which envisages labor merely as an "abstract mass in the grip of an abstract force."

Labor's own "home grown" ideology is disclosed only through a study of the "working rules" of labor's own "institutions." The trade unions are the institutions of labor today, but much can be learned also from labor's institutions in the past, notably the gilds.

It is the author's contention that manual groups, whether peasants in Russia, modern wage earners, or medieval master workmen, have had their economic attitudes basically determined by a consciousness of scarcity of opportunity, which is characteristic of these groups, and stands out in contrast with the business men's "abundance consciousness," or consciousness of unlimited opportunity. Starting with this consciousness of scarcity, the "manualist" groups have been led to practising solidarity, to an insistence upon an "ownership" by the group as a whole of the totality of economic opportunity extant, to a "rationing" by the group of such opportunity among the individuals constituting it, to a control by the group over its members in relation to the conditions upon which they as individuals are permitted to occupy a portion of that opportunity—in brief, to a "communism of opportunity." This differs fundamentally from socialism or communism, which would "communize" not only "opportunity," but also production and distribution —just as it is far removed from "capitalism." Capitalism started from the premise of unlimited opportunity, and arrived, in its classical formulation, at "laissez faire" for the individual all along the line—in regard to the "quantity" of opportunity he may appropriate, the price or wage he may charge, and in regard to the ownership of the means of production. "Communism of opportunity" in the sense here employed existed in the medieval gilds before the merchant capitalists had subverted them to the purposes of a protected business men's oligarchy; in Russian peasant land communities with their periodic redivisions, among the several families, of the collectively owned land, the embodiment of the economic opportunity of a peasant group; and exists today in trade unions enforcing a "job control" through union "working rules."

But, in this country, due to the fact that here the "manualist" had found at hand an abundance of opportunity, in unoccupied land and in a pioneer social condition, his economic thinking had therefore issued, not from the scarcity premise but from the premise of abundance. It thus resulted in a social philosophy which was more akin to the business men's than to the trade unionists' or gildsmen's. Accordingly, the American labor movement, which long remained unaware of any distinction between itself and the "producing classes" in general,—which included also farmers, small manufacturers, and small business men,—continued for many decades to worship at the shrine of individualistic "antimonopoly." "Anti-monopoly" was a program of reform, through politics and legislation, whereby the "producing classes" would apply a corrective to the American social order so that economic individualism might become "safe" for the producers rather than for land speculators, merchant capitalists, and bankers. Unionism, on the contrary, first became a stabilized movement in America only when the abundance consciousness of the pioneer days had been replaced in the mind of labor by a scarcity consciousness—the consciousness of job scarcity. Only then did the American wage earner become willing to envisage a future in which his union would go on indefinitely controlling his relation to his job rather than endeavoring to afford him, as during the anti-monopoly stage of the labor movement, an escape into free and unregulated self-employment, by winning for him a competitive equality with the "monopolist."

In America, the historical struggle waged by labor for an undivided expression of its own mentality in its own movement was directed against the ideology of "anti-monopoly." But in Europe the antithesis to the labor mentality has been the mentality of the intellectual.

Twenty-five years ago, Nicolai Lenin clearly recognized the divergence which exists between the intellectual and the trade unionist, although not in terms of an inevitable mutual antagonism, when he hurled his unusual polemical powers against those in the Social-Democratic Party, his own party at the time, who would confine their own and the party's agitational activities to playing upon labor's economic grievances. He then said that if it had not been for the "bourgeois intellectuals" Marx and Engels, labor would never have got beyond mere "trifling,"—going after an increase in wage here and after a labor law there. Lenin, of course, saw labor and the trade union movement, not as an aggregation of concrete individuals sharing among themselves their collective job opportunity, as well as trying to enlarge it and improve it by joint effort and step by step, but rather as an abstract mass which history had predetermined to hurl itself against the capitalist social order and demolish it. Lenin therefore could never have seen in a non-revolutionary unionism anything more than a blind groping after a purpose only vaguely grapsed, rather than a completely self-conscious movement with a full-blown ideology of its own. But to see "labor" solely as an abstract mass and the concrete individual reduced to a mere mathematical point, as against the trade unionists' striving for job security for the individual and concrete freedom on the job, has not been solely the prerogative of "determinist-revolutionaries" like Lenin and the Communists. The other types of intellectuals in and close to the labor movement, the "ethical" type, the heirs of Own and the Christian Socialists, and the "social efficiency" type, best represented by the Fabians—to mention but English examples,—have equally with the orthodox Marxians reduced labor to a mere abstraction, although each has done so in his own way and has pictured "labor" as an abstract mass in the grip of an abstract force, existing, however, only in his own intellectual imagination, and not in the emotional imagination of the manual worker himself.

■   ■   ■

A theory of the labor movement should include a theory of the psychology of the laboring man. The writings of socialists, syndicalists, anarchists, communists, and "welfare" capitalists abound in embroideries on the theme of "what labor wants" or "what labor aspires to." But the safest method is to go to the organizations of labor's own making, shaped and managed by leaders arisen from labor's own ranks, and to attempt to discover "what's really on labor's mind" by using as material the "working rules," customs and practices of these organizations. A study of such "rules" and customs, the products of long drawn out, evolutionary developments, will aid in distinguishing fundamental from accidental purposes. No such certainty can attach, of course, to the formulations by the "ideologists" of labor, just because these latter, being intellectuals and without the workingman's shop experience, are unable, for all their devotion, to avoid substituting their own typical attitudes and wishes for the genuine philosophy of the laboring man.

There are, by and large, three basic economic philosophies: the manual laborers', the business men's, and the intellectuals'. Werner Sombart, in his definitions of "handicraft" and of capitalism, offers the best clue to an explanation of the essential psychologies of the "manualist" and of the business man. He points out in these definitions the wide gulf between economic motives in the mediæval economy and in modern business. A secure livelihood for everyone was the aim of the gilds, but the business man has from the first been inspired by a boundless desire to amass wealth. This thought, which is one of Sombart's many illuminating contributions to economic history, can be made the starting point of a more comprehensive theory of economic group psychology. It can be done by showing, first, how the psychological contrast between the two historical epochs, the gild and the capitalistic, continues in our own day, in the contrast between the psychology of trade unionism and the psychology of buisness, and second, how each and every type of such group psychology, past and present, can be explained through a common theory.

In an economic community, there is a separation between those who prefer a secure, though modest return,—that is to say, a mere livelihood,—and those who play for big stakes and are willing to assume risk in proportion. The first compose the great bulk of manual workers of every description, including mechanics, laborers, farmers, small manufacturers, and shopkeepers (since petty trade, as Sombart correctly points out, is also a manual occupation); while the latter are, of course, the entrepreneurs and the big business men. The limited or unlimited purpose is, in either case, the product of a simple survey of accessible economic opportunity and of a psychic self-appraisal. The manual worker is convinced by experience that he is living in a world of limited opportunity. He sees, to be sure, how others, for instance business men, are finding the same world a storehouse of apparently unlimited opportunity. Yet he decisively discounts that, so far as he is himself concerned. The business man, on the contrary, is an eternal optimist. To him the world is brimful of opportunities that are only waiting to be made his own.

The scarcity consciousness of the manualist is a product of two main causes, one lying in himself and the other outside. The typical manualist is aware of his lack of native capacity for availing himself of economic opportunities as they lie amidst the complex and ever shifting situations of modern business. He knows himself neither for a born taker of risks nor for the possessor of a sufficiently agile mind ever to feel at home in the midst of the uncertain game of competitive business. Added to this is his conviction that for him the world has been rendered one of scarcity by an institutional order of things, which purposely reserved the best opportunities for landlords, capitalists and other privileged groups. It may also be, of course, that the manual worker will ascribe such scarcity to natural rather than to institutional causes, say, to a shortage of land brought on by increase of population, or, like mediæval merchants and master workmen, to the small number of customers and the meagre purchasing power of these. At all events, whether he thought the cause of the apparent limitations to be institutional or natural, a scarcity consciousness has always been typical of the manual worker, in direct contrast to the consciousness of an abundance of opportunity, which dominates the self-confident business man.

By correlating economic types, as we do here, with an abundance or a scarcity consciousness, respectively, we are enabled to throw a bridge between our own time and earlier periods. The mediæval craftsman and gild master, notwithstanding his economic "independence," was of the same economic type as the wage earner of today. The gildsman maintained his independence solely because his rudimentary business psychology sufficed for an age when the market was limited to the locality, and the tools of production were primitively simple. Put the average wage earner back into the Thirteenth Century, and he would set up as a master; transfer a gild master into the age of modern business, and he would fall into the ranks of wage labor. While, to be sure, the economic historian was justified in refusing to see any historical continuity between gilds and trade unions, he often overlooked their common fundamental psychology: the psychology of seeking after a livelihood in the face of limited economic opportunity. Just as, to the gildsman, opportunity was visibly limited to the local market, so, to the industrial wage earner, it is limited to the number of jobs available, almost always fewer than the number of job seekers.

The economic pessimism of the manual group is at the bottom of its characteristic manner of adjusting the relation of the individual to the whole group. It prompts also the attitude of exclusion which manual groups assume towards those regarded as "outsiders." Again the manualist's psychology can best be brought out by contrast with that of the fully developed business man. Basically the business man is an economic individualist, a competitor *par excellence*. If opportunity is plentiful, if the enterprising person can create his own opportunity, what sane object can there be in collectively controlling the extent of the individual's appropriation of opportunity, or in drastically excluding those from other localities? Nor will this type of individual submit to group control, for he is confident of his ability to make good bargains for himself. If, on the contrary, opportunity is believed to be limited, as in the experience of the manual worker, it then becomes the duty of the group to prevent the individual from appropriating more than his rightful share, while at the same time protecting him against oppressive bargains. *The group then asserts its collective ownership over the whole amount of opportunity*, and, having determined who are entitled to claim a share in that opportunity, undertakes to parcel it out fairly, directly or indirectly, among its recognized members, permitting them to avail themselves of such opportunities, job or market, only on the basis of a "common rule." Free competition becomes a sin against one's fellows, anti-social, like a self indulgent consumption of the stores of a beleaguered city, and obviously detrimental to the individual as well. A collective disposal of opportunity, including the power to keep out undesirables, and a "common rule" in making bargains are as natural to the manual group as *"laissez-faire"* is to the business man.

■   ■   ■

Does this opportunity theory explain the business man's conduct through the several stages of economic society? His individualism shows up clearest during periods of great economic expansion. When markets are becoming rapidly extended and technology revolutionized; in other words, when opportunity is expanding by leaps and bounds, then his competitiveness approaches the ruthlessness of a Darwinian struggle for existence. The elder Rockefeller and Andrew Carnegie, moral men who raised competitiveness to an ethic, are indeed excellent examples. This is not to say that business men will not form "rings" even in the midst of economic revolution, nor that they cannot be taught to abate their competition in the common interest. Yet, on the whole, the "new competition" or "co-operative competition," may be said to have been given its chance only after the rush for new opportunities had already subsided of itself, due to a slackening in the opportunity-creating economic expansion.

Furthermore, notwithstanding this "new competition" on the modern commodity market, there always remains a vital difference between a business men's group, with the characteristic consciousness of abundance which is normal to that economic type, co-operating to a common end, and the solidarity in action manifested by genuine "scarcity" groups. When a business men's group has been led, through fear of cutthroat competition and price wars, to resort directly or indirectly, to the rationing of market opportunity among its members, this movement has always sprung from the "head," but never spontaneously nor from the "heart," as it were, in contrast with the gilds, peasant land communities, or trade unions, which have usually taken to sharing opportunity even long before becoming formally organized. For the same reason, we never find individual business men anxious to emulate the manualist's willingness, nay, even burning zeal as shown during strikes, literally to sacrifice his own interest for the good of his group as a whole.

■ ■ ■

What relation has this opportunity theory of the labor group psychology to the plans of the socialists, to "workers' control," to the "abolition of wagery," and so forth?

Socialism, in its many varieties, while correctly grasping a part of the true psychology of the worker—his desire for solidarity—overlooks his unwillingness to become completely merged with his own class. Whenever and wherever full "workers' control" has been tried, by "self-governing workshops" and like organizations, history shows that sooner or later the workers have, consciously or unconsciously, opposed the creation of a solidarity exceeding a common control of opportunity and common "working rules,"— that is, if the undertaking did not die at birth, or, surviving, experience a conversion, materially prosperous but spiritually degrading, into a capitalist enterprise owned by a few of the "smarter" co-operators. For, the workers, it seems, will cheerfully submit to an almost military union discipline in their struggles against the employer; they will be guided by the union working rules in seeking and holding jobs; but they will mistrust and obstruct their union leaders who have become shop-bosses under whatever scheme of "workers' control." Perhaps in abstract reasoning, the wage earner might be expected to envisage the whole of the economic organization of society as the ultimate source of his job opportunity; and therefore wish for a complete "workers' control" of industry. Actually, however, the typical wage earner, when he can express himself in and through his trade union free of domination by intellectuals, who are never too bashful to do his thinking for him, seldom dreams of shouldering the risks of management. Ordinarily he traces the origin of his opportunity not much farther back than the point where it materializes in jobs, and will grasp and support only such union policies as will enable or force the employers to offer more jobs, equally available to all fellow craftsmen, and upon improved terms.

■ ■ ■

In the unionism of the printers' organization we have encountered a truly stable and mature type of collective behavior by labor. The printers' union qualifies as stable and mature, because it has been led by men risen from its own ranks, because it has evolved a complete "law of the job," but in a still deeper sense, because it has mastered the dilemma of serving simultaneously the individual member and the group as a whole. Such unionism is individualistic and collectivistic at the same time. It is individualistic in the sense that it aims to satisfy the individual aspirations of Tom, Dick, and Harry for a decent livelihood, for economic security, and for freedom from tyranny on the part of the boss. But such unionism is also collectivistic, since it aspires to develop in the individual a willingness to subordinate his own interests to the superior interests of the collectivity. It may be true, as Whiting Williams pointed out in his *Mainsprings of Men*, that the majority of workingmen are "on the fence," deliberately weighing the relative advantages from following the employer or the union leader, each one arriving at his own decision only after a cold-blooded calculation. However, such "Whiting Williams unionists" resemble real unionists no more than a resident of Upper Silesia would have resembled a true national of either country, had he stopped to weigh, on the memorable day of the

Plebiscite, the relative material advantage from voting himself either a German or a Pole. Consequently, while it is true that a union can never become strong or stable except by attaching the individual to itself through the tangible benefits accruing to him from its administration of the job opportunities of the group as a whole, neither can it be a union in the full sense of the word unless it has educated the members to put the integrity of the collective "job-territory" above the security of their individual job tenure. Unionism is, in this respect, not unlike patriotism which may and does demand of the citizen the supreme sacrifice, when the integrity of the national territory is at stake. Just as a mere pooling by forty million Frenchmen of their individualistic self-interests will not yet produce a patriotic France, so a bare adding together of the individual job interests of five million wage earners, united in a common organization, will scarcely result in a labor movement. To have a really stable unionism and a really stable labor movement, the individual members must evince a readiness to make sacrifices on behalf of the control by their union of their collective "job-territory," without stopping to count too closely the costs involved to themselves. And like nationalism, unionism is keenly conscious of a "patria irredenta" in the non-union portion of its trade or industry.

But if unionism means an idealistic readiness on the part of the individual to offer, as the need arises, unstinted sacrifices for the group as a whole, what then of "business unionism"? May even such a unionism have an "ideology"? To many, of course, any "ideology" whatsover in a unionism which is merely "business" and which avowedly limits its objective to a mere control of jobs, is entirely and definitely precluded. However, upon closer examination, it would seem that if, by naming the predominant type of American unionism "business unionism," it was meant to bring out that it had no "ideology," then the name was clearly a misnomer. The difficulty arises from a disposition to class as idealistic solely the professions of idealistic aims—socialism, anarchism, and the like,—but to overlook the unselfconscious idealism in the daily practice of unionism. In truth, unionism, even "business unionism," shows idealism both in aim and in method; only it does so in the thoroughly unsophisticated way of "Tom, Dick, and Harry idealism." All unions sooner or later stress "shop rights," which, to the workingman at the bench, are identical with "liberty" itself,—since, thanks to them, he has no need to kowtow to foreman or boss, as the price of holding his job. And, after all, is not this sort of liberty the only sort which reaches the workman directly and with certainty and that can never get lost *en route*, like the "broader" liberty promised by socialism? For, in practice, that other liberty may never succeed in straining through the many layers of the socialistic hierarchy down to the mere private in industry. Secondly, a union which expects its members to sacrifice for the group on a scale almost commensurate with the sacrifices which patriotism evokes, cannot be without its own respectable ideology. Frequently, therefore, the "materialism" of unionism proves only the one-sidedness of the view of the particular observer.

Yet, granting that even "business unionism" possesses ideology after a fashion, might it not be that, after all, the conception of unionism advanced here could fit only a narrow craft unionism, not a unionism with a wider conception of labor solidarity? True, the more distinct the trade identity of a given group and therefore the clearer the boundaries of its particular "job-territory," the stronger are normally the bonds which tie the members together in a spontaneous solidarity. Yet, on the other hand, the specific area of that common job-territory, or of the common opportunity which a group considers its own, is seldom fixed, but is constantly tending to widen, just as the numerical size and the composition of the group itself is constantly tending to grow. When accumulated technological changes have undermined the partitions between the several grades of labor in an industry and have thus produced a virtually undivided "job-territory" for all employed in it, the function of framing "rules of occupancy and tenure" for the job opportunities included within the now expanded job-territory will sooner or later be taken over by an *industrial* union or by an *amalgamated* union bordering upon the industrial type. And that union, when it will come to face the common enemy, will display a solidarity no less potent than the solidarity of the original craft unions, although as a job administrator the new and expanded union will endeavor to give recognition, so far as it will still remain possible, to the original particularistic job claims.

Nor need a job conscious unionism, with respect to many portentous issues, arrest the growth of its solidarity, short of the outer boundaries of the wage earning class as a whole. Many are the influences affecting union job control: the legal status of unionism, the policies of the government, a favorable public opinion, and others. Thus every union soon discovers that the integrity of its "job-territory," like the integrity of the geographic territory of a nation, is inextricably dependent on numerous wide relationships. And the very consciousness of the scarcity of opportunity, which is basic to labor's thinking, engenders in individual unions, labor's original organic cells, a wish for mutual cohesion, a common class-consciousness, and eventually a readiness to subordinate the interests of the individual cell to the aspirations of the whole labor organism. We know from history that the most craft-conscious bodies that ever existed, the mediæval gilds, left nothing to be desired so far as solidaristic action against the common overloads was concerned. There is, however, a practical limitation upon labor's solidarity, and this limitation is a very vital one, namely that, in a labor movement which has already gone beyond the emotional stage and acquired a definite *rationale* of its own, an appeal for common class action, be it through a sympathetic strike or through joint political action, will only be likely to evoke the response which is desired if the objective of the proposed common undertaking be kept so close to the core substance of union aspiration that Tom, Dick, and Harry could not fail to identify it as such.

Just as we find job conscious unionism far from devoid of idealism of a kind, so its ultimate industrial vision need not at all be limited to the job itself. In truth, such a unionism might easily acquire a lively interest in problems of management without previously undergoing mutation. It is not at all unnatural that a unionism which is intent upon job opportunities should join with management in a joint campaign to reduce the cost of operation and raise efficiency—all for the "conservation" of the current job opportunities. However, to grant so much is far from making the claim that labor might be brought to embrace "efficiency" as its primary concern instead of merely pursuing it secondarily to the primary interest in jobs. Thus it grows out of the preceding that whether one is trying to "improve" labor's "ideology," to broaden its solidarity, or to awaken its interest in "efficiency," one will indeed do well, in order to avoid wasted efforts, to steer close to the fundamental scarcity consciousness of the manual workers, which rules unionism today as it ruled the gilds of the past.

What the true purposes of unionism are (distinguished from mere verbal pronunciamentos, in which the preambles to the constitutions of some "socialistic" unions abound), and what a union does when it applies a scientific rationalism to its problems, have best been shown by the Amalgamated Clothing Workers of America. Although it is the outstanding "socialistic" union in America, it has, in practice, turned its efforts not to fighting capitalism in its industry, but to securing a thorough-going job control. As an organization of quite recent origin, the Clothing Workers' union lacked the advantage which the printers' union had derived from the long, evolutionary growth of a union "common law," which enforced itself almost automatically, as it were, upon the employers, through the sheer weight of trade custom. The Clothing Workers' union was therefore obliged to acquire the same control of the job through a system of *unrestricted* collective bargaining, and to secure the upbuilding of a common law, similar to that in the printing trade, through a shrewd use of the machinery for continuous arbitration, functioning under the joint agreements in that industry. The "rules of occupancy and tenure" of the employment opportunities are in the clothing industry practically identical with the printers', and, for that matter, with the rules of the railwaymen, of the miners, and of the other organized trades,—showing the same "union control of opportunity" and the same united bargaining front. But in Chicago, the Clothing Workers' union has gone a step farther, and has taken over the employment work for the whole local industry. It has installed to that end a modern employment office, originally under the management of a former chief of the Canadian system of government employment offices.

In Chicago, too, the Clothing Workers have led the way in perfecting a new method of "job preservation," rejecting both the cruder "making work" devices of the older unions and the employer's cure-all, a wage reduction. During the depression after 1920, which has not yet ended, the union has come to the employers' aid in a way altogether novel. Without itself going into business, but letting the employer remain the risk-taker and the responsible manager, this union has contrived materially to lighten his burden by considering and helping solve the problems of each concern on their merits,— up to the point of assuming responsibility for the supervision of the work. In this manner the union, through co-operating with the employer in reducing his costs and enabling him to continue in business, has saved many jobs for its members and has substantially protected the wage scale.

■ ■ ■

In marked contrast to the actual behavior of "organic" labor groups, peasant communities, gilds and trade unions, stand the several programs for labor action mapped out by the intellectuals. This contrast is, in the last analysis, a product of two opposite ways of looking at labor. It has already been brought out how the organic groups, notwithstanding that they rigorously enforce, upon their individual members, collectively framed rules for the "occupancy and tenure of economic opportunity," yet at each turn keep in sight the concrete individual, with his very tangible individual interests and aspirations. But it has always been the main characteristic of the intellectual to think of labor as an abstract "mass" in the grip of an abstract "force." By the intellectual is meant, of course, the educated non-manualist, who has established a contact with the labor movement, either indirectly, through influence acquired over trade union bodies, or else as a leader of labor in his own right, as Lassalle was in Germany and as the leading Communists are in Russia today.

So long as the intellectual is investigating specific subjects, which have definite and calculable bearings upon the workers' welfare,—for instance, industrial accidents, unemployment, wage trends, and the like, his tendency to reduce labor in the concrete to an abstraction is restrained. But let the intellectual's thought turn from relatively prosaic matters like the above mentioned to the infinitely more soul-stirring one of "labor and the social order," and it is the rare intellectual who is able to withstand an onrush of overpowering social mysticism. Labor then ceases to be an aggregation of individuals seeking as a group to control their common economic opportunity in accord with common rules, as well as to enlarge that opportunity. Instead, labor takes on the aspect of a "mass" driven by a "force" towards a glorious "ultimate social goal." The intellectual, to be sure, is unconscious of his mysticism. On the contrary, he is generally careful to connect every move of labor towards the "new social order" which he prognosticates, with definite changes in labor conditions, with a growing wastefulness of competition, or with an equally comprehensible urge within the workingman to a greater freedom in the shop, due to an awakened self-consciousness. Yet, at bottom, the intellectual's conviction that labor must espouse the "new social order" rests neither on statistically demonstrable trends in conditions nor on labor's stirrings for the sort of liberty expressed through the control of the job, which anyone who knows workingmen will recognize and appreciate, but on a deeply rooted faith that labor is somehow the "chosen vessel" of whatever may be the power which shapes the destiny of society. The best evidence that one is here dealing with the psychological phenomenon of faith is the intellectual's persistence in that faith regardless of labor's repeated refusals to reach out for its appointed destiny and to advance materially in that direction, even when opportunity appears to beckon most promisingly. When brought face to face with evidence of this sort, the typical intellectual rather than admit that his original conception of labor's psychology was wrong, will take refuge in an explanation that what has occurred is merely a temporary "delay," and he will account for that delay by calling attention to the rise of a reactionary trade union bureaucracy, through whose machinations the grip of the "force" upon the labor "mass" has temporarily become weakened and its movement thus been deflected in an illegitimate direction.

While the concept of labor as a "mass" in the grip of a "force" is the common basis of all intellectualist theories of the labor movement, intellectuals fall into three distinct groupings, depending on what they take the nature of that "force" to be. The Marxian, who is a "determinist-revolutionary," pictures it as the ever growing force of material production, embodied in the tools of production and in technological methods. This "force," in seeking to break through the capitalist strait jacket which encases it and impedes its further growth, is inevitably hurling the labor "mass" against the political and legal régime established and defended by the capitalist class. Secondly, we have the "ethical" intellectual to whom the "force" that grips the labor "mass" is the force of labor's own awakened ethical perception. This "ethical" force causes labor to strive for the fullest ethical self-realization, which in turn is conditional upon labor's escape from the degradation of "wagery" into "freedom." And "freedom" is found either in the self-governing workshop of the Christian Socialist, in the "labor commune" of the Anarchist, or in the "national gild" of the Gild Socialist. Finally, there is the "efficiency" intellectual with his vision of society advancing from a state of disorganization to one of "order," meaning a progressive elimination of waste and the abolition of destitution. This type of intellectual, who is best exemplified by the Fabians, sees labor as a "mass" propelled by the force of its awakened burning interest in a planned economic order yielding a maximum technical and social efficiency.

Every one of these three types of "intellectuals" projects from his own abstract conception of "labor as a mass in the grip of a force" a mental picture of the workingman as an individual. Consequently, every one of these pictures differs widely from the real person whom employers and union leaders know. The Marxian pictures the workingman as a class-conscious proletarian who, at the dawn of a real revolutionary opportunity such as a world war or a similar upheaval, will unhesitatingly scorn all the gains in his material conditions and in his individual status which as a trade unionist he has already conquered from the employers, and will buoyantly face an uncertain future—all for the sake of the dictatorship of his class.

Unlike the Marxian, who makes a virtue of thinking in terms of the "mass," the "ethical" intellectual places the highest value upon the liberated human personality and consequently is obliged to keep the individual in the center of his vision. Yet he too falls short of a true vision, since he arrives at his individual workingman by separating him out as a molecule from the abstract labor "mass." By this process, curiously enough, the individual workingman emerges bearing a very striking spiritual resemblance to his maker, the "ethical" intellectual. To the latter, industrial freedom means the complete disappearance of all authority from above, and an opportunity for everyone to participate in the total creative planning of industry. So his "workingman," too, feels that he is still being denied his rightful chance for development of personality, if he has merely been given the opportunity, under the protection of his union, to enjoy an inalienable right to his job.

Lastly, the individual workingman of the "efficiency" intellectual, as we shall come to see, is a creature who has forever given up any claim to a vested right in any particular job, or, in common with the others in his group, to any particular "job-territory"; but is, on the contrary, totally indifferent as to who gets the job or jobs, so long as the employer observes the union standards of wages and hours. This "workingman" has presumably arrived at such a thorough oblivion of self and of his nearest group in the vital matter of securing his opportunity, because he has realized that, with such an arrangement, the employer would be free to select the fittest worker for the job and that hence the way would be opened to the highest "efficiency." Truly, the "workingman" of the "efficiency" intellectual should have no trouble in getting admitted to the Fabian Society or even perhaps into a somewhat reconstituted Taylor Society of America.

All intellectuals, whether of the "ethical," or the "efficiency," or the "deterministic-revolutionary" type, are alike desirous to make their own ideology also the ideology of labor. However, the methods which they will pursue to gain this ascendency and the lengths to which they will go, generally vary with the particular ideology each professes.

■ ■ ■

Labor history cannot deny to the revolutionary intellectual a truly pivotal part in the labor struggles of the past. Only in English-speaking countries did the labor movement show the capacity to arise without his leadership. On the Continent, it was from the intellectual that the philosophy and program of the budding labor movements came, just as it was the intellectual who built up the first labor organizations and directed their first campaigns. And where, as in Germany, his hegemony was long and undisputed, he managed to leave upon the labor movement an indelible imprint of idealism and of an unquestioned class solidarity, regardless of distinctions of craft and of wage levels, a solidarity which has survived, to the great advantage of the movement, even after his predominant influence had long passed. Thus few indeed will assert that without the early leadership of Lassalle and of those intellectuals upon whom fell his mantle and the mantle of Marx, German labor would have been what it is today. English labor, which lacked the intellectuals' contribution during most of its history, long retained an ingrained narrow craft consciousness; while American labor, which has never come under his influence, largely remains even today in the stage of mere craft consciousness.

Nevertheless, the basic contradiction which exists between the mentality of organic labor and that of the revolutionary intellectual must, in every instance, sooner or later become strikingly plain. The trade union leader sees the labor movement climbing a difficult road, beset with many pitfalls, towards a civilized level of existence for oneself and one's dependents. Some of these pitfalls are of the employers' making, while others are unwittingly dug by labor's devoted but impractical friends. With every stretch of the road that has been covered, labor is acquiring an ever stronger incentive to turn a deaf ear to the preachers of a complete upsetting of the established poltical and industrial order. Labor leaders know that if with such a revolution there should come a disruption of production, a consequence which to practical unionists seems not at all unlikely, the hard-won labor standards would be just as much a thing of the past as the employers' profits. Furthermore, organized labor is under no illusion as to the sort of resistance that would be offered by a capitalism fighting for its very existence. But to the way of thinking of the intellectual of the "determinist-revolutionary" category, the labor movement is only an instrument of the inevitable revolution. History has irrevocably determined that the proletariat must follow the revolutionary path. The capitalists might throw labor back, but that can be only temporary. In the end, the revolutionary proletariat must win against all obstacles. If, however, organized labor hesitates and turns from the revolutionary course, the Simon-pure Marxian will admit only one conclusion: labor has fallen under a treacherous or cowardly leadership. To remove that corrupt and corrupting leadership, by whatever expedient means lie at hand, then becomes the revolutionist's first and foremost duty. If that means an inevitable factional fight within the organization, which may threaten its very existence, the risk is still worth taking. If the revolution and the ensuing dictatorship mean a more or less prolonged period of industrial disorganization fraught with fatal dangers in the case of an industrialized country depending upon exports for its food supply, the risk still remains worth taking.

This ruthless philosophy, ruthless not only towards the "bourgeoisie," but to the labor movement and to the laboring people as well, was originally the product of the "will to revolution" of the intellectual who, like the prophet of old, has heard the voice of God and has dedicated his life to making God's will prevail on earth—except that the "God" of the "determinist-revolutionary" intellectual is not a personal God but the "law" of the development of society. But, under certain circumstances, the non-intellectual, the manualist, may be made to worship the same God, and with the same fervor. Given a Marxian training and a pronounced susceptibility to the lure of Messianism, especially when unchecked by a sense of personal responsibility for keeping one's trade union organization intact, many a young workingman or workingwoman will display the selfsame mentality. Moreover, in numerous cases, that mentality may even become permanent, showing how an early and decisive commitment to a "foreign" philosophy, reinforced no doubt by a suitable temperament, may block the growth of an "organic" labor outlook.

---

[1]This article was reprinted as Chapter XIV in his *Labor and Administration* (Macmillan, 1913).

[2]Trade unionists and intellectuals use alike the term "labor," which has an abstract connotation. But, to the trade unionists, "labor" means nothing more abstract or mystical than the millions of concrete human beings with their concrete wants and aspirations. And it is in this sense that the author uses it. . . .

# 23
## Insight and Illusion in Perlman's Theory of the Labor Movement
### CHARLES A. GULICK AND MELVIN K. BERS                      1953

### Structure of the Perlman System

We understand the essential question to which Perlman sought to provide an answer to be: Why is the labor movement in a given country what it is? Or, put in a more "historical" way, what have been the crucial influences or factors shaping the development and form of labor movements? Perlman reveals his approach in his Preface, where he reports that during the course of his researches,

> . . . three factors emerged as basic in any modern labor situation: first, the resistance power of capitalism, determined by its own historical development; second, the degree of dominance over the labor movements by the intellectual's "mentality," which regularly underestimates capitalism's resistance power and overestimates labor's will to radical change; and, third, the degree of maturity of a trade union "mentality."[1]

These "factors" are amplified in the chapter entitled "Toward a Theory of the Labor Movement." In succeeding chapters, special attention is given to an evaluation of each of them, as the histories of the labor movements in Russia, Great Britain, Germany, and the United States are reviewed. The broad implication of the approach is that different values attributable to the three factors account for the different observed results in the countries under examination. In Russia, for example, Perlman found: (a) the resistance power of capitalism at a low level, (b) a labor movement dominated by the intellectualist "mentality," (c) a low degree of "maturity" of the trade union "mentality." Result: overthrow of the system and establishment of a society framed in terms of the intellectualist mentality. In the United States he found: (a) a very high resistance power of capitalism, (b) a small and diminishing intellectualist influence upon the labor movement, (c) a completely "mature" trade union "mentality." Result: a stable capitalism and a stable job-conscious trade unionism.

■   ■   ■

### Interdependence of Three Factors

With these general comments behind us, it is possible to sketch in the basic criticism of Perlman's three-factor system. As he presents them, the factors appear to be independent forces, each contributing an influence upon the developing labor movement; but on closer analysis they are seen to be inextricably interrelated and are, in fact, partly identities by definition. This is illustrated as follows:

1. The "resistance power of capitalism" is enhanced when the greater part of society (especially the greater part of the manualists and their leaders) accepts fundamental capitalist principles, as for example, the principle of private property, the principle of private initiative in economic affairs, and the principle that capitalists "alone . . . know how to operate" modern economies. But the very acceptance of these principles is a rejection of the "intellectualist" position, which is characteristically anti-capitalist. To the

extent, therefore, that such principles are accepted by the labor movement, it is not domi-nated by the intellectualist mentality. Thus, Perlman's first factor is in large measure defined in terms of his second, and vice versa.

2. When the so-called trade union mentality is fully matured, job-consciousness is the rock upon which labor action is based. But making job-consciousness the focus of attention means ipso facto the rejection of class consciousness as the prime basis for action. Further, it is said to imply a limited sphere for political activity. But to state that the likelihood of a concerted political effort by the working class to secure basic social changes is very small is merely to describe one aspect of a well-entrenched capitalism. Thus, Perlman's first factor and his third factor are in part defined in terms of each other.

3. The second and third factors are merely opposite sides of the same coin. This is clear from the very way in which they are stated. The second factor is the degree of intel-lectualist domination of the labor movement. The third factor is the degree of maturity of trade union mentality. Both are in terms of degree of domination of the labor move-ment, and since they are revealed to be polar opposites they are "independent" factors precisely in the same sense in which "two factors" may be said to determine a man's height, namely, his tallness and his shortness. When the trade union mentality is fully "matured," the degree to which the intellectualist mentality guides the actions of work-ers is, *by definition*, nil. Where the intellectualist mentality dominates, the trade union mentality has not "matured." Reference is being made to an objective condition which can be described in terms of either the second or the third factor.

4. The factors are not independent of each other even apart from definition. One element of the resistance power of capitalism as described by Perlman is the actual power wielded by the capitalist class and its will to use it in its own interest. When both the power and the will are very strong, it follows that efforts of the working class (or seg-ments thereof) to enlarge its position in society will encounter obstacles and frictions at every turn. Faced with this sort of resistance, it is less than surprising that laborers see something of a "limited-opportunity" world. Nor is it surprising that the path of least resistance—job-conscious unionism—should appear to be the most feasible alternative to large segments of the wage-earning class. Moreover, if the prevailing capitalism should be operating so successfully that at the same time it yielded a rising level of income, shorter hours of work, and a rising social and political status for most members of the working class, it is not difficult to see how a program designed to sweep away the exist-ing order might lack a mass following. Depending upon one's definition and evaluation of the "resistance power of capitalism," there are certain specific implications for the other two "factors."

The relationships exposed above illustrate two important properties of Perlman's formulation. The first is that his "factors" are so *defined* that attributing a value or strength to any one of them immediately implies, and may define, a value for the other two. The three-factor schema therefore represents a unity in a very fundamental sense.

The second is that confusions are inherent because of the indiscriminate merger of an elaborate system of purely descriptive and/or definitional categories with certain explanatory principles and the designation of the resultant mixture as a "theory" of the labor movement. It is necessary to point out that the three-factor schema taken as a whole does not constitute a theory of the labor movement in any meaningful sense, although it appears to pass as one. This is true because the schema is essentially a defini-tional system which represents, at best, an intricate restatement of the questions to which it apparently addresses itself.

## The Basic Questions

What are these questions? The first, and most important, is the basic attitude (as expressed in the program which it follows) of the labor movement toward capitalism as a system. It is with respect to this question that Perlman took issue with Marxist and other theorists; it is upon this question that his attention is clearly focused in the definition of his "factors." Marxist theorists had propounded an answer which designated the labor movement as the primary force for social change. The change anticipated was the overthrow of capitalism by an alienated working class. In the Perlman *terminology*, the Marxists predicted a labor movement dominated by the "intellectual's mentality." Perlman, in challenging the adequacy of the Marxian analysis, cites, on the other hand, a working class which is "content to leave the employer in the unchallenged possession of his property and business." The prediction implicit in the Perlman theory and expressed in the Perlman *terminology* is that of a labor movement dominated by the "trade union mentality."

As was pointed out previously and as we have just indicated again, the two "factors" which figure here represent two alternative programs which labor movements *could* adopt. Which of the two outcomes will be realized is, of course, one issue on which Perlman and his rival theorists differ. It is a little weird, therefore, to find *both outcomes* incorporated as "factors" in a "theory" presumably endeavoring to explain why one of the outcomes is to be anticipated.

Let us turn briefly to a second question. Marxists and Perlman also differ in their estimate of the stability of capitalism as a system. Marxists "saw" its weakness and decline. Perlman, writing in 1928, cited its great strength and resilience. The issue, it would seem to us, was clear-cut. It is again somewhat weird, therefore, to find the whole controversy incorporated as a "factor" (the "resistance power of capitalism") in the Perlman "theory." It is, after all, that very resistance power which was at issue.

Some of the confusion is eliminated, however, when it is recognized that the three-factor schema is primarily a system of definitions and not a theory. It is the purely terminological property of such a system that it cannot be "wrong." This explains why Perlman is always able to apply his system of descriptive categories in a way to give the impression that his "theory" is correct. Any "labor situation" of the type in which Perlman was interested can be described in terms of it. Thus, in describing developments in Russia leading up to the 1917 revolution, he could say that the "resistance power of capitalism" turned out to be weak; whereas, in describing the United States, it was possible to say that the "resistance power of capitalism" turned out to be strong. Similarly, he could refer to the Russian labor movement as dominated by the "intellectual's mentality" and to the American labor movement as dominated by the "trade union mentality." It could also have been said that in Russia the trade union mentality did not "mature," and that in America the labor movement "freed itself" of the domination of intellectuals. One might even go so far as to say that in Russia and in pre-AFL America, manualists had been hypnotized, in some sense, by "intellectuals."

But all of this is mere description. A theory of the labor movement must answer *why* all this occurred. It should explain, for example, *why* manualists are attracted to "intellectualist" programs in some instances and *why* they are indifferent to them in others. The three-factor schema does not offer such an explanation.

## Scarcity Consciousness

Leaving behind the three-factor schema, which does not constitute a theory, we turn now to a consideration of the unique ingredient of the Perlman system which does.

The basic proposition is that the most compelling force operating upon the development of labor movements is the "psychology" of the laboring man himself, and that given certain preconditions, this "psychology" will express itself in the type of movement already described as dominated by a "trade union mentality." The general claim is that previous theorists, notably Marxists and the Webbs, have erred because they failed to grasp the nature of this "psychology," and a considerable portion of the *Theory* is devoted to an exposition of its principal qualities. In this section, therefore, we shall examine closely the case for the unique "psychology"—characterizable as "scarcity consciousness"—in connection with the consequences which are said to flow from it.

The scarcity of which manualists are said to be conscious refers to economic opportunity. Important as this concept of economic opportunity is in Perlman's system, his definition, and even more his usage, of it are elusive. There appear to be three distinct types of opportunity, although Perlman does not trouble to draw precise distinction among them. The first type may be designated as "mass-worker" opportunity. It is with this type that the average wage earner, the rank-and-file manualist, is associated. This is what Perlman has in mind when he refers to "job opportunity." The second type may be called "bright-worker" opportunity and refers to the possibilities of advancement and improvement open to individuals who are somewhat above the average in "ability and ambition," although not blessed with the spark of entrepreneurial genius or the ownership of much property or wealth. Perlman speaks of opportunities to get ahead by selling "on the commission basis," by entering (very) small business, by climbing into "minor supervisory positions in the large manufacturing establishments," or by migrating from "older to newer and less developed sections."[2] The third type may be called "entrepreneurial" or "producer" opportunity. It refers to the availability of resources and markets and the freedom to link them together. It refers also to land and other assets and the possibility of attaining ownership of them.

These distinctions having been made, it is possible now to pass to a consideration of the "scarcity consciousness of the manualist" which, according to Perlman, "is a product of two main causes, one lying in himself and the other outside." The "inside" cause, corresponding to the manualist's "psychic self-appraisal," is described as follows:

> The typical manualist is aware of his lack of native capacity for availing himself of economic opportunities as they lie amidst the complex and ever shifting situations of modern business. He knows himself neither for a born taker of risks nor for the possessor of a sufficiently agile mind ever to feel at home in the midst of the uncertain game of competitive business.[3]

Two important points are to be noted in this formulation. The first is that it refers exclusively to entrepreneurial or producer opportunity. The second is that the manualist's lack of native ability is *in itself* the creator of scarcity. For it would make little difference whether producer opportunity were abundant or limited in the real world. If it were abundant, the manualist's self-recognized impotence in the face of it contrives to prevent him from exploiting it. He would not know what to do with this welter of resources and potential markets. The "typical manualist," thus shut off from producer opportunity and presumably also from "bright-worker" opportunity (we take this to be implicit in "typical," especially in view of Perlman's comment that the "great mass of the wage earners . . . will die wage earners"),[4] finds himself limited to job opportunity over which he and his fellows seek to impose a control. The control instrument is, of course, the trade union.

The second source of "scarcity consciousness," designated by Perlman as the "outside" cause and evidently representing the conclusions drawn from a "simple survey of accessible economic opportunity," is the manualist's

> ... conviction that for him the world has been rendered one of scarcity by an institutional order of things, which purposely reserved the best opportunities for landlords, capitalists, and other privileged groups. It may also be, of course, that the manual worker will ascribe such scarcity to natural rather than to institutional causes, say, to a shortage of land brought on by increase of population, or, like mediaeval merchants and master workmen, to the small number of customers and the meagre purchasing power of these. At all events, whether he thought the cause of the apparent limitations to the institutional or natural, a scarcity consciousness has always been typical of the manual worker, in direct contrast to the consciousness of an abundance of opportunity, which dominates the self-confident business man.[5]

This passage, too, refers exclusively to "producer" opportunity, but an additional reason for its "scarcity" is adduced. This time it is attributed to "natural" causes (such as might yield a shortage of land), or to the "institutional order of things" which manualists learn from experience has operated to reserve producer opportunity for others. Barred from producer opportunity for a second reason, manualists are, by another route, led to control of "job opportunity" and hence the creation of a union.

Implicit in all this, of course, is a scarcity of job opportunity. Otherwise there would appear to be little need for unions. A scarcity of job opportunity is appropriately introduced—"the number of jobs available [is] almost always fewer than the number of job seekers"[6]—and the system is complete.

### Function of a Labor Theory

It should be noticed that what has been provided by this excursion into manualist "scarcity consciousness" is merely a rationale for unionism per se. The large question to which Perlman addressed himself (and to which anyone professing to offer a "theory of the labor movement" must address himself) remains unanswered. Why is the labor movement in a given country what it is? For the United States, this means that what has to be explained is the appearance and persistence of job-conscious unionism as *the* labor movement. That American unions are job conscious is not a controversial matter. That manualists are conscious of a scarcity of economic opportunity (of any or all types) and that they have been impelled to seize and control the distribution of opportunity available to them—this, too, is not a controversial matter. No one denies these facts. And nothing is "proved" by incessant reference to them. What a *theory* has to explain is why the nature of the American labor movement involves: (1) the renunciation of any broad program of social reorganization designed to improve the status and economic condition of the group involved; (2) the renunciation of political activity in a predominantly "labor" party as a major weapon for the institution of such a program or, at least, for economic betterment of the group involved; and (3), possibly only a corollary of the first item in this series, apparent contentment with the existing framework of economic institutions and relationships, which reserves to another group ("businessmen") the privilege of making many of the crucial decisions for the community as a whole in the vital spheres of output and employment.

### Manualist Psychology

Now it is somewhere in the "psychology of the laboring man" that Perlman claims to find support for this type of labor movement. For the manualist "psychology" (usually the *foundation of*, but frequently *synonymous with*, manualist "mentality" or "ideology" in the Perlman terminology) is supposed to yield the "mature" trade unionism which is precisely this type of labor movement. We are obliged to probe further into Perlman's notion of the manualist "psychology."

The first matter to be questioned is the origin of the notion itself. What is it that convinced Perlman that the manualist "psychology" (or "mentality" or "ideology") really is what he describes it to be? His answer is that the "psychology" is to be *deduced* from the system of shop rules (and the like) of labor's own making.

> Labor's own "home grown" ideology is disclosed only through a study of the "working rules" of labor's own "institutions."[7]

> A theory of the labor movement should include a theory of the psychology of the laboring man. The writing of socialists, syndicalists, anarchists, communists, and "welfare" capitalists abound in embroideries on the theme of "what labor wants" or "what labor aspires to." But the safest method is to go to the organizations of labor's own making, shaped and managed by leaders arisen from labor's own ranks, and to attempt to discover "what's really on labor's mind" by using as material the "working rules," customs and practices of these organizations.[8]

Immediately the question arises: Is it possible to deduce from labor's "working rules" what Perlman has in fact deduced? Do imposition of collective ownership over limited job opportunities and the disposition of these jobs in accordance with certain traditionally derived equity principles prove or imply anything about psychic predilections for, or antipathy to, capitalism as a system? Do monopoly and subsequent distribution of job opportunity prove or imply anything about manualist attitudes respecting any particular type or extent of political activity?

Undoubtedly what has greatly impressed Perlman is American labor's preoccupation with control over jobs and wage rates to the exclusion of other types of activity, e.g., formation of a labor party, agitation for basic reforms of the social and economic system, and so on. But if this is the main evidence for the existence of a manualist "psychology" of the kind described by Perlman, the "theory of the psychology of the working man" boils down to a piece of circular reasoning. The "psychology" is inferred from the observed fact of almost exclusive preoccupation with control of job opportunities and the renunciation of other types of activity. On the other hand, the "psychology" is in turn defined as that which is typically preoccupied with "job control" to the exclusion of other types of activity. This kind of logic chases its tail forever. Of course, it does not follow from this that a "psychology" so deduced is necessarily false. But unless a great deal of *positive* evidence is supplied, there is little reason to believe it to be correct. Any number of other deductions are equally possible.

### Economic Opportunity

As noted above, an adequate theory of the American labor movement must explain why it is that broad schemes of social reorganization have been rejected in favor of a narrowly oriented job-conscious unionism. Perlman's explanation runs largely in terms of the alleged "psychology of the laboring man." In this a serious logical inconsistency is involved. One might wonder, for example, why it is that unionists halt at monopoly of "job opportunity." Why is it that the whole amount of the community's economic opportunity does not present itself to them as suitable for control? This problem is explicitly recognized by Perlman, but his answer is painfully lame.

Perhaps in abstract reasoning, the wage earner might be expected to envisage the whole of the economic organization of society as the ultimate source of his job opportunity; and therefore wish for a complete "workers' control" of industry. Actually, however, the typical wage earner, when he can express himself in and through his trade union free of domination by intellectuals, who are never too bashful to do his thinking for him, seldom dreams of shouldering the risks of management. Ordinarily he traces the origin of his opportunity not much farther back than the point where it materializes in jobs, and will grasp and support only such union policies as will enable or force the employers to offer more jobs, equally available to all fellow craftsmen, and upon improved terms.[9]

A footnote to the excerpt quoted makes it clear that the term "risks of management" refers to the risk of loss of privately invested capital. The assertion that the manualist "seldom dreams" of shouldering these risks may be seen to be an expansion of the idea expressed in Perlman's statement of the "inside" source of "scarcity consciousness"; namely, that manualists are aware of a lack of entrepreneurial ability. Assuming for the moment that they are, it may be asked what the risks of management have to do with the case. The question to be answered is why manualists have not supported a program of socialism and the answer which has been given is that they do not see themselves as efficient capitalists. This is a roaring *non sequitur*. There is no problem of risk in this sense in a socialist system.

If another kind of risk is envisioned, the statement is equally questionable. Perhaps it may be suggested that risk of failure to perform efficiently in a managerial or administrative capacity is implied. But this presents no problem. The average trade unionist "seldom dreams" of managing his own union; yet this does not prevent him from supporting it. He elects someone with the requisite skills to do the managing.

The mere fact that there have been millions of manualist Socialists, manualist anarchists, manualist Communists, manualist syndicalists, and, for that matter, manualist "free homesteaders" throughout the Western world should be sufficient to call into question Perlman's rather glib treatment of this important issue. If American manualists of recent times have been, in the main, supporters of "free enterprise," the reasons are more fruitfully sought in the modern American environment than in their manualism per se. For there is nothing in the concept of "scarcity consciousness" as developed by Perlman which throws any light on this subject.

The weakness of Perlman's case for the particular worker "psychology" he describes is sharply revealed in his distinction between manualist "psychology" and businessman "psychology." Whereas "scarcity consciousness" and (hence) "pessimism" are said to characterize the former,

The business man, on the contrary, is an eternal optimist. To him the world is brimful of opportunities that are only waiting to be made his own.[10]

Perlman's businessman appears to be the personification of Sombart's spirit of enterprise. We have presented to us the portrait of the born taker of risks, the purely rapacious entrepreneur, the man with unlimited horizons, the maximizing buccaneer with the steely eyes—this is the romantic vision evoked by the writings of Sombart and Perlman.

At the other pole stand the manualists, whose group psychology is representative of the mediaeval spirit. There is the insistence on stability, the appeal to equalitarianism (within the group), the emphasis upon security of livelihood, the resistance to radical change—all, according to Perlman, growing out of a fundamentally pessimistic appraisal of available economic opportunity. The trade union "mentality" is said to be the gild "mentality" in modern guise.

We submit that neither of these conceptualizations adequately reflects the real world phenomena to which they refer. They are rather ideal types, useful for some purposes perhaps, but hardly valid as accurate descriptions of either businessman or manualist psychology. It may be asked, for example, what basic difference from the viewpoint of "opportunity" appraisal can be read from pools, gentlemen's agreements, Gary dinners, and a basing point price system on the one hand, and efforts to establish a union shop in the steel industry on the other? Both envision a limited opportunity and both represent attempts to monopolize it or to control its distribution. What essential difference lies between "Checking the race for employment opportunity," and ". . . a business men's group [which] has been led, through fear of cutthroat competition and price wars, to resort directly or indirectly, to the rationing of market opportunity among its members . . ."? In the actions and motives involved there appears to be little difference. Yet, Perlman feels there is one. His dictum is that such collusive activity when undertaken by businessmen ". . . has always sprung from the 'head,' but never spontaneously nor from the 'heart'. . . ."[11] But this flows directly from his having *defined* the businessman's "heart" in a way that excludes a propensity for collusion or a yearning for stability. The "heart" defined in this way is nothing more than the "spirit of enterprise"—that idealization which was postulated at the beginning of the argument.

∎ ∎ ∎

The point which we are attempting to establish here (at the cost perhaps of somewhat cavalier treatment of a complex process in the development of capitalism) is that the essential "psychologies" of wage earner and businessman cannot be split into polar opposites. Each appears to strive for economic or social advancement or self-betterment, and each employs the methods which give promise of achieving this end. . . .

We hope by the foregoing to have indicated that the "scarcity consciousness" of the "manualists," which leads them to impose a collective control over "opportunity" accessible to the group, is only a species of a far more general phenomenon. The so-called "psychology" which Perlman ascribes to "peasants in Russia, modern wage earners, or medieval master workmen"; and later to "farmers, small manufacturers, and shop-keepers"; and, finally, to "all scarcity groups throughout history"[12] appears to express itself in activities not essentially different from those of bankers, industrialists, and "capitalists" of every type.

It is in the term "scarcity group" that the key to Perlman's confusion lies. For what he describes as a "scarcity group" is nothing more than a group which recognizes a community of interest with respect to limited available means to achieve common ends. There is no *essential* difference between the process Perlman describes for his manualists and the process by which residents in a cooperatively administered apartment house impose the rule that no radios shall be left on after midnight. What is monopolized here is "sleep opportunity." This "shop rule" recognizes limitations of space and time in the face of given biological needs and imposes a common mode of action on all participants. It would be interesting to make a collection of such apartment house rules. From a study of them it might be possible to deduce a "mentality" or "psychology," the essential nature of which would indicate beyond question that the residents, being so thoroughly occupied in "controlling" their limited "opportunity," are psychically committed to (a) living in apartment houses and (b) endorsement of the prevailing distribution of real-estate ownership.

## Political Activity

Further doubt—extremely strong doubt—is cast upon Perlman's position by the vaguely defined role attributed to political activity in "mature" trade unionism. Logical consistency demands that relegation of political action to a secondary or tertiary role in manualist efforts to improve their positions be somehow traceable to the basic "psychology" of the laboring man. Yet, on this score, Perlman provides no causal link. There is nothing in his entire discussion of "scarcity consciousness"—the key to worker psychology—which specifies a definite role for political action, either large or small.

A final criticism of Perlman's attempt to attribute to manualists some deep-lying and unique "psychology" (and thus to establish this "psychology" as an independent force influencing labor movement development) rests upon his treatment of the shift in the orientation of American labor in the period marked by the decline of the Knights of Labor and the rise of the AFL. The transition period is characteristically described by Perlman as an "evolution of the psychology of the American wage earner,"[13] and the completed process is described as the belated "fruition" of job-and-wage conscious unionism. If it be asked why the "psychology" which Perlman says has "always been typical of the manual worker"[14] was not always typical of the American manualist, the only reply which can be made (and the one which Perlman makes) is that the American case was an "exception to the general rule."[15] But an exception, rather than proving the rule, invariably calls the rule into question, and such an important "exception" as this bids fair to refute it. It does no good to refer to pre-AFL labor activity as some kind of perversion of the "true psychology of the working man," or to represent it as having been "mentally tied to a 'foreign' [non-manualist] philosophy."[16] For this is merely to affirm in different words that the American case *was* an exception.

## Economic Progress

The emergence of a "job-conscious" labor movement in the United States was a phenomenon almost unique in labor history. Yet without resorting to an analysis the essence of which is to divide Western humanity into spurious psychological categories it is possible to find an explanation of it.

There is in the American experience one colossal datum which has stood above all the rest. It has been the fact of a tremendously growing level of material well-being yielded by the system as a whole. The truth is that whether resulting from the "free air" of competitive enterprise, or from native "know-how," or from the context of fabulously rich resources in which the whole system has been immersed, the American wage earner has experienced over a seventy-five year period a rate of economic betterment which has made him labor aristocrat of the world. America is rich, and from this fact flows much of the strength of the going system, for it has enabled: (a) widespread holding of wealth, thus reinforcing general sentiment supporting the principle of private property; (b) high living standards—an objective factor incuding strong passive support of the system as a whole; or, what amounts to the same thing, apathetic response to programs of broad-scale change; as a corollary of these, but most important for our purposes, (c) it has enabled a job-conscious labor movement to demonstrate tangible successes, thus discouraging the pursuit of alternative types of labor activity designed to achieve the same or more comprehensive goals. The essential point here is that "job-consciousness" must be seen as a *means*, and that only when a job-conscious labor movement is associated with substantial progress toward the attainment of the prevailing income and status goals of most of its constituents does it have an effective claim on their allegiance. In a very general way, this has been the experience in the United States.

Of course, attention to the level of economic well-being or the rate of its growth cannot constitute the whole of a theory which aims to explain why the labor movement in a particular country is what it is or to predict what it is likely to become. It represents a keystone, however, and it is interesting to note the degree to which the three presumably independent factors mentioned by Perlman as "basic characteristics of the American community" rest upon it. . . .

## Class Consciousness

Greater attention must be directed to the "lack of a class consciousness among American labor" which is, in fact, a crucial factor. European labor movements, such as those of Germany and Austria, drew much of their strength from a pervasive class consciousness, and the direction almost invariably taken by these movements—broad programs of social reform implemented by strong political party structures—is roughly the opposite of that taken by the "mature" manualist organizations of Perlman's description. It is revealing that Perlman's "mature" labor activity—"job-conscious unionism"— growing out of a "psychology" said to be characteristic of *all* manual groups, should have emerged from a context in which one of the "basic characteristics" is a *unique* lack of class consciousness among the laboring group. The essential absence in the United States of class consciousness, which is, after all, a powerful organizing and mobilizing force, helps to explain the failure of a broadly oriented labor movement to emerge. And it should be observed that this factor, too, is not independent of what we have cited as the colossal datum in the American experience.

■    ■    ■

## Conclusions

It is in terms such as the foregoing that an explanation of the appearance and persistence of a job-conscious labor movement in the United States has to be undertaken. Analysts attached to Perlman's "theory of the psychology of the laboring man," if they could bring themselves to reject it, might console themselves with the thought that sufficient objective factors exist to explain what has to be explained.

Now it follows from this type of analysis that there is little that is intrinsically unalterable in the present basic orientation of American labor. A shift in underlying conditions could inspire important changes in labor's policy. Another severe depression, another situation of mass unemployment, or the appearance of other oppressive conditions could give rise to pressures for a labor program departing significantly from the present one. It would be folly to predict an indefinite extension of job-conscious unionism as "the" labor movement in this country. Yet such a prophecy appears to flow directly from Perlman's theory of the "psychology" of the laboring man.

We may summarize our analysis of the Perlman contribution in this way. The three-factor schema directs attention to important questions but does not provide the explanatory principles required of a theory. The assertions with respect to the "psychology" of the laboring man do constitute a theory, but it is a fallacious one. Even if taken at its face value, the so-called "psychology" provides only a rationale for unionism; under no circumstances does it actually explain what it is called upon to explain in the *Theory*.

But it can not be taken at its face value, and as has been demonstrated, it falls apart completely under close scrutiny.

If we abandon the attempt to make something of the highly complicated formulation presented by Perlman, and fall back upon a "common sense" interpretation, the "psychology" reduces merely to a desire on the part of workingmen to improve their conditions of labor and their standard of living, *plus* a determination to use whatever means are at their disposal to achieve it. The union is such a means. But a political party, cooperative societies, and other traditional instrumentalities or agencies are also such means. To adopt this procedure, therefore, is to junk the "theory," for there is not enough in it to provide answers to the questions which have to be answered by a theory of the labor-movement, and it certainly is not productive of the specific kind of answer which Perlman wanted to give.

It is possible that all Perlman wished to do was to debunk the idea that laborers are in some sense *by nature* embryonic Socialists. If this was his purpose, he went to the other extreme by attempting to show that they are *by nature* unionists and nothing but unionists. Now the facts are that they are sometimes unionists, sometimes Socialists, sometimes both, and sometimes neither. An adequate theory has to explain the facts.

■   ■   ■

Our chief complaint must be lodged against the most ardent followers of Perlman who, having absorbed without evident discomfiture the "theory of the psychology of the laboring man" and all the *non sequiturs* committed in its name, the dubious terminology, the argument by definition, and the crucifixion of the "intellectual," continue to endorse, nay, to laud a "theory" which is patently contradicted by almost every labor movement outside the United States. Is it too much to charge that such steadfast allegiance to a logically deficient and empirically discredited theory "rests on a species of faith"? We think not.

---

[1] Selig Perlman, *A Theory of the Labor Movement* (New York: Macmillan, 1928), p. x.
[2] *Ibid.*, pp. 165–166.
[3] *Ibid.*, p. 239.
[4] *Ibid.*, p. 165.
[5] *Ibid.*, pp. 239–240.
[6] *Ibid.*, p. 241.
[7] *Ibid.*, p. 6. Just below the sentence quoted, Perlman proceeds to base the "ideology" on the "psychology" of "consciousness of scarcity of opportunity."
[8] *Ibid.*, p. 237.
[9] *Ibid.*, pp. 246–247.
[10] *Ibid.*, p. 239.
[11] *Ibid.*, pp. 243, 244.
[12] *Ibid.*, pp. 6, 239, 304.
[13] *Ibid.*, p. 198.
[14] *Ibid.*, p. 240.
[15] *Ibid.*, n. 2.
[16] *Ibid.*, p. 182.

# FOUR

**The Labor Movement as an Agent of Industrial Reform**

# Introduction

Sidney and Beatrice Webb were leading supporters of British industrial reform and influential members of the Fabian Society, a socialist group which advocated an evolutionary path to socialism. They provided the intellectual and theoretical underpinnings to British social welfare organization and developed an understanding of the development of the British labor movement. Their study was based on a careful and systematic analysis of British industrial society and trade unions. The pioneer work of the Webbs in interpreting the labor movement has been a major influence on other theorists up to the present time. Their methodology and general formulations had a significant effect on the work of John R. Commons and the Wisconsin school of labor history. In concert with Karl Marx and John R. Commons, they viewed the rise of labor unions as the by-product of the emergence of a working class whose functions were separate and distinct from that of the capitalist.

While the Webbs accepted the Marxian concept of a class struggle, they disagreed with Marx that the conflict could only be resolved by force or with the elimination of one of the classes. Unlike Marx, but like Commons and Selig Perlman, the Webbs held that labor unions were essentially economic institutions. They did not interpret labor organization in moral, psychological, and revolutionary terms. Their main objective, they wrote, was to maintain and improve the conditions of life of wage earners. This entailed not only material betterment and job security but also the extension of democratic principles to the workplace, and ultimately throughout British industrial society.

Labor unions, according to the Webbs, evolved along evolutionary lines. Influenced by the prevailing political, economic, and cultural norms in each social epoch, labor organizations developed an underlying theme or thrust, labeled a *doctrine,* which in turn determined their immediate goals, termed *devices,* and the methods utilized to achieve their aims. In the eighteenth century, for example, unionists clung to the belief that workers had a legal right or vested interest in a trade, a sole and exclusive claim to a particular job. Workers, therefore, had a natural right to protect their property by any lawful means. To safeguard their members' "right to a trade," unions attempted to control the labor market by restricting the number of entrants into the trade. This, however, had the distinct disadvantage of hindering the selection of the most capable manual workers and thus promoted industrial inefficiency. The union had to seek other means to attract hesitating recruits and to bind its members more closely to the union. The method devised was one of mutual insurance. Members were offered protection against personal affliction such as sickness, accident, and old age on the one hand, and the stoppage of income through unemployment, strikes, or lockouts on the other. These benefits were a poignant reminder to the members of the benefits of trade union membership.

With the advent of capitalism and a market economy in the nineteenth century, the doctrine of supply and demand occupied a dominant place in the thinking of most trade union leaders. Laborers were looked upon as any other commodity and, like the sellers of goods, claimed the best they could extract from buyers. The conditions of employment corresponded to the strength of the parties in the marketplace. To protect the worker from being seriously disadvantaged, unions employed the device of the common rule—the establishment of standard rates of wages and conditions of employment for wage earners in a particular trade or industry. The method employed to achieve this goal was collective bargaining. However, if the "freedom to contract" between capitalists and wage earners ran counter to the interests of the majority, then some form of community intervention in the process was considered necessary.

With the coming of the twentieth century, public opinion began to question the belief that working and living conditions should be determined by the relative strategic position of the parties at the bargaining table. In the first place, it was unjust to those who lacked the strength to extract a fair price for their labor; second, it was in the interest of the community to see that all workers secured those conditions necessary to their function in society. Trade unionists now began to veer toward the doctrine of a living wage, which held that workers ought to earn wages sufficient to acquire the basic necessities of life and that no worker should be reduced to a condition inconsistent with industrial efficiency and civic responsibility. This goal could be met by establishing a national minimum which would guarantee to each citizen a minimum level of existence. A resort to the law seemed the only way to bring such minimums into effect and to achieve a degree of permanence and universality. Organized labor, therefore, had to shift its attention to the legislative halls to ensure passage of measures which would bring the idea of a national minimum into reality.

The Webbs did not view trade unions as temporary organizations to be dissolved when capitalism is terminated and a socialist society instituted. "Trade unionism," they insisted, "is not merely an incident of the present phase of capitalist industry, but has a permanent function to fulfill in the democratic state." Whether capitalist society was dominated by immense trusts or small business enterprises or by what the Webbs expected—government agencies and administrators—unions were necessary to protect workers from social oppression and the community from industrial parasitism. Trade unions, they maintained, were an essential force for democracy. As public control of industry expanded, the functions of trade unions would also undergo change. The Webbs saw the present adversarial role of trade unions gradually replaced by institutional concern with the professional standards and education of its members. Unions, in other words, would eventually assume the character of professional associations.

# 24
## *The Origins of Trade Unionism*
SIDNEY AND BEATRICE WEBB                                                     1894

A Trade Union, as we understand the term, is a continuous association of wage-earners for the purpose of maintaining or improving the conditions of their working lives. This form of association has, as we shall see, existed in England for over two centuries, and cannot be supposed to have sprung at once fully developed into existence. . . .

■   ■   ■

The explanation of the tardy growth of stable independent combination among hired journeymen is, we believe, to be found in the prospects of economic advancement which the skilled handicraftsman still possessed. We do not wish to suggest the existence of any Golden Age in which each skilled workman was his own master, and the wage system was unknown. The earliest records of English town history imply the presence of *hired* journeymen who were not always contented with their wages. But the apprenticed journeyman in the skilled handicrafts belonged, until comparatively modern times, to the same social grade as his employer, and was indeed usually the son of a master in the same or an analogous trade. So long as industry was carried on mainly by small masters, each employing but one or two journeymen, the period of any energetic man's service as a hired wage-earner cannot normally have exceeded a few years, and the industrious apprentice might reasonably hope, if not always to marry his master's daughter, at any rate to set up in business for himself. Any incipient organization would always be losing its oldest and most capable members, and would of necessity be confined, like the Coventry journeymen's Gild of St. George, to "the young people," or like the ephemeral fraternity of journeymen tailors of 1415–17, to "a race at once youthful and unstable," from whose inexperienced ranks it would be hard to draw a supply of good Trade Union leaders. We are therefore able to understand how it is that, whilst industrial oppression belongs to all ages, it is not until the changing conditions of industry had reduced to an infinitesimal chance the journeyman's prospect of becoming himself a master, that we find the passage of ephemeral combinations into permanent trade societies. . . .

■   ■   ■

If we examine the evidence of the rise of combinations in particular trades, we see the Trade Union springing, not from any particular institution, but from every opportunity for the meeting together of wage-earners of the same occupation. Adam Smith remarked that "people of the same trade seldom meet together, even for merriment and diversion, but the conversation ends in a conspiracy against the public, or in some contrivance to raise prices." And there is actual evidence of the rise of one of the oldest of the existing Trade Unions out of a gathering of the journeymen "to take a social pint of porter together." More often it is a tumultuous strike, out of which grows a permanent organisation. Elsewhere, as we shall see, the workers meet to petition the House of Commons, and reassemble from time to time to carry on their agitation for the enactment of some new regulation, or the enforcement of an existing law. In other instances we shall find the journeymen of a particular trade frequenting certain public-houses, at

Sidney and Beatrice Webb, *History of Trade Unionism* (New York: Longmans, Green & Co., 1894), pp. 1, 5–6, 21–25, 35, 37–39. Footnotes in the original have been eliminated.

which they hear of situations vacant, and the "house of call" becomes thus the nucleus of an organisation. Or we watch the journeymen in a particular trade declaring that "it has been an ancient custom in the kingdom of Great Britain for divers Artists to meet together and unite themselves in societies to promote Amity and true Christian Charity," and establishing a sick and funeral club, which invariably proceeds to discuss the rates of wages offered by the employers, and insensibly passes into a Trade Union with friendly benefits. And if the trade is one in which the journeymen frequently travel in search of work, we note the slow elaboration of systematic arrangements for the relief of these "tramps" by their fellow-workers in each town through which they pass, and the inevitable passage of this far-extending tramping society into a national Trade Union.

All these, however, are but opportunities for the meeting of journeymen of the same trade. They do not explain the establishment of continuous organisations of the wage-earners in the seventeenth and eighteenth rather than in the fifteenth or sixteenth centuries. The essential cause of the growth of durable associations of wage-earners must lie in something peculiar to the later centuries. This fundamental condition of Trade Unionism we discover in the economic revolution through which certain industries were passing. In all cases in which Trade Unions arose, the great bulk of the workers had ceased to be independent producers, themselves controlling the processes, and owning the materials and the product of their labour, and had passed into the condition of life-long wage-earners, possessing neither the instruments of production nor the commodity in its finished state. "From the moment that to establish a given business more capital is required than a journeyman can easily accumulate within a few years, gild mastership— the mastership of the masterpiece—becomes little more than a name. . . . Skill alone is valueless, and is soon compelled to hire itself out to capital. . . . Now begins the opposition of interest between employers and employed, now the latter begin to group themselves together; now rises the trade society." Or, to express this Industrial Revolution in more abstract terms, we may say, in the words of Dr. Ingram, that "the whole modern organisation of labour in its advanced forms rests on a fundamental fact which has spontaneously and increasingly developed itself—namely, the definite separation between the functions of the capitalist and the workman, or, in other words, between the direction of industrial operations and their execution in detail."

■   ■   ■

It is easy to understand how the massing together in factories of regiments of men all engaged in the same trade facilitated and promoted the formation of journeymen's trade societies. But with the cotton-spinners, as with the tailors, the rise of permanent trade combinations is to be ascribed, in a final analysis, to the definite separation between the functions of the capitalist *entrepreneur* and the manual worker—between, that is to say, the direction of industrial operations and their execution. It has, indeed, become a commonplace of modern Trade Unionism that only in those industries in which the worker has ceased to be concerned in the profits of buying and selling—that inseparable characteristic of the ownership and management of the means of production —can effective and stable trade organisations be established.

The positive proofs of this historical dependence of Trade Unionism upon the divorce of the worker from the ownership of the means of production are complemented by the absence of any permanent trade combinations in industries in which the divorce had not taken place. The degradation of the Standard of Life of the skilled manual worker on the break-up of the mediæval system occurred in all sorts of trades, whether the operative retained his ownership of the means of production or not, but Trade Unionism followed only where the change took the form of a divorce between capital and labour. . . .

■   ■   ■

We do not contend that the divorce supplies, in itself, a complete explanation of the origin of Trade Unions. At all times in the history of English industry there have existed large classes of workers as much debarred from becoming the directors of their own industry as the eighteenth-century tailor or woolcomber, or as the modern cotton-spinner or miner. Besides the semi-servile workers on the land or in the mines, it is certain that there were in the towns a considerable class of unskilled labourers, excluded, through lack of apprenticeship, from any participation in the gild. By the eighteenth century, at any rate, the numbers of this class must have been largely swollen, by the increased demand for common labour involved in the growth of the transport trade, the extensive building operations, etc. But it is not among the farm servants, miners, or general labourers, ill-paid and ill-treated as these often were, that the early Trade Unions arose. We do not even hear of ephemeral combinations among them, and only very occasionally of transient strikes. The formation of independent associations to resist the will of employers requires the possession of a certain degree of personal independence and strength of character. Thus we find the earliest Trade Unions arising among journeymen whose skill and Standard of Life had been for centuries encouraged and protected by legal or customary regulations as to apprenticeship, and by the limitation of their numbers which the high premiums and other conditions must have involved. It is often assumed that Trade Unionism arose as a protest against intolerable industrial oppression. This was not so. The first half of the eighteenth century was certainly not a period of exceptional distress. For fifty years from 1710 there was an almost constant succession of good harvests, the price of wheat remaining unusually low. The tailors of London and Westminster united, at the very beginning of the eighteenth century, not to resist any reduction of their customary earnings, but to wring from their employers better wages and shorter hours of labour. The few survivors of the hand woolcombers still cherish the tradition of the eighteenth century, when they styled themselves "gentlemen woolcombers," refused to drink with other operatives, and were strong enough, as we have seen, to give "laws to their masters." The very superior millwrights, whose exclusive trade clubs preceded any general organisation of the engineering trade, had for "their everyday garb" a "long frock coat and tall hat." And the curriers, hatters, woolstaplers, shipwrights, brushmakers, basketmakers, and calico-printers, who furnish prominent instances of eighteenth-century Trade Unionism, all earned relatively high wages, and long maintained a very effectual resistance to the encroachments of their employers.

It appears to us from these facts that Trade Unionism would have been a feature of English industry, even without the steam-engine and the factory system. Whether the association of superior workmen which arose in the early part of the century would, in such an event, ever have developed into a Trade Union Movement is another matter. The typical "trade club" of the town artisan of this time was an isolated "ring" of highly skilled journeymen, who were even more decisively marked off from the mass of the manual workers than from the small class of capitalist employers. The customary enforcement of the apprenticeship prescribed by the Elizabethan statutes, and the high premiums often exacted from parents not belonging to the trade, long maintained a virtual monopoly of the better-paid handicrafts in the hands of an almost hereditary caste of "tradesmen" in whose ranks the employers themselves had for the most part served their apprenticeship. Enjoying, as they did, this legal or customary protection, they found their trade clubs of use mainly for the provision of friendly benefits, and for "higgling" with their masters for better terms. We find little trace among such trade clubs of that sense of solidarity between the manual workers of different trades which afterwards became so marked a feature of the Trade Union Movement. Their occasional disputes with their employers resembled rather family differences than conflicts between distinct social classes. They exhibit more tendency to "stand in" with their masters against the community, or to back them against rivals or interlopers, than to join their fellow-workers of other trades in an attack upon the capitalist class. In short, we have industrial society still divided vertically trade by trade, instead of horizontally between employers and wage-earners. This latter cleavage it is which has transformed the Trade Unionism of petty groups of skilled workmen into the modern Trade Union Movement.

# 25
## *The Assumptions of Trade Unionism*
**SIDNEY AND BEATRICE WEBB** 1897

It is important to drag into full light the assumptions on which the Trade Union-ists habitually base both their belief in Trade Unionism itself and their justification of particular demands.

We have first the typical assumption of all reformers in all ages—the conviction that economic and social conditions can, by deliberate human intervention, be changed for the better. Trade Unionists have never even understood the view—still occasionally met with—that there is an absolutely predetermined "Wage-Fund," and that the average workman's share of the produce depends exclusively on the arithmetical proportion between the total of this fund and the number of wage-earners. They assume, on the con-trary, that the ratio in which the total product of industry is shared between the prop-erty-owners, the brain-workers, and the manual laboring class respectively, is a matter of human arrangement, and that it can be altered, effectively and permanently, to the advantage of one class or another, if the appropriate action be taken. . . .

For the improvement of the conditions of employment, whether in respect of wages, hours, health, safety, or comfort, the Trade Unionists have, with all their multi-plicity of Regulations, really only two expedients, which we term, respectively, the Device of the Common Rule, and the Device of Restriction of Numbers. The Regula-tions . . . are but different forms of one principle—the settlement, whether by Mutual Insurance, Collective Bargaining, or Legal Enactment, of minimum conditions of employment, by Common Rules applicable to whole bodies of workers. All these Regula-tions are based on the assumption that when, in the absence of any Common Rule, the conditions of employment are left to "free competition," this always means, in practice, that they are arrived at by Individual Bargaining between contracting parties of very unequal economic strength. Such a settlement, it is asserted, invariably tends, for the mass of the workers, towards the worst possible conditions of labor—ultimately, indeed, to the barest subsistence level—whilst even the exceptional few do not permanently gain as much as they otherwise could. We find accordingly that the Device of the Common Rule is a universal feature of Trade Unionism, and that the assumption on which it is based is held from one end of the Trade Union world to the other. The Device of Restriction of Numbers stands in a different position. . . . The Regulations embodying this device, once adopted as a matter of course, have successively been found inapplicable to the circumstances of modern industry. The assumption on which they are based—that better conditions can be obtained by limiting the number of competitors—would not be denied by any Trade Unionist, but it cannot be said to form an important part in the working creed of the Trade Union world. . . .

But these initial assumptions as to the need for Trade Unionism and the efficacy of its two devices do not, of themselves, account for the marked divergence between differ-ent Unions, alike in the general character of their policy and in the Regulations which they enforce. . . . The Trade Unionists . . . are influenced by three divergent conceptions of the principle upon which wages, hours, and other terms of the labor contract ought to be determined. These three assumptions, which we distinguish as the Doctrine of Vested

Sidney and Beatrice Webb, *Industrial Democracy* (New York: Longmans, Green & Co., 1897), pp. 559–563, 565–566, 570–575, 580–582, 584, 590–591, 595–597, 807–810, 812–830, 832–834, 838–842. Footnotes in the original have been eliminated.

Interests, the Doctrine of Supply and Demand, and the Doctrine of a Living Wage, give us the clue to the conflicting policies of the Trade Union world.

By the Doctrine of Vested Interests we mean the assumption that the wages and other conditions of employment hitherto enjoyed by any section of workmen ought under no circumstances to be interfered with for the worse. It was this doctrine . . . which inspired the long struggle, lasting down to about 1860, against the introduction of machinery, or any innovation in processes. It is this doctrine which to-day gives the bitterness to demarcation disputes, and lies at the back of all the Regulations dealing with the "right to a trade." It does more than anything else to keep alive the idea of "patrimony" and the practice of a lengthened period of apprenticeship, whilst it induces the workmen of particular trades to cling fondly to the expedient of limiting the numbers entering those trades, even after experience has proved such a limitation to be impracticable. But the Doctrine of Vested Interests extends much further than these particular Regulations. There is scarcely an industry in which it will not be found, on one occasion or another, inspiring the defence of the customary rates of wages or any threatened privilege. . . .

It is difficult for middle-class observers, accustomed to confine the doctrine of "vested interests" to "rights of property," to understand the fervor and conviction with which the skilled artisan holds this doctrine in its application to the "right to a trade." This intuitive conviction of natural right we ascribe, in great part, to the long and respectable history of the idea. Down to the middle of the eighteenth century it was undisputed. To the member of a Craft Gild or Incorporated Company it seemed as outrageous, and as contrary to natural justice, for an unlicensed interloper to take his trade as for a thief to steal his wares. Nor was this conception confined to any particular section of the community. To the economists and statesmen of the time the protection of the vested interests of each class of tradesmen appeared a no less fundamental axiom of civilised society than the protection of property in land or chattels. . . .

■　■　■

But this conception of a vested interest in a trade, though it derives sanction among an essentially conservative class from its long and venerable history, does not rest upon tradition alone. To men dependent for daily existence on continuous employment, the protection of their means of livelihood from confiscation or encroachment appears as fundamental a basis of social order as it does to the owners of land. What both parties claim is security and continuity of livelihood—that maintenance of the "established expectation" which is the "condition precedent" of civilised life. . . .

■　■　■

Amid the rush of new inventions, a legal "right to a trade," or a legal limitation of apprentices, whilst it remained an irksome restriction, ceased to safeguard the workman's livelihood. The only remedy for the consequent disturbance of vested interests would have been to have stereotyped the existing industrial order, by the absolute prohibition of machinery or any other innovation. To the statesman, keen on securing the maximum national wealth, any such prohibition appeared suicidal. To the new class of enterprising captains of industry, all restrictions stood in the way of that free use of their capital from which they could derive private wealth. The dispossessed craftsmen could themselves devise no feasible alternative to *laisser faire,* and no one among the dominant classes thought of any means of compensation. As the Industrial Revolution progressed, the objection to any interference with mobility increased in strength. New armies of workpeople grew up without vested interests of their own, and accordingly opposed to any conception of society which excluded them from the most profitable occupations. Finally, we have the rise in influence of the great body of consumers, loth to admit that the disappointment of the "established expectation" of particular sections of workers is any adequate ground for refraining from the cheapest method of satisfying their ever-changing desires. The result is that even Trade Unionists feel the Doctrine of Vested Interests to be out of date. It is still held with fervor by the more conservative-minded members of every trade, to whom it fully justifies such restrictive regulations as they are able to maintain. It is naturally strongest in the remnants of the time-honored ancient handicrafts. . . . [But] the old Doctrine of Vested Interests has, in fact, lost its vitality. It is still secretly cherished by many workmen, and its ethical validity is, in disputes between different Trade Unions, unhesitatingly assumed by both sides. But we no longer find it dominating the mind of Trade Union leaders, or figuring in their negotiations with employers, and appeals for public support. Whatever fate may be in store for other forms of vested interests, the modern passion for progress, demanding the quickest possible adaptation of social structure to social needs, has effectually undermined the assumption that any person can have a vested interest in an occupation.

When, at the beginning of this century, the Doctrine of Vested Interests was, as regards the wage-earners, definitely repudiated by the House of Commons, the Trade Unionists were driven back upon what we have termed the Doctrine of Supply and Demand. Working men were told, by friends and foes alike, that they could no longer be regarded as citizens entitled to legal protection of their established expectations; that labor was a commodity like any other, and that their real position was that of sellers in a market, entitled to do the best they could for themselves within the limits of the law of the land, but to no better terms than they could, by the ordinary arts of bargaining, extract from those with whom they dealt. It was the business of the employer to buy "labor" in the cheapest market, and that of the workman to sell it in the dearest. It followed that the only criterion of justice of any claim was ability to enforce it, and that the only way by which the workmen could secure better conditions of employment was by strengthening their strategic position against the employer. . . .

Between 1843 and 1880 the Doctrine of Supply and Demand, though never universally accepted, occupied a dominant place in the minds of most of the leaders of Trade Union thought. Viewed in the light of the workmen's experience of the evils of Individual Bargaining, and of the weakness of merely local unions, it meant the establishment of strong national societies, heaping up great reserve funds, and seeking to control the supply of labor in a whole industry from one end of the kingdom to the other. It involved, moveover, the gradual substitution of a policy of inclusion for that of exclusion. Instead of jealously restricting Trade Union membership to men who had "earned" a right to the trade by a definite apprenticeship under restrictive conditions, the unions came more and more to use all lawful means of enforcing membership on every competent workman whom they found actually working at their trade, however questionable might have been the means by which he had acquired his skill. The policy with regard to apprenticeship underwent, accordingly, a subtle change. The ideas of patrimony, of the purchase and sale of "the right to a trade," and of a traditional ratio between learners and adepts, gradually faded away, to be replaced by a frank and somewhat cynical policy of so regulating the entrance to an industry as to put the members of the union in the best possible position for bargaining with the employers. . . . But the most obvious result of the change of doctrine was a revolution in policy with regard to wages and hours. Under the influence of the Doctrine of Vested Interests, the eighteenth-century Trade Unionists had confined themselves, in the main, to protecting their customary livelihood; asking advances, therefore, not when profits were large, but when the cost of living had risen. Under the influence of the view that wages should be determined by the strategic position of the combined wage-earners, the Trade Unionists of the middle of the present century boldly asserted a claim, in times of good trade, to the highest possible rates that they could exact from employers eager to fulfil immensely profitable orders. . . .

■ ■ ■

We see, therefore, that the Doctrine of Supply and Demand differs in the most practical way from the Doctrine of Vested Interests. Instead of being inconsistent with the facts of modern industry, it seems capable of indefinite development to meet the changing conditions of the world-commerce. Far from being antagonistic to the business spirit of the present century, it falls in with the assumption that the highest interests of Humanity are best attained by every one pursuing what he conceives to be his own interest in the manner, within the limits of the law of the land, that he thinks best for himself. It is, moreover, merely applying to the relations of capital and labor the principles which already govern the business relations of commercial men to each other. Whether the capitalist can bargain individually with his workpeople, or is forced by their combination to deal with them collectively, the Doctrine of Supply and Demand seems to put the matter on a strictly business footing. The relation between employer and wage-earner, like that between buyer and seller, becomes, in fact, merely an incident in the "beneficent private war which makes one man strive to climb on the shoulders of another and remain there.". . . . We find, in fact, that a complete intellectual acceptance of the Doctrine of Supply and Demand has much the same results upon the attitude of Trade Unionism as it has upon commercial life, and that it throws up, as leaders, much the same type of character in the one case as in the other. Those who know the Trade Union world will have no difficulty in recognizing, in certain of its sections, both in corporate policy and in the characters of individual leaders, the same strong, self-reliant, and pugnacious spirit; the same impatience of sentiment, philanthropy, and idealism; the same self-complacency at their own success in the fight, and the same contempt for those who have failed; above all, the same conception of the social order, based on the axiom that "to him that hath shall be given, and from him that hath not shall be taken away even that which he hath." To the idealist who sees in Trade Unionism a great class upheaval of the oppressed against the oppressors, it comes as a shock to recognise, in the Trade Union official of this type, pushing the interests of his own clients at the expense of everybody else, merely another embodiment of the "spirit of the bagman." Nor has the believer in individual self-help any right to complain when the "spirit of the bagman" leads, not to free competition and war, but to close corporations and monopoly. . . .

But though the Doctrine of Supply and Demand is now accepted by a large section of the Trade Union world, as regards the amount of money wages, there is a strong and, as we think, a growing protest against it. The assumption that the conditions of employment should vary according to the strategic position of each section of the wage-earners, obviously works out disadvantageously for the weaker sections. . . .

■ ■ ■

We reach here a point on which the community has long since become convinced

195

that neither the Doctrine of Vested Interests, nor that of Supply and Demand affords any guide in determining the conditions of employment. In all that concerns the sanitary condition of the workplace, or the prevention of accidents, we are not content merely to protect the "established expectation" of the workmen, nor yet to leave the matter to settle itself according to the strategic position of each section. By common consent the employer is now required, in all this range of conditions, to give his workpeople, not what has been customary, nor yet what they can exact, but what, in the opinion of Parliament and its expert advisers, is necessary for their health and efficiency. . . .

■   ■   ■

We can now form a definite idea of the assumption which this generation has set up against the Doctrine of Supply and Demand, and which we have termed the Doctrine of a Living Wage. There is a growing feeling, not confined to Trade Unionists, that the best interests of the community can only be attained by deliberately securing, to each section of the workers, those conditions which are necessary for the continuous and efficient fulfilment of its particular function in the social machine. From this point of view, it is immaterial to the community whether or not a workman has, by birth, servitude, or purchase, acquired a "right to a trade," or what, at any given moment, may be his strategic position towards the capitalist employer. The welfare of the community as a whole requires, it is contended, that no section of workers should be reduced to conditions which are positively inconsistent with industrial or civic efficiency. Those who adopt this assumption argue that, whilst it embodies what was good in the two older doctrines, it avoids their socially objectionable features. Unlike the Doctrine of Vested Interests, it does not involve any stereotyping of industrial processes, or the protection of any class of workers in the monopoly of a particular service. It is quite consistent with the freedom of every wage-earner to choose or change his occupation, and with the employer's freedom to take on whichever man he thinks best fitted for his work. Thus it in no way checks mobility or stops competition. Unlike the Doctrine of Supply and Demand it does not tempt the workmen to limit their numbers, or combine with the employers to fix prices, or restrict output. It avoids, too, the evil of fluctuations of wages, in which the income of the workers varies, not according to their needs as citizens or producers, nor yet to the intensity of their exertion, but solely according to the temporary and, as far as they are concerned, fortuitous position of their trade. On the other hand, the Doctrine of a Living Wage goes far in the direction of maintaining "established expectation." Whilst it includes no sort of guarantee that any particular individual will be employed at any particular trade, those who are successful in the competition may feel assured that, so long as they retain their situations, the conditions of an efficient and vigorous working life will be secured to them.

■   ■   ■

The foregoing exposition of the assumptions of Trade Unionism will have given the reader the necessary clue, both to the historical changes in Trade Union policy from generation to generation, and also to the diversity at present existing in the Trade Union world. As soon as it is realised that Trade Unionists are inspired, not by any single doctrine as to the common weal, but more or less by three divergent and even contradictory views as to social expediency, we no longer look to them for any one consistent and uniform policy. The predominance among any particular section of workmen, or at any particular period, of one or other of the three assumptions which we have described—the Doctrine of Vested Interests, the Doctrine of Supply and Demand, and the Doctrine of a Living Wage—manifests itself in the degree of favor shown to particular Trade Union Regulations. The general faith in the Doctrine of Vested Interests explains why we find Trade Unionism, in one industry, or at one period, expressing itself in legally enforced terms of apprenticeship, customary rates of wages, the prohibition of new processes, strict maintenance of the lines of demarcation between trades, the exclusion of "illegal men," and the enforcement of "patrimony" and entrance fees. With the acceptance of the Doctrine of Supply and Demand we see coming in the policy of inclusion and its virtually compulsory Trade Unionism, Sliding Scales, the encouragement of improvements in machinery and the actual penalising of backward employers, the desire for a deliberate Regulation of Output and the establishment of alliances with employers against the consumer. Finally, in so far as the Doctrine of a Living Wage obtains, we see a new attention to the enforcement of Sanitation and Safety, general movements for the reduction of hours, attempts by the skilled trades to organise the unskilled laborers and women workers, denunciation of Sliding Scales and fluctuating incomes, the abandonment of apprenticeship in favor of universal education, and the insistence on a "Moral Minimum" wage below which no worker should be employed. Above all, these successive changes of faith explain the revolutions which have taken place in Trade Union opinion as to the relation of Labor to the State. When men believe in the Doctrine of Vested Interests, it is to the common law of the realm that they look for the protection of their rights and possessions. The law alone can secure to the individual, whether with regard to his right to a trade or his right to an office, his privilege in a new process or his title to property, the fulfilment of his "established expectation." Hence it is that we find eighteenth-century Trade Unionism confidently taking for granted that all its regulations ought properly to be enforced by the magistrate, and devoting a large part of its funds to political agitations and legal proceedings. When the Doctrine of Vested Interests was replaced by that of Supply and Demand, the Trade Unionists naturally turned to Collective Bargaining as their principal method of action. Instead of going to the State for protection, they fiercely resented any attempt to interfere with their struggle with employers, on the issue of which, they were told, their wages must depend. The Common Law, once their friend, now seemed always their most dangerous enemy, as it hampered their freedom of combination, and by its definitions of libel and conspiracy, set arbitrary limits to their capacity of making themselves unpleasant to the employers or the non-unionists. Hence the desire of the Trade Unionists of the middle of this century, whilst sweeping away all laws against combinations, to keep Trade Unionism itself absolutely out of the reach of the law-courts. The growth of the Doctrine of a Living Wage, resting as this does on the assumption that the conditions of employment require to be deliberately fixed, naturally puts the State in the position of arbitrator between the workman who claims more, and the employer who offers less, than is consistent with the welfare of other sections. But the appeal is not to the Common Law. It is no longer a question of protecting each individual in the enjoyment of whatever could be proved to be his customary privileges, or to flow from identical "natural rights," but of prescribing, for the several sections, the conditions required, in the interest of the whole community, by their diverse actual needs. We therefore see the Common Rules for each trade embodied in particular statutes, which the Trade Unionists, far from resisting, use their money and political influence to obtain. The double change of doctrine has thus brought about a return to the attitude of the Old Unionists of the eighteenth century, but with a significant difference. To-day it is not custom or privilege which appeals to the State, but the requirements of efficient citizenship. Whenever a Trade Union honestly accepts as the sole and conclusive test of any of its aspirations what we have termed the Doctrine of a Living Wage, and believes that Parliament takes the same view, we always find it, sooner or later, attempting to embody that aspiration in the statute law.

■  ■  ■

It might easily be contended that Trade Unionism has no logical or necessary connection with any particular kind of state or form of administration. If we consider only its fundamental object—the deliberate regulation of the conditions of employment in such a way as to ward off from the manual-working producers the evil effects of industrial competition—there is clearly no incompatibility between this and any kind of government. Regulations of this type have existed, as a matter of fact, under emperors and presidents, aristocracies and democracies. . . .

The problem of how far Trade Unionism is consistent with autocratic government . . . is not of practical concern to the Anglo-Saxon. In the English-speaking world institutions which desire to maintain and improve their position must at all hazards bring themselves into line with democracy. The wise official who has to function under the control of a committee of management, carefully considers its modes of action and the interests and opinions of its members, so that he may shape and state his policy in such a way as to avoid the rejection of the measure he desires. In the same way each section of Trade Unionists will have to put forward a policy of which no part runs counter to the interests and ideals of the bulk of the people. . . .

We see at once that the complete acceptance of democracy, with its acute consciousness of the interests of the community as a whole, and its insistence on equality of opportunity for all citizens, will necessitate a reconsideration by the Trade Unionists of their three Doctrines—the abandonment of one, the modification of another, and the far-reaching extension and development of the third. To begin with the Doctrine of Vested Interests, we may infer that, whatever respect may be paid to the "established expectations" of any class, this will not be allowed to take the form of a resistance to inventions, or of any obstruction of improvements in industrial processes. Equitable consideration of the interests of existing workers will no doubt be more and more expected, and popular governments may even adopt Mill's suggestion of making some provision for operatives displaced by a new machine. But this consideration and this provision will certainly not take the form of restricting the entrance to a trade, or of recognising any exclusive right to a particular occupation or service. Hence the old Trade Union conception of a vested interest in an occupation must be entirely given up. . . .

Coming now to the Doctrine of Supply and Demand we see that any attempt to better the strategic position of a particular section by the Device of Restriction of Numbers will be unreservedly condemned. Not only is this Device inconsistent with the democratic instinct in favor of opening up the widest possible opportunity for every citizen, but it is hostile to the welfare of the community as a whole, and especially to the manual workers, in that it tends to distribute the capital, brains, and labor of the nation less productively than would otherwise be the case. Trade Unionism has, therefore, absolutely to abandon one of its two Devices. This throwing off of the old Adam of monopoly will be facilitated by the fact that the mobility of modern industry has, in all but a few occupations, already made any effective use of Restriction of Numbers quite impracticable. . . .

■   ■   ■

Thus, the Doctrine of Supply and Demand will have to manifest itself exclusively in the persistent attempts of each trade to specialise its particular grade of skill, by progressively raising the level of its own Common Rules. In so far as this results in a corresponding increase in efficiency it will . . . not only benefit the trade itself, but also cause the capital, brains, and labor of the community to be distributed in the most productive way. And the demands of each grade will, in the absence of any Restriction of Numbers or resistance to innovations, be automatically checked by the liberty of the customer to resort to an alternative product and the absolute freedom of the directors of industry to adopt an alternative process, or to select another grade of labor. Thus, the permanent bias of the manual worker towards higher wages and shorter hours of labor is perpetually being counteracted by another—his equally strong desire for continuity of employment. If the Common Rule in any industry at any time is pressed upward further or more quickly than is compensated for by an equivalent advance in the efficiency of the industry, the cost of production, and, therefore, the price, will be raised, and the consumers' demand for that particular commodity will, in the vast majority of cases, be thereby restricted. The rise of wages will, in such a case, have been purchased at the cost of throwing some men out of work. And though the working-class official cannot, any more than the capitalist or the economist, predict the effect on demand of any particular rise of wages, even the most aggressive members of a Trade Union discover, in an increase of the percentage of unemployed colleagues whom they have to maintain an unmistakable and imperative check upon any repetition of an excessive claim. . . .

So far democracy may be expected to look on complacently at the fixing, by mutual agreement between the directors of industry and the manual workers, of special rates of wages for special classes. But this use of the Method of Collective Bargaining for the advantage of particular sections—this "freedom of contract" between capitalists and wage-earners—will become increasingly subject to the fundamental condition that the business of the community must not be interfered with. When in the course of bargaining there ensues a deadlock—when the workmen strike, or the employers lock out—many other interests are affected than those of the parties concerned. We may accordingly expect that, whenever an industrial dispute reaches a certain magnitude, a democratic state will, in the interests of the community as a whole, not scruple to intervene, and settle the points at issue by an authoritative fiat. The growing impatience with industrial dislocation will, in fact, when Collective Bargaining breaks down, lead to its supersession by some form of compulsory arbitration; that is to say, by Legal Enactment. And when the fixing of the conditions on which any industry is to be carried on, is thus taken out of the hands of employers and workmen, the settlement will no longer depend exclusively on the strategic position of the parties, or of the industry, but will be largely influenced by the doctrine of a living wage. The Trade Union official would then have to prove that the claims of his clients were warranted by the greater intensity of their effort, or by the rareness of their skill in comparison with those of the lowest grade of labor receiving only the National Minimum; whilst the case of the associated employers would have to rest on a demonstration, both that the conditions demanded were unnecessary, if not prejudicial, to the workmen's efficiency, and that equally competent recruits could be obtained in sufficient numbers without the particular "rent of ability," demanded by the Trade Union over and above the National Minimum.

It is accordingly on the side of the Doctrine of a Living Wage that the present policy of Trade Unionism will require most extension. Democratic public opinion will expect each trade to use its strategic position to secure the conditions necessary for the fulfilment of its particular social function in the best possible way—to obtain, that is to say, not what will be immediately most enjoyed by the "average sensual man," but what, in the long run, will most conduce to his efficiency as a professional, a parent, and a citizen. This will involve some modification of Trade Union policy. Powerful Trade Unions show no backwardness in exacting the highest money wages that they know how to obtain; but even the best organised trades will at present consent, as a part of their bargain with the employer, to work for excessive and irregular hours, and to put up with unsafe, insanitary, indecent, and hideous surroundings. In all the better-paid crafts in the England of to-day, shorter and more regular hours, greater healthfulness, comfort, and refinement in the conditions of work, and the definite provision of periodical holidays for recreation and travel, are, in the interests of industrial and civic efficiency, more urgently required than a rise in the Standard Rate. . . .

Nor is it enough for each trade to maintain and raise its own Standard of Life. Unless the better-paid occupations are to be insidiously handicapped in the competition for the home and foreign market, it is . . . essential that no one of the national industries should be permitted to become parasitic by the use of subsidised or deteriorating labor. Hence the organised trades are vitally concerned in the abolition of "sweating" in all occupations. . . . And this self-interest of the better-paid trades coincides, as we have seen, with the welfare of the community, dependent as this is on securing the utmost development of health, intelligence, and character in the weaker as well as in the stronger sections. Thus we arrive at the characteristic device of the Doctrine of a Living Wage, which we have termed the National Minimum—the deliberate enforcement, by an elaborate Labor Code, of a definite quota of education, sanitation, leisure, and wages for every grade of workers in every industry. This National Minimum the public opinion of the democratic state will not only support, but positively insist on for the common weal. But public opinion alone will not suffice. To get the principle of a National Minimum unreservedly adopted . . . requires persistent effort and specialised skill. For this task no section of the community is so directly interested and so well-equipped as the organised trades, with their prolonged experience of industrial regulation and their trained official staff. It is accordingly upon the Trade Unions that the democratic state must mainly rely for the stimulus, expert counsel, and persistent watchfulness, without which a National Minimum can neither be obtained nor enforced.

■   ■   ■

To obtain for the community the maximum satisfaction it is essential that the needs and desires of the consumers should be the main factor in determining the commodities and services to be produced. . . . One thing is certain, namely, that the several sections of manual workers, enrolled in their Trade Unions, will have, under private enterprise or Collectivism, no more to do with the determination of what is to be produced than any other citizens or consumers. As manual workers and wage-earners, they bring to the problem no specialised knowledge, and as persons fitted for the performance of particular services, they are even biassed against the inevitable changes in demand which characterise a progressive community. This is even more the case with regard to the second department of industrial administration—the adoption of material, the choice of processes, and the selection of human agents. Here, the Trade Unions concerned are specially disqualified, not only by their ignorance of the possible alternatives, but also by their overwhelming bias in favor of a particular material, a particular process, or a particular grade of workers, irrespective of whether these are or are not the best adapted for the gratification of the consumers' desires. On the other hand, the directors of industry, whether thrown up by the competitive struggle or deliberately appointed by the consumers or citizens, have been specially picked out and trained to discover the best means of satisfying the consumers' desires. Moreover, the bias of their self-interest coincides with the object of their customers or employers—that is to say, the best and cheapest production. Thus, if we leave out of account the disturbing influence of monopoly in private enterprise, and corruption in public administration, it would at first sight seem as if we might safely leave the organisation of production and distribution under the one system as under the other to the expert knowledge of the directors of industry. But this is subject to one all-important qualification. The permanent bias of the profit-maker, and even of the salaried official of the Co-operative Society, the Municipality, or the Government Department, is to lower the expense of production. So far as immediate results are concerned, it seems equally advantageous whether this reduction of cost is secured by a better choice of materials, processes, or men, or by some lowering of wages or other worsening of the conditions upon which the human agents are employed. But the democratic state is . . . vitally interested in upholding the highest possible Standard of Life of all its citizens, and especially of the manual workers who form four-fifths of the whole. Hence the bias of the directors of industry in favor of cheapness has, in the interests of the community, to be perpetually controlled and guided by a determination to maintain, and progressively to raise, the conditions of employment.

This leads us to the third branch of industrial administration—the settlement of the conditions under which the human beings are to be employed. The adoption of one material rather than another, the choice between alternative processes or alternative ways of organising the factory, the selection of particular grades of workers, or even of a particular foreman, may affect, for the worse, the Standard of Life of the operatives concerned. This indirect influence on the conditions of employment passes imperceptibly into the direct determination of the wages, hours, and other terms of the wage contract. On all these matters the consumers, on the one hand, and the directors of industry on the other, are permanently disqualified from acting as arbiters. . . . In the elaborate division of labor which characterises the modern industrial system, thousands of workers co-operate in the bringing to market of a single commodity; and no consumer, even if he desired it, could possibly ascertain or judge of the conditions of employment in all these varied trades. Thus, the consumers of all classes are not only biassed in favor of low prices: they are compelled to accept this apparent or genuine cheapness as the only practicable test of efficiency of production. And though the immediate employer of each section of workpeople knows the hours that they work and the wages that they receive, he is precluded by the stream of competitive pressure, transmitted through the retail shopkeeper and the wholesale trader, from effectively resisting the promptings of his own self-interest towards a constant cheapening of labor. Moreover, though he may be statistically aware of the conditions of employment, his lack of personal experience of those conditions deprives him of any real knowledge of their effects. To the brain-working captain of industry, maintaining himself and his family on thousands a year, the manual-working wage-earner seems to belong to another species, having mental faculties and bodily needs altogether different from his own. Men and women of the upper or middle classes are totally unable to realise what state of body and mind, what level of chracter and conduct result from a life spent, from childhood to old age, amid the dirt, the smell, the noise, the ugliness, and the vitiated atmosphere of the workshop; under constant subjection to the peremptory, or, it may be, brutal orders of the foreman; kept continuously at laborious manual toil for sixty or seventy hours in every week of the year; and maintained by the food, clothing, house-accommodation, recreation, and family life which are implied by a precarious income of between ten shillings and two pounds a week. If the democratic state is to attain its fullest and finest development, it is essential that the actual needs and desires of the human agents concerned should be the main considerations in determining the conditions of employment. Here, then, we find the special function of the Trade Union in the administration of industry. The simplest member of the working-class organisation knows at any rate where the shoe pinches. The Trade Union official is specially selected by his fellow-workmen for his capacity to express the grievances from which they suffer, and is trained by his calling in devising remedies for them. But in expressing the desires of their members, and in insisting on the necessary reforms, the Trade Unions act within the constant friction-brake supplied by the need of securing employment. It is always the consumers, and the consumers alone, whether they act through profit-making entrepreneurs or through their own salaried officials, who determine how many of each particular grade of workers they care to employ on the conditions demanded.

Thus, it is for the consumers, acting either through capitalist entrepreneurs or their own salaried agents, to decide what shall be produced. It is for the directors of industry, whether profit-makers or officials, to decide how it shall be produced, though in this decision they must take into account the objections of the workers' representatives as to the effect on the conditions of employment. And, in the settlement of these conditions, it is for the expert negotiators of the Trade Unions, controlled by the desires of their members, to state the terms under which each grade will sell its labor. But above all these, stands the community itself. To its elected representatives and trained Civil Service is entrusted the duty of perpetually considering the permanent interests of the State as a whole. When any group of consumers desires something which is regarded as inimical to the public wellbeing . . . the community prohibits or regulates the satisfaction of these desires. When the directors of industry attempt to use a material, or a process, which is regarded as injurious . . . their action is restrained by Public Health Acts. And when the workers concerned, whether through ignorance, indifference, or strategic weakness, consent to work under conditions which impair their physique, injure their intellect, or degrade their character, the community has, for its own sake, to enforce a National Minimum of education, sanitation, leisure, and wages. . . . In each of its three divisions, the interests and will of one or other section is the dominant factor. But no section wields uncontrolled sway even in its own sphere. The State is a partner in every enterprise. In the interests of the community as a whole, no one of the interminable series of decisions can be allowed to run counter to the consensus of expert opinion representing the consumers on the one hand, the producers on the other, and the nation that is paramount over both.

It follows from this analysis that Trade Unionism is not merely an incident of the present phase of capitalist industry, but has a permanent function to fulfil in the democratic state. Should capitalism develop in the direction of gigantic Trusts, the organisation of the manual workers in each industry will be the only effective bulwark against social oppression. If, on the other hand, there should be a revival of the small master system, the enforcement of Common Rules will be more than ever needed to protect the community against industrial parasitism. And if, as we personally expect, democracy moves in the direction of superseding both the little profit-maker and the Trust, by the salaried officer of the Co-operative Society, the Municipality, and the Government

Department, Trade Unionism would remain equally necessary. For even under the most complete Collectivism, the directors of each particular industry would, as agents of the community of consumers, remain biassed in favor of cheapening production, and could, as brainworkers, never be personally conscious of the conditions of the manual laborers. And though it may be assumed that the community as a whole would not deliberately oppress any section of its members, experience of all administration on a large scale, whether public or private, indicates how difficult it must always be, in any complicated organisation, for an isolated individual sufferer to obtain redress against the malice, caprice, or simple heedlessness of his official superior. Even a whole class or grade of workers would find it practically impossible, without forming some sort of association of its own, to bring its special needs to the notice of public opinion, and press them effectively upon the Parliament of the nation. Moreover, without an organisation of each grade or section of the producers, it would be difficult to ensure the special adaptation to their particular conditions of the National Minimum, or other embodiment of the Doctrine of a Living Wage, which the community would need to enforce; and it would be impossible to have that progressive and experimental pressing upward of the particular Common Rules of each class, upon which, as we have seen, the maximum productivity of the nation depends. In short, it is essential that each grade or section of producers should be at least so well organised that it can compel public opinion to listen to its claims, and so strongly combined that it could if need be, as a last resort against bureaucratic stupidity or official oppression, enforce its demands by a concerted abstention from work, against every authority short of a decision of the public tribunals, or a deliberate judgment of the Representative Assembly itself.

But though, as industry passes more and more into public control, Trade Unionism must still remain a necessary element in the democratic state, it would, we conceive, in such a development, undergo certain changes. The mere extension of national agreements and factory legislation has already, in the most highly regulated trades, superseded the old guerilla warfare between employers and employed, and transformed the Trade Union official from a local strike leader to an expert industrial negotiator, mainly occupied, with the cordial co-operation of the secretary of the Employers' Association and the Factory Inspector, in securing an exact observance of the Common Rules prescribed for the trade. And as each part of the minimum conditions of employment becomes definitely enacted in the regulations governing the public industries, or embodied in the law of the land, it will tend more and more to be accepted by the directors of industry as a matter of course, and will need less and less enforcement by the watchful officials concerned. The Trade Union function of constantly maintaining an armed resistance to attempts to lower the Standard of Life of its members may be accordingly expected to engage a diminishing share of its attention. On the other hand, its duty of perpetually striving to raise the level of its Common Rules, and thereby increasing the specialised technical efficiency of its craft, will remain unabated. We may therefore expect that, with the progressive nationalisation or municipalisation of public services, on the one hand, and the spread of the Co-operative movement on the other, the Trade Unions of the workers thus taken directly into the employment of the citizen-consumers will more and more assume the character of professional associations. . . . They may even come to be little concerned with any direct bargaining as to sanitation, hours, or wages, except by way of redressing individual grievances, or supplying expert knowledge as to the effect of proposed changes. The conditions of employment depending on the degree of expert specialisation to which the craft has been carried, and upon public opinion as to its needs, each Trade Union will find itself . . . more and more concerned with raising the standard of competency in its occupation, improving the professional equipment of its members, "educating their masters" as to the best way of carrying on the craft, and endeavoring by every means to increase its status in public estimation.

So far our review of the functions of Trade Unionism in the democratic state has taken account only of its part in industrial organisation. But the Trade Unions are turned also to other uses. At present, for instance, they compete with the ordinary friendly societies and industrial insurance companies in providing money benefits in cases of accident, sickness, and death, together with pensions for the aged. This is the side of Trade Unionism which commonly meets with the greatest approval, but it is a side that, in our opinion, is destined to dwindle. As one class of invalids after another is taken directly under public care, the friendly benefits provided by the Trade Unions will no longer be necessary to save their members from absolute destitution. With any general system of compensation for industrial accidents, provided or secured by the state itself, the costly "accident benefit" hitherto given by Trade Unions will become a thing of the past. . . . But in the democratic state these adventitious aids will no longer be necessary. The Trade Union will be a definitely recognised institution of public utility to which every person working at the craft will be imperatively expected, even if not . . . legally compelled to contribute. With Trade Union membership thus virtually or actually compulsory, Trade Union leaders will find it convenient to concentrate their whole attention on the fundamental purposes of their organisation, and to cede the mere insurance business to the Friendly Societies. . . .

■　■　■

But whilst Trade Unionism may be expected to lose some of its present incidental functions, we suggest that the democratic state will probably find it new duties to fulfil. . . . The technical instruction of our craftsmen would, for instance, gain enormously in vigor and reality if the Trade Unions were in some way directly associated with the administration of the technological classes relating to their particular trades. . . . In other directions, too, such as the compilation of statistics relating to particular occupations, and the dissemination of information useful to members of particular crafts, the democratic state will probably make increasing use of Trade Union machinery.

Finally, there is the service of counsel. On all issues of industrial regulation, whether in their own or other trades, the Trade Union officials will naturally assume the position of technical experts, to whom public opinion will look for guidance. But industrial regulation is not the only matter on which a democratic state needs the counsels of a working-class organisation. Whenever a proposal or a scheme touches the daily life of the manual-working wage-earner, the representative committees and experienced officials of the Trade Union world are in a position to contribute information and criticism, which are beyond the reach of any other class. . . .

■　■　■

Now, Trade Unionism has no logical connection with any particular form of ownership of land and capital, and the members of British Trade Unions are not drawn, as Trade Unionists, unreservedly either towards Individualism or towards Collectivism. Certain sections of the Trade Union world . . . find that they can exact better terms from the capitalist employer than would be likely to be conceded to them by a democratic government department. Other sections, on the contrary, see in the extension of public employment the only remedy for a disastrous irregularity of work and all the evils of sweating. . . . It is in their capacity of citizens, not as Trade Unionists, that the manual workers will have to decide between the rival forms of social organisation, and to make up their minds as to how they wish the economic rent of the nation's land and capital to be distributed. And though, in this, the most momentous issue of modern democracy, the manual workers will be influenced by their poverty in favor of a more equal sharing of the benefits of combined labor, they will, by their Trade Unionism, not be biassed in favor of any particular scheme of attaining this result outside their own Device of the Common Rule. And when we pass from the ownership of the means of production and the administration of industry to such practical problems as the best form of currency or the proper relation between local and central government, or to such vital questions as the collective organisation of moral and religious teaching, the provision for scholarship and science and the promotion of the arts—not to mention the sharper issues of "Home Rule" or foreign affairs—the members of the Trade Union world have no distinctive opinion, and their representatives and officials no special knowledge. We may therefore infer that the wage-earners will, in the democratic state, not content themselves with belonging to their Trade Union, or even to any wider organisation based on a distinction of economic class. Besides their distinctive interests and opinions as wage-earners and manual workers, they have others which they share with persons of every grade or occupation. The citizen in the democratic state, enrolled first in his geographical constituency, will take his place also in the professional association of his craft; but he will go on to combine in voluntary associations for special purposes with those who agree with him in religion or politics, or in the pursuit of particular recreations or hobbies.

These considerations have a direct bearing on the probable development of Trade Union structure. . . . The Trade Union world has, throughout its whole history, manifested an overpowering impulse to the amalgamation of local trade clubs into national unions, with centralised funds and centralised administration. The economic characteristics of Trade Unionism revealed to us the source of this impulse in the fundamental importance to each separate class of operatives that its occupation should be governed by its own Common Rules, applicable from one end of the kingdom to the other. This centralisation of administration, involving the adoption of a national trade policy, and, above all, the constant levelling-up of the lower-paid districts to the higher standard set in more advantageous centres, requires . . . the development of a salaried staff, selected for special capacity, devoting their whole attention to the commercial position and technical details of the particular section of the industry that they represent, and able to act for the whole of that section throughout the nation. It is . . . because of the absence of such a staff that so few of the Trade Unions of the present day secure national agreements, or enforce with uniformity such Common Rules as they obtain. The Trade Union of the future will, therefore, be co-extensive with its craft, national in its scope, centralised in its administration, and served by an expert official staff of its own.

■  ■  ■

Our vision of the sphere of Trade Unionism in the democratic state . . . gives us also its political programme. . . . In spite of the fact that Trade Unionists include men of all shades of political opinion, . . . the federal organisations of the British Trade Unions of to-day are perpetually meddling with wide issues of general politics, upon which the bulk of their constituents have either no opinions at all, or are marshalled in the ranks of one or another of the political parties. . . . This waste of time and dissipation of energy over extraneous matters arises, we think, mainly from the absence of any clearly conceived and distinctive Trade Union programme. In the democratic state of the future the Trade Unionists may be expected to be conscious of their own special function in the political world, and to busy themselves primarily with its fulfilment. First in importance to every section we put the establishment of a National Minimum of education, sanitation, leisure, and wages, its application to all the conditions of employment, its technical interpretation to fit the circumstances of each particular trade, and, above all, its vigorous enforcement, for the sake of the whole wage-earning world. . . . Upon this fundamental ground level each separate craft will need to develop such technical regulations of its own as are required to remove any conditions of employment which can be proved to be actually prejudicial to the efficiency of the operatives concerned. . . . And since the utmost possible use of the Method of Legal Enactment will . . . still permanently leave a large sphere for the Method of Collective Bargaining, there must be added to the political programme of the federated unions all that we have described as the Implications of Trade Unionism. The federal executive of the Trade Union world would find itself defending complete freedom of association, and carefully watching every development of legislation or judicial interpretation to see that nothing was made criminal or actionable, when done by a Trade Union or its officials, which would not be criminal or actionable if done by a partnership of traders in pursuit of their own gain. And the federal executive would be on its guard, not only against a direct attack on the workmen's organisations, but also against any insidious weakening of their influence. . . .

. . . The "dim, inarticulate" multitude of manual-working wage-earners have . . . felt . . . [that] the uncontrolled power wielded by the owners of the means of production, able to withhold from the manual worker all chance of subsistence unless he accepted their terms, meant a far more genuine loss of liberty, and a far keener sense of personal subjection, than the official jurisdiction of the magistrate, or the far-off, impalpable rule of the king. . . . Against this autocracy in industry, the manual workers have, during the century, increasingly made good their protest. . . . The democratic idea which rules in politics has no less penetrated into industry. The notion of a governing class, exacting implicit obedience from inferiors, and imposing upon them their own terms of service, is gone, never to return. Henceforward, employers and their workmen must meet as equals. What has not been so obvious to middle-class observers is the necessary condition of this equality. Individual Bargaining between the owner of the means of subsistence and the seller of so perishable a commodity as a day's labor must be, once for all, abandoned. In its place, if there is to be any genuine "freedom of contract," we shall see the conditions of employment adjusted between equally expert negotiators, acting for corporations reasonably comparable in strategic strength, and always subject to and supplemented by the decisions of the High Court of Parliament, representing the interests of the community as a whole. Equality in industry implies, in short, a universal application of the Device of the Common Rule.

. . . Political democracy will inevitably result in industrial democracy. . . .

# FIVE

**The Labor Movement as a Psychological Reaction to Industrialism**

# Introduction

In Part V we include several theories that explain the emergence and characteristics of the labor movement primarily in psychological terms. Carleton Parker did not develop anything even approaching a complete theory of the labor movement, but he did exert an important influence on later thinking. Drawing on a theory of psychological instincts similar to Sigmund Freud's, Parker saw life as less morally rigorous for working-class children than for upper-middle-class children. Thus working-class children would be less instinctually repressed, and psychically healthier, than their upper-middle-class counterparts. However, upon encountering the grown-up world of work, the working-class child discovers strong discipline, monotonous, boring, dirty, and hard work, and other impediments to free expression of his or her instincts. The resulting psychic repression causes a psychological pathology, one of whose outlets is industrial strife. Strikes, sabotage, and irrational actions follow. Although he died prematurely and never drew out the full implications of his observations, Parker implied that labor unrest and probably even unionism itself were psychological abnormalities that would be cured by proper and humane treatment of the worker at work. He is thus an early forerunner to personnel management schools of thought which stress human relations and welfare measures as a counter to the labor movement.

Robert Hoxie is another important labor theorist within the psychological tradition. Hoxie was a very careful researcher who analyzed the labor movement thoroughly from a variety of viewpoints. One of his major contributions was the application of the methodology of the social sciences—particularly sociology—to the study of the labor movement. Hoxie concluded that there is no one unitary labor movement, but a wide variety of trade unions exhibiting a wide variety of characteristics. Unions are formed and respond according to the social psychology of workers; since workers in different situations have different psychological outlooks, they will develop unions with widely varying structures and functions.

Hoxie looks at unions in terms of both their structure and their function. Structurally, he finds (1) *craft* unions, (2) *federations* of unions (such as the AFL), (3) *industrial* unions, (4) all-inclusive *labor* unions (such as the Knights of Labor and the IWW), and a number of cross-combinations of the four basic types. But it is his functional analysis of unions which has become most famous. Hoxie finds four basic functional types of unionism: (1) *business* unionism, (2) friendly, or *uplift* unionism, (3) *revolutionary* unionism, and (4) *predatory* unionism. His description of the social outlook and practice of each type can be easily supplemented with examples from American labor history.

Hoxie's overall conclusions about American trade unionism and a proper theoretical understanding of it are as follows: (a) unions can be analyzed by both their structure and their function, but the key is their function; (b) the functional type of a union will depend on the group psychology of the workers forming the unions, and the union structure is merely a means to satisfy that group psychology; (c) group psychology is not the same for all workers in a society as diverse as ours; (d) previous historical and economic analyses of unionism were too narrow because they overlooked the background and temperament of workers; and (e) there is no *one* labor movement, but many different types of unions which require a knowledge of many factors if one is to understand them.

Frank Tannenbaum sees the labor movement as a reaction to the atomization of workers which accompanied the industrial revolution and to the subsequent growth of capitalism as a system. In reaction to the extreme individualism and isolation they faced, workers formed associations to recreate the sense of society they had lost. In an early work titled *The Labor Movement* (1921), Tannenbaum considered the labor movement inherently revolutionary; the new "society" being created in the trade unions was a revolutionary challenge that must eventually eliminate capitalism. At this point Tannenbaum was somewhat taken with the IWW, and his theory had definite syndicalist overtones. By the time of his later book, *A Philosophy of Labor* (1951), Tannenbaum had changed this aspect of his theory. He now felt that the labor movement was counterrevolutionary, moving us back to a society based on "status" and explicit moral values such as obtained in the Middle Ages. The psychological values of the workers, Tannenbaum feels, will express themselves through the trade unions and ultimately create a society of joint corporation-union ownership with enterprises run according to the workers' need for a sense of dignity and belonging.

Thorstein Veblen, the final psychological theorist in Part V, is an important and original thinker who merits close consideration. We reproduce below portions of *The Theory of Business Enterprise* (1904), *The Vested Interests and the Common Man* (1919), and *Absentee Ownership* (1923). Because Veblen's thinking and terminology changed over time, some explanation is necessary if the reader is to fully understand his thinking. In the *Theory* selection, Veblen posits that a new psychological outlook is growing among workers. The industrialized machine process creates a scientific, cause-and-effect viewpoint in the modern worker. This outlook clashes with the anthropomorphic, "natural rights" outlook of the businessmen (whom he terms the "pecuniary interests"), which grounds all thinking on private property rights. The new scientific attitude of the worker demands production for the sake of production (highest efficiency) or at least production for the sake of use. The obvious corollary is a rational, planned economy which puts to use all modern engineering and scientific techniques for maximum productivity and satisfaction of human needs irrespective of pecuniary matters such as ability to pay. Thus the machine process is slowly creating a subversive, socialist outlook on the part of the worker; respect for private property is being undermined by the industrial machine process. Trade unions are a halfway house in this psychological change, according to Veblen. Trade unionism also attacks private property and the natural rights tradition, but only partially. But the more mature and developed trade unionism becomes, the more radical it gets. Trade unionism logically passes over to socialism, which is the culmination of the industrial psychology of the worker.

In response to this subversion of the established order, businessmen search for a cultural force to counteract the deterioration of respect for private property and traditional values. Veblen asserts that they can find it only in war or preparation for war. Militarization fulfills most of the needs of the established interests: it disciplines workers, abridges civil rights, establishes unquestioning obedience, drives the political spectrum to the right, creates unthinking jingoistic patriotism, legitimizes rank differences in life situations, diverts attention from class inequities, and in general conduces to subordination of the producing classes.

But the authoritarian, semibarbaric, warlike state Veblen prescribes for capitalism's ills is also incompatible in the long run with the survival of business dominance, he argues. It too would undermine our modern business system by fostering a reversion to medieval and ancient patterns of life and thought. So according to Veblen, the modern business system is caught between two unpalatable and subversive alternatives: continued growth of materialistic and scientific patterns of thought culminating in socialism, or a reversion to a pre-scientific, intentionally antirational social order of extremely warlike and authoritarian dimensions which also undermines business hegemony. From the left, trade unionism, as a pale reflection of socialism, weakens the system by undermining private property rights.

Fifteen years later, Veblen had modified his theory somewhat to account for the business unionism of the AFL. In *The Vested Interests* Veblen calls businessmen or capitalists "vested interests" rather than "pecuniary intersts." To be a vested interest means to have an established right to get something for nothing. Businessmen have this through their legal rights based on private ownership of property. Standing against the vested interests is the common man, who has no such presumptive rights. However, the craft unions of the AFL have come to act like vested interests, despite the material circumstances of their members being much closer to those of the common man than to those of the wealthy. By forming labor market monopolies and squeezing an extremely small margin of wages above that dictated by the market, the AFL unions are quasi-vested interests—at least in behavior—and ally themselves with (and behave like) business interests in our society. At this time Veblen did not think there was much material basis for the AFL's behavior, though, and he asserted that the IWW was much more likely to be the vanguard of future labor developments.

By 1923, Veblen had changed his perspective on unions considerably. The IWW was all but destroyed; a declining but resilient AFL was all that remained. In *Absentee Ownership*, Veblen sees the AFL acting as any business does: creating profit for itself by sabotaging output, restricting and cartelizing the market, creating artificial scarcities and intentional shortages. These are all sound and standard business practices for obtaining a profit, Veblen asserts; what is new is that *unions* are learning to use these techniques. Although compared to businessmen unions are at a disadvantage in this pursuit, they have a certain ability to carry it off, especially in the most highly skilled crafts. By the twenties Veblen had given up on unions as a subversive force undermining the business system. His attention turned to engineers and others as the agents of social change. However, his earlier work has a number of striking similarities to—and equally striking divergences from—the revolutionary theories in Part II of this book.

# 26
## *Understanding Labor Unrest*

CARLETON PARKER                                                                    1920

I come now to the character of evolution in the field of modern industrialism. Children of the middle class without doubt have a more unhealthy psychic life than those of the working class. But following the statistics of evident malnutrition, short school experience, and the abnormally high death rate of children of mill towns, our conventional mores have moved us to general if mild conviction that children of the working class are woefully badly off. It seems, however, that the necessary laxness of working home discipline, the decay among the working population of respect for conventional rules and law, the favorable opportunities for the children to quit school, the plasticity of the codes governing street social life, all work in an important manner towards allowing a relatively free and healthy psychic development of the children affected by it. Working mothers have not the time to enforce minutely the best current moral standards, for it takes much of the day's energies of the upper middle class mother to create by such an enforcement that atmosphere whose frequent and almost normal product is the above analyzed sexual and economic abnormalities.

However, at a later date in the life of these working class children, certain powerful forces in their environment, though they work on the less susceptible and less plastic natures of mature individuals, produce obsessions and thwartings which function at times, exclusively almost, in determining the behavior of great classes of the industrial population. The powerful forces of the working class environment which thwart and balk instinct expression are suggested in the phrases monotonous work, dirty work, simplified work, mechanized work, the servile place of labor, insecure tenure of the job, hire and fire, winter unemployment, the ever found union of the poor district with the crime district, and the restricted district with prostitution, the open shop, and labor turnover, poverty, the breadlines, the scrap heap, destitution. If we postulate some twenty odd unit psychic characters which are present under the laborer's dirty blouse and insistently demand the same gratification that is with painful care planned for the college student, in just what kind of perverted compensations must a laborer indulge to make endurable his existence? A western hobo tries in a more or less frenzied way to compensate for a general all embracing thwarting of his nature by a wonderful concentration of sublimation activities on the wander instinct. The monotony, indignity, dirt and sexual apologies of, for instance, the unskilled worker's life bring their definite fixations, their definite irrational inferiority obsessions. The balked laborer here follows one of the two described lines of conduct:

First, either weakens, becomes inefficient, drifts away, loses interest in the quality of his work, drinks, deserts his family, or,

Secondly, he indulges in a true type-inferiority compensation and in order to dignify himself, to eliminate for himself his inferiority in his own eyes, he strikes or brings on a strike, he commits violence or he stays on the job and injures machinery, or mutilates the materials; he is fit food for dynamite conspiracies. He is ready to make sabotage a part of his regular habit scheme. His condition is one of mental stress and unfocussed psychic unrest, and could in all accuracy be called a definite industrial psychosis. He is neither wilful nor responsible, he is suffering from a stereotyped mental disease.

If one leaves the strata of unskilled labor and investigates the higher economic classes he finds parallel conditions. There is a profound unrest and strong migratory tendency among department store employees. One New York store with less than three thousand employees has thirteen thousand pass in a year through its employ. Since the establishment in American life of "big business" with its extensive efficiency systems, its order and de-humanized discipline, its caste system, as it were, there has developed among its highly paid men a persistent unrest, a dissatisfaction and decay of morale which is so notable and costly that it has received repeated attention. Even the conventional competitive efficiency of American Business is in grave question. I suggest that this unrest is a true psychosis, a definite mental unbalance, an efficiency psychosis, as it were, and has its definite psychic antecedents—and that our present moralizing and guess-solutions are both hopeless and ludicrous. We blindly trust that a ten per cent wage increase will cure that breakdown which a sympathetic social psychiatrist might, if given all power, hope merely to alleviate. . . .

The most notable inferiority compensation in industrial life is the strike. The strike has two prerequisites,—a satisfactory obsession in the labor mind, and a sufficient decay in the eyes of labor of the prestige of social norms, to allow the laborer to make those breaches of law and convention which a well run strike of today demands. The violence of the strike varies directly with both the psychic annoyance due to the obsession and with the extent of decay in the striker's eyes of conventional mores. Veblen has shown how modern machine technology gives a causal, deterministic bias to labor class thinking and how this bias makes impossible the acceptance at face value of the mystic, anthropomorphic pretensions of law and business rights. These pretensions seem fitted to endure only in a society experiencing a placid, unaroused and ox-like existence, or in one where the prestige of law and order is maintained by a large professional army and a policy of frightfulness not rendered inefficient by the inopportune presence of emotional religions. Neither of these prerequisites is present in America, so our strikes tend to reflect without serious modification both the psychic ill-health generated by the worker's experience, and the rapid and interesting decay of the respect and popularity of the law, the courts, property, and the rich man. Trotter has described modern social revolt as the war between man stimulated by his sore psychical experiences and the Power of the Herd. This is but a Veblenesque description of the strike.

My main thesis might be stated as a plea to consider the states of conventional "Willfulness," such as laziness, inefficiency, destructiveness in strikes, etc., as ordinary mental disease of a functional kind, a sort of industrial psychosis. If we accept this approach then the cure for these menacing social ailments beckons to us from the field of abnormal and comparative psychology. . . .

■   ■   ■

In industrial labor and in business employments a new concept, a new going philosophy must unreservedly be accepted which has, instead of the ideal of forcing human beings to mould their habits to assist the continued existence of the inherited order of things, an ideal of moulding all business institutions and ideas of prosperity in the interests of scientific evolutionary aims and large human pleasures. As Pigou has said, "Environment has its children as well as men." Monotony in labor, tedium in office work, time spent in business correspondence, the boredom of running a sugar refinery, would be asked to step before the bar of human affairs and get a health standardization. Today industry produces goods that cost more than they are worth, are consumed by persons who are degraded by the consuming of them, destroying permanently the raw material source which science has painfully explained could be made inexhaustible. Some intellectual revolution must come which will de-emphasize business and industry and re-emphasize most other ways of self expression. . . .

So the problem of industrial labor is one with the problem of the discontented business man, the indifferent student, the unhappy wife, the immoral minister,—it is one of mal-adjustment between a fixed human nature and a carelessly ordered world. The result is suffering, insanity, racial perversion, and danger. The final cure is gaining acceptance for a new standard of normality. The first step towards this is to break down the mores-inhibitions to free experimental thinking.

# 27
## *Trade Unionism in the United States*

**ROBERT HOXIE**                                               1917

Trade unionism may be after all, not a simple, consistent entity, but a complex of the utmost diversity, both structurally and functionally. . . .

There are in the United States today hundreds of union organizations, each practically independent or sovereign, and each with its own and often peculiar aims, policies, demands, methods, attitudes and internal regulations. Nor is there any visible or tangible bond, however tenuous, that unites these organizations into a single whole. Groups there are indeed with overstructures and declared common aims and methods. But group combats group with the bitterness that can arise only out of the widest diversity of ideals and methods.

A slight acquaintance with the history of organized labor shows that this situation is not unique, and at the same time furnishes the apparent clews to its explanation. It reveals the fact that unionism has not a single genesis, but that it has made its appearance time after time, independently, wherever in the modern industrial era a group of workers, large or small, has developed a strong internal consciousness of common interests. It shows, moreover, that each union and each union group has undergone a constant process of change or development, functionally and structurally, responding apparently to the group psychology and therefore to the changing conditions, needs, and problems of its membership. In short, it reveals trade unionism as above all else essentially an opportunistic phenomenon.

For, if the history of unionism seems to admit of any positive generalizations, they are that unionists have been prone to act first and to formulate theories afterward, and that they have acted habitually to meet the problems thrust upon them by immediate circumstances. Everywhere they have done the thing which under the particular circumstances has seemed most likely to produce results immediately desired. Modes of action which have failed, when measured by this standard, have been rejected and other means sought. Methods that have worked have been preserved and extended, the standards of judgment being always most largely the needs and experiences of the group concerned. So that, prevailingly, whatever theory unionists have possessed has been in the nature of group generalization, slowly developed on the basis of concrete experience.

■   ■   ■

Thus the scope and character of union ideals and methods have been as broad and diverse as the conscious common needs and conditions of the groups of workers entering into organization. Some unions have confined themselves to attempts to deal directly with their immediate employers and their immediate conditions of work and pay; others have emphasized mutual aid and education; still others have enlarged their field of thought and action to include all employers and all conditions—economic, legal, and social. In other words, the union program, taking it with all its mutations and contradictions, comprehends nothing less than all the various economic, political, ethical and social viewpoints and modes of action of a vast and heterogeneous complex of working class groups, molded by diverse environments and actuated by diverse motives; it expresses nothing less than the ideals, aspirations, hopes, and fears, modes of thinking

Robert Hoxie, *Trade Unionism in the United States* (New York: Appleton, Century, Crofts Inc., 1921) pp. 33–51, 55–67. Footnotes in the original have been eliminated or renumbered.

and action of all these working groups. In short, if we can think of unionism as such, it must be as one of the most complex, heterogeneous and protean of modern social phenomena.

But can we thus think of it? If all that has been said be true, are we not forced to this pregnant conclusion as the basic hypothesis of our study—namely: that there is no such thing as unionism, either in the sense of an abstract unity, or of a concrete, organic, and consistent whole, which can be crowded within the confines of a narrow definition or judged sweepingly as good or bad, right or wrong, socially helpful or harmful? If, then, we dispense with narrow preconceptions and face things as they actually are, and are becoming, it is impossible to say that unionism as such is artificial or natural, revolutionary or conservative, violent or law-abiding, monopolistic or inclusive, boss-ridden or democratic, opposed to industrial progress or favorable to efficiency, the spontaneous outgrowth of legitimate needs or the product and tool of selfish and designing individuals. In short, there is unionism and unionism. But looking at matters concretely and realistically, there is no single thing that can be taken as unionism *per se*.

It follows as a corollary that the union problem is neither simple nor unitary. It is not a mere question of wages and hours, of shop conditions, and of narrow economic rights of employer and employee, and it cannot be solved by a mere resort to economic theory. On the contrary, it is a complex of economic, legal, ethical, and social problems, which can be understood and met only by knowing the facts and the genesis of the viewpoint of organized labor in all its reach, diversity, contradictoriness, and shifting character, and by considering this viewpoint in relation to developing social conditions and social standards.

. . . Unionism is what it is and not what any advocate or opponent would have it to be. It is a matter of fact in the same sense that institutions, animal and plant species, or any other organic manifestations are matters of fact. There is no normal or abnormal unionism; no unionism that is artificial as distinguished from that which is natural. In short, there is no fixed union norm by which any concrete case is to be tested. . . .

The master key to the real character of unionism and union problems is to be found apparently in the existence of distinct union types. Though unionism itself is so pragmatic and therefore so protean as to warrant the rejection of all attempts to characterize and judge it as a whole, it has seemingly developed along certain fairly distinct general lines, giving rise thus to types sufficiently definite to allow of legitimate generalization in regard to them. It appears possible to distinguish such types, both as to function and structure. . . .

Naming the structural types in what hypothetically may perhaps be considered their natural sequence of development, we find, first, what is ordinarily called the craft union. This is an organization of wageworkers engaged in a single occupation, as, for example, in glass bottle blowing, horseshoeing, locomotive engineering. The occupation may be limited strictly to one simple task, or may include a number of closely allied tasks or crafts. The strict test of a craft union seems to be that each member of the organization performs or may perform all the tasks included in the occupation. Usually a craft union covers but a fraction of the work of a given industry. The craft organization has developed two principal units, or appears in two main forms; the *local craft union*, which usually unites the members of the craft or occupation working in a particular locality—a town, a city, or a section of a city; the *national or international craft union*, which unites into one organization the local units of a single craft or occupation throughout the country or neighboring countries.

Secondly, there appears what may be termed the *crafts* or *trades union*. This organization is a *federation* of unions in different crafts or industries. It has developed three principal forms or units: the *local trades union*, or *city federation*; the *state federation*; and the *national* or *international federation*, which unite through delegate organizations, respectively, the unions of a locality, a state, or a larger territorial area. Examples are the Chicago Federation of Labor, The Illinois Federation of Labor, and the American Federation of Labor. The essential characteristic of the trades union is that the constituent organizations retain their individual independence or sovereignty.

Thirdly, we may distinguish the *industrial union*. This type, as the name implies, is organized on the basis of the industry rather than the craft. That is to say, it attempts to unite into one homogeneous organic group all the workers, skilled and unskilled, engaged in turning out and putting on the market a given finished product or series of closely related products. For example, this type of union would unite all the craftsmen in the direct employ of brewing concerns, including not only actual brewers, maltsters, bottlers, and packers, but the engineers, firemen, teamsters, watchmen, etc.; or, again, it would organize into one union all the workmen in and about a coal mine, including actual miners, miners' helpers, shot firers, drivers, spraggers, trappers, trackmen, timbermen, hoisting engineers, check-weighmen, dumpers, etc. The actual connotation of this type of unionism varies in different productive lines and with the integration of productive enterprise, but the essential test of industrial unionism seems to be that the industrial scope or area of the workers' organization shall be coterminous with that of the capitalistic enterprise or series of closely related enterprises. The main forms or units of this type of unionism thus far are: the *local industrial union*, a combination of all the employees of a single local industrial plant or of all the industrial enterprises of a like character in a given locality; the *national or international industrial union*, a combination of all the workers in a given industry throughout the nation or the international economic unit; the *district industrial union*, an organization covering an area within which productive and market conditions are essentially similar. Thus, for example, the coal mine workers are organized into local unions at the mines, into an international union including workers in the mines of the United States and Canada, and into district organizations covering adjacent bituminous or anthracite mines or fields.

Fourthly, there exists what is technically known as the *labor union*. This type of unionism proposes the organization of all workers regardless of craft or industrial division into homogeneous groups by localities, by districts, and throughout the nation or largest possible international area. At present the *local labor union* is the only existing unit of importance in the United States which realizes this ideal of organization, though attempts have been made, notably in the case of the Knights of Labor, to establish and maintain labor unionism in all its ideal forms, *local, district*, and *national*.

Besides these four structural types of unionism, there exist in this country at least two varieties which can hardly be designated as distinct types, but which, strictly speaking, are apparently neither craft, trades, industrial, nor labor unions. The first of these varieties may be called the *compound craft* or *crafts union*. It is a centralized, homogeneous organization of the workers in a number of related crafts. It differs from the craft union in that it includes workers who do not engage in the same tasks or occupations. But it is not an industrial union, since it may be one of several labor organizations whose workers are engaged in turning out a given finished product, or are in the employ of a single capitalistic enterprise. On the other hand, it may overlap industrial divisions. It may be the outcome of a formal consolidation of two or more crafts or compound craft unions, in which case it is usually known as an *amalgamated* craft or crafts union. Examples of this variety of unionism are to be found in the Amalgamated Association of Iron,

Tin, and Steel Workers of North America, the Amalgamated Meat Cutters and Butcher Workmen of North America, the International Association of Machinists, and the Amalgamated Association of Street and Electrical Employees of America. In fact, a large proportion of the unions, *local* and *national*, in the United States are today compound or amalgamated craft unions, whether or not so designated by title. As this variety of union has special representatives in all the intermediate structural stages between strict craft unionism and industrial unionism, it would perhaps be not unreasonable to regard it, provisionally at least, as a mode of transition between these two distinct types. . . .

The second structural variety of unionism which is difficult to classify may, in the absence of any generally accepted designation, be termed the *quasi industrial federation*. It is generally a federation of industrially related craft and compound craft unions, appearing in *local, district* or *state*, and *national* units. Examples of it are to be seen in local printing trades, and local building trades councils, in state building trades councils and system federations of railway employees, and in the building trades, metal trades and railroad employees' departments of the American Federation of Labor. This variety of unionism is one in which the constituent craft or amalgamated craft unions retain their individual sovereignty, yet appear and act as a single organization with respect to designated affairs of common interests. It resembles both the trades union and the industrial union types, but differs from each essentially. It is a narrower and closer association than the trades union and is vitally unlike it in the scope and character of its activities. On the other hand, it lacks the organic homogeneity and centralization of the industrial union. As it is in every case, roughly speaking, an organization within a particular industry, and as its aims and activities approximate—as far as they go—those of the industrial union type, it may perhaps be regarded also as an intermediate phase—a mode of transition between the craft and the industrial union. . . .

As we have said, the existence of distinct structural types and varieties of unionism has quite generally been recognized, and it has been noted further that union function tends to vary somewhat with the variation in structure. It seems possible, however, to go much further than this in the general functional analysis of unionism. A penetrating study of the union situation, past and present, seems, in fact, to warrant the recognition of functional types quite as distinct in their essential characteristics as the diverse structural manifestations. It is true that these functional types do not in practice represent exactly and exclusively the ideas and activities of any particular union organization or group. That is to say, no union organization functions strictly and consistently according to type. Yet as representing as fairly distinct alternative programs of union action, and as guides to the essential character and significance of the diverse organizations and groups included in the heterogeneous union complex, these functional types apparently do exist, and are of the most vital concern to the student of unionism. There are seemingly four of these distinct types, two of which present dual variations.

The first and perhaps most clearly recognizable functional type may be termed *business unionism*. Business unionism appears most characteristically in the programs of local and national craft and compound craft organizations. It is essentially trade-conscious, rather than class-conscious. That is to say, it expresses the viewpoint and interests of the workers in a craft or industry rather than those of the working class as a whole. It aims chiefly at more, here and now, for the organized workers of the craft or industry, in terms mainly of higher wages, shorter hours, and better working conditions, regardless for the most part of the welfare of the workers outside the particular organic group, and regardless in general of political and social considerations, except in so far as these bear directly upon its own economic ends. It is conservative in the sense that it professes belief in natural rights, and accepts as inevitable, if not as just, the existing capitalistic organization and the wage system, as well as existing property rights and the binding force of contract. It regards unionism mainly as a bargaining institution and seeks its ends chiefly through collective bargaining, supported by such methods as experience from time to time indicates to be effective in sustaining and increasing its bargaining power. Thus it is likely to be exclusive, that is, to limit its membership, by means of the apprenticeship system and high initiation fees and dues, to the more skilled workers in the craft or industry, or even to a portion of these; though it may, where immediate circumstances dictate, favor a broadly inclusive policy—when, for example, the unregulated competition of the unorganized and the unskilled seriously threatens to sweep aside the trade barriers and break down the standards of wages, hours and shop conditions it has erected. Under these circumstances it tends to develop a broad altruism and to seek the organization of all the workers in the craft or industry. In harmony with its business character it tends to emphasize discipline within the organization, and is prone to develop strong leadership and to become somewhat autocratic in government, though government and leaders are ordinarily held pretty strictly accountable to the pragmatic test. When they fail to "deliver the goods" both are likely to be swept aside by a democratic uprising of the rank and file. In method, business unionism is prevailingly temperate and economic. It favors voluntary arbitration, deprecates strikes, and avoids political action, but it will refuse arbitration, and will resort to strikes and politics when such action seems best calculated to support its bargaining efforts and increase its bargaining power. This type of unionism is perhaps best represented in the program of the railroad brotherhoods, though these organizations . . . present some characteristics of a vitally different nature.

The second union functional type seems best designated by the terms, *friendly* or *uplift unionism*. Uplift unionism, as its name indicates, is characteristically idealistic in its viewpoint. It may be trade-conscious, or broadly class-conscious, and at times even claims to think and act in the interest of society as a whole. Essentially it is conservative and law-abiding. It aspires chiefly to elevate the moral, intellectual, and social life of the worker, to improve the conditions under which he works, to raise his material standards of living, give him a sense of personal worth and dignity, secure for him the leisure for culture, and insure him and his family against the loss of a decent livelihood by reason of unemployment, accident, disease, or old age. Uplift unionism varies greatly in degree of inclusiveness, and in form of government. But the tendency seems to be toward the greatest practicable degree of mutuality and democracy. In method, this type of unionism employs collective bargaining, but stresses mutual insurance, and drifts easily into political action and the advocacy of coöperative enterprises, profit-sharing, and other idealistic plans for social regeneration. The nearest approach in practice to uplift unionism is perhaps to be found in the program of the Knights of Labor, though that organization has varied in many respects from the strict type.

As a third distinct functional type, we have what most appropriately may be called *revolutionary unionism*. Revolutionary unionsim, as the term implies, is extremely radical both in viewpoint and in action. It is distinctly class-conscious rather than trade-conscious. That is to say, it asserts the complete harmony of interests of all wageworkers as against the representatives of the employing class, and seeks to unite the former, skilled and unskilled together, into one homogeneous fighting organization. It repudiates, or tends to repudiate, the existing institutional order and especially individual ownership of productive means, and the wage system. It looks upon the prevailing modes of right and rights, moral and legal, as, in general, fabrications of the employing class, designed to secure the subjection and to further the exploitation of the workers. In government it aspires to be democratic, striving to make literal application of the phrase *vox populi, vox Dei*. In method, it looks askance at collective bargaining and mutual insurance as making for conservatism and hampering the free and united action of the workers.

Of this revolutionary type of unionism there are apparently two distinct varieties. The first finds its ultimate ideal in the socialistic state and its ultimate means in invoking class political action. For the present it does not entirely repudiate collective bargaining or the binding force of contract, but it regards these as temporary expedients. It would not now amalgamate unionist and socialist organizations, but would have them practically identical in membership and entirely harmonious in action. In short, it looks upon unionism and socialism as the two wings of the working class movement. The second variety of revolutionary unionism repudiates altogether socialism, political action, collective bargaining, and contract. Socialism is to it but another form of oppression, political action a practical delusion, collective bargaining and contract schemes of the oppressor for preventing the united and immediate action of the workers. It looks forward to a society based upon free industrial association, and finds its legitimate means in agitation, rather than in methods which look to immediate betterment. Direct action and sabotage are its accredited weapons, and violence its habitual resort. These varieties of the revolutionary type may be termed respectively *socialistic* and *quasi anarchistic unionism*. The former is perhaps most clearly represented in the United States by the Western Federation of Miners, the latter by the Industrial Workers of the World.

Finally, in the union complex, it seems possible to distinguish a mode of action sufficiently definite in its character and genesis to warrant the designation, *predatory unionism*. This type, if it be truly such, cannot be set apart on the basis of any ultimate social ideals or theory. It may be essentially conservative or radical, trade-conscious or class-conscious. It appears to aim solely at immediate ends and its methods are wholly pragmatic. In short, its distinguishing characteristic is the ruthless pursuit of the thing in hand by whatever means seem most appropriate at the time, regardless of ethical and legal codes or effect upon those outside its own membership. It may employ business, friendly, or revolutionary methods. Generally, its operations are secret, and apparently it sticks at nothing.

Of this assumed union type also there appear to be two varieties. The first may be termed *hold-up unionism*. This variety is usually to be found in large industrial centers, masquerading as business unionism. In outward appearance it is conservative; it professes a belief in harmony of interests between employer and employee; it claims to respect the force of contract; it operates openly through collective bargaining, and professes regard for law and order. In reality it has no abiding principles, and no real concern for the rights or welfare of outsiders. Prevailingly it is exclusive and monopolistic. Generally it is boss-ridden and corrupt, the membership for the most part being content to follow blindly the instructions of the leaders so long as they "deliver the goods." Frequently it enters with the employers of the group into a double-sided monopoly intended to eliminate both capitalistic and labor competition, and to squeeze the consuming public. With the favored employers, it bargains not only for the sale of its labor, but for the destruction of the business of rival employers and the exclusion of rival workmen from the craft or industry. On the whole its methods are a mixture of open bargaining coupled with secret bribery and violence. This variety of unionism has been exemplified most frequently among the building trades organizations under the leadership of men like the late notorious "Skinney" Madden.

The second variety of predatory labor organization may be called, for want of a better name, *guerilla unionism*. This variety resembles the first in the absence of fixed principles and in the ruthless pursuit of immediate ends by means of secret and violent methods. It is to be distinguished from hold-up unionism, however, by the fact that it operates always directly against its employers, never in combination with them, and that it cannot be bought off. It is secret, violent, and ruthless, seemingly because it despairs of attaining what it considers to be legitimate ends by business, uplift, or revolutionary methods. This union variant has been illustrated recently in the campaign of destruction carried on by the Bridge and Structural Iron Workers.[1]

■    ■    ■

Students in general have approached unionism on the structural side, and have treated it as though the union were essentially an organic unit with certain functional attributes; and hitherto we have spoken of the functional and structural forms as though they were independent and coördinate expressions of unionism. Both of these attitudes are untenable. From the standpoint of motives and ends, as well as from that of its character and significance as a social problem, the real unionism—its primary and essential expression—is functional. The structural form is altogether secondary and dependent. This will be made evident by a brief analysis of the motives which actuate prospective unionists and the manner and purposes for which the union is brought into being.

What concerns men primarily in their social relationships as ends to be striven for is not forms of organizations but standards of living—using this phrase to cover not merely the narrow economic aspect of life but social standards generally, including moral and judicial as well as material conditions, rights, and privileges. As social beings we are all concerned primarily with the problem of living as presented by these conditions and standards; and our attention is focused on the solution of this problem in terms of our particular needs and the peculiar circumstances which we have to face and overcome. In our efforts to comprehend and solve this problem each of us develops more or less completely and systematically an interpretation of life—an explanation of things as they are in terms of the conditions and relationships of which we are conscious and the forces which determine these. And along with this interpretation there tends to grow up in the mind of each some plan or scheme for the modification or complete alteration of the situation in the furtherance of his special ideals or interests.

The wageworker is no exception in respect to all this. His hopes and fears center primarily about such matters as employment, wages and hours, conditions of work, modes of remuneration—in short, the most vital concerns which immediately touch his present and future well-being—and the economic, ethical, and juridical conditions, standards, and forces that practically determine these matters; and his mind focuses on the problem of living as presented in these terms. In his attempt to comprehend and solve this problem he also develops some sort of social viewpoint—an interpretation of the social situation as viewed from the standpoint of his peculiar experiences and needs—and a set of beliefs concerning what should and can be done to better the situation, especially as it bears upon the conditions of living which he faces.

The scope and character of this viewpoint and the mode of its development in the mind of the worker vary with the individual. If he is by nature and training thoughtful and independent, he may work out his own conclusions, subject of course to the unconscious influence of the general body of opinion about him, and his interpretation and solution may cover the widest range, including not only the immediate economic conditions and relationships which confront him, but the ethical and legal foundations upon which these rest. One indeed frequently encounters workmen who have thus possessed themselves of a complete and often esoteric social philosophy.

If, on the other hand, the individual worker is intellectually untrained and sluggish, his view is likely to be relatively narrow, concerned mainly with his own immediate conditions and relationships, and taken over bodily from the current opinion of his associates. In such cases he is likely to reflect merely the opinions of some stronger or more expansive personality who has constituted himself a leader. But whatever its range or quality, and however it may have been acquired, each worker possesses and is guided by some sort of social philosophy rooted in his peculiar temperament and in his immediate experiences and relationships.

It is evident that under these circumstances workers similarly situated economically and socially, closely associated and not too divergent in temperament and training, will tend to develop a common interpretation of the social situation and a common solution of the problem of living. This may come about gradually and spontaneously, or it may be the apparently sudden outcome of some crisis in the lives of the men concerned. It may, for example, result immediately from some alteration for the worse in the conditions of living, or an interference with what are considered established rights and modes of action, of which cases in point would be wholesale discharges from employment or the discharge of favorite individuals, a lowering of the wage rate, the requirement of more onerous or more dangerous conditions of work, a sudden rise in the prices of necessities, some police action or legal decision which touches the workers on the raw with respect to modes of action or their assumed dignity and rights as men. Or this crystallization of sentiment may come about as the result of the appearance from without or the rise from within the group of a purposeful agitator and leader—a man whose personality or position commands attention, who is capable of putting into general form the discontents of the individuals and offering a positive solution of their difficulties. But whatever the immediate cause, the result is the same. A social group is thus constituted, marked off by a more or less unified and well-developed but effective viewpoint or group psychology.

As soon as this state of affairs has been reached group action is a natural consequence. Those whose interpretations of the situation and solutions of the problem are sufficiently alike to make coöperation apparently possible, spontaneously or under purposeful leadership band themselves together for common effort and mutual assistnace. They come together thus, not primarily to establish and vindicate a form of organization —the organization is merely means to end—but to establish and maintain certain conditions of living—to put through a remedial program based on their common interpretation of the social situation viewed from the standpoint of their immediate conditions and needs.

Thus the union comes into existence. It goes back in its genesis ultimately to the common needs and problems of the wageworkers; it arises immediately out of the consciousness of the common or group character of those needs and problems; it exists for common action looking to the betterment of the living conditions; it appears primarily as a group interpretation of the social situation in which the workers find themselves, and a remedial program in the form of aims, policies, and methods; the organization and the specific form or structure which it takes are merely the instruments which the group adopts for propagating its viewpoint and putting its program into effect. In short, looking at it from the standpoint of motives and ends, as well as from that of its character as a social problem, the heart and core of the thing—its essential aspect or expression—is functional. Its structural or organic expression is secondary and dependent.

If, then, functional and structural types of trade unionism exist, we have here the most definite indications of what must be their nature and relationships. Assuming their existence, the functional type is simply a specific case of group psychology. It is a social interpretation and remedial program held by a group of wageworkers. Obviously there may be as many of these functional types as there are groups of workers with vitally different social viewpoints and plans of action. The structural type, on the other hand, is simply one of the organic methods by means of which the functional types seek to maintain discipline among their members and to put into effect their programs of action. Evidently there may be as many structural types as there are distinct organic modes of combination effective for these purposes. The functional type *is* unionism of a certain species. The structural type is öne organic form in which it may clothe itself. In other words, the structural type is related to the functional type somewhat as government is related to the nation. It is altogether a subordinate and dependent manifestation.

But do such types exist? So far as concerns structural types, this has been generally conceded. What can we say, then, in regard to the functional aspect of the case? Let us carry the analysis a step farther. It is evident that, once the viewpoint stated above is comprehended and accepted, we should look for distinct and conflicting varieties of unionism, functionally speaking. We should expect these to appear wherever and whenever there exist groups of workers with well-defined and conflicting social viewpoints. Moreover, we should expect to find them existing not only in succession but concurrently, and not only in different industries but among the workers in the same industry and even in the same craft. For as soon as we concede that the union is in essence an expression of group psychology we realize that it will get its specific character not merely from environmental conditions but from these in conjunction with the temperamental characteristics of the workers concerned, and that consequently union variants are likely to appear with a variation in either of these factors. In short, we should expect to find concurrent functional variation and conflict to be among the chief features of contemporary unionism in a country like our own, with its diversity of environmental conditions and its richness of racial and temperamental contrasts.

And the facts amply confirm the deduction: not only does the student of American unionism encounter different union groups in different industries with widely varying viewpoints and interpretations, but different unions with varying aims, policies, and methods contending for the domination of the same industry. And nothing is more characteristic of the situation than the descent of this form of conflict into the particular union where rival groups or factions struggle for the control of the organization in the interests of conflicting interpretations and programs. The bitterness of these contests and their continuance over long periods and under different sets of leaders leave no doubt that they spring, in part at least, from the existence of irreconcilable viewpoints.

If the validity of the preceding analysis be conceded, it is evident that the orthodox causal and historical interpretation of unionism must be abandoned or thoroughly revised. It has been the habit of students to look upon trade unionism as fundamentally an economic manifestation and to interpret it almost exclusively, or at least primarily, in terms of industrial or economic factors. Thus one school would explain unionism in terms of the development of the process of production in its narrow sense, making of it a succession of organic adaptations to the conditions and needs of the workers produced immediately by the successive types or units of capitalistic enterprise, e.g., the small craft unit, the industrial unit, and the enlarged industrial unit or trust. Unionism thus appears ultimately as the organic corollary of the form of the tool or machine. Another school insists that unionism is to be explained primarily in terms of the development of markets and the character and scope of market competition, endeavoring to show that the different forms of unionism correspond naturally to the conditions existing in conjunction with the customs market, the retail competitive market, and the wholesale market. Here transportation is perhaps the most potent underlying determinant. It is not denied that other factors have a formative influence, especially, for example, the presence or absence of free land, the political ideals and situation, and the state of public education. But these factors are looked upon as modifiers. Environment is practically the sole, and economic environment the chief, formative force, and unionism is again regarded as a series of successive adaptations of one and the same thing to the changing environmental conditions.

These attempts at explanation simply or mainly in industrial or economic terms result largely from the habit of regarding unionism primarily as an organic phenomenon and thus centering the attention on structural forms and changes, and are the chief cause for failure to recognize the possible nonunitary character of unionism. For as soon as we discard the older mode of approach and look at unionism as primarily functional in character, the appearance of orderly succession vanishes, and the simple modes of interpretation described above are seen to be altogether inadequate to account for the facts. We have then to explain chiefly the existence of contradictory group interpretations and programs which succeed each other apparently in no order accountable for by changes in the economic situation, and which appear, as we have pointed out, not only consecutively in conjunction with different systems of production and marketing, but concurrently, and not merely in the same general industrial and social *milieu*, but among workers in the same trade and even in the same union.

Evidently functional variations thus existing and persisting cannot be explained in economic or even in environmental terms alone. They can be accounted for only on the supposition that primary forces besides the industrial and environmental are vitally responsible for their genesis and being. In short, an interpretation of unionism, not in monistic, but in dualistic or pluralistic terms is required.

What then conceivably are these relatively permanent, non-industrial factors which enter into the determination of the primary or functional character of unionism? Since these diverse viewpoints and interpretations which make up unionism are obviously specific cases of group or social psychology, we have merely to inquire what are the determining factors of the psychology of social groups. This query the social psychologist stands ready to answer with considerable assurance. He assures us that one of these factors is environment—not economic environment merely, but political, social, and traditional as well, in the sense of the whole body of transmitted sentiments, ideas, and precepts—moral, religious, and customary. But he assures us also that over against environment as thus broadly interpreted is another factor, perhaps equally potent and certainly more permanent. This is the subjective factor. It includes temperament and aptitudes, both personal and racial, which show themselves as between different races and individuals in relatively permanent and conflicting feelings, ideals, and attitudes. It is these temperamental differences plus environmental influences that at any moment cause individuals to differ in respect to what is good and bad, right and wrong, just and unjust; which mold and color their social interpretations, and thus, through the primal forces of association, bring about psychological groups with diverse and conflicting viewpoints and programs of action. We may then reasonably conclude that the existence of concurrent and conflicting functional variants is to be explained as the outcome of different combinations of all these relatively permanent forces that affect the psychology of group membership, both environmental and subjective or temperamental, and since the functional aspect of unionism is its primary and essential expression it also is to be explained causally and historically in the same terms.

---

[1]It has been suggested that there is still another functional union type which might be called *dependent unionism*. It is well known that there are unions whose existence is dependent wholly or in large part upon other unions or upon the employers. Some unions, for example, could not exist except for their labels, which secure a special market among other unionists or union sympathizers for the goods which they turn out. Such unions are sometimes demanded or initiated by the employers, who see in the label a good commercial asset. Again, there are unions instigated and practically dominated by employers, organized and conducted on especially conservative lines with the purpose of combating or displacing independent unionism. We may then, perhaps, be justified in recognizing here a fifth functional type with two subordinate varieties.

# 28
## *A Philosophy of Labor*

FRANK TANNENBAUM                                                               1951

Trade-unionism is the conservative movement of our time. It is the counterrevolution. Unwittingly, it has turned its back upon most of the political and economic ideas that have nourished western Europe and the United States during the last two centuries. In practice, though not in words, it denies the heritage that stems from the French Revolution and from English liberalism. It is also a complete repudiation of Marxism. This profound challenge to our time has gone largely unnoticed because the trade-union's preoccupation with the detailed frictions that flow from the worker's relation to his job seemed to involve no broad program. In tinkering with the little things—hours, wages, shop conditions, and security in the job—the trade-union is, however, rebuilding our industrial society upon a different basis from that envisioned by the philosophers, economists, and social revolutionaries of the eighteenth and nineteenth centuries.

The importance of trade-unionism has been obscured until recently by the claims upon public attention of movements of lesser historical significance. The Communist, Fascist, and Nazi eruptions are secondary outcroppings of the same social rift that has brought trade-unionism into being. These popular upheavals are of passing import because they rest upon formal ideologies, subject to modification as the fashions in ideas change. Their dependence upon dogma reveals their inner debility, and their weakness is attested by their readiness to use force to impose upon society the design their ideology calls for. This assumes an ability to model and freeze man within some preconceived mold, which is contrary to experience. The unending flux of the people of the earth cannot be contained in an ideological straitjacket, and those who use violence toward that end are merely digging their own graves, as they always have done.

In contrast with these self-conscious and messianic political movements, the trade-union has involved a clustering of men about their work. This fusion has been going on for a long time. It has been largely unplanned, responsive to immediate needs, irrepressible, and inarticulate of its own ends because, on the whole, it had no general purposes. A sparsity of general ideas and a lack of any "ideology" kept the trade-union movement from being obtrusively vocal and permitted mesmeric political groups to look upon it as something of no great importance. But its very lack of ideas made it strong and enabled it to concentrate upon immediate ends without wasting its energies in a futile pursuit of Utopia. The trade-union movement could go on for generation after generation despite many failures, gradually accommodating itself to a changing industrial environment. It could do that without challenging the political or moral ideas current at the time, all the while slowly shaping new institutions, habits, and loyalties. It has gathered power within the community until it has suddenly dawned upon men that a new force—not an idea, but a new force—has come into being. This force is changing the structure of our economy and redistributing power in our society.

The emphasis in trade-unionism is upon the fusion of men in their respective trades or industries, and upon *movement*. There is nothing static about it, and calling this profound social drift "a problem to be solved" is a quaint commentary upon our optimism. The trade-union movement is not a problem. It is a process giving rise to innumerable conflicts because it has incalculable consequences. Its influence is felt at every point

Frank Tannenbaum, *A Philosophy of Labor* (New York: Alfred A. Knopf, 1951), pp. 3–14, 32–34, 44–46, 58–61, 105–107, 140–143, 162–164, 169, 198–199. Footnotes in the original have been eliminated or renumbered.

because it affects every aspect of modern society. The trade-union movement—*movement*—is not soluble. There is nothing in modern political wisdom or skill that can write *finis* to this flux, or even give it permanent direction. It is no more a soluble "problem" than the rise of the "middle class"[1] was a "problem" that could have been solved by a feudal society. As we look back upon the centuries of conflict that record the slow and at times violent transition from a feudal to a commercial and industrial commonwealth, it is clear that there was nothing the older society could have done to prevent the newer design from taking shape. In time the middle class came to have a special law of its own, and to be organized into a distinct body, the incorporated town with its own charter. It is important for purposes of comparison with the trade-union movement to remember that these changes were not the result of a plan, a philosophy, or even a theory. The rising merchants had no revolutionary objectives. "They only asked of society to make for them a place compatible with the sort of life they were leading."[2]

What the merchants and traders asked from their contemporary feudal institutions was the freedom to come and go as their business required. They wanted their own law, and they urged the "abolition of protestations most incompatible" with their way of life as citizens of a chartered town. Obviously, medieval society was faced with a stubborn "problem," but the real problem was how to meet the newer needs with the least possible violence. So it has been with the trade-union movement. What the workers asked for when the factory had welded them into coherent groups were a few changes in the rules governing their daily labor.

The workers wanted the right: (1) to organize; (2) to bargain collectively; (3) to keep nonmembers off the pay roll; (4) to participate in fixing wages and conditions of labor; (5) to meet freely for their purposes; (6) to define the jurisdiction of their jobs.

Like the rising towns that imposed new rules upon medieval society, the trade-unions are forcing basic changes in the laws, practices, and habits that welded modern society into a going concern. The implementation of these union rules has so changed the character of our society as to be comparable to the rise of the bourgeoisie. The growth of the middle class was more significant than the French Revolution, the Reform Bill in Great Britain, the revolutions of 1848 in central Europe, or the hundreds of other political upheavals from the period of the Reformation down to our own time. It is in this sense that the Communist movement in Russia and the Nazi upheaval in Germany are merely incidents in a wider drift of which they are unconscious manifestations.

This wider drift is reflected in the new "society" formed by the workers of the mill, mine, and factory, for whom the trade-union has proved the "natural" instrument, just as the town proved the fitting vehicle for the rising merchants and traders.

The full measure of the trade-union movement can be appreciated only by seeing the role it has played in the lives of the workers in the transition from a simple society to a complex industrial and urban economy. The Industrial Revolution destroyed the solid moorings of an older way of life, and cast the helpless workers adrift in a strange and difficult world. The peasant who had been reared in the intimacy of a small village, where customary values prescribed for every act between the cradle and the grave and where each man played a role in a drama known to all, now found himself isolated and bewildered in a city crowded with strangers and indifferent to a common rule. The symbolic universe that had patterned the ways of men across the ages in village, manor, or guild had disappeared.

This is the great moral tragedy of the industrial system. It destroyed the symbolic and meaningful world that had endowed the life of the individual with an ethical character. The individual worker now had no recognizable place that he could call his own, no society to which he "naturally" belonged, and no values by which he was expected to live. The ordinary meanings that make life acceptable had evaporated. His economic insecurity was but part of a larger perplexity. The rapid growth of factory, town, and city had brought a new world into being.

■　　■　　■

A hundred and fifty years ago the vast majority of the people in the United States and in the rest of the world lived in rural districts and were self-employed. The cities were small, the markets chiefly parochial; and the families supplied a large part of their own needs by direct and immediate production. Perhaps not more than ten per cent of the people who earned their living by labor were dependent upon a money wage for all of their real income. In the last hundred and fifty years the Industrial Revolution has stripped the mass of men in western Europe and the United States of their self-sufficiency and has driven them from the country and the village to the larger towns and cities. At the same time it has made them dependent on a money wage, not as a supplement to goods they produced themselves, but as the source of all their income. . . .

This change is unique for both its rapidity and its inclusiveness. Today in the United States, out of a working population of over 60,000,000, approximately 12,000,000 work for themselves. We have become a nation of employees. We are dependent upon others for our means of livelihood, and most of our people have become completely dependent upon wages. If they lose their jobs they lose every resource, except for the relief supplied by the various forms of social security. Such dependence of the mass of the people upon others for *all* of their income is something new in the world. *For our generation, the substance of life is in another man's hands.*

This dependence upon a job has been a cumulative process, and has been growing with increasing speed and intensity. In the last two generations the urban drift has become most evident. In 1870, in the United States, 53 per cent of those working for a living were engaged in agriculture. Today only some 13 per cent are working as farmers or farm hands. This unforeseen and unplanned transformation has modified the nature of the society man has always known. The city has disintegrated the extended family that cushioned and protected the individual between the cradle and the grave, served him in his need, and shared with him the pleasures and the sorrows of life. What is left of the family in the urban community is a weak and unstable makeshift for what the race has always known as its most basic and stable institution.

It is against this background that the role of the trade-union must be examined. In terms of the individual, the union returns to the worker his "society." It gives him a fellowship, a part in a drama that he can understand, and life takes on meaning once again because he shares a value system common to others. Institutionally the trade-union movement is an unconscious effort to harness the drift of our time and reorganize it around the cohesive identity that men working together always achieve.

That is why the trade-union is a repudiation of the individualism of the French Revolution and of the liberalism of English utilitarian philosophers. It rests upon the group, upon the organized "society" forged by the mine, mill, and factory. Trade-unionism is a repudiation of Marxism because its ends are moral rather than economic. It is a social and ethical system, not merely an economic one. It is concerned with the whole man. Its ends are the "good life." The values implicit in trade-unionism are those of an older day, antedating the grating modern political slogans. It is an unwitting effort to return to values derived from the past: security, justice, freedom, and faith. It is in those values, explicit and inherent, that man had found his human dignity.

Trade-unionism is counterrevolutionary because it contrives to build these values into our industrial society by working at them specifically and in detail, without any commitment to a general theory or an ideology, and even without a sense of direction. But the sum of these thousands of little acts, precedents, rights, and privileges adds up to a rebuilding of our industrial system along different lines from those on which it first developed and contrary to the designs the social revolutionaries would impose upon it. The trade-union movement is conservative and counterrevolutionary just because it is creative. It builds step by step, and the design expands as a series of new institutions that govern the entire man and increasingly rule the world wherein he has his being. He who would understand the labor movement must look backward and see where it came from. The future direction is to be discerned in the institutional pattern resting on previously established rule, habit, and commitment.

The trade-union's concern with detail is the most important point because it is an attempt to bridge the gap between labor on the one hand and freedom and security on the other. This gap has been one of the prime characteristics of urban industrial society. The union is faced with the question: how can the daily task be made coterminous with the good life, as it always had been until the machine came to make work and life separate things. If man cannot once again make freedom, security, and work synonymous, he will destroy the machine. Our industrial civilization will not survive state planning, Socialist control, Communist bureaucracy, or Fascist moral perversion, for they all postulate this disparity between labor and freedom.

The separation between life and labor, from which so many of our difficulties stem, is implicitly accepted by liberalism and Marxism and explains their failure to develop a satisfying theory for our time. They both assume that the good society can be built upon economic motives. The free competition of the economists and the classless society of the Communists have this in common. They are caught up in the endless beneficence of a money economy. But the bane of our industrial society lies in making income in money coterminous with the ends of life itself. A widening money economy increases the complexity of our society, standardizes the objectives, multiplies the dissatisfactions of all men, drives the society toward equalitarian ends in monetary terms, and universalizes individual insecurity.

If the possession of money is the goal of all our efforts, the lack of it is complete failure, for without it nothing is to be had, not even the barest subsistence. The moral inadequacy of industrialism lies in substituting a "good wage" for the good life.

The trade-union stepped into this breach between the good life and work for a money wage that resulted from the destruction of the earlier cohesive society, and the reduction of man to an isolated individual, hired as a "hand," and paid in cash. Its interests in the detailed relationships between the worker and his employer saved the trade-union from a commitment to any general formula and made it possible for the economists, the liberals, and the Marxists to deny its intrinsic importance. If the economists and liberals considered the trade-union a hindrance to a possible competitive harmony, the Marxists believed that unless they could secure control of the trade-union movement it would prove an impediment in the way of the revolution that would create heaven upon earth by abolishing the source of all evil. The early economists would have put an end to the movement; the Marxists sought to capture it for their own purposes.

Neither have had their way. The trade-union movement has survived because it satisfies the human craving for moral status in a recognizable society.

■　　■　　■

The trade-union movement is an unconscious rebellion against the atomization of industrial society. It suggests that the men, skilled and unskilled, who do the labor of the world want to return to an older and socially "normal" way of life. If the historical record has any meaning, a sense of identity among men laboring at a common task is "natural" and inevitable. Men identified with one another in their daily work develop a sense of their part of the social universe which is peculiarly their own and which they share with no one else. How otherwise explain the world-wide spread of the guild for traders, craftsmen, and artisans? . . .

■　　■　　■

The village, the manor, and the guild provided both a "society" and a way of life, which were little affected by the doings of kings and nobles. Centuries might pass and dynasties disappear, but the ways of the community remained much as they always had been. The changes that brought modern industry into being, however, destroyed the habits that had maintained an orderly community. In the earlier days "custom was the shield of the poor." The new factories, with their insistence upon an individual wage bargain, threw this precious heritage to the winds, and man found himself in a world without a definition of right respected by the whole community. What the Industrial Revolution did to the individual in general and to the laborer in particular was to disrupt his society and undermine the customary law he lived by. It threw him upon his own resources. Man was now "free" in a way he had never been previously. There had been unfortunate "masterless" men before, and itinerant tinkers and scholars, but here, for the first time, man in general was made independent. If he could get a job, he could live by himself, without a family, friends, guild, or craft.

The complex forces that wrought these changes are well known, but the long-run consequences of this loosening of the moorings were unforeseen. The weakening of the community adversely affected not only men, but also women and children, old and young, skilled and unskilled. Its effects reached all groups in the community, so that a society of traditional "status" melted away and became increasingly composed of isolated, equal, and independent individuals. For the first time men became responsible to themselves alone, and irresponsible for the well-being of anyone else, even their closest relatives. Even if this splintering of the community was never completed, because there is no absolute logic to a social movement except in theory, it still remains true that its effects were sufficiently broad to describe an age. It laid the basis for a series of political upheavals of which we in our own time are the unwitting heirs.

It was the payment of a money wage to each separate worker, man, woman, or child, that became the immediate cause of the breakdown of the older society. The payment of a money wage detached children from their parents and made old and young equal. By means of a separate money wage, the younger could be better off than their elders, and sons could lord it over their fathers. Under the new dispensation even daughters were free to abandon the family roof and live "independent" lives. Hordes of individual men, women, and children, drawn from other towns, and in the United States from different countries, were thrown together in city slums to find for themselves the key to the good life that had in the past been provided by the family, the church, the guild, and the community. The isolated worker, free and irresponsible, dominated the scene. A steel center such as Pittsburgh could be described as a city of single men, each of whom was free, independent, and equal. Every man was free if he had a job, independent because he could leave it, and equal because he had an opportunity to be measured by his ability to earn a living.

Equality for the worker took a new and strange form: the earning of a money wage. It came to mean equality for competitive strife. To secure a job and hold it proved to be the test of all else and the very means of survival. A kind of free-for-all became the prevailing rule among men, and the social milieu was sufficiently fluid to make room at the top for many who had the energy, skill, or shrewdness to swim with the tide and outstrip their opponents. But that was for the fortunate, the strong, and the ruthless. The mass of men found the going hard, the life a lonely one, and the boasted freedom something of a burden.

■ ■ ■

The new factories that worked this change in men's lives also stirred great hope for mechanical improvement and economic progress. By a curious turn, however, the hope of improvement was not for the laborer. The workers' poverty and misery, it was said, were due to their own shortcomings. Their poverty was the natural result of their laziness and lack of thrift, but it was said to serve a good end. The indigence of the worker was considered necessary to social stability and economic progress. Recreation was a waste of time, amusement was a sin, and rest was synonymous with idleness.

Pessimism over human destiny seemed natural to the age. Time and circumstances had combined to weaken the church and undermine the family. The crowded towns had demoralized the working people. The crowded towns had demoralized the working people. Drunkenness and immorality had increased and become notorious. The tavern, with its profanity and its obscenity, became a conspicuous feature of urban life. Murder, robbery, and assault increased; the jails were crowded; and transportation and hanging were commonplace.

The new industrial society, so full of promise for the future, had little to offer in the way of immediate consolation. The doctrines of individualism proved a poor substitute for the older values. To the workers, individualism, in so far as they had heard of it, was just a word. It embodied no tradition and provided no comfort. To the workers, who needed succor the most, the new doctrine had least to offer. The workers required, as all men do, a society of which they were members and in which they played a role. They wanted, once again, an opportunity to act out their humble parts in some recognizable drama and to be members of some organized group. Without knowing it, they wanted to re-create a "society."

■ ■ ■

There is no simple logic to a broad economic and political movement. Thus, while prevailing theory and public policy were preoccupied with the expanding individualism, another and unheralded movement came into being. This new movement denied the theory without repudiating it and, where it could, counteracted in its own way the process of atomization.

As the Industrial Revolution became more inclusive, more and more individuals had to depend upon a wage-paying job, and their helplessness in relation to it increased. It was not theirs to keep and to hold. As business enterprises grew larger, contact between the worker and his employer became less frequent, and the opportunities for understanding and identity between the two decreased. A new phase in the structure of the economy had developed. The factory system contained numerous individually helpless persons, each dependent upon a common employer. Men were not competent to assert either moral or economic influence upon the conditions of their labor, or to influence the retention of their jobs. They were individually helpless, and equal in their helplessness.

What the workers had in common was their employer, the industry they worked in, the hours they labored, the bench or the machine they worked at, the wage rate they received, the foreman who ruled over them, the materials they worked with, the whistle that called them from their beds in the morning or brought a halt to their labors. In addition, they had each other in common. They worked together at the same bench, inside the same mill or mine, struggled with the same refractory materials, and were dependent upon one another's co-operation. Here was a new social factor. The same process that had gathered these laborers together had forged a "society" in which a sense of identity became inevitable. Their personal helplessness was apparent to each. Their collective strength was yet to be revealed, but it could be discovered in the fact that they were all equally dependent upon the power that had brought them together. Their mutual association and experience, their similar skills, their relationship at the work bench, the tools they used, and the materials with which they worked gave them a common language. They acquired the language of the craft, the job, the shop, and the industry. They shared the special points of pride and shame that can have only specific and local meaning. They could complain about light and heat, or cold and dampness. They could indulge in interminable talk about the job, infinitely interesting in its repetitious monotony because it detailed the daily round of the little things men share. It gave them a common, if local, vocabulary. The employer became the catalytic agent that crystallized them into a self-conscious group. When a conflict stirred, this provided the stimulus to bring it to the surface.

Thus the social atomization resulting from the payment of an individual money wage was in time to be defeated by the fusing of men together functionally, and this functional coalescence became the firm foundation upon which the trade-union movement grew, and which, in fact, made it inevitable.

The original organizer of the trade-union movement is the shop, the factory, the mine, and the industry. The agitator or the labor leader merely announces the already existing fact. This is true in spite of the many instances of workers refusing to join a union. The process has gone on for so long a time, and over so wide an area, that it must be looked upon as an organic phenomenon, naturally following the spread of modern industry. The union is the spontaneous grouping of individual workers thrown together functionally. It reflects the moral identity and psychological unity men always discover when working together, because they need it and could not survive without it. There is nothing new about this. The fact that it takes the form of a trade-union is a historical accident, determined by the type of association the machine imposes. The theory which insisted that labor was a commodity like any other made collective action the only means of asserting the moral status of the individual. The trade-union was the visible evidence that man is not a commodity, and that he is not sufficient unto himself.

■　■　■

In its essence, trade-unionism is a revulsion against social atomization on the one hand, and the divorce of owner and worker from their historical function as moral agents in industry on the other. If there is any meaning that can be derived from the persistent grouping of men about their tools or within their industry, it is that work must fill a social and moral as well as an economic role. The vacuum created between the job and the man has proved intolerable; and it cannot be filled by higher wages, shorter hours, better conditions of labor, music in the shops, or baby clinics. Man has to belong to something real, purposeful, useful, creative; he must belong to his job and to his industry, or it must belong to him. There is no way of permanently separating the two. What gnaws at the psychological and moral roots of the contemporary world is that most urban people, workers and owners, belong to nothing real, nothing greater than their own impersonal pecuniary interests. To escape from this profound tragedy of our industrial society is the great issue of our time, for a world in which neither the owner nor the worker is morally identified with his source of income has no principle of continuity. No institution can survive for long in a moral vacuum. For the worker the trade-union has represented an unwitting attempt to escape from this dilemma.

There is a continuing failure to recognize that the trade-union, like the corporation, represents a structural change within the economy. The trade-union is not a reform movement; it is not a political party; it is not revolutionary in intent; it is not a legislative activity. It may at times contribute to all of these, but it is none of them. It is the formal expression of the socially inevitable grouping of men in modern industry, just as the corporation and the holding company are new ways of organizing capital for industry. The trade-union is the opposite side of the medal. Where you have corporate industry, there you have the modern national labor union. As long as industry and commerce were small and proprietary the very nature of the trade-union was different.

■　■　■

As long as the union can limit the number of workers it will admit, and insist upon membership as a condition of receiving or keeping a job, it can control the workers within the industry. The courts, under the common law, have upheld the right of the unions to exclude new members on the grounds that they are voluntary associations. But they are voluntary associations with compulsive powers over both the employer and the worker. They are, in fact, private lawmaking bodies whose rules affect the lives of millions of human beings and thousands of industrial plants. This is evidenced by the more than fifty thousand collective labor agreements existing in the country. The unions that sign these contracts acquire an influence over the activities of their members which in time circumscribe their daily lives and redefines the privileges of men who, under the law, are equal to each other. Without intent or plan, the trade-union movement is integrating the workers into what in effect amounts to a series of separate social orders. It is re-creating a society based upon status and destroying the one we have known in our time—a society based upon contract.

If membership in a union is essential to an opportunity to work, and if every union has its own rules of admission, apprenticeship, dues, initiation fees, promotion, wages, retirement funds, and social benefits, then every union becomes in effect a differentiated order within the community, endowing its own members with rights and immunities shared only among themselves. Moreover, a member finds it increasingly difficult to leave his union, because the penalties for desertion are severe. These penalties include the loss of a job, the impossibility of securing other employment in the same industry, the lost of seniority and possible promotion, and the surrender of accumulated retirement, sickness, and old-age benefits. A new body of rights and disciplines, which greatly change the substance of a free society, has come into being. A single bargaining agency collects dues (its own form of taxation) from the worker, without his consent, through the check-off, and has enforceable union security provisions so that the worker must end by being a member of the union. In the spread of such industry-wide agreements we have the making of a new social design in which status rather than contract is the governing rule.

In theory, this status is voluntarily assumed. In fact, the penalties for not accepting the "voluntary" status become unavoidable. This compulsory membership is now to be found in a vast number of industries, occupations, and professions, from barbers to steel-workers, from musicians to airplane pilots, from chorus girls to sailors. Skilled and unskilled, professional and learned occupations, small and large plants, highly mechanized and semi-mechanized industries, are being incorporated into and made part of this pattern, and there is no prospect of an immediate end to the movement. If the history of trade-unionism demonstrates anything at all, it is that restrictive legislation, or other opposition, which proved ineffectual when the movement was new will not bring it to a halt now.

It is noteworthy that the growth of these stratifications has been justified and defended in the name of freedom, equality, and justice.The freedom, equality, and justice here spoken of have a functional rather than a political or civil context. One of the long-run and unforeseen by-products of the individual worker's attempt to achieve "economic security" is the gradual remolding of industrial society on the older order of "estates." The Industrial Revolution destroyed a social system in which each man had a place in a "society" and in which he could fulfill his role as a human being. It gradually tore that "society" apart and robbed man of his traditional responsibilities and duties. But membership within a social group, so necessary to man, reappeared in a new form when the workers were congregated into industries. Here a common setting made the strangers of yesterday the companions of today. All that has followed in the structure and impact of the trade-union movement was a necessary sequence to the organic relationship the factory imposed. The industrialism that destroyed a society of status has now re-created it. The last one hundred and fifty years are a strange interlude in the history of man in the Western World, a period in which man was "freed" from one age-old association and, after a lapse, gradually reidentified with another one. If there is anything to this view of the matter, the system of "estates" now being developed is a necessary and logical outcome of the Industrial Revolution.

■　■　■

The worker, once organized and integrated into the industrial structure, tends to surrender his freedom to separate himself from the industry. The union increasingly ties the worker to the industry and tends to convert a contract terminable at will into one terminable only at death. His union gives him his freedoms within the industry, but it hedges his "freedom" to abandon the industry within which he makes his living.

The developing situation is lost sight of in the persistent argument over wages, as if the union were chiefly occupied with pecuniary income. That is not the case. The overemphasis of economic ends has obscured the real issues. The economic ends are there, but there are also the purposes embraced by membership in a "society," and these include the broad ethical objectives that define the good life. The form the argument between management and labor takes is in some ways irrelevant to the inner bent of the union. Each dispute is over a specific issue. The underlying drive is increased participation in management, because whatever management does has its bearing not merely upon the future economic security of the members and the future role of the union, but also upon the undefinable but very real sense of membership in a going concern. The union may talk the language of the market and be obsessed by economic objectives. That is part of the milieu as given, and it is a language that both labor and management understand. But the underlying theme is the drive for moral status within the industry. A commitment to spend one's life in a job where no moral status was achievable would not be tolerable; it would be equivalent to slavery.

The union, if it is to survive, must maintain the fealty of its members, and it can do that only by giving them a sense of dignity and standing, not only within the union, but also within the industry. Such a sense of dignity can only be had if the workers have a concern for all the issues and difficulties of the enterprise. Identity on both a moral and a psychological basis is a condition of peaceful friction within the industrial system, and cannot be had as long as the workers and their unions are treated as outsiders. It is this underlying necessity that shapes the continuing pressure for increased participation in management. In gradually expanding the range of its responsibilities, the union satisfies the only irreducible expectancy of the worker: a growing moral status within the industry. The union thus gives the worker something he must have, a place in which he can feel at home; and only by doing this can the union be sure of that loyalty of its members which it must have to survive.

The growth of labor responsibility in management is inevitable under contemporary industrial conditions because the trade-union represents all of the life interests of its members. It is, in fact, a "society" with powers of "governance." Management's definition of its own role as that limited by the satisfaction of profit motives places it at a moral and psychological disadvantage and puts it on the defensive.

The major error of the last century has been the assumption that a total society can be organized upon an economic motive, upon profit. The trade-union has proved that notion to be false. It has demonstrated once again that men do not live by bread alone. Because the corporation can offer only bread or cake, it has proved incompetent to meet the demands for the good life. The union, with all its faults, may yet save the corporation and its great efficiencies by incorporating it into its own natural "society," its own cohesive labor force, and by endowing it with the meanings that all real societies possess, meanings that give some substance of idealism to man in his journey between the cradle and the grave. . . .

If this analysis has any meaning, the trade-union is the conservative force of our time. It is conservative because through bickering over details and by continuous compromise it seeks to preserve the older values by integrating a nonmoral, and therefore essentially corrosive, power (the corporation) into a "society" possessed of an ethical basis for survival. This forced conversion of an institution devoted to the increase of profit as an end is a more promising route for a change-over by the corporation to the values essential to any "society" than is likely to be found through the recently proclaimed doctrines of public responsibility and public service now being avowed in professional management associations.

■ ■ ■

The trade-union is the real alternative to the authoritarian state. The trade-union is our modern "society," the only true society that industrialism has fostered. As a true society it is concerned with the whole man, and embodies the possibilities of both the freedom and the security essential to human dignity. The corporation and the union will ultimately merge in common ownership and cease to be a house divided. It is only thus that a common identity may once again come to rule the lives of men and endow each one with rights and duties recognized by all.

---

[1] I use the term "middle class" in its conventional sense, but I use it reluctantly. It seems to me one of those clichés in the "social sciences," like the word "problem," that we would do better without if we could get rid of it. The whole concept of "class" is a hindrance to social analysis.

[2] Henri Pirenne: *Medieval Cities* (translated from the French by Frank D. Halsey, Princeton University Press, 1925), p. 176.

# 29

## *The Theory of Business Enterprise*

THORSTEIN VEBLEN                                                         1904

Within the comprehensive situation of to-day there is this new factor, the machine process. . . . The machine process pervades the modern life and dominates it in a mechanical sense. Its dominance is seen in the enforcement of precise mechanical measurements and adjustment and the reduction of all manner of things, purposes and acts, necessities, conveniences, and amenities of life, to standard units. . . . The point of immediate interest here is the further bearing of the machine process upon the growth of culture,—the disciplinary effect which this movement for standardization and mechanical equivalence has upon the human material.

This discipline falls more immediately on the workmen engaged in the mechanical industries, and only less immediately on the rest of the community which lives in contact with this sweeping machine process. Wherever the machine process extends, it sets the pace for the workmen, great and small. The pace is set, not wholly by the particular processes in the details of which the given workmen is immediately engaged, but in some degree by the more comprehensive process at large into which the given detail process fits. It is no longer simply that the individual workman makes use of one or more mechanical contrivances for effecting certain results. Such used to be his office in the earlier phases of the use of machines, and the work which he now has in hand still has much of that character. But such a characterization of the workman's part in industry misses the peculiarly modern feature of the case. He now does this work as a factor involved in a mechanical process whose movement controls his motions. It remains true, of course, as it always has been true, that he is the intelligent agent concerned in the process, while the machine, furnace, roadway, or retort are inanimate structures devised by man and subject to the workman's supervision. But the process comprises him and his intelligent motions, and it is by virtue of his necessarily taking an intelligent part in what is going forward that the mechanical process has its chief effect upon him. The process standardizes his supervision and guidance of the machine. Mechanically speaking, the machine is not his to do with it as his fancy may suggest. His place is to take thought of the machine and its work in terms given him by the process that is going forward. His thinking in the premises is reduced to standard units of gauge and grade. If he fails of the precise measure, by more or less, the exigencies of the process check the aberration and drive home the absolute need of conformity.

There results a standardization of the workman's intellectual life in terms of mechanical process, which is more unmitigated and precise the more comprehensive and consummate the industrial process in which he plays a part. This must not be taken to mean that such work need lower the degree of intelligence of the workman. No doubt the contrary is nearer the truth. He is a more efficient workman the more intelligent he is, and the discipline of the machine process ordinarily increases his efficiency even for work in a different line from that by which the discipline is given. But the intelligence required and inculcated in the machine industry is of a peculiar character. The machine process is a severe and insistent disciplinarian in point of intelligence. It requires close and unremitting thought, but it is thought which runs in standard terms of quantitative precision. Broadly, other intelligence on the part of the workman is useless; or it is even

Reprinted from Thorstein Veblen, *The Theory of Business Enterprise* (1904; repr. 1965, A. M. Kelley, Publishers), pp. 306–309, 314–318, 327–332, 335–336. Footnotes in the original have been eliminated.

worse than useless, for a habit of thinking in other than quantitative terms blurs the workman's quantitative apprehension of the facts with which he has to do.

In so far as he is a rightly gifted and fully disciplined workman, the final term of his *habitual* thinking is mechanical efficiency, understanding "mechanical" in the sense in which it is used above. But mechanical efficiency is a matter of precisely adjusted cause and effect. What the discipline of the machine industry inculcates, therefore, in the habits of life and of thought of the workman, is regularity of sequence and mechanical precision; and the intellectual outcome is an habitual resort to terms of measurable cause and effect, together with a relative neglect and disparagement of such exercise of the intellectual faculties as does not run on these lines.

■　■　■

Leaving aside the archaic vocations of war, politics, fashion, and religion, the employments in which men are engaged may be distinguished as pecuniary or business employments on the one hand, and industrial or mechanical employments on the other hand. In earlier times, and indeed until an uncertain point in the nineteenth century, such a distinction between employments would not to any great extent have coincided with a difference between occupations. But gradually, as time has passed and production for a market has come to be the rule in industry, there has supervened a differentiation of occupations, or a division of labor, whereby one class of men have taken over the work of purchase and sale and of husbanding a store of accumulated values. Concomitantly, of course, the rest, who may, for lack of means or of pecuniary aptitude, have been less well fitted for pecuniary pursuits, have been relieved of the cares of business and have with increasing specialization given their attention to the mechanical processes involved in this production for a market. In this way the distinction between pecuniary and industrial activities or employments has come to coincide more and more nearly with a difference between occupations. . . .

■　■　■

The everyday life of those classes which are engaged in business differs materially . . . from the life of the classes engaged in industry proper. There is an appreciable and widening difference between the habits of life of the two classes; and this carries with it a widening difference in the discipline to which the two classes are subjected. It induces a difference in the habits of thought and the habitual grounds and methods of reasoning resorted to by each class. There results a difference in the point of view, in the facts dwelt upon, in the methods of argument, in the grounds of validity appealed to; and this difference gains in magnitude and consistency as the differentiation of occupations goes on. So that the two classes come to have an increasing difficulty in understanding one another and appreciating one another's convictions, ideals, capacities, and shortcomings.

The ultimate ground of validity for the thinking of the business classes is the natural-rights ground of property,—a conventional, anthropomorphic fact having an institutional validity, rather than a matter-of-fact validity such as can be formulated in terms of material cause and effect; while the classes engaged in the machine industry are habitually occupied with matters of causal sequence, which do not lend themselves to statement in anthropomorphic terms of natural rights and which afford no guidance in questions of institutional right and wrong, or of conventional reason and consequence. Arguments which proceed on material cause and effect cannot be met with arguments from conventional precedent or dialectically sufficient reason, and conversely.

■ ■ ■

The industrial classes appear to be losing the instinct of individual ownership. The acquisition of property is ceasing to appeal to them as a natural, self-evident source of comfort and strength. The natural right of property no longer means so much to them as it once did.

A like weakening of the natural-rights animus is visible at another point in the current frame of mind of these classes. The growth of trade-unionism and of what is called the trade-union spirit is a concomitant of industry organized after the manner of a machine process. Historically this growth begins, virtually, with the industrial revolution, coming in sporadically, loosely, tentatively, with no precise assignable date, very much as the revolution does. England is the land of its genesis, its "area of characterization," and the place where it has reached its fullest degree of specification and its largest force; just as England is the country in which the modern machine industry took its rise and in which it has had the longest and most consistent life and growth. In this matter other countries are followers of the British lead and apparently borrowers of British precedents and working concepts. Still, the history of the trade-union movement in other countries seems to say that the working classes elsewhere have not advisedly borrowed ideals and methods of organization from their British congeners so much as they have been pushed into the same general attitude and line of conduct by the same general line of exigencies and experiences. Particularly, experience seems to say that it is not feasible to introduce the trade-union spirit or the trade-union rules into any community until the machine industry has had time extensively to standardize the scheme of work and of life for the working classes on mechanical lines. Workmen do not take to full-blown trade-union ideals abruptly on the introduction of those modern business methods which make trade-union action advisable for the working class. A certain interval elapses between the time when business conditions first make trade-union action feasible, as a business proposition, and the time when the body of workmen are ready to act in the spirit of trade-unionism and along the lines which the union animus presently accepts as normal for men in the mechanically organized industries. An interval of discipline in the ways of the mechanically standardized industry, more or less protracted and severe, seems necessary to bring such a proportion of the workmen into line as will give a consensus of sentiment and opinion favorable to trade-union action.

The pervading characteristic of the trade-union animus is the denial of the received natural-rights dogmas wherever the mechanical standardization of modern industry traverses the working of these received natural rights. Recent court decisions in America, as well as decisions in analogous cases in England at that earlier period when the British development was at about the same stage of maturity as the current American situation, testify unequivocally that the common run of trade-union action is at variance with the natural-rights foundation of the common law. Trade-unionism denies individual freedom of contract to the workman, as well as free discretion to the employer to carry on his business as may suit his own ends. Many pious phrases have been invented to disguise this iconoclastic trend of trade-union aims and endeavors; but the courts, standing on a secure and familiar natural-rights footing, have commonly made short work of the shifty sophistications which trade-union advocates have offered for their consideration. They have struck at the root of the matter in declaring trade-union regulations inimical to the natural rights of workman and employer alike, in that they hamper individual liberty and act in restraint of trade. The regulations, therefore, violate that system of law and order which rests on natural rights, although they may be enforced by that *de facto* law and order which is embodied in the mechanical standardization of the industrial processes.

Trade-unionism is an outgrowth of relatively late industrial conditions and has come on gradually as an adaptation of old methods and working arrangements carried over from the days of handicraft and petty trade. It is a movement to adapt, construe, recast, earlier working arrangements with as little lesion to received preconceptions as the new exigencies and the habits of thought bred by them will permit. It is, on its face, an endeavor of compromise between received notions of what "naturally" ought to be in matters of industrial business, on the one hand, and what the new exigencies of industry demand and what the new animus of the workman will tolerate, on the other hand. Trade-unionism is therefore to be taken as a somewhat mitigated expression of what the mechanical standardization of industry inculcates. Hitherto the movement has shown a fairly uninterrupted growth, not only in the numbers of its membership, but in the range and scope of its aims as well; and hitherto it has reached no halting-place in its tentative, shifty, but ever widening crusade of iconoclasm against the received body of natural rights. The latest, maturest expressions of trade-unionism are, on the whole, the most extreme, in so far as they are directed against the natural rights of property and pecuniary contract.

The nature of the compromise offered by trade-unionism is shown by a schedule of its demands: collective bargaining for wages and employment; arbitration of differences between owners and workmen; standard rates of wages; normal working day, with penalized regulation of hours for men, women, and children; penalized regulation of sanitary and safety appliances; mutual insurance of workmen, to cover accident, disability, and unemployment. In all of this the aim of unionism seldom goes the length of overtly disputing the merits of any given article of natural-rights dogma. It only endeavors to cut into these articles, in point of fact, at points where the dogmas patently traverse the conditions of life imposed on the workmen by the modern industrial system or where they traverse the consensus of sentiment that is coming to prevail among these workmen.

When unionism takes an attitude of overt hostility to the natural-rights institutions of property and free contract, it ceases to be unionism simply and passes over into something else, which may be called socialism for want of a better term. Such an extreme iconoclastic position, which would overtly assert the mechanical standardization of industry as against the common-law standardization of business, seems to be the logical outcome to which the trade-union animus tends, and to which some approach has latterly been made by more than one trade-unionist body, but which is, on the whole, yet in the future, if, indeed, it is to be reached at all. On the whole, the later expressions go farther in this direction than the earlier; and the animus of the leaders, as well as of the more wide-awake body of unionist workmen, appears to go farther than their official utterances.

■     ■     ■

The above presentation of the case of trade-unionism is of course somewhat schematic, as such a meagre, incidental discussion necessarily must be. It takes account only of those features of trade-unionism which characteristically mark it off from that business scheme of things with which it comes in conflict. There are, of course, many survivals, pecuniary and others, in the current body of trade-union demands, and much of the trade-union argument is carried on in business terms. The crudities and iniquities of the trade-union campaign are sufficiently many and notorious to require no rehearsal here. These crudities and iniquities commonly bulk large in the eyes of critics who pass an opinion on trade-unionism from the natural-rights point of view; and, indeed, they may deserve all the disparaging attention that is given them. Trade-unionism does not fit into the natural-rights scheme of right and honest living; but therein, in great part, lies its cultural significance. It is of the essence of the case that the new aims, ideals, and expedients do not fit into the received institutional structure; and that the classes who move in trade-unions are, however crudely and blindly, endeavoring, under the compulsion of the machine process, to construct an institutional scheme on the lines imposed by the new exigencies given by the machine process.

# 30
## *The Vested Interests*

THORSTEIN VEBLEN                                                    1919

The new order has brought the machine industry, corporation finance, big business, and the world market. Under this new order in business and industry, business controls industry. Invested wealth in large holdings controls the country's industrial system, directly by ownership of the plant, as in the mechanical industries, or indirectly through the market, as in farming. So that the population of these civilised countries now falls into two main classes: those who own wealth invested in large holdings and who thereby control the conditions of life for the rest; and those who do not own wealth in sufficiently large holdings, and whose conditions of life are therefore controlled by these others. It is a division, not between those who have something and those who have nothing—as many socialists would be inclined to describe it—but between those who own wealth enough to make it count, and those who do not.

And all the while the scale on which the control of industry and the market is exercised goes on increasing; from which it follows that what was large enough for assured independence yesterday is no longer large enough for tomorrow. Seen from another direction, it is at the same time a division between those who live on free income and those who live by work,—a division between the kept classes and the underlying community from which their keep is drawn. It is sometimes spoken of in this bearing—particularly by certain socialists—as a division between those who do no useful work and those who do; but this would be a hasty generalisation, since not a few of those persons who have no assured free income also do no work that is of material use, as e.g., menial servants. But the gravest significance of this cleavage that so runs through the population of the advanced industrial countries lies in the fact that it is a division between the vested interests and the common man. It is a division between those who control the conditions of work and the rate and volume of output and to whom the net output of industry goes as free income, on the one hand, and those others who have the work to do and to whom a livelihood is allowed by these persons in control, on the other hand. In point of numbers it is a very uneven division, of course.

A vested interest is a legitimate right to get something for nothing, usually a prescriptive right to an income which is secured by controlling the traffic at one point or another. The owners of such a prescriptive right are also spoken of as a vested interest. Such persons make up what are called the kept classes. But the kept classes also comprise many persons who are entitled to a free income on other grounds than their ownership and control of industry or the market, as, e.g., landlords and other persons classed as "gentry," the clergy, the Crown—where there is a Crown—and its agents, civil and military. Contrasted with these classes who make up the vested interests, and who derive an income from the established order of ownership and privilege, is the common man. He is common in the respect that he is not vested with such a prescriptive right to get something for nothing. And he is called common because such is the common lot of men under the new order of business and industry; and such will continue (increasingly) to be the common lot so long as the enlightened principles of secure ownership and self-help handed down from the eighteenth century continue to rule human affairs by help of the new order of industry

The kept classes, whose free income is secured to them by the legitimate rights of the vested interests, are less numerous than the common man—less numerous by some ninety-five per cent or thereabouts—and less serviceable to the community at large in perhaps the same proportion, so far as regards any conceivable use for any material purpose. In this sense they are uncommon. But it is not usual to speak of the kept classes as the uncommon classes, inasmuch as they personally differ from the common run of mankind in no sensible respect. It is more usual to speak of them as "the better classes," because they are in better circumstances and are better able to do as they like. Their place in the economic scheme of the civilised world is to consume the net product of the country's industry over cost, and so prevent a glut of the market.

But this broad distinction between the kept classes and their vested interests on the one side and the common man on the other side is by no means hard and fast. There are many doubtful cases, and a shifting across the line occurs now and again, but the broad distinction is not doubtful for all that. The great distinguishing mark of the common man is that he is helpless within the rules of the game as it is played in the twentieth century under the enlightened principles of the eighteenth century.

There are all degrees of this helplessness that characterises the common lot. So much so that certain classes, professions, and occupations—such as the clergy, the military, the courts, police, and legal profession—are perhaps to be classed as belonging primarily with the vested interests, although they can scarcely be counted as vested interests in their own right, but rather as outlying and subsidiary vested interests whose tenure is conditioned on their serving the purposes of those principal and self-directing vested interests whose tenure rests immediately on large holdings of invested wealth. The income which goes to these subsidiary or dependent vested interests is of the nature of free income, in so far that it is drawn from the yearly product of the underlying community; but in another sense it is scarcely to be counted as "free" income, in that its continuance depends on the good will of those controlling vested interests whose power rests on the ownership of large invested wealth. Still it will be found that on any test vote these subsidiary or auxiliary vested interests uniformly range themselves with their superiors in the same class, rather than with the common man. By sentiment and habitual outlook they belong with the kept classes, in that they are staunch defenders of that established order of law and custom which secures the great vested interests in power and insures the free income of the kept classes. In any twofold division of the population these are therefore, on the whole, to be ranged on the side of the old order, the vested interests, and the kept classes, both in sentiment and as regards the circumstances which condition their life and comfort.

Beyond these, whose life-interests are, after all, closely bound up with the kept classes, there are other vested interests of a more doubtful and perplexing kind; classes and occupations which would seem to belong with the common lot, but which range themselves at least provisionally with the vested interests and can scarcely be denied standing as such. Such, as an illustrative instance, is the A. F. of L. Not that the constituency of the A. F. of L. can be said to live on free income, and is therefore to be counted in with the kept classes—the only reservation on that head would conceivably be the corps of officials in the A. F. of L., who dominate the policies of that organisation and exercise a prescriptive right to dispose of its forces, at the same time that they habitually come in for an income drawn from the underlying organisation. The rank and file assuredly are not of the kept classes, nor do they visibly come in for a free income. Yet they stand on the defensive in maintaining a vested interest in the prerogatives and perquisites of their organisation. They are apparently moved by a feeling that so long as the established arrangements are maintained they will come in for a little something over and above what would come to them if they were to make common cause with the undistinguished common lot. In other words, they have a vested interest in a narrow margin of preference over and above what goes to the common man. But this narrow margin of net gain over the common lot, this vested right to get a narrow margin of something for nothing, has hitherto been sufficient to shape their sentiments and outlook in such a way as, in effect, to keep them loyal to the large business interests with whom they negotiate for this narrow margin of preference. As is true of the vested interests in business, so in the case of the A. F. of L., the ordinary ways and means of enforcing their claim to a little something over and above is the use of a reasonable sabotage, in the way of restriction, retardation, and unemployment. Yet the constituency of the A. F. of L., taken man for man, is not readily to be distinguished from the common sort so far as regards their conditions of life. The spirit of vested interest which animates them may, in fact, be nothing more to the point than an aimless survival.

■  ■  ■

Such a vested right to free income, that is to say this legitimate right of the kept classes to their keep at the cost of the underlying community, does not fall in with the lines of that mechanistic outlook and mechanistic logic which is forever gaining ground as the new order of industry goes forward. Such free income, which measures neither the investor's personal contribution to the production of goods nor his necessary consumption while engaged in industry, does not fit in with that mechanistic reckoning that runs in terms of tangible performance, and that grows ever increasingly habitual and convincing with every further habituation to the new order of things in the industrial world. Vested perquisites have no place in the new scheme of things; hence the new scheme is a menace. It is true, the well stabilised principles of the eighteenth century still continue to rate the investor as a producer of goods; but it is equally true that such a rating is palpable nonsense according to the mechanistic calculus of the new order, brought into bearing by the mechanical industry and material science. This may all be an untoward and distasteful turn of circumstances, but there is no gain of tranquillity to be got from ignoring it.

So it comes about that, increasingly, throughout broad classes in these industrial countries there is coming to be visible a lack of respect and affection for the vested interests, whether of business or of privilege; and it rises to the pitch of distrust and plain disallowance among those peoples on whom the preconceptions of the eighteenth century sit more lightly and loosely. It still is all vague and shifty. So much so that the guardians of law and order are still persuaded that they "have the situation in hand." But the popular feeling of incongruity and uselessness in the current run of law and custom under the rule of these timeworn preconceptions is visibly gaining ground and gathering consistency, even is so well ordered a republic as America. A cleavage of sentiment is beginning to run between the vested interests and the variegated mass of the common lot; and increasingly the common man is growing apathetic, or even impervious, to appeals grounded on these timeworn preconceptions of equity and good usage.

The fact of such a cleavage, as well as the existence of any ground for it, is painstakingly denied by the spokesmen of the vested interests; and in support of that comfortable delusion they will cite the exemplary fashion in which certain monopolistic labor organisations "stand pat." It is true, such a quasi-vested interest of the A. F. of L., which unbidden assumes to speak for the common man, can doubtless be counted on to "stand pat" on that system of imponderables in which its vested perquisites reside. So also the kept classes, and their stewards among the keepers of law and custom, are inflexibly content to let well enough alone. They can be counted on to see nothing more to the point than a stupidly subversive rapacity in that loosening of the bonds of convention that so makes light of the sacred rights of vested interest. Interested motives may count for something on both sides, but it is also true that the kept classes and the businesslike managers of the vested interests, whose place in the economy of nature it is to make money by conforming to the received law and custom, have not in the same degree undergone the shattering discipline of the New Order. . . .

But a large fraction of the people in the industrial countries is visibly growing uneasy under these principles as they work out under existing circumstances. So, e.g., it is evident that the common man within the United Kingdom, in so far as the Labor Party is his accredited spokesman, is increasingly restive under the state of "things as they are," and it is scarcely less evident that he finds his abiding grievance in the Vested Interests and that system of law and custom which cherishes them. And these men, as well as their like in other countries, are still in an unsettled state of advance to positions more definitely at variance with the received law and custom. In some instances, and indeed in more or less massive formation, this movement of dissent has already reached the limit of tolerance and has found itself sharply checked by the constituted keepers of law and custom.

It is perhaps not unwarranted to count the I. W. W. as such a vanguard of dissent, in spite of the slight consistency and the exuberance of its movements. After all, these and their like, here and in other countries are an element of appreciable weight in the population. They are also increasingly numerous, in spite of well-conceived repressive measures, and they appear to grow increasingly sure. And it will not do to lose sight of the presumption that, while they may be gravely in the wrong, they are likely not to be far out of touch with the undistinguished mass of the common sort who still continue to live within the law. It should seem likely that the peculiar moral and intellectual bent which marks them as "undesirable citizens" will, all the while, be found to run closer to that of the common man than the corresponding bent of the law-abiding beneficiaries under the existing system.

Vaguely, perhaps, and with a picturesque irresponsibility, these and their like are talking and thinking at cross-purposes with the principles of free bargain and self-help. There is reason to believe that to their own thinking, when cast in the terms in which they conceive these things, their notions of reasonable human intercourse are not equally fantastic and inconclusive. So, there is the dread word, Syndicalism, which is quite properly unintelligible to the kept classes and the adepts of corporation finance, and which has no definable meaning within the constituent principles of the eighteenth century. But the notion of it seems to come easy, by mere lapse of habit, to these others in whom the discipline of the New Order has begun to displace the preconceptions of the eighteenth century.

# 31
## *Absentee Ownership*

THORSTEIN VEBLEN                                                        1923

That period which has here been called the "era of free competition" was marked by a reasonably free competitive production of goods for the market, the profits of the business to be derived from competitive underselling. It is for such a "competitive system" that the economists have consistently spoken, through the nineteenth century and after, and the rehabilitation of it is still the abiding concern of many thoughtful persons. In practical effect it tapered off to an uncertain close in England about the middle of the century, in America something like a quarter-century later. So that it is a past phase. It meant a competition between producing-sellers, and so far as the plan was operative it inured to the benefit of the consumers.

Doubtless, such freely competitive production and selling prevailed only within reasonable bounds even in the time when it may be said to have been the rule in industrial business, and with the passage of time and the approaching saturation of the market the reasonable bounds gradually grew narrower and stricter. The manner of conducting the business passed by insensible degrees into a new order, and it became an increasingly patent matter-of-course for business enterprise in this field consistently to pursue the net gain by maintaining prices and curtailing the output.

It is not that competition ceased when this "competitive system" fell into decay, but only that the incidence of it has shifted. The competition which then used to run mutually between the producing-sellers has since then increasingly come to run between the business community on the one side and the consumers on the other. Salesmanship, with sabotage, has grown gradually greater and keener, at an increasing cost. And the end of this salesmanship is to get a margin of something for nothing at the cost of the consumer in a closed market. Whereas on the earlier plan the net gain was sought by underselling an increased output of serviceable goods in an open market. The old-fashioned plan, so far as it was effective, might be called a competition in workmanship; the later plan, so far as it has gone into effect, is a competition in publicity and scarcity.

■  ■  ■

Among these circumstances that so made for a new order in industrial business the one which is, presumably, the decisive one beyond the rest is the growing productive capacity of industry wherever and so far as the later advances in industrial process are allowed to go into effect. By about the middle of the nineteenth century it can be said without affectation that the leading industries were beginning to be inordinately productive, as rated in terms of what the traffic would bear; that is to say as counted in terms of net gain. Free-swung production, approaching the full productive capacity of the equipment and available man-power, was no longer to be tolerated in ordinary times. It became ever more imperative to observe a duly graduated moderation, and to govern the volume of output, not by the productive capacity of the plant or the working capacity of the workmen, nor by the consumptive needs of the consumers, but by what the traffic would bear; which was then habitually and increasingly coming to mean a modicum of unemployment both of the plant and the available man-power. It was coming to be true, increasingly, that the ordinary equipment of industry and the available complement of workmen were not wanted for daily use, but only for special occasions and during seasons of exceptionally brisk trade. Unemployment, in other words sabotage, to use a word of later date, was becoming an everyday care of the business management in the mechanical industries, and was already on the way to become, what it is today, the most engrossing care that habitually engages the vigilance of the business executive. And sabotage can best be taken care of in the large; so that the corporations, and particularly the larger corporations, would be in a particularly fortunate position to administer the routine of salutary sabotage. And when the Captain of Industry then made the passage from industrial adventurer to corporation financier it became the ordinary care of his office as Captain to keep a restraining hand on employment and output, and so administer a salutary running margin of sabotage on production, at the cost of the underlying population.

■   ■   ■

To do a profitable business one should buy cheap and sell dear, as all reasonable men know. In its dealings with the underlying population the business community buys their man-power and sells them their livelihood. So it is incumbent on the business men in the case to buy the industrial man-power as cheap as may be, and to sell the means of living to the ultimate consumer as dear as may be. All of which is a platitudinous matter of course.

■   ■   ■

In these endeavours to sell dear the farmers have hitherto met with no measurable success, apparently for want of effectual collusion. In effect and in the common run the farm population and its work and livelihood are a species of natural resources which the business community holds in usufruct, in the nature of inert materials exposed to the drift of circumstances over which they have no control, somewhat after the analogy of bacteria employed in fermentation.

The case of the industrial man-power in the narrower sense is somewhat different, the case of the specialised workman engaged in the mechanical industries. In great part, and more or less effectually, these have been drawn together in craft-unions to do their bargaining on a collusive plan for the more profitable sale of their man-power. In the typical case these unions are businesslike coalitions endeavoring to drive a bargain and establish a vested interest, governed by the standard aims and methods of the price-system.[1] The unions habitually employ the standard methods of the merchandising business, endeavoring to sell their vendible output at the best price obtainable; their chief recourse in these negotiations being a limitation of the supply, a strategic withdrawal of efficiency by means of strikes, union rules, apprenticeship requirements, and devices for consuming time unproductively. The nature of the business does not admit the use of sales-publicity in this traffic in anything like the same measure in which that expedient is employed in ordinary merchandising. Hence the strategic stress of their salesmanship falls all the more insistently and effectually on the limitation of the vendible supply; a running balance of unemployment and orderly inefficiency under union rules, rising promptly to the proportions of an embargo on productive work in any emergency. The aim being a scarcity-price for work done, quite in the spirit of business-as-usual.

Meantime the continued flow of credits and capitalisations continues to expand the volume of purchasing-power in the market, and so continues to enhance the price-cost of living for the workmen, along with the rising level of general prices. Which provokes the organised workmen to a more assiduous bargaining for higher wages; which calls for a more exacting insistence on mediocrity and obstruction in the day's work and a more instant mobilisation in the way of strikes. On sound business principles, the organised workmen's remedy for scarcity of livelihood is a persistent curtailment of output.

As a secondary effect—which may presently, in the course of further habituation, turn out to be its gravest consequence—this struggle for existence by way of sabotage fosters a rising tide of hostility and distrust between the parties to the bargain. There would seem to be in prospect a progressively settled and malevolent hostility on the part of the embattled workmen over against their employers and the absentee owners for whose ease and gain they are employed; which should logically be counted on to rise in due course to that pitch of vivacity where it will stick at nothing. But in the mean time the logical recourse of the workmen in their negotiations for wages and livelihood, according to the logic of sound business under the price-system, is a strategic withdrawal of efficiency, of a passive sort, increasing in frequency and amplitude to keep pace with the increasing urgency of their case.

■   ■   ■

In the negotiations between owners and workmen there is little use for the ordinary blandishments of salesmanship. The two parties to the quarrel—for it is after all a quarrel—have learned to know what to count on. And the bargaining between them therefore settles down without much circumlocution into a competitive use of unemployment, privation, restriction of work and output, strikes, shut-downs and lockouts, espionage, pickets, and similar manoeuvres of mutual derangement, with a large recourse to menacing language and threats of mutual sabotage. The colloquial word for it is "labor troubles." . . .

■   ■   ■

The official personnel of civil government, the constituted authorities who have had the making and surveillance of precedents and statutory regulations touching these matters in recent times, have necessarily been persons of businesslike antecedents, imbued with an inveterate businesslike bias, governed by business principles, if not also by business interests. Business exigencies, borne along on this habitual bent of the legislators and judiciary, and enforced by the workday needs of the substantial citizens, have decided that such collusion, conspiracy, or coalition as takes the form of (absentee) ownership is right and good, to be safeguarded in all the powers and immunities of ownership by the constituted authorities at any cost to the community at large. So that any strategic withdrawal of efficiency incident to the conduct of business by such an organisation of collusive ownership, any restriction of output to what the traffic will bear, any unemployment of equipment and man-power with a view to increased earnings on capital, has the countenance of the constituted authorities and will be defended by a suitable use of force in case of need.

It is otherwise, in a degree, with the collusive organisations of workmen. Being not grounded in ownership, their legal right of conspiracy in restraint of trade is doubtful at the best. It has also not the countenance of the substantial citizens or of the minor business men, of the pulpit, or the public press. The effectual limits on strikes are somewhat narrower than on lockouts. Boycotts in support of strikes are illegal, and the more effectual methods of picketing are disallowed by courts and police, except in negligible cases. Since the striking workmen are not owners of the plant that is to be laid idle by their striking, they are excluded from the premises, and they are therefore unable to watch over the unemployment which they have precipitated, and to see to its unbroken continuance. This is a grave disability. The owners are more fortunate in this respect. The power to dispose of matters in the conduct of industry commonly attaches to ownership, and is not legally to be claimed on other grounds. The employer-owners are in a much better position to take care of any desired unemployment, as in case of a lockout. In the same connection it should be recalled that effectual collusion and concert of action is more a matter of routine and takes effect in a more compact and complete fashion on the side of the owners, who are already organised as a corporate unit. The block of ownership embodied in any ordinary business corporation of the larger sort covers a larger segment of the industrial processes involved in any given strike or lockout than does the body of industrial man-power with which the corporation is contending. This will more particularly be the case where and in so far as the old-fashioned craft-unions have not been displaced by an industrial union. It comes to a conflict between a corporate whole on the side of the owners against a fragment of the working forces on the side of the workmen.

So again, in any eventual resort to force, the workmen are under a handicap as against the owners,—a handicap due to law and precedent as well as to the businesslike predilections that are habitual among the personnel of the constituted authorities. Labor troubles are disorders of business, and business is a matter of ownership, while work and livelihood are not. The presumption, in law and custom and official predilection, is against the use of force or the possession or disposal of arms by persons or associations of persons who are not possessed of appreciable property. It is assumed, in effect, that the use of weapons is to protect property and guard its rights; and the assumption applies to the use of weapons by private persons as well as to the armed forces of government. . . .

■　■　■

But whatever may be the relative strength of the two parties to this controversy, present or prospective, the negotiations between them are visibly falling into more tangible and more standardised shape and are conducted on increasingly businesslike principles of what the traffic will bear, and on both sides alike the negotiations as to what the traffic will bear are carried on in terms of competitive unemployment, mutual defeat, designed to hold the work and output down to such a minimum as will yield the most profitable price per unit to one party or the other. In due consequence, as the contending forces achieve a more effectual mobilisation on a larger scale, and as these tactics of inaction and retardation take effect with greater alacrity and consistency, the practicable minimum of work and output should logically become the ordinary standard practice. So that in "ordinary times" the effectual volume of work and output should run at a minimum.

■　■　■

In the long run, so soon as the privation and chronic derangement which follows from this application of business principles has grown unduly irksome and becomes intolerable, there is due to come a sentimental revulsion and a muttering protest that "something will have to be done about it,"—as, e.g., in the case which has arisen in the coal industry. Thoughtful persons will then devise remedial measures. As a matter of course, in a community which is addicted to business principles, the remedial measures which are brought under advisement in such a case by responsible citizens and officials are bound to be of a businesslike nature; designed in all reason to safeguard the accomplished facts of absentee ownership in the natural resources involved and in the capitalised overhead charges which have been incorporated in the business. Necessarily so, for the community at large is addicted to business principles, and the official personnel is so addicted in an especial degree, in the nature of things.

Yet all the while there are certain loose ends in this fabric of business convictions which binds the mentality of these peoples. There is always the chance, more or less imminent, that in time, after due trial and error, on duly prolonged and intensified irritation, some sizable element of the underlying population, not intrinsically committed to absentee ownership, will forsake or forget their moral principles of business-as-usual, and will thereupon endeavor to take this businesslike arrangement to pieces and put the works together again on some other plan, for better or worse.

---

[1]The American Federation of Labor may be taken as a type-form; although it goes perhaps to an extreme in its adherence to the principles and procedure of merchandising, in all its aims and negotiations, its constant aim being an exclusive market and a limitation of supply.

# SIX

The Labor Movement as a Moral Force

## Introduction

The theorists represented in Part VI view the labor movement as a moral institution based on Protestant Christian Socialist or Roman Catholic social movement principles. They see the solution to social and industrial questions in the application of religious morality to societal problems with the church overseeing and monitoring its use. The labor movement is looked upon as a moral contributor to or detractor from the spiritual betterment of the human race. Religious theorists rarely developed a complete theory of the labor movement. Nevertheless, these theorists have contributed to the overall body of theory on the subject. And in several instances—most notably with the papal encyclicals reprinted below—they have had a large impact on the actual history of trade unionism, including that within the United States.

One of the early leading members of this group was Richard T. Ely, a prominent Christian Socialist in the late nineteenth century, and a professor of political economy at Johns Hopkins University and later at the University of Wisconsin. According to Ely, labor organizations came into existence to counter the disadvantages faced by the worker in the labor market: unequal bargaining power in negotiating the labor contract and uncertainty in eking out an existence through the sale of their labor power. Ely views unions as enabling the laborer to counterbalance the bargaining advantages of the employer and consequently to mitigate the effects of the free market system on workers. Furthermore, labor organizations raise the moral standards of their members by teaching self-restraint and self-discipline, by developing in the individual workers a sense of responsibility toward their work and society, and by teaching workers to exercise greater care in family matters. Finally, Ely believes labor unions will lead us to a morally superior form of society based on cooperation between labor and capital and concern for all humanity. This cooperative society exhibiting Christian moral principles will be a form of socialism which will elevate the level of political discourse and lead away from poverty, wars, and conflicts. Ely saw unions as the strongest force outside of the Christian church for social reform and the brotherhood of mankind.

Scholars have only recently begun to assess the impact of the Catholic church on the ideology of American labor. Catholic social thought was formulated and given widespread acceptance through the issuance of papal encyclicals, written messages by the pope setting forth church doctrine. The various social encyclicals on labor form an integrated body of thought which defines church doctrine concerning the workers' relationship to work, the employer, labor organizations, and the state.

*Rerum Novarum,* the first great social encyclical which became known as "the social Magna Carta of Catholicism" and which won for Pope Leo XIII the name of "the workingman's pope," laid the cornerstone of Catholic social thought on labor. Written at a time when civic strife was threatening to transform the existing social and political order, the encyclical sets forth a set of basic principles pertaining to the rights and obligations of workers, employers, and the states. Its ideas run counter to prevailing thought based on classical economic doctrine. Pope Leo XIII, cognizant of the mass unrest, was critical of those practices which led to the increasing misery of the working class and resulted in discontent, disorder, and revolution. Coupled with such criticism is a vehement rejection of any remedy based on socialist ideas or practices. The abolition of private property, declared the pope, violates the natural rights of man. Thus it is not capitalism as a system which is responsible for the economic problems of the masses but a handful of the very rich who are misled by greed. No socioeconomic classes are in conflict. Individuals rather than classes are the root cause of the problems.

Any solution to the problems of the working masses must be based on justice and morality, and none can be found without the intervention of the church, the pope held. The church, in the eyes of the pope, is an indispensable remedial agency in bringing about cooperation between employees, employers, and the state. *Rerum Novarum* rejects the idea that the state is only a passive observer in the marketplace and supports the right of the state to intervene to remove industrial evils, prevent injustice to any group, and contribute to the betterment of workers' lives. Finally, the encyclical emphasizes the natural right of wage earners to live humanely and decently and to join labor associations for their mutual benefit. However, workers also have an obligation to see that these associations are not controlled by subversive elements but develop along lines drawn by the church. If unions in accordance with the teachings of the church cannot be formed, Leo XIII urges Catholics to form their own Catholic unions.

*Quadragesimo Anno,* issued by Pope Pius XI in 1931, developed further the principles of *Rerum Novarum.* The encyclical reaffirms the teaching of Leo XIII: private property is natural and must be maintained, the wage system must be humanized and made more just, and all socialist ideology must be rejected. The original contribution of the encyclical is its outline for a new Christian social order. In the United States this became known as the Industry Council Plan. The plan envisions the construction of a syndical or corporative society. It would comprise industries and professions, including unions and associations in each industry, which are to establish joint boards or councils in a common field of production. These industries and professions are to be federated in a national economic council which will be responsible for overall economic planning. All distinctions between workers and employers will be eliminated and a true partnership of capital and labor will be established. The result will be harmony among the classes and the suppression of socialism. Hostile critics have noted similarities between Pius XI's plan and some variants of fascism, but the church has constantly asserted that a very different form of corporate organization was intended. This particular element of the Pope's encyclical has not had much impact on subsequent Catholic theory and practice.

In his encyclical *Laborem Exercens* (1981), Pope John Paul II extends Catholic labor theory on several fronts. Several shifts in emphasis are obvious: the theory centers on the worker rather than on questions about private property or economic systems; the focus is shifted to a worldwide frame; there is a definite distancing of the church from capitalism as well as communism; for the first time legitimacy is given to a possible socializing of the means of economic production; unemployment and its many evils are extensively discussed; and a strong emphasis is placed on the need for labor unions and worker "solidarity." Worker rights are also strengthened by being placed within the framework of human rights and made an essential condition for industrial peace in the modern world. The concept of the indirect employer is first introduced. Not only is the direct employer responsible for the labor relationship but the indirect employers—agents on a national or international level which condition the action of the direct employer— must also undertake responsibility for creating the conditions where the needs of wage earners can be satisfied. Planning on an international level thus becomes necessary if progress is to be made in achieving justice for the working masses. All these changes together have led some to assert that John Paul II is moving the Catholic church further to the left than its traditional, rather conservative role in labor affairs. It is difficult to tell if that will be the long-term impact of *Laborem Exercems,* but it is clear that some changes—at least of emphasis—are present in this latest encyclical.

# 32
## *The Labor Movement in America*

RICHARD T. ELY                                                                1886

While labor is a commodity, it is an expenditure of human force which involves the welfare of a personality. It is a commodity which is inseparably bound up with the laborer, and in this it differs from other commodities. The one who offers other commodities for sale reserves his own person. The farmer who parts with a thousand bushels of wheat for money reserves control of his own actions. They are not brought in question at all. Again, the man of property who sells other commodities has an option. He may part with his wares and maintain his life from other goods received in exchange, or he can have recourse to his labor-power. The laborer, however, has, as a rule, only the service residing in his own person with which to sustain himself and his family. Again, a machine, a locomotive, for example, and a workingman resemble each other in this: they both render services, and the fate of both depends upon the manner in which these services are extracted. But there is this radical difference: the machine which yields its service to man is itself a commodity, and is only a means to an end, while the laborer who parts with labor is no longer a commodity in civilized lands, but is an end in himself, for man is the beginning and termination of all economic life. The consequences for the great mass of laborers possessed of only average qualities are as follows, provided there is no intervention of legislation, and provided the working classes are not organized. While those who sell other commodities are able to influence the price by a suitable regulation of production, so as to bring about a satisfactory relation between supply and demand, the purchaser of labor has it in his own power to determine the price of this commodity and the other conditions of sale. There may be exceptions for a time in a new country, but these are temporary and often more apparent than real. Even now in the United States the right of capital to rule is generally assumed as a matter of course, and when labor would determine price and conditions of service, it is called dictation. The reason is that man comes to this world without reference to supply and demand, and the poverty of the laborer compels him to offer the use of his labor-power unreservedly and continuously. The purchase of labor gives control over the laborer and a far-reaching influence over his physical, intellectual, social, and ethical existence. The conditions of the labor-contract determine the amount of this rulership. Again, while illness, inability to labor, by reason of accident or old age and death, do not destroy other commodities or their power to support life, when these misfortunes overtake the person of the laborer, he loses his power to sell his only property, the commodity labor, and he can no longer support himself and those dependent on him. These consequences of the peculiarity of labor may be summed up as follows:—

1. The absence of actual equality between the two parties to the labor-contract, and the one-sided determination of the price and other conditions of labor.
2. The almost unlimited control of the employer over the social and political life, the physical and spiritual existence, and the expenditures of his employees.
3. The uncertainty of existence which, more than actual difference in possessions, distinguishes the well-to-do from the poor.

Richard T. Ely, *The Labor Movement in America* (New York: Thomas Y. Crowell Co., 1886), pp. 98–100, 114–115, 117–118, 136–139. Footnotes in the original have been eliminated.

■ ■ ■

The disadvantages under which those are placed who live by the sale of the commodity labor have been briefly examined. It remains to show the manner in which trades-unions and labor organizations may operate to counteract these economic evils.

The labor organizations enable the laborer to withhold his commodity temporarily from the market, and to wait for more satisfactory conditions of service than it is possible for him to secure when he is obliged to offer it unconditionally. They further enable him to gain the advantages of an increased demand for his commodity, to bring about a more satisfactory relation than would otherwise be possible between the supply and the demand for labor, and also to exercise an influence upon the supply in the future market. These organizations are calculated to do away with the injurious consequences of the peculiarities of labor as a commodity to be sold, and "through them labor for the first time becomes really a commodity, and the laborer a man."

The trades-unions, and other agencies of the labor movement, such as the labor press, assist the laborer to find the best market for his commodity; and as the best market usually means the most productive market considered from a politico-economic standpoint, this is of benefit to society as a whole.

■ ■ ■

Finally, the trades-unions educate the laborers to prudence in marriage. They accustom their members to overlook the field of labor, to pass judgment on the prospect of satisfactory remuneration for their commodity in the future; they help them to secure higher wages than would otherwise be possible, so that they have something to lose; they awaken in them a regard for the welfare of others, and cultivate a feeling of duty with respect to their conduct toward others; finally, the limitation of the number of apprentices is a guarantee—imperfect, to be sure, still a guarantee of some value—that those who are prudent and restrain their desires will reap the benefit of their sacrifices. "Experience teaches that the trades-unionists of England are more prudent in regard to marriage than the unskilled laborers who belong to no organizations."

■ ■ ■

The laboring classes, through their unions, are learning discipline, self-restraint, and the methods of united action, and are also discovering whom they can trust, finding out the necessity of uniting great confidence in leaders with strict control of them, and with the aid of their press are building up a great market for the products of co-operative enterprise.

Thus the labor movement is preparing the way for that goal which has for many years been the ideal of the best thinkers on labor problems,—the union of capital and labor in the same hands, in grand, wide-reaching, co-operative enterprises, which shall embrace the masses. Formerly it was an argument in favor of slavery that in that way only could labor and capital be united in the same hands and disastrous conflicts be prevented; but up from the people there comes a voice, crying, "We will show you a more excellent way." The movement has already begun,—co-operative enterprises, productive and distributive, are springing up in every part of the land. Co-operation is urged by a united labor press, and labor societies set it before the masses as an ultimate goal. One of the objects of the Knights of Labor is stated thus in their official declaration: "To establish co-operative institutions, such as will tend to supersede the wage system by the introduction of a co-operative industrial system."

■   ■   ■

But our picture will not be complete until we have shown the still wider ethical significance of the labor-movement. First, there is rational ground to hope that it will in the end introduce a higher tone into our political life, though it has scarcely done so up to the present time. The labor organizations have certain practical aims in politics, often very definite, and they will hereafter attempt to gain these by sending honest men to our legislatures to represent them. Year by year they are becoming increasingly restive under the attempted control of the professional politician; in many cases they have entirely emancipated themselves from party prejudice, and have already learned that only sharp, vigorous, honest, and independent political action can ever bring them as a class anything worth having. There is said to be quite a strong feeling among the Knights of Labor in favor of civil service reform; and it can never gain a firm foothold in this country until it is supported by a strong popular sentiment. Second, it is worthy of notice that those in the organizations call one another brother and sister, and that many of the unions are called brotherhoods; as, for example, The Brotherhood of Locomotive Firemen of North America, The Grand International Brotherhood of Locomotive Engineers, The Brotherhood of Carpenters and Joiners of America.

The labor movement, as the facts would indicate, is the strongest force outside the Christian Church making for the practical recognition of human brotherhood; and it is noteworthy that, at a time when the churches have generally discarded brother and sister as a customary form of address, the trades-unions and labor organizations have adopted the habit. And it is not a mere form. It is shown in good offices and sacrifices for one another in a thousand ways every day, and it is not confined to those of one nation. It reaches over the civilized world; and the word international as a part of the title of many unions, and the fact that their membership is international, are quite as significant as they appear to be at first sight....

The laborers are the most thorough-going peace-men to be found, and I am often inclined to think that they are the only large class who really and truly desire peace between nations, the abandonment of armies, the conversion of spears into pruning-hooks, and swords into ploughshares. At the time of the Franco-German war, German laborers alone protested against the slaughter of their French brothers; at the beginning of our late war, American laborers met in convention, to protest against hostilities between the sections; and in the fall of 1885 the veterans of the Union and Confederate armies among the Knights of Labor formed an organization called The Gray and the Blue of the Knights of Labor, and took the motto, "Capital divided, labor unites us." Its object, says *John Swinton's Paper,* "is to teach the toilers who make up the armies of the world, that in peace, not in war, is the worker's emancipation." I sincerely believe that the time is not so far distant as one might think, when organized labor will force the governments of earth to substitute arbitration for war, will compel them to live peaceably, each with the other, to devote their forces to the fruitful pursuit of art, industry, and science, and in a vast international parliament to lay the foundations of a federated world state. But even this is not the whole of their high mission of peace; for they are, in our South, bringing about an amicable understanding between black and white, since it is necessary that they should unite and act in harmony to accomplish their common ends.

Thus they bring an elevating influence to bear upon the more ignorant blacks, and help to solve the vexed problem of race in the United States. Strange, is it not? that the despised trades-union and labor organizations should have been chosen to perform this high duty of conciliation! But hath not God ever called the lowly to the most exalted missions, and hath he not ever called the foolish to confound the wise?

# 33
## *Rerum Novarum*

POPE LEO XIII                                                                                    1891

1. It is not surprising that the spirit of revolutionary change, which has long been predominant in the nations of the world, should have passed beyond politics and made its influence felt in the cognate field of practical economy. The elements of a conflict are unmistakable: the growth of industry, and the surprising discoveries of science; the changed relations of masters and workmen; the enormous fortunes of individuals and the poverty of the masses; the increased self-reliance and the closer mutual combination of the working population; and, finally, a general moral deterioration. The momentous seriousness of the present state of things just now fills every mind with painful apprehension. . . .

■  ■  ■

All agree, and there can be no question whatever, that some remedy must be found, and quickly found, for the misery and wretchedness which press so heavily at this moment on the large majority of the very poor. The ancient workmen's Guilds were destroyed in the last century, and no other organization took their place. Public institutions and the laws have repudiated the ancient religion. Hence by degrees it has come to pass that Working Men have been given over, isolated and defenseless, to the callousness of employers and the greed of unrestrained competition. The evil has been increased by rapacious Usury, which, although more than once condemned by the Church, is nevertheless, under a different form but with the same guilt, still practiced by avaricious and grasping men. And to this must be added the custom of working by contract, and the concentration of so many branches of trade in the hands of a few individuals, so that a small number of very rich men have been able to lay upon the masses of the poor a yoke little better than slavery itself.

3. To remedy these evils the *Socialists,* working on the poor man's envy of the rich, endeavor to destroy private property, and maintain that individual possessions should become the common property of all, to be administered by the State or by municipal bodies. They hold that, by thus transferring property from private persons to the community, the present evil state of things will be set to rights, because each citizen will then have his equal share of whatever there is to enjoy. But their proposals are so clearly futile for all practical purposes, that if they were carried out the working man himself would be among the first to suffer. Moreover they are emphatically unjust, because they would rob the lawful possessor, bring the State into a sphere that is not its own, and cause complete confusion in the community.

### Private Ownership

4. It is surely undeniable that, when a man engages in remunerative labor, the very reason and motive of his work is to obtain property, and to hold it as his own private possession. If one man hires out to another his strength or his industry, he does this for the purpose of receiving in return what is necessary for food and living; he thereby expressly proposes to acquire a full and real right, not only to the remuneration, but also to the disposal of that remuneration as he pleases. Thus, if he lives sparingly, saves money, and

Reprinted by permission of the publisher from *Seven Great Encyclicals,* pp. 1–12, 16–25, 27. Mahwah, N.J.: Paulist Press, 1963. Footnotes in the original have been eliminated.

invests his savings, for greater security, in land, the land in such a case is only his wages in another form; and, consequently, a working man's little estate thus purchased should be as completely at his own disposal as the wages he receives for his labor. But it is precisely in this power of disposal that ownership consists, whether the property be land or movable goods. The *Socialists,* therefore, in endeavoring to transfer the possessions of individuals to the community, strike at the interests of every wage earner, for they deprive him of the liberty of disposing of his wages, and thus of all hope and possibility of increasing his stock and of bettering his condition in life.

5. What is of still greater importance, however, is that the remedy they propose is manifestly against justice. For every man has by nature the right to possess property as his own. This is one of the *chief points of distinction* between man and the animal creation. . . . It is the mind, or the reason, which is the chief thing in us who are human beings; it is this which makes a human being human, and distinguishes him essentially and completely from the brute. And on this account—*viz.,* that man alone among animals possesses reason—it must be within his right to have things not merely for temporary and momentary use, as other living beings have them, but in stable and permanent possession; he must have not only things which perish in the using, but also those which, though used, remain for use in the future.

■ ■ ■

### The Law of Nature

Here, again, we have another proof that private ownership is according to nature's law. For that which is required for the preservation of life and for life's well-being, is produced in great abundance by the earth, but not until man has brought it into cultivation and lavished upon it his care and skill. Now, when man thus spends the industry of his mind and the strength of his body in procuring the fruits of nature, by that act he makes his own that portion of nature's field which he cultivates—that portion on which he leaves, as it were, the impress of his own personality; and it cannot but be just that he should possess that portion as his own, and should have a right to keep it without molestation.

■ ■ ■

### A Family Right

■ ■ ■

That right of property . . . which has been proved to belong naturally to individual persons must also belong to a man in his capacity of head of a family; nay, such a person must possess this right so much the more clearly in proportion as his position multiplies his duties.

10. For it is a most sacred law of nature that a father must provide food and all necessaries for those whom he has begotten; and, similarly, nature dictates that a man's children, who carry on, as it were, and continue his own personality, should be provided by him with all that is needful to enable them honorably to keep themselves from want and misery in the uncertainties of this mortal life. Now, in no other way can a father effect this except by the ownership of profitable property, which he can transmit to his children by inheritance. A family, no less than a State, is, as we have said, a true society, governed by a power within itself, that is to say, by the father. Wherefore, provided the

limits be not transgressed which are prescribed by the very purposes for which it exists, the family has, at least, equal rights with the State in the choice and pursuit of those things which are needful to its preservation and its just liberty.

■ ■ ■

### Socialism Rejected

11. The idea, then, that the civil government should, at its own discretion, penetrate and pervade the family and the household, is a great and pernicious mistake. True, if a family finds itself in great difficulty, utterly friendless, and without prospect for help, it is right that extreme necessity be met by public aid; for each family is a part of the commonwealth. In like manner, if within the walls of the household there occur grave disturbance of mutual rights, the public power must interfere to force each party to give the other what is due; for this is not to rob citizens of their rights, but justly and properly to safeguard and strengthen them. But the rulers of the State must go no further: nature bids them stop here. Paternal authority can neither be abolished by the State nor absorbed; for it has the same source as human life itself. . . . The Socialists, therefore, in setting aside the parent and introducing the providence of the State, act *against natural justice,* and threaten the very existence of family life.

■ ■ ■

Thus it is clear *that the main tenet of Socialism, the community of goods, must be utterly rejected;* for it would injure those whom it is intended to benefit, it would be contrary to the natural rights of mankind, and it would introduce confusion, and disorder into the commonwealth. Our first and most fundamental principle, therefore, when We undertake to alleviate the condition of the masses, must be the inviolability of private property. This laid down, We go on to show where we must find the remedy that We seek.

### The Church Is Necessary

13. We approach the subject with confidence, and in the exercise of the rights which belong to Us. For no practical solution of this question will ever be found without the assistance of Religion and the Church. It is We who are the chief guardian of religion, and the chief dispenser of what belongs to the Church, and We must not by silence neglect the duty which lies upon Us. We affirm without hesitation that all the striving of men will be vain if they leave out the Church. It is the Church that proclaims from the Gospel those teachings by which the conflict can be brought to an end, or at least made far less bitter; the Church uses its efforts not only to enlighten the mind, but to direct by its precepts the life and conduct of men; the Church improves and ameliorates the condition of the working man by numerous useful organizations; does its best to enlist the services of all ranks in discussing and endeavoring to meet, in the most practical way, the claims of the working classes; and acts on the decided view that for these purposes recourse should be had, in due measure and degree, to the help of the law and of State authority.

14. Let it be laid down, in the first place, that humanity must remain as it is. It is impossible to reduce human society to a level. The *Socialists* may do their utmost, but all striving against nature is vain. There naturally exists among mankind innumerable differences of the most important kind; people differ in capability, in diligence, in health, and in strength; and unequal fortune is a necessary result of inequality in condition. . . .

In like manner, the other pains and hardships of life will have no end or cessation on this earth; for the consequences of sin are bitter and hard to bear, and they must be with man as long as life lasts. To suffer and to endure, therefore, is the lot of humanity, let men try as they may, no strength and no artifice will ever succeed in banishing from human life the ills and troubles which beset it. If any there are who pretend differently—who hold out to a hard-pressed people freedom from pain and trouble, undisturbed repose, and constant enjoyment—they cheat the people and impose upon them, and their lying promises will only make the evil worse than before. There is nothing more useful than to look at the world as it really is—and at the same time look elsewhere for a remedy to its troubles.

### Employer and Employee

15. The great mistake that is made in the matter now under consideration, is to possess oneself of the idea that class is naturally hostile to class; that rich and poor are intended by nature to live at war with one another. So irrational and so false is this view, that the exact contrary is the truth. Just as the symmetry of the human body is the result of the disposition of the members of the body, so in a State it is ordained by nature that these two classes should exist in harmony and agreement, and should, as it were, fit into one another, so as to maintain the equilibrium of the body politic. Each requires the other; capital cannot do without labor nor labor without capital. Mutual agreement results in pleasantness and good order; perpetual conflict necessarily produces confusion and outrage. Now, in preventing such strife as this, and in making it impossible, the efficacy of Christianity is marvelous and manifold.

16. First of all, there is nothing more powerful than Religion (of which the Church is the interpreter and guardian) in drawing rich and poor together, by reminding each class of its duties to the other, and especially of the duties of justice. Thus Religion teaches the laboring man and the workman to carry out honestly and well all equitable agreements freely made, never to injure capital, nor to outrage the person of an employer; never to employ violence in representing his own cause, nor to engage in riot and disorder; and to have nothing to do with men of evil principles, who work upon the people with artful promises, and raise foolish hopes which usually end in disaster and in repentance when too late. Religion teaches the rich man and the employer that their work people are not their slaves; that they must respect in every man his dignity as a man and as a Christian; that labor is nothing to be ashamed of, if we listen to right reason and to Christian philosophy, but is an honorable employment, enabling a man to sustain his life in an upright and creditable way; and that it is shameful and inhuman to treat men like chattels to make money by, or to look upon them merely as so much muscle or physical power. Thus, again, Religion teaches that, as among the workmen's concerns are Religion herself, and things spiritual and mental, the employer is bound to see that he has time for the duties of piety; that he be not exposed to corrupting influences and dangerous occasions; and that he be not led away to neglect his home and family or to squander his wages. Then, again, the employer must never tax his work-people beyond their strength, nor employ them in work unsuited to their sex or age.

17. His great and principal obligation is to give to every one that which is just. Doubtless before we can decide whether wages are adequate many things have to be considered; but rich men and masters should remember this—that to exercise pressure for the sake of gain, upon the indigent and destitute, and to make one's profit out of the need of another, is condemned by all laws, human and divine. To defraud any one of wages that are his due is a crime which cries to the avenging anger of Heaven. . . . Finally, the

rich must religiously refrain from cutting down the workman's earnings, either by force, fraud, or by usurious dealing; and with the more reason because the poor man is weak and unprotected, and because his slender means should be sacred in proportion to their scantiness.

Were these precepts carefully obeyed and followed would not strife die out and cease?

■  ■  ■

19. The chief and most excellent rule for the right use of money is one which the heathen philosophers indicated, but which the Church has traced out clearly, and has not only made known to men's minds, but has impressed upon their lives. It rests on the principle that it is one thing to have a right to the possession of money, and another to have a right to use money as one pleases. Private ownership, as we have seen, is the natural right of man; and to exercise that right, especially as members of society, is not only lawful but absolutely necessary. . . . But if the question be asked, How must one's possessions be used? the Church replies without hesitation . . . : "Man should not consider his outward possessions as his own, but as common to all, so as to share them without difficulty when others are in need." . . . True, no one is commanded to distribute to others that which is required for his own necessities and those of the household; nor even to give away what is reasonably required to keep up becomingly his condition in life; "for no one ought to live unbecomingly." But when necessity has been supplied, and one's position fairly considered, it is a duty to give to the indigent out of that which is over. . . .

■  ■  ■

**The Dignity of Labor**
20. As for those who do not possess the gifts of fortune, they are taught by the Church that, in God's sight poverty is no disgrace, and that there is nothing to be ashamed of in seeking one's bread by labor. This is strengthened by what we see in Christ Himself, "Who whereas He was rich, for our sakes became poor"; and who, being the son of God, and God Himself chose to seem and to be considered the son of a carpenter—nay, did not disdain to spend a great part of His life as a carpenter Himself. "Is not this the Carpenter, the Son of Mary?" From the contemplation of this Divine example, it is easy to understand that the true dignity and excellence of man lies in his moral qualities, that is, in virtue; that virtue is the common inheritance of all, equally within the reach of high and low, rich and poor; and that virtue, and virtue alone, wherever found, will be followed by the rewards of everlasting happiness. . . .

■  ■  ■

**Justice Toward All**
To the State the interests of all are equal whether high or low. The poor are members of the national community equally with the rich; they are real component parts, living parts, which make up, through the family, the living body; and it need hardly be said that they are by far the majority. It would be irrational to neglect one portion of the citizens and to favor another; and therefore the public administration must duly and solicitously provide for the welfare and the comfort of the working people, or else that law of justice will be violated which ordains that each shall have his due. . . . Among the many

and grave duties of rulers who would do their best for their people, the first and chief is to act with strict justice—with that justice which is called in the schools *distributive*—toward each and every class.

But although all citizens, without exception, can and ought to contribute to that common good in which individuals share so profitably to themselves, yet it is not to be supposed that all can contribute in the same way and to the same extent. No matter what changes may be made in forms of government, there will always be differences and inequalities of condition in the State. Society cannot exist or be conceived without them. Some there must be who dedicate themselves to the work of the commonwealth, who make the laws, who administer justice, whose advice and authority govern the nation in times of peace, and defend it in war. Such men clearly occupy the foremost place in the State, and should be held in the foremost estimation, for their work touches most nearly and effectively the general interests of the community. Those who labor at a trade or calling do not promote the general welfare in such a fashion as this; but they do in the most important way benefit the nation, though less directly. We have insisted that, since it is the end of Society to make men better, the chief good that Society can be possessed of is virtue. Nevertheless, in all well-constituted States it is by no means an unimportant matter to provide those bodily and external commodities, "the use of which is necessary to virtuous action." And in the provision of material well-being, the labor of the poor—the exercise of their skill and the employment of their strength in the culture of the land and the workshops of trade—is most efficacious and altogether indispensable. Indeed, their co-operation in this respect is so important that it may be truly said that it is only by the labor of the working man that States grow rich. Justice, therefore, demands that the interests of the poorer population be carefully watched over by the administration, so that they who contribute so largely to the advantage of the community may themselves share in the benefits they create—that being housed, clothed, and enabled to support life, they may find their existence less hard and more endurable. It follows that whatever shall appear to be conducive to the well-being of those who work, should receive favorable consideration. Let it not be feared that solicitude of this kind will injure any interest; on the contrary, it will be to the advantage of all; for it cannot but be good for the commonwealth to secure from misery those on whom it so largely depends.

## The First Law of Government

28. We have said that the State must not absorb the individual or the family; both should be allowed free and untrammelled action as far as is consistent with the common good and the interests of others. Nevertheless, rulers should anxiously safeguard the community and all its parts; the community, because the conservation of the community is so emphatically the business of the supreme power, that the safety of the commonwealth is not only the first law, but is a Government's whole reason of existence; and the parts, because both philosophy and the Gospel agree in laying down that the object of the administration of the State should be not the advantage of the ruler, but the benefit of those over whom he rules. . . .

Whenever the general interest of any particular class suffers, or is threatened with, evils which can in no other way be met, the public authority must step in to meet them.

29. Now, among the interests of the public, as of private individuals, are these: that peace and good order should be maintained; that family life should be carried on in accordance with God's laws and those of nature; that Religion should be reverenced and obeyed; that a high standard of morality should prevail in public and private life; that the sanctity of justice should be respected, and that no one should injure another with impu-

nity: that the members of the commonwealth should grow up to man's estate strong and robust, and capable, if need be, of guarding and defending their country. If by a strike, or other combination of workmen, there should be imminent danger of disturbance to the public peace; or if circumstances were such that among the laboring population the ties of family life were relaxed; if Religion were found to suffer through the workmen not having time and opportunity to practice it; if in workshops and factories there were danger to morals through the mixing of the sexes or from any occasion of evil; or if employers laid burdens upon the workmen which were unjust, or degraded them with conditions that were repugnant to their dignity as human beings; finally, if health were endangered by excessive labor, or by work unsuited to sex or age—in these cases there can be no question that, within certain limits, it would be right to call in the help and authority of the law. The limits must be determined by the nature of the occasion which calls for the law's interference—the principle being this, that the law must not undertake more, nor go further, than is required for the remedy of the evil or the removal of the danger.

## The Right of Protection

Rights must be religiously respected wherever they are found; and it is the duty of the public authority to prevent and punish injury, and to protect each one in the possession of his own. Still, when there is question of protecting the rights of individuals, the poor and helpless have a claim to special consideration. The richer population have many ways of protecting themselves, and stand less in need of help from the State; those who are badly off have no resources of their own to fall back upon, and must chiefly rely upon the assistance of the State. And it is for this reason that wage-earners, who are, undoubtedly, among the weak and necessitous, should be specially cared for and protected by the commonwealth.

30. Here, however, it will be advisable to advert expressly to one or two of the more important details.

It must be borne in mind that the chief thing to be secured is the safeguarding, by legal enactment and policy, of private property. Most of all it is essential in these times of covetous greed, to keep the multitude within the line of duty; for if all may justly strive to better their condition, yet neither justice nor the common good allows anyone to seize that which belongs to another, or, under the pretext of futile and ridiculous equality, to lay hands on other people's fortunes. It is most true that by far the larger part of the people who work prefer to improve themselves by honest labor rather than by doing wrong to others. But there are not a few who are imbued with bad principles and are anxious for revolutionary change, and whose great purpose it is to stir up tumult and bring about a policy of violence. The authority of the State should intervene to put restraint upon these disturbers, to save the workmen from their seditious arts, and to protect lawful owners from spoliation.

## The Workman's Rights

31. When work-people have recourse to a strike, it is frequently because the hours of labor are too long, or the work too hard, or because they consider their wages insufficient. The grave inconvenience of this not uncommon occurrence should be obviated by public remedial measures; for such paralysis of labor not only affects the masters and their work-people, but is extremely injurious to trade, and to the general interests of the public; moreover, on such occasions, violence and disorder are generally not far off, and thus it frequently happens that the public peace is threatened. The laws should be beforehand, and prevent these troubles from arising; they should lend their influence and

authority to the removal in good time of the causes which lead to conflicts between masters and those whom they employ.

32. But if the owners of property must be made secure, the workman, too, has property and possessions in which he must be protected; and, first of all, there are his spiritual and mental interests. . . .

From this follows the obligation of the cessation of work and labor on Sundays and certain festivals. This rest from labor is not to be understood as mere idleness; much less must it be an occasion of spending money and a vicious excess, as many would desire it to be; but it should be rest from labor consecrated by Religion. . . .

## Hours of Labor

33. If we turn now to things exterior and corporal, the first concern of all is to save the poor workers from the cruelty of grasping speculators, who use human beings as mere instruments for making money. It is neither justice nor humanity so to grind men down with excessive labor as to stupefy their minds and wear out their bodies. Man's powers, like his general nature, are limited, and beyond these limits he cannot go. His strength is developed and increased by use and exercise, but only on condition of due intermission and proper rest. Daily labor, therefore, must be so regulated that it may not be protracted during longer hours than strength admits. How many and how long the intervals of rest should be, will depend upon the nature of the work, on circumstances of time and place, and on the health and strength of the workman. . . .

## Just Wages

34. We now approach a subject of very great importance and one on which, if extremes are to be avoided, right ideas are absolutely necessary. Wages, we are told, are fixed by free consent; and, therefore, the employer when he pays what was agreed upon, has done his part, and is not called upon for anything further. The only way, it is said, in which injustice could happen, would be if the master refused to pay the whole of the wages, or the workman would not complete the work undertaken; when this happens the State should intervene, to see that each obtains his own, but not under any other circumstances.

This mode of reasoning is by no means convincing to a fairminded man, for there are important considerations which it leaves out of view altogether. To labor is to exert one's self for the sake of procuring what is necessary for the purposes of life, and most of all for self-preservation. "In the sweat of they brow thou shalt eat bread." Therefore, a man's labor has two notes or characters. First of all, it is *personal;* for the exertion of individual power belongs to the individual who puts it forth, employing this power for that personal profit for which it was given. Secondly, a man's labor is *necessary;* for without the results of labor a man cannot live; and self-conservation is a law of nature, which it is wrong to disobey. Now, if we were to consider labor merely so far as it is *personal,* doubtless it would be within the workman's right to accept any rate of wages whatever; for in the same way as he is free to work or not, so he is free to accept a small remuneration or even none at all. But this is a mere abstract supposition; the labor of the working man is not only his personal attribute, but it is *necessary;* and this makes all the difference. The preservation of life is the bounden duty of each and all, and to fail therein is a crime. It follows that each one has a right to procure what is required in order to live; and the poor can procure it in no other way than by work and wages.

Let it be granted, then, that, as a rule, workman and employer should make free agreements, and in particular should freely agree as to wages; nevertheless, there is a dictate of nature more imperious and more ancient than any bargain between man and man, that the remuneration must be enough to support the wage-earner in reasonable and frugal comfort. If through necessity or fear of a worse evil, the workman accepts harder conditions because an employer or contractor will give him no better, he is the victim of force and injustice. In these and similar questions, however—such as, for example, the hours of labor in different trades, the sanitary precautions to be observed in factories and workshops, etc.—in order to supersede undue interference on the part of the State, especially as circumstances, times and localities differ so widely, it is advisable that recourse be had to societies or boards such as We shall mention presently, or to some other method of safeguarding the interests of wage-earners; the State to be asked for approval and protection.

### Benefits of Property Ownership

35. If a workman's wages be sufficient to enable him to maintain himself, his wife, and his children in reasonable comfort, he will not find it difficult, if he is a sensible man, to study economy; and he will not fail, by cutting down expenses, to put by a little property: nature and reason would urge him to do this. We have seen that this great labor question cannot be solved except by assuming as a principle that private ownership must be held sacred and inviolable. The law, therefore, should favor ownership, and its policy should be to induce as many people as possible to become owners.

Many excellent results will follow from this; and first of all, property will certainly become more equitably divided. For the effect of civil change and revolution has been to divide society into two widely different castes. On the one side there is the party which holds the power because it holds the wealth; which has in its grasp all labor and all trade; which manipulates for its own benefit and its own purposes all the sources of supply, and which is powerfully represented in the councils of the State itself. On the other side there is the needy and powerless multitude, sore and suffering, always ready for disturbance. If working people can be encouraged to look forward to obtaining a share in the land, the result will be that the gulf between vast wealth and deep poverty will be bridged over, and the two orders will be brought nearer together. Another consequence will be the great abundance of the fruits of the earth. Men always work harder and more readily when they work on that which is their own; nay, they learn to love the very soil which yields in response to the labor of their hands, not only food to eat, but an abundance of the good things for themselves and those that are dear to them. It is evident how such a spirit of willing labor would add to the produce of the earth and to the wealth of the community. And a third advantage would arise from this: men would cling to the country in which they were born; for no one would exchange his country for a foreign land if his own afforded him the means of living a tolerable and happy life. These three important benefits, however, can only be expected on the condition that a man's means be not drained and exhausted by excessive taxation. The right to possess private property is from nature, not from man; and the State has only the right to regulate its use in the interests of the public good, but by no means to abolish it altogether. The State is, therefore, unjust and cruel, if, in the name of taxation, it deprives the private owner of more than is just.

### Workmen's Associations

36. In the first place—employers and workmen may themselves effect much in the

matter of which We treat, by means of those institutions and organizations which afford opportune assistance to those in need, and which draw the two orders more closely together. Among these may be enumerated: societies for mutual help; various foundations established by private persons for providing for the workman, and for his widow or his orphans, in sudden calamity, in sickness, and in the event of death; and what are called "patronages," or institutions for the care of boys and girls, for young people, and also for those of more mature age.

The most important of all are Workmen's Associations; for these virtually include all the rest. History attests what excellent results were effected by the Artificer's Guilds of a former day. They were the means not only of many advantages to the workmen, but in no small degree of the advancement of art, as numerous monuments remain to prove. Such associations should be adapted to the requirements of the age in which we live—an age of greater instruction, of different customs, and of more numerous requirements in daily life. It is gratifying to know that there are actually in existence not a few societies of this nature, consisting either of workmen alone, or of workmen and employers together; but it were greatly to be desired that they should multiply and become more effective. We have spoken of them more than once; but it will be well to explain here how much they are needed, to show that they exist by their own right, and to enter into their organization and their work.

37. The experience of his own weakness urges man to call in help from without. We read in the pages of Holy Writ: "It is better that two should be together than one; for they have the advantage of their society. If one fall he shall be supported by the other. Woe to him that is alone, for when he falleth he hath none to lift him up." And further: "A brother that is helped by his brother is like a strong city." It is this natural impulse which unites men in civil society; and it is this also which makes them band themselves together in associations of citizen with citizen; associations which, it is true, cannot be called societies in the complete sense of the word, but which are societies nevertheless.

These lesser societies and the society which constitutes the State differ in many things, because their immediate purpose and end is different. Civil society exists for the common good, and, therefore, is concerned with the interests of all in general, and with the individual interests in their due place and proportion. Hence, it is called *public* society. . . . But the societies which are formed in the bosom of the State are called *private,* and justly so, because their immediate purpose is the private advantage of the associates. . . .

38. Particular societies, then, although they exist within the State, and are each a part of the State, nevertheless cannot be prohibited by the State absolutely and as such. For to enter into a "society" of this kind is the natural right of man; and the State must protect natural rights, not destroy them; and if it forbids its citizens to form associations, it contradicts the very principle of its own existence; for both they and it exist in virtue of the same principle, *viz.,* the natural propensity of man to live in society.

There are times, no doubt, when it is right that the law should interfere to prevent association; as when men join together for purposes which are evidently bad, unjust, or dangerous to the State. In such cases the public authority may justly forbid the formation of association, and may dissolve them when they already exist. But every precaution should be taken not to violate the rights of individuals, and not to make unreasonable regulations under the pretense of public benefit. For laws only bind when they are in accordance with right reason, and therefore with the eternal law of God.

■  ■  ■

### Violent Oppression

40. Associations of every kind, and especially those of working men, are now far more common than formerly. In regard to many of these there is no need at present to inquire whence they spring, what are their objects or what means they use. But there is a good deal of evidence which goes to prove that many of these societies are in the hands of invisible leaders, and are managed on principles far from compatible with Christianity and the public well-being; and that they do their best to get into their hands the whole field of labor and to force workmen either to join them or to starve. Under these circumstances the Christian workmen must do one of two things; either join associations in which their religion will be exposed to peril or form associations among themselves—unite their forces and courageously shake off the yoke of an unjust and intolerable oppression. No one who does not wish to expose man's chief good to extreme danger will hesitate to say that the second alternative must by all means be adopted.

■  ■  ■

### Religion First

. . . Speaking summarily, we may lay it down as a general and perpetual law, that Workmen's Associations should be so organized and governed as to furnish the best and most suitable means for attaining what is aimed at, that is to say, for helping each individual member to better his condition to the utmost, in body, mind and property. It is clear that they must pay special and principal attention to piety and morality, and that their internal discipline must be directed precisely by these considerations; otherwise they entirely lose their special character, and come to be very little better than those societies which take no account of Religion at all.

# 34
## *Quadragesimo Anno*

POPE PIUS XI 1931

In order that what has been well begun may be rendered stable, that what has not yet been accomplished may now be achieved, and that still richer and brighter blessings may descend upon mankind, two things are particularly necessary: the reform of institutions and the correction of morals.

78. When We speak of the reform of institutions it is principally the State We have in mind. Not indeed that all salvation is to be hoped for from its intervention, but because on account of the evil of "individualism," as We called it, things have come to such a pass that the highly developed social life which once flourished in a variety of prosperous and interdependent institutions, has been damaged and all but ruined, leaving virtually only individuals and the State, with no little harm to the latter. But the State, deprived of a supporting social structure, and now encumbered with all the burdens once borne by the disbanded associations, is in consequence overwhelmed and submerged by endless affairs and responsibilities.

79. It is indeed true, as history clearly shows, that owing to the change in social conditions, much that was formerly done by small bodies can nowadays be accomplished only by large organizations. Nevertheless, it is a fundamental principle of social philosophy, fixed and unchangeable, that one should not withdraw from individuals and commit to the community what they can accomplish by their own enterprise and industry. So, too, it is an injustice and at the same time a grave evil and a disturbance of right order, to transfer to the larger and higher collectivity functions which can be performed and provided for by lesser and subordinate bodies. Inasmuch as every social activity should, by its very nature, prove a help to members of the body social, it should never destroy or absorb them.

80. The State authorities should leave to other bodies the care and expediting of business and activities of lesser moment, which otherwise become for it a source of great distraction. It then will perform with greater freedom, vigor and effectiveness, the tasks belonging properly to it, and which it alone can accomplish, directing, supervising, encouraging, restraining, as circumstances suggest or necessity demands. Let those in power, therefore, be convinced that the more faithfully this principle of "subsidiarity" is followed and a hierarchical order prevails among the various organizations, the more excellent will be the authority and efficiency of society, and the happier and more prosperous the condition of the commonwealth.

### Harmony between Ranks in Society

81. Now this is a major and pressing duty of the State and of all good citizens: to get rid of conflict between "classes" with divergent interests, and to foster and promote harmony between the various "ranks" or groupings of society.

82. It is necessary, then, that social policy be directed toward the re-establishment of functional groups. Society today continues in a strained and hence unstable and uncertain condition, for it relies upon "classes" with diverse interests and opposing each other, and hence prone to enmity and strife.

83. Labor, indeed, as has been well said by Our Predecessor in his Encyclical, is not a mere chattel, since the human dignity of the workingman must be recognized in it,

---

Reprinted by permission of the publisher from *Seven Great Encyclicals,* pp. 147–151. Mahwah, N.J.: Paulist Press, 1963. Footnotes in the original have been eliminated.

and consequently it cannot be bought and sold like any piece of merchandise. None the less the demand and supply of labor divides men on the labor market into two classes, as into two camps, and the bargaining between these parties transforms this labor market into an arena where the two armies are engaged in combat. To this grave disorder which is leading society to ruin a remedy must evidently be applied as speedily as possible. But there cannot be question of any perfect cure, except this opposition be done away with, and well ordered members of the social body come into being: functional "groups," namely, binding men together not according to the position they occupy in the labor market, but according to the diverse functions which they exercise in society. For as nature induces those who dwell in close proximity to unite into municipalities, so those who practice the same trade or profession, economic or otherwise, constitute as it were fellowships or bodies. These groupings, autonomous in character, are considered by many to be, if not essential to civil society, at least a natural accompaniment thereof.

84. Order . . . is unity arising from the apt arrangement of a plurality of objects; hence, true and genuine social order demands various members of society, joined together by a common bond. Such a bond of union is provided on the one hand by the common effort to employers and employees of one and the same "group" joining forces to produce goods or give service; on the other hand, by the common good which all "groups" should unite to promote, each in its own sphere, with friendly harmony. Now this union will become powerful and efficacious in proportion to the fidelity with which the individuals and the "groups" strive to discharge their professional duties and to excel in them.

85. From this it is easy to conclude that in these associations the common interest of the whole "group" must predominate: and among these interests the most important is the directing of the activities of the group to the common good. Regarding cases in which interests of employers and employees call for special care and protection against opposing interests, separate deliberation will take place in their respective assemblies and separate votes will be taken as the matter may require.

■    ■    ■

87. Just as the citizens of the same municipality are wont to form associations with diverse aims, which various individuals are free to join or not, similarly, those who are engaged in the same trade or profession will form free associations among themselves, for purposes connected with their occupations. Our Predecessor explained clearly and lucidly the nature of free associations. We are content, therefore, to emphasize this one point: not only is man free to institute such associations, legally and functionally of private character, but he also has the right of "freely adopting such organization and such rules as are judged best for the end in view." The same liberty must be claimed for the founding of associations which extend beyond the limits of a single trade. Let those free associations which already flourish and produce salutary fruits make it the goal of their endeavors, in accordance with Christian social teaching to prepare the way and to do their part toward the realization of those more ideal vocational fellowships or "groups" which We have mentioned above.

### Restoration of the Guiding Principle of Economic Life
88. Another and closely related aim should be kept in view. Just as the unity of human society cannot be built upon "class" conflict, so the proper ordering of economic affairs cannot be left to the free play of rugged competition. From this source, as from a

polluted spring, have proceeded all the errors of the "individualistic" school. This school, forgetful or ignorant of the social and moral aspects of economic activities, regarded these as completely free and immune from any intervention by public authority, for they would have in the market place and in unregulated competition a principle of self-direction more suitable for guiding them than any created intellect which might intervene. Free competition, however, though justified and quite useful within certain limits, cannot be an adequate controlling principle in economic affairs. This has been abundantly proved by the consequences that have followed from the free rein given to these dangerous individualistic ideals. It is therefore very necessary that economic affairs be once more subjected to and governed by a true and effective guiding principle. Still less can this function be exercised by the economic supremacy which within recent times has taken the place of free competition: for this is a headstrong and vehement power, which, if it is to prove beneficial to mankind, needs to be curbed strongly and ruled with prudence. It cannot, however, be curbed and governed by itself. More lofty and noble principles must therefore be sought in order to regulate this supremacy firmly and honestly: to wit, social justice and social charity.

To that end all the institutions of public and social life must be imbued with the spirit of justice, and this justice must above all be truly operative. It must build up a juridical and social order able to pervade all economic activity. Social charity should be, as it were, the soul of this order. It is the duty of the State to safeguard effectively and to vindicate promptly this order, a task it will perform the more readily if it free itself from those burdens which, as We stated above, are not properly its own.

■ ■ ■

91. Within recent times, as all are aware, a special syndical and corporative organization has been inaugurated which, in view of the subject of the present Encyclical, should now be briefly outlined and commented upon.

92. The State here grants legal recognition to the syndicate or union, and thereby confers on it some of the features of a monopoly, for in virtue of this recognition, it alone can represent respectively workingmen and employers, and it alone can conclude labor contracts and labor agreements. Affiliation to the syndicate is optional for everyone; but in this sense only can the syndical organization be said to be free, since the contribution to the union and other special taxes are obligatory for all who belong to a given branch, whether workingmen or employers, and the labor contracts drawn up by the legal syndicate are likewise obligatory. True, it has been authoritatively declared that the juridically established syndicate does not preclude the existence of trade or professional associations not recognized in law.

93. The corporations are composed of representatives of the unions of workingmen and employers of the same trade or profession, and as genuine and exclusive instruments and institutions of the State they direct and co-ordinate the activities of the syndicates in all matters of common interest.

94. Strikes and lock-outs are forbidden. If the contending parties cannot come to an agreement, public authority intervenes.

95. Little reflection is required to perceive advantages in the institution thus summarily described: peaceful collaboration of the classes, repression of socialist organizations and efforts, the moderating authority of a special ministry.

But in order to overlook nothing in a matter of such importance, and in the light of the general principles stated above, as well as that of which We are now about to formulate, We feel bound to add that to Our knowledge there are some who fear that the State is substituting itself in the place of private initiative, instead of limiting itself to necessary and sufficient help and assistance. It is feared that the new syndical and corporative order possesses an excessively bureaucratic and political character, and that, notwithstanding the general advantages referred to above, it risks serving particular political aims rather than contributing to the restoration of social order and the improvement of the same.

# 35
## *Laborem Exercens*

POPE JOHN PAUL II                                                     1981

If one studies the development of the question of social justice, one cannot fail to note that, whereas during the period between *Rerum Novarum* and Pius XI's *Quadragesimo Anno* the church's teaching concentrates mainly on the just solution of the "labor question" within individual nations, in the next period the church's teaching widens its horizon to take in the whole world. The disproportionate distribution of wealth and poverty and the existence of some countries and continents that are developed and of others that are not call for a leveling out and for a search for ways to ensure just development for all. . . .

This trend of development of the church's teaching and commitment in the social question exactly corresponds to the objective recognition of the state of affairs. While in the past the "class" question was especially highlighted as the center of this issue, in more recent times it is the "world" question that is emphasized. Thus, not only the sphere of class is taken into consideration, but also the world sphere of inequality and injustice and, as a consequence, not only the class dimension, but also the world dimension of the tasks involved in the path toward the achievement of justice in the modern world. . . .

■   ■   ■

Man has to subdue the earth and dominate it, because as the "image of God" he is a person, that is to say, a subjective being capable of acting in a planned and rational way, capable of deciding about himself and with a tendency to self-realization. As a person, man is therefore the subject of work. As a person he works, he performs various actions belonging to the work process; independently of their objective content, these actions must all serve to realize his humanity, to fulfill the calling to be a person that is his by reason of his very humanity. . . .

■   ■   ■

This truth, which in a sense constitutes the fundamental and perennial heart of Christian teaching on human work, has had and continues to have primary significance for the formulation of the important social problems characterizing whole ages.

■   ■   ■

The sources of the dignity of work are to be sought primarily in the subjective dimension, not in the objective one.

. . . However true it may be that man is destined for work and called to it, in the first place work is "for man" and not man "for work." Through this conclusion one rightly comes to recognize the pre-eminence of the subjective meaning of work over the objective one. Given this way of understanding things and presupposing that different sorts of work that people do can have greater or lesser objective value, let us try nevertheless to show that each sort is judged above all by the measure of the dignity of the subject of work, that is to say, the person, the individual who carries it out. On the other hand, independent of the work that every man does, and presupposing that this work constitutes a purpose—at times a very demanding one—of his activity, this purpose does not possess a definitive meaning in itself. In fact, in the final analysis it is always man who is the purpose of the work, whatever work it is that is done by man—even if the common scale of values rates it as the merest "service," as the most monotonous, even the most alienating work.

■ ■ ■

In the last century . . . "the worker question," sometimes described as "the proletariat question" . . . and the problems connected with it gave rise to a just social reaction and caused the impetuous emergence of a great burst of solidarity between workers, first and foremost industrial workers. The call to solidarity and common action addressed to the workers—especially to those engaged in narrowly specialized, monotonous and depersonalized work in industrial plants, when the machine tends to dominate man—was important and eloquent from the point of view of social ethics. It was the reaction against the degradation of man as the subject of work and against the unheard-of accompanying exploitation in the field of wages, working conditions and social security for the worker. This reaction united the working world in a community marked by great solidarity.

Following the lines laid down by the encyclical *Rerum Novarum* and many later documents of the church's magisterium, it must be frankly recognized that the reaction against the system of injustice and harm that cried to heaven for vengeance and that weighed heavily upon workers in that period of rapid industrialization was justified from the point of view of social morality. . . .

■ ■ ■

In order to achieve social justice in the various parts of the world, in the various countries and in the relationships between them, there is a need for ever new movements of solidarity of the workers and with the workers. This solidarity must be present whenever it is called for by the social degrading of the subject of work, by exploitation of the workers and by the growing areas of poverty and even hunger. . . .

We must first of all recall a principle that has always been taught by the church: the principle of the priority of labor over capital. This principle directly concerns the process of production: In this process labor is always a primary efficient cause, while capital, the whole collection of means of production, remains a mere instrument or instrumental cause. This principle is an evident truth that emerges from the whole of man's historical experience.

■ ■ ■

This truth, which is part of the abiding heritage of the church's teaching, must always be emphasized with reference to the question of the labor system and with regard to the whole socioeconomic system. We must emphasize and give prominence to the primacy of man in the production process, the primacy of man over things. Everything contained in the concept of capital in the strict sense is only a collection of things. Man, as the subject of work and independent of the work he does—man alone is a person. This truth has important and decisive consequences.

■   ■   ■

. . . The encyclical *Rerum Novarum,* which has the social question as its theme, stresses . . . the right to private property even when it is a question of the means of production. . . .

The above principle, as it was then stated and as it is still taught by the church, diverges radically from the program of collectivism as proclaimed by Marxism and put into practice in various countries in the decades following the time of Leo XIII's encyclical. At the same time it differs from the program of capitalism practiced by liberalism and by the political systems inspired by it. In the latter case, the difference consists in the way the right to ownership or property is understood. Christian tradition has never upheld this right as absolute and untouchable. On the contrary, it has always understood this right within the broader context of the right common to all to use the goods of the whole of creation: The right to private property is subordinated to the right to common use, to the fact that goods are meant for everyone.

Furthermore, in the church's teaching, ownership has never been understood in a way that could constitute grounds for social conflict in labor. As mentioned above, property is acquired first of all through work in order that it may serve work. This concerns in a special way ownership of the means of production. Isolating these means as a separate property in order to set it up in the form of "capital" in opposition to "labor"—and even to practice exploitation of labor—is contrary to the very nature of these means and their possession. They cannot be possessed against labor, they cannot even be possessed for possession's sake, because the only legitimate title to their possession—whether in the form of private ownership or in the form of public or collective ownership—is that they should serve labor and thus by serving labor that they should make possible the achievement of the first principle of this order, namely the universal destination of goods and the right to common use of them. From this point of view, therefore, in consideration of human labor and of common access to the goods meant for man, one cannot exclude the socialization, in suitable conditions, of certain means of production. . . .

In the present document, which has human work as its main theme, it is right to confirm all the effort with which the church's teaching has striven and continues to strive always to ensure the priority of work and thereby man's character as a subject in social life and especially in the dynamic structure of the whole economic process. From this point of view the position of "rigid" capitalism continues to remain unacceptable, namely the position that defends the exclusive right to private ownership of the means of production as an untouchable "dogma" of economic life. The principle of respect for work demands that this right should undergo a constructive revision both in theory and in practice. If it is true that capital, as the whole of the means of production, is at the same time the product of the work of generations, it is equally true that capital is being unceasingly created through the work done with the help of all these means of production, and these means can be seen as a great workbench at which the present generation of workers is working day after day. Obviously we are dealing here with different kinds of work, not only so-called manual labor, but also the many forms of intellectual work, including white-collar work and management.

In the light of the above, the many proposals put forward by experts in Catholic social teaching and by the highest magisterium of the church take on special significance:

proposals for joint ownership of the means of work, sharing by the workers in the management and-or profits of businesses, so-called shareholding by labor, etc. Whether these various proposals can or cannot be applied concretely, it is clear that recognition of the proper position of labor and the worker in the production process demands various adaptations in the sphere of the right to ownership of the means of production. This is so not only in view of older situations but also, first and foremost, in view of the whole of the situation and the problems in the second half of the present century with regard to the so-called Third World and the various new independent countries that have arisen, especially in Africa but elsewhere as well, in place of the colonial territories of the past.

Therefore, while the position of "rigid" capitalism must undergo continual revision in order to be reformed from the point of view of human rights, both human rights in the widest sense and those linked with man's work, it must be stated that from the same point of view these many deeply desired reforms cannot be achieved by an *a priori* elimination of private ownership of the means of production. For it must be noted that merely taking these means of production (capital) out of the hands of their private owners is not enough to ensure their satisfactory socialization. They cease to be the property of a certain social group, namely the private owners, and become the property of organized society, coming under the administration and direct control of another group of people, namely those who, though not owning them, from the fact of exercising power in society manage them on the level of the whole national or the local economy.

This group in authority may carry out its task satisfactorily from the point of view of the priority of labor; but it may also carry it out badly by claiming for itself a monopoly of the administration and disposal of the means of production and not refraining even from offending basic human rights. Thus, merely converting the means of production into state property in the collectivist systems is by no means equivalent to "socializing" that property. We can speak of socializing only when the subject character of society is ensured, that is to say, when on the basis of his work each person is fully entitled to consider himself a part owner of the great workbench at which he is working with everyone else. A way toward that goal could be found by associating labor with the ownership of capital, as far as possible, and by producing a wide range of intermediate bodies with economic, social and cultural purposes; they would be bodies enjoying real autonomy with regard to the public powers, pursuing their specific aims in honest collaboration with each other and in subordination to the demands of the common good, and they would be living communities both in form and in substance in the sense that the members of each body would be looked upon and treated as persons and encouraged to take an active part in the life of the body.

■  ■  ■

While work, in all its many senses, is an obligation, that is to say a duty, it is also a source of rights on the part of the worker. These rights must be examined in the broad context of human rights as a whole, which are connatural with man and many of which are proclaimed by various international organizations and increasingly guaranteed by the individual states for their citizens. Respect for this broad range of human rights constitutes the fundamental condition for peace in the modern world: peace both within individual countries and societies and in international relations. . . . The human rights that flow from work are part of the broader context of those fundamental rights of the person.

However, within this context they have a specific character corresponding to the specific nature of human work as outlined above. It is in keeping with this character that we must view them. Work is, as has been said, an obligation, that is to say, a duty, on the part of man. This is true in all the many meanings of the word. Man must work both because the Creator has commanded it and because of his own humanity, which requires work in order to be maintained and developed. Man must work out of regard for others, especially his own family, but also for the society he belongs to, the country of which he is a child and the whole human family of which he is a member, since he is the heir to the work of generations and at the same time a sharer in building the future of those who will come after him in the succession of history. All this constitutes the moral obligation of work, understood in its wide sense. When we have to consider the moral rights corresponding to this obligation of every person with regard to work, we must always keep before our eyes the whole vast range of points of reference in which the labor of every working subject is manifested.

For when we speak of the obligation of work and of the rights of the worker that correspond to this obligation, we think in the first place of the relationship between the employer, direct or indirect, and the worker.

The distinction between the direct and the indirect employer is seen to be very important when one considers both the way in which labor is actually organized and the possibility of the formation of just or unjust relationships in the field of labor.

Since the direct employer is the person or institution with whom the worker enters directly into a work contract in accordance with definite conditions, we must understand as the indirect employer many different factors, other than the direct employer, that exercise a determining influence on the shaping both of the work contract and consequently of just or unjust relationships in the field of human labor.

■   ■   ■

The concept of indirect employer includes both persons and institutions of various kinds and also collective labor contracts and the principles of conduct which are laid down by these persons and institutions and which determine the whole socioeconomic system or are its result. The concept of "indirect employer" thus refers to many different elements. The responsibility of the indirect employer differs from that of the direct employer—the term itself indicates that the responsibility is less direct—but it remains a true responsibility: The indirect employer substantially determines one or other facet of the labor relationship, thus conditioning the conduct of the direct employer when the latter determines in concrete terms the actual work contract and labor relations. This is not to absolve the direct employer from his own responsibility, but only to draw attention to the whole network of influences that condition his conduct. When it is a question of establishing an ethically correct labor policy, all these influences must be kept in mind. A policy is correct when the objective rights of the worker are fully respected.

The concept of indirect employer is applicable to every society and in the first place to the state. For it is the state that must conduct a just labor policy. However, it is common knowledge that in the present system of economic relations in the world there are numerous links between individual states, links that find expression, for instance, in the import and export process, that is to say, in the mutual exchange of economic goods, whether raw materials, semimanufactured goods or finished industrial products. These links also create mutual dependence, and as a result it would be difficult to speak in the case of any state, even the economically most powerful, of complete self-sufficiency or autarky.

Such a system of mutual dependence is in itself normal. However it can easily become an occasion for various forms of exploitation or injustice and as a result influence the labor policy of individual states; and finally it can influence the individual worker who is the proper subject of labor. For instance the highly industrialized countries, and even more the businesses that direct on a large scale the means of industrial production (the companies referred to as multinational or transnational), fix the highest possible prices for their products, while trying at the same time to fix the lowest possible prices for raw materials or semimanufactured goods. This is one of the causes of an ever increasing disproportion between national incomes. The gap between most of the richest countries and the poorest ones is not diminishing or being stabilized, but is increasing more and more to the detriment, obviously, of the poor countries. Evidently this must have an effect on local labor policy and on the worker's situation in the economically disadvantaged societies. Finding himself in a system thus conditioned, the direct employer fixes working conditions below the objective requirements of the workers, especially if he himself wishes to obtain the highest possible profits from the business which he runs (or from the businesses which he runs, in the case of a situation of "socialized" ownership of the means of production).

It is easy to see that this framework of forms of dependence linked with the concept of the indirect employer is enormously extensive and complicated. It is determined, in a sense, by all the elements that are decisive for economic life within a given society and state, but also by much wider links and forms of dependence. The attainment of the worker's rights cannot however be doomed to be merely a result of economic systems which on a larger or smaller scale are guided chiefly by the criterion of maximum profit. On the contrary, it is respect for the objective rights of the worker—every kind of worker: manual or intellectual, industrial or agricultural, etc.—that must constitute the adequate and fundamental criterion for shaping the whole economy, both on the level of the individual society and state and within the whole of the world economic policy and of the systems of international relationships that derive from it.

■  ■  ■

When we consider the rights of workers in relation to the "indirect employer," that is to say, all the agents at the national and international level that are responsible for the whole orientation of labor policy, we must first direct our attention to a fundamental issue: the question of finding work or, in other words, the issue of suitable employment for all who are capable of it. The opposite of a just and right situation in this field is unemployment, that is to say, the lack of work for those who are capable of it. It can be a question of general unemployment or of unemployment in certain sectors of work. The role of the agents included under the title of indirect employer is to act against unemployment, which in all cases is an evil and which, when it reaches a certain level, can become a real social disaster. It is particularly painful when it especially affects young people, who after appropriate cultural, technical and professional preparation fail to find work and see their sincere wish to work and their readiness to take on their own responsibility for the economic and social development of the community sadly frustrated. The obligation to provide unemployment benefits, that is to say, the duty to make suitable grants indispensable for the subsistence of unemployed workers and their families, is a duty springing from the fundamental principle of the moral order in this sphere, namely the principle of the common use of goods or, to put it in another and still simpler way, the right to life and subsistence.

In order to meet the danger of unemployment and to ensure employment for all, the agents defined here as "indirect employer" must make provision for overall planning with regard to the different kinds of work by which not only the economic life, but also the cultural life of a given society is shaped; they must also give attention to organizing that work in a correct and rational way. In the final analysis this overall concern weighs on the shoulders of the state, but it cannot mean one-sided centralization by the public authorities. Instead, what is in question is a just and rational coordination, within the framework of which the initiative of individuals, free groups and local work centers and complexes must be safeguarded, keeping in mind what has been said above with regard to the subject character of human labor.

The fact of the mutual dependence of societies and states and the need to collaborate in various areas mean that, while preserving the sovereign rights of each society and state in the field of planning and organizing labor in its own society, action in this important area must also be taken in the dimension of international collaboration by means of the necessary treaties and agreements. Here too the criterion for these pacts and agreements must more and more be the criterion of human work considered as a fundamental right of all human beings, work which gives similar rights to all those who work in such a way that the living standard of the workers in the different societies will less and less show those disturbing differences which are unjust and are apt to provoke even violent reactions. The international organizations have an enormous part to play in this area. They must let themselves be guided by an exact diagnosis of the complex situations and of the influence exercised by natural, historical, civil and other such circumstances. They must also be more highly operative with regard to plans for action jointly decided on, that is to say, they must be more effective in carrying them out.

■  ■  ■

As we view the whole human family throughout the world, we cannot fail to be struck by a disconcerting fact of immense proportions: the fact that while conspicuous natural resources remain unused there are huge numbers of people who are unemployed or underemployed and countless multitudes of people suffering from hunger. This is a fact that without any doubt demonstrates that both within the individual political communities and in their relationships on the continental and world levels there is something wrong with the organization of work and employment, precisely at the most critical and socially most important points.

■  ■  ■

All these rights, together with the need for the workers themselves to secure them, give rise to yet another right: the right of association, that is, to form associations for the purpose of defending the vital interests of those employed in the various professions. These associations are called labor or trade unions. The vital interests of the workers are to a certain extent common for all of them; at the same time, however, each type of work, each profession, has its own specific character which should find a particular reflection in these organizations.

In a sense, unions go back to the medieval guilds of artisans, insofar as those organizations brought together people belonging to the same craft and thus on the basis of their work. However unions differ from the guilds on this essential point: The modern unions grew up from the struggle of the workers—workers in general but especially the industrial workers—to protect their just rights vis-a-vis the entrepreneurs and the owners of the means of production. Their task is to defend the existential interests of workers in all sectors in which their rights are concerned. The experience of history teaches that organizations of this type are an indispensable element of social life, especially in modern industrialized societies. Obviously this does not mean that only industrial workers can set up associations of this type. Representatives of every profession can use them to ensure their own rights. Thus there are unions of agricultural workers and of white-collar workers; there are also employers' associations. All, as has been said above, are further divided into groups or subgroups according to particular professional specializations.

Catholic social teaching does not hold that unions are no more than a reflection of the "class" structure of society and that they are a mouthpiece for a class struggle which inevitably governs social life. They are indeed a mouthpiece for the struggle for social justice, for the just rights of working people in accordance with their individual professions. However, this struggle should be seen as a normal endeavor "for" the just good: In the present case, for the good which corresponds to the needs and merits of working people associated by profession; but it is not a struggle "against" others. Even if in controversial questions the struggle takes on a character of opposition toward others, this is because it aims at the good of social justice, not for the sake of "struggle" or in order to eliminate the opponent. It is characteristic of work that it first and foremost unites people. In this consists its social power: the power to build a community. In the final analysis, both those who work and those who manage the means of production or who own them must in some way be united in this community. In the light of this fundamental structure of all work—in the light of the fact that, in the final analysis, labor and capital are indispensable components of the process of production in any social system—it is clear that even if it is because of their work needs that people unite to secure their rights, their union remains a constructive factor of social order and solidarity, and it is impossible to ignore it.

Just efforts to secure the rights of workers who are united by the same profession should always take into account the limitations imposed by the general economic situation of the country. Union demands cannot be turned into a kind of group or class "egoism," although they can and should also aim at correcting—with a view to the common good of the whole of society—everything defective in the system of ownership of the means of production or in the way these are managed. Social and socioeconomic life is certainly like a system of "connected vessels," and every social activity directed toward safeguarding the rights of particular groups should adapt itself to this system.

In this sense, union activity undoubtedly enters the field of politics, understood as prudent concern for the common good. However, the role of unions is not to "play politics" in the sense that the expression is commonly understood today. Unions do not have the character of political parties struggling for power; they should not be subjected to the decision of political parties or have too close links with them. In fact, in such a situation they easily lose contact with their specific role, which is to secure the just rights of workers within the framework of the common good of the whole of society; instead they become an instrument used for other purposes.

Speaking of the protection of the just rights of workers according to their individual professions, we must of course always keep in mind that which determines the subjective character of work in each profession, but at the same time, indeed before all else, we must keep in mind that which conditions the specific dignity of the subject of the work. The activity of union organizations opens up many possibilities in this respect, including their efforts to instruct and educate the workers and to foster their self-education. Praise is due to the work of the schools, what are known as workers' or people's universities and the training programs and courses which have developed and are still developing this field of activity. It is always to be hoped that, thanks to the work of their unions, workers will not only have more, but above all be more: in other words that they will realize their humanity more fully in every respect.

One method used by unions in pursuing the just rights of their members is the strike or work stoppage, as a kind of ultimatum to the competent bodies, especially the employers. This method is recognized by Catholic social teaching as legitimate in the proper conditions and within just limits. In this connection workers should be assured the right to strike, without being subjected to personal penal sanctions for taking part in a strike. While admitting that it is a legitimate means, we must at the same time emphasize that a strike remains, in a sense, an extreme means. It must not be abused; it must not be abused especially for "political" purposes. Furthermore, it must never be forgotten that when essential community services are in question, they must in every case be ensured, if necessary by means of appropriate legislation. Abuse of the strike weapon can lead to the paralysis of the whole of socioeconomic life, and this is contrary to the requirements of the common good of society, which also corresponds to the properly understood nature of work itself.

# SEVEN

## The Labor Movement as a Pernicious Monopoly

# Introduction

In Part VII we present theories hostile to the labor movement. The most influential theory opposed to the labor movement comes from the neoclassical tradition in economics. Written within this tradition in 1944, Henry Simons's "Some Reflections on Syndicalism" is probably the most complete and hostile attack on trade unions. Portions of this essay are reprinted below.

Simons sees trade unions as organized monopolies of the most dangerous sort. They operate to restrict output and raise costs, he asserts. As consumers we all lose due to the resulting inefficiency. But labor unions are not simply monopolies—they are a particularly harmful kind. According to Simons they enjoy an unprecedented freedom and ability to engage in violence to attain their ends. Furthermore, their virtually unlimited power enables them to hold industrial capital hostage while they progressively destroy the industry through excessive labor costs. The consumer is exploited through the exorbitant cost of the final product. Eventually the democratic system of government is undermined; unions form a violent, aggressive special interest which usurps all substantive power. The resulting unstable economy and social system is not compatible with democracy.

Ten years later, Orme Phelps wrote a reply to Simons which briefly summarizes many of the objections to Simons's theory. Phelps argues that Simons is factually incorrect in many of his key assertions. His underlying theoretical model of trade unionism is fundamentally mistaken because it misses the *political* character of unions. Phelps concludes that Simons's theory has very little relationship to reality.

Simons's pupil and protégé, Milton Friedman, and his wife Rose, although less extreme than Simons in their pronouncements, make very similar arguments. They see unions solely as monopolies harming the consumer and other workers; there is no difference between a typical union and the American Medical Association, they claim. Monopolization at the expense of everybody else is the goal. The Friedmans and like-minded conservative economists in the neoclassical tradition are the modern day upholders of Simons's basic theory.

The final selection by Freeman and Medoff criticizes the anti-union theories for being one-sided and factually incorrect. Freeman and Medoff argue that unions have two "faces": the *monopolistic* one so prominently featured in anti-union theories, and a *collective voice/institutional response* face. While the monopolistic role of unions is undeniable, it has been greatly exaggerated, they claim. In fact, unions overall are a force for equality. Furthermore, unions provide a voice for workers in corporate decision-making. This union voice in turn alters the operations of the workplace and the enterprise in virtually every other measurable way, and the vast majority of these changes are positive from the point of view of social policy.

Although Freeman and Medoff do not put forth a labor theory of their own, they do cast serious doubt on the claims of anti-union theorists. The strength of their research lies in the amount of empirical evidence they have marshalled in support of their argument. Despite such evidence, however, anti-union theories remain popular in many business and academic circles, as well as with much of the general public in the United States today.

# 36
## *Some Reflections on Syndicalism*

**HENRY SIMONS**                                                                    1944

Questioning the virtues of the organized labor movement is like attacking religion, monogamy, motherhood, or the home. Among the modern intelligentsia any doubts about collective bargaining admit of explanation only in terms of insanity, knavery, or subservience to "the interests." Discussion of skeptical views runs almost entirely in terms of how one came by such persuasions, as though they were symptoms of disease. One simply cannot argue that organization is injurious to labor; one is either for labor or against it, and the test is one's attitude toward unionism. But let me indicate from the outset that my central interest, and the criterion in terms of which I wish to argue, is a maximizing of aggregate labor income and a minimizing of inequality. If unionism were good for labor as a whole, that would be the end of the issue for me, since the community whose welfare concerns us is composed overwhelmingly of laborers.

Our problem here, at bottom, is one of broad political philosophy. Advocates of trade-unionism are, I think, obligated morally and intellectually to present a clear picture of the total political-economic system toward which they would have us move. For my part, I simply cannot conceive of any tolerable or enduring order in which there exists widespread organization of workers along occupational, industrial, functional lines. Sentimentalists view such developments merely as a contest between workers who earn too little and enterprises which earn too much; and, unfortunately, there has been enough monopsony in labor markets to make this view superficially plausible, though not enough to make it descriptively important. What we generally fail to see is the identity of interest between the whole community and enterprises seeking to keep down costs. Where enterprise is competitive—and substantial, enduring restraint of competition in product markets is rare—enterprisers represent the community interest effectively; indeed, they are merely intermediaries between consumers of goods and sellers of services. Thus we commonly overlook the conflict of interest between every large organized group of laborers and the community as a whole. What I want to ask is how this conflict can be reconciled, how the power of strongly organized sellers can be limited out of regard for the general welfare. No insuperable problem arises so long as organization is partial and precarious, so long as most unions face substantial nonunion competition, or so long as they must exercise monopoly powers sparingly because of organizational insecurity. Weak unions have no large monopoly powers. But how does a democratic community limit the demands and exactions of strong, secure organizations? Looking at the typographers, the railway brotherhoods, and metropolitan building trades, among others, one answers simply: "It doesn't!"

In an economy of intricate division of labor, every large organized group is in a position at any time to disrupt or to stop the whole flow of social income; and the system must soon break down if groups persist in exercising that power or if they must continuously be bribed to forgo its disastrous exercise. There is no means, save internal competition, to protect the whole community against organized labor minorities and, indeed, no other means to protect the common interests of organized groups themselves. The dilemma here is not peculiar to our present economic order; it must appear in any kind of system. This minority-monopoly problem would be quite as serious for a democratic socialism as it is for the mixed individualist-collectivist system of the present. It is the

Reprinted by permission of the University of Chicago Press from Henry Simons, "Some Reflections on Syndicalism," *Journal of Political Economy* 52 (1944): 1–25. Footnotes in the original have been eliminated.

rock on which our present system is most likely to crack up; and it is the rock on which democratic socialism would be destroyed if it could ever come into being at all.

All the grosser mistakes in economic policy, if not most manifestations of democratic corruption, arise from focusing upon the interests of people as producers rather than upon their interests as consumers, that is, from acting on behalf of producer minorities rather than on behalf of the whole community as sellers of services and buyers of products. One gets the right answers usually by regarding simply the interests of consumers, since we are all consumers; and the answers reached by this approach are presumably the correct ones for laborers as a whole. But one does not get elected by approaching issues in this way! People seldom vote in terms of their common interests, whether as sellers or as buyers. There is no means for protecting the common interest save in terms of rules of policy; and it is only in terms of general rules or principles that democracy, which is government by free, intelligent discussion, can function tolerably or endure. Its nemesis is racketeering—tariffs, other subsidies, and patronage dispensations generally and, outside of government, monopoly, which in its basic aspect is impairment of the state's monopoly of coercive power.

Trade-unionism may be attacked as a threat to order under any kind of system. The case against it is crystal clear if one thinks in terms of purer types of systems like democratic collectivism. A socialist government, faced with numerous functional minorities each organized to disrupt the whole production process unless its demands are met, would be exactly in the position of recent Chinese governments faced with great bandit armies continuously collecting ransom from the nominal sovereign. It would either deprive such minorities of the power to act as units in withholding services or be displaced by a nondemocratic authority which could and would restore monopoly of violence. There is no place for collective bargaining, or for the right to strike, or for effective occupational organization in the socialist state, save in the sense that revolution against established authority is an undeniable privilege and violent chaos always an imminent possibility; and every intelligent socialist, whatever his public utterances, knows as much.

I am arguing, however, not as a socialist, but as an advocate of the elaborate mixed system of traditional economic liberalism. The essence of this practical political philosophy is a distrust of all concentrations of power. No individual may be trusted with much power, no organization, and no institution save the state itself. The state or sovereign must, of course, possess great reserves of power, if only to prevent other organizations from threatening or usurping its monopoly of violence. But the exercise of power inherent in government must be rigidly economized. Decentralization of government is essential. Indeed, the proper purpose of all large-scale organization or federation—as should be obvious to people facing the problem of world order—is that of dispersing power.

■   ■   ■

Along these lines we may reconstruct a total political system in which organization becomes progressively looser and functions increasingly narrow and negative as one moves from local government (counties?) to states, to nations, and to supranational agencies. The good political order is one in which small nations and governments on the scale of American states are protected in their autonomy against neighbors and protected against federalisms or unions which appropriate their powers, take positive government farther from the people, and systematically subordinate common to special interests.

The great sins against world order, by way of trade restraint and military activity, are those of great, not small, nations. In spite of popular impressions to the contrary, the worst breaches of political morality, the worst patronage corruption, and the most glaring weakness against organized minorities are characteristic of great national or federal governments far more than of smaller units—and of our federal government, with all its "respectability" and "efficiency," especially.

Governments can be trusted to exercise large power, broad functions, and extensive control only at levels of small units like American states and under the limitations imposed by freedom of external trade. Especially in the higher levels or larger units of government, action must follow broad general rules or principles. Only by adherence to "constitutional" principles of policy can the common interest be protected against minorities, patronage, and logrolling; and only in terms of issues of broad principle can government by free, intelligent discussion (democracy) prevail. Most important here are the presumptions in favor of free trade and against dispensations to producer minorities. Constitutional principles or accepted norms are also peculiarly important, and lacking, in fiscal (monetary, budgetary) policy.

Other implications of this older liberalism may be mentioned briefly. The government must not tolerate erection of great private corporate empires or cartel organizations which suppress competition and rival in power great governmental units themselves. . . . It must guard its powers jealously both against the combination of numerous pressure groups and against powerful lobbies like the present federal lobby of landowners. . . . It must hold in check organizations designed for raiding the Treasury (witness the history of pension legislation and the political power of veterans' organizations). Finally, and most important for the future, it must guard its powers against great trade-unions, both as pressure groups in government and as monopolists outside.

The danger here is now most ominous, in the very nature of such agencies and also because the danger is least well recognized and commonly denied entirely. In other areas we are, if diffident and careless, at least on our guard; nothing is likely to happen that cannot be undone if we will; but labor monopolies and labor "states" may readily become a problem which democracy simply cannot solve at all. There must be effective limitations upon their powers; but I do not see how they can be disciplined democratically save by internal competition or how that discipline can be effected without breaking down organization itself. Here, possibly, is an awful dilemma: democracy cannot live with tight occupational monopolies; and it cannot destroy them, once they attain great power, without destroying itself in the process. If democratic governments cannot suppress organized extortion and preserve their monopoly of violence, they will be superseded by other kinds of government. Organized economic warfare is like organized banditry and, if allowed to spread, must lead to total revolution, which will, on very hard terms, restore some order and enable us to maintain some real income instead of fighting interminably over its division among minorities.

Monopoly power must be abused. It has no use save abuse. Some people evidently have believed that labor organizations should have monopoly powers and be trusted not to use them. Collective bargaining, for the Webbs, was evidently a scheme whereby labor monopolies were to raise wages to competitive levels, merely counteracting monopsony among buyers, but eschewing further exercise of organizational powers. A trade-unionism, affecting wages and working rules only within such limits, and doing all the many other good things that unions can do, would be a blessing all around. No one could seriously question its merits in the abstract. But monopsony in the labor market is, I think, very unsubstantial or transitory; and it is romantic and unreasonable to expect organizations to exercise powers only within limits consistent with the common interest. All bargaining power is monopoly power. Such power, once attained, will be used as fully as its conservation permits and also used continuously for its own accretion and consolidation. The skin disease of monopsony is certainly a poor excuse for stopping the peaceful and productive game of free enterprise and free exchange in favor of the violent contest of organized producer-minorities.

I do not assert that our only monopoly problems lie in the labor market. Save for the monopolies which government is promoting in agriculture, however, no others seem comparably important for the future. It is shameful to have permitted the growth of vast corporate empires, the collusive restraint of trade by trade associations, and the gross abuse of patent privilege for extortion, exclusion, and output restriction. But enterprise monopoly is also a skin disease, easy to correct when and if we will, and usually moderate in its abuses, since its powers are necessarily small, and since the danger of political reckoning is never very remote. Enterprise monopoly, enjoying very limited access to violence and facing heavy penalties for unfair methods against rivals, is always plagued by competition, actual and potential, and must always operate against a deeply hostile, if lethargic, attitude of courts, legislatures, and the public. In exceptional cases it has acquired vast power and sustained power over long periods. In many cases it has transformed salutary price competition into perverse and wasteful "competition" in merchandising and advertising. But, to repeat, the proper remedies here are not very difficult technically or politically.

Labor monopolies are, now or potentially, a different kind of animal. If much violence has been used against them as they struggled into existence, this should not obscure the fact that, once established, they enjoy an access to violence which is unparalleled in other monopolies. If governments have tolerated flagrant violations of law by employers, they are nearly impotent to enforce laws against mass minorities even if majority opinion permitted it. Thus, unions may deal with scabs in ways which make even Rockefeller's early methods seem polite and legitimate. They have little to fear from chiselers in their own midst; and they have now little to fear from Congress or the courts.

Patently restrictive practices are now commonly deplored and, perhaps because unnecessary, seem somewhat on the wane. But there have been many cases of severe limitations upon entry—high initiation fees, excessive periods of apprenticeship and restrictions upon numbers of apprentices, barriers to movement between related trades, and, of course, make-work restrictions, cost-increasing working rules, and prohibition of cost-reducing innovations, notably in the building trades—not to mention racial and sex discriminations against which effective competition in labor markets is probably a necessary, if not a sufficient, protection.

It is not commonly recognized, however, that control of wage rates *is* control of entry, especially where seniority rules are in force and, even failing such rules, where qualitative selection is important and turnover itself very costly to firms. If able to enforce standard rates, experienced, established workers can insulate themselves from the competition of new workers merely by making their cost excessive, that is, by establishing labor costs and wage expectations which preclude expansion of production or employment in their field. New and displaced workers typically migrate, not to high-wage occupations but to places where employment opportunities exist; high wages are less attractive if jobs cannot be had. Wage control, determining a major element in operating cost, also determines the rate at which a whole industry will expand or, more likely, with strong organization, the rate of contraction.

Frankly, I can see no reason why strongly organized workers, in an industry where huge investment is already sunk in highly durable assets, should ever permit a return on investment sufficient to attract new capital or even to induce full maintenance of existing capital. If I were running a union and were managing it faithfully in the interest of the majority of its members, I should consistently demand wage rates which offered to existing firms no real net earnings but only the chance of getting back part of their sunk investment at the cost of the replacement outlays necessary to provide employment for most of my constituents during their own lifetimes as workers. In other words, I should plan gradually to exterminate the industry by excessive labor costs, taking care only to prevent employment from contracting more rapidly than my original constituents disappeared by death and voluntary retirement.

If I were operating, as labor leader, without the valuable hostages of large sunk investment, I should be obliged to behave more moderately. But I should still seek, controlling prices via labor costs, to restrict production as rapidly as consistent with decline of my membership by death and retirement and, while permitting some return to investors, should try always to induce only as much employment and production as my original constituents could take care of without new members. If investors disliked my high wages, they would like the high prices which I could assure them by excluding lower-wage competitors. In both cases I should, of course, not serve my constituents well toward the end unless I utilized the opportunity of permitting some newcomers, by payment of heavy tribute, to enter, to acquire skill and experience, and to become established with my older cronies; for the initiation fees would contribute handsomely to our retirement annuities.

The situation is more complicated, of course, where unions do permit and facilitate entry, that is, where work is shared equally between newcomers and others. Here the advantages of high wages are dissipated by the sharing of unemployment; and annual wages may even drop below a competitive level, if workers value leisure highly or are usually able to find other remunerative work during their periods of layoff. The outcome resembles that of the pure cartel among enterprises, where price is fixed by voluntary agreement, output divided by quotas, and newcomers admitted freely and granted quotas on the same basis as old firms. No one gains, and everybody as consumer loses. There is great social wastage of resources, of labor in one case, of investment in the other; and the two wastes are likely to occur together, as in coal-mining.

But free entry and division of work are not likely to characterize unionism of the future and have rarely prevailed in the past. Employees increasingly seek seniority rights; employers prefer to exercise qualitative selection; and the demands from both sides are roughly consistent, especially in large established firms where workers are carefully selected in the first place and experience is important. Some conflict arises, fortunately, between the rank and file, who want the highest possible wage rates, and labor leaders, whose power and influence, in government and in labor circles, depends on the number of their constituents; but this conflict will usually be reconciled in favor of the interests of the rank and file or avoided via organizational imperialism (jurisdictional conquests). Sentimentalists will urge that strong unions should moderate wage demands, recognizing an obligation to permit entry of young workers and workers displaced in decadent industries; but I should not expect them to behave so or blame them for using power, if they have it, in their own interest; and I see no way to avoid severely restrictive policies save by depriving them of control over wages, that is, of bargaining power.

■   ■   ■

I am here arguing merely the classical case for free trade, free markets, and free occupational migration. The argument is equally sound whether invoked against external or internal barriers, against governmental restrictions on trade, or against those imposed by private monopolies. . . . The public interest demands free exchange and free movement of workers among occupations. Above all, it demands the easiest possible access by workers in low-wage occupations to highly productive and unusually remunerative employment. Unionism implies ability of established workers in high-wage areas and occupations to insulate themselves from competition, excluding inexperienced new workers and qualitatively inferior labor from their markets. It enables an aristocracy of labor to build fences around its occupations, restricting entry, raising arbitrarily the costs and prices of its products, and lowering the wages and incomes of those outside, and of the poor especially.

■   ■   ■

Freedom of entry is peculiarly essential in the case of unusually remunerative employments, if one believes in greater equality of opportunity. Only by permitting the freest movement upward through wage categories can we minimize economic inequality and maximize incomes at the bottom of the scale. But it is exactly the high-wage industries which invite and facilitate organization; and it is the favorably situated who have most to gain by exclusion, restriction, and monopolistic practices. At best, no labor organization is likely to be more unselfish or to make less use of its powers than the American Medical Association; and, considering its loose organization and small power, the comparison is surely alarming.

Organization is a device by which privilege may be intrenched and consolidated. It is a device by which the strong may raise themselves higher by pressing down the weak. Unionism, barring entry into the most attractive employments, makes high wages higher and low wages lower. Universally applied, it gets nowhere save to create disorder. Surely we cannot all get rich by restricting production. Monopoly works when everyone does not try it or when few have effective power. Universally applied it is like universal, uniform subsidy paid out of universal, uniform taxation, save that the latter is merely ridiculous while the former is also incompatible with economy of resources and even with order. But the dictator will be installed long before monopoly or functional organization becomes universal. Must we leave it to the man on horseback, or to popes of the future, to restore freedom of opportunity and freedom of occupational movement?

Unionism is only incidentally a means for raising labor incomes at the expense of profits or property income. Profits are usually a small moiety, sometimes positive and often negative; and all property income is a margin whose reduction by particular wage increases reacts promptly and markedly upon employment, production, and product price. Increased labor cost in particular areas has its impact upon earnings; but, as with excise taxes, the burden or incidence quickly transfers to the buyer of products, if not to sellers of services, via output changes.

Labor demands may be rationalized and popularized as demands for a larger share of earnings—as part of a contest over the shares of labor and capital in particular outputs. But enterprises remain essentially intermediaries between sellers of services and buyers of product. The semblance of struggle between labor and capital conceals the substantial conflict between a labor monopoly and the community; between organized workers and consumers; and especially between established workers in more remunerative occupations and workers elsewhere. The masses of the unorganized and unorganizable lose as consumers; they lose by being denied access to higher-wage areas; and they lose by an artificial abundance of labor in the markets where they must sell, that is, by being forced to compete with workers who should have been drawn off into the higher-wage occupations. And let no one infer that their problem would be solved if they too were organized. The monopoly racket, like that of tariffs and subsidies, works only so long as it is exceptional—works only to advantage minorities relatively, with over-all diseconomy and loss.

■    ■    ■

In the name of equalizing bargaining power we have sanctioned and promoted the proliferation of militant labor monopolies whose proper, natural function is exploitation of consumers. The ultimate burden of their exactions will not fall mainly upon industrial investors or enterprises; but enterprises, as intermediaries, will bear the impact of new exactions and may expect to see earnings continuously pressed down to such extent that average expectations are utterly discouraging. For industrial investors, the result is much the same as though the state had promoted organized banditry and denied them all protection against it—while offering unusual safeguards to holders of idle funds (deposits) and large new investment outlets in government bonds (not to mention "tax-exempts").

We face a real problem in economic inequality. This problem can be handled easily and without serious diseconomies, if one is not hysterically in a hurry, by progressive taxation of income and inheritance. Merely by repairing a few structural flaws in our income tax, we could assure steady reduction of inequality in property incomes and continuous correction of wide disparities in nonproperty incomes. But radicals and power-seekers have little interest in such dull, peaceful, orderly, efficient, gradualist methods. So they have simply ignored critical issues in tax reform and plumped for labor organization. They have promoted the organization of innumerable industrial armies, with implicit sanction to employ force, coercion, and violence to the full extent of their power, at least to prevent competing sales of services at rates below their own offers. We are told that violence is essential only in the organizing phase; that it will disappear afterward as organization is achieved and recognized—which, of course, is true. Organizations which have attained power need use little overt violence to maintain it. However, it is only the middle phase of unionism or syndicalism which is nonviolent. There is much violence at the start inevitably; but there is more and worse violence at the end, involving total reconstitution of the political system. Somehow, sometime, the conflict between the special interests of labor monopolies and the common interest must be reconciled. Beyond some point their exactions become insufferable and insupportable; and their power must be broken to protect the general welfare.

■    ■    ■

Few Americans will straightforwardly espouse syndicalism or look with approval on Il Duce's corporative state. Few likewise will face the patent fact that we are rushing pell-mell toward and into that political order in the United States. Our formal political structure, of course, retains its traditional character. Our legislators, state and federal, still represent geographic sections of the nation. But alongside this formal political structure arises now a structure of powerful organizations of labor, immune to prosecution as monopolies and largely immune to the proscriptions or penalties of other laws. An essentially syndicalist order (or disorder) may, of course, evolve or arise without formal participation of industrial or occupational organizations in the legislative process. Indeed, such organizations may exercise greater power as extra-constitutional political agencies than they could if they had direct representation in Congress, in state assemblies, and in county and local government.

The intricate pluralism of modern democracies is, of course, a commonplace among students of sociology and politics. Equally commonplace, however, is the fact that organized minorities are a continuing threat to democratic order and internal peace. The danger may arise dramatically in the case of churches, secret societies, vigilante movements, a Ku Klux Klan, or less dramatically in the case of political machines, tariff lobbies, silver senators, veterans' organizations, and farm blocs. In the main, however, we have rarely or briefly endured political usurpation by minorities practicing violence and intimidation; and (save at federal levels!) we manage somehow to stop corruption and vote-buying short of insolvency and short of disintegration in political morality.

But, to repeat, we have never faced the kind of minority problem which widespread, aggressive, national and regional unions and their federations present. They are essentially occupational armies, born and reared amidst violence, led by fighters, and capable of becoming peaceful only as their power becomes irresistible. Other groups practice violence, of course; but few others practice it with general public approbation or employ it at all without grave risks of punishment or loss of power. Peaceful strikes, even in the absence of overt violence or intimidation, are a meaningless conception when they involve disruption of an elaborate production process with intricate division of labor. What is obvious in the case of railways and utilities is similarly true of coal-mining, steel production, and ultimately of every important industry and occupation.

Some conservatives will defend labor organization in terms of the right of voluntary association as a basic privilege in a democratic system, while deploring the use of violence and intimidation. Obviously, the practical problem would largely disappear if laws protecting persons and property were enforcible and enforced against strikers, pickets, and labor organizers. But there are no absolute rights; and the right of voluntary association must always be qualified, *inter alia,* by prohibitions against monopolizing— against collusive action among sellers. Failing ability to use violence or to threaten it effectively, particular organizations could not practice heavy extortion or sustain it indefinitely; but they could often tax the community substantially for a time and subject it to substantial, if minor, disturbances. The grave diseconomies of the theorist's pure cartel situation, in labor and other markets, are relevant to real situations, actual and possible; and protection of the public interest demands limitation of the right of association where the association is of people as suppliers of particular commodities or services.

The point, in any case, is rather academic, for labor organization without large powers of coercion and intimidation is an unreal abstraction. Unions now have such powers; they always have had and always will have, so long as they persist in their present form. Where the power is small or insecurely possessed, it must be exercised overtly and extensively; large and unchallenged, it becomes like the power of strong government, confidently held, respectfully regarded, and rarely displayed conspicuously. But, to repeat, this apparent peacefulness of a maturing syndicalism is unsubstantial and deceptive. It marks a fundamental disintegration of the very bases of political order—a disappearance of free exchange and of the state's monopoly of coercion. Individual groups, securely organized and secure in their monopoly positions, may levy their exactions without overt violence and merely through peaceful political maneuvering (via the arbitration device especially). However, they necessarily restrict drastically the normal flows of trade, destroying general prosperity in their struggle for relative advantage, and reducing enterprisers and investors to a defensive, defeatist task of withdrawing their property, on the least unfavorable terms obtainable politically, into the dubious security of government bonds. Ultimately, this means disappearance of all opportunities for remunerative enterprise and investment, governmental or private, via excessive costs, actual and prospective. Moreover, it means a drying-up of government revenues, whether derived by taxes from return on private propety or from socialized enterprise. It means also vastly increasing dispensations by way of unemployment relief and other meliorative measures.

A maturing syndicalism is the mature economy of our monetary and fiscal extremists. It is inherently unstable and unmanageable. It may be kept going, at income levels far short of our potentialities, by sufficiently large fiscal and monetary stimulation; and no one may wisely condemn policies which postpone revolutionary upheaval if postponement alone is possible. But we should face the fact that nothing else is ahead along this route. Especially, we should be skeptical of economic analysis and prescription which rests on the political premise that mass monopolies (and increasing enterprise monopoly) are ordained and assured for the future beyond any recourse of democratic discussion and orderly political process.

Our great minority and monopoly problem of the present and of the discernible future is the problem of labor organization. One may stress the right of voluntary association or, rather, the right of free entry into occupations. One may stress the right to bargain collectively on a national or regional scale or, rather, the right of free occupational migration. In neither case can one sensibly defend both categorically. If one is accorded and exercised, the other is curtailed or destroyed. The issue is simply whether wage rates should be determined competitively or monopolistically.

# 37
## The Trade Unionism of Henry Simons
**ORME W. PHELPS**                                                            1954

After ten years, Henry Simons' "Reflections on Syndicalism" is still the high-water mark of anti-union denunciation in economic literature, and the standard periodically invoked by fellow theorists when criticizing the labor movement. In Simons' eyes, trade unionism has nothing but pernicious effects upon the distribution of income and the allocation of resources, and is also an encouragement to business monopoly, the primary threat to democracy, and perhaps the most important cause of war. The route by which he reaches his conclusions is made perfectly clear. His standard is the free, competitive economy, with concentration upon the general welfare (of consumers) instead of the special interests of producers, whereas for labor, his criterion is "a maximizing of aggregate labor income and minimizing of inequality." The major premise and the conclusions are connected in the Simons analysis by the middle term "organized labor." We must therefore examine with care the author's account of the institution itself.

In about the order of their importance, Simons denounces: 1) labor monopoly, or bargaining power; 2) the union's "access to" and reliance upon violence; 3) unionized "control of wage rates"; 4) union responsibility for increased labor costs; and 5) union restrictive practices.

What this adds up to is "syndicalism." According to Simons:

Few Americans will straightforwardly espouse syndicalism. . . . Few likewise will face the patent fact that we are rushing pell-mell toward and into that political order in the United States. . . . Alongside [our] formal political structure arises now a structure of powerful organizations of labor, *immune to prosecution as monopolies and largely immune to the proscriptions or penalties of other laws.* (italics supplied.)

The syndicalist character of the labor movement is primarily an outgrowth of two things: monopoly and violence. Compared to organized labor, business monopoly is "a skin disease, easy to correct when and if we will," and employer monopsony in the labor market another "skin disease," unsubstantial and transitory. Labor monopolies, on the other hand, are:

A different kind of animal. If much violence has been used against them as they struggled into existence, this should not obscure the fact that, once established, they enjoy an access to violence which is unparalleled in other monopolies.

They are essentially occupational armies born and reared amidst violence, led by fighters, and capable of becoming peaceful only as their power becomes irresistible. Other groups practice violence, of course; but few others practice it with general public approbation or employ it at all without grave risks of punishment or loss of power. Peaceful strikes, even in the absence of overt violence or intimidation, are a meaningless conception when they involve disruption of an elaborate production process with intricate division of labor. What is obvious in the case of railways and utilities is similarly true of coal-mining, steel production, and ultimately of every important industry and occupation.

From *Proceedings of the Seventh Annual Meeting of Industrial Relations Research Association,* December 28–30, 1954 (Madison, WI: The Association, 1955), pp. 280–285. Footnotes in the original have been eliminated or renumbered.

In an economy of intricate division of labor, *every* large organized group is in a position at any time to disrupt or to stop *the whole flow* of social income; and the system must soon break down if groups persist in exercising that power or if they must continuously be bribed to forego its disastrous exercise. (italics supplied.)

With these key passages, Simons describes the organized labor movement in America. Are they accurate?

First, with respect to violence. In the roughly 100 years of continuous, organized union activity in the United States, all the great picket-line massacres have been on the side of "law-and-order," which is to say, the employers, with a single exception—the Herrin affair in Illinois in 1922. Compared to the mass assaults of the Pinkertons, the Bergoffs, and the thousands of deputized company guards, union violence has been casual, incidental, and ineffective. Where really violent retaliation by workers has occurred, it has usually been against armed strikebreakers imported into the community to force the issue. Herrin is a perfect illustration.

Nor is there any evidence that I am aware of to support Simons' contention of "general public approbation" of what union violence there is. There undoubtedly is general public approbation of unionism as such and often of specific union acts such as strikes, even when the latter cause the public great inconvenience. Insofar as Simons equated strikes which "involve disruption of an elaborate production process" with "violence," the conclusion may stand as a logical proposition, but it seems a rather tortured way to make a point. In my opinion, the general public does not approve of or even condone union violence, and the proposition is in a class which calls for substantial proof.

Do unions practice violence "without . . . risks of punishment or loss of power"? Is it true that "they have now little to fear from Congress or the courts"? The reader is referred to the War Labor Disputes Act of 1943, the Taft-Hartley Act of 1947, and state labor legislation of recent years, including the 17 state right-to-work laws. The question might even be put to Mr. Meany, Mr. Reuther, and their colleagues. If the answer is "Yes," then labor leaders have been wasting a lot of time and energy along lines which directly contradict it.

It will come as news to students of labor relations that the many long histories of peaceful union-management negotiation and contract administration in the United States have been conditioned upon the irresistible power of the unions involved. Few unions are irresistible. It is a strong word and a highly inaccurate one, as the record of organized industry clearly bears out, though perhaps necessary to support Simons' most extreme conclusion of all. This was the remarkable statement that *any* large organized group can stop the *whole flow* of social income at its pleasure in "an economy of intricate division of labor," which I am sure the author meant to be descriptive of the United States of America in 1944. If it was so then, it is far more so now. Was it so then? Is it so now?

If we take the gross national product as a reasonable approximation of the flow of social income at the material level only, then how large and how powerful an organized group would be required to bring its rate to zero? One can only wonder how a serious writer is led to make the statements he does. There has never been a time in the history of the country when a labor dispute has interrupted a significant fraction of the flow of social income, taken whole, nor is there any plan, policy, or program of organized labor in process to make it a possibility. A concerted work stoppage by every union member in the country, inconceivable as it may be, would certainly have a significant impact—and bring immediate reprisals of a most serious sort—but it would not cut national income to zero or to any conceivable approximation to it. The assertion is nonsense, explainable on grounds of carelessness or exaggeration for rhetorical effect.

In sum, Simons does not make his case that labor monopoly is more brutal, more powerful, more independent, or more widely condoned than other forms of combination.

Granted that unions are monopolies, in some respects and some very substantial respects as subversive of the economic order as any other type of combination. Nonetheless, monopoly has other uses than abuse and one of these is defense. With buyers uniformly organized into large economic units, made even larger and more powerful by formal association and "understandings" with respect to existing scales, then formal combination of sellers to match them in bargaining power may well be a useful counterweight in the market. Unions are the appropriate organizations to help decide whether lower wages-lower costs-lower prices (assuming an unbroken sequence, of course) are better for the community than higher consumption standards for the workers involved, along with the increased costs, higher prices, and fewer sales which may be imputed to them. The answer surely will not be the same in every case.

For myself, I am sure that labor monopoly has been carried to the point many times where it unduly raised costs, lowered sales, and restricted employment opportunities. I am equally sure that in many other cases these effects have been counterbalanced by a substantial equalization of labor costs between firms and between industries, by the correction of inequities within firms, by concrete improvement of conditions of work, and by a rise in morale and productivity of the working force. There are both gains and losses to be considered and no single answer will suffice for all cases.

Nothing is more revealing of Simons' grasp of unions as operating organizations than his proposals for union management:

> If I were running a union and were managing it faithfully in the interest of the majority of its members, I should consistently demand wage rates which offered to existing firms no real net earnings but only the chance of getting back part of their sunk investment at the cost of replacement outlays necessary to provide employment for most of my constituents during their own lifetimes as workers. In other words, I should plan gradually to exterminate the industry by excessive labor costs, taking care only to prevent employment from contracting more rapidly than my original constituents disappeared by death and voluntary retirement.

This might be called "The Pure Economic Union, Simons Model": 100 per cent organization, the closed shop, an industrial union which permits no replacement of dying or departing employes, the strict shortrun viewpoint with collapse of the industry scheduled to coincide with superannuation of the last man. Would it work?

We are unlikely to find out, since no union management would for a moment entertain a policy like that described. Stated in economic terms, it would maximize neither membership, employment, nor income. On the other hand, reassuring as it may be to economic readers, any talk of maximization is probably beside the point. Unions are not economic organizations; they are "political agencies operating in an economic environment."[1] Their objectives are power and influence. One of their purposes, perhaps their major purpose, is to influence the distribution of income, but they do not hesitate to sacrifice the latter if it conflicts with the true goal of security and authority of the organization. Furthermore, a union is an organization with a life and character of its own, apart and distinct from its membership. The leaders serve the permanent organization first and the membership, which is transitory, second. Simons' naivete consisted of judging the union as a collection of individuals concerned solely with maximizing their personal life-time receipts. It is immaterial that the method proposed would be an obvious failure along these lines as well.

On union "control of wage rates," the Simons' analysis clearly implies a competitive, or "normal" wage with the union "standard rate" in every case forced above this level. It happens that labor organization occurred first and has been most complete in industries characterized by extensive labor-market monopsony: large employers, vigorous employer associations, *and* in the absence of unions, not only low wages and long hours, but in many cases really vicious working conditions. I cite you, in the memory of many still living: coal mining, metal mining, the railroads, shipping, the waterfront, the steel mills, the garment trades, and so on. Monopsony, like monopoly, is also subject to abuse. There is sufficient evidence in various investigations conducted during the 20th century in this country to raise plenty of doubts that these strongly organized employers, many of them maintaining an employers' closed shop by fair means or foul, were setting wages at the competitive level. There is a strong possibility that wages are nearer "normal" (if there is such a thing) in these industries today than prior to recognition and union contract.

The unionist of course is deeply concerned with economic inequality. As economist, Simons was too. His solution was the elegantly simple one of progressive taxation of the well-to-do and socialized consumption at the bottom of the income scale. The idea was to redistribute income without disturbing the "competitive productivity norms" of the free market.

To this there are several answers. First, there should be wide agreement that "competitive productivity norms" are operating in the labor market. There are others besides trade unionists who doubt this. Secondly, this brand of paternalism (relief, family allowances, etc.) sounds dreadfully dull. It promises much more fun to negotiate a few fringe benefits for yourself, rather than wait for the manna to be distributed from Heavenly, D. C. Thirdly, there is the pragmatic approach: How soon and how much and for whom? I suspect that, confronted with a choice between waiting for the government to act and reliance upon the maxim "The Lord helps those who help themselves," most economists would act like unionists.

Last, and probably most important of all, the unionist speaks by proxy to his employer as an equal. He may not get what he asks for. Strikes often cost more in wages than can be recouped in the differential gain, a fact which is solemnly recounted in employer publicity and newspaper headlines time after time. What is overlooked is that it may be a small price to pay for self-respect, and self-respect is a value in American life, for unionists as well as economists.

---

[1]Arthur M. Ross, *Trade Union Wage Policy* (Berkeley: University of California Press, 1948), p. 12.

# 38

## *Free to Choose: A Personal Statement*

MILTON AND ROSE FRIEDMAN                                                           1980

Given that members of strong unions are highly paid, the obvious question is: are they highly paid because their unions are strong, or are their unions strong because they are highly paid? Defenders of the unions claim that the high pay of their members is a tribute to the strength of union organization, and that if only all workers were members of unions, all workers would be highly paid.

The situation is, however, much more complex. Unions of highly skilled workers have unquestionably been able to raise the wages of their members; however, people who would in any event be highly paid are in a favorable position to form strong unions. Moreover, the ability of unions to raise the wages of some workers does not mean that universal unionism could raise the wages of all workers. On the contrary, and this is a fundamental source of misunderstanding, *the gains that strong unions win for their members are primarily at the expense of other workers.*

The key to understanding the situation is the most elementary principle of economics: the law of demand—the higher the price of anything, the less of it people will be willing to buy. Make labor of any kind more expensive and the number of jobs of that kind will be fewer. Make carpenters more expensive, and fewer houses than otherwise will be built, and those houses that are built will tend to use materials and methods requiring less carpentry. Raise the wage of airline pilots, and air travel will become more expensive. Fewer people will fly, and there will be fewer jobs for airline pilots. Alternatively, reduce the number of carpenters or pilots, and they will command higher wages. Keep down the number of physicians, and they will be able to charge higher fees.

A successful union reduces the number of jobs available of the kind it controls. As a result, some people who would like to get such jobs at the union wage cannot do so. They are forced to look elsewhere. A greater supply of workers for other jobs drives down the wages paid for those jobs. Universal unionization would not alter the situation. It could mean higher wages for the persons who get jobs, along with more unemployment for others. More likely, it would mean strong unions and weak unions, with members of the strong unions getting higher wages, as they do now, at the expense of members of weak unions.

Union leaders always talk about getting higher wages at the expense of profits. That is impossible: profits simply aren't big enough. About 80 percent of the total national income of the United States currently goes to pay the wages, salaries, and fringe benefits of workers. More than half of the rest goes to pay rent and interest on loans. Corporate profits—which is what union leaders always point to—total less than 10 percent of national income. And that is before taxes. After taxes, corporate profits are something like 6 percent of the national income. That hardly provides much leeway to finance higher wages, even if all profits were absorbed. And that would kill the goose that lays the golden eggs. The small margin of profit provides the incentive for investment in factories and machines, and for developing new products and methods. This investment, these innovations, have, over the years, raised the productivity of the worker and provided the wherewithal for higher and higher wages.

Higher wages to one group of workers must come primarily from other workers.

Nearly thirty years ago one of us estimated that on the average about 10 to 15 percent of the workers in this country had been able through unions or their equivalent, such as the American Medical Association, to raise their wages 10 to 15 percent above what they otherwise would have been, at the cost of reducing the wages earned by the other 85 to 90 percent by some 4 percent below what they otherwise would have been. More recent studies indicate that this remains roughly the order of magnitude of the effect of unions. Higher wages for high-paid workers, lower wages for low-paid workers.

All of us, including the highly unionized, have indirectly been harmed as consumers by the effect of high union wages on the prices of consumer goods. Houses are unnecessarily expensive for everyone, including the carpenters. Workers have been prevented by unions from using their skills to produce the most highly valued items; they have been forced to resort to activities where their productivity is less. The total basket of goods available to all of us is smaller than it would have been.

## The Source of Union Power

How can unions raise the wages of their members? What is the basic source of their power? The answer is: the ability to keep down the number of jobs available, or equivalent, to keep down the number of persons available for a class of jobs. Unions have been able to keep down the number of jobs by enforcing a high wage rate, generally with assistance from government. They have been able to keep down the number of persons available, primarily through licensure, again with government aid. They have occasionally gained power by colluding with employers to enforce a monopoly of the product their members help to produce.

*Enforcing a high wage rate.* If, somehow or other, a union can assure that no contractor will pay less than, say, $15 an hour for a plumber or a carpenter, that will reduce the number of jobs that will be offered. Of course, it will also increase the number of persons who would like to get jobs.

Suppose for the moment that the high wage rate can be enforced. There must then be some way to ration the limited number of lucrative jobs among the persons seeking them. Numerous devices have been adopted: nepotism—to keep the jobs in the family; seniority and apprenticeship rules; featherbedding—to spread the work around; and simple corruption. The stakes are high, so the devices used are a sensitive matter in union affairs. Some unions will not permit seniority provisions to be discussed in open meetings because that always leads to fistfights. Kickbacks to union officials to secure preference for jobs are a common form of corruption. The heavily criticized racial discrimination by unions is still another device for rationing jobs. If there is a surplus of applicants for a limited number of jobs to be rationed, any device to select the ones who get the jobs is bound to be arbitrary. Appeals to prejudice and similar irrational considerations often have great support among the "ins" as a way of deciding whom to keep out. Racial and religious discrimination have entered also into admissions to medical schools and for the same reason: a surplus of acceptable applicants and the need to ration places among them.

To return to the wage rate, how can a union enforce a high wage rate? One way is violence or the threat of violence: threatening to destroy the property of employers, or to beat them up if they employ nonunion workers or if they pay union members less than the union-specified rate; or to beat up workers, or destroy their property, if they agree to work for a lower wage. That is the reason union wage arrangements and negotiations have so often been accompanied by violence.

An easier way is to get the government to help. That is the reason union headquarters are clustered around Capitol Hill in Washington, why they devote so much money and attention to politics. In his study of the airline pilots' union, Hopkins notes that "the union secured enough federal protective legislation to make the professional airline pilots practically a ward of the state."

A major form of government assistance to construction unions is the Davis-Bacon Act, a federal law that requires all contractors who work on a contract in excess of $2,000 to which the U.S. government or the District of Columbia is a party to pay wage rates no less than those "prevailing for the corresponding classes of laborers and mechanics" in the neighborhood in question, as "determined by the Secretary of Labor." In practice the "prevailing" rates have been ruled to be union wage rates in "an overwhelming proportion of wage determinations . . . regardless of area or type of construction." The reach of the act has been extended by the incorporation of its prevailing wage requirement in numerous other laws for federally assisted projects, and by similar laws in thirty-five states (as of 1971) covering state construction expenditures. The effect of these acts is that the government enforces union wage rates for much of construction activity.

Even the use of violence implicitly involves government support. A generally favorable public attitude toward labor unions has led the authorities to tolerate behavior in the course of labor disputes that they would never tolerate under other circumstances. If someone's car gets overturned in the course of a labor dispute, or if plant, store, or home windows get smashed, or if people even get beaten up and seriously injured, the perpetrators are less likely to pay a fine, let alone go to jail, than if the same incident occurred under other circumstances.

■   ■   ■

*Restricting numbers.* An alternative to enforcing a wage rate is to restrict directly the number who may pursue an occupation. That technique is particularly attractive when there are many employers—so that enforcing a wage rate is difficult. Medicine is an excellent example, since much of the activity of organized medicine has been directed toward restricting the number of physicians in practice.

Success in restricting numbers, as in enforcing a wage rate, generally requires the assistance of the government. In medicine the key has been the licensure of physicians— that is, the requirement that in order for any individual to "practice medicine," he must be licensed by the state. Needless to say, only physicians are likely to be regarded as competent to judge the qualifications of potential physicians, so licensing boards in the various states (in the United States licensure is under the jurisdiction of the state, not the federal government) are typically composed wholly of physicians or dominated by physicians, who in turn have generally been members of the AMA.

The boards, or the state legislatures, have specified conditions for the granting of licenses that in effect give the AMA the power to influence the number of persons admitted to practice. They have required lengthy training, almost always graduation from an "approved" school, generally internship in an "approved" hospital. By no accident, the list of "approved" schools and hospitals is generally identical with the list issued by the Council on Medical Education and Hospitals of the American Medical Association. No school can be established or, if established, long continue unless it can get the approval of the AMA Council on Medical Education. That has at times required limiting the number of persons admitted in accordance with the council's advice.

Striking evidence of the power of organized medicine to restrict entry was provided during the depression of the 1930s when the economic pressure was particularly great.

Despite a flood of highly trained refugees from Germany and Austria—at the time centers of advanced medicine—the number of foreign-trained physicians admitted to practice in the United States in the five years after Hitler came to power was no larger than in the preceding five years.

Licensure is widely used to restrict entry, particularly for occupations like medicine that have many individual practitioners dealing with a large number of individual customers. As in medicine, the boards that administer the licensure provisions are composed primarily of members of the occupation licensed—whether they be dentists, lawyers, cosmetologists, airline pilots, plumbers, or morticians. There is no occupation so remote that an attempt has not been made to restrict its practice by licensure. According to the chairman of the Federal Trade Commission: "At a recent session of one state legislature, occuptional groups advanced bills to license themselves as auctioneers, well-diggers, home improvement contractors, pet groomers, electrologists, sex therapists, data processors, appraisers, and TV repairers. Hawaii licenses tattoo artists. New Hampshire licenses lightning-rod salesmen." The *justification* offered is always the same: to protect the consumer. However, the *reason* is demonstrated by observing who lobbies at the state legislature for the imposition or strengthening of licensure. The lobbyists are invariably representatives of the occupation in question rather than of the customers. True enough, plumbers presumably know better than anyone else what their customers need to be protected against. However, it is hard to regard altruistic concern for their customers as the primary motive behind their determined efforts to get legal power to decide who may be a plumber.

To reinforce the restriction on numbers, organized occupational groups persistently strive to have the practice of their occupation legally defined as broadly as possible in order to increase the demand for the services of licensed practitioners.

One effect of restricting entry into occupations through licensure is to create new disciplines: in medicine, osteopathy and chiropractic are examples. Each of these, in turn, has resorted to licensure to try to restrict its numbers. The AMA has engaged in extensive litigation charging chiropractors and osteopaths with the unlicensed practice of medicine, in an attempt to restrict them to as narrow an area as possible. Chiropractors and osteopaths in turn charge other practitioners with the unlicensed practice of chiropractic and osteopathy.

■    ■    ■

*Collusion between unions and employers.* Unions have sometimes gained power by helping business enterprises combine to fix prices or share markets, activities that are illegal for business under the antitrust laws.

The most important historical case was in coal mining in the 1930s. The two Guffey coal acts were attempts to provide legal support for a price-fixing cartel of coal mine operators. When, in the mid-thirties, the first of the acts was declared unconstitutional, John L. Lewis and the United Mine Workers that he headed stepped into the breach. By calling strikes or work stoppages whenever the amount of coal above the ground got so large as to threaten to force down prices, Lewis controlled output and thereby prices with the unspoken cooperation of the industry. As the vice-president of a coal company put it in 1938, "They [the United Mine Workers] have done a lot to stabilize the bituminous coal industry and have endeavored to have it operate on a profitable basis, in fact though one dislikes to admit it their efforts along that line have in the main . . . been a bit more efficacious . . . than the endeavors of coal operators themselves."

301

The gains were divided between the operators and the miners. The miners were granted high wage rates, which of course meant greater mechanization and fewer miners employed. Lewis recognized this effect explicitly and was more than prepared to accept it—regarding higher wages for miners employed as ample compensation for a reduction in the number employed, provided those employed were all members of his union.

The miners' union could play this role because unions are exempt from the Sherman Anti-Trust Act. Unions that have taken advantage of this exemption are better interpreted as enterprises selling the services of cartelizing an industry than as labor organizations. The Teamsters' Union is perhaps the most notable. There is a story, perhaps apocryphal, about David Beck, the head of the Teamsters' Union before James Hoffa (both of whom ultimately went to jail). When Beck was negotiating with breweries in the state of Washington about wages for drivers of brewery trucks, he was told that the wages he was asking were not feasible because "eastern beer" would undercut local beer. He asked what the price of eastern beer would have to be to permit the wage he demanded. A figure, X dollars a case, was named, and he supposedly replied, "From now on, eastern beer will be X dollars a case."

Labor unions can and often do provide useful services for their members—negotiating the terms of their employment, representing them with respect to grievances, giving them a feeling of belonging and participating in a group activity, among others. As believers in freedom, we favor the fullest opportunity for voluntary organization of labor unions to perform whatever services their members wish, and are willing to pay for, provided they respect the rights of others and refrain from using force.

However, unions and comparable groups such as the professional associations have not relied on strictly voluntary activities and membership with respect to their major proclaimed objective—improving the wages of their members. They have succeeded in getting government to grant them special privileges and immunities, which have enabled them to benefit some of their members and officials at the expense of other workers and all consumers. In the main, the persons benefited have had decidedly higher incomes than the persons harmed.

# 39
## *What Do Unions Do?*

RICHARD B. FREEMAN AND JAMES L. MEDOFF                    1984

Many economists view unions largely as monopolies in the labor market whose primary economic impact is to raise members' wages at the expense of unorganized labor and of the efficient functioning of the economy. These analysts stress the adverse effects of union work rules on productivity, the loss of employment in the organized sector due to union wage effects, and the consequent crowding of the nonunion sector with displaced workers. Consistent with this view, managers frequently complain about inflexible operations and work disruptions due to unions, while many social critics paint unions as socially unresponsive, elitist, non-democratic, and crime-riddled institutions.

■　　■　　■

During the past twenty-five years . . . the negative view of trade unions has become increasingly dominant. While there are notable exceptions, many on both the right and left now doubt the social relevance and value of America's organized labor movement. The widespread, one might say textbook, picture of U.S. unions today is of institutions adept at advancing their own interests at the public's expense. Economists concerned with quantifying the economic effects of collective bargaining have focused almost exclusively on the monopoly wage impact of unions, developing a large and valuable literature on the differences in wages paid to organized and unorganized labor. Because monopolistic wage increases are socially harmful—in that they can be expected to induce both inefficiency and inequality—most economic studies, implicitly or explicitly, have judged unions as being a negative force in society.

■　　■　　■

### The "Two Faces" Debate

The meaning of the results of our study of U.S. trade unionism can best be understood by recognizing that unions have two faces, each of which leads to a different view of the institution: a *monopoly* face, associated with their monopolistic power to raise wages; and a *collective voice/institutional response* face, associated with their representation of organized workers within enterprises.

#### The Monopoly Face

Most, if not all, unions have monopoly power, which they can use to raise wages above competitive levels. Assuming that the competitive system works perfectly, these wage increases have harmful economic effects, reducing the national output and distorting the distribution of income. The analysis of unions as monopolies focuses on the magnitude of the union markup of wages and traces the ways in which this markup causes firms to lower employment and output, thereby harming economic efficiency and altering the distribution of income.

Despite the attention economists give to the monopoly face of unionism, analysis of union monopoly behavior is much less fully developed than is the analysis of monopolistic enterprises. The principal reason is that unions are not the simple monopolies of economics textbooks but rather collective organizations of workers with diverse interests. Unlike the monopoly firm that sets prices to maximize profits, unions rarely set wages; they bargain over wages with employers. Unless one believes that the process of collective bargaining is a sham, the wages obtained by unions must be viewed as the joint responsibility of management and labor: the stronger management resistance to union wage goals is, the smaller union wage gains will be. Moreover, unions' ability to raise wages is limited by the fact that, all else the same, higher union wages will induce employers to reduce employment. Some members gain when wages are very high; others lose. Despite decades in which unions have been part of the economic scene, economists lack an accepted maximizing theory of union behavior that would predict the results of bargaining within the union over wage goals. Under some circumstances a union may seek a high wage at the cost of unemployment; under others, it may be more moderate in its wage demands to preserve jobs. This union concern is quite distinct from the worries of a monopolist, whose sole goal is to maximize profits, regardless of what happens to the number of units sold.

Analysis of the monopoly face of unionism must confront the important issue of the source of union monopoly power. If unions operated in perfectly competitive markets, and if *all* they did were to raise wages above competitive levels, unions would have a very difficult time surviving, for organized firms would necessarily have higher costs of production than other firms. One way unions could survive in such markets would be organizing the entire industry or sector. If production costs are higher for all establishments in a sector, output and employment will be lower than they would be in the absence of unionism, but the sector will survive. Alternatively, if unions operate in markets where firms have different cost structures (for reasons unassociated with unionism), unions could survive by organizing firms with the lowest costs of production, raising wages at the expense of above-normal profits or "rent." Perhaps most importantly, union monopoly power is likely to be closely related to the market power of the sector it organizes. When unions organize noncompetitive firms, they are able to raise wages without endangering the life of the firm. In sum, from the monopoly perspective, unions are likely to exist in industries where new firms have difficulty entering and/or where some enterprises have cost advantages over their competitors.

The fact that union monopoly power is likely to be important only when unionized firms either completely dominate a market or operate in a non-competitive market has created an interesting intellectual anomaly. Some economists of a strong free-enterprise bent, who one might expect to be strongly opposed to unions, are in fact rather indifferent. They believe that markets are competitive enough to give unions little or no power to extract monopoly wage gains.

### The Collective Voice / Institutional Response Face

As Hirschman pointed out in his important book *Exit, Voice, and Loyalty*, societies have two basic mechanisms for dealing with social or economic problems.[1] The first is the classic market mechanism of exit-and-entry, in which individuals respond to a divergence between desired and actual social conditions by exercising freedom of choice or mobility: the dissatisfied consumer switches products; the diner whose soup is too salty seeks another restaurant; the unhappy couple divorces. In the labor market, exit is synonymous with quitting, while entry consists of new hires by the firm. By leaving less desirable for more desirable jobs, or by refusing bad jobs, individuals penalize the bad employer and reward the good, leading to an overall improvement in the efficiency of the economic system. The basic theorem of neoclassical economics is that, under well-specified conditions, the exit and entry of persons (the hallmark of the free-market system) produces a situation in which no individual can be made better off without making someone worse off. Much economic analysis can be viewed as a detailed study of the implications of this kind of adjustment and of the extent to which it works out in real economies. As long as the exit-entry market mechanism is viewed as the *only* adjustment mechanism, institutions like unions are invariably seen as impediments to the optimal operation of the economy.

The second mode of adjustment is the political mechanism that Hirschman termed "voice." "Voice" refers to the use of direct communication to bring actual and desired conditions closer together. It means talking about problems: complaining to the store about a poor product rather than taking business elsewhere; telling the chef that the soup had too much salt; discussing marital problems rather than going directly to the divorce court. In a political context, "voice" refers to participation in the democratic process, through voting, discussion, bargaining, and the like.

The distinction between the two mechanisms is best illustrated by a specific situation—for instance, concern about the quality of schools in a given locality. The exit solution to poor schools would be to move to a different community or to enroll one's children in a private school, thereby "taking one's business elsewhere." The voice solution would involve political action to improve the school system through schoolboard elections, Parent Teacher Association meetings, and other channels of communication.

In the job market, voice means discussing with an employer conditions that ought to be changed, rather than quitting the job. In modern industrial economies, and particularly in large enterprises, a trade union is the vehicle for collective voice—that is, for providing workers as a group with a means of communicating with management.

Collective rather than individual bargaining with an employer is necessary for effective voice at the workplace for two reasons. First, many important aspects of an industrial setting are "public goods," that is, goods which will affect the well-being (negatively or positively) of every employee in such a way that one individual's partaking of the good does not preclude someone else from doing so. Safety conditions, lighting, heating, the speed of the production line, the firm's formal grievance procedure, pension plan, and policies on matters such as layoffs, work-sharing, cyclical wage adjustment, and promotion all obviously affect the entire workforce in the same way that defense, sanitation, and fire protection affect the community at large. One of the most important economic theorems is that competitive markets will not provide enough of such goods; some form of collective decision making is needed. Without a collective organization, the incentive for the individual to take into account the effects of his or her actions on others, or to express his or her preferences, or to invest time and money in changing conditions, is likely to be too small to spur action. Why not "let Harry do it" and enjoy the benefits at no cost? This classic "free-rider" problem lies at the heart of the so-called "union-security" versus "right-to-work" debate.

A second reason why collective action is necessary is that workers who are tied to a firm are unlikely to reveal their true preferences to an employer, for fear the employer may fire them. In a world in which workers could find employment at the same wages immediately, the market would offer adequate protection for the individual, but that is not the world we live in. The danger of job loss makes expression of voice by an individual risky. Collective voice, by contrast, is protected both by the support of all workers and by the country's labor law: "It shall be an unfair labor practice for an employer by discrimination in regard to hire or tenure or employment or any term or condition of employment to encourage or discourage membership in any labor organization" (National Labor Relations Act, Section 7a of the 1935 law). Court interpretation of U.S. labor law makes a sharp distinction between collective and individual actions at the workplace: even nonunion workers acting in a concerted fashion are protected from managerial retaliation. However, the nonunion protester acting alone and not seeking a union is "terminable at will" and must speak very carefully.

The collective nature of trade unionism fundamentally alters the operation of a labor market and, hence, the nature of the labor contract. In a nonunion setting, where exit-and-entry is the predominant form of adjustment, the signals and incentives to firms depend on the preferences of the "marginal" worker, the one who might leave because of (or be attracted by) small changes in the conditions of employment. The firm responds primarily to the needs of this marginal worker, who is generally young and marketable; the firm can to a considerable extent ignore the preferences of typically older, less marketable workers, who—for reasons of skill, knowledge, rights that cannot be readily transferred to other enterprises, as well as because of other costs associated with changing firms—are effectively immobile. In a unionized setting, by contrast, the union takes account of *all* workers in determining its demands at the bargaining table, so that the desires of workers who are highly unlikely to leave the enterprise are also represented. With respect to public goods at the workplace, the union can add up members' preferences in much the same manner as a government can add up voters' preferences for defense, police protection, and the like to determine social demand for them. In sum, because unions are political institutions with elected leaders, they are likely to respond to a different set of preferences from those that prevail in a competitive labor market.

In a modern economy, where workers tend to be attached to firms for many years, younger and older workers are likely to have different preferences (for instance, regarding pension or health insurance plans versus take-home pay, or layoffs ordered inversely to seniority versus cuts in wage growth or work sharing). The change from an approach that focuses only on workers at the coming-or-going margin to one that considers all employees is likely to lead to a very different labor contract. Under some conditions, the union contract—by taking account of all workers and by appropriately considering the sum of preferences for work conditions that are common to all workers—can be economically more efficient than the contract that would result in the absence of unions.

Finally, as a collective voice unions also fundamentally alter the social relations of the workplace. The essence of the employment relationship under capitalism—as stressed by such diverse analysts as Karl Marx, Herbert Simon, and Ronald Coase—is the payment of money by the employer to the employee in return for the employer's control over a certain amount of the employee's time. The employer seeks to use his employee's time in a way that maximizes the profitability of the enterprise. Even in the case of piece rates, employers monitor employee activity to assure the quality of output, prevent the wastage of materials, and protect the stock of capital. As a result, the way in which the time purchased is utilized must be determined by some interaction between workers and their employer. In the absence of unionism, the worker has limited responses to orders that he feels are unfair: the worker can quit, or he can perhaps engage in quiet sabotage or shirking, neither of which is likely to alter the employer's actions. In the union setting, by contrast, the union constitutes a source of worker power, diluting managerial authority and offering members protection through both the "industrial jurisprudence" system, under which many workplace decisions are based on rules (such as seniority) instead of supervisory judgment or whim, and the grievance and arbitration system, under which disputes over proper managerial decision making on work issues can be resolved. As a result, management power within enterprises is curtailed by unionism, so that workers' rights are likely to be better enforced. Consider, for example, a firm that decides to fire senior workers immediately before they become eligible for pension rights. In the nonunion setting, a firm may be able to get away with such a maneuver; in the union setting, it is unlikely to have such power. Economic theorists of all persuasions have increasingly recognized that unions' ability to enforce labor agreements, particularly those with deferred claims, creates the possibility for improved labor contracts and arrangements and higher economic efficiency.

■   ■   ■

## The Study and Its Findings

. . . We have studied a wide variety of data that distinguish between union and nonunion establishments and between union and nonunion workers, and we have interviewed representatives of management, labor officials, and industrial-relations experts. Although additional study will certainly alter some of the specifics, we believe that the results of our analysis provide a reasonably clear and accurate picture of what unions do —a picture that stands in sharp contrast to the negative view that unions do little more than win monopoly wage gains for their members.

Our most far-reaching conclusion is that, in addition to well-advertised effects on wages, unions alter nearly every other measurable aspect of the operation of workplaces and enterprises, from turnover to productivity to profitability to the composition of pay packages. The behavior of workers and firms and the outcomes of their interactions differ substantially between the organized and unorganized sectors. On balance, unionization appears to improve rather than to harm the social and economic system. . . . Our analysis shows that unions are associated with greater efficiency in most settings, reduce overall earnings inequality, and contribute to, rather than detract from, economic and political freedom. This is not to deny the negative monopoly effects of unions. They exist. They are undesirable. But they are not the only ways in which unions affect the society. Our analysis indicates that, in fact, focusing on them leads to an exceedingly inaccurate representation of what unions do. In the United States in the period we have studied, the voice/response face of unions dominates the monopoly face, though we stress that an accurate portrait must show both faces.

Following is a capsule summary of the more specific findings that underlie this broad conclusion:

1. On the wage side, unions have a substantial monopoly wage impact, but there is no single union/nonunion wage differential. The union wage effect is greater for less educated than more educated workers, for younger than for prime-age workers, and for junior than for senior workers, and it is greater in heavily organized industries and in regulated industries than in others. It increased in the 1970s as unionized workers won wage gains exceeding those of their nonunion peers. Most importantly, the social costs of the monopoly wage gains of unionism appear to be relatively modest, on the order of .3 percent of gross national product, or less.

2. In addition to raising wages, unions alter the entire package of compensation, substantially increasing the proportion of compensation allotted to fringe benefits, particularly to deferred benefits such as pensions and life, accident and health insurance, which are favored by older workers. These changes are, on balance, to be viewed as a social plus.

3. The claim that unions increase wage inequality is not true. It is true that unions raise the wages of organized blue-collar workers relative to the wages of unorganized

blue-collar workers, and thus increase that aspect of inequality. But they also raise blue-collar earnings relative to the higher white-collar earnings, thus reducing inequality between those groups. Moreover, by adopting pay policies that limit managerial discretion in wage-setting, they reduce inequality among workers in the same establishments and among different establishments. Quantitatively, the inequality-reducing effects of unionism outweigh the inequality-increasing effects, so that on balance unions are a force for equality in the distribution of wages among individual workers.

4. By providing workers with a voice in determining rules and conditions of work, by instituting grievance and arbitration procedures for appealing supervisors' decisions, and by negotiating seniority clauses desired by workers, unionism greatly reduces the probability that workers' will quit their jobs. As a result, unionized work forces are more stable than nonunion workforces paid the same compensation.

5. Unionism alters the way in which firms respond to swings in the economy. In cyclical downturns, unionized firms make more use of temporary layoffs and less use of cuts in wage growth than do nonunion firms, while in cyclical upturns, unionized firms recall relatively more workers and nonunion firms tend to hire new employees. In a decline that threatens the jobs of senior employees, unions negotiate wage and work-rule concessions of substantial magnitudes.

6. Union workplaces operate under rules that are both different from and more explicit than nonunion workplaces. Seniority is more important in union settings, with unionized senior workers obtaining relatively greater protection against job loss and relatively greater chance of promotion than nonunion senior workers. In addition, management in union companies generally operates more "by the book," with less subjectivity and also less flexibility, than does management in nonunion companies, and in more professional, less paternalistic or authoritarian ways.

7. Some nonunion workers, namely those in large nonunion firms that are trying to avoid unions through "positive labor relations," obtain higher wages and better working conditions as a result of the existence of trade unions. The average employed nonunion blue-collar worker may enjoy a slight increase in well-being because the threat of unionism forces his or her firm to offer better wages and work conditions, but the average white-collar worker appears essentially unaffected by the existence of blue-collar unionization. Some workers, however, may suffer from greater joblessness as a result of higher union wages in their city or their industry.

8. Paradoxically, while unionized workers are less willing to leave their employers than nonunion workers, unionized workers often report themselves less satisfied with their jobs than nonunion workers. Unionists are especially dissatisfied with their work conditions and their relations with supervisors. One explanation is that unions galvanize worker discontent in order to make a strong case in negotiations with management. To be effective, voice must be heard.

9. The view of unions as a major deterrent to productivity is erroneous. In many sectors, unionized establishments are more productive than nonunion establishments, while in only a few are they less productive. The higher productivity is due in part to the lower rate of turnover under unionism, improved managerial performance in response to the union challenge, and generally cooperative labor-management relations at the plant level. When labor-management relations are bad, so too is productivity in organized plants.

10. Unionized employers tend to earn a lower rate of return per dollar of capital than do nonunion employers. The return is lower under unionism because the increase in wages and the greater amount of capital used per worker are not compensated for by the

higher productivity of labor associated with unionism. The reduction in profitability, however, is centered in highly concentrated and otherwise historically highly profitable sectors of the economy.

11. Unions have had mixed success in the political arena. Legislators representing highly unionized districts or receiving considerable union campaign support tend to support unions' political goals in the Congress, but legislators representing less unionized districts or receiving more support from business and other interest groups often oppose union political goals. In the important area of major labor legislation, bills opposed by unions have been enacted while bills favored by unions have been voted down. In general unions have managed to *preserve* laws augmenting monopoly powers in specific sectors but have not been able to use the law to *expand* their monopoly power. Most union political successes have come in the areas of general labor and social goals that benefit workers as a whole rather than unionists alone.

12. The picture of unions as nondemocratic institutions run by corrupt labor bosses is a myth. Most unions are highly democratic, with members having access to union decision-making machinery, especially at the local level. While corruption exists in some unions, its occurrence seems to be highly concentrated in a few industries.

13. The percentage of the U.S. private-sector work force that is in trade unions has declined precipitously since the mid 1950s. The decline is due largely to a dramatic increase in the amount and sophistication of both legal and illegal company actions designed to forestall the organization of workers, and reduced union organizing activity per nonunion worker.

Some of our findings are controversial. They challenge the prevailing negative assessment of the economic and political impact of unions. Not surprisingly, they have engendered considerable critical comment. It is therefore important to understand the strengths and weaknesses of the evidence on which they are based.

The distinctive feature of the evidence presented . . . is that it is derived largely from quantitative analyses of data from many sources. Some of this information is from samples of thousands of individuals or establishments, some from companies, and some from industries. While labor economists have been using similar data for over a decade to estimate the effect of unions on wages, it is only in the past few years that we and others have used this sort of information to examine the effects of unions on the nonwage outcomes central to the voice/response face of unionism.

■  ■  ■

We believe that the results . . . raise a lot of important issues for public policy regarding the key worker institution in the American capitalist system. While some of our specific results will surely be altered by additional research and some (few, we hope) may even be proven wrong, we do believe that our findings present a reasonably valid picture of what unions do in the United States. It stands in sharp contrast to the unidimensional monopoly view of trade unions and to many popular opinions about them. According to our analysis, in most settings the positive elements of the voice/response face of unions offset or dominate the negative elements of the monopoly face. As a result we come out with the following assessment—generally positive though not uniformly so —of what unions do to the three major outcomes about which debate has raged: efficiency, distribution of income, and social organization.

• Efficiency. Our analysis has shown that unionism does three things to efficiency: on the monopoly side, it reduces employment in the organized sector; on the voice/ response side, it permits labor to create, at no extra cost to management, workplace practices and compensation packages more valuable to workers; and in many settings it is associated with increased productivity. Although it is difficult to sum up these three effects, our evidence suggests that unionism on net probably raises social efficiency, and if it lowers it, it does so by minuscule amounts except in rare circumstances. This conclusion contradicts the traditional monopoly interpretation of what unions do to efficiency.

- Distribution of Income. On the question of distribution, we have found a definite dominance for the voice/response face of unions, with unions reducing wage inequality and lowering profits, which generally go to higher-income persons. For readers to whom greater economic equality is a plus, what unions do here is definitely good. For readers to whom greater equalization of incomes is undesirable, what unions do is definitely bad.

- Social Organization. Our analysis of the internal affairs of unions has dispelled some of the negative myths about undemocratic practices and discriminatory and corrupt behavior. It has shown that unions, for the most part, provide political voice to all labor and that they are more effective in pushing general social legislation than in bringing about special interest legislation in the Congress.

All our conclusions are based, we stress, on comparisons of what happens under trade unions with what happens in comparable nonunion settings, not on comparisons with some theoretical construct the real world has yet to witness. In an economy where governments, business, and unions work imperfectly—sometimes for, sometimes against the general welfare—there is a place for unions to improve the well-being not only of their members but of the entire society, to increase the total amount of goods and services, including the dignity and rights of workers.

While our research suggests that unionism generally serves as a force for social and economic good, it has also found that unions benefit labor at the expense of capital. Unions reduce the profitability of organized firms, particularly those in concentrated sectors where profits are abnormally high. In addition, while some nonunion workers lose from unionism, our investigations indicate that many nonunion workers, especially those in large firms, benefit from the threat of organizing and from the information about workers' desires that comes from unionism.

Should someone who favors, as we do, a thriving market economy, also favor a strong union movement and be concerned with the ongoing decline in private sector unionism? According to our research findings, yes.

Should someone who wants a thriving, profitable company, as managers and stockholders rightly do, oppose the unionization of his or her firm? According to our research findings, the answer is generally yes.

The paradox of American unionism is that it is at one and the same time a plus on the overall social balance sheet (in most though not all circumstances) and a minus on the corporate balance sheet (again, in most though not all circumstances). We believe that this paradox underlies the national ambivalence toward unions. What is good for society at large is not necessarily good for GM (or any other specific company).

---

[1] See Albert O. Hirschman, *Exit, Voice, and Loyalty* (Cambridge, Mass.: Harvard University Press, 1971).

# EIGHT

**The Labor Movement in a Pluralist Industrial Society**

# Introduction

Four leading American economists—Clark Kerr, John Dunlop, Frederick Harbison and Charles Myers—dissatisfied with current explanations of the labor movement, have staked out new paths in explaining the origin and development of labor unions worldwide. They are critical of Commons' and Perlman's attempts to interpret labor unions through the prism of "job control" or business unionism, which they view as inapplicable outside the North American continent. In addition, they offer their thesis as a rejection not only of Marxian labor theory but also of the theoretical imperatives which underlie communism as a worldwide system.

Marx, they hold, erred in a number of important aspects. Instead of the escalating misery and poverty of the working class under capitalism which Marx predicted, they see workers enjoying ever-higher living standards as industrialism progresses. The result is dwindling discontent among the workers and a decline in protest against workplace or societal rules. Protest, therefore, does not arise from the capitalist relations of production but from early stages of industrialization when the factory worker was unaccustomed to urban life and demands of factory discipline. The decisive element in future historical change is not the proletariat but the industrial managers and their technical and professional associates. It is this group which becomes the vanguard of change. As a result, labor unions in the future industrial society will play a secondary and passive role whose main function is to monitor the acts of the state and the managerial class and point out their insufficiencies and wrongdoing. It will be the managerial elite who initiate while the unions merely observe.

Contrary to Marxian thinking about the withering away of the state, Kerr et al. hold that in an increasingly industrialized society the role of the government will be enhanced and expanded. Finally, they reject Marx's contention that as capitalism matures workers will develop a stronger sense of class consciousness. They claim that advancing industrialism, with the increasing educational level of the workers and more leisure time, leads to proliferating interests and diversities of occupation, culture and associational activities. Pluralism rather than class solidarity characterizes the new industrial society.

The nature of group protest is not the result of worker reaction to capitalism but varies depending on the character of those individuals, termed "elites," who are the initiators and directors of the industrializing process. Five generalized types of "industrializing elites" and the kind of society they established are mentioned:

(1) The middle-class elite is drawn primarily from the existing commercial and artisan groups. Pragmatic and less rigid ideologically, they construct a highly individualistic society in which self interest is the prime motivating factor to stimulate economic growth. Industry is dispersed rather than under centralized control. A set of rules and institutions is created to manage industrial conflict, which is built into the system.

(2) Members of the dynastic elite, formed in the landed and commercial aristocracy, are held together by a firm belief in maintaining the status quo and preserving tradition. Family and class are the essential ingredients in upward mobility. This elite accepts the task of building the industrializing process if necessary to preserve their personal and family power. The economic and political system is paternalistic, and authority is solely in the hands of the state and government. Conflict, therefore, is unacceptable and suppressed.

(3) The colonial elite introduces industrialization in areas of the world in which they are outsiders representing an external power. Colonial administrators, therefore,

owe their loyalty to the mother country rather than to the indigenous population. They create a political, economic and social system which is largely under alien control. Management is viewed as representing a superior culture while workers are regarded as subordinate beings dependent on the colonial power for guidance and survival. Conflict between labor and management is controlled or suppressed. Labor organizations, where allowed to exist, evolve in the direction of nationalist goals.

(4) The revolutionary industrial elite, in seizing control and leadership of the industrializing process, eliminates the old elite and their cultural traditions and replaces them with a new leadership and newly fashioned culture. Guided by a theory of history which sets for them a specific course of action and a predestined vision of a future society, they create a highly centralized state economy and political system. Managers are the dominant class in industry. Workers are dependent on management which, in turn, is dependent on the state.

(5) The nationalistic elite is composed of charismatic leaders who guide the masses in struggle against the old order or the colonial rules. The state controls all aspects of the economy, dominates existing labor organizations, and makes workers dependent on it for economic benefits and political direction. Rules governing industrial organization and labor relations are largely in the hands of the state. Conflict between labor and management is controlled or suppressed.

Industrializing elites seldom appear in a pure or ideal state. They are often found in mixed form combining characteristics from any of the aforementioned ideal types. Each ideal type has its own evolutionary path so that nations whose ideal types have similar characteristics are likely to develop along parallel lines.

Dynastic elites, if they govern effectively, move toward a middle-class society where class divisions are minimized and labor organizations and political parties become less ideological and labor organizations have greater input into decision-making; ineffectual leadership will bring the country under the sway of nationalist or revolutionary intellectual leadership. The middle class is seen as the most stable of all types. All elite groups tend to move gradually into its orbit. Once in full control of the industrializing process, it has never in history had its authority successfully challenged internally. Colonialism is the most transient of all the societal types. Its type of rule is unadaptable to the needs of an advanced industrial society. It eventually gives way to nationalism or rule by the revolutionary intellectuals. The revolutionary intellectuals come to power at a moment of crisis in the old order. However, with the advance of industrialization ideological considerations diminish and class stratification declines. Eventually industrial society moves toward some form of middle-class pattern. Nationalist leaders, if successful, move toward a society dominated by the middle class; if unsuccessful, the leadership eventually passes to the revolutionary intellectuals.

Industrialization has a logic of its own. All nations from diverse geographical areas eventually fall victim to its enticements. Once underway, it sets in motion forces for uniformity and consensus which eventually overpower those elements promoting diversity or dissension. The age of ideology gives way to realism and pragmatism. Disruption of the industrializing process is of concern to all. Since each part of the process is dependent on the other, this interdependence leads to cooperation rather than dissension if each is to attain its desired goal. The labor force accepts the web of rules and the goals of the new industrial society. Managers are less harsh in their treatment of labor. Many of the amenities of life are provided by the state.

Technological advances also call for higher levels of skill. Workers assume more responsibility for expensive equipment and operational tasks. This consent can only be obtained willingly. As a consequence, the workers' influence and responsibility expand. An industrial society needs trained and educated workers. It acts as a leveling agent by drawing workers from the least-skilled occupations and propelling them into positions with higher wage levels. The result is greater equality among people economically and greater similarity in political outlook.

Kerr et al. describe their future society as one based on "pluralistic industrialism." The state will assume greater power in such a society, moderating conflicts between managers and the managed, producers and consumers, and preventing collusion by labor and management against the public. Power in the new society will be shared by the state, the industrial enterprise, and the professional association. The latter organization will be grouped around skill and occupation. Uniting all the groups and institutions will be a web of rules developed primarily by the state. Labor will not be an advocate of class struggle urging the total reform of society but will instead assume the form of professional associations. They will revolve primarily around craft or occupation. Their principal duties will be to improve the income and status of their occupational group and to provide the necessary information about latest developments and advances in the field. In a society based on consensus, rigid political control is unnecessary. Rebellion will become antiquated and disagreements will take the form of petty bureaucratic struggles. Marx's class struggle is nonexistent and the age of the classless society emerges.

Part VIII contains two essays critical of the work of Kerr et al. In his review of their work, economist Neil Chamberlain argues that Kerr and associates fail to develop a theory at all. The use of "ideal types," an elusive (and basically useless) "logic of industrialism," and a prediction that all societies will eventually end up looking like 1960 middle-class America are all criticized. British sociologist Michael Mann criticizes Kerr et al. for belonging to an "end of ideology" school of thought containing an unwarranted harmonistic tinge to all their theorizing.

John Kenneth Galbraith develops industrial pluralist theory in a slightly different direction from that of Kerr et al. Galbraith argues that unions have lost their original reason for being; what's more, they are unlikely to appeal to the new breed of workers in advanced industrial societies. He does find that they serve useful functions for the economic system, but most of these are incidental to the unions' purposes and hardly constitute grounds for optimism about the labor movement's future. Galbraith finds that, like Jonah's triumph over the whale, unions have finally been accepted into the industrial system as they are swallowed up within it.

In the final selection, British sociologist John Goldthorpe and his associates disagree with the predictions of both Kerr et al. and Galbraith. On the basis of a major study of British blue collar workers in the most technologically advanced industrial sectors, Goldthorpe and associates argue that, while the pluralist industrialist theorists *could* be correct in their predictions, the evidence is far from decisive. Although he is not a Marxist or a revolutionary, Goldthorpe finds class-based movements in radical opposition to be a distinct possibility—contrary to the other theories in Part VIII.

## 40
### *Industrialism and Industrial Man*
CLARK KERR, JOHN T. DUNLOP,
FREDERICK H. HARBISON, AND CHARLES A. MYERS                1960

#### The Necessity for a New View

A century or more has passed since the early stages of the first instance of industrialization under middle-class leadership which so influenced Marx's formulations. Also, a century of advance in theoretical economics has replaced the Ricardian system which Marx adopted as a starting point. The intervening years have seen industrialization take an increasing variety of economic and political forms. There are infinitely more data on which to formulate a general view of the industrialization process and its impacts upon workers, managers, and governments. The advantage of first-hand observation and detailed discussions in a number of industrializing countries now provides a more solid basis for valid generalization.

The following points compare and contrast the major features of the Marxian interpretation of the capitalist process with the analytical framework to be developed in this volume. . . .

*Industrialization Rather Than Capitalism.* This volume is concerned with the industrialization process rather than with the "Process of Capitalist Production" which was the subtitle to Marx's *Capital.* It is not the process of capitalist production but rather industrialization in many guises which is of contemporary interest. In our times it is no longer the specter of Communism which is haunting Europe, but rather emerging industrialization in many forms that is confronting the whole world. The giant of industrialization is stalking the earth, transforming almost all the features of older and traditional societies.

*Rising Levels of Skill and Responsibility.* The technology of modern industry tends to raise substantially and progressively the average levels of skills and responsibilities of a work force. It also tends to raise the proportion of highly skilled and responsible employees. While some older handicraft skills may be destroyed and the transitions may be painful, new skills and new responsibilities are created. Modern technology is displacing highly repetitive tasks with new machinery and processes and is creating new skills at high levels to design, install, maintain and service such automatic processes. The distinction between machine operatives and attendants tends to disappear. New industries and occupations are continually being created by modern industry, and white-collar and service occupations, outside a factory milieu, come to bulk very large.

*Growing Proportion of Technical and Managerial Personnel.* Modern industry requires a rapidly increasing number and a high proportion of technical, professional, and managerial personnel. This is equally true whether ownership is private or public. This staff is concerned with the functions of planning, organization, direction, training, and research that have become indispensable to modern factory production and to urban communities. Neither this group, nor the skilled manual workers, can be referred to as "a numerically unimportant class of persons." On the contrary, they are a group continu-

Excerpted by permission of the publishers from *Industrialism and Industrial Man* by Clark Kerr, John T. Dunlop, Frederick H. Harbison, and Charles A. Myers, pp. 28–32, 48–52, 74–76, 215–233, 288–296 Cambridge, Mass.: Harvard University Press. Copyright © 1960 by the President and Fellows of Harvard College. Footnotes in the original have been eliminated.

ously increasing in size and significance. They require an ever higher degree of formal education and training, and substantial resources in the community tend to be devoted to their development.

*New Wealth and Leisure.* Industrialization is technically so superior to earlier forms of production that it tends under any political and economic system to raise materially the level of wages, to reduce the hours of work, and to raise living standards as measured by such conventional means as life expectancy, health, and education. While policies of rapid industrialization may divert for a period all "surplus" to further industrial expansion in heavy industry, eventually improvements in living standards cannot be longer delayed. The prospects are for increased well-being rather than for increased misery. Indeed, much of the early resistance to industrialization has disappeared, even in economically backward countries, as economic development has become a policy of these regions and as individuals seek and expect the benefits associated with industrialization.

*The Decline of Overt Protest.* The discontent of workers, reflected in disruptive forms of protest, tends to be greatest in the early stages of industrialization and tends to decline as workers become more accustomed to industrialization. The partially committed industrial worker, with strong ties to the extended family and village, unaccustomed to urban life and to the discipline and mores of the factory, is more likely to reflect open revolt against industrial life than the seasoned worker more familiar with the ways of the factory, more understanding of the reasons for the web of factory rules, more reconciled to factory life, more motivated by urban and monetary considerations and less attached to the traditional and rural society. The worker in process of the early stages of industrialization is more prone to absenteeism, prolonged and sporadic withdrawal from industrial work, wildcat stoppages, naked violence, and destruction of machines and property. In later periods, industrial workers tend to be more disciplined in their withdrawal of effort and in the use of the strike. The extent of protest does not tend to rise with increasing industrialization, reaching the crescendo of revolution with a mature work force fully committed to factory and urban life. Rather, turning Marx on his head, protest tends to peak early. The initial generations of industrial workers tend to be critical from the perspective of concern with the revolutionary consequences of the transition to the industrial society.

*Greater Role of Enterprise Managers.* Industrial managers, private or public, and their technical and professional associates, rather than industrial workers, have the more significant and decisive role in industrialization. Again, turning Marx on his head, they are the "vanguard" of the future. It is they who largely create and apply the new technology, who determine the transformations in skills and responsibilities, who influence the impact of such changes upon the work force and who exercise leadership in a technological society. This is not to imply that workers and their organizations exercise no influence on the course of industrialization. They perform the vital role of protest, of calling attention to both the direct and unforeseen consequences of managerial decisions upon workers and the larger community. But, except for crisis periods, this is essentially a more restricted and passive role. The initiative for the technological revolution and its consequences for the work force are concentrated more largely in the hands of managers. This view places an even heavier responsibility upon industrial managers, upon their selection, training, and norms of conduct, be they private or public.

*The Omnipresent State.* Industrialization involves a large role for government not only to treat with the technological complexities of modern industry, or with developmental programs, but also as a consequence of the goods and services demanded in the industrializing society, such as education and health services, and directly in the regulation of the relations between managers and workers. Modern industrialization does not see the withering away of the state and its bureaucracy; rather the role of governmental agencies is expanded and enhanced. Industrial relations seldom concern the relations of workers (and their organizations) and managers solely. Typically, there is a three-way relation, including state agencies.

*The Eternal Classes.* No classless society arises under industrialism, even if a revolution is executed to eliminate a class. Workers are never freed from restraints; they never lose their "chains" in the work place. Industrialization requires and develops a distinctive web of rules to constrain and to direct the industrial work force, and workers have or may have more or less influence in shaping these rules. The industrializing society whatever its political form, demands high-skilled technologists and lower-skilled manual workers, and requires managers and the managed.

*Many Roads to Industrialism.* The course of industrialization does not follow a single mold or prescribed pattern. Underdeveloped countries need not grow in all important respects in "the image" of any particular advanced country. There is a variety of leaders of industrialization movements, with different objectives, starting with societies at varying degrees of backwardness, confronting different obstacles, proceeding at quite different rates of speed, and using a variety of political and social forms. Nor does the industrialization process end in a single stereotype revolution.

*Pluralistic Industrialism.* The industrializing society does not in the end create political uniformity and standardized interests. Workers do not develop a monolithic solidarity, although the advanced industrializing society eliminates many of the regional, linguistic, and nationalist internal differences of an earlier stage of development. New differentiations appear as diverse occupational, cultural, and associational interests arise in a society of higher incomes, more leisure, and higher standards of education. The society nearing industrialism is pluralistic in its interests, with a wide range for individual freedom outside the work place.

An interpretation of the industrialization process developed during the early stages of the first instance of industrialization is not likely to be appropriate or applicable after a century of experience. No rigid model or dogma is satisfying to the dynamic industrialization process in new settings, in new and varied forms and with new leaders. There is need to rethink the logic of the industrialization process and its consequences for workers, managers, and their interrelations with governments. . . .

■      ■      ■

## The Dynamic Elites and Social Conquest

Industrialization is always at first of necessity undertaken by a minority group— the colonial company, the indigenous entrepreneur, the government agency, the military unit. It cannot come into full bloom overnight except, perhaps, in small societies with unusual natural resources which attract external capital, like Kuwait; but even there an initiating human agent is requisite. Usually industrialization starts in a restricted geographical area or sector of a society as a small subculture initiated by a subordinated group which then spreads into new areas and new sectors until it is the dominating system of production affecting almost all the relations of men within the society.

The subordinated group which initiates the industrialization process is, of course, a product of the particular culture found in the pre-industrial society or is a foreign elite. The range of issues which confronts the leaders of industrialization are shaped, in part, by and are seen through cultural and economic constraints. . . . Members of the various elites do make choices, but they are shaped by their strategies and their values and by the fact that the culture, the economic environment and history have made these persons leaders. The conjuncture of these cultural and economic variables is, in fact, implicit in the concept of an elite, and the typology of elites which is used throughout this volume reflects this interrelatedness.

There are at the start of the march toward industrialism some important minorities, of course, who do not wish to move in this direction at all, but their influence can only be local and relatively temporary. They are usually found among the leaders of the older society, the land owners, the "medicine men," the higher artisans, the aristocrats. They are the static minorities. They can delay and by their delay affect the location within society of the new initiative, but they cannot prevent the transformation in the long run; and their delaying efforts are only likely to make the inevitable transition more traumatic.

The technology of industrialization requires dynamic elites for its introduction and extension into a society. The human agents who successfully introduce and extend the new technology have great influence in the society. They can guide and direct it within reasonable limits to suit their wishes. Consequently it is of considerable significance who introduces the new systems and what their wishes may be.

Thus a crucial factor in any industrializing society is which elites become the initiators of industrialization, and how they view their role and the nature of the "good society." The universal questions are these:
(1) Who leads the march to industrialism?
(2) What is the purpose of the march?
(3) How is the march organized?

The answers to these three basic questions depend in part on cultural and economic preconditions; they also depend in some measure on the aspirations of the newly emerging group of industrial employees, ever more numerous and more powerful. They wish progress, and they also wish participation. Some elites promise more of one or the other or of both than do others. And promise and delivery do not always coincide. Consequently the routes the industrial workers prefer to take are subject to change—now one and now another; here one and here another. Much of the turmoil of the last century was caused, and much of the turmoil of the next century will be caused, as this group debates its preferences, changes or is led to change its preferences, and attempts to assert them. The industrial workers, however, are a conditioning, not a determining influence. But they can have a clear impact on the election, the performance, and the survival of the dynamic elites. The peasants, also, are, except at certain times of crisis, an even more passive force in the industrialization process but, unlike the workers, they are a declining element.

At this juncture in history there are five ideal types of elites who customarily and variously take the leadership of the industrialization process. These are the initiators, the manipulators, the prime movers:
(1) Dynastic elite
(2) The middle class
(3) The revolutionary intellectuals
(4) The colonial administrators
(5) The nationalist leaders

The fourth group, at least in its pure form, is particularly transitory in its span of leadership; and the longer range competitors are probably found among the other four.

They have the greater survival value but they also may turn out to be, as history unfolds, transient instruments of the transformation; for industrialization is relatively new to man and what form it will finally take cannot yet be clearly seen.

It should be understood that each of these elite groups may have associated with it or indeed may be composed of several elements—political leaders, industrial managers, military officers, religious figures, top civil servants, leaders of labor organizations, associated intellectuals, among others; and thus when we speak of a certain type of elite we refer more to the character of its central orientation than to the specific individuals who constitute it at any moment of time.

Each of these elite groups has a strategy by which it seeks to order the surrounding society in a consistent and compatible fashion. This strategical perspective, if the society is to end up with a cultural consistency, must pervade the entire culture. It needs to penetrate and order the cultural totality; to become the dominant theme in the culture. Otherwise there is internal tension, conflict, and restlessness. It is partly because the colonial managers do not have in their positions and in their outlooks the possibilities for developing a cultural consistency that they are perishable elements; their base of operation is too foreign and too narrow.

An internal conflict between the new culture, with its dominant theme set by the industrializing elite, and the old culture is inevitably fought on many fronts—the economic, political, religious, intellectual; and an external conflict between alternative ideologies of industrialism tends to be fought on all fronts at once. Consistency at home and compatibility abroad, since industrialism will inevitably in the end be a world-wide system, are two insistent imperatives felt in greater or lesser degrees by each dominant group; imperatives which press on the instinct to survive. Each industrializing system becomes a "way of life," no matter what its specific form, and a "way of life" demands internal acceptance and external protection if it is to function successfully in the long run. The only ultimate external protection is a world organized along reasonably compatible lines. These are the internal and external aspects of the historical battle over the character of the industrial society—the effort to secure internal consistency and to assure external compatibility.

Management types, protest forms, labor organization typologies, rule-making relationships, all relate to the central themes of industrialization and cannot be fully understood outside the context of these themes; else the individual phenomena appear largely unrelated to each other and are explained singly only by history. But there is a consistency which binds them all more or less firmly together and the elucidation of this consistency is the first, but not the last, step in the analysis of the separate types, forms, typologies, and relationships. All things are not possible in all situations.

These five types of industrialization, it should be noted, are "ideal" situations, and, as such, no individual historical case corresponds fully to any one of them. But most individual cases may be understood better in relation to one of these types. They abstract from reality, but by reducing complexity and by making comparisons they can also illuminate reality. They give order to our task of comprehending the forms of industrialization and their varying impacts in the labor-management-state area.

It should be borne in mind that these five ideal types of industrialization ignore much important detail in individual cases; they do not correspond exactly to any single actual case; many cases are, to a degree, mixtures; and several societies have changed, and will continue to change, their essential type over time. Moreover, some elites have developed at an earlier point in history than others; consequently comparisons at the same point of time are hazardous.

■   ■   ■

### The Decisive Questions

We started with three questions (Who leads the march? What is the purpose of the march? How is the march organized?); we identified four systems which apparently have or may have some survival value (the dynastic elite, the middle class, the revolutionary intellectuals, and the nationalist leaders). Another system (that of the colonial administrators), it was suggested, does not have such survival value and will be effective only in the short run. Colonialism is either overthrown or it ceases to be colonialism. Two other elements (the intellectuals and the generals) were presented as factors of importance in crisis periods, but not as groups which in themselves provide a stable base for industrial advance.

If it takes a reasonably consistent strategic approach to be able to run an industrializing society effectively, then the four major contenders at this moment in history are the dynastic elite, the middle class, the revolutionary intellectuals, and the nationalist leaders. Their respective answers to the three questions might be summarized as follows:

*Who leads the march?* The dynastic elite answers, those born to lead and they are identified by family and by class. Their rule should be a personal one based on tradition and backed, if necessary, by force. The middle class answers, those who through competitive education and competitive experience most merit leadership responsibility; and their leadership should be based on consent and take place within certain generalized rules of the game. The revolutionary intellectuals reply that it should be those persons who have the superior theory of history and superior strategy for organizing a society in keeping with the demands of industrial technology; and they rest their leadership on force. The nationalist leaders say that it should be the men who through their vision and courage represent the future of the nation; and their power is based on the sense of patriotism they can arouse in the citizens of the nation.

*What is the purpose of the march? And how is the march organized?* The dynastic elite sees the goal as the preservation of the old order, with its emphasis on the paternal community, to the extent possible, while still keeping control of the new method of production. The method of the paternal community calls for a reasonably strong state intent on preserving internal order and stability, very substantial rule-making authority in the hands of the enterprise managers, and dependent workers owing loyalty to the managers. The middle class understands the goal to be a method which it is expected will, over time, bring the greatest welfare to individuals—the method of the open market in political and economic affairs. The open market entails a heavy emphasis on private as against public effort, a pluralistic distribution of rule-making authority in the industrial relations area among management, labor organizations, and the state, and independent workers motivated by self-interest and capable of undertaking conflict with the employers in the name of this self-interest. The revolutionary intellectuals envision the goal as a totally new society fully compatible with the new technology. This calls for a powerful centralized state which holds in its hands all rule-making authority and which expects the worker to perform his duty and to accept without conflict the decisions of the state, which is held to be acting in his interest. The nationalist leaders see the goal to be the independence and progress of the nation to be achieved under the guidance of the state.

The dynastic elite offers continuity; the middle class, individual choice; the revolutionary intellectuals, high velocity industrialization; and the nationalist leaders, the integrity and advancement of the nation. None of them, however different their essential emphasis, can escape the imperatives of consensus and assimilation. In each case, starting as a minority, they must get the acceptance of the society and become broadly based within a culture which is compatible with their strategic approach. Once this has been done the society becomes internally largely ideologically barren, for there no longer is a basic conflict over the strategic approach to industrial society. The decline of ideology in a society marks the rise in acceptance of the dominant strategy. The decline of ideology in the world will come when there is only one accepted approach to industrialism; and that eventuality, if it ever comes, is still a long distance away.

This chapter has been largely concerned with "ideal types," but each actual situation has grown within a preexisting culture and been affected by it; each has encountered a series of historical and economic facts and been molded by them. The almost infinite variety of realistic experience can only be understood by reference to the variety of cultural, historical, and economic settings. Industrialism in the end may become one, but it certainly will have found its initial beginnings in the many.

■ ■ ■

### Worker Organizations and the Elites

In the community led by each ideal type of industrializing elite distinctive worker organizations develop in conformity to the elite's grand strategy of the great transition and reinforcing its other policies. Industrialization everywhere creates organizations of workers, but they differ widely in their functions, structure, leadership, and ideology. Indeed, the term "labor organizations" is used here rather than "labor unions" to emphasize more generality and to avoid implications of forms and functions peculiar to the middle-class ideal type.

The general relationship between each of the ideal types of elites and the labor organizations which arise in the societies they seek to industrialize may be briefly characterized at the outset. The dominant labor organizations in the dynastic-led society remain foreign to the elite; they do not fit nor do they readily conform to the paternal view of the elite. The labor organizations of the middle-class elite conform and are consonant with the market. In the industrialization program of the revolutionary intellectuals the labor organizations are consistent with and conform to the state. The labor organizations of the colonial elite are not congenial to the dominant elite; they tend to be nationalist and press for independence. They are foreign to the colonialist vision of industrialization. The labor organizations under the nationalist elite are beset by a deep dilemma and divided loyalties in shaping their policies. . . . These general relationships between the ideal types of elites and their labor organizations suggest that greatest conflict and tension would characterize the dynastic and colonial-led industrialization.

■ ■ ■

*The Dynastic Elite.* The dynastic community is characterized by workers personally dependent upon the enterprise manager. The worker looks to the paternal manager for guidance in personal, economic and social problems; community affairs are not properly his concern, but the province of the paternal elite.

The dynastic elite does not in principle encourage labor organizations. At the plant level, organizations of workers supplement and help to administer the paternal activities of the managers and the state, but they provide little effective constraint on the decisions of management. At the industry level they provide a broad form of minimum regulation which the enterprise managers often find congenial to the support of cartels or associations. These standards have little relevance to actual plant conditions, and there is little connection between the plant level and the industry level of workers' organizations. In the society led by the dynastic elite, political organizations of workers emerge which often have only indirect connections with the plant and industry levels of workers' organizations, and they seek detailed government regulation of compensation and working conditions to offset plant and industry-level weaknesses and division of workers. These political organizations also seek to challenge the established elite and conduct political demonstrations.

In the traditional society led by the dynastic elite there are frequently deep social distinctions, religious, racial, nationalist, linguistic, and political party divisions among workers. There tends to be multiple representation of workers at the plant level, as in workers' councils, and at the industry level, as in negotiations for agreements signed by several overlapping workers' organizations. Among these organizations at the plant and industry level, and in political activities, there may be keen rivalry and competition. In the absence of exclusive jurisdiction or exclusive representation for the majority organization, the rivalry is limited since it need not end in extinction for any of the competitors. Majority rule does not apply with the winner-take-all. Changing conditions lead to relative shifts in workers' support, but the existence of the organizations is not endangered. There may also be keen competition between organizations at the plant level and at the national level over the distribution of functions. Any competition among workers' organizations is lamented; it is tolerated as an unavoided consequence of historical divisions in the traditional society.

The dynastic elite tends to build organizations which provide minimum regulation on an industry basis, without a direct line of control to the plant level. The labor organization is constricted on the one hand by work-level groups, such as workers' councils, over which it has little, if any, control, and the political organs which seek regulative legislation. The labor organization operates in a relatively narrow corridor between plant groups and the political parties. There is strong internal confederation control which may be further limited by rival confederations.

The operations of labor organizations, as any other, are much influenced by the funds at their disposal and the source of their finances. Under the dynastic elite labor organizations tend to be relatively poorly financed. There are a variety of competitors for support by the workers—work-level organizations, national level groups, and political parties—and their access to workers for funds is not often coordinated. The paternal characteristics of the system are not congenial to large dues payments. The focus of the society around the family, state, and religion is not congenial to the financial support of vigorous voluntary associations. Labor organizations do not place a high preference upon building strong financial positions in view of their major activities. Labor organizations are a movement, and movements are not primarily concerned with finances. At times the government may provide some resources in the form of buildings, a subsidy for the operation of labor exchanges, or social insurance services, or pay the salaries of some leaders who may fill some nominal public function in exchange for loyalty.

Leadership of labor organizations may be drawn from the ranks or from intellectuals outside the organizations or be imposed from a party or subject to government approval. The leadership of labor organizations in the country under the dynastic elite tends to be drawn from those ideologically oriented toward political activities and from intellectuals. The activities of the labor organizations, as opposed to works councils and enterprise or plant bodies, are primarily at the industry and national level. The emphasis upon social policy and law places a relative premium upon learning. The absence of

## Worker organizations and the elites.

| Industrializing Elite | Dynastic | Middle-Class | Revolutionary-Intellectuals | Colonials | Nationalists |
|---|---|---|---|---|---|
| View toward workers | Personally dependent upon managers in time of need. | Independent workers. | Class of dependent workers. | Dependent upon foreigners. | Partners in the new nation. |
| Functions of workers' organizations | Social functions at plant level; little constraint upon management. Provides minimum industry conditions by legislation. Political activity challenges the elite. | Regulates management at the local and industry level. Independent political activity accepted. Does not challenge the elite. | Instrument of party to educate, lead workers and to stimulate production. No political activity except through the party. | Largely a part of the independence and nationalist movement. | Confronts the conflicting objectives of economic development and protection of workers. |
| Competition among workers' organizations | Limited rivalry at the plant level and the distribution of functions between the local and industry levels. No exclusive representation. | Exclusive representation and keen competition. Some rivalry between plant and industry levels over allocation of functions. | No rivalry or competition allowed. | Divided by ideological, tactical, regional and personal leadership factions. | Tendency for consolidation among organizations recognized as loyal by nationalistic elite. Advantage over those not so recognized. |
| Structure of worker organizations | Relatively large number of industrial unions. Centralized confederation often limited by rival confederations. Unions perform narrow range of functions. | A variety of structural forms. Confederations not so centralized. Organizations perform a wide range of functions. | A few industrial unions. Centralized confederation. Organizations perform a narrow range of functions. | A wide variety of structures. Organizations not well developed, often personal. | Tendency toward industrial unions with one confederation acceptable to elite. |
| Sources of funds | Meager resources from irregular dues payments and indirect government allowances. Financial success not highly regarded by workers' organizations. | Substantial resources secured by regular dues; regulatory functions require administrative organizations and large budgets. | Substantial resources secured by assessment of all workers; financial resources present no problem with support of regime. | Meager funds often raised outside workers' organizations. | Funds often secured indirectly from government in addition to meager dues. Officers receive other salaries. |
| Sources of leadership | Intellectuals and those ideologically oriented toward political activity. The leaders income position is often insecure. | The ranks through lower levels of workers' organizations. They have an established career. | Reliable party leaders with experience in worker organizations. They have an established career. | Nationalist and independence leaders. Intellectuals with a personal following. | National leaders and intellectuals except where confined to manual workers. |
| Ideology | Class-conscious and revolutionary except for a minority. | Reformist. | Preserve the true revolution. | Independence. | Nationalism. |

plant level problems as a concern in these organizations decreases the need for leadership more familiar with the actual work processes. The income of such leaders may not always depend solely upon the labor organization, but may be based also upon political activity, legal practice, journalism, and other activities. It should not be inferred that leaders do not arise from the ranks, but the dynastic arrangements tend to favor the intellectual type for labor leadership.

The labor organizations which emerge in the course of industrialization under each ideal type of elite tend to develop a distinctive ideology or view of their place in the community. Under the dynastic elite the dominant labor organizations tend to be class-conscious and revolutionary; they advocate the drastic overhaul of the traditional society. There may also be labor organizations, particularly organized along religious lines, which are more loyal to the traditional society.

*The Middle-Class Elite.* The middle-class case is characterized by the independent worker. While the worker is required to follow the directions of management at the work place, as are workers everywhere, his personal affairs are his own concern within a system of rules, and in community life his vote is the equal of the manager's.

The middle-class elite is more readily reconciled to the principle of workers' organizations than the dynastic elite and supports the principle of their affirmative public value. At the plant and industry level the organizations regulate relationships with managements. There is closer coordination and often direct lines of authority in these workers' organizations between the industry and the plant level; in some cases this authority extends to a single national center, as in Sweden, at least on some questions. The political organization of workers is less concerned with detailed regulation of managements and more preoccupied with community issues. The middle-class elite regards such organized political activity as legitimate, and the workers' political organizations are less dedicated to challenge or to displace the industrializing elite.

In the society led by the middle class there is typically supposed to be one workers' organization for each type of worker by craft or industry. The scope of labor organizations often conforms to the contour of the market. There tends to be competition among contending organizations since the triumph of one means the loss of recognition to the rivals among a particular group of workers, at least for a period. A degree of competition among workers' organizations, moreover, is regarded as an affirmative good to stimulate more responsiveness to the wishes of the workers. There is relatively little overt competition, however, between organizations over the distribution of functions at the plant and industry levels, although there is internal tension in workers' organizations over the extent of centralization and decentralization of functions.

The labor organizations under the middle-class-led industrialization tend to build a variety of unions: craft, industrial, and general. The range of functions is broad, not constricted by other forms of worker organizations. The diversity in structure represents a response to a gradual historical development, to a lesser degree of confederation centralization, and to a greater responsiveness to the preferences of particular sectors and groups of workers. It also reflects an economy with more reliance upon the market mechanism under which the pattern of union growth may have had to conform to market constraints to survive. The powers of the the confederation often tend to be lesser than in the other ideal types; the principles of decentralization and autonomy are highly regarded values.

The country led by the middle-class elite develops labor organizations that tend to be relatively well financed by dues regularly collected from the membership. The labor organizations seek to build strong financial positions, partly to provide more effective services to the members and partly to provide security in case of struggle with managements. The labor organizations typically receive little, if any, support or subsidy from the government (save in a few cases related to social services). Financial independence from government is a cherished value. The emphasis upon regulatory functions, in constraining management through rules at the work place, operates to create modern administrative organizations which require large-scale budgets.

The leadership of labor organizations in the middle-class-led country tends to be drawn almost exclusively from the ranks of workers. The predominate concern with rules constricting enterprise managers and the direct interest in the immediate work place necessarily place a premium upon leadership seasoned in the practical operating problems of enterprises. The intellectual would be out of place. The more direct organizational tie between plant and industry or confederation levels of workers' organizations creates more of a ladder on which leadership starts at the bottom. Full-time officers arise who regard the labor organizations as a career; they are in a sense professionals or bureaucrats of the labor organizations with a primary concern for administering and negotiating agreements with professionals in management.

The middle-class elite leads a society in which labor organizations are bargaining institutions primarily; they are mildly reformist in their ideology and attitudes toward the larger community.

*The Revolutionary Intellectual.* This elite regards workers as a dependent class. Industrial workers as a group are subject to managerial direction which is regarded as an expression of the elite leadership. The personal conditions of individual workers are not the concern of managers, and workers do not look to them personally, as with the dynastic elite, but the rules of the work place are paternal rather than market oriented. In community affairs the worker is to look to the leadership of the party.

The revolutionary intellectual elite regards organizations of workers at the plant or industry level as its own preserve. The purpose of the workers' organizations is less to constrain managements than to educate, to stimulate production, and to lead the industrial workers on behalf of the ruling elite. They are agents of the state to insure industrial production. Independent political organization or activity is precluded except through and under the direction of the party.

In the society led by the revolutionary intellectuals there is no room for competition between contending labor organizations at the plant level, nor is there any contention over functions to be performed by rival workers' organizations. Since the organization of workers is an instrument of the ruling party to educate and to lead workers, discordant tones serve no purpose and are not tolerated. Labor organizations are agents of the state; and there is only one state. A degree of tension may arise between plant-level representatives and those higher in the hierarchy. Competition among workers' organizations, however, is seen only as an evil, weakening the regime.

The revolutionary intellectual elite tends to create a limited number of labor organizations, industrial in form, with a high degree of centralization over district and local groups and at the confederation level. The structure reflects the deliberate design of labor organizations by the elite rather than more gradual evolution or conformance to the market. This structure also reflects the function of the organizations: to serve as the organ of education and communication between the party and the industrial workers and to stimulate industrial output. This narrow range of functions reflects a design in which the party and the state fulfill the functions of regulating or constraining managers which is elsewhere performed by labor organizations and the market. This type of organizational structure may be vulnerable to the rise of plant-level worker organizations from below as illustrated by works councils in Hungary.

In the country led by the revolutionary intellectual elite, labor organizations are relatively well financed by assessments levied upon all workers. The organizations are particularly well supplied with buildings appropriate to their status as an arm of the regime. Finances and resources are no problem.

The leadership of the labor organizations in the revolutionary-intellectual-led country tends to be drawn from reliable party leaders, many of whom have devoted a career to the work of the party in labor organizations. They are financially secure and are in a sense (with a different type of assignment) professionals or bureaucrats of the labor organization and the party. They are concerned with the administration and implementation of policy and ideology developed by the party.

Labor organizations under the revolutionary intellectuals have no ideology apart from the ruling elite. They seek to preserve the true revolution envisaged by the elite.

*The Colonial Elite.* The indigenous worker is envisaged as personally dependent upon the foreign manager as the agent of the colonial power. The role of labor organizations of indigenous workers tends to be largely a part of the nationalist and independence movement. After a country has passed through the portals of political independence, the dilemma of the function of labor organizations arises with perplexing urgency. There is, of course, the purpose to "consolidate independence," to "liquidate the evil remains of colonialism," and to push for the more practical objectives, in foreign firms particularly, of training local citizens to replace foreigners in managerial, technical, and highly skilled positions. . . .

Labor organizations under the colonial elite tend to be united on the theme of independence, but they are likely to be divided on a wide range of ideological, regional, and tactical grounds, as well as on the basis of personal leadership. The rivalry is one of slogans, programmes, and personal leadership rather than of representation or constraints on management. Under the colonial elite the workers' organizations among the indigenous workers tend to reflect a wide variety of structures. Organizations are not well developed, and they are often the reflection of personal leadership.

Labor organizations have no systematic dues collection, and they are poorly supplied with funds. Their funds may come largely from other nationalist groups. The leaders of labor organizations in the colonial community are drawn from the nationalist and independence movement; they tend to be intellectuals with a personal following. The ideology of these labor organizations is built around independence and anticolonialism.

*Nationalist Leaders.* Workers in the new nationalist state regard foreign managers as a lingering vestige of colonialism and indigenous managers ideally as partners in the new nation.

The nationalist leader seeks the support of the rising group of industrial workers and is concerned to insure their reliability. Industrial workers are a strategic group to the nationalist elite. The elite tends to bestow favors upon reliable organizations and to assist in the opposition to rivals for worker support in exchange for subordination to the nationalist objectives.

This elite tends to develop more explicit and more advanced organizational structures than under the colonial elite, largely industrial in form. The tendency is to adopt the organizational forms of labor organizations from some more economically advanced country held in high prestige by the nationalist elite. The nationalist elites tend to promote reliable and loyal labor organizations and encourage the collection of membership dues for them. These dues may even be required of all workers. The elite may also provide funds directly for local organizations, and it may support reliable groups by government grants to worker education and by employment on public payrolls of a number of leaders of labor organizations.

The reliable leadership of labor organizations is drawn from nationalist leaders in the first generation after independence. The leadership includes many intellectuals responsive to the nationalist elite, except in cases in which leadership is specifically confined to manual workers. The ideology of labor organizations under the nationalist elites is that of partners in development.

## The Dilemmas of Labor Organizations in Early Industrialization

Labor organizations in newly industrializing countries, particularly with a new nationalist elite, confront four questions of fundamental significance to the elites and to the labor organizations:

(1) *Wages vs. Capital Formation.* There are conflicting claims of economic development and immediately improved wages and other benefits for workers. The nationalist labor leaders' dedication to industrialization, which requires increased savings, conflicts with the labor organizations' declared purpose and their often promised gains from independence, to provide immediately improved wages and working conditions. Within some limits, higher wages may increase worker productivity, but this is likely to be a narrow and a difficult range of wage policy to find.

(2) *Strikes vs. Production.* The nationalist labor leader must choose again on strike policy. Strike action tends to decrease production where successful and may make development investments less attractive to foreign investors, but strike action may be necessary to achieve economic objectives of the labor organization, to build disciplined labor organizations, and to retain the interest of the membership.

(3) *Grievance-handling vs. Discipline.* Individual workers and small groups in an emerging industrial work force have numerous complaints, grievances, and frustrations. The national labor leader must choose in some degree between supporting the immediate reactions and grievances of workers or supporting the insistence upon higher standards of discipline, a faster pace, training, and production which are vital to economic development.

(4) *Organizational Prestige vs. Political Subservience.* The labor organization is often long on political influence and short on economic power. It must weigh the costs of faithful support and dependence on a political party or government against the benefits of governmental recognition and support in a variety of ways, including exclusive labor rights and favoritism in treating rival labor organizations and outright financial support. The immediate attractiveness of a strong legal position in dealing with managements, members, and rivals and financial solvency is to be balanced against the loss in independence of action in being subservient to the government.

These basic policy decisions, which are most difficult for labor organizations in a country led by a democratic and middle-class elite, present few difficulties for the labor organizations under the revolutionary intellectual elite. Economic development takes first priority over wage increases; production cannot be interfered with by strikes; labor organizations are designed to increase labor productivity, and they are always subservient to the party and government. There is more of a problem in a country under the dynastic elite, but in the main wages cannot be raised very much in the face of the slow rate of development, and strikes are little more than demonstrations. The labor movement cannot secure many concessions from the government or ruling elite, although individual leaders or factions of labor organizations may secure benefits in exchange for political support.

It is easy to understand why many leaders of industrializing countries and their labor organizations in countries outside the Eastern orbit find the choices posed above to be very hard, and they talk of ways to develop labor organizations that will make a more affirmative contribution to the national objective of industrialization. Neither the elite nor the leaders of labor organizations find congenial the traditional model of the "free trade union" drawn from advanced Western countries. As Dr. Nkrumah has said, ".... The trade union movement has a great part to play and a far wider task to perform than merely the safeguarding of the conditions and wages of its members." The debate and the experimentation over the role of labor organizations in recently industrializing countries is one of the focal points of the competition among groups for leadership in the process of industrialization.

The distinctive characteristics of the labor organizations created in the industrialization process by each ideal type of elite indicate the interdependence of each separate feature. The functions exercised by labor organizations, for instance, are closely related to their structure, leadership, financial arrangements, and ideology. Further, the labor organizations that arise in a society in transition led by an ideal type of elite fit into the full range of policies of that industrializing elite. The universals of worker protest and organization are molded to conform and contribute to the grand strategy of the industrializing elite.

## Worker Protest and Pressure as an Historical Force

Worker protest to Marx was not just *the* labor problem but, indeed, *the* important social force at a certain stage in history. It was the peaking of labor protest in a revolution that ushered in the new society. But it was not only Marx who thus raised the historical import of worker protest to a dominant position. In the century from 1850 to 1950, worker protest was often as feared by the conservatives as it was worshipped by the radicals.

As noted earlier ... , however, theories to the contrary, worker protest has been a declining not an increasing force as the evolution of industrialization has unfolded; and it has seldom, in fact, occupied the center of the stage. This does not mean, however, that it has been of little or no significance. Nearly everywhere it has been a social force to be reckoned with and in a few situations it has been the critical social force.

The main impact of worker protest has been its glacial impact—this is the central observation. In certain specific cases, worker protest has additionally played a large role in revolutionary transformation.

*Glacial impact.* Everywhere workers have a sense of protest in the course of the changes that industrialization brings in its wake. Everywhere, or nearly everywhere, they organize or are organized. Through organization, whether autonomous or controlled, they bring pressures to bear on enterprise managers and the ruling elite—pressures through grievances, negotiations, strikes, elections. These pressures work in the direction of more formal rules, more equality of treatment, more checks and balances on managers, more accumulated rights for workers and, generally, toward a sharing of power—toward the "constitutional" approach to authority over workers. These pressures also lead toward the greater intervention of neutrals, usually through actions of the state, the greater development of formal procedures to settle controversies, the creation of experts to handle industrial relations problems. Whether faster or slower, deeper or shallower, this is the direction of penetration of the impact of worker protest.

This glacial pressure can bring substantial changes over a period of years. It can help change the nature of the strategy of a dynastic elite from unadulterated paternalism toward pluralism, as in Germany; soften the policies of a middle class society toward labor, as in England and the United States; lead a nationalist drive toward industrialization in the direction of more consideration for the workers, as in Egypt; and even bring greater consideration for the wishes of the masses as against the requirements of the ideology, as in Poland and Yugoslavia. It can be an evolutionary force of some consequence helping to change in essential ways the strategies of elite groups.

*Revolutionary transformation.* There are exceptional cases where worker protest has played a major role in a social transformation—in the rise of a new elite or the shift of power from one elite to another. Not all such social transformations, however, inherently involve a role for labor protest. The rise of a dynastic elite to control the industrialization process or the introduction of a foreign elite into control of a colony, are not processes in which worker protest can normally play an affirmative role. Also, the rise to supremacy of a middle class elite is usually achieved without the assistance of worker protest, although the case of England shows how worker protest may aid the new middle class in reducing the authority of the old society.

The only two elites which can count on worker protest as a key to their assumption of supremacy are the revolutionary intellectuals and the nationalist leaders. Both are likely to rely on force in taking over from an ineffective dynastic elite or from a colonial regime; and part of the force they may muster is the force of worker protest through the general strike, the urban mob, the revolution. This worker violence helped weaken and then displace the old regimes in Russia, Argentina, Iraq, Indonesia. If the old regime is not actually destroyed, as in Argentina, the organizations of workers may be held in readiness to descend again into the streets to preserve the new regime.

These revolutionary transformations, with the aid of labor protest, not only can occur only in some places (the taking over of power from a dynastic elite or a colonial regime) but also only at some times—those turning points in history when social change is made posssible by the decay of an old system and often only when such decay is made more evident by the effects of depression or of war.

These are the specific cases, not the general rule; the specific cases where worker protest can be a climactic force in changing the rule from one elite to another. The general rule is that worker protest is available as a revolutionary force only in certain situations and at certain times, and also only to certain people—the revolutionary intellectuals and the nationalist leaders.

*Alliances.* Worker protest, by itself, has never brought a change in the ruling elite. Workers and the middle class, with the role of the new middle class quite dominant, helped end the old regime in England. Workers and intellectuals and sometimes army officers and peasants have joined under Communist or Nationalist auspices to supplant a dynastic elite or a colonial power in a number of countries. Worker organizations may even be the source of the leadership of such movements, as in Kenya and Guinea.

But ruling elites may form alliances with worker organizations and direct the sense of worker protest to the purposes of the regime; and this has been one of the significant historical discoveries of the revolutionary intellectuals and the nationalist leaders in a number of countries—Russia, China, Brazil, Pakistan, Mexico. Worker protest need not be against the ruling regime; it can be turned against the defunct regime, the foreigners, backwardness, national degradation; it can be turned in favor of mutual goals of industrial progress, military power, national self-sufficiency. Thus it need not be destructive of the existing regime.

The ruling elites may also form their own alliances against protesting worker organizations when these exist; alliances with the army, the middle class, the Church.

And they may seek to split the workers, as in Germany, into white collar versus manual, Catholic versus Socialist, officials against subordinates; and to isolate them from the middle class and the peasants. Only the colonial administrators are really bereft of possible alliances with a long-term base; much as they may try to rely on tribal chiefs and "tame" native leaders.

Thus protest can be owned by many people; even by the ruling elite as well as by its opponents. Least of all is it likely to be solely owned by the workers themselves, since to be effective they must make alliances with others. Worker protest seldom loses its chains.

*The lessons of the past century.* The next century of industrialization as compared with the first century of world-wide industrialization (1850–1950) may see an even less central role reserved for social protest.

(1) Workers now protest more in favor of industrialization than against it. "Machine breakers" are no longer heroes. Thus the new protest can be constructive toward industrialization and its ruling elites instead of destructive. The relations of leaders and led in the march to industrialization can be positive as well as negative.

(2) Workers have proved themselves much more adjustable to the impacts of industrialization on their technical and social skills, and much more agreeable to the imposition of the web of rules than was once suspected. The led are more easily led.

(3) The elites have gained experience alike in the means of reducing protest—better housing, better personnel practices, greater social security—and in the means of controlling it—grievance procedures, incentives, development of joint goals—than they were a century ago. They appreciate more the need for consensus in society and understand better the ways to achieve it.

(4) The organizations of workers and their leaders have proved quite susceptible to the guidance involved in the development of consensus in an industrializing society; and even to more direct guidance by the elite through selection of goals and of men. Most labor organizations are, in fact, to one degree or another, a part of the established system. This explains, in part, the increasingly constant threat to them from "shop steward movements."

Earlier views on the role of worker protest reflected the facts of earlier times; periods when protest was more frequently against an authoritarian dynastic elite, a hard pushing middle class, harsh colonial masters; periods when protest was against the new technology itself. It then seemed reasonable to suggest the universal nature of class warfare, with the possibility of a few exceptions (Netherlands and the United States).

The conditions for class warfare still exist; but they are increasingly the exception. These exceptions are most likely to rest on the failure of an elite group—a dynastic elite that does not adapt fast enough or a colonial regime that does not transfer power fast enough. A related but separable phenomenon is where the incompetence of particular leaders among the revolutionary intellectuals or the nationalists created the basis for violent worker protest against those leaders.

The general phenomenon now to be explained is class collaboration on the road to industrialization; the collaboration of the new dynastic elite, the new middle class, the new revolutionary intellectuals, the new nationalists, with the workers and their organizations. What were thought to be the exceptions have become the rule; what was thought to be the rule, has become the exception. The road to industrialization is paved less with class warfare and more with class alliances.

The role of worker protest is both different and more complex than has been postulated in the past. It can affect the selection, the performance and the survival of each of the elites, but more frequently through its steady impact than through sudden exertion of massive force. It may also be a supportive feature to the elites more often than a destructive one. Thus the direction of its impact may be different as well as the force of its influence on history less decisive. Worker protest is more the fruit of the past, than the seed of the future. As a seed of the future, it leads both to more industrial progress and to more worker participation in society.

Industrialization does have an impact on workers. They do protest some aspects of this impact. Their protest does in turn have an impact on the course of history, but seldom as the single decisive force. This protest gets organized, channeled, controlled; and this is part of the larger process of the structuring of the labor force. The end result is the creation in each society of an industrial relations system. . . .

■    ■    ■

## The Road Ahead: Pluralistic Industrialism

The future can be really penetrated only when it becomes the present, but visions of the future also help determine the future by the time it has become the present. So men attempt to peer ahead, to understand the structure of history, to alter the process of history, if possible, in accord with their preferences. As we have seen, the history of industrialization to date has not been a smoothly unilinear one; it has been uneven and multilinear. It is likely that in the future it will continue to be both somewhat uneven and multilinear; and there will continue to be some latitude for choice and for chance. Chance may elude man, but choice need not; and the choice of men, within fairly broad limits, can shape history. To predict the future with any accuracy, men must choose their future. The future they appear to be choosing and pressing for is pluralistic industrialism.

Industrialism is a system of social organization where industries, including many large-scale industries, are the dominant method of production. Such a system cannot be an atomistic one with infinite fractionalization of power and distribution of decision making. Authority must be concentrated, although individuals may still have areas in which they can make free choices. Authority may be concentrated in a monistic or pluralistic arrangement. It is our view that the dominant arrangement will be pluralistic. Where there is one locus of power, there will come to be several; where there are many, there will come to be fewer.

Among the factors discussed above pressing for uniformity in industrialization, several push for uniformity in the direction of pluralistic industrialism. The complexity of the fully developed industrial society requires, in the name of efficiency and initiative, a degree of decentralization of control, particularly in the consumer goods and service trades industries; but it also requires a large measure of central control by the state and the conduct of many operations by large-scale organizations. Industrialism cannot function well according to either the monistic or atomistic models.

As the skill level rises and jobs become more responsible, as noted before, any regime must be more interested in consent, in drawing forth relatively full cooperation. For the sake of real efficiency, this must be freely given. The discipline of the labor gang no longer suffices. Higher education and research become two of the larger and more important industries. In them, in particular, the consent and cooperation of the individual producer is particularly important; but more and more other industries take on some of the aspects of the university with its faculty. The university becomes more the model for the enterprise than the enterprise for the university. With skill and responsibility go the need for consent, and with consent goes influence and even authority. Occupational and professional groups, of necessity, achieve some prestige and authority as against both the central organs of society and the individual members of the occupation or profession.

Education brings in its wake a new economic equality and a consequent new equality of political outlook; the universal industrial mass. This in turn, along with many other developments, helps bring consensus to society. The harsh use of power by the state is not so necessary to hold society together by the seams. Education also opens the mind to curiosity and to inquiry, and the individual seeks more freedom to think and to act. Education brings a demand for liberty and can help create conditions in which it is safe to grant it. Education leads to comparisons among nations; to comparisons of progress which often rests on central control and of participation which always rests on a distribution of authority.

This is industrialism at work; centralizing and decentralizing at the same time; creating areas of control and areas of freedom; weaving a web of rules and liberating the individual. No one of these contrary tendencies reigns supreme, many visions of the future to the contrary. An uneasy balance arises among these tendencies; in one situation, one is stronger; in another, another. The fully developed industrial society is too dynamic and complex to yield to the dictates of a single imperative; and a theory about it which yields sole place to any single imperative is too simple to do more than mislead.

Industrialism is so complex and subject to such contrary internal pressures that it never can assume a single uniform unchanging structure; but it can vary around a general central theme and that theme is pluralism. It will, however, take generations before this theme will become universal in societies around the world; but the direction of the movement seems already sufficiently clear. The complexity of industrial society, the ever higher skill levels, the impacts of universal education all work in this direction.

*The State That Does Not Wither Away.* The state will be powerful. It will, at the minimum, have the responsibility in an industrial society for the rate of growth of the economy; the over-all distribution of income among uses and among individuals; the basic security of individuals thus replacing the family as the basic security unit; the stability of the system; the provision of the essential public services of education, transportation, recreational areas, cultural facilities, and the like, which will become more important as the standard of living rises, leisure increases, education improves, and men multiply in numbers; particularly the state will take on the responsibility of providing a favorable physical environment for urban man.

Any pluralistic society is subject to three great potential internal problems and the state is responsible for handling each. One is the conflict among the several power elements in a pluralistic society. The state must set the rules of the game within which such conflict will occur, enforce these rules, and act as mediator; conflicts between managers and the managed are the most noticeable, but by no means the only ones. Another is the control of collusion by producers against consumers, by a profession against its clients, by labor and management against the public. The undue aggrandizement of sectional interests is always endemic if not epidemic in a pluralistic society; in fact, one of the arguments for monism and atomism alike is the avoidance of sectionalism. Additionally, the state will come generally, under pluralistic industrialism, to set the rules relating members to their organizations—who may get in, who may stay in, what rights and obligations the members have, what are the boundaries for the activities of the organization. It will, almost of necessity, be against too much conflict among or collusion between or domination of the members by the subsidiary organizations in society.

All these responsibilities mean the state will never "wither away"; that Marx was more utopian than the despised utopians. It will be the dominant organization in any industrial society. It may, however, itself be less than fully unitary; itself be subject to checks and balances including the check of public acceptance of its current leadership and policies.

*The Crucial Role of the Enterprise—The Middle Class and the Middle Bureaucracy.* The productive enterprise under pluralistic industrialism, whether it is private or public, will be in a dominant position. It will often be large and it must always have substantial authority in order to produce efficiently. This authority will not be complete for it will be checked by the state, by the occupational association, by the individual employee; but it will be substantial.

The managers, whether private or public, will be professionals, technically trained and carefully selected for their tasks. They will be bureaucratic managers, if private, and managerial bureaucrats, if public; each responding to the rules and the technical requirements of the job. The distinction between the private and the public manager will decrease just as the distinction between the private and the public enterprise; distinction among managers will be more according to the size, the product, and the nature of their enterprise. The controlled market and the controlled budget will bring more nearly the same pressures on the managers. The private enterprise, however, will usually have more freedom of action than the public enterprise; but the middle class and the middle bureaucracy will look much alike.

*Associated Man.* The occupational or professional association will range alongside the state and the enterprise as a locus of power in pluralistic industrialism; and there will be more occupations and particularly more professions seeking association. Group organizations around skill and position in the productive mechanism will be well-nigh universal. These organizations will affect output norms, comparative incomes, access to employment, codes of ethics in nearly every occupational walk of life. Their containment within reasonable limits will be an all-enduring and all-pervading problem; and some of the groups will always seek to invade and infiltrate the government mechanisms which are intended to supervise them. Class warfare will be forgotten and in its place will be the bureaucratic contest of interest group against interest group. The battles will be in the corridors instead of the streets, and memos will flow instead of blood.

*The Web of Rules.* Uniting these organizations—the state, the enterprise, the association—will be a great web of rules set by the efforts of all the elements but particularly the state. This web of rules will also relate the individual to each of these elements. In the contest over who should make the web of rules, the end solution will be that they will be made or influenced by more than one element; they will not be set by the state alone or the enterprise alone, or by the association alone. The web of rules will not equally cover all aspects of life.

*From Class War to Bureaucratic Gamesmanship.* Conflict will take place in a system of pluralistic industrialism, but it will take less the form of the open strife or the revolt and more the form of the bureaucratic contest. Groups will jockey for position over the placement of individuals, the setting of jurisdictions, the location of authority to make decisions, the forming of alliances, the establishment of formulas, the half-evident withdrawal of support and of effort, the use of precedents and arguments and statistics. Persuasion, pressure, and manipulation will take the place of the face-to-face combat of an earlier age. The conflict also will be, by and large, over narrower issues than in earlier times when there was real disagreement over the nature of and the arrangements within industrial society. It will be less between the broad programs of capital and labor, and of agriculture and industry; and more over budgets, rates of compensation, work norms, job assignments. The great battles over conflicting manifestos will be replaced by a myriad of minor contests over comparative details.

*From Class Movement to Special Interest Group.* Labor-management relations will conform to this new context. Labor organizations will not be component parts of class movements urging programs of total reform, for the consensus of a pluralistic society will have settled over the scene. Nor may they be very heavily identified by industry, particularly with the increasing multiplication and fractionalization of industries. Rather they may tend to take more the craft, or perhaps better, the occupational form. With skills more diverse, at a generally higher level and obtained more through formal education, and with geographical mobility greatly increased, the professional association may become the most common kind of organization, like those of doctors, lawyers, teachers, nurses, airline pilots in many countries already. These occupational and professional associations will not be united by a single program of social reform, but rather divided by the separate and often conflicting interests of their occupational or professional groups. The day of ideological labor movements as we have known them will have passed.

The purpose of these occupational and professional associations will be relatively narrow, mostly the improvement of the status of the occupation in terms of income, prestige, and specification of the rights and duties that accompany it. Generally these organizations will be a conservative force in society, opposed to new ways of doing things, resistant to increased efforts by members of the occupation. The enterprise managers will be the more progressive elements in the society, although they too may become heavily weighted down by checks and balances and rules.

The techniques of the professional associations for achieving their ends will be those of the bureaucratic organization everywhere; a far cry from the individual withdrawal, or the guerilla warfare, or the strike or the political reform movement of earlier times. They will constitute the quarrels between the semimanaged and the semimanagers.

Individuals will identify themselves more closely with their occupation, particularly if it involves a formal training period for entry, and mobility will follow more the lines of the occupation than the lines of the industry or the job possibilities of the immediate geographical area. In terms of identification, the orientation will be more nearly that of the member of a guild than of a class or of a plant community. Mayo will turn out to be as wrong as Marx. Just as the class will lose its meaning, so also will the plant community fail to become the modern counterpart of the primitive tribe. The occupational interest group will represent the employee in his occupational concerns and the occupation will draw his allegiance. Status in the tribe will not give way to status in the plant; nor will status have given way to the individual contract through the march of civilization; rather interest identification will take the place of both status and individual contract in ordering the productive arrangements of men.

Education, occupation, occupational organization will all be drawn together to structure the life-line and the economic interests of many if not most employees.

*Organization Man and the New Bohemianism.* The individual will be in a mixed situation far removed either from that of the independent farmer organizing most aspects of his own life or from that of the Chinese in the commune under total surveillance. In his working life he will be subject to great conformity imposed not only by the enterprise manager but also by the state and by his own occupational association. For most people, any true scope for the independent spirit on the job will be missing. However, the skilled worker, while under rules, does get some control over his job, some chance to organize it as he sees fit, some possession of it. Within the narrow limits of this kind of "job control," the worker will have some freedom. But the productive process tends to regiment. People must perform as expected or it breaks down. This is now and will be increasingly accepted as an immutable fact. The state, the manager, the occupational association are all disciplinary agents. But discipline is often achieved by a measure of persuasion and incentive. The worker will be semi-independent with some choice among jobs, some control of the job, and some scope for the effects of morale; but he will also be confined by labor organizations, pensions, and seniority rules, and all sorts of rules governing the conduct of the job.

Outside his working life the individual may have more freedom under pluralistic industrialism than in most earlier forms of society. Politically he can be given some influence. Society has achieved consensus and it is perhaps less necessary for Big Brother to exercise political control. Nor in this Brave New World need genetic and chemical means be employed to avoid revolt. There will not be any revolt, anyway, except little bureaucratic revolts that can be handled piecemeal. An educated population will want political choice and can be given it. There will also be reasonable choice in the controlled labor market, subject to the confining limits of the occupation, and in the controlled product market.

The great new freedom may come in the leisure of individuals. Higher standards of living, more leisure, more education make this not only possible but almost inevitable. This will be the happy hunting ground for the independent spirit. Along with the bureaucratic conservatism of economic and political life may well go a New Bohemianism in the other aspects of life and partly as a reaction to the confining nature of the productive side of society. There may well come a new search for individuality and a new meaning to liberty. The economic system may be highly ordered and the political system barren ideologically; but the social and recreational and cultural aspects of life diverse and changing.

The world will be for the first time a totally literate world. It will be an organization society, but it need not be peopled by "organization men" whose total lives are ruled by their occupational roles.

The areas closest to technology will be the most conformist; those farthest from the requirements of its service, the most free. The rule of technology need not, as Marx thought it would, reach into every corner of society. In fact, there may come a new emphasis on diversity, on the preservation of national and group traits that runs quite counter to the predictions of uniform mass consumption. The new slavery to technology may bring a new dedication to diversity and individuality. This is the two-sided face of pluralistic industrialism that makes it forever a split personality looking in two directions at the same time. The new slavery and the new freedom go hand in hand.

Utopia never arrives, but men may well settle for the benefits of a greater scope for freedom in their personal lives at the cost of considerable conformity in the working lives. If pluralistic industrialism can be said to have a split personality, then the individual in this society will lead a split life too; he will be a pluralistic individual with more than one pattern of behavior and one dominant allegiance.

Social systems will be reasonably uniform around the world as compared with today's situation; but there may be substantial diversity within geographical and cultural areas as men and groups seek to establish and maintain their identity. The differences will be between and among individuals and groups and subcultures rather than between and among the major geographical areas of the world. Society at large may become more like the great metropolitan complexes of Paris or London or New York or Tokyo, urbanized and committed to the industrial way of life, but marked by infinite variety in its details.

Pluralistic industrialism will never reach a final equilibrium. The contest between the forces for uniformity and for diversity will give it life and movement and change. This is a contest which will never reach an ultimate solution. Another eternal battle will be between the manager and the managed all up and down the line of all the hierarchies that will mark the world; quiet but often desperate little battles will be fought all over the social landscape. The themes of uniformity and diversity, and manager and managed which mark the world today will characterize it in the future as well. There will be constant adjustments between these eternally conflicting themes, but no permanent settlement. They will constitute the everlasting threads of history: the uniformity that draws on technology and the diversity that draws on individuality; the authority that stems from the managers and the rebellion, however muted, that stems from the managed. These threads of conflict will continue when class war, and the contest over private versus public initiative, and the battle between monistic and atomistic ideologies have been left far behind in the sedimentary layers of history.

## PLURALISTIC INDUSTRIALISM.

| | |
|---|---|
| Industrial leadership | Professional managers—private and public. |
| Central purpose of industrial leadership | Effectiveness of the enterprise. |
| Central characteristics of the society | Checks and balances and the web of rules in a society of ever-changing technology. |
| Sources of variation in approach | Shifting balance between forces of uniformity and diversity. |
| Basic rule-making authority in labor-management relations | State, manager, associations. |
| View of worker | Semi-independent. |
| Attitude toward conflict | Bureaucratic quarrels within highly structured situations. |

# 41

## *Review of* Industrialism and Industrial Man

NEIL W. CHAMBERLAIN                                                    1961

This book is elusive, both in purpose and in execution. The concern of the four authors is with the process of industrialization, and particularly with the relationships which it creates between workers and managers. They propose "to create a framework of our own . . . which is, in its totality, new and different" (p. 2). They offer "an approach to an understanding of industrial relations which seeks to draw on the experience of several countries" (p. 12). An "approach" implies a choice of issues, and on pages 20–21 they have listed ten "central questions" to which they intend to address themselves, ranging from what contributions have been made by previous interpretations of industrialization, to whether industrializing societies tend to become more similar to each other. But they also assert that "the discussion of these questions as a whole is designed to provide a coherent and general theory of industrialization and its impact on managers and workers" (p. 21).

A framework of analysis and an approach to a denationalized understanding of industrial relationships is here, but I have searched in vain for the theory. The book is long on categories and classifications and impressionistic observations, but it is short on analysis. It is perhaps best described as a latter-day descendant of the 19th century German school of economic history, whose hallmark was a literary exposition of the transition from one idealized state of economic development to another.

The general theme of this study, as I reconstruct it, is that first comes pre-industrialism, which has its setting in a variety of cultures with differing forms of economic organization. "Into the midst of this disparity of systems there [then] intruded a new and vastly superior technique of production" (p. 279), embodied in the industrialization process. "Once unleashed on the world, the new technique kept spreading and advancing." The manner of its spread was determined, however, by the nature of the "elite" group dominating a particular society.

These elites can be grouped into five "ideal types," whose names are sufficiently self-descriptive for purposes of this review. These types are the dynastic elite, the middle class, the revolutionary intellectuals, the colonial administrators, and the nationalist leaders. In each country where industrialization appears, it is sponsored by an elite which falls into one of these ideal types, with that elite seeking "to organize society in such a way as both to use the new technique and to serve their own goals." Although other forces help to shape the industrializing society, the dominant influences are the sponsoring leadership group and the society's own culture patterns. "The inherent logic of industrialism interacts with the diversity of cultural factors, economic constraints, and the strategies of the industrializing elites."

The result is a process which in its earlier stages differs among countries by virtue of the dissimilar influences playing on it, but one which itself becomes increasingly influential as it spreads through a society, its own technical requirements—uniform across cultural boundaries—overshadowing the distinctive character imparted by its elite sponsors and cultural traits. In this conflict between elitist control of the process and its own self-determining qualities (here the line of argument seems occasionally to shift and is not wholly clear), the elitist group can hope to ride the industrializing wave only if it adapts to the necessities which the process imposes. But, in adapting, its own character is

Reprinted by permission from *American Economic Review* 51 (June 1961), pp. 475–480.

changed, and over time all elitist groups tend to become more and more similar. So do their industralized societies. In future generations the world will become one more or less homogenized ball of industrialism except for minor cultural variations of a "Bohemian" nature.

This broadly stated thesis makes an arresting point of departure for the construction of a conceptually-based theory which might then have been tested by reference to the course of development in particular countries. Considering the fact that this volume constitutes the capstone of a five-year project involving 78 persons of 11 nationalities, sponsoring 40 projects in 35 countries, and producing 12 books with 14 more to come, not to mention more than 21 articles, this might not have been out of the question. But no such attempt has been made. There are a few—surprisingly few—casual references to the country studies, but no systematic exploitation of that mountain of material. But perhaps this failure to use the country data systematically in exploring the challenging thesis posed is not so surprising in view of the fact that, in its present vague and unclear statement, it would be impossible to test for anything.

The two key "concepts" in the argument are (1) the industrializing process and (2) the industrializing elites. The relationship (one might almost say the contest) between these two constitutes the leitmotif of the whole volume. It is a fascinating theme—if I seem to be unduly critical of the result it is only because so much promising material has been allowed to go to waste. The notion of a technological movement spreading over the world like some irresistible glacier, transforming societies by the strength of its own "logic," with five types of leader groups in country after country around the world seeking to harness its tremendous powers for their own ends, only themselves to be swept aside or transformed in the process, is a conception as breathtaking as Marx's. But Marx's conclusions rested on concept and theory, however much these erred in particulars. The present study has substituted categories for concepts, assertions for analysis, and impressionistic observation for theoretical abstraction.

Consider "the industrializing process," one of the two "conceptual" bases on which this edifice is built. How do the authors define it? Gertrude Stein could have done no better. "Industrialization refers to the actual course of transition from the traditional society toward industrialism. Industrialism is an abstraction, a limit approached through historical industrialization. Industrialism is the concept of the fully industrialized society, that which the industrialization process inherently tends to create" (p. 33).

It is clear by referring to this as a process and by mention of its historical epochs and the stages of its development that the authors conceive of industrialization as something evolutionary. "However, no country is yet fully industrialized; all economies, including the United States and Great Britain, are still to some extent underdeveloped" (p. 18). What is it then that we in this country are still in the process of becoming? What constitutes "full" or "successful" or "complete" industrialization—adjectives which appear from time to time in the book? How does industrialization differ from the post-agricultural, postcommercial phases of economic development? If it is not equivalent to economic growth (excepting its farming and mercantile aspects), how is it distinguished? Is "full industrialization" the end of the econommic road, beyond which no other stages lie, as it seems to be implied?

What is the "logic" of industrialism, to which the authors devote a chapter? The question is answered there only in terms of a list of characteristics rationally or empirically presumed to be associated with that phenomenon which is left so undefined: a high degree of occupational and social mobility in an open society; an enveloping system of education but geared to technological processes; a highly differentiated labor force subject to a web of rules and structured in occupational and professional associations; an urban dominance of the society; a large role for government by way of regulating and coordinating relationships; a society largely governed by consensus, worldwide in its orientation, and a population whose numbers have been brought under control.

The grounds for associating these traits with industrialism (whose nature we must intuitively grasp or deduce from bits of evidence scattered through the book) are developed in the literate style to which we have become accustomed from each of the authors. But nothing in the chapter builds up to a concept of the "logic" of that irresistible force which is destined to transform the world. There is no sense of an inherent nature of an evolutionary process which builds on itself and which has these characteristics out of some inner necessity. It is almost as though the authors were defining an "ideal" industrialism in terms of these traits. Other writers might "define" it by a different set of characteristics. And this is not the kind of situation where one social scientist can properly ask of another, "Grant me my definition and see what follows," for here "what follows" has been made part of the "definition."

Now, briefly, as to the ideal types of industrializing elites. Of these the authors say (p. 272): "The actual industrializing elites are seldom, if ever, as we have noted earlier, pure or ideal types. They are often both mixed and changing by type, although there is enough of the central theme of the ideal type to permit differentiation and classification of systems. At this stage in history, in the middle of the twentieth century, we can still identify many countries which adhere to one or another of these types; but relatively few of them illustrate the particular type in all its purity. Each type, however, seems to have its own natural tendencies for evolution and thus there exist more or less parallel evolutions for countries equally patterned after a certain type."

The uselessness of this kind of approach to a process analysis is easily demonstrable. If a type has any conceptual usefulness, its counterpart in the real world must be sufficiently akin to it that results which are deduced from the type apply to a real world situation. But if the types overlap, if they are "mixed and changing," application becomes a neat trick, the first aspect of which is to identify to what ideal type (or types) a given society at a given time corresponds. Presumably this cannot always be done, since it is said that in this century we can "still identify many countries" (not all) in this way. Parenthetically, it may be noted, however, that nowhere has any effort been made to establish such identification, except as casual example of some (partial) aspect of a society at some point in its history. The industrialization process has not been traced out in any country in terms of the pattern set forth in this book.

But the difficulties run deeper. With each ideal type there are associated (and described at some length) certain strategies and policies of industrialization, cultural factors, types of management, forms of worker protest, worker organizations, and industrial relations systems. What happens to these associated aspects of industrial society when each elite type follows its "natural tendencies for evolution?" Not until the last chapter, after the basic portions of the framework have all been filled in, are we treated to some speculative and impressionistic observations as to how these changes may take place.

What happens when one of these types succeeds another in the same society, as the last chapter admits not only can happen but avers will happen? Does the whole bundle of associated social characteristics change along with the ideal type of governing elite? Or, as is implied, may certain characteristics implanted by an earlier elite persist even after it has been supplanted by another elite? If so, what does this do to any "natural tendency for evolution," or to any correspondence between actual characteristics of a society and those associated with its ideal type? If we are eventually led to say that no correlation may exist, then of what value as analytical tool is the typology?

The essence of the difficulty lies in the fact that the authors' unfortunate absorption with the ideal-type approach leads them into the necessity of intruding the dynamics of change into a methodological device that is inescapably static. Once they have constructed a roster of the social and institutional characteristics associated with a given type of elite, they are left with the necessity of maintaining that those characteristics are always associated with that type (regardless of how it comes to power or what other elite it succeeds), or else they are faced with the necessity of explaining changes in institutions and elites (which influences the other?) by some form of causal analysis which their typology nowhere provides. Or is it that the succession (evolution?) of elites is brought about by that onsweeping and homogenizing (but still obscure) industrialization process itself? We are left in the realm of speculation for lack of a set of concepts which lend themselves to analysis.

Finally, with respect to the elite types, we are told that of the five, only two are "basic," the dynastic and the middle class. These two plant the colonial type (which is doomed to disappear) and they provoke the nationalistic and revolutionary intellectual types. But then, as we follow with pencil and paper to see where the "natural" evolutionary tendencies of these types will take us, we wind up with a surprising result. We are told (1) that the dynastic type, if it is ineffective, gives way to the nationalistic or intellectual revolutionary. If effective, it develops into a middle-class elite. (2) The colonial type precedes the nationalistic. (3) The nationalistic elite, if ineffective, leads to revolutionary intellectualism, and if effective, to a modified middle class. (4) The revolutionary intellectuals are historically dated, useful only for transitional purposes, and must give way too to a modified middle class. (5) The middle-class elite itself, however, is the most stable of the lot. It changes, but never in history has it been displaced once it was "in full control of the industrialization process."

Tracing these evolutionary paths out to their end results, we discover that the fate of all countries is to wind up under a modified version of the middle-class type. If we can reasonably presume that this type accords most closely with our society, and that our society is the closest prototype extant or emergent of this ideal type, then we are left with the heartening conclusion that given a few generations the whole world will be modeled after what we shall look like at that time.

Let me conclude by saying that there is a great deal in this book which will stimulate one's thinking and lead him off into interesting intellectual paths. The central theme of the book is, as I have said, provocative and exciting. The execution betrays the difficulties of four-author collaboration in reducing a wealth of ideas to a systematic analysis resting on a clearly defined conceptual basis. But let us thank them for reaching for the stars!

# 42

## *Consciousness and Action among the Western Working Class*

MICHAEL MANN                                                                                    1973

The main disadvantage of asking the question, "Is the working class still a force for revolutionary change in the West?" is that most readers will already have decided on an answer. Yet the nature of this answer will vary according to the reader's political persuasion and nationality. Whereas Marxists and many Frenchmen and Italians might be inclined to answer "yes," those to the political Right and to the north-west (in Britain and the United States especially) are more likely to answer "no." Clearly, both groups cannot be correct, though each may be reflecting accurately a segment of the reality of the West today. For, whereas a proletarian revolution seems inconceivable in the United States, only slightly less so in Western Germany and improbable in Great Britain, in France and Italy it appears a distinct possibility, as the dramatic events of May–June 1968 showed. . . . All of these countries are capitalist liberal democracies, at a more or less comparable level of overall technological development and with identifiably "Western" cultural values. Why then the apparent differences between their class relations?

There are two conventional though opposed ways of interpreting these differences coming from the "Right" and from the "Left" of modern class theory—respectively, *the end of ideology thesis* and *Marxism*. Whereas the former views class conflict as decreasing with the development of mature capitalist societies, the latter predicts its increase. Their mutual confidence in predicting comes from a shared quality of economic determinism. Both view the economic process as determining the structure of modern societies, but one sees this as producing class compromise, the other conflict and revolution.

By the label "end of ideology theorists" I describe those American writers, loosely connected with each other and with functionalism, who analysed in the 1950s and 1960s what they saw as a secular and continuing decline in socialist ideology among most of the Western working class. The principal figures were Daniel Bell, Clark Kerr and S. M. Lipset, while much of the detailed research was carried out at the Berkeley Institute of Industrial Relations. Their writings differed, particularly in the extent to which they were willing to predict boldly the future of the West, but it is possible to construct from their themes an "artificial end of ideology" theory. Its central tenet would be that there is an inherent strain in the industrialisation process toward the compromise of class interests and the institutionalisation of conflict. For Clark Kerr and his collaborators this is even part of the "logic" of industrialisation. Unlike Marxists, they see the conflict between capital and labour as being essentially a quantitative economic dispute about "who should get how much" of the surplus. And for some of them a rising standard of prosperity is itself conducive to a decline in conflict. The general view of the group is that, though economic conflict cannot be eliminated, it can be channelled into compromise bargaining which then reinforces its own precondition, the growth of the surplus available for distribution. In this way conflict becomes *functional*. Thus, for example, the militancy of American trade unions is regarded as pressurising management into cost-reduction and greater efficiency, to the potential benefit of both capital and labour. Institutionalisation also isolates each type of conflict from other types, and class conflict is fragmented into separate industrial, political, etc., disputes. "Class" conflict consequently does not threaten social stability and may be actually functional for the existing

---

Reprinted from *Consciousness and Action among the Western Working Class* by Michael Mann, pp. 9–11, 68–69. By permission of Humanities Press International, Inc., Atlantic Highlands, N.J.

structure of society. In this way the economic determinism of Marxism has been turned against itself, and most "end of ideology" theorists paint the institutionalised politics and the industrial relations of the West in fairly rosy colours. It should also be noted that phenomena such as work deprivation or alienation rarely appear in their analyses, and we are generally left with the impression that the working class is reasonably content with its role in existing society.

These writers are well aware that some Western countries still exhibit an apparently high level of class conflict. But they argue that this is caused by extra-industrial elements of society. France and Italy are their normal examples, and the turbulence of French and Italian class relations are attributed to such factors as "dynastic" or tradition-minded *élites,* a religion which disparages economic activity and a labour force recently uprooted from a rural setting. As Lipset expresses it, class conflict there is "a function of the extent to which the enduring economic struggle among the classes overlapped with the issues concerning the place of religion and the traditional status structure".... And the persistent economic determinism of these writers generally leads them to predict, more or less boldly, that "tradition" will give way before the modernising, secular, urban and democratic influence of industry and thus precipitate a decline in class conflict and in the ideology of socialism (among the working class). From "the end of ideology" perspective, therefore, we would conclude that severe class conflict is a product of extra-industrial elements of society and will decline with further industrialisation.

■　■　■

Before turning to more complex questions of theory we can quickly dismiss the harmonistic tinge of the more extreme versions of "the end of ideology" thesis. Even relatively successful bargaining between employer and worker does not answer all the important needs of workers. Whatever other industrial attitudes they may hold, workers show unmistakable signs of conscious deprivation which we might well wish to term *alienation.* This holds for all the countries we have examined.

Yet alienation does not express the worker's total consciousness or explain his behaviour fully. Indeed, at every turn we have been confronted by a profound *dualism* in the worker's situation and his consciousness. Co-existing with a normally passive sense of alienation is an experience of (largely economic) interdependence with the employer at a factual, if not a normative, level. Surges of class consciousness are continually undercut by economism, and capitalism survives. Yet this is a much less even and harmonistic process than "the end of ideology" implies. There is a distinct lack of fit between the two halves of consciousness, producing erratic and often chaotic industrial relations punctuated by genuine "explosions" of consciousness. Action cannot be consistent when consciousness is contradictory, and this is the obstacle to revolution as well as to harmony.

In short, we must reject both rival claims that the Capital–Labour relationship contains an inherent tendency toward either revolution or harmonistic stability. Once we do this, we can see that the "end of ideology" theorists have practised a sleight-of-hand (I hope an unconscious one) upon us. While correctly pointing out the way in which extra-industrial factors have heightened class conflict in countries like France or Italy, they have drawn attention away from the fact that the relative industrial peace of countries such as the United States may be equally produced by extra-industrial causes (such as, for example, racial divisions in the American working class). A genuine multi-factor explanation is needed on this side, too.

# 43

## *The Industrial System and the Union*

**JOHN KENNETH GALBRAITH**          1967

Unions within the industrial system have long since ceased to expand and have, indeed, lost ground. In almost any view they are less militant in attitude and less powerful in politics than in earlier times. Industrial relations have become markedly more peaceful as collective bargaining has come to be accepted by the modern large industrial enterprise. Unions and their leaders are widely accepted and on occasion accorded a measure of applause for sound social behavior both by employers and the community at large. All this suggests some change.

The present analysis foretells further such change and leads to the conclusion that it has durable significance. The loss of union membership is not a temporary setback pending the organization of white-collar employees and engineers but the earlier stages of a permanent decline. The increasingly conciliatory character of modern industrial relations, especially in the larger corporation, has come about not because labor leaders and vice presidents in charge of labor relations have entered upon an era of pacific enlightenment, the operative agent being the rise of industrial statesmanship and the somewhat delayed triumph of Judeo-Christian ethics and the golden rule. It has come about because interests that were once radically opposed are now much more nearly in harmony. Behavior is not better; it is merely that interests are concordant. Were interests still opposed, labor relations would still be characterized by argument and invective, accented on occasion by clubs, stones, and low-yield explosives. The unquestioned expertise of the modern industrial relations man would not appreciably ease the passion.

All of the changes here examined—the shift in power from ownership and the entrepreneur to the technostructure,[1] technological advance, the regulation of markets and aggregate demand, and the imperatives of price and wage regulation—have had an effect on the position of the union. In every case they have subtracted from its role.

The employee was linked to the entrepreneurial firm by pecuniary motivation. There was an unquestioned conflict in pecuniary interest between the employee and employer. . . . An increase in labor costs, when the firm was already maximizing profits, could only reduce profits. These profits, or a substantial share of them, accrued to the entrepreneur. And his interest in pecuniary return, since among other things it rewarded the capital he supplied or commanded, was also strong.

The union, in these circumstances, had the power, unavailable to the individual worker, of forcing the employer to accept the higher costs and reduced profits, by threatening the even greater cost and profit reduction of a strike. It follows that the employer had every reason to resist the union and regret its existence. And the worker had equal reason for wanting it. The resistance of the employer might keep the union from gaining a foothold. But its importance to the worker was equally a factor in giving it strength. Additionally, the man who sided with the employer was abetting the income of another man instead of his own. If he was rewarded he was a fink and if not he was a fool. In either case any tendency he might have to identify himself with the goals of the employer could be regarded with contempt and be, by the union, so characterized.

In the United States the classic last-ditch battles against the unions . . . were all waged by entrepreneurs. All these were in industries in which mature corporations led the way in surrender.

The first goal of the technostructure is its own security. Profits, provided that they are above the minimum necessary for security, are secondary to growth. Labor relations, naturally enough, are conducted in accordance with the goals of the technostructure.

This means that the technostructure may readily trade profits for protection against such an undirected event with such an unpredictable outcome as a strike. Once again there is the important fact that those who make the decision during union negotiations do not themselves have to pay.

But no reduction in profits may be required from yielding to the union. Since the mature firm does not maximize profits, it can maintain income by increasing its prices. The wage settlement, since it affects all or most firms in the industry, provides all with a common signal to consider such action. Its effect on growth will, of course, be considered. But since this will be the same for all firms in the industry, and since the regulation of aggregate demand keeps the latter at a high level, price increases will often seem allowable.

No absolute rule can be laid down on the reaction of the technostructure to a union demand. It will depend on the existing level of prices and earnings, the effectiveness of the management of demand for the products or product, the importance of wage costs and other factors. But in general the mature corporation in the pursuit of its own goals will accede far more readily than the entrepreneurial enterprise to the demands of the union, and accordingly, is much less averse to its existence. It may even pay something for what is called a good employer image. These tendencies, far more than Christian revelation, explain the harmony that increasingly characterizes the labor relations of the mature corporation, to the pride of all concerned.

But while the task of the union is much easier, the union is also much less essential for the worker. What the technostructure gives to the union, it can also give without a union or to avoid having a union. At a minimum the union shrinks in stature. A fighting lawyer is a figure of great majesty before a hanging judge. His stature is less before one who places everyone on probation.

It has long been a minor tenet of trade union doctrine that all employers are essentially alike. All seek their own best gain. All, accordingly, are inimical to the interest of the worker. Thus any worker who identifies his interest with that of his boss is making a mistake. The vehemence with which this doctrine has been enunciated in modern times may indicate uneasiness as to the truth of the proposition in the case of the mature corporation. Such teaching was not so necessary in the age of the Homestead massacre and the Pullman strike. In any case it is not true.

As compared with the entrepreneurial firm, not only is there a much less flat opposition of interest between workers in the mature corporation and those who have the power of decision on matters relating to wages and other conditions of employment, but identification is part of the established and accepted system of motivation. And, although identification is most important in the technostructure, its existence there serves to make it a more general tendency. Loyalty to the firm will often be part of the general mood. This is adverse to the union. Additionally, in the earlier stages of industrial technology— in the early steel mills or on the early automobile assembly lines—hard, repetitive and tedious work acted as a barrier to identification. Among machinists, toolmakers, steam fitters and other skilled workers there was the sense of common interest arising from a shared skill. As machinery replaces both repetitive and drudging work and eliminates skilled occupations, it lowers these barriers to identification. This increases the difficulties of organization and thus adds to the problems of the union.

But much more important, modern technology opens the way for a massive shift from workers who are within the reach of unions to those who are not. Both the capital resources and the goals of the technostructure of the mature corporation strongly facilitate and encourage such a shift. . . . In its planning, the technostructure seeks to minimize the number of contingencies that are beyond its control. Labor costs and supply are significantly of this character and more so when there is a union. To substitute capital, in the form of machinery, the supply and cost of which are wholly or largely under control, for labor which is not and which can strike, is an admirable bargain. It is worth the sacrifice of some earnings. It is also adverse to the union for that is the purpose.

The substitution, as earlier noticed, has been proceeding rapidly. In the eighteen years from 1947 to 1965, white-collar workers in the United States—professional, managerial, office and sales workers—increased by 9.6 million. In these years blue-collar workers—craftsmen, operatives, and laborers, farmers and miners apart—decreased by 4 million. By 1965 there were nearly 8 million more white- than blue-collar workers—44.5 million as compared with 36.7 million. During these years the number of professional and technical workers, the category most characteristic of the technostructure, approximately doubled. No other group had increased so rapidly. In industries strongly typical of the industrial system the change has been much more dramatic. Between 1947 and 1965 the number of white-collar workers increased from 16.4 to 25.6 per cent of employed workers in manufacturing. In the primary metal industries the increase was from 12.9 to 18.3 per cent; in fabricated metal products from 16.5 to 22.6 per cent; in transportation equipment (automotive and aircraft) it was from 18.5 to 28.7 per cent; in electrical equipment it was from 21.7 to 31.5 per cent.

White-collar workers have rarely been susceptible to organization in the United States and, with the rise of the technostructure, they are almost certainly less so. In the entrepreneurial corporation a visible line divided the bosses—those whose position depended on ownership or their ability to produce profits for the owners—from clerks, bookkeepers, timekeepers, secretaries, salesmen and others who were purely employees. In the mature corporation this line disappears. Decision is divorced from ownership; the location of decision moves in the direction of the body of white-collar workers. Distinctions between those who make decisions and those who carry them out, and between employer and employee, are obscured by the technicians, scientists, market analysts, computer programmers, industrial stylists and other specialists who do, or are, both. A continuum thus exists between the center of the technostructure and the more routine white-collar workers on the fringe. At some point, power or the chance for moving toward the center becomes negligible. But it is no longer possible to recognize that point.

In consequence, white-collar workers identify themselves with the technostructure from which they are not visibly distinct. A survey of such workers in 1957 showed that more than three-quarters regarded themselves as being more closely associated with management than with production workers. As a result, they have remained unorganized. For them, "Persuasion, pressure, and manipulation [and bureaucratic gamesmanship] . . . take the place of the face-to-face combat of an earlier age."

. . . If unemployment is endemic and incomes are close to the minimum required for physical survival, men are held to their jobs by the threat of physical suffering. In these circumstances the union greatly enhances the liberty of the worker. The worker cannot walk off the job by himself. But he knows that if things become intolerable he can walk off with all of the others. Shared privation is easier to bear than individual privation. And a union may have strike pay or a soup kitchen to mitigate, however slightly, the hardship involved.

Both high employment and high income are solvents for the sense of compulsion and thus are substitutes for the union. If employment is high, there will be alternative jobs. Accordingly, a man can quit. It is the high employment, not the union, that rescues him from his slavish dependence on the job he holds. In the United States, as in Britain, Canada and elsewhere, the regulation of aggregate demand to insure high employment was strongly pressed by the unions. It was the accommodation of the state to the needs of the industrial system that the labor movement most sought. It was the thing most designed to make unions less needed.

High income also lessens the danger of fear of physical privation. Thus it accords the worker liberty that he once obtained from the union. And, therefore, it too weakens dependence on the union. . . .

■   ■   ■

The industrial system, it seems clear, is unfavorable to the union. Power passes to the technostructure and this lessens the conflict of interest between employer and employee which gave the union much of its reason for existence. Capital and technology allow the firm to substitute white-collar workers and machines that cannot be organized for blue-collar workers that can. The regulation of aggregate demand, the resulting high level of employment together with the general increase in well-being all, on balance, make the union less necessary or less powerful or both. The conclusion seems inevitable. The union belongs to a particular stage in the development of the industrial system. When that stage passes so does the union in anything like its original position of power. And, as an added touch of paradox, things for which the unions fought vigorously—the regulation of aggregate demand to insure full employment and higher real income for members—have contributed to their decline.

Yet it would be premature to write off the union entirely. Numerous organizations —the Fishmongers and the Cordwainers in the City of London, the House Un-American Activities Committee in Washington—regularly survive their function. Once a union is in being there is nothing in continuing its existence—the collection or deduction of dues, the enrollment of newly hired members, the holding of conventions and the designation of officers—that is nearly so difficult as bringing it to an end. And while the industrial system undermines old functions, it does not eliminate them entirely, and it does add some new ones. Finally, not all unions are within the industrial system and those outside have a better prospect. The overall effect of the rise of the industrial system is greatly to reduce the union as a social force. But it will not disappear or become entirely unimportant.

The trend in union strength is clearly adverse. After 1957, total union membership in the United States began to fall and in the next five years, although the number of workers in nonagricultural employment increased by more than four million, the number enrolled in unions fell by 1.7 million. . . . The decline was especially severe in manufacturing, and within manufacturing the unions suffering the most severe losses were the Automobile Workers and the Steelworkers. Both are in industries strongly characteristic of the industrial system. . . .

. . . White-collar workers including technical and professional workers are a rapidly expanding proportion of the labor force. . . . Only about 12 per cent of all white-collar workers belong to unions and in manufacturing the proportion is only about 5 per cent.

Nor is the white-collar worker the only problem. Production workers in areas of advanced technology—computer and data-processing industries, instrumentation, telemetry, specified electronics, and the like—are not easily organized. If the number of production workers is large and the firm has closely related branches that have unions, the new workers are often added to the existing unions without difficulty. In isolated branches or otherwise unorganized firms, or where the proportion of engineers and technicians is high, the unions do not make headway. The workers, in effect, become an extension of the technostructure and evidently so see themselves.

However, there are opposing trends. In the early stages of industrialization the working force was, as previously noted, a homogeneous mass. Members could be paid and treated alike or, at most, they fell into a few simple classifications. The modern working force, by contrast, is highly differentiated. The rules that regulate pay, other benefits, seniority and conditions of promotion and retirement for the various classes of workers are voluminous. Any unilateral application of such rules would, however meticulous, seem arbitrary or unjust to some. By helping to frame the rules and by participating in their administration through the grievance machinery, the union serves invaluably to mitigate the feeling that such systems or their administration are arbitrary or unjust. It is a measure of the importance of this function that, where the union does not exist, good management practice calls for the development of some substitute. In helping to prevent discontent and, therewith, a sense of alienation, the union also removes barriers to identification—barriers which once contributed to its own power.

Also, while some unions have resisted technological change, others have greatly helped it by aiding the accommodation to change. They have helped to arrange a trade of higher pay, a shorter week, severance pay or other provision for those sacrificed for smaller employment. And they have persuaded their members to accept the bargain. The industrial system attaches great importance to such help. The union leader who provides it is accorded its highest encomium, that of labor statesman.

In the Soviet-type economies, the union has long had an ambiguous and somewhat unsettled role. As the historic voice of the worker in the class struggle, it had to exist and be nurtured. But unions could not be accorded any role which was inconsistent with the full identification of their members with the goals of the firm by which they were employed. In the end their functions have been much the same as those just mentioned. Along with educational and welfare activities, which are also of some importance in some American and Western European unions, the Soviet unions serve as a channel of communications between the firm and its workers and a way of according the latter a voice in the framing of rules and in their administration.

However, in the non-Soviet systems the union renders a further service; it is an important factor in planning and, therewith, in the relations of the industrial system with the state.

We have already noticed that the unions assumed the principal role in winning approval of the policy of regulating aggregate demand. Though commonly billed as having the objective of providing full employment, this policy is also essential for the planning of the industrial system. Unions furthermore have a potentially important role in stabilizing demand for particular products procured by the state. Such procurement, that for defense needs in particular, cannot be claimed as something that serves the needs of the firm. It must be regarded strictly as an outgrowth of broad public policy. So, in seeking contracts, the technostructure cannot publicly plead the pressure of its own convenience, necessity or earnings. But it can with more decency plead the adverse effect of contract termination, or failure to win renewal, or denial of a new contract on its workers or the community. Here the union can be a valuable seconding voice. Such cooperation between unions and technostructure is by no means complete; in all legislative matters there is a good deal of traditional hostility to overcome.

The much more important service of the union to planning is to standardize wage costs between different industrial firms and to insure that changes in wages will occur at approximately the same time. This greatly assists price control by the industry. And it also greatly facilitates the public regulation of prices and wages. Both services are far more important than is commonly recognized.

Specifically, if there is an industry-wide union, one of its tasks will be to insure that rates of pay will be more or less the same for the same kinds of work. This is done in the name of fairness and equity but it means too that no firm can reduce prices because of lower wage rates and none will be impelled to seek higher prices because its rates of pay are higher. Price-setting and maintenance where there are a number of firms are thus facilitated. So is planning.

Rates will also change when the labor contract for the industry expires. This change will affect all firms at approximately the same time and by approximately the same amount. All accordingly have a common signal to adjust their prices; the same change is called for by all. So wage adjustment and related changes, which might otherwise be a threat to minimum price setting in the industry, cease to be a serious problem.

At the same time the union contract brings wage levels within the purview of the state. The situation here is akin to that of diplomacy. It may be difficult to do business with a strong government such as that of the Soviet Union. But when business is done, something is accomplished. This is not the case where, as with the Congo, Laos or South Viet Nam, the writ of the government runs only to the airport. There is no way of enforcing that to which governments agree. Similarly wage control may be difficult with a union. The latter may resist energetically the terms. But it also brings workers within the ambit of control.

The union negotiates a bargain that is binding on all of its members. If this bargain can be influenced by the state then the level of wages is subject to influence—or control. And since collective bargaining contracts are for some period of time—a period that, in yet another accommodation to the industrial system, is tending to become longer—the number of occasions when the state must intervene is kept down to a practical number. In between, the contract acts as a ceiling on wage payments. Were wage bargains struck by individuals or for a vast number of small categories of workers, and were they of indeterminate duration, control and surveillance would be impossible.

The union renders a yet further service. The commonplace strategy of wage and price stabilization is to hold wage increases within the amounts that can be paid from gains in productivity. The amount of the productivity gain—the increase in output per worker—only becomes known over time. And it differs for different firms. The period of the contract allows time for knowledge of the gains in productivity to accumulate and for calculation as to what increase can be afforded without prejudice to price stability. The union, since it bargains for an industry-wide membership, settles not for what the individual firm can afford, which would mean different wage rates for different firms, which would be an impossible complication, but for what all can afford as an average. This is an invaluable simplification.

The union does not render these services to wage and price stabilization deliberately or even willingly. It has no choice. Should it refuse to conform to a broad strategy of stabilization, the firms with which it has contracts would, in turn, raise their prices. If an appreciable number of unions get wage advances greater than justified by gains in productivity, then all must be accorded them. Responding price increases will then be general. And part of all of the gains from wage increases will be lost in price increases. The union will have opposed public authority, and perhaps risked popular displeasure, for gains that its own members will recognize to be transitory. This alternative may, on occasion, be tried. But it is not an attractive alternative. Nor is it one that strengthens the union.

In fact the industrial system has now largely encompassed the labor movement. It has dissolved some of its most important functions; it has greatly narrowed its area of action; and it has bent its residual operations very largely to its own needs. Since World War II, the acceptance of the union by the industrial firm and the emergence thereafter of an era of comparatively peaceful industrial relations have been hailed as the final triumph of trade unionism. On closer examination it is seen to reveal many of the features of Jonah's triumph over the whale.

---

[1][Galbraith defines the technostructure as "all who participate in group decision-making or the organization which they form."—*Eds.*]

# 44

## The Affluent Worker in the Class Structure

JOHN H. GOLDTHORPE, DAVID LOCKWOOD,
FRANK BECHHOFER, AND JENNIFER PLATT                    1969

Outside the circle of 'fundamentalist' believers, the continuing lack of historical validation for Marx's theory of the working class encouraged numerous more critical appraisals. Sympathisers as much as adversaries attempted to identify the particular deficiencies in Marx's analysis of capitalism which could be related to developments within modern western society that he had manifestly failed to anticipate. . . .

■    ■    ■

Thus, . . . not only a systematic critique of Marx but also an alternative theory of the evolution of the working class became possible. That is, a theory asserting not the inevitable transformation of a "class in itself" into a "class for itself"—which would then, until the day of reckoning, encamp within capitalist society like a hostile army—but rather a theory of the progressive *integration* of the working class into the institutional structure of capitalism; this being brought about on the one hand by the purposive modification of this structure and on the other by the "natural" development of the capitalist economy. A theory on these lines, although never fully worked out by any one writer, could in fact be regarded as at least the implicit basis of the case against Marx as this stood around the mid-point of the twentieth century.[1] What essentially was called into question was the *revolutionary potential* of the working class—it's mission to act as the gravedigger of capitalism: what was emphasised was the apparent readiness of the mass of wage workers under capitalism to accept the responsibilities along with the rights of national citizenship and to pursue their objectives through organisations which recognised "the rules of the game" within both the industrial and political sectors.

This, then, was the stage which the debate on the working class had reached by the time that the advanced societies of the West began to recover from the effects of the second world war. From this period onwards, however, it is important to recognise that a further distinctive phase in the debate commences. Against a background of sharply accelerating social change, new issues were opened up and old ones appeared in different forms.

In the years in question, economic growth, in North America and western Europe in particular, went rapidly ahead. The era of "high mass consumption" was generally achieved and the coming of the "affluent society" was, at all events, frequently proclaimed. At the same time further important, if less widespread, changes were occurring on the side of production. The second industrial revolution was sweeping aside the satanic mills of the first and creating new types of factory. Managements were becoming increasingly concerned with "human relations," while automated or process production systems gave rise to conditions of work which, from both a physical and a social point of view, differed markedly from those characteristic of an earlier age of industry. Further still, extensive changes were also in progress in patterns of residence and community life.

Reprinted with permission of the publisher from *The Affluent Worker in the Class Structure* by John H. Goldthorpe, David Lockwood, Frank Bechhofer, and Jennifer Platt, pp. 4–12, 162–163, 165–166, 178–179, 195. Copyright © 1969 by Cambridge University Press. Footnotes in the original have been eliminated or renumbered.

On the one hand, the movement of population from rural to urban areas continued, and at an increasing rate in many regions; on the other, the great towns and cities in all the advanced societies of the West spilled out the inhabitants of their older, more central districts into the suburbs or rapidly expanding fringe areas and commuter belts. Thus, many long-established communities were disrupted and many new ones created, together with their distinctive opportunities and problems.

Under the impact of changes of these kinds, new lines of thought emerged concerning the destiny of the working class, and ones which went clearly beyond the former, negative argument that this class could no longer be realistically considered, even in potential, as a revolutionary force. Rather, a major and recurrent theme—and most notably in liberal quarters—was that of the incipient *decline* and *decomposition* of the working class. As the development of industrial societies continued, it was suggested, the working class, understood as a social stratum with its own distinctive ways of life, values and goals, would become increasingly eroded by the main currents of change. The very idea of a working class had been formed in, and in fact belonged to, the infancy of industrial society: in the era to come it would steadily lose its empirical referent. Social inequalities would no doubt persist; but these would be modified and structured in such a way that the society of the future would be an overwhelmingly "middle-class" society, within which the divisions of the past would no longer be recognisable.

In other words, the developmental—even, perhaps, the historicist—perspectives of Marx and the Marxists were revived. But in place of a theory of working-class revolution as the inevitable culmination and conclusion of capitalism, there was proposed a theory of the progressive disappearance of the working class as part of the inherent logic of industrialism. The Marxist claim that the development of the forces of production is the ultimate determinant of the pattern of stratification and of the balance of cohesive and disruptive forces within society was generally accepted: but a radically different view was taken of the consequences of this relationship in the past and for the future. In brief, the contention was that, as expressed by one prominent author, "history has validated a basic premise of Marxist sociology, at the expense of Marxist politics."[2]

What, then, in more detail are the arguments that have been advanced in support of this theory of the working-class in decline? Three main types of change which stimulated new thinking have been alluded to: economic, technological and managerial, and ecological. The ways in which each of these have been seen as shaping and defining the future of the working class may be usefully considered in turn.

So far as the consequences of economic changes are concerned, the particular development to which most importance has been attached is that usually referred to as the "homogenisation" of incomes and living standards. In the course of the 1950s, statistics became available in most of the advanced societies of the West which suggested that, concomitantly with the general increase in prosperity, a significant expansion was taking place in the numbers of individuals or families in receipt of middle-sized incomes. Quite apart from the degree to which the overall range of economic inequality was being reduced, an increasing proportion of the population appeared to be falling into the intermediate brackets of the income scale—to the extent, in fact, that several writers referred to the need to discard the old idea of an income pyramid and to think rather of a "diamond-shaped" distribution.[3] Moreover, the major source of this expansion it could be claimed, lay in the marked increase in incomes that had been achieved, from around the end of the 1940s, among many sections of the working class: that is to say, the new middle-income group was to be seen as largely the result of the relatively rapid economic

*351*

advance of substantial numbers of manual workers and their families who had been able to secure incomes comparable to those of many white-collar employes and smaller independents.

Consistently with this, statistics on consumption patterns could also be adduced as evidence of the blurring of class differences, in economic terms at least. For example, the possession of various kinds of consumer durables—television sets, record players, vacuum cleaners, washing machines—was evidently becoming fairly general, while increasingly too manual workers were invading the hitherto almost exclusively middle-class preserves of car- and house-ownership. Surveys carried out by consumers research agencies led to enthusiastic reports on the immense possibilities offered by the newly emergent "middle market."

On this basis, it became possible to argue that one defining characteristic of the working class, as traditionally conceived, was fast being obliterated: that is, its clearly inferior position in terms of economic resources and consumer power. The existence of a large class of "have-nots," it could be held, was a necessary feature of industrial society in its early phases; but at the stage of development now being attained, the nature of the economy ensures—and indeed requires—that the bulk of the population enjoy middle-class living standards. Severe economic deprivation may still exist in the case of certain special groups, but this can no longer be the lot of the mass of the manual labour force. In the words of one exponent of this point of view: "A mass-oriented economy depends on a mass-market . . . The very existence of families able to afford Cadillacs depends on the existence of millions of families able to buy Chevrolets."[4]

Furthermore, arguments concerning the homogenisation of living standards have typically led on to claims concerning homogenisation at a cultural level also. The achievement by increasing numbers of manual workers of middle-sized incomes has been widely regarded as providing them with their *entrée* into middle-class worlds from which they were previously excluded; as enabling them to participate in middle-class life-styles which were previously beyond their means and to share in values that were hitherto inappropriate to their material conditions and expectations. In regard to modes of speech and dress, eating habits and styles of décor, entertainment, leisure activities, child-rearing practices and parental aspirations—to mention only some topics—it has been argued that the more affluent sections of the working class at least are taking over middle-class models, norms and attitudes. As the working class ceases to be distinctive in terms of its economic position, so its distinctiveness as a cultural entity is also steadily diminished.

In this way, then, the Marxian notion of the *embourgeoisement* of the manual worker re-appears: this process being now understood, however, not as some temporary irregularity, occasioned by the uneven development of capitalism, but rather as an integral part of the evolution of industrial society in its post-capitalist phase. Indeed, what is being claimed is another complete reversal of a Marxian prediction: instead of salaried employees becoming homogeneous in all important respects with the proletariat and joining the latter in its political struggle, "the 'proletarian' workers are becoming homogenous with the white-collar workers and are joining the middle class."[5]

Turning next to changes in technology and industrial management, the implications of these have been seen as reinforcing the process of *embourgeoisement* in two major ways. In the first place, a connection is made between technological progress in industry and the sharp increase in incomes experienced by certain groups within the labour force; that is, by those workers who are employed in the most advanced sectors and plants and who benefit from the fact that in the enterprises in which they work productivity is exceptionally high and labour costs represent only a relatively low proportion of total costs. Furthermore, with some forms of advanced technology, the work-tasks employees perform do not require great physical exertion and the level of output is not primarily determined by the degree of effort they expend. This is so, for example, where their work is mainly concerned with the monitoring or regulating of largely automatic or "continuous flow" production systems. Consequently, it has been also argued that men performing such tasks are differentiated from the traditional type of industrial worker in more than economic terms alone. While the latter earns his livelihood through selling his labour power—through engaging in a direct "money for effort" bargain—these new workers are employed chiefly to exercise their knowledge and experience and, above all, to act responsibly in regard to the requirements of the production process. They perform therefore the functions of technicians rather than of hands or operatives; and increasingly too, it is claimed, this is being recognised by mangement in that these workers are often accorded virtually white-collar status within the plant including conditions of service of a "staff" character.

In sum, then, the contention here is that in the most progressive branches of industry—those which may be expected to set the pattern for the future—the division between manual and nonmanual grades, between "works" and "staff," is breaking down. The work situation of the majority of employees is such that these categories no longer apply: it was through the development of the "forces of production" that such categories were initially created and it is through this development too that they are now being outmoded.⁶

Secondly, technological change has also been seen as having an important influence within the enterprise in altering attitudes to work and in restructuring social relationships at shop-floor level. As industrial technology goes beyond conventional mass production methods, it is held, not only do work-tasks become in general less stressful and more inherently rewarding but, in addition, advanced production systems and the progressive management policies associated with them are such as to further encourage the "integration" of rank-and-file workers into their employing organisations.

For instance, while mass production typically involves individuals working at fragmented and repetitive work-tasks under restrictive conditions, automated or process production often brings men together in relatively small and tightly-knit teams within which they can perform a variety of tasks. At the same time, such workers usually enjoy greater autonomy in planning and organising their work and greater freedom of movement about the plant. Then again, most advanced production systems make it likely that both specialist staff and operating managers will be brought into direct and frequent contact with members of the rank-and-file, and on an essentially consultative and collaborative basis. The primary function of works management is no longer that of maintaining discipline or extracting effort but that of collecting and disseminating information and of giving expert advice and assistance: consequently, the possibility of relatively harmonious and co-operative management-worker relations is significantly enhanced. Finally, it is suggested that the social integration of the enterprise is further aided by the fact that the operation of a highly complex technology imposes a *common* discipline upon superiors and subordinates alike. In, say, a fully automatic factory or a chemical plant or refinery, the system of control which bears upon employees is recognised by them as being inherent in the production process itself and as applying to the enterpise as a whole. It is not interpreted as an exercise of managerial authority in pursuit of specifically managerial interests. Once more, then, the likelihood of harmony rather than of conflict is favoured; workers are helped to *identify* with their enterprise instead of viewing the employment relationship in the old oppositional terms of "us" and "them."

353

In these several ways, therefore, it is claimed that the alienation of the industrial worker is being progressively overcome. As one author, Robert Blauner, has expressed it, alienation in industry is to be seen as following "a course that could be charted on a graph by means of an inverted U-curve." That is to say, alienation was at its most extreme in the period which followed the disruption of craft industry and which saw the introduction of large-scale mass production based on the assembly-line principle. But, with the still further technological advances of recent years, conditions have again been created under which men can perform "meaningful work in a more cohesive, integrated industrial climate." As a result, the "social personality" of workers in the most evolved types of enterprise now "tends toward that of the new middle class, the white-collar worker in bureaucratic industry . . . Generally lukewarm to unions and loyal to his employer, the blue-collar employee in the continuous process industries may be a worker 'organisation man' in the making."[7]

Lastly, then, in regard to what we have termed ecological changes, we can again distinguish two main lines of argument that have been advanced in support of the thesis of "the worker turning middle class." As was noted earlier, the changes in question involved the continuing expansion of the urban population as a result of the "drift" from the countryside and at the same time the spread of urban areas as central districts are redeveloped and new suburbs, estates and satellite communities are created. A variety of writers have sought to show that through both of these processes the distinctiveness of the working class as a cultural and social entity is being reduced and further that the merging of working class and middle class is thereby facilitated.

■  ■  ■

We regard with some scepticism the broad evolutionary perspectives on western industrialism in which the emergence of a "middle-class" society is seen as a central process, resulting more or less automatically from continuing economic growth. In particular, we must be sceptical of the reliance that is placed on rising affluence, advances in technical organisation in industry and changing patterns of urban residence as forces likely in themselves to bring about a radical restructuring of the stratification hierarchy. Such developments may certainly be expected to have a powerful effect on the material conditions of life and on the material attributes of members of the working class, as indeed of all strata; for example, on their incomes and possessions, on the kinds of job they do, on the kinds of houses and localities they live in, and so on. But, as we understand it, social stratification is ultimately a matter of sanctioned social relationships; and while major changes in the respects above mentioned will obviously exert an influence on such relationships, this is not *necessarily* one which transforms class and status structures or the positions of individuals and groups within these structures. A factory worker can double his living standards and still remain a man who sells his labour to an employer in return for wages; he can work at a control panel rather than on an assembly line without changing his subordinate position in the organisation of production: he can live in his own house in a "middle-class" estate or suburb and still remain little involved in white-collar social worlds. In short, class and status relationships do not change entirely *pari passu* with changes in the economic, technological and ecological infrastructure of social life: they have rather an important degree of autonomy, and can thus accommodate considerable change in this infrastructure without themselves changing in any fundamental way.

However, while our main point remains that the *embourgeoisement* thesis, and the general view of industrialism of which it forms part, seriously exaggerate the changes in stratification that have accompanied the development of industrial economies, this point should perhaps be accompanied by two disclaimers. First, we do not, of course, seek to rule out the possibility of more basic changes occurring in the pattern of social stratification, and conceivably ones in the direction of a more "middle-class" society, at some future stage. In this regard we would only observe that such changes would appear to depend on certain fairly radical institutional alterations—in industrial organisation, in educational systems and so on—of a kind which have not yet occurred to any marked extent, and which are unlikely to do so unless purposive action of a political character is undertaken to that end. Secondly, and more importantly, in rejecting the idea of *embourgeoisement* as part of a logic of industrialism we in no way wish to imply that the effect of economic development on working-class social life has been a negligible one. On the contrary, our own research indicates clearly enough how increasing affluence and its correlates can have many far-reaching consequences—both in undermining the viability or desirability of established life-styles and in encouraging or requiring the development of new patterns of attitudes, behaviour and relationships.

■  ■  ■

The idea that under the economic and social conditions of advanced industrialism trade unions begin to lose their functions and thus their appeal for the industrial labour force is one which has by now gained some prominence in the American literature. It is argued, for example, that especially in the presence of the modern large-scale enterprise, the collective protection of workers' interests becomes less and less necessary; that affluent workers develop a preference for individual independence; and that employees at all levels tend increasingly to identify with their firms and their managements. . . .[8]

■  ■  ■

How, then, can we best draw together the diverse observations that we have been led to make on the whole question of the probable future modes of action of the new working class in both the industrial and political spheres? While the complexity of the matter is obviously such as to make any simple statement perilous, the results of our study would appear to offer grounds for at least the two following conclusions as regards the British case. First: that it is mistaken to suppose that the economic and social attributes characteristic of "vanguard" groups within the industrial labour force are incompatible with their continued adherence to the traditional *forms* of working-class collectivism; that is, trade unionism and electoral support for the Labour Party. Secondly, however, that although these groups may still regard the unions and the Labour Party as organisations which have some special claim on their allegiance, their attachment to them *could* certainly become an increasingly instrumental—and thus conditional —kind, and one devoid of all sense of participation in a class *movement* seeking structural changes in society or even pursuing more limited ends through concerted class action. In short, the idea of any necessary decline in working-class collectivism within the affluent society may be rejected as theoretically and empirically unsound: but the meaning of this collectivism and the nature of its objectives are clearly not impervious to those changes in working-class life with which our study has been centrally concerned.

■  ■  ■

Thus, our conclusion must be that if the working class does in the long term become no more than one stratum within a system of "classless inegalitarianism," offering no basis for or response to radical initiatives, then this situation will not be adequately explained either as an inevitable outcome of the evolution of industrialism or as reflecting the ability of neo-capitalism to contain the consequences of its changing infrastructure by means of mass social-psychological manipulation. It will to some degree be also attributable to the fact that the political leaders of the working class *chose* this future for it.

---

[1]As among the most important of the works in which this case is embodied, although in different contexts and with differing emphases, one could cite the following: Theodor Geiger, *Die Klassengesellschaft im Schmelztiegel* (Cologne and Hagan, 1949); T. H. Marshall, *Citizenship and Social Class* (Cambridge,1950); Dahrendorf, *Class and Class Conflict in Industrial Society*; and Reinhard Bendix, *Work and Authority in Industry* (New York, 1956). See also the important essay by Bendix, "Transformations of Western European Societies since the Eighteenth Century," in his *Nation Building and Citizenship* (New York, 1964).

[2]S. M. Lipset, "The Changing Class Structure of Contemporary European Politics," *Daedalus*, vol. 63, no. 1 (1964). Probably the most comprehensive statement of the theory in question is to be found in Clark Kerr, John T. Dunlop, Frederick H. Harbison and Charles A. Myers, *Industrialism and Industrial Man* (London, 1962). Also influential, though containing few direct references to changes in class structure, has been W. W. Rostow, *The Stages of Economic Growth: A Non-Communist Manifesto* (Cambridge, 1960). For a critique of the view of Kerr and his associates as a form of "evolutionary para-Marxiasm," see John H. Goldthorpe, "Social Stratification in Industrial Society" in P. Halmos (ed.), *The Development of Industrial Societies*, Sociological Review Monograph no. 8 (Keele, 1964).

[3]See, for example, Kurt Mayer, "Recent Changes in the Class Structure of the United States," *Transactions of the Third World Congress of Sociology*, vol. 3 (London, 1956); "Diminishing Class Differentials in the United States," *Kyklos*, vol. 12 (October 1959); and "The Changing Shape of the American Class Structure," *Social Research*, vol. 30 (Winter 1963). Cf. also Robert Millar, *The New Classes* (London, 1966), pp. 27-8.

[4]Jessie Bernard, "Class Organisation in an Era of Abundance," *Transactions of the Third World Congress of Sociology*, vol 3 (London, 1956), p. 27. Cf. also the discussion of the process of *embourgeoisement* in Raymond Aron, *La Lutte de Classes* (Paris, 1964), pp. 205-13.

[5]Mayer, "Recent Changes in the Class Structure of the United States," p. 78.

[6]For argument on these lines, see in particular M. M. Postan, *An Economic History of Western Europe, 1945-1964* (London, 1967), pp. 320-6, 335-6; and for considered statements, Millar, *The New Classes*, pp. 81-5; and J. K. Galbraith, *The New Industrial State* (London, 1967), chs. 23 and 24 esp.

[7]Robert Blauner, *Alienation and Freedom: the Factory Worker and his Industry* (Chicago and London, 1964), pp. 181-2. Cf. Galbraith, *The New Industrial State*, pp. 226-7, 276. Blauner is the most notable exponent of the view that the evolution of industrial technology will lead workers to adopt distinctively middle-class attitudes towards their work and their employing organisations, but a number of other industrial sociologists have argued that the more advanced types of production system tend to be associated with more harmonious work relations and with the greater normative integration of the industrial enterprise. See, for example, for Great Britain, Joan Woodward, *Management and Technology* (London, H.M.S.O., 1958); "Industrial Behaviour—Is there a Science?" *New Society*, 8 October 1964; and *Industrial Organisation: Theory and Practice* (Oxford, 1965), pp. 160-8, 198-205.

[8]These arguments are most forcefully expressed in Galbraith, *The New Industrial State*, chs. 22 and 24. See also Blauner, *Alienation and Freedom*, pp. 154, 162-5, 181; and, for a somewhat different perspective, S. Barkin, "The Decline of the Labor Movement," in Andrew Hacker (ed.), *The Corporation Takeover* (New York, 1964). Clark Kerr *et al.*, *Industrialism and Industrial Man*, pp. 292-3, offer a more sophisticated view of unions being transformed into specialised interest groups operating in a context of "bureaucratic gamesmanship." Galbraith, as an arch-exponent of the view that industrial societies are following convergent paths of development, clearly anticipates that his analysis will come to have relevance for more than the American case alone.

# NINE

**Labor Theory: A Reassessment**

## Introduction

In Part IX John H. M. Laslett reviews the major theories of the labor movement and looks at future prospects for new developments in the field. While he finds major weaknesses in previous theories, he also argues that there is room for optimism concerning our present ability to overcome those weaknesses. Laslett's essay is a useful guide which the reader can use to judge the theoretical adequacy of the theories presented in this volume.

## 45

## *The American Tradition of Labor Theory and Its Relevance to the Contemporary Working Class*

JOHN H. M. LASLETT                                                                 1979

In a review of academic literature on the American working class published in February 1970, the conservative social critic Irving Kristol claimed that aside from a number of valuable industry-wide studies, the subject of labor theory had become a dull and unfashionable topic on which little that was really new or creative had been written in the United States for a number of years. This was surprising, Kristol added, in view of the perennial importance of labor unions in American society, and the growing signs of tension, both within the official labor movement and in its relations with the outside world. "The membership is restless and increasingly contemptuous of its leadership," he wrote. "The leaders are bewildered, insecure, and increasingly contemptuous of the public. As for the public, it is beginning to wonder whether the institution of trade unionism itself is really 'relevant' to the emerging American society of the 1970's."[1]

Kristol should not have been so surprised. Because of its relatively small size and heavily "economist" tradition, the American labor movement, unlike that in Europe, has never attracted men and women of genius such as Lenin, Gramsci, Rosa Luxemburg, Sorel, or Marx himself into thinking and writing deeply and creatively about the historical role of the working class. As a result, when they have thought about labor at all, the dominant tradition of American social theorists—influenced by a history of pluralist thought stretching back at least to James Madison's treatment of "factions" in *Federalist Paper* No. 10—has tended to treat it as one among a broad range of essentially equal social groupings, each vying for a share in an apparently limitless supply of wealth, status, and power. American Marxists, however, have hardly done better. With some notable exceptions, they have until recently tended to regard American labor within a narrow, deterministic, and vulgar-Marxist form of perspective. Deriving virtually all of their ideas from Europe, they have so far failed to devise an "American" form of Marxism which would serve at once as a viable call to action, and at the same time create a comprehensible model of behavior which can take each of the "exceptionalist" elements in the history of American industrialization into account.

Aside from the Socialist Scholars' conferences, which have produced a number of highly valuable papers on topics associated with labor theory in the past few years,[2] and which have met regularly since 1964, the last major conference to concern itself explicitly with the theory of the labor movement was held by the Industrial Relations Research Association at the University of Wisconsin in December 1950, more than twenty-five years ago. A review of its proceedings[3] indicates that it devoted itself almost wholly to an uncritical reaffirmation of the conservative, job-conscious labor union philosophy of Selig Perlman, the Wisconsin school's most famous product. His book, *A Theory of the Labor Movement*, which was published in 1928, had by then become by far the most influential attempt to provide a general theoretical explanation of the particular characteristics and behavior of the American working class. Almost no attempt was made at that conference to reexamine the basic tenets of Perlman's *Theory*, despite the tremendous expansion of the labor movement which had taken place in the 1930s and the growth of a more pro-

Published by permission of Transaction, Inc. from *The American Working Class: Prospects for the 1980s*, ed. Irving Louis Horowitz, John C. Leggett, and Martin Oppenheimer, pp. 3–30. New Brunswick, N.J.: Transaction Books, 1979. Copyright © 1979 by Transaction.

gressive social philosophy under the leadership of the CIO. Since that time, although several scholars have criticized Perlman's work, very little has been done, either by its supporters or by its critics, to evaluate his theory in the light of further historical developments, or to test it against the vast body of empirical research which has since been conducted into various aspects of American working class life.

The purpose of this essay, therefore, is twofold. First, to review briefly and in historical sequence the four or five most important general theories which have been advanced to account for the particular character and outlook of American labor as it has developed over the past one hundred years. Second, to make a preliminary attempt to see what value, if any, these theories may still have in explaining the behavior of American workingmen today.

Two general remarks about the works to be reviewed are in order. First, no proper attempt was made by any of the authors under review to define properly what they meant by labor theory. In most cases, what the various theorists found was a set of rather simple observable patterns in the behavior of small groups of workingmen in their public roles as trade unionists, not an operational model for American working-class behavior as a whole. They made little or no attempt, as social scientists are doing today, to enquire into the private beliefs of workers, or into their views on matters of race, status, religion, or family. Nor did they even examine in detail the attitude of American workers toward politics, beyond certain generalizations concerning old-party loyalty, or expressions of skepticism about undertaking third-party political action. Where no pretense was made at a general theory which went beyond these observable patterns of trade-union behavior no particular harm was done, although this fact in itself sets strict limits to the applicability of their findings to the working class considered as a whole. But where a claim *was* made to a more universal theory which sought to explain working-class behavior generally, but which was in fact based on nothing more than these observed patterns of trade-union activity, unsubstantiated generalizations were made—as I shall suggest in the case of Perlman's theory in particular—which should make us extremely wary of elevating them to the status of a general theory, if we do so at all.

The second remark, which is a corollary of the first, is that until approximately the Second World War, most labor theorists looked at the working class from the point of view of the role played by labor unions viewed as institutional mechanisms for achieving certain social or economic goals. In conducting their research they also examined only the views of a small group of labor leaders, with little regard for the opinions or activities either of the unorganized workers, or of the organized rank and file. Part of the reason for this was that most of them (John R. Commons, Jacob Hollander, George Barnett, and Robert F Hoxie, to name only a few) were professional academics who—unlike most labor theorists in Europe—rarely played a role within the labor movement itself. It was partly because, in addition to being academics, they were also often social-scientific or Taylor-oriented labor economists. They saw their role as part of an attempt to "solve," or at least to come to grips with, the "labor problem" (as it was called in the nineteenth century) instead of viewing trade-union behavior as part of working-class culture as a whole. In the United States this meant describing and assessing the effectiveness of labor unions as the most characteristic device which working people had developed to cope with the problems created by rapid industrialization and governmental laissez-faire.[4] In view of the fact that up until the 1930s, unlike Germany or England, less than twenty percent of the total American labor force was organized into trade unions, this approach was perhaps understandable. Nevertheless, it limited still further the value of their work for the study of working-class behavior generally, considered either in historical or in sociological terms.

Despite this, however, the remarkable fact is that the small body of theory we are about to examine represents the only coherent set of attempts to examine the behavior of American workingmen within some sort of generalized framework. If it achieves nothing else, this review should enable the contemporary social observer to decide what, from the earlier body of theory, is relevant to the situation of the working class today, and what can safely be assigned to the lumber room of history.

The first major school of American labor theory was the so-called moral uplift or moral conditioning school, which flourished from about 1880 to 1920.[5] This school saw labor unions primarily as manifestations of the worker's desire to improve his intellectual and moral standing vis-à-vis the community as a whole, rather than as protective devices to shelter workers against the effects of industrialization (a view shared by Marxist and job-conscious theorists alike). The moral uplift school was led by two Christian Socialists, Richard T. Ely (1854–1943), of Johns Hopkins University, and Father John Ryan (1896–1945), a Catholic cleric and teacher whose thinking was heavily influenced by papal encyclicals on the subject of labor, such as *Rerum Novarum* (1891), as well as by Ely's views. Although they were concerned with such characteristic economic functions of trade unions as arbitration, wage negotiations and strike action, the main contribution of these authors was to emphasize the educational value of labor organizations. In *The Labor Movement in America*, first published in 1886, Ely argued that throughout American history unions had led the fight for free public schooling, political participation, and land reform, and that they were now "perhaps the chief power in this country for temperance." They taught "true politeness and grace in manners." Best of all, the labor movement advocated international peace and social harmony, or as he put it: "The labor movement, as the facts would indicate, is the strongest force outside the Christian Church making for the practical recognition of human brotherhood."[6]

This educational function of trade unions, raising the consciousness level, as we might put it today, was not simply designed for the moral improvement of the individual. Both Ely and Ryan believed in producers' cooperation and public ownership as a more just way of distributing wealth. They evidently thought, moreover, that unions would train their members to believe it also. "Through this process of training," Father Ryan wrote in 1927, "the wage earners will be able in due time to demand a share in the surplus profits and a share in determining all the policies of the industrial concern, and will become fitted to carry on cooperative industries and to sit on the directing boards of publicly owned and democratically managed industrial enterprises."[7]

Although much of this undoubtedly seems quaint and anachronistic to contemporary ears—especially the references to temperance and the cultivation of "true politeness and grace in manners"—the moral uplift school sheds light on the historical antecedents for at least two areas of labor activity which are still of great contemporary concern. One is the traditional role which American labor unions have played in socializing and assimilating a largely immigrant work force to a number of commonly accepted American norms and social goals. Since the decline of massive European immigration caused by the 1924 Immigration Restriction Act, there has been less obvious scope for this particular function of the labor movement. Nevertheless, current attempts to unionize previously neglected domestic or native-born ethnic groups—such as Mexican-Americans into Cesar Chavez's United Farm Workers in California, or former southern blacks into the Detroit

UAW[x]—raise once more the issue of what values such groups bring with them to modern industrial society and on what terms they allow themselves to be socialized. Historically speaking, for example, the respectable English-speaking founders of the United Mine Workers of America, although freely admitting blacks and southern-European immigrants into their union, balked at some of the social habits which peasant migrants brought with them from the countryside.[9] If, as I believe, social outlook is as important as institutional tradition in creating proletarian forms of counterculture which can challenge the hegemony of bourgeois rule, then this question is as important in the United States today as it was a hundred years ago. For example, is racial pride to be a positive influence in helping blacks to humanize the degrading and trivializing effects of assembly-line production as socialist ideals once were to poor Jewish garment workers on the Lower East Side? Or is it to continue to be lost and wasted in apathy, submission, or sectarian intraunion quarrels?

Ely's and Ryan's analysis of the progressive social philosophy of the American labor movement also included support for free public schools, land reform, and even some measure of socialization of industry. This serves to remind us that even at the leadership level, American labor unions have by no means always had the narrow job-conscious outlook which they developed under the American Federation of Labor in the early years of the twentieth century, and which in some respects they have reverted to since the decline of the CIO. The dominant interpretation of Selig Perlman and the Wisconsin school of labor economists, which we shall analyze at greater length later on, appeared for some years to convince all but a small group of radicals and social historians that American workers were an exceptionally selfish, narrow-minded lot who had never been interested in anything more than shorter hours and higher wage levels. This outlook also affected the "working class authoritarianism" school of labor sociologists, of which S. M. Lipset still remains the leading expositor. Such an approach has always been unfair, especially during the heyday of the IWW between 1905 and 1917, and in the early years of the history of the CIO. It was especially untrue during the period of the Knights of Labor, which was dominant in the labor movement at the time when Ely wrote *The Labor Movement in America* in 1886, and which, although it was never in any real sense socialist, upheld producer's and consumer's cooperation, equal pay for women, and "a proper share of the wealth that they [the workers] create."[10] Of course, none of this means that we should expect the AFL-CIO to turn suddenly toward socialism. The official labor movement seems just now to be moving even further to the right. It does mean however, that there is nothing inevitable about the way labor ideology has developed in this country, either in the past or by extension in the future. Hence the interesting point for comparative analysis is not why "economism" has played a major role in the American labor movement. It has done so in all labor movements. The question is why it has done so to the exclusion of almost everything else. Part of the answer, I believe, lies in the ongoing influence in this country of a peculiarly tenacious form of labor aristocracy which defeated the Knights of Labor in a struggle for control in the labor movement in the 1880s, and which—because of ethnic, racial, and ideological unpreparedness on the part of unskilled elements in the labor force—has since rarely been effectively challenged.

The second influential school of labor research, the so-called economic-welfare school led by the economist George E. Barnett (1873–1938), who was also of Johns Hopkins, took for granted (without ever defining it) a "general dissatisfaction" with industrialism which caused workingmen to band together and demand greater job security, higher wages, and improved working conditions. The only real question for Barnett—who was heavily influenced by the Webbs in England—was whether economics or politics, that is, trade-union or legislative action, was the more rational, efficient way of securing labor's ends. This raises, indirectly, an issue which has always been important in American labor theory. That is whether, if workers take the legislative route, they will choose to pursue it through one of the two major parties or through a third party of their own making. They have nearly always done the former in the United States, unlike their counterparts in Germany or England, who have established political parties of their own. Barnett, however, did not consider the problem in these terms. Instead, he and his followers conducted a great deal of empirical research into the effects on workingmen of the nationalization of the labor market, and into the characteristics of trade-union members. They also produced the first systematic study of trade-union structure to appear in America, *The Printers*, published in 1909. The main interests of Barnett's work lies in the investigations which he conducted into the internal dynamics and functions of trade unions—a tradition which was to be taken up later by scholars such as Lloyd Ulman, Walter Galenson, or Lipset, Coleman, and Trow in their *Union Democracy* (1956)—not in any fundamental contribution which he made to the theory of the working class.

The third group of American labor theorists, although connected with no single place or university, is somewhat more interesting than the second. Influenced by the instinctual psychology of Thorstein Veblen, and also by the recently translated works of Sigmund Freud, Carleton Parker (1878–1918), Robert F. Hoxie (1868–1916), and Frank Tannenbaum (b. 1893) were together responsible for what came to be called the psychological-environment theory. This school was influential in the years immediately before and after World War I. Like their predecessors, these writers tended to treat workingmen as a single, abstract mass, and to make few differentiations among them on the basis of occupation, race, or social origin. Nevertheless, the psychological-environment school demonstrated more explicit concern than its predecessors for the more general, underlying, preinstitutional concerns and aspirations of workingmen, which they conceived of in psychological terms. Their analysis, although it was in some respects simplistic and monocausal, did make it possible to distinguish between the general characteristics and motives of working-class behavior, on the one hand, and the institutional manifestations of it, on the other. It also made it possible to perceive trade unions as only one among a variety of responses of the working class to general problems of industrialization and technological change.

In some ways the most interesting of these three men was Carleton H. Parker, whose *The Casual Laborer and Other Essays*, published posthumously in 1920, saw the labor movement arising partly out of economic degradation and the loss of economic independence occasioned by industrial and urban developments, but mainly out of a psychological maladjustment to the life of the factory and the large-scale farm. In the relatively undemanding atmosphere of home and school, Parker argued, the antisocial elements among man's instincts (which include anger or pugnacity, revulsion, and revolt at confinement) were either moderated or controlled. But in the sudden transition to the rigid, confining, and degrading work of factory or large-scale ranch, man's antisocial instincts create acute dissatisfaction or frustration with his lot, which is manifested in the creation of unions which serve either as defensive mechanisms or as agents of social revolt. "The problem of industrial labor," he wrote in one essay, "is one with the problem of the discontented businessman, the indifferent student, the unhappy wife, the immoral minister—it is one of maladjustment between a fixed human nature and a carelessly ordered world. The result is suffering, insanity, racial perversion, and danger. The final cure is gaining acceptance for a new standard of normality."[11] Among the programs which Parker advocated to cure the problem were measures for industrial decasualization, and the encouragement of group relationships in industry which would break down the traditional barriers between employer and employee. He also suggested that government and industry should make use of university- and hospital-trained psychologists for advice on ways to overcome worker hostility toward their position.

One difficulty with Parker's theory, aside from its transparently manipulative character, is that it was predicated primarily upon his observations among wandering western mineworkers, lumberjacks, or bums, few of whom followed more traditional occupational pursuits, and many of whom joined the IWW. Hence it may be wondered whether Parker's pseudo-anthropological conclusions concerning the "culture of poverty" out of which many of these migrant workers came (and which have been put to interesting use in Melvyn Dubofsky's recent *We Shall Be All: A History of the IWW*) can equally well be applied to the allegedly more settled, factory-oriented labor force in the East. To what degree the eastern, urban labor force is actually more settled in its occupational or geographical mobility patterns than its supposedly more volatile western, or frontier counterpart, has recently become a matter of important historical debate.[12] However, in Frank Tannenbaum's *The Labor Movement: Its Conservative Functions and Social Consequences*, published in 1921, as well as in Robert F. Hoxie's *Trade Unionism in the United States*, published in the same year, the leaders of the psychological-environment school went on to apply their theories to the whole American labor force. Their central idea remained that workingmen had become maladjusted by the dehumanizing effects of the machine process, and that the function of trade unions was not simply to improve their economic position, but to reassert some semblance of control by the individual over his own fate.[13] Robert F. Hoxie, in particular, elaborated a whole pantheon of different types of labor organizations ranging from craft, quasi-industrial, compound craft and industrial unions, to friendly-benefit, revolutionary, and what he called "hold-up" or "guerrilla" unions. He argued that the particular form a labor organization took depended upon the particular constellation of environmental and psychological factors involved.[14]

The great weakness of this body of work, as with most of the theories we are dealing with, is that with the partial exception of Hoxie it was written almost entirely in abstract terms, and made no serious attempt to apply the analytical scheme which it had elaborated to any specific body of workingmen. The central issue with which the psychological-environment school was concerned was, after all, the problem of alienation, although they tended to see it in psychological terms rather than, as a Marxist would, in economic terms. This is, of course, an extremely important issue in discussions of the working class today, as may be seen in a whole series of recent works ranging from Ely Chinoy's *Automobile Workers and the American Dream* (1955), through Robert Blauner's *Alienation and Freedom: The Factory Worker and His Industry* (1964), to Louise Kapp Howe's more recent *The White Majority: Between Poverty and Affluence* (1970). More recently have come still more sensitive, although even less theoretical, compilations of interviews and biographies from the experiences of ordinary workingmen and women both in and out of the work situation, deriving part of their technique from the methods of social survey research, and part from the newly burgeoning field of oral history. Two examples are *Rank and File: Personal Histories by Working Class Organizers*, by Alice and Staughton Lynd (1973), and Studs Terkel's impressive *Working* (1972). The fact that neither Parker's, nor Tannenbaum's, nor Hoxie's work rates even a footnote in any of these volumes indicates what little influence the psychological-environment school now exerts.

The fourth group of American labor theorists is the Marxist school. Numerous writers have, of course, attempted Marxist or neo-Marxist interpretations of the American labor movement, ranging from class conflict interpretations of the workingman's role in the American revolution, to Communist analyses of the New Deal in the 1930s. They have predicated the rise of the labor movement upon technological advances in production which have caused changes in the property relationships between the bourgeois, property-holding class and the working, property-less class. However muted or transmogrified in the American context, the ultimate cause of unionism is class conflict; the ultimate cause of class conflict is capitalist control of the means of production [which must be taken] away from the bourgeoisie, in the interests of production for use instead of profit and the establishment of a more just society. Either explicitly or implicitly, Marxist accounts repudiate what they regard as the utopian or romantic notions of the moral-conditioning theory; the nonrevolutionary (although somewhat more scientific) Fabianism of the economics-welfare school; and the manipulative implications of the psychological-environment school; as well as, of course, the job-conscious theories of the Wisconsin-Perlman school, which limits the worker's response simply to the nature of the opportunity market in which he finds himself, without any deeper analysis of his ultimate destiny or condition.

The recent revival of labor militancy among teamsters, white-collar workers, farm workers, longshoremen and coal miners may well lead the contemporary analyst of the labor movement to this Marxist tradition of labor-union theory with high expectations for its relevance and cogency. If so, he is likely to be disappointed—at least if he reads what may be called the Old Left, or vulgar-Marxist school of labor historiography. There have, of course, been numerous distinguished efforts by individual scholars to apply a general Marxist framework to problems which are either peripherally or centrally concerned with aspects of working class life. One thinks here of the historian Eugene Genovese, or the sociologist C. Wright Mills. But until quite recently those labor theorists who have discussed the American labor movement as such in Marxist terms have nearly always taken each of the Marxist categories of analysis uncritically as givens without any real attempt to examine the theoretical difficulties posed for the model by relatively high wage levels, ethnic or racial fragmentation of the labor force, or a fluid system of social stratification including the very rapid (and un-Marxist) growth in the size of the American middle class.[15] Little effort has been made to rethink Marx's concepts of proletarianization (in terms of Edouard Bernstein's Revisionist argument over upward occupational mobility), or of the dominance in America of bourgeois ideology and values (in terms of arguments by others over embourgeoisement) in relation to the actual circumstances and environment of any significant body of the American working class. Although as works of history they are often competent, the main theoretical interest in reading traditional or Old Left Marxist interpretations of the American labor movement, from William Z. Foster to Philip Foner,[16] is to review the numerous changes in tactics through which revolutionaries active in the labor movement have gone, and to impart blame for their limited success upon leadership sellouts, or "incorrect" tactics on the part of the rank and file.

To give two brief examples, the first Communist *History of the American Working Class*, written in 1928 by Anthony Bimba, begins by giving an interesting chronological account of the development of American working-class movements, only to become progressively more factional as it approaches contemporary times. After generously praising the activities of the American anarchists in the 1880s, for example, Bimba goes on to derogate all opponents of "boring from within" (the Communist tactic at the time his book was written), and to manipulate much of the history of the pre-1914 labor movement in the interests of a proper "line."[17] A more moderate example of this is Nathan Fine's *Farmer and Labor Parties in the United States* which was, as Paul Buhle has pointed out,[18] in many ways the Socialist counterpart of Bimba's work. After cataloging the institutional history of various reform movements in the nineteenth century, Fine turned to a lengthy defense of conservative trade-union Socialists against Left Socialists in the Debs period, and then to a further defense of both against the Communists in the 1920s. Although Fine closes with a clarion call of confidence in the future of the Socialist movement in America, his study is of little more than academic interest to those who would formulate a viable Marxist framework for understanding the present condition of the American working class. As Gabriel Kolko pointed out as long ago as 1966, Old Left Marxism, both in Europe and America, "accepted a paralysing and debilitating optimism which was inherited from the intellectual tradition of the idea of Progress. Defeat as a possibility . . . was never entertained, and a social theory that cannot consider this notion is not merely intellectually unsatisfactory but misleading as a basis of political analysis and action."[19]

The persistence of this narrow vulgar-Marxist school of analysis, seen today perhaps most characteristically in the work of Herbert Aptheker and Philip Foner, is all the more disappointing in view of the mass of evidence now being brought to light concerning the repressed early condition, and present dissatisfied status, of much of the American working class. This work is being carried out by a newer generation of sociologists, economists, and historians represented—to take a few random examples—by Herbert Gutman, James Weinstein, Harry Braverman, David Montgomery, Andrew Levinson, and James R. Green.[20] Braverman's and Levinson's work we will refer to again later on. The historians among this group fall into no readily identifiable theoretical category. Certainly not all of them are in any strict sense New Left. What unites them, however, is a common desire to go beyond the narrow, mechanistic perspectives of Old Left, vulgar-Marxist history, and to examine the interplay between community, ideology, family, race, and social class in ways which promise to tell us something in detail for the first time about the difficulties which have inhibited the development of a common working-class culture in the United States.

And yet, to repeat, neither Old nor New Left forms of Marxist social enquiry have so far come near to formulating an "American Marxism" capable at the same time of explaining the "exceptionalist" character of the American industrial experience, and of providing a coherent guide to social action. Some among the Old Left school, indeed, persist in denying that there is anything really "exceptionalist" about American industrialization at all. Part of the reason for this has to do with the inherent difficulty of the subject; part with a "cult of proletarianism" in the radical movement which reinforced native American traditions of antiintellectualism, and discouraged original thought; and part, as we have seen, with the failure of the labor movement itself to make new demands on the body of Marxist theory because of its own inability or unwillingness to present any serious threat to the social system. A further difficulty, I would suggest—and one whose importance has become increasingly noticed as blacks and other minority groups take up an even larger share of jobs among the factory working class—has to do with still unresolved weaknesses in the Marxist schema itself concerning the two areas of enquiry which are likely to be the most critical for the future growth of class consciousness among the American proletariat: Marxist attitudes toward the issue of race and the issue of nationality.

In the 1930s, thousands of black workers joined the American Communist party because it seemed to be the only one which genuinely cared about their fate. But aside from paternalism, white chauvinism, and the great difficulty which the Communist party itself had in overcoming its early use as an arm of Soviet foreign policy, neither it nor its successors have yet been able to resolve the fundamental dilemma created for Marxist theory by conflicts between blacks and other racial minorities' legitimate desires for self-determination, on the one hand, and Marxist analyses of society based upon social class, on the other. In revolutionary Russia, Lenin made use of Ukrainian, Hungarian, and other forms of east-European nationalism as a device to enhance Bolshevism's popular appeal. This tactic was condemned at the time by Rosa Luxemburg as inconsistent with Marxism's class basis. Nevertheless, it was temporarily adopted by the American Communist party in its 1930s proposal for a territorially independent Southern Black Belt. Not only did the Old Left fail to recognize that the desire for self-determination among American blacks (unlike east Europeans) was rarely linked to the land question, it also found itself, as a consequence of its views in conflict with petty bourgeois pan-African nationalists such as Marcus Garvey, who for all his racial demagoguery succeeded in developing a militant mass black movement where the Communist party failed.[21] Nothing that has happened since, from the Black Panthers to minority movements to end racial discrimination in the labor movement, suggests that this aspect of the problem has been resolved.

We now come to the fifth, and historically speaking, still the most influential theory of the American labor movement; namely the job-conscious theory elaborated by Selig Perlman and the Wisconsin school. In light of the great influence which it has exerted on teaching and research into the fields of labor economics and labor history, somewhat more attention will be paid to its actual content than to that of its predecessors. Strictly speaking, the Wisconsin school was founded not by Perlman but by the eminent progressive and leader of the research team at the University of Wisconsin, of which Selig Perlman was a member, John R. Commons (1862–1945). Commons's numerous empirical investigations led him (most notably in his celebrated article, "American Shoemakers, 1648–1895," first published in 1909) to locate the origins of the labor movement, not as with Marx, in changes in the mode of production. Insead, Commons placed it in the more limited but still vast changes in the nature of the market for labor and for goods which took place as a result of the rapid expansion of the American economy after the Civil War. In this period, the functions of merchant, manufacturer, and worker, which had hitherto been combined in one person, were divided and the individual worker was forced to combine with others to defend the interests of his own separate craft or trade. This laid the intellectual foundations for Perlman's *Theory of the Labor Movement* (1928), much the most celebrated monograph in our literature on the behavior of the American working class.

There are really two parts to Perlman's theory. One takes up the question of why the American labor movement has not adopted socialism, or independent labor politics which Perlman attributes in a rather tautologous fashion to the strength of the institution of private property, to the lack of class-consciousness in America, and to the difficulties of practicing third-party politics in a federal electoral system. The other concerns the issue of what labor's own "organic" or "home-grown" philosophy will be when it is left free from the interference of revolutionary intellectuals. The chief characteristic of the latter, Perlman argued, was to regard labor "merely as an abstract mass in the grip of an abstract force," and to attempt to manipulate it in the direction of revolutionary goals in which, he blithely asserts, it has no intrinsic interest. In America, however (and potentially in Europe also, where Perlman suggested that the influence of intellectuals over the labor movement was in decline), the worker had been able to develop his own organic philosophy. This consisted essentially in dividing control between himself and the employer over the limited opportunities afforded to him by the job in which he was employed. "The safest way to assure this group control over opportunity," Perlman argued, was for the union to "seek, by collective bargaining with the employers, to establish 'rights' on the job, . . . by incorporating, in the trade agreement, regulations applying to overtime, to the 'equal turn,' to priority and seniority in employment, to apprenticeship, to the introduction and utilization of machinery, and so forth."[22]

Perlman's answer to the question of why workers conceived of their opportunities as limited was twofold. First, a survey of the changes which had taken place in the nature of the market in the nineteenth century—essentially, as far as the United States was concerned, the post-Civil War decades—convinced him that he could no longer operate as a would-be entrepreneur attempting by means of land or currency reform to restore his position as an autonomous economic unit. Instead, he had accepted his position as a wage-earner, seeking by means of collective bargaining, instead of the largely political or legislative means which he had used earlier, to make his position as secure as possible within the particular trade or calling in which he was employed. "The trade unionism of the American Federation of Labor," Perlman wrote, "was a shift from an optimistic psychology, reflecting the abundance of opportunity in a partly settled continent, to the more pessimistic trade union psychology, built upon the premise that the wage earner is faced by a scarcity of opportunity."

Second, this scarcity consciousness just referred to derived from what Perlman conceived of as a universal psychology among manual workers or workingmen—universal throughout Europe as well as America, once the interfering influence of the intellectual had been withdrawn—according to which the worker accepts inherent limitations in his ability to manipulate the economic world. "The typical manualist is aware of his lack of native capacity for availing himself of economic opportunities as they lie amidst the complex and ever shifting situations of modern business." In contrast, a psychology of unlimited opportunity characterized the entrepreneur, whom Perlman, like Schumpter, thought of as a born risk-taker who could impose his will upon the vagaries of the capitalist system. "Whether he thought the cause of the apparent limitations to be institutional or natural," Perlman concluded, "a scarcity consciousness has always been typical of the manual worker, in direct contrast to the consciousness of abundance of opportunity, which eminates the self-conscious businessman."[23] From a job-conscious psychology created by an age of allegedly shrinking job opportunities, and the development of labor institutions and policies responsive to a wage-earning constituency which was free from the influence of middle-class intellectuals, all else flowed in the shaping of American trade unionism.

It is not difficult to point out the basic weaknesses in Perlman's *Theory*, both in historical and in theoretical terms. Perlman wrote from the perspective of the 1920s, when the conservative craft unionism of the American Federation of Labor was still firmly entrenched. A year after he published his *Theory* in 1928, the Great Depression began, and American capitalism foundered to a degree never before anticipated. The labor movement broke out of its craft-union mold and swiftly encompassed the mass production workers in the years after 1935. Given its commitment to broader social objectives, its willingness to engage in partisan politics, and its encouragement of government involvement in the labor sphere, could the CIO be characterized as pure-and-simple trade unionism? More fundamentally, have not the changes since the 1920s—the incorporation into the labor movement of millions of mass production workers, the development of an economy in which job scarcity no longer seems inevitable, and the immense expansion of the public role of the labor movement—been so far-reaching as to render Perlman's analysis inapplicable? Perlman himself stood by his ealier views. At the 1950

Industrial Relations Research Association symposium, (which took place nine years before his death), he remarked: "In the grasp of the Wisconsin school, the American labor movement, indicative of its basic philosophy, has shown remarkable steadfastness through times of rapid external change. The objective . . . is unaltered from Gompers' day; the methods, even outside the immediate vicinity of the job, show no more change than could be accounted for by the changing environment."[24]

The AFL-CIO, particularly after the two halves of the labor movement reunited in 1955, has continued to reveal the powerful grip which the job-conscious philosophy still exerts. Its social idealism has faltered badly, particularly on matters of race and of organizing the marginal and minority workers who lie beyond the mass production industries; its central concern has remained the exercise of control over wage levels, fringe benefits, and other elements in the American worker's general terms of employment. On the other hand, we should ask whether labor's political role, its community involvement, and its abandonment of voluntarism (or aversion to state interference in the affairs of trade unions) do not demand a major reassessment of Perlman's *Theory* on strictly empirical grounds.

Even so, there are fundamental theoretical weaknesses in Perlman's *Theory*. Adolph Sturmthal, for example, taking up an argument earlier disputed at great length between Lenin and the economist school of Russian orthodox Marxists, has pointed out that the radicalization of labor as such by no means always depends upon the external prompting of intellectuals. This is in itself a more orthodox Marxist view which I myself have attempted to elaborate in a recent work on the American labor movement.[25] However, this still leaves open the question of how far a successful socialist party depends upon an alliance being established *between* the two groups, which in many ways it clearly does.

Close study of Perlman's monograph, moreover, reveals that the celebrated scarcity consciousness of the worker—although supposedly deriving from a survey of available economic opportunity and from the worker's inherent awareness of his lack of capacity as an entrepreneur[26]—was in fact deduced solely from a limited number of union contracts and bargaining documents, which in themselves tell us very little either about the worker's psychic predispositions towards capitalism, or about his self-awareness as a putative entrepreneur. In addition, Perlman used both arguments (that based on a supposed survey of available opportunity, and the one based on the worker's inherent limitations as entrepreneur) interchangeably and indiscriminately, without apparently being aware of the enormous implications of the differences between them. It is one thing to assert that the American worker is job-conscious because he has surveyed his range of available opportunities and decided that this is the best tactic for him to pursue. It is even more breathtaking to suggest (with all due respect to Lenin) that all workers everywhere and at all times are *inherently* incapable of anything other than a job-conscious philosophy. Aside from anything else, most historians who have studied the problem would surely agree that such a rigid distinction is implausible, and that at least since the eighteenth century both businessmen *and* manual workers have operated within a framework of limited opportunity, in which the former seeks to impose order on the economic world by means of monopolies and price-fixing, while the latter seeks to do so through trade agreements and work rules.

This is not, of course, to say that the range of opportunities open to the businessman is not always greater than those available to the worker, or that the industrial revolution did not force the worker to defend himself against the depredations of the entrepreneur. The central point to grasp, however, is that whatever name one gives to the predicament, or variety of predicaments, which face the manual worker (whether it be scarcity consciousness, bourgeois exploitation, or psychological maladjustment), those predicaments simply provide a rationale for some form of labor movement. They do not dictate either its philosophy or its form. On the question of form or structure, for example, there is nothing inherent in the predicament of the American manual worker to explain why the American Federation of Labor chose craft unionism as its dominant mode of organization, or resisted mass, industrial unionism for so long. Nor does the predicament of the worker in itself dictate that labor unions should be job-conscious rather than class-conscious in their orientation, or that they should stop short at job-monopoly, instead of reaching for total worker control of industry. One must turn for an explanation to the actual historical influences which have affected the outlook of the American worker, such as ethnic and racial difficulties, high real wage levels, leadership characteristics, or a relatively fluid stratification system, instead of relying on a spurious and deterministic concept of worker psychology, the validity of which has yet to be demonstrated either as a category of actual historical experience or as a viable sociological research tool.

What, then, is the relevance of all this to present studies of the contemporary character and development of the American working class? Before concluding our observations on that question we ought perhaps first to ask whether there has been, since the 1950s, any further contribution to labor theory which represents a major advance over the theories which we have just reviewed. My answer would be that while a number of extremely interesting new areas for research have recently been opened up by social scientists (or, perhaps, taken seriously for the first time), none of them so far have yielded a set of generalizations which can in any sense be called a general theory.

From one direction, we have seen a rapidly growing sensitivity, on the part of sociologists as well as of historians, toward the importance of new or previously neglected minorities or ethnic minorities in the labor force, ranging from C. Wright Mills's and Everett Kassalow's very different studies of the white-collar worker, to the work, respectively, of Joan Moore. Harry Kitano, and Julius Jacobson or Herbert Hill on the increasing importance of Mexican-Americans, Japanese-Americans, and blacks in the labor force.[27] Given their larger numbers and an already strategic position in key industries such as autos, steel, and meatpacking—there are 2.5 million black workers in the AFL-CIO, and they already control most of the UAW local offices in Detroit—it is perhaps natural that the blacks should so far have received the greatest amount of attention. But the developing importance of white-collar and ethnic minority groups of all kinds (even though the latter, of course, have always been part of the traditional working class) has raised issues of status versus class analysis, or of race versus job consciousness, which were almost never considered by the earlier tradition of labor theorists. From the point of view of labor militancy, the Mexican-American farm workers of Texas and California have succeeded in recapturing something of the spirit of the early CIO by integrating national pride with social idealism in their struggle for union recognition. But so far, politically, they show no signs of going beyond the liberal Democratic posture of their earlier New Deal comrades.

From another direction has come a burgeoning and increasingly sophisticated sociological literature on the attitudes, problems, and behavior of contemporary working-class groups at the rank and file level, and sometimes outside of the workplace altogether. Within the union context, we have had Joel Seidman's *The Worker Views His*

*Union* (1958), containing interviews and reflections on the attitudes toward their unions of workers in six different industries; Sidney Peck's *Rank and File Leader* (1963), an analysis of levels of consciousness among shop stewards in a Milwaukee plant in the late 1950s, indicating some degree of anti-Semitism, male chauvinism, and status resentment toward younger workers on the part of the older employees; and John C. Leggett's *Class, Race and Labor* (1968), which correlates regional background, ethnicity, and economic insecurity with the persistence of working-class consciousness in the Detroit work force in the 1960s, to mention only three of the most important works. Outside the union context, there has been Bennett Berger's *Working Class Suburb* (1960), demonstrating the persistence of a sense of working class identity among Ford workers despite the transition from Richmond, California to a San Jose suburb; and Mirra Komarovsky's saddening, but at the same time highly illuminating *Blue Collar Marriage* (1962), showing the loneliness and frustration visited by economic insecurity and traditional assumptions of masculinity upon innumerable working-class wives. Outside formal academic circles, the New Left magazines—*Radical America, Guardian, Socialist Revolution*, Radical Education Project pamphlets—and sometimes even Old Left journals such as *Dissent* or *Science and Society*, have poured forth a veritable flood of reports, opinions, and views.

None of this new literature, with its conflicting and different ideological points of view, has presented any new general theory of the American labor movement, nor has it even attempted to do so. Some of it, however, has provided ammunition for two interrelated sets of debates from which such new theoretical perspectives as we now have can be said to have come. The first of these debates concerns the general political and ideological outlook of the American working class, or what, given present trends in the labor force, its philosophical outlook is likely to become in the future. In itself this is, of course, an old issue. To a great extent in the 1960s, however, it revolved around the hotly debated end-of-ideology thesis—or explanations of American labor moderation in terms of certain recent changes in the American economy and social structure. The second debate, which in part helps to account for and in part itself derives from the first, turns on the equally hotly debated issue of whether, given these same trends in the economy towards a postindustrial society, an industrial working class in the sense that we have hitherto known it will continue to exist at all.

The end-of-ideology argument, although it is usually associated with conservative social theorists such as Seymour Lipset and Daniel Bell—whose book, *The End of Ideology*, was published in 1960—in fact also derives from positions taken by radicals such as Barrington Moore and Herbert Marcuse. Thus Marcuse in his book *One Dimensional Man* (1964), and in numerous statements since, argues that the American working class has been integrated into the affluent society and "shares in large measure the needs and aspirations of the dominant class."[28] Paul Sweezy and the late Paul Baran, writing in 1966, also came to the conclusion that organized workers in the United States had been "integrated into the system as consumers and ideologically conditioned members of the society."[29] Essentially, however, they assert that the main consequence of the remarkable productivity of American capitalism (and, indeed, of western capitalism generally) since World War II, coupled with the development of sophisticated and successful collective bargaining techniques, has been, to quote Lipset, to "undercut many of the conditions which earlier had led workers to support different forms of class-conscious radical ideology."[30] According to this school, what we should now be concerned with is not the traditional economic grievances of artisans and blue-collar workers (which save for ethnic minorities and other marginal groups are no longer a serious issue) but with the status anxieties, racial attitudes, and—according to Lipset at least—the simplistic, authoritarian attitudes towards politics on the part of the white working class, which survey research techniques allegedly show to be extensive.[31]

One response to this type of argument, put forward in an interesting paper given by Richard Hamilton to the Socialist Scholars' Conference in 1965,[32] has been to challenge the alleged racism and authoritarianism of blue-collar workers suggested by the conservative sociologists on purely empirical grounds. Hamilton argued, for example, correctly in my view, that the working class is no more afflicted by this type of prejudice than are other elements in the American community. Another approach, which has so far been developed more fully in England than in the United States (in John Goldthorpe's *Affluent Worker*, although Bennett Berger's *Working Class Suburb* represents an interesting corollary in the United States) has been to deny that affluence, improved wages and conditions of work, and the benefits of a consumer society have necessarily led to *embourgeoisement* along the lines described.[33] Still a third response, to be seen in the work of Martin Glaberman, Stanley Weir, and numerous other radical commentators, has been to acknowledge that collective bargaining techniques, at least for that portion of the labor force which is organized, may have been able to meet the demands of the contemporary labor aristocracy as regards wages, living standards or working conditions. But this still leaves out many ethnic minorities and other hitherto marginal elements which conservative theorists ignore.[34] The obvious corollary to this argument, which is also in my view well taken, is that collective bargaining is inherently unable to solve problems created by alienation, fragmentation of the work process, bureaucracy, and automation, factors which in the presence of a national crisis—but only then—might still lead to some form of traditional labor revolt. Much the most sensitive treatment of this latter aspect of the problem has been that in Harry Braverman's recent book, *Labor and Monopoly Capital* (1974), which discusses Taylorism, absenteeism, job rationalization, and a whole host of other aspects of the alienation question under the general rubric of "the degradation of work in the twentieth century." The weakness of Braverman's work, although it sets the discussion more firmly than any of its predecessors within Marx's own analytic framework as seen in volume one of *Capital*, is that it offers us no way of judging whether the degradation of the work process in the last generation or so—in what is still, save Japan, technologically the most rapidly changing industrial economy in the world—has been more or less acute than it has been throughout the whole history of industrialization. Thus we are left unable to answer the question posed by Braverman himself in his introduction, whether the recent flurry of rank and file discontent in the labor movement has been "at the usual level, endemic to life under capitalism, or whether it was rising threateningly."[35] The failure of the recent growth of mass unemployment to generate more than a very limited radical response in the United States makes it very difficult, so far at least, to answer Braverman's question with anything other than a negative.

In Italy, in France, in Portugal, and in Great Britain we are, of course, faced with a very different story; perhaps the best refutation of the "end of ideology" argument is simply to point to the rising Communist vote and the ongoing labor unrest among blue-collar workers in these countries, even if it were not easily refuted as nonsensical on other grounds as well. Strictly speaking, however, Bell addressed himself only to advanced industrial societies, which leaves out Portugal, and possibly even Italy, although most assuredly not Great Britain. How far the current British crisis will turn itself from an advanced case of inflation-fueled "economist" discontent into something greater—my own hunch is that it won't—is at this point no more than idle speculation. But to return to the United States, the debate over ideology, although cast in very different terms from that between the earlier job-conscious and Marxist schools, would at least have been recognizable to the pre-1950s tradition of American labor theory. But the second debate, over whether structural changes now occurring in the economy may lead to the creation of a postindustrial (but still capitalist) society in which the very existence of an industrial working class as we have hitherto known it may be called into question, would have been incredible, as well as incomprehensible, to most of the earlier American theorists. They worked and wrote in a context in which the presence of some kind of industrial proletariat could be taken for granted. Now, however, the conservative school of pluralist sociologists, led again by Daniel Bell, have begun to suggest that changes in technology and in the pattern of consumer demand now taking place will in the long run be so far-reaching as to abolish altogether the traditional concept of a blue-collar proletariat.

The issue has arisen, clearly enough—although so far largely only in America—because of structural change in patterns of employment. As a result of these changes, the proportion of workers employed in goods-producing, mostly blue-collar occupations, while still continuing to rise somewhat in absolute terms (except for those in mining or in agriculture, who continue to decline rapidly in number) is now falling markedly relative to the numbers employed in service, largely white-collar occupations. The effect of this will be, according to one estimate,[36] that by 1980 the proportion of workers employed in the blue-collar field will fall to less than 32 percent of the total work force (it was well over 60 percent in 1935), while the proportion of white-collar workers, especially among government employees (already 7 million in 1968), teachers (already 2 million), scientists and engineers (already about 1.4 million), and engineering and science technicians (already about 900,000 in 1968), will continue to rise sharply. Thus what we may now see emerging is a bifurcated working population, in which the old industrial working class is diminishing in importance and is in any event, according to the end-of-ideology argument, largely satisfied; and a new, better educated, rapidly growing white-collar element which will be largely nonmilitant in its outlook because it already has middle-class status and aspirations.

This latter point has caused perhaps the greatest amount of controversy. Initially, Marxist analysts of this new phenomenon such as C. Wright Mills in his already cited *White Collar* (1951), tended to argue that the new semiprofessional and technical cadres could not be thought of as an autonomous independent class, but would eventually have to move in one direction or another and give their support either to the old industrial working classes or to the business community. But more recently, beginning with French analysts such as Serge Mallet and Andre Gorz, radical American critics of the postindustrial society thesis argued that these new cadres would not simply by virtue of their somewhat higher income become another version of the old and largely conservative aristocracy of labor which had developed in the industrial working class at an earlier period. They argued that these new groups had considerable revolutionary potential—which could be exploited for organizing purposes—because their skills had been broken down and compartmentalized, and they were no longer able to fulfill the creative role for which they had been trained.[37] Thus Herbert Gintis, to take one example, saw the student rebellions of the late 1960s as foreshadowing the revolt of "educated labor" as a whole against capitalism. Even within the New Left, however, there was sharp debate as to what the future loyalties and ideological outlook of these white-collar groups was likely to be. Stanley Aronowitz pointed out, for example, the need to distinguish carefully between the roles of technocrats and technicians, and between those of teachers and governmental employees, before coming to any definitive conclusions. In an essay published in 1971, he questioned the assumption, which had been advanced by a number of other New Left critics, that a rise in educational levels would necessarily lead to mass radicalization among white-collar workers, and concluded rather sharply that at present, "the United States does *not* have a new working class."[38]

But as in the "end of ideology" debate, perhaps the simplest and the most effective response to the postindustrial thesis has come from those who have pointed out that its champions have either anticipated far too much in consigning the traditional proletariat to oblivion, or have simply got their facts wrong. In a remarkable book published in 1974 called *The American Working Class Majority*, Andrew Levinson set out to show, with considerable success, not that Bell's projections concerning the overall future shape were completely out of kilter (that would be impossible) but that his and others' use of figures to show a relative increase in affluence among blue-collar workers, a relative decline in their liberal political outlook, as well as an overall decline in their numbers within the work force, has been much exaggerated. "The majority of Americans are not white-collar, or well off," he writes. "Thirty per cent of blue collar workers are poor and another 30 per cent cannot earn enough to reach the very modest government definition of a middle-class standard of living. . . . American workers are a class apart," Levinson concludes, "with real and legitimate problems and discontents. And unlike the abstract paper coalitions of wildly disparate groups which Liberals have proposed, they are united by common interests and constitute a majority of the American people."[39] If Levinson's analysis is correct, as careful perusal by the reader will, I believe, convince him that it is, it has profound implications for the "embourgoisement," "the end of ideology," "the working class authoritarianism," and "the post-industrial society" schools of analysis. At the very least it has thrown the ball back into their proponents' court.

During the earlier part of this essay we reviewed the previous body of American labor-union theory to see what relevance it had, if any, to the present problems and characteristics of the American working class. Save for Perlman's *Theory*, which is fundamentally shallow, and Marxist theory, which is of course the opposite of shallow but which has so far been incapable of developing an American version of anything like the depth and profundity which Antonio Gramsci, for example, developed for Italy,[40] the value of the remainder for contemporary analysis is extremely limited. Our final purpose is to see what lessons, if any, can be gained for the future by juxtaposing the methodological approach taken to problems of labor theory by the post-1950s generation of analysts, with that taken by scholars of the pre-1950s era, in the light of a brief review of the American tradition of labor theory taken as a whole. On this point, although as I suggested earlier no new theoretical framework has yet emerged which can be said to have entirely displaced those which went before, the greater methodological sophistication of the new group of labor analysts, coupled with their willingness to treat workers as individual human beings with interests and commitments that go beyond their role as members of a labor union, give grounds for hope that a new general theory of the labor movement, if and when it does emerge, will at least be based on both a sounder and a broader range of evidence than the old.

Methodologically speaking, the earlier body of labor theory suffered, in my view, from four main sets of weaknesses which the more recent efforts of labor analysts show signs of being able to overcome. The pre-1950s tradition was guilty, first, of an almost universal tendency (for which both the Perlmanites and their Marxist opponents can equally be blamed) to treat the labor force as a single, abstract entity, or at most as two or three abstract entities, with little attempt to break down into its component parts, or to examine factors which may have influenced the behavior of workingmen other than those which developed out of the workplace. Robert F. Hoxie of the psychological-environment school was a partial exception here, but he went little further than to recognize the issue. Even a brief review of the mass of empirical work now being done on the racial, ethnic, familial and extra-union roles of working people given in the previous section, however, should convince any future labor theorist that he can no longer afford to ignore the wide variety of contexts, aside from the workplace itself, in which working people operate.

Second, as already suggested, most earlier theorists suffered from an equally debilitating tendency to concentrate upon the trade union as the single most obviously characteristic institution of the working-class movement, and to treat labor theory as though it were confined to a study of the origins, characteristics, and advantges of trade unions. This led, owing largely to the baleful influence of the Wisconsin school of labor economists, to the writing of an extremely narrow, rigid, and dull type of labor history in this country, and to a split between the study of labor-union theory, on the one hand, and the general study of working-class culture, on the other, which has had unfortunate consequences for both. Such tendencies reinforced the predilection of labor theorists either to ignore the pre- or noninstitutional concerns and aspirations of working people (as in the economics-welfare school of George E. Barnett), or (as in the case of Perlman) to base their views upon an explicit or implicit set of assumptions which were set forth in largely abstract terms, and for which they presented very little empirical evidence. Here again, the detailed work now being done on the non- or extra-union activities of working people should enable us to prevent a repeat of this kind of performance.

Third, the pre-1950s tradition of labor-union theory developed generalizations based upon a static model of the labor force which took little, if any, account of changes in its occupational shape or character over time. Elementary statistics concerning changes in patterns of migration, for instance, or changes in the demands of industry for different kinds of labor, such as are now being used as ammunition in the "old"-working-class/"new"-working-class debate should also enable any new labor theorist to avoid that particular pitfall.

Finally, there has been a tendency toward a rigid or deterministic view of labor ideology which I would label ahistorical, not only because it gives us an oversimplified picture of the past, but also because it limits the predictive value of labor theory for the future. Contemporary labor theorists are certainly not wholly free of this tendency, as may be seen in the highly dogmatic assertions concerning working class authoritarianism made by the Lipset school of sociologists, or in the equally elitist and contemptuous attitude toward the working class adopted by such left-wing critics as Marcuse. Generally speaking, however, there has been a much greater degree of sympathy and sophistication in the way in which the various positions adopted by contemporary commentators have been argued. Selig Perlman, for example, dismissed the antimonopoly, producer-oriented consciousness of the pre-Civil War labor movement as irrelevant and anachronistic to a modern labor movement based upon job-consciousness and a factory economy. It may well be, however, that antimonopolism was indeed appropriate to the labor movement of the early part of the nineteenth century, situated as it was in a relatively small-scale, workshop-oriented economy still largely imbued with rural values. In the same way, a "labor aristocracy" form of explanation may well have been appropriate to the skill-oriented economy of the latter part of the nineteenth century; and an industrial union form of explanation appropriate to the mass-production industries of the first half of this century. Now, as we have seen, the economy is changing again. The predominantly white, blue-collar worker no longer occupies the center of the stage, and in the last years of the twentieth century, assembly-line processes will be largely taken care of by blacks, Chicanos, and other hitherto marginal elements in the labor force, while an increasing number of service, managerial, and technical jobs are filled by white-collar workers with very different backgrounds and skills. Who can say what will happen to the supposedly universal job-conscious theory of labor organization then?

Yet if Perlman put the issue too simply, and if there are many other questions in our study of the working class that we would want to ask besides those concerning job-consciousness, the relevance of his original question still remains. For despite major depressions, active repression by both government and employers, revolutionary changes in the character and types of rewards offered by employment, and appeals from all sides to adopt a different course of action, most American workers have not been willing so far to go beyond the pursuit of rather limited bread-and-butter aims. I have tried to suggest that Perlman's method of establishing the reasons for this was methodologically unsound, and based upon so little empirical evidence as to create doubt in the reader's mind whether he had answered the question at all. But until the unlikely event that the American working class chooses to adopt a different course of action, we must continue to ask why.

[1]Irving Kristol, "Writing about Trade Unions," *New York Times Book Review:* February 1, 1970, pp. 2, 24. See also Paul Jocobs, *The State of the Unions* (New York, 1963). The most recent general survey, with essays on various aspects of the subject, is *Dissent's* special issue "The World of the Blue Collar Worker" (Winter 1972).

[2]The most important of these have been collected in George Fischer, ed., *The Revival of American Socialism: Selected Papers of the Socialist Scholars' Conference* (New York, 1971).

[3]Industrial Relations Research Association, *Interpreting the Labor Movement* (Champaign, 1952) pp. 1–69, 83–109.

[4]For a further discussion of the role of labor economists in the writing of labor theory and of labor history, see Paul J. McNulty, "Labor Problems and Labor Economics: The Roots of an Academic Discipline," *Labor History* 9 (1968): 239–61.

[5]This summary of the views of the early American labor theorists is taken from Mark Perlman (Selig's son), *Labor Union Theories in America: Background and Development* (Evanston, 1958), except where otherwise indicated.

[6]Richard T. Ely, *The Labor Movement in America* (New York, 1886), p. 138.

[7]John A. Ryan, *Declining Liberty and Other Papers* (New York, 1927), p. 218.

[8]For insight into these two groups, see Petro Matthiessen, *Sol Si Puedes: Cesar Chavez and the New American Revolution* (New York, 1969); B. J. Widick, "Black City, Black Unions?" *Dissent* (Winter 1972): 138–45; or numerous pamphlets published by the Radical Education Project in Detroit on DRUM (Dodge Revolutionary Union Movement) and FRUM (the equivalent for Ford), in the late 1960s. One example of the latter is Robert Dudnick, "Black Workers in Revolt" (1969).

[9]See, for example, Frank J. Warne, *The Slav Invasion and the Mine Workers: A Study in Immigration* (Philadelphia, 1954), pp. 65–71.

[10]*Preamble to the Constitution of . . . the Knights of Labor*. In John H. M. Laslett, ed., *The Workingman in American Life: Selected Readings* (New York, 1968), p. 41.

[11]Carleton H. Parker, *The Casual Laborer and Other Essays* (New York, 1920), p. 59.

[12]See, for example, Stephan Thernstrom, "Urbanization, Migration, and Social Mobility in Late Nineteenth Century America," in Barton J. Bernstein, ed., *Towards a New Past: Dissenting Essays in American History (New York, 1967), pp. 158–75.*

[13] Tannenbaum went on to argue (although his views on the radical potential of the labor movement were considerably modified in his late book, *A Philosophy of Labor,* 1957), that the worker's desire for security was so great that he would not stop, as Perlman was to argue later, at attempting to share control with the employer over the immediate rewards and character of the job, but would seek to supplant the employer entirely. However, this did not lead Tannenbaum into the Marxist position of arguing for proletarian seizure of the entire means of production, but instead to a more limited form of guild socialism (after G. D. H. Cole, in England) which would be more satisfying to the individual's desire for controlling his own fate.

[14]Robert F. Hoxie, *Trade Unionism in the United States* (New York, 1921), pp. 67ff.

[15]For an interesting review of Old Left Marxist writing on American Labor, see Paul Buhle, "American Marxist Historiography, 1900-1940," *Radical America* 4 (1970): 5-35.

[16]For example, William Z. Foster, *American Trade Unionism* (New York, 1950), or his *Misleaders of Labor* (1927). Philip Foner's major work is *The History of the Labor Movement in the United States*, 4 vols. (New York, 1947-65).

[17]Anthony Bimba, *History of the American Working Class* (New York, 1937), pp. 10-45, 68-69, 115, 122, 232.

[18]Buhle, "American Marxist Historiography," p. 17.

[19]Quoted from Gabriel Kolko, "The Decline of American Radicalism in the Twentieth Century," in James Weinstein and David W. Eakins, eds., *For a New America* (New York, 1970), p. 198.

[20]For Gutman's work, see various references attached to his "Work, Culture, and Society in Industrializing America, 1815-1919," *American Historical Review* 78 (1973): 531-87. Weinstein has written *The Decline of Socialism in America, 1912-1925* (New York, 1967), and *The Corporate Ideal and the Liberal State, 1900-1918* (New York, 1968); Montgomery, *Beyond Equality* (New York, 1967); and Green, "The Brotherhood of Timber Workers 1910-1913: A Radical Response to Industrial Capitalism in the U.S.A.," in *Past and Present*, 60 (August 1973).

[21]Robert L. Allen, *Reluctant Reformers* (New York, 1975), pp. 227-59.

[22]Selig Perlman, *A Theory of the Labor Movement* (New York, 1928), pp. 6, 199.

[23]Ibid., pp. 214, 239-40.

[24]Industrial Relations Research Association, *Interpreting the Labor Movement*, p. 52.

[25]In a study of the sources of radicalism in six leading American trade unions at the turn of the century, I found evidence of radicalization resulting from technological displacement, low wages, slum conditions, and other forms of capitalist exploitation. See John H. M. Laslett, *Labor and the Left: A Study of Socialist and Radical Influences in the American Labor Movement, 1881-1924* (New York, 1970), pp. 291-93 ff. For other critiques of Perlman, see Adolph Sturmthal, "Comments on Selig Perlman's 'A Theory of the Labor Movement,' " *Industrial and Labor Relations Review* 4 (1951): 483-96; Charles A. Gulick and Melvin K. Bers, "Insight and Illusion in Perlman's Theory of the Labor Movement," *Industrial and Labor Relations Review* 68 (1953): 510-31.

[26]Aside from anything else, both of these concepts assume far too great a degree of rational self-awareness in the decision-making processes of both worker and entrepreneur.

[27]C. Wright Mills, *White Collar: The American Middle Class* (New York, 1951); Everett M. Kassalow, "White Collar Unionism in the United States," in Adolph Sturmthal, ed., *White Collar Trade Unions: Contemporary Developments in Advanced Countries* (Urbana, 1966), pp. 305-64; Joan Moore and Afredo Cuellar, *Mexican Americans* (Englewood Cliffs, 1970); Harry Kitano, *Japanese Americans: The Evolution of a Subculture* (Englewood Cliffs, 1969); essays by Julius Jacobson and Herbert Hill in Julius Jacobson, ed., *The Negro and the American Labor Movement* (New York, 1968).

[28]Cited in Ernest Mandel and George Novack, "On the Revolutionary Potential of the Working Class," Merit pamphlet (New York, 1969), p. 24.

[29]Paul Sweezy and Paul Baran, *Monopoly Capital* (New York, 1966), p. 363.

[30]John H. M. Laslett and Seymour Martin Lipset, *Failure of A Dream? Essays in the History of American Socialism* (New York, 1974), p. 27.

[31]The initial statement of this position, so far as Lipset is concerned, came in his *Political Man: The Social Bases of Politics* (New York, 1960), ch. 4. His most recent reformulation is to be found in S. M. Lipset and E. Raab, *The Politics of Unreason: Right Wing Extremism in America* (New York, 1970), chs. 1, 9-12.

[32]Richard Hamilton, "Class and Race in the United States," in Fischer, *The Revival of American Socialism*, pp. 81-106.

[33]John H. Goldthorpe et al. *The Affluent Worker in the Class Structure* (Cambridge, 1969).

[34]Martin Glaberman, "Marxism, the Working Class and the Trade Unions," in *Studies on the Left* 4 (1964): 65-72; Stanley Weir, "The Labor Revolt," *International Socialist Journal* (April and June 1967).

[35]Harry Braverman, *Labor and Monopoly Capital* (New York, 1974), p. 34.

[36]Figures here are taken from Daniel Bell, "Labor in the Post-Industrial Society," *Dissent* (Winter 1972): 170-73 ff. For a more extended analysis see various chapters in his *The Coming of Post-Industrial Society* (New York, 1973).

[37]Mills, *White Collar*, p. 342; Serge Mallet, *La Nouvelle Classe Ouvrière* (Paris, 1963), pp. 69 ff; André Gorz, *Strategy for Labor* (Boston, 1967), pp. 104-6 ff (first published as *Strategie Ouvrière et Néo-Capitalisme* (1964). See also Alain Touraine, *The Post-Industrial Society* (New York, 1971), first published as *La Société Post-industrialle*, 1969.

[38]Herbert Gintis, "The New Working Class and Revolutionary Youth," in *Socialist Revolution* 1 (1970): 13-43; Stanley Aronowitz, "Does the United States have a New Working Class?" in Fischer, *The Revival of*

*American Socialism*, pp. 188-216. For other contributions to the "old"-working-class/"new"-working-class debate, see Donald C. Hodges, "Old and New Working Classes," in *Radical America* 5 (1971): 11-32; and the essays by Bell and Michael Harrington in *Dissent* (Winter 1972): 146-89.

[39]Andrew Levinson, *The American Working Class Majority* (New York, 1974), p. 51.

[40]See the recently translated works of Gramsci, edited together with an introduction by Quintin Hoare and Geoffrey Nowell Smith in *Selections from the Prison Notebooks of Antonio Gramsci* (New York, 1971), which also, incidentally, includes a highly illuminating chapter on the United States entitled "Americanism and Fordism."

# Selected Bibliography

## Part I

Dunlop, John T. "The Development of Labor Organization: A Theoretical Framework." In Richard A. Lester and Joseph Shister, eds., *Insights into Labor Issues.* New York: Macmillan Co., 1948, pp. 163–193.
_____. *Industrial Relations Systems.* New York: Henry Holt & Co., 1958.

## Part II

### Marxism

Blackburn, Robin, and Alexander Cockburn, eds. *The Incompatibles: Trade Union Militancy and the Consensus.* Harmondsworth, England: Penguin in association with *New Left Review,* 1967.
Clarke, Tom, and Laurie Clements, eds. *Trade Unions Under Capitalism.* Atlantic Highlands, N.J.: Humanities Press, 1978.
Debs, Eugene. *Unionism and Socialism: A Plea for Both.* Terre Haute, Ind.: Standard Publishers, 1904.
DeLeon, Daniel. *The Burning Question of Trade Unionism.* New York: New York Labor News Co., 1960.
_____. *Industrial Unionism: Selected Editorials.* New York: New York Labor News Co., 1963.
Draper, Hal. *Karl Marx's Theory of Revolution.* Vol. 2, *The Politics of Social Classes.* Chapters 4 and 5. New York: Monthly Review Press, 1978.
Engels, Frederick. *The Condition of the Working Class in England.* Moscow: Progress Publishers, 1973.
Gordon, David M. "The Best Defense Is a Good Defense: Toward a Marxian Theory of Labor Union Structure and Behavior." In Michael Carter and William Leahy, eds., *New Directions in Labor Economics and Industrial Relations.* Notre Dame, Ind.: University of Notre Dame Press, 1981, pp. 167–214.
Green, Gil. *What's Happening to Labor.* New York: International Publishers, 1976.
Hammond, Thomas Taylor. *Lenin on Trade Unions and Revolution, 1893–1917.* New York: Columbia University Press, 1957.
Hinton, James and Richard Hyman, *Trade Unions and Revolution.* London: Pluto Press, 1975.
Hyman, Richard. *Marxism and the Sociology of Trade Unionism.* London: Pluto Press, 1971.
_____. *Industrial Relations: A Marxist Introduction.* London: The Macmillan Co., 1975.
Lenin, V. I. *On Trade Unions.* Moscow: Progress Publishers, 1970.
_____. *What Is To Be Done?* New York: International Publishers, 1969.
Lozovsky, A. *Marx and the Trade Unions.* Westport, Ct.: Greenwood Press, 1976.
Mandel, Ernest and George Novack. *On the Revolutionary Potential of the Working Class.* New York: Merit Publishers, 1969.
Mann, Michael. *Consciousness and Action among the Western Working Class.* Atlantic Highlands, N.J.: Humanities Press, 1981.
Marx, Karl and Frederick Engels. *The Communist Manifesto.* New York: Monthly Review Press, 1964.
Marx, Karl. *Capital.* 3 vols. New York: International Publishers, 1967.
_____. *Value, Price and Profit.* New York: International Publishers, 1935.

Sweezy, Paul. "Marx and the Proletariat." In *Modern Capitalism and Other Essays*. New York: Monthly Review Press, 1972.

Trotsky, Leon. *Leon Trotsky on the Trade Unions*. New York: Pathfinder Press, 1969.

## IWW and Syndicalism

Brissenden, Paul Frederick. *The I.W.W., a Study of American Syndicalism*. 2d ed. New York: Russell & Russell, 1957.

Brooks, John Graham. *American Syndicalism: The I.W.W.* New York: Macmillan Co., 1913.

Conlin, Joseph Robert. *Bread and Roses Too: Studies of the Wobblies*. Westport, Ct.: Greenwood Press, 1969.

DeCaux, Len. *The Living Spirit of the Wobblies*. New York: International Publishers, 1978.

Dubofsky, Melvyn. *We Shall Be All: A History of the Industrial Workers of the World*. New York: Quadrangle Books, 1969.

Foner, Philip. *The Industrial Workers of the World 1905-1917*. New York: International Publishers, 1965.

Kornbluh, Joyce L. *Rebel Voices: An I.W.W. Anthology*. Ann Arbor: University of Michigan Press, 1964.

Levine, Louis. "Development of Syndicalism in the United States." *Political Science Quarterly* 28 (September 1913): 451-479.

Lorwin, Lewis. *Syndicalism in France*. New York: AMS Press, 1970.

Lorwin, Val R. *The French Labor Movement*. Cambridge, Mass.: Harvard University Press, 1966.

Renshaw, Patrick. *The Wobblies: The Study of Syndicalism in the United States*. Garden City, N.Y.: Doubleday Co., 1967.

Saposs, David J. *Left Wing Unionism: A Study of Radical Policies and Tactics*. New York: Russell & Russell, 1967.

Sorel, Georges. *Reflections on Violence*. New York: AMS Press, 1975.

Tyler, Robert L. *Rebels of the Woods: The I.W.W. in the Pacific Northwest*. Eugene, Ore.: University of Oregon Press, 1967.

Weistein, Irving. *Pie in the Sky, an American Struggle: The Wobblies and Their Time*. New York: Delacorte Press, 1969.

## New Left

Aronowitz, Stanley. "Does the United States Have a New Working Class?" In George Fischer, ed., *The Revival of American Socialism*. New York: Oxford University Press, 1971, pp. 199-216.

——. *False Promises*. New York: McGraw Hill, 1973.

Gorz, André. "The Working Class and Revolution in the West." *Liberation*, Sept. 1971, pp. 31-37.

——. *Strategy for Labor*. Boston: Beacon Press, 1967.

Harrington, Michael. "The Old Working Class." *Dissent*, Winter 1972, pp. 146-158.

Marcuse, Herbert. *One Dimensional Man*. Boston: Beacon Press, 1964.

## Part III

Commons, John R., ed. *A Documentary History of American Industrial Society*. 11 vols. Cleveland: A. H. Clark Co., 1910-1911.

——. "The American Shoemakers, 1648-1895." In *Labor and Administration*. New York: Macmillan Co., 1913.

——. *Institutional Economics: Its Place in Political Economy*. 2 vols. Madison, Wis.: University of Wisconsin Press, 1961.

Commons, John R. et al. *History of Labor in the United States*. 2 vols. New York: Macmillan Co., 1918; Lescohier and Brandeis, *Working Conditions and Labor Legislation* (vol. 3). New York: Macmillan Co., 1935; Perlman and Taft, *Labor Movements* (vol. 4). New York: Macmillan Co., 1935.

Dawley, Alan. *Class and Community: The Industrial Revolution in Lynn*. Cambridge, Mass.: Harvard University Press, 1976.

De Brizzi, John A. *Ideology and the Rise of Labor Theory in America*. Westport, Ct.: Greenwood Press, 1983.

Harter, Lafayette. *John R. Commons: His Assault on Laissez-Faire*. Corvallis, Oregon: Oregon State University Press, 1962.

Industrial Relations Research Association. "A Reappraisal of Commons-Perlman Theory." In *Proceedings of the Third Annual Meeting of the IRRA, 1950*. Madison, Wis.: IRRA, 1951, pp. 140-183.

——. *Interpreting the Labor Movement*. Madison, Wis.: IRRA, 1952.

Kaiser, Philip M. "Experience Abroad Supports Commons-Perlman Theory." *Labor and Nation* 7, no. 1 (Winter 1951): 52-53.

Kaplan, David. "Broad Appeal of Commons-Perlman Theory." *Labor and Nation* 7, no. 1 (Winter 1951): 50-51.

Kassalow, Everett M. "Commons-Perlman Theory Needs to be Revised." *Labor and Nation* 7, no. 1 (Winter 1951): 54–56.

Peck, Sidney. "Fifty Years After *A Theory of the Labor Movement*: Class Conflict in the United States," *The Insurgent Sociologist* 8, nos. 2 & 3 (Fall 1978): 4–13.

Perlman, Selig. *A Theory of the Labor Movement*. New York: Macmillan Co., 1928.

———. *A History of Trade Unionism in the United States*. New York: Augustus M. Kelley, 1922.

———. "The Objective Is Unaltered from Gompers' Day." *Labor and Nation* 7, no. 1 (Winter 1951): 56–57.

Sturmthal, Adolf. "Comments on Selig Perlman's 'A Theory of the Labor Movement.' " *Industrial and Labor Relations Review* 4 (July 1951): 483–496.

Taft, Philip. "Commons-Perlman Theory Rooted in Workers' Expectations." *Labor and Nation* 7, no. 1 (Winter, 1951): 44–46.

———. "A Rereading of Selig Perlman's 'A Theory of the Labor Movement.' " *Industrial and Labor Relations Review*, 4 (October 1950): 70–77.

Ulman, Lloyd. "Some Theories of the Labor Movement." Chapter 18 in *The Rise of the National Trade Union*. Cambridge, Mass.: Harvard University Press, 1955.

## Part IV

Bauder, Russell. "Three Interpretations of the American Trade Union Movement." *Social Forces* 22 (1943–1944): 215–224.

Cole, Margaret, ed. *The Webbs and Their Work*. Westport, Ct.: Greenwood Press, 1985.

———. *The Story of Fabian Socialism*. Stanford, Cal.: Stanford University Press, 1961.

McBriar, A. M. *Fabian Socialism and English Politics, 1884–1918*. Cambridge, England: Cambridge University Press, 1962.

Webb, Sidney, and Beatrice Webb. *The History of Trade Unionism*. London and New York: Longmans, Green & Co., 1920.

———. *Industrial Democracy*. London and New York: Longmans, Green & Co., 1920.

## Part V

Anderson, Karl L. "The Unity of Veblen's Theoretical System." *Quarterly Journal of Economics* 47 (1932–33): 598–626.

Dorfman, Joseph. *Thorstein Veblen and His America*. New York: Augustus M. Kelley, 1972.

Frey, John P. "Robert F. Hoxie: Investigator and Interpreter." *Journal of Political Economy* 24 (1916): 884–893.

Hardman, J. B. S. "Critique of Frank Tannenbaum's *Philosophy of Labor*," with reply by Tannenbaum. *Labor and Nation* 7, no. 1 (Winter 1951): 67–71.

Parker, Carleton H. *The Casual Laborer and Other Essays*. Seattle: University of Washington Press, 1972.

Tannenbaum, Frank. *The Labor Movement: Its Conservative Functions and Social Consequences*. New York: Arno Press, 1969.

———. *A Philosophy of Labor*. New York: Alfred A. Knopf, 1962.

Veblen, Thorstein. *The Theory of Business Enterprise*. New York: Augustus M. Kelley, 1965.

———. *Absentee Ownership and Business Enterprise in Recent Times: The Case of America*. Boston: Beacon Press, 1967.

———. *The Vested Interests and the Common Man*. New York: Capricorn Books, 1969.

———. "The Preconceptions of Economic Science." *Quarterly Journal of Economics* 13 (January 1899): 121–150; 13 (July 1899): 396–426; 14 (February 1900): 240–269.

## Part VI

Baum, Gregory. *The Priority of Labor: A Commentary on "Laborem Exercens," Encyclical Letter of Pope John Paul II*. New York: Paulist Press, 1982.

Donahue, Thomas R. "A Trade Union Perspective of 'Laborem Exercens.' " Pamphlet issued by the AFL-CIO, n.d.

Ely, Richard T. *The Labor Movement in America*. New York: Arno Press, 1969.

Fine, Sidney. "Richard T. Ely: Forerunner of Progressivism, 1880–1901." *Mississippi Valley Historical Review* 37 (1951): 599–624.

———, ed. "The Ely-Labadie Letters." *Michigan History* 36 (1952): 1–32.

Fox, Mary Harrita. *Peter E. Dietz, Labor Priest*. Notre Dame, Ind.: University of Notre Dame Press, 1953.

Gearty, Patrick W. *The Economic Thought of Monsignor John A. Ryan*. Washington, D.C.: Catholic University of America Press, 1953.

Higgins, Monsignor George. *On Human Work: A Resource Book for the Study of Pope John Paul II's Third Encyclical.* Washington, D.C.: U.S. Catholic Conference, 1982.

Houck, John W., and Oliver F. Williams, eds. *Co-Creation and Capitalism: John Paul II's "Laborem Exercens."* Lanham, Md.: University Press of America, 1983.

Hoxie, Robert F. Review of Ryan, *A Living Wage. Journal of Political Economy* 15 (1907): 641–642.

John Paul II. " 'Laborem Exercens': On Human Work." *Origins,* September 24, 1981, pp. 1, 227–243.

John XXIII. " 'Mater et Magistra': Christianity and Social Progress." In *Seven Great Encyclicals.* New York: Paulist Press, 1963.

Karson, Marc. "The Catholic Church and the Political Development of American Trade Unionism (1900–1918)." *Industrial and Labor Relations Review 4 (July 1951): 527–542.*

Leo XIII. " 'Rerum Novarum,' The Condition of Labor." In *Seven Great Encyclicals.* New York: Paulist Press, 1963.

Pius XI. " 'Quadregesimo Anno': Reconstructing the Social Order." In *Seven Great Encyclicals.* New York: Paulist Press, 1963.

Ryan, John A. *The Church and Socialism, and Other Essays.* Washington, D.C.: The University Press, 1919.

————. *The Church and Labor.* New York: Macmillan Co., 1920.

————. *Declining Liberty and Other Papers.* New York: Da Capo Press, 1972.

————. *Distributive Justice.* New York: Arno Press, 1978.

————. *A Living Wage: Its Ethical and Economic Aspects.* New York: Arno Press, 1971.

————. "Moral Aspects of Labour Unions." In *Catholic Encyclopedia,* Vol. VIII (1910), pp. 724–728.

————. "The Morality of the Aims and Methods of Labor Unions." *American Catholic Quarterly Review,* April 1904, pp. 326–355.

————. *Seven Troubled Years, 1930–1936.* Ann Arbor, Mich.: Edwards Brothers, 1937.

————. *Social Doctrine in Action.* New York: Harper & Bros., 1941.

Ryan, John A., and Morris Hillquit. *Socialism: Promise or Menace?* Westport, Ct.: Hyperion Press, 1975.

Seaton, Douglas P. *Catholics and Radicals: The Association of Catholic Trade Unionists and the American Labor Movement, from Depression to Cold War.* Lewisburg, Pa.: Bucknell University Press, 1981.

Smith, William J. *The Pope Talks about Labor Relations.* St. Paul, Mn.: Catechetical Guild Educational Society, 1955.

## Part VII

Freeman, Richard B., and James L. Medoff. *What Do Unions Do?* New York: Basic Books, 1984.

————. "The Impact of Collective Bargaining: Can the New Facts Be Explained by Monopoly Unionism?." In Joseph D. Reid, ed., *Research in Labor Economics: New Approaches to Labor Unions,* Supp. 2. Greenwich, Ct.: JAI Press, 1983.

Friedman, Milton. *Capitalism and Freedom.* Chicago: University of Chicago Press, 1962.

Friedman, Milton, and Rose Friedman. *Free to Choose.* New York: Harcourt Brace Jovanovich, 1980.

Haberler, Gottfried. "Wage Policy and Inflation." In Philip D. Bradley, ed., *The Public Stake in Union Power.* Charlottesville, Va.: University of Virginia Press, 1959, pp. 63–85.

Hutt, W. H. *The Theory of Collective Bargaining.* Glencoe, Ill.: The Free Press, 1954.

Machlup, Fritz. *The Political Economy of Monopoly.* Baltimore: Johns Hopkins University Press, 1952.

Petro, Sylvester. *The Labor Policy of the Free Society.* New York: The Ronald Press, 1957.

Phelps, Orme W. "The Trade Unionism of Henry Simons." *Proceedings of the Seventh Annual Meeting of the IRRA,* 1954, pp. 280–285.

Simons, Henry. "Some Reflections on Syndicalism." *Journal of Political Economy* 52, no. 1 (March 1944): 1–25.

————. *Economic Policy for a Free Society.* Chicago: University of Chicago Press, 1948.

## Part VIII

Bell, Daniel. *The End of Ideology.* New York: The Free Press, 1966.

————. *The Coming of Post-Industrial Society.* New York: Basic Books, 1973.

————. "Labor in the Post-Industrial Society." *Dissent,* Winter 1972, pp. 163–189.

Galbraith, John Kenneth. *The New Industrial State.* Boston: Houghton Mifflin Co., 1967.

Goldthorpe, John H., David Lockwood, Frank Bechhofer, and Jennifer Platt. *The Affluent Worker in the Class Structure.* New York: Cambridge University Press, 1969.

Heilbroner, Robert. "Economic Problems of a 'Postindustrial' Society." *Dissent,* Spring 1973, pp. 163–176.

Kerr, Clark, John T. Dunlop, Frederick H. Harbison, and Charles A. Myers. *Industrialism and Industrial Man.* Cambridge, Mass.: Harvard University Press, 1960.

———. *Industrialism and Industrial Man Reconsidered.* Princeton, N.J.: The Inter-University Study of Human Resources in National Development, 1975.

Lester, Richard. *As Unions Mature.* Princeton, N.J.: Princeton University Press, 1958.

Mann, Michael. *Consciousness and Action among the Western Working Class.* Atlantic Highlands, N.J.: Humanities Press, 1981.

Schmidman, John. *Unions in Post-Industrial Society.* University Park, Pa.: Penn State University Press, 1979.

Touraine, Alain. *The Post-Industrial Society.* New York: Random House, 1971.

## Part IX

Bauder, Russell. "Three Interpretations of the American Trade Union Movement." *Social Forces,* December 1943, pp. 215–224.

Cartter, Allan and Ray Marshall. "Theories of Labor Movements." Chapter 3 of *Labor Economics.* Homewood, Ill.: Richard Irwin, 1972.

Mills, C. Wright. *The New Men of Power: America's Labor Leaders.* New York: Augustus M. Kelley, 1971.

Perlman, Mark. *Labor Union Theories in America: Background and Development.* Westport, Ct.: Greenwood Press, 1976.

———. "Labor Movement Theories: Past, Present and Future." *Industrial and Labor Relations Review* 13, no. 3 (April 1960): 338–348.

Poole, Michael. *Theories of Trade Unionism: A Sociology of Industrial Relations.* London and Boston: Routledge & Kegan Paul, 1981.

Taft, Philip. "Theories of the Labor Movement," in George Brooks et al., eds., *Interpreting the Labor Movement.* Madison, Wis.: Industrial Relations Research Associaton, 1952, pp. 1–38.

# Index

CPSIA information can be obtained
at www.ICGtesting.com
Printed in the USA
JSHW031227080920
7720JS00002B/11